MAUI

AND LANA'I

Making the Most of Your Family Vacation

by Dona Early & Christie Stilson

Prima Publishing in affiliation with
Paradise Publications

Maui and Lana'i, Making the Most of Your Family Vacation
Copyright © 1999 Paradise Publications, Portland, Oregon

First Edition:	Dec 1984	Fifth Edition:	Oct 1992
Second Edition:	May 1986	Sixth Edition:	Nov 1994
Third Edition:	May 1988	Seventh Edition:	Nov 1996
Fourth Edition:	May 1990	Eighth Edition:	Oct 1998

Prima Publishing and colophon are registered trademarks of Prima Communications, Inc.

Illustrations: Janora Bayot
Maps: Tom Spaulding
Layout & Typesetting: Paradise Publications
Published by Prima Publishing, Rocklin, California

ISBN 0-7615-1480-5

International Standard Serial Number Pending

98 99 00 01 02 H H 10 9 8 7 6 5 4 3 2 1
Printed in the United States of America

WARNING DISCLAIMER
Prima Publishing in affiliation with Paradise Publications has designed this book to provide information in regard to the subject matter covered. It is sold with the understanding that the publishers and authors are not liable for the misconception or misuse of information provided. Every effort has been made to make this book as complete and as accurate as possible. The purpose of this book is to educate. The authors, Prima Publishing and Paradise Publications shall have neither liability nor responsibility to any person or entity with respect to any loss, damage, or injury caused or alleged to be caused directly or indirectly by the information contained in this book. They shall also not be liable for price changes, or for the completeness or accuracy of the contents of this book.

HOW TO ORDER
Quantity discounts are available from the publisher, Prima Publishing, PO Box 1260BK, Rocklin, CA; telephone (916) 632-4400. On your letterhead, include information concerning the intended use of the books and the number of books you wish to purchase.

Visit Prima online at: www.primapublishing.com

"Maui No Ka Oi"

(Maui is the Best)

Dedicated to Maren and Jeffrey, two terrific travelers.

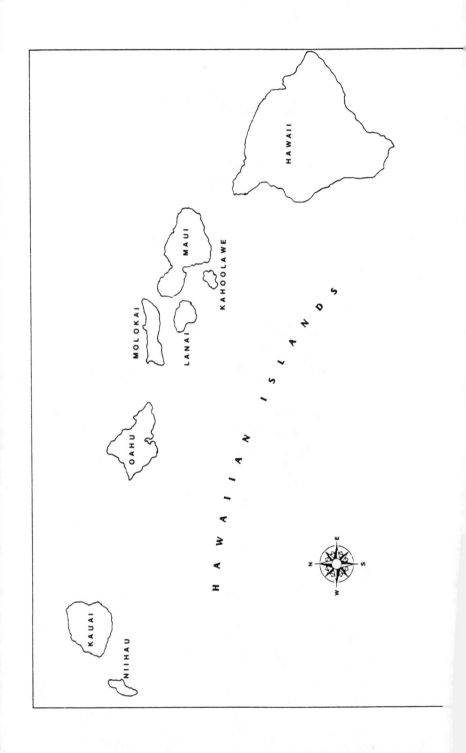

TABLE OF CONTENTS

IV. RESTAURANTS (continued)

V. BEACHES AND BEACH ACTIVITIES

VI. RECREATION AND TOURS

VII.   THE ISLAND OF LANA'I

VIII.   RECOMMENDED READING

IX.   ORDERING INFORMATION

X.   INDEX

MAP INDEX

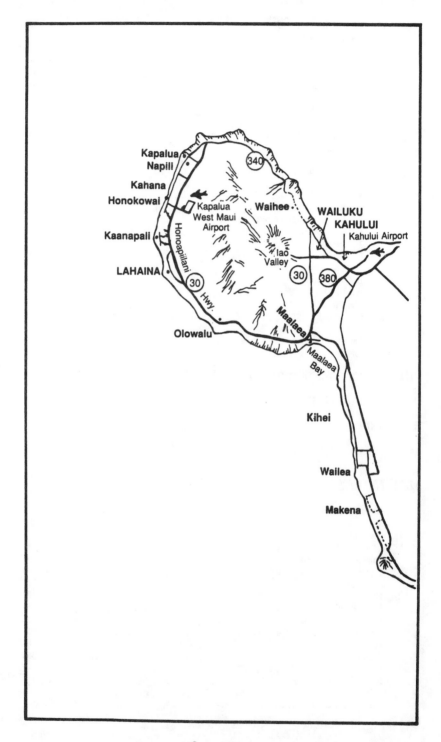

Kapalua
Napili

Kahana

Honokowai

Kaanapali

LAHAINA

Kapalua
West Maui
Airport

Waihee

WAILUKU
KAHULUI

Kahului Airport

Honoapiilani Hwy.

Iao
Valley

340

30

30

380

Olowalu

Maalaea

Maalaea
Bay

Kihei

Wailea

Makena

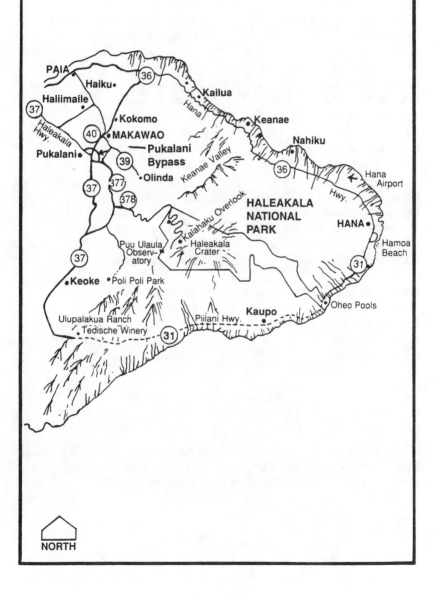

MAUI

PAIA
Haiku
Haliimaile
(37)
(36)
Kailua
Haleakala Hwy.
Kokomo
Keanae
(40) MAKAWAO
Nahiku
Pukalani
Pukalani Bypass
(39)
Keanae Valley
(36)
Hana Airport
Olinda
(37)
(377)
Hana Hwy.
(378)
Kalahaku Overlook
HALEAKALA NATIONAL PARK
Puu Ulaula Observatory
Kalahaku Overlook
Haleakala Crater
HANA
(37)
Hamoa Beach
Keoke
Poli Poli Park
(31)
Ulupalakua Ranch
Tedische Winery
Piilani Hwy.
Kaupo
Oheo Pools
(31)

NORTH

9

KAWAIPUNAHELE

No e Kawaipunahele	For you Kawaipunahele
Ku'u le aloha mae'ole	My never-fading lei
Pili hemo'ole, pili pa'a pono	Never separated, firmly united
E huli ho'i kaua	Come, let's go back
E Kawaipunahele	O Kawaipunahele
Ku 'oe me ke ki'eki'e	You stand majestically
I ka nani a'o Wailuku	In the splendor of Wailuku
Ku'u ipo henoheno,	My cherished sweetheart
Ku'u wehi o ka po	My adornment of the night
E huli ho'i kaua	Come, let's go back
E Kawaipunahele	O Kawaipunahele
Eia ho'i 'o Keali'i	Here is Keali'i
Kali'ana i ka mehameha	Waiting in loneliness
Mehameha ho'i au, 'eha'eha ho'i au	I am lonely, I hurt
E huli ho'i kaua	Come, let's go back
E kawaipunahele	O Kawaipunahele
Puana 'ia ke aloha	Tell of the love
Ku'u le aloha mae 'ole	Of my never-fading lei
Pili hemo'ole, pili pa'a pono	Never separated, firmly united
Ke pono ho'i kaua	When it's right, we'll go back
E Kawaipunahele	O Kawaipunahele

Music and lyrics by Keali'i Reichel, Arrangement by Moon Kauakahi. Used with the permission of Punahele Productions, Wailuku, Maui. From Keali'i Reichel's CD recording, *Kawaipunahele*.

Although the islands have changed greatly during the century since Mark Twain visited the islands, there remains much to fall in love with. The physical beauty and seductiveness of the land remains despite what may seem rampant commercialism, and the true aloha spirit does survive. We are confident that as you explore these islands, you too will be charmed by their magic. Keep in mind the expressive words used by Twain over 100 years ago when he visited and fell in love with Hawai'i.

"No alien land in all the world has any deep strong charm for me but that one, no other land could so longingly and so beseechingly haunt me, sleeping and waking, through half a lifetime, as that one has done. Other things leave me, but it abides; other things change, but it remains the same. For me its balmy airs are always blowing, its summer seas flashing in the sun; the pulsing of its surfbeat is in my ear; I can see its garlanded crags, its leaping cascades, its plumy palms drowsing by the shore, its remote summits floating like islands above the cloud wrack; I can feel the spirit of its woodland solitudes, I can hear the splash of its brooks; in my nostrils still lives the breath of flowers..."

ALOHA!

Congratulations on choosing Maui as the site of your vacation. You will soon see why it has the deserved slogan, *Maui No Ka Oi* (Maui is the Best). The sun and lush tropicalness, and some of the finest accommodations, blend sublimely together to create a perfect holiday paradise - a place both magical and beautiful. While this guide is dubbed a *Family Travel Guide* -- it is aimed for any kind of family, from a single traveler to a family reunion. It is for you the traveler who wishes to be in control of his/her vacation plans. From the family values "buzz words" of the 90's we know that "family" can mean anything. *Ohana*, the Hawaiian word for relative or family, is also used for an extended family of friends, neighbors or co-workers. Even visitors who share a common love and respect for the islands are often described as "part of the *ohana*." Your co-authors for this book have felt this "*ohana*" ever since they first visited the islands. Christie first visited the islands in 1978, and became so infatuated that she kept returning each year. In 1983, Dona moved to Maui permanently.

As authors who travel in very different modes (Christie, who travels with a family with two children, and Dona as a single adult), we can share our island experiences from different "family" viewpoints. Maui offers a perfect location for a romantic interlude, a vacation with family or a wonderful destination to spend time relaxing with friends. There is plenty of information on traveling with children, as well as older adults who might be a part of your family. (If you don't have children or seniors to travel with, you might want to consider renting one after you read up on some of the freebies & discounts they get!)

We work continually to update our information, discover new things, rediscover old things and to thoroughly enjoy the tropical energy and seductive charm of Maui. While first-time visitors will delight in the diversity of activities that Maui has to offer, those making a return visit can enjoy discovering new sights and adventures on this magnificent island.

KOI

The chapters on accommodations and sights, restaurants, and beaches are conveniently divided into areas with similar characteristics and indexes are provided for each chapter. This allows a better feel for, and access to, the information on the area in which you are staying, and greater confidence in exploring other areas. Remember that, except for Hana, most of the areas are only a short drive and worth a day of sightseeing, beach exploring, or a meal at a fine restaurant.

Maui can be relatively inexpensive, or extravagantly expensive, depending on your preference in lodgings, activities, and eating arrangements. Therefore, we have endeavored to give complete and detailed information covering the full range of budgets. The opinions expressed are based on our personal experiences, and while the positive is emphasized, it is your right to know, in certain cases, our bad experiences. To aid you, a *BEST BET* summary is included at the beginning of the GENERAL INFORMATION chapter. Refer to individual chapters for additional Best Bets and check for ★'s which identify our special recommendations.

Our guide is as accurate as possible at the time of publication, however, changes seem extremely rapid for an island operating on "Maui Time." Ownerships, managements, names, and menus do change frequently, as do prices. For the latest information on the island, Paradise Publications has available *THE MAUI UPDATE*, a quarterly newsletter. We invite you to receive a complimentary issue or to order a yearly subscription; see ORDERING INFORMATION at the back of this guide. If your itinerary includes visits to the other islands, the Paradise Family Guide Series includes *Kaua'i, A Paradise Family Guide* by Christie Stilson and Dona Early and *Hawai'i: The Big Island, A Paradise Family Guide* by John Penisten. These essential travel accessories not only contain details on all the condos, hotels, and restaurants (along with specific recreational activity information), but also inside tips and advice that most visitors never receive, shared by authors who know and love the islands. These titles also feature their own Update newsletters.

A special mahalo to Maren Stilson for editorial consultation. And sincere thanks to J, T and K for their friendship and support at a time when it was needed most.

Our thanks also to all of you who have written sharing your trip experiences. (Yes! We read them all!) It is a delight to be invited to share your trip through your letters.

Aloha and happy travels to you!

Dona and Christie

GENERAL
INFORMATION

OUR BEST BETS

For Our Best Bets on Dining, see the beginning of the RESTAURANT section. And For Best Recreation and Tours see beginning of Recreation and Tours chapter for ideas!

BEST ALOHA WEAR: The traditional tourist garb is available in greatest supply at the 17,000 square foot Hilo Hattie factory in the Lahaina Center at the Kaanapali end of Lahaina.

BEST CHEAP ALOHA WEAR: While not for every traveler, the Salvation Army can be a great place to pick up some Hawaiian clothes to wear on your vacation. A muu muu for less than $5 is great for a beach cover-up or for wearing to a luau. Their Thrift Stores are located in Lahaina, Kihei, and Kahului. There is also a Savers located in Kahului.

BEST SHOPPING: *Affordable and fun* - Kahului Swap Meet each Saturday and Lahaina's Front Street at any time; *Practical* - Kaahumanu Shopping Center in Kahului; *Extravagant* - Any of the gift shops at the fine resorts on Maui; *Odds 'n Ends* - Longs Drug Store (Kahului, Lahaina and Kihei) and Costco or Kmart in Kahului. For the adventurous there are dozens of thrift and consignment shops, *Encore* in Lahaina has some particularly nice clothes and good values. *Least fun* - Whalers Village has gone off the deep end. Most of the shops here are now expensive designer boutiques with little for the average visitor.

MOST SPECTACULAR RESORT GROUNDS: The Hyatt Regency Maui at Kaanapali and the Grand Wailea Resort & Spa in Wailea tie for first place. The Westin Maui is a close second.

BEST EXCURSIONS: *Most spectacular* - a helicopter tour. *Most unusual* - a bike trip down Haleakala or around Upcountry. *Best adventure on foot* -a personalized hike with Hike Maui. *Best sailing* - a day-long snorkel and picnic to Lana'i with the congenial crew of the Trilogy.

BEST BEACHES: *Beautiful and safe* - Kapalua Bay and Ulua Beach. *Unspoiled* -Oneloa (Makena) and Mokuleia (Slaughterhouse) Beaches. For young kids - try Puunoa Beach near Lahaina.

BEST MAUI GET AWAY FROM IT ALL RESORT: The Hotel Hana-Maui or on Lana'i either the Lodge at Koele or Manele Bay Resort.

MOST INTIMATE ACCOMMODATIONS: The Victorian-style Lahaina Inn is a step back into time. No ocean view here (or televisions for that matter) but wonderful and romantic. Plantation Inn (just up the street) is equally charming with more of a tropical feel and the added amenities of air-conditioning, a pool and televisions.

BEST CONDOS IF YOU CAN SPLURGE: South Maui - Makena Surf is a terrific, luxury property: elegant, ideally located and beautifully appointed units. You can really get away from it here. West Maui - The Kaanapali Alii has long been one of our favorites.

BEST ACCOMMODATIONS DISCOUNT: Entertainment book discounts offer half price at some Maui hotels and condominiums. The ***Entertainment book*** is printed in most major cities around the country and contains coupons for dining and activities in that area. In addition, they carry discounts for accommodations in other regions of the U.S., including Hawai'i. The books are sold by non-profit organizations as fund-raisers. Check your phone book under Entertainment, Inc. There is also a Hawai'i edition which carries coupons for dining and attractions, largely for O'ahu, but the outer islands are included as well. Restrictions are plenty, with limited times for availability and allowable only on certain categories of rooms. They only offer a few rooms at these discounts, so make your travel plans well in advance to take advantage of this vacation bargain! Be sure to be informed and know what standard room rates are so you'll know if you are really getting a good discount! Call ***Entertainment Publications*** at their Honolulu office at (808) 737-3252 or write them at 4211 Waialae Ave., Honolulu, HI 96816. There is a fee for these books (about $40.)

The complimentary services of ***Concierge Connection*** can provide you with both accommodation only and package discounts; coupons and percentage off cards for restaurants & activities - even resort guest prices for golf courses or the Grand Wailea Spa! They offer free advice, information, and recommendations on all other aspects of your Maui vacation - with discounts on those, too! Call toll-free 1-800-961-9196, (808) 875-9366 on Maui or Email them at: connect@maui.net

BEST BODY SURFING: Slaughterhouse in winter (only for experienced and strong swimmers).

BEST SURFING: Honolua Bay in winter (for experienced surfers only!)

BEST SNORKELING: North end - Honolua Bay in summer. Kapalua area - Kapalua Bay and Namalu Bay. Kaanapali - Black Rock at the Sheraton. Olowalu at Mile Marker 14. Wailea - Ulua Beach. Makena - Ahihi Kinau Natural Reserve. Island of Lana'i - Hulopoe Beach Park. And Molokini Crater.

BEST WHALE WATCHING: From the shore it is definitely the Pali on the road to West Maui and Lahaina. While whale watch boat excursions are great, you'll be in for a real thrill if you can view them from a helicopter! Sign up for a helicopter excursion to Moloka'i which crosses the Pailolo (which translates to "slap crazy") Channel. You won't believe your eyes! We have also found that off Makena Beach seems to be another good location in the early evening.

BEST WINDSURFING: Hookipa Beach Park (for experienced windsurfers).

MOST UNUSUAL VISUAL ADVENTURE: The Hawaii Experience Domed Theater in Lahaina.

BEST POSTCARD HOME: Write your personal greetings on a coconut, mail it and surprise someone back home! Hana Gardenland has the best prices (about $10 for a plain coconut, $15 for a painted one) though you can sometimes find inexpensive ones at the Kahului Swap Meet.

UNUSUAL GIFT IDEAS: For the green thumb, be sure to try Dan's Green House on Prison Street in Lahaina for a Fuku-Bonsai planted on a lava rock. They are specially sprayed and sealed for either shipping or carrying home.

Maui's Kaanapali Estate Coffee is the only authentic Maui coffee grown right here. Not to be confused with "blends," it's available at most grocery stores (in the gold package) or you can order by phone at 1-800-99MAUI-9.

If you'd like to bring home a deed for property on Maui, it's only $15.99 for "Maui by the Inch" 1-800-300MAUI PO Box 779, Kihei, HI 96753.

Roy's Do-It Yourself Chocolate Souffle kit for making his signature dish.

Kmart has mouse pads with Hawaiian designs - the perfect gift for all your Internet friends.

Specialty breads from Mama Ding's (the Puerto Rican pasteles restaurant) in Kahului come in Hawaiian flavors like coconut-papaya-pineapple, strawberry-guava, and Portuguese sweetbread.

Maui Crafts Guild at 43 Hana Highway in Paia (579-9697) has some unusual handcrafted, albeit expensive, gifts.

Antique maps and prints make an unusual and prized gift for yourself or a family member or friend. Visit Lahaina Printsellers galleries for a piece of history.

If you'd like to share a little Hawai'i with friends back home, consider a CD of Hawaiian music. A good selection and the best prices in town are at Costco in Kahului. We'd recommend any of Keali'i Reichel's albums; also Hapa and Israel Kamakawiwo'ole are fabulous.

The Maui Onion Cookbook ($4.95) is a great little book, die-cut in the shape of an onion and filled with recipes from Maui chefs and residents. It's unusual, inexpensive and easy to pack - or mail! (Tip: Bring home a few Kula onions to go with it!)

If you love Kona coffee, you'll love the *coffee bean jewelry* made by Heart Springs of Maui. They make earrings out of real Kona coffee beans, but add a variety of colored stones so you don't have to wear brown clothes all the time! They're $9.95 and you can find them at all of The Coffee Store locations (Kahului, Kihei, Napili), at Anthony's in Paia, or Makani Hou Gifts in Haiku at the Pauwela Cannery.

For years it has been well-known that the red dirt from the Kalaheo area of Kaua'i would permanently stain whatever it touched. The idea to use the dirt as a dye was born and with it, the russet-colored ***Red Dirt Shirt***! The prices vary considerably, but the best we found was at their factory outlet at Azeka Place in Kihei. Tees and tanks run $20. Also available are socks, shorts, hats, and bags plus sweat shirts, polo shirts and kid's shirts. We prowled through a box of irregular shirts and discovered a couple of great finds for only $10, but **WARNING!** *Orange Undie Alert*: Watch the washings or you might wind up with 'em! Although Red Dirt Shirts are (literally) a good way to bring some of Maui home with you, you'll find a more "flavorful" selection of T-shirts at Crazy Shirts. The coffee, chocolate and *Li Hing Mui* (local Chinese plum) colored tee's look - and smell - yummy! They come in clever packages (the coffee shirt comes in a coffee bag); they're preshrunk - and colorfast! What's more, you can accessorize: If you love your coffee earrings, you can wear them with your coffee t-shirt (or your chocolate one if you're feeling kind of "mocha") AND now you can even get jewelry to match your Red Dirt Shirt! Heart Springs is now the "authorized dirt dealer," making Red Dirt earrings and necklace pendants from tiny "flasks" that hold real, authentic Red Dirt! Currently only available at the Red Dirt Stores (Lahaina Center and the factory outlet at Azeka Place, Kihei), but soon you'll be able to find it anywhere you can buy Red Dirt Shirts.

And if you can wear coffee and chocolate (and dirt!), why not cook and serve your food with a coconut? The *Coconut Cookery* collection includes ladles, spoons, spatulas, bowls - even chopsticks - all made from the shell of a coconut. Pieces and prices vary. Ka Honu Gift Gallery (Whalers Village, Kaanapali), Maui to Go (Lahaina), The Import Store (Kihei), Collections (Makawao), Hana Treasures and Lamont's Sundries (Kea Lani or Hyatt Regency)and both Lana'i hotels. For kids who like coconut (but don't cook!), McConnell's Ice Cream in the Lahaina Cannery offers an original selection of items, all hand-carved from and coconut shells and husks: Mask ($8), Puppy ($10), China doll ($15).

BEST T-SHIRTS: Our favorites are *Crazy Shirts* (regular or "flavored"), more expensive than the run of the mill variety, but excellent quality and great designs. There is a Crazy Shirts outlet at most malls and several in Lahaina. A huge selection of inexpensive shirts are available at the *T-Shirt Factory* near the Kahului Airport. Sizes range from infants to XL adults and, with plenty to choose from, it is easy to mix and match styles and sizes. Also check the Kahului Swap Meet.

BEST TAKE-HOME FOOD PRODUCTS: Tropical fruit, macadamia nuts, Maui chips and Maui onions ready to ship or take on the plane at Take Home Maui, Inc. at 121 Dickenson St., Lahaina. Or wait till you get home and have Hawaii Tropical Express mail them to you. Call 1-888-826-3444.

BEST FLOWERS: For best flower values visit the Maui Swap Meet in Kahului (to make your own arrangements). Leis are sometimes available here also. Check Ooka's grocery in Wailuku (enroute to the airport) for fresh flowers and leis to take home. Safeway in Lahaina also has a fair selection. Or order from Hawaii Tropical Express (here or when you get home) and receive a free video on "Tropical Flower Arrangements." For a free catalog call 1-888-826-1444 (or 661-1111 on Maui.)

BEST FREE (OR ALMOST FREE) STUFF: *Around the island* - Free introductory scuba instruction offered poolside at many of the major resorts. A self-guided tour of the Grand Wailea, Hyatt Regency Maui or Westin Maui Resorts. Public beaches with their free parking. Free snorkel guide from Maui Dive Shop in Lahaina or Kihei. (Lahaina Divers has a free map of some of the most popular beach diving and snorkeling sights on Maui. It advises divers as to the special features and facilities of each beach and the suitability for diving or snorkeling. Stop by the headquarters of Lahaina Divers at 143 Dickenson St. in Lahaina, or contact them at (808) 667-7496.) Country Western Dancing at locations island-wide. (Nominal charge) Call 669-8343 for schedule. Free hikes with Sierra Club. Or just go to church! Churches in Hawai'i have less to do with "religion" than with fellowship, celebration, wonderful music and - aloha! See Annual Events for more *free* stuff!

Lahaina-Kaanapali-Kapalua - Friday night is "art night" in Lahaina when the Front Street galleries have their openings and special exhibits. You may have an opportunity to meet the artists and possibly get some free refreshment! Also on Front Street, the Halloween Parade, Kamehameha Day Parade (June) or Festival of Arts & Flowers (Nov). Visit Pioneer Inn, now an official U.S. Historic Landmark. Canoe races held at Honoka'o'o Park. The shuttle bus in West Maui (which used to be free) is now $1, but the routes have been extended for travel between Lahaina, Kaanapali, and The Ritz-Carlton. Free admission to Wo Hing Temple in Lahaina. There are free Hawaiian shows and musical entertainment around Maui. The times and days change, so please check. Watch *Hula Kahiko* (Ancient Dance) at the Kapalua Shops (669-5433) Thursdays at 10 am or enjoy Hawaiian ukulele and slack key guitar music every Tuesday, 10am-noon. Whalers Village (661-4567) offers hula performances nightly at 7pm.

The Lahaina Center (667-9216) has hula shows Wed & Fri at 2pm in their *Hale Kahiko* Hawaiian village. A Keiki Hula Show is presented there Fri at 6pm with Tues & Wed rehearsals open to the public from 5-6pm. The Lahaina Cannery Mall (661-5304) also has a keiki hula show (Sat & Sun at 1pm), a Polynesian show on Tues & Thurs at 7pm and arts & crafts Mon-Fri 9:30am-4pm.

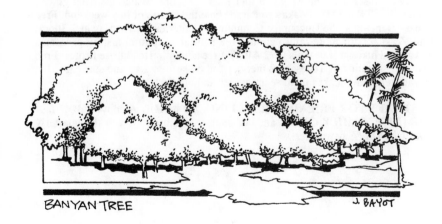

BANYAN TREE   J. BAYOT

Free Hula Show at the Kaanapali Beach Hotel (661-0011) held nightly at 6:30pm with Hawaiian Arts & Crafts on display on Mon-Wed-Fri. Whale presentations with naturalist Phil Secretario or Martha Simonsen are presented seasonally (whale season, of course!). See the amazing sand sculptures on the beach at Whalers Village in Kaanapali. Award-winning artist Billy Lee creates a new design each week which remains on display for all to enjoy and take pictures. The Whalers Village Whaling Museum is great and free to the public. A whale slide presentation is shown here Thursdays at 8pm. The Crazy Shirts shop located on the north end of Lahaina town has a nice display of whaling memorabilia and a big cannon sits out behind the shop. Free tour of the artwork at the Westin Maui. "Live on the Beach" -- a free concert of contemporary and Hawaiian music at Whalers Village the last Sunday of the month.

Kihei-Wailea-Makena - Free hula show every Tues & Fri in the Molokini Lounge at the Maui Prince Resort. Free guided tour, twice weekly, of the artwork at the Grand Wailea Resort. Free hula show Thurs and Sun (6:30-9:30pm) at the Oasis Pool Bar (Maui Coast Hotel). A pleasant surprise along the Wailea Beach Walk is the reconstruction of a stone foundation for an original Hawaiian dwelling. Charle's House of Miniatures (Kihei Industrial Center) is fast becoming a "mini" museum of ethnic and period dolls, (with appropriate clothes, houses and furniture) and an electric train set in an historic Maui landscape.

Wailuku-Waikapu-Kahului - Visit the Iao Needle located near Wailuku. Watch windsurfing at Hookipa Beach on Maui's windward shore. See the Maui Botanical Gardens in Wailuku. Ooka's Market in Wailuku is worth a visit just to see the varied island foods available, from breadfruit to flying fish eggs! The Maui Tropical Plantation has free admission to their marketplace; a charge to tour their grounds. Free behind-the-scenes tours of the Maui Arts & Cultural Center, Wed 11 am. Free Hawaiian entertainment at the Maui Mall on the 2nd & 4th Friday of each month, 6-8:30pm.

Upcountry - No charge to visit Hui No'eau Visual Arts Center in Makawao; special events may require a fee (572-6560). Visit Hot Island Glass Studio in Makawao to see glass blowing and tour their art shops. Watch the hang gliders from Polipoli Road. The Makawao Parade held the Fourth of July weekend. Free Square Dancing at the Upcountry Community Center every Tuesday at 7:30pm. Call 572-1721 for more information. Free natural & cultural history programs and guided hikes at Haleakala (572-4400). Free admission to Sunrise Protea. Free tour and sampling at Tedeschi Winery. (And be sure to stay and star gaze: the elevation at Kula makes them seem bigger and clearer!)

BEST GIFT FOR FRIENDS TRAVELING TO MAUI: A copy of *MAUI, A PARADISE FAMILY GUIDE* and, of course, a subscription to the quarterly *MAUI UPDATE* newsletter!

HISTORY

Far beneath the warm waters of the Pacific Ocean is the Pacific Plate, which moves constantly in a northwest direction. Each Hawaiian island was formed as it passed over a hot vent in this plate. Kaua'i, the oldest of the major islands in the Hawai'i chain was formed first and has since moved away from the plume, the source of the lava, and is no longer growing. Some of the older islands even farther to the northwest have been gradually reduced to sandbars and atolls. The Big Island is the youngest in the chain and is continuing to grow. A new island called Lo'ihi (which means "prolonged in time"), southeast of the Big Island is growing and expected to emerge from the oceanic depths in about a million years.

It was explosions of hot lava from two volcanoes that created the island of Maui. Mauna Kahalawai (Ma-ow-na Ka-HA-la-why) is the oldest, creating the westerly section with the highest point (elevation 5,788 ft.) known as Pu'u Kukui (Poo'oo koo-KOO-ee). The great Haleakala (HAH-leh-AH-kuh-LAH), now the world's largest dormant volcano, created the southeastern portion of the island. (The last eruption on Maui took place about 1789 and flowed over to the Makena area.) A valley connects these two volcanic peaks, hence the source of Maui's nickname, "The Valley Isle."

The first Hawaiians came from the Marquesa and Society Islands in the central Pacific. (Findings suggest that their ancestors came from the western Pacific, perhaps as far away as Madagascar.) The Polynesians left the Marquesas about the 8th century and were followed by natives from the Society Islands sometime between the 11th and 14th centuries. The Hawaiian population may well have been as high as 300,000 by the 1700's, spread throughout the chain of islands. Fish and poi were diet basics, supplemented by various fruits and occasionally meat from chickens, pigs and even dogs.

Four principal gods formed the basis of their religion until the missionaries arrived. The stone foundations of heiaus, the ancient religious temples, can still be visited on Maui.

The islands were left undisturbed by western influence until the 1778 arrival of James Cook. He spotted and visited Kaua'i and O'ahu first and is believed to have arrived at Maui on November 25 or 26, 1778. He was later killed in a brawl on the Big Island of Hawai'i.

The major islands had a history of independent rule with, at times, open warfare. On Maui, Kahului and Hana were both sites of combat between the Maui islanders and the warriors from neighboring islands.

Kamehameha the First was born on the Big Island of Hawai'i about 1758. He was the nephew of Kalaiopi who ruled the Big Island. Following the King's death, Kalaiopi's son came to power, only to be subsequently defeated by Kamehameha in 1794. The great chieftain Kahekili was Kamehameha's greatest rival. He ruled not only Maui, but Lana'i and Moloka'i, and also had kinship with the governing royalty of O'ahu and Kaua'i. King Kahekili died in 1794 and left control of the island to his son. A bloody battle (more like a massacre since Kamehameha used western technology, strategy, and two English advisors) in the Iao Valley resulted

King Kamehameha I

in the defeat of Kahekili's son, Kalanikupule, in 1795. Kamehameha united all the islands and made Lahaina the capital of Hawai'i in 1802. It remained the capital until the 1840's when Honolulu became the center for government affairs. Lahaina was a popular resort for Hawaiian royalty who favored the beaches in the area. Kaahumanu, the favorite wife of Kamehameha was born in Hana, Maui, and spent much of her time there. (Quiet Hana was another popular spot for vacationing royalty.)

Liholiho, the heir of Kamehameha the Great, ruled as Kamehameha II from 1819 to 1824. Liholiho was not a strong ruler so Kaahumanu proclaimed herself prime minister during his reign. She ended many of the kapus of the old religion, thus creating a fortuitous vacuum which the soon-to-arrive missionaries would fill. These New England missionaries and their families arrived in Lahaina in the spring of 1823 at the invitation of Queen Keopuolani. They brought drastic changes to the island with the education of the natives both spiritually and scholastically. The first high school and printing press west of the Rockies was established at Lahainaluna. Built just outside of Lahaina, it now houses a museum, and is open to the public. Liholiho and his wife were the first Hawaiian royalty to visit the United States. When their travels continued to Europe, they succumbed to the measles while in London. Liholiho was succeeded by Kauikeaouli (the youngest son of Kamehameha the Great) who ruled under the title of Kamehameha the III from 1824 to 1854.

Beginning in 1819 and continuing for nearly 40 years, whaling ships became a frequent sight, anchored in the waters off Lahaina. The whalers hunted their prey north and south of the islands, off the Japanese coast, and in the Arctic. Fifty ships were sometimes anchored off Lahaina, and during the peak year of whaling, over 400 ships visited Lahaina with an additional 167 in Honolulu's harbor. Allowing 25 to 30 seamen per ship you can quickly see the enormous number of sailors who flooded the area.

While missionaries brought their Christian beliefs, the whaling men lived under their own belief that there was "No God West of the Horn." This presented a tremendous conflict between the sailors and missionaries, with the islanders caught right in the middle. After months at sea, sailors arrived in Lahaina anxious for the grog shops and native women. It was the missionaries who set up guidelines that forbade the island girls to visit the ships in the harbor. Horrified by the bare-breasted Hawaiian women, the missionary wives quickly set about to more thoroughly clothe the native ladies. The missionary women realized that their dresses would not be appropriate for these more robust woman and using their nightwear as a guideline, fashioned garments from these by cutting the sleeves off and enlarging the armholes. The muumuu was the result, and translated means "to amputate or to cut short."

In 1832, a coral fort was erected near the Lahaina harbor following an incident with the unhappy crew of one vessel. The story goes that a captain, disgruntled when he was detained in Lahaina for enticing "base women," ordered his crew to fire shots at the homes of some Lahaina area missionaries. Although the fort was demolished in 1854, remnants of the coral were re-excavated and a corner of the old fort reconstructed. It is located harborside by the Banyan Tree.

An interesting fact is reported in the 1846 Lahaina census. The count included 3,445 Hawaiians, 112 foreigners, 600 seamen, 155 adobe houses, 822 grass houses, 59 stone and wooden houses, as well as 528 dogs!

The *whaling era* strengthened Hawaii's ties with the United States economically, and the presence of the missionaries further strengthened this bond. A combination of things brought the downfall of the whaling industry: The onset of the Civil War depleted men and ships, (one Confederate warship reportedly set 24 whaling vessels ablaze), and the growth of the petroleum industry lessened the need for whale oil. Lastly, the Arctic freezes of 1871 and 1876 resulted in many ships being crushed by the ice. Lahaina, however, continues to maintain the charm and history of those bygone whaling days. (Ironically, Maui is now the headquarters for the Hawaiian Island Humpback Whale National Marine Sanctuary, the nations's 12th and the only one dedicated to one species: the humpback whale. Encompassing waters from Kaua'i to the Big Island, the Sanctuary was designated in February, 1998.)

The last monarch was Liliuokalani, who ruled from 1891 to 1893. Hawai'i became a territory of the United States in 1900 and achieved statehood in 1959.

Sugar cane brought by the first Hawaiians was developed into a major industry on Maui. Two sons of missionaries, Henry P. Baldwin and Samuel T. Alexander, as well as Claus Spreckels played notable roles and their construction of a water pipeline to irrigate the arid central isthmus of Maui secured the future of the sugar industry and other agricultural development on the island.

Pineapple, another major agricultural industry, has played an important role in the history of Maui. Historians believe that pineapple may have originated in Brazil and was introduced to the modern world by Christopher Columbus on return from his second visit to the Americas. When it arrived in the islands is uncertain, but Don Francisco de Paula y Marin writes in his diary on January 21, 1813 that "This day I planted pineapples and an orange tree." The first successful report of pineapple agriculture in Hawai'i is attributed to Captain James Kidwell, an English horticulturist. He brought the smooth cayenne variety of pineapple from Jamaica and began successfully cultivating and harvesting the fruit on O'ahu in 1886.

Since the fresh fruits perished too quickly to reach the mainland, Captain Kidwell also began the first cannery, called Hawaiian Fruit and Packing Company, which operated until 1892 when it was sold to Pearl City Fruit Company. James Dole, a young Harvard graduate, arrived on O'ahu from Boston in 1899, and by 1901 had established what has today become known as the Dole Pineapple Company.

Grove Ranch and Haleakala Ranch Company both began pineapple cultivation on Maui in 1906. Baldwin Packers began as Honolua Ranch and was owned by Henry Baldwin who started it in 1912. The Grove Ranch hired David T. Fleming as company manager and began with several acres in Haiku which soon increased to 450 acres. W. A. Clark succeeded Fleming as Grove Ranch manager and while the acreage increased, for some unknown reason the pineapples failed. For ten years the fields were leased to Japanese growers who were successful.

During these early years Haleakala Ranch Company continued to expand their acreage and to successfully produce pineapples. J. Walter Cameron arrived from Honolulu to become manager of Haleakala Ranch Company in about 1925. In 1929 the ranch division was separated from the pineapple division and the company became Haleakala Pineapple Company. In 1932 the Company and Grove Ranch merged, forming Maui Pineapple Company Limited and thirty years later in 1962, Baldwin Packers merged with Maui Pineapple Company to form what we know today as Maui Land and Pineapple. Maui Land and Pineapple continues to raise pineapples as well as develop land into the fine resort area known as Kapalua. The company owns 29,800 acres of land and uses 7,300 acres for company operations while employing approximately 1,800 people on a year-round or seasonal basis. While competition from abroad (particularly Thailand) has been fierce, Maui Land and Pineapple has chosen to maintain their market by supplying a quality product. Maui Land and Pineapple Company is the only 100% Hawaiian producer of canned pineapple in the world.

It was about 100 years ago that the first macadamia nut trees arrived from Australia. They were intended to be an ornamental tree since they had nuts that were extremely difficult to crack. It was not until the 1950's that the development of the trees began to take a commercial course. Today, some sugar cane fields are being converted to macadamia. It is a slow process, taking seven years for the grafted root (they do not grow from seed) to become a producing tree. While delicious, beware of their hazards: 1/2 ounce of nuts contains 100 calories!

The Kula area of Maui has become the center for many delicious fruits and vegetables as well as the unusual Protea flower, a native of South Africa. Wineries have also made a comeback with the success of the Tedeschi Winery at Ulupalakua. They started by producing an unusual pineapple wine followed by a champagne in 1984 and a red table wine in 1985. Be sure to also sample the very sweet Kula onions raised in this area (these are not the same as "Maui onions" that can be grown anywhere in Maui County) that are available for shipping home. In recent years coffee has proved to be a successful and popular new crop for Maui. Amfac currently has more than 500 acres (planted on a single-estate site of former sugar cane land) in Kaanapali for coffee production.

UPCOUNTRY PRODUCE

MAUI'S NAMES AND PLACES

Haiku (HAH-ee-KOO) abrupt break
Haleakala (HAH-leh-AH-kuh-LAH) house of the sun

Hali'imaile (HAH-LEE-'ee-MAH-ee-leh) maile vines spread
Hana (HAH-nuh) rainy land

Honoapiilani (HOH-noh-AH-PEE-'ee-LAH-nee) bays of Pi'ilani
Honolua (HOH-noh-LOO-uh) double bay

Hookipa (HOO-keep-pah) welcome
Iao (EE-AH-oh) cloud supreme, name of star

Kaanapali (KAH-AH-nuh-PAH-lee) land divided by cliffs
Kahana (Kuh-HAH-nuh) meaning unknown, of Tahitian origin

Kaho'olawe (kuh-Ho-'oh-LAH-veah) taking away by currents
Kahului (Kah-hoo-LOO-ee) winning

Kapalua (KAH-puh-LOO-uh) two borders
Kaupo (KAH-oo-POH) night landing

Ke'anae (keh-'uh-NAH-eh) the mullet
Keawakapu (Keh-AH-vuh-KAH-poo) sacred harbor

Kihei (KEE-HEH-ee) shoulder cape
Kula (Koo-la) open country, school

Lahaina (LAH-HAH-ee-NAH) unmerciful sun
Lana'i (LAH-NAH-ee) meaning lost

Maala'ea (MAH-'uh-LAH-eh-uh) area of red dirt
Makawao (mah-kah-wah-oh) forest beginning

Makena (Mah-KEH-nuh) abundance
Napili (NAH-PEE-lee) pili grass

Olowalu (oh-loh-wah-loo) many hills
Paia (PAH-EE-uh) noisy

Pukalani (poo-kah-lah-nee) sky opening
Ulupalakua (OO-loo-PAH-luh-KOO-uh) ripe breadfruit

Waianapanapa (WAH-ee-AH-NAH-puh-NAH-puh) glistening water
Wailea (WAH-ee-LEH-uh) water Lea (Lea was the canoe maker's goddess)

Wailua (WAH-ee-LOO-uh) two waters
Wailuku (WAH-ee-LOO-KOO) water of slaughter

HAWAIIAN WORDS - MEANINGS

alii (ah-lee-ee) chief
aloha (ah-loh-hah) greetings

hale (Hah-lay) house
hana (HAHA-nah) work

heiau (heh-ee-ah-oo) temple
ipo (ee-po) sweetheart

kai (kye) ocean
kahuna (kah-HOO-nah) teacher, priest

Kamaaina (Kah-mah-AI-nuh) native born
kane (kah-nay) man

kapu (kah-poo) keep out
keiki (kayee-kee) child

lanai (lah-nah-ee) porch or patio
lomi lomi (loh-mee-LOH-mee) to rub or massage

luau (loo-ah-oo) feast
mahalo (mah-ha-low) praise, thanks

makai (mah-kah-ee) toward the ocean
mauka (mah-oo-kah) toward the mountain

mauna (MAU-nah) mountain
mele (MAY-leh) Hawaiian song or chant

menehune (may-nay-hoo-nee) Hawaiian dwarf or elf
moana (moh-ah-nah) ocean

nani (NAH-nee) beautiful
ono (oh-no) delicious

pali (PAH-lee) cliff, precipice
paniolo (pah-nee-oh-loh) Hawaiian cowboy

pau (pow) finished
pua (POO-ah) flower

puka (POO-ka) a hole
pupus (poo-poos) appetizers

wahine (wah-hee-nay) woman
wiki wiki (wee-kee wee-kee) hurry

WHAT TO PACK

When traveling to paradise, you won't need too much. Comfortable shoes are important for all the sightseeing and shopping! Sandals are the norm for foot-wear. Dress is casual for dining. Many restaurants require men to wear sport shirts with collars, but only one or two require a tie. Clothes should be light-weight and easy care. Cotton and cotton blends are more comfortable for the tropical climate than polyesters. Shorts and bathing suits are the dress code here! A lightweight jacket with a hood or sweater is advisable for evenings and the occasional rain showers.

The only need for warmer clothes is if your plans should include hiking or camping in Haleakala Crater or seeing the sunrise. While it may start out warm and sunny, the weather can change very quickly Upcountry. Even during the daytime, a sweater or light jacket is a good idea when touring Upcountry. (The cooler weather here is evidenced on the roofs of the homes where chimney stacks can be spotted.) Tennis shoes or hiking shoes are a good idea for the rougher volcanic terrain of Haleakala or hiking elsewhere as well. Sunscreens are a must. A camera, of course, needs to be tucked in. Many visitors are taking their memories home on video tape. Binoculars are an option and may be well used if you are traveling between December and May when the whales arrive for their winter vacation. Special needs for traveling with children are discussed in the next section. Anything that you need can probably be purchased once you arrive. Don't forget to leave some extra space in those suitcases for goodies that you will want to take back home!

TRAVEL WITH CHILDREN

Traveling with children can be an exhausting experience for parents and children alike. There are a number of direct flights to Maui out of Seattle, San Francisco, Los Angeles, Chicago and Dallas, which saves stopping over in Honolulu. These flights are very popular and fill up well in advance. Young children may have difficulty clearing their ears when the plane lands. Many people don't realize that cabins are pressurized to approximately the 6,000 foot level during flight.

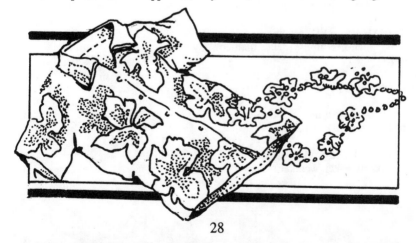

To help relieve the pressure of descent, have infants nurse or drink from a bottle, and older children may benefit from chewing gum. If this is a concern of yours, consult with your pediatrician about the use of a decongestant prior to descent.

Packing a child's goody bag for the long flight is a must. A few new activity books or toys that can be pulled out enroute can be sanity-saving. Snacks (boxes of juice or Capri Sun) can tide over the little ones at the airport or on the plane while awaiting your food/drink service. A thermos with a drinking spout works well and is handy for use during vacations. A change of clothes and a swim suit for the kids can be tucked into your carry-on bag. (Suitcases have been known to be lost or delayed.) Another handy addition is a small nightlight as unfamiliar accommodations can be somewhat confusing for children during the bedtime hours. And don't forget a strong sunscreen!

CAR SEATS: By law, children under 4 must travel in child safety seats in Hawai'i. While most rental agencies do have car seats for rent, you need to request them well in advance as they have a limited number. The one, and only, car seat we have rented had seen better days, and its design was only marginal for child safety. Prices run about $24 per week, $36 for two weeks or $6 per day. You may wish to bring your own with you. Several styles are permitted by the airlines for use in flight, or it may be checked as a piece of baggage. Or call *Kids Closet* in Lahaina - you might be able to buy a used one ($20-40), then sell it back to them when you leave! Call Tracy at (808) 661-9520.

BABYSITTING: Most hotels have some form of babysitting service which runs about $10 an hour. Check with your condo office as they sometimes have numbers of local sitters. As you can easily figure from the rates, spending much time away from your children can be costly. Consider the feasibility of bringing your own sitter, it may actually be less expensive, and certainly much more convenient (and your sitter will love you forever). This has worked well for us on numerous occasions.

With any of these agencies, or through your hotel, at least a 24 hour notice is requested. We suggest phoning them *as soon* as you have set up your plans. At certain times of the year, with the limited number of sitters available, it can be nearly impossible to get one. If you can plan out your entire vacation babysitting needs, it might also be possible to schedule the same sitter for each occasion.

A few years back there were a number of childcare services. The field has dwindled to just a couple. One reason might have been simply too much competition. Another might be the increased number of resorts and hotels that are now offering half, full day and evening childcare programs year round. A few even offer evening programs. Previously, many of the resorts had only offered them during holidays and summer months. With only a couple of exceptions, most programs don't accept children younger than four or five years.

Our recommendation for your childcare needs is *The Nanny Connection.* They began serving Maui in 1991. Owners Thomas and Patricia Seider are licensed, bonded and insured and personally interview each nanny. All nannies have CPR and First Aid certification. They offer personal pager service (at an extra charge) for those who would be more comfortable knowing the nanny could reach them.

Rates are $10 per hour for one or two children with a three hour minimum. Extra child from the same family is an additional $1 per hour, from a different family $3 per hour per child. No travel fee, no tax. Extra charge past midnight or holidays. PO Box 477, Puunene, Maui, HI 96784. (808) 875-477 or (808) 667-5777.

CRIBS: Most condos and hotels offer cribs for a rental fee that may vary from $2 to $10 per night. Companies such as *Maui Rents* (877-5827) charge $6 a day, $30 a week and $36 for two weeks. *Kids Closet* (669-0145) rents play pens for the same price with the advantage that you can take them with you to the beach or other outings. They also rent strollers ($30 week/$5 day) as well as walkers, swings or backpacks ($15 week). For an extended stay you might consider purchasing one of the wonderful folding cribs that pack up conveniently. There are several varieties which fold up into a large duffle bag. At around $60, and depending on the length of your stay, they might be worth bringing along.

EMERGENCIES: There are several clinics around the island which take emergencies or walk-in patients. Your condominium or hotel desk can provide you with suggestions, or check the phone book. Kaiser Permanente Medical Care Facilities are located in Wailuku (243-6000); Lahaina (661-7400) and now Kihei (891-3000). Doctors on Call (Hyatt, Westin or Ritz: 667-7676) and Dr. Ben Azman, (Whalers Village: 667-9721) all specialize in visitor care. See the section on Helpful Information for additional numbers. Calling 911 will put you in contact with local fire, police and ambulances.

BEACHES - POOLS: Among the best beaches for fairly young children are the Lahaina and Puunoa beaches in Lahaina, where the water is shallow and calm. Kapalua Bay is also well protected and has fairly gentle wave action. Remember to have children well supervised and wearing flotation devices for even the calmest beaches can have a surprise wave. Several of the island's beaches offer lifeguards, among these are the Kamaole I, II, and III beaches in Kihei. Kamaole III Park also has large open areas and playground equipment. In the Ma'alaea area, follow the road down past the condominiums to the public access for the beach area. A short walk down the kiawe-lined beach - to the small rock jetty with the large pipe - and you'll discover a seawater pool on either side that is well protected and ideal for the younger child. Another precaution on the beach that is easily neglected is the application of a good sunscreen; reapply after swimming.

A number of complexes have small shallow pools designed with the young ones in mind. These include the Maui Marriott, Kaanapali Alii, Sands of Kahana, Grand Wailea Resort and the Kahana Sunset. We recommend taking a life jacket or water wings (floaties). Packing a small inflatable pool for use on your lanai or courtyard may provide a cool and safe retreat for your little one. Typically Maui resorts and hotels DO NOT offer lifeguard services. Older children will be astounded by the labyrinth of pools and rivers at the Grand Wailea Resort. The Hyatt Regency has a great waterslide; the Westin Maui has recently added one. To inquire about public pools (e.g. Lahaina's Aquatic Center and the brand new Kihei community pool), lifeguard status and information on county beaches, call (808) 871-2944.

A number of children's programs at resorts around the island are open to non-resort guests. Some of these youth programs are seasonal, offered just summer, spring and Christmas holidays. Many are available year round.

ENTERTAINMENT: The 112 acre *Maui Tropical Plantation* has become one of the top visitor attractions in the state. We find it "touristy," but an interesting stop anyway. Surrounding the visitor center are acres planted in sugar cane, macadamia, guava, mango, banana, papaya, pineapple, passion fruit, star fruit, and coffee in addition to an array of flowers. There are also displays of Hawai'i's agricultural history throughout the grounds. Admission to the plantation market and restaurant are free, but there is a charge for the tram which takes visitors through the functioning mini-plantation.

Movies: There is a six-plex cinema at the Kaahumanu Center and a four-plex in Kihei's Kukui Mall. In Lahaina, there is a tri-cinema at The Wharf Cinema (Shopping) Center and another set of four theaters at the Lahaina Center. All offer a $4 admission for matinees and all-day Tuesdays. Children and Seniors are $3.75 anytime. There are also a number of video stores which rent movies and equipment. An all new 12-screen movie theater with stadium seating was expected to move into the former Woolworth's location by the end of 1998.

The Napili Kai Beach Club's Sea House Restaurant has for years been involved with local performers. They offer a Friday evening dinner show where children perform Hawaiian songs and dances. The *Napili Kai Foundation Dinner Show* costs $35 for adults and $20 for children.

Keiki Tours specializes in trips for whole families (or just children) for full or half-days tours to the Maui Ocean Center, Keiki Zoo, Hawai'i Nature Center, Hawaiian history museums, tide pools and more. The Fun Bus is equipped for fun *and* safety with seat belts, a/c, TV/VCR and complete communications equipment; guides are educated professionals with CPR and first aid training. Call (808) 874-5561 for rates or Email: mauitour@juno.com

In addition to baseball and mini-soccer fields, the new $11 million, 110-acre *Maui Central Park* (*Keopuolani*) offers playgrounds (by ages) and picnic tables (50 of them!) throughout. Proposals are under consideration that the park (or portions) be alcohol and tobacco-free. The adjoining *Maui Botanical Gardens* is undergoing extensive renovation with complete expansion and revitalization expected by the year 2000. During the process, the playground and garden are still open to the public - free. They no longer have a zoo, but it's still a great stop-off so bring along a picnic lunch! For more information see WHERE TO STAY - WHAT TO SEE, Wailuku & Kahului.

Keiki Zoo Maui will also become part of the new park by the end of 1999, but in the meantime, continues to offer tours by appointment (Tuesday-Friday 10am; Saturday noon) at their Kula facility. Interact "eyelash to eyelash" with a Hawaiian hawk or nene, a cow, owl, or Belgian horse, but watch out for Louie De Llama - he loves to kiss the ladies! Admission $2-4. Call (808) 878-2189.

The Hawai'i Nature Center at Iao Valley now offers a new interactive Science Arcade and Gift Shop. There are more than 30 exhibits focusing on Hawaii's natural history. A towering glass solarium presents an ever-changing view of the valley, rushing water flowing over impressive rock formations into touch pools and aquariums of native streamlife. Rainforest explorations, live insect and stream animal exhibits provide adventuresome and educational attractions. They also offer weekly guided "themed" hikes for children where they can go worm hunting, learn about forest plants, make a tree rubbing, have a bug bash, recycle with "garbage games and trash tricks," get wet, sing bird songs, make a mask, or just play in the mud! Hours are 10am-4pm daily and admission to the interactive center is $6 adults and $4 children. (Call for current schedule on other events.) Call (808) 244-6500. FAX (808) 244-6525.

Allow a minimum of two hours to visit the new *Maui Ocean Center* which offers tours, films, and classes on their exhibits which include an aquarium - the only one of its kind in Hawai'i; reef, turtle, and ray pools (plus an outdoor "Touch Pool"); a shark tank; and Whale Center. Oceanview restaurant plus kiosk for fast food and snacks. Open 9am-5pm. Admission: $17.50A; $12C. Phone (808) 270-7000. See RECREATION chapter for more information.

Take a self-guided tour of the coastal wetlands and sand dunes of the *Kealia Pond National Wildlife Refuge*. You'll see turtles (and whales) from the elevated vantage point - with the aid of interpretive signs along the newly constructed boardwalk (3/4 mile) on the tour trail. (808) 875-1582. Or for a guided tour, check with Arnold DeClercq of Hidden Adventures (808) 264-1423 who specializes in family adventures.

In the Lahaina-Kaanapali area, the colorful *Sugar Cane Train* runs a course several times a day along Honoapiilani Highway from Kaanapali to Lahaina. Transportation can be purchased alone or in combination with one of several excursions in Lahaina. After arrival in Lahaina, you will board a red, double decker bus for the short drive to the Lahaina Harbor. (See Land Tours for additional details.) There is time for a stroll or a visit to the Baldwin missionary home before returning to the train for the trip home or combine your train excursion with a trip to the Hawaii Experience Domed Theater.

The *Whaling Museum,* renovated and better than ever at Whalers Village in Kaanapali, is a most informative stop. And the weekly sand sculptures are a real treat! The annual *Keiki Fishing Tournament* is held during July each year in Kaanapali. The large pond in the golf course is stocked with fish for the event.

Wailea Golf Course offers seasonal specials including Parent-Child golf rates! 879-7450.

Kaanapali Kalikimaka kicks off the holiday season in early December. Arrival of Santa class, free rides on the Sugar Cane Train, puppet shows, magic, and more. Call (808) 661-3271 for dates and information.

There are plenty of great opportunities to enjoy free *Hula Shows and Polynesian revues* - some that feature keiki (child) performers. See Our Personal Best Bets for these listings - and other free things to do with kids!

The *Hawaii Experience Domed Theatre* is an interesting, educational and "cool" way to spend an hour on a warm Lahaina afternoon.

Several *submarines* and a number of boats offer the young and young at heart a chance to tour the underwater wonders of the Pacific without getting wet. The boats depart from Lahaina Harbor, see RECREATION section for more details.

A new public tour program of the *Maui Space Surveillance Complex* began in late 1997. Eight telescopes (located on the top of Haleakala) perform work for the Department of Defense in space surveillance and in optical research and development. Two tours are given the last Friday of the month and last approximately 90 minutes. Groups are limited to 16 people. Due to length of tour and altitude, visitors must be ages 13 and up. For more information call (808) 874-1601 or visit their website at: < http://ulua.mhpcc.af.mil/ ~ det3 >

Theatre Theatre Maui is a community and youth-oriented theater organization in West Maui offering summer workshops for children and teens. For more information contact Nancy Sherman (661-1168) 505 Front St., #226 (PO Box 12318), Lahaina, Maui, HI 96761. The *Maui Arts & Cultural Center* has some great opportunities to enjoy a variety of family entertainment. Among performance groups is the *Maui Academy of Performing Arts*. For schedules call (808) 244-8760. See Theater section for more information.

Kalama Park, (874-6834), Kihei's in-line hockey rink, is open to the public for rollerblading from 4-8pm on the weekends. A new skateboard park is expected to be completed there by the year 2000. *Maui Raceway* (on Mokulele Highway, just above Kihei) has drag races nine times a year (they're off December, January and June). For more information and exact schedules, given them a call at (808) 579-9493 or visit their website at < www.mrp.org >

Using the "Discover" technique (so kids can learn on their own), Ron Bass offers special *kayaking classes* with appropriately smaller-sized equipment. He also coordinates special drug-free trips for youth to pick up litter and plant trees. Call to see when the next one is scheduled. (808) 572-6299; FAX 572-6151.

Kids (and their parents) will love learning to *surf* with Goofy Foot. An easy land lesson prepares you before you get wet. The dry lessons are done in front of 505 Front Street and the wet lessons are just off shore in the gentle waves of the Lahaina Harbor. Tim offers a Goofy Foot plus. The opportunity to come back at any time and for a $10 board rental fee and you can join any existing class. Not only does this give you a chance to rest up for a day or two and try again, but you're able to give it a second chance with some supervision on-hand. There isn't any limit to the times you can return during your stay. What a deal for those teenagers! (However, they should call it "paddling" -- you'll spend more time doing that than surfing!) Tim has also just initiated large group surfing beach parties for a full day of surfing, food and games at beach. Call (808) 244-WAVE or page Tim locally at 229-6737. < WWW >

SchinDola Farms offers horse-drawn wagon rides through the "wine country" of Ulupalakua. Tues-Sun, 9am/11am/1pm. 1 1/2 hour tours, $45 (or $55 with meal at Deli.) Every third child (under 12) free with paying adult. (808) 573-9174.

Embassy Vacation Resort, in Honokowai above Kaanapali, has an 18-hole *miniature golf course* on their roof-top. The only such course on the island, it is open 9am to 10pm daily, $5 for adults, $2.50 for guests 12 and under. 661-2000. The island's only *bowling alley*, Aloha Bowling Center, is in Wailuku.

Inside *Global Books* at 71 Baldwin Avenue in Paia, you'll find *The Keiki Learning Center*, offering childcare for children ages 2-6 years. You visitors may be interested in knowing that their non-scheduled (drop-in) students will be charged $6 per hour for the class. Class sessions include story-telling and arts and crafts. Open 10am-5pm. (808) 579-8990. The local bookstores offer a wealth of wonderful *Hawaiian books* for children. There are some delightful books with factual information designed to stimulate each child with a fundamental knowledge of Hawaii's birds, reptiles, amphibians and mammals. A collection of colorful Hawaiian folk tales may be a perfect choice to take home for your own children to enjoy or as a gift for others. *Borders* bookstore in Kahului has an outstanding selection for children with a special area and "Kidstaff" to provide story telling, arrange book character visits and present special programs.

The *Paper Airplane Museum* in the Maui Mall features the unique juice can creations of the Tin Can Man along with aviation model exhibits and pictures depicting the history of aviation in the Hawaiian Islands. Tin can and paper airplane demonstrations, too! (808) 877-8916.

Upcountry Toys (Pukalani Shopping Center) is a great place to stop with the kids on your way back from the crater. They have an old-fashioned drugstore soda fountain with milk shakes, banana splits, shave ice, and freshly-made burgers. Open 9am-8pm, Monday-Friday; till 5 on Saturday.

You can't walk by *Kite Fantasy* in the Cannery without stopping to watch the swimming frog or the weasel ball. Display tables in front have a great selection of puzzles, activity books, magic tricks, and other keep-em-occupied-on-the-way-to-Hana ideas; inside are Beanie Babies, water and beach toys, dolls, and of course, kites!

Call the *Kid's Shop* in Kihei (808) 874-5437 to find out when they'll be presenting their next balloon artist, yo-yo demonstration or jumping castle. They're open till 7pm, Mon-Sat, in the Dolphin Plaza.

Maui Mike's Goofshop - The Wailuku Toy Store specializes in gags, novelties and other goofy stuff! Stop by 1500 Lower Main (at Mill St.) or call BIG-GOOF (808) 244-4663.

You'll find *keiki* (children's) menus at restaurants as diverse as Kimo's, Charthouse, Mango Cafe, Sam Choy's, Pauwela Cafe, Kobe, Buzz's Wharf, Kihei Caffe, Seahouse, Tony Roma's, Cafe Kiowai and Kincha. Polli's has keiki meals for $1 on Tuesdays, SharRon's offers child-size dinners for $1.99-3.99 (depending on age), Cascades offers both a separate keiki menu or 1/2 off/1/2 portion adult entrees, and Koho's will even cut the crusts off their "sammiches!" There are also an assortment of Burger Kings and McDonald's on the island.

Flashlights can turn the balmy Hawaiian evenings into adventures! One of the most friendly island residents is the Bufo (Boof-oh). In 1932 this frog was brought from Puerto Rico to assist with insect control in the cane fields. Today this large toad still emerges at night to feed or mate and seems to be easier to spot during the winter months, especially after rain showers. While they can be found around most condominiums, Kawiliki Park (the area behind the Luana Kai, Laule'a and several other condominium complexes with access from Waipulani Road off South Kihei Road) seems to be an especially popular gathering spot. We suggest you don't touch them, however. The secretions may cause skin irritation. We also enjoy searching for beach crabs and the African snails which have shells that may grow to a hefty five inches.

The other Hawaiian creature that cannot go without mention is the gecko. They are finding their way into the suitcases of many an island visitor, in the form of tee-shirts, sun visors and jewelry. This small lizard is a relative of the chameleon and grows to a length of three or four inches. They dine on roaches, termites, mosquitos, ants, moths, and other pesky insects. While there are nearly 800 species of geckos found in warm climates around the world, there are only about five varieties found in Hawaii. The house gecko is the most commonly found, with tiny rows of spines that circle its tail, while the mourning gecko has a smooth, satiny skin and along the middle of its back, it sports pale stripes and pairs of dark spots. The mourning gecko species is parthenogenic. That means that there are only females which produce fertile eggs -- no need for a mate! The stump-toed variety is distinguished by its thick flattened tail. The tree gecko enjoys the solitude of the forests, and the fox gecko, with a long snout and spines along its tail, prefers to hide around rocks or tree trunks. The first geckos may have reached Hawai'i with early voyagers from Polynesia, but the house gecko may have arrived as recently as the 1940s, along with military shipments to Hawaii. Geckos are most easily spotted at night when they seem to enjoy the warm lights outside your door. We have heard they each establish little territories where they live and breed so you will no doubt see them around the same area each night. They are very shy and will scurry off quickly. Sometimes you may find one living in your hotel or condo. They're friendly and beneficial animals and are said to bring good luck, so make them welcome. As for snakes, there are only two male specimens on display in the Honolulu zoo, Hawai'i has no snakes ... and they hope to keep it that way!

If you headquarter your stay near the Papakea Resort in Honokowai, you might take an adventurous nighttime reef walk. If an evening low tide does not conflict with your children's bedtime, put on some old tennis shoes and grab a flashlight. (Flashlights that are waterproof or at least water resistant are recommended.) The reef comes right into shore at the southern end of Papakea where you can walk out onto it like a broad living sidewalk. Try and pick a night when the low tide is from 9-11pm (tide information is available in the *Maui News* or call the recorded weather report) and when the sea is calm. Searching the shallow water will reveal sea wonders such as fish and eels that are out feeding. Some people looked at us strangely as we pursued this new recreation, but our little ones thought it an outstanding activity. Shoes (we recommend old sneakers) are a must as the coral is very sharp. Afterwards, be sure to thoroughly clean your shoes promptly with fresh water or they will become horribly musty smelling.

Check with your resort concierge for additional youth activities. During the summer months, Christmas holidays, and Easter, many of the resort hotels offer partial or full day activities for children. Rates range from free to $65 per day. Following are a few of the programs offered by some Maui resorts. Please be sure to check with the resort to see the current schedules, availability and prices for their children's programs.

As we mentioned previously, some of these *children's programs* are available to non-hotel or resort guests. Check to see if the Ritz-Kids at The Ritz Carlton, Kapalua still allows non-resort guests. Camp Grande at the Grand Wailea Resort & Spa will take non-resort guests. Even more good news is the fact that more and more of them appear to be heading to year-round and evening programs.

The resort programs for kids range from half day to full day, a few days a week or all week and some even offer evening programs. Each resort generally has a theme and since these change very often, we'll summarize what you might be offered. Lei making and other Hawaiiana arts and crafts, sandcastle building, nature walks, picnics, swimming, Olympic-like games, scavenger hunts and some even provide tours to places such as the Whalers Museum at Kaanapali or taking a trip on the Sugar Cane Train. Most properties tend to center their operations outside, but a few, like the Grand Wailea have very impressive indoor facilities. The following are properties which offer children's programs on a regular basis. Many include lunch and a few give the kids a free T-shirt! Call to check on current prices.

Aston Kaanapali Shores Resort features a year-round program for children ages 3-10 years. "Camp Kaanapali" is offered from 8am-3pm Monday thru Friday. A $10 initial registration covers you regardless of the length of your stay and includes a camp T-shirt. Three sessions available each day and the cost is $5 per session. Choose a morning 8-11am session, or a lunch 11am-noon session, or afternoon activities 12-3pm. Program available for resort guests only. (808) 667-2211.

Aston Wailea Resort (formerly Maui Inter-Continental) in Wailea offers the "Keiki's Club Gecko Program" for children age 5 and older. Second child in same family at half price. Activities include Hawaiian arts & crafts, and off-property tours. Special activities for holidays. Children's menus available in restaurants. The program is open to guests and non-guests. Programs Tuesday, Thursday, and Saturday. 9am-3pm. (808) 879-1922.

Embassy Vacation Resort children's program, "Beach Buddies," operates year round, seven days a week from 8:15-2:30pm. Activities are designed to keep the children ages 4-10 years entertained as well as acquainting them with the Hawaiian way of life. Daily rate includes a T-shirt and lunch. (808) 661-2000.

The Four Seasons Wailea features "Kids for all Seasons," a daily complimentary program for youths age 5-12 years with year round supervised activities from 9am-5pm. (808) 874-8000.

Grand Wailea Resort & Spa offers the most incredible 20,000 sq. foot space devoted to their youthful guests ages 4-12 years. The program is also available to non-resort guests for an additional fee. When we called to inquire about the current rate schedule, hours of operation etc. they suggested that they FAX me the information. A half mile of fax paper later... well, okay, it was only seven pages... we had enough information to start another book! They have it all covered, including handicapped children, illnesses, early or late drop offs, and even swim requirements. So here is a synopsis. (This one is pricey!) Day camp from 9am-3pm includes lunch ($65!). A half day is 9am to noon including lunch or from noon to 4pm. There is an evening camp (5-10pm including dinner), one to three times each week, depending on the season. Half days and evenings, $40. Packages are available at a special rate and must be purchased in advance. The program has structured activities in the morning and free play in the afternoon. The camp facility has a video room, arts & crafts center, special kiddie pool, and movie theater. Guests of the resort may accompany (and stay) with their children and enjoy the facilities of Camp Grande, but you still pay the child's camp fees. Ask about one hour workshops on authentic lei making, computer graphics, pottery, tile painting and more. Nanny services can be arranged. The Camp Video Arcade and Escapades are open several days a week. Candy, chips, juice, and ice cream can be purchased. Parental supervision is required for children under 10 years of age. The arcade is complimentary to hotel guests. The whale wading pool, playground & kiddieland is complimentary to hotel guests, accompanied by their children! (808) 875-1234.

Hyatt Regency Maui operates Camp Hyatt, for youth age 3-12 years, daily from 9am-3pm ($50). Camp is also offered nightly from 6pm-10pm. Evening activities include table games, movies, video games and light snacks. Cost is $10 per hour per child. (808) 661-1234.

Kaanapali Beach Hotel features a Kalo (Taro) Patch Kids program. This is offered only seasonally (summer & holidays), but is generally very inexpensive. (808) 661-0011.

Kapalua Bay Hotel and Villas offers Camp Kapalua for kids 5-12 years. The full-day program runs Monday to Friday, year-round, for Kapalua guests. Discount for second child in the same family. (808) 669-5656.

GRAND WAILEA RESORT & SPA

GENERAL INFORMATION_____
Travel with Children

Kea Lani Hotel offers "Keiki Lani" (Heavenly Kids) for youths of hotel guests age 5-11 years. This program services hotel guests year-round, seven days a week, from 9am-3pm. (808) 875-4100.

Maui Marriott Resort offers their "Kaanapali Kids," a children's activity and adventure program, Monday-Friday, year round, for guests aged 6-12 years. Marriott guests only. 8am-2pm. (808) 667-1200.

Maui Prince Hotel offers a program year-round called the "Prince Kids Club." Children ages 5-12 years can have hours of fun with activities such as bamboo pole fishing, sand castle building, pool swims, Hawaiian arts and crafts, or treasure hunts. Three sessions are offered to hotel guests throughout the day. A morning session (9 am to noon) is free. There is a fee for the afternoon session (noon until 3pm) which includes lunch. Or combine the two sessions for a full day. (808) 874-1111.

Napili Kai Beach Club offers a Keiki Club for youth ages 6-12 years during spring, summer and winter breaks. The complimentary camp is one to two hours daily, except Sunday. Activities include Hawaiian games, hula, hot dog barbecues and nature walks. (808) 669-6271

Renaissance Wailea Beach Resort (formerly Stouffer) provides "Camp Wailea" for kids 5 - 12 years. Currently offered five days a week, 9am-1pm. Lunch included. 1-800-468-3571 or (808) 879-4900.

The Ritz-Carlton, Kapalua provides a children's program for hotel and non-hotel guests. One of the few to do so. (We'd recommend that non-hotel guests call to confirm). Their "Ritz Kids" program explores the earth, sea and sky with full-day and half-day programs for keikis 5-12 years of age. The theme varies each day of the week with topics such as Whale Day, Ocean Day or Volcano Day setting the focus for the activities. The program is 9am-4pm daily, $15 for resort guests. The half-day program, from 9am-noon or from 1-4pm is complimentary for resort guests. (808) 669-6200.

Sheraton Maui offers their Keiki Aloha program each summer for children 5-12 years of age. (808) 661-0031.

Wailea Golf Course has golf instruction, summer only, for 6-12 year olds. The 6 week program runs two hours per session. (808) 879-2966.

Wailea Resort Company offers junior tennis clinics and golf lessons during various weeks in the summer months, as well as tennis camps. Ages 4-13 years, the program charges a registration fee and then a charge per each session. Some single lessons or play. (808) 879-1958.

Westin Maui offers Keiki Kamp Kaanapali for 5-12 year olds. The program runs daily from 9am-3pm, $45. An evening program is also offered at $20. Discount for siblings. (808) 667-2525.

The Whaler on Kaanapali Beach provides a program during summer, Christmas, and spring break sessions. Call for current information. (808) 661-4861.

TRAVEL TIPS FOR THE PHYSICALLY IMPAIRED

Make your travel plans well in advance and inform hotels and airlines when making your reservations that you are a person with a disability. Bring along your medical records in the event of an emergency. It is recommended that you bring your own wheelchair and notify the airlines in advance that you will be transporting it. There are no battery rentals available on Maui. Additional information can be obtained from the State Commission on Persons with Disabilities, c/o State Department of Health, 54 High St., Wailuku, Maui 96793 (984-8219 V-TT; FAX 808-984-8222). Or call the State Commission on Persons with Disabilities on O'ahu: 808-586-8121 V-TT; FAX 808-586-8129. They offer a book entitled *Aloha Guide to Accessibility* which is divided into sections that provides services information and advises persons with disabilities on the accessibility features of hotels, beaches, parks, shopping centers, theaters & auditoriums, and visitor attractions. They will send specific sections or the entire guide for the cost of postage. ($3-5 per section; $15 complete).

ARRIVAL AND DEPARTURE: On arrival at the Kahului airport terminal, you will find the building easily accessible for mobility impaired persons. Parking areas are located in front of the main terminal for disabled persons. Restrooms with handicapped stalls (male and female) are also found in the main terminal.

TRANSPORTATION: There is no public transportation on Maui (although there is an airport shuttle) and taxi service can be spendy. For short hops, the Lahaina-Kaanapali route of the "West Maui Shopping Express" has a wheelchair accessible bus. The only car rental companies providing hand controls are Avis and Hertz. See the Rental Car listing for phone numbers. They need some advance notice to install the equipment. Accessible Vans of Hawai'i offers wheelchair accessible van rentals with hand controls, and delivery and pick up of island visitors. Phone 1-800-303-3750, (808) 879-5521 or FAX 879-0649. Hawai'i Care Van Shuttle and Tour (Kapalua Executive Transportation) at 10 Hoohui Rd., #306, Lahaina, HI 96761 offers airport transports island-wide and tour services. Phone (808) 669-2300 or FAX (808) 669-3811. The Maui Economic Opportunity Center operates a van with an electric lift for local residents.

ACCOMMODATIONS: Each of the major island hotels offer one or more handicapped rooms including bathroom entries of at least 29" to allow for wheelchairs. Due to the limited number of rooms, reservations should be made well in advance. Information on condominium accessibility is available from the Commission on Persons with Disabilities (see above). Accessible Vans of Hawai'i also has condo listings as well as additional information on the availability of roll-in showers and wheelchair-accessible bathrooms.

ACTIVITIES: Accessible Vans of Hawai'i and Hawai'i Care Van Shuttle and Tour offer wheelchair accessible touring and can provide information on recreational activities for the traveler. Among the options are wheelchair tennis or basketball, bowling and swimming. Contact them in advance of your arrival. Wheelchair access to some of the tourist attractions may be limited. One of the few boats to offer access for the handicapped is *The Pride of Maui*.

Maui County continues to make the beaches more accessible for disabled travelers with handicapped designations at beach parking lots, sidewalks and curb cuts, comfort stations, picnic tables, showers, and an accessible pathway onto the beach. Currently beaches that have been made accessible include Kamaole I, II and III, Hanaka'o'o Beach and Kanaha Beach.

Renaissance Wailea is one of the few resorts that has been wheelchair-accessible since its inception (as the Westin Wailea!), but with ADA requirements now governing new and remodeled shopping centers, new recreation complexes like the Maui Ocean Center and Maui Central Park, and renovation of sightseeing destinations (like Lahaina's Front Street), Maui is becoming more accessible than ever before! American-Hawaii now offers fully handicapped-accessible suites on its *Independence* cruise ship.

Ron Bass is an independent tour guide who specializes in kayaking and snorkeling for the disabled. His special equipment includes three-person kayaks, view boards and beach-access wheelchairs. Call (808) 572-6299 or FAX (808) 572-6151. <http://maui.net/ ~kayaking> Ron also operates "Wilderness Wish," a non-profit organization that assists disabled folks to experience new adventures by discovering and exploring out-of-the-way places.

MEDICAL SERVICES AND EQUIPMENT: Maui Memorial Hospital is located in Wailuku and there are also good clinics in all areas of the island. Check the local directory. Several agencies can assist in providing personal care attendants, companions, and nursing aides while on your visit. Maui Center for Independent Living (808) 242-4966 provides personal care attendants, as does Aloha International Employment Service (808) 871-6373, and Interim Health Care (808) 877-2676.

Lahaina Pharmacy (Old Lahaina Center) (808) 661-3119 has wheelchairs, crutches, canes, and walkers. Gammie Home Care, located in the Kahului Industrial Center, 292 Alamaha, Kahului, HI 96732, can provide medical equipment rentals, from walking aides to bathroom accessories or wheelchairs as well as oxygen services (808) 877-4032 or FAX (808) 877-3359. It is again recommended that you contact them well in advance of your arrival.

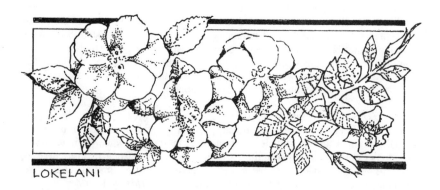

LOKELANI

Accessible Vans of Hawai'i is the only travel, tour and activity agency on Maui that specializes in assisting the disabled traveler. "Imagination is your limit" they report when it comes to the activities they offer. They can assist in making reservations at a condominium or hotel to fit the needs of the traveler, make airport arrangements including wheelchair-accessible vans with lifts and arrange for personal care such as attendants, pharmacists, or interpreters. They can arrange for rental cars with hand controls, make airport arrangements including ticketing, and provide "doctors on call." Owner David McKown is a one-stop shopping connection for the disabled traveler and the Maui (and State of Hawaii) Representative for Accessible Vans of America. As a quadriplegic, their Travel Counselor, Vicky Allen, can understand and assist you with accommodations, activities and personal care needs. (Call her direct at (808) 875-9599; FAX (808) 875-6016.) As for recreation, how about snorkeling, scuba diving, helicopter tours, bowling, golf, horseback riding, boating, luaus, tennis (disabled opponent available), tours, jet skiing, or ocean kayaking! Wedding and honeymoon arrangements, too. Accessible Vans of Hawai'i can also provide sand/beach wheelchairs with big inflatable rubber tires. Write or call for their free brochure: 186 Mehani Circle, Kihei, Maui, HI 96753. (808) 879-5521 or 1-800-303-3750 for reservations. FAX: (808) 879-0649.

Hearing Impaired: Both the Wallace and Consolidated movie theater chains have "assisted listening devices" available at their Lahaina, Kihei, and Kahului theaters. The headsets increase the volume (or decrease the noise!) on an individual basis. The Maui Arts & Cultural Center also provides the headsets for their plays and concerts and, as one of Maui's newer constructions, is completely ADA accessible. Steve Marceno, CSC, is a nationally certified sign language interpreter who can assist the deaf or hard of hearing on an individual basis or as part of a group to interpret guided tours, boat trips, luaus or even weddings! (Although it does seem almost redundant to have sign language at a luau when that's the language of hula anyway!) You can reach him at (808) 878-3020 (Voice or TTY) or write: 109-A Akea Place, Kula, HI 96790.

Vision Impaired: New legislation will allow seeing eye dogs to travel to Hawai'i without quarantine providing that current proof of vaccinations is provided.

ESPECIALLY FOR SENIORS

More and more businesses are beginning to offer special savings to seniors. RSVP booking agency offers special rates for seniors who book their accommodations through them. They are listed in the Rental Agents section of our accommodations chapter. Remember that AARP members get many travel discounts for rooms, cars and tours. Whether it is a boating activity, an airline ticket or a condominium, be sure to ask about special senior rates. And be sure to travel with identification showing your birthdate. Check the yellow pages when you arrive on Maui for the senior discount program logo. Look for a black circle with white star in the ads.

A number of airlines have special discounts for seniors. Some also have a wonderful feature which provides a discount for the traveling companion that is accompanying the senior. Coupon books for senior discounts are also available from a number of airline carriers.

Pleasant Hawaiian Holidays features a "Makua Club" with special rates for seniors. Outrigger offers a "Fifty-Plus Program;" Aston calls theirs the "Senior Sun Club." Maui Condo & Home, Destination Resorts Hawaii, Kumulani Vacations, and Condominium Rentals Hawaii offer economy rates and discounts for seniors. Three Kihei properties - Kamaole Sands, Maui Coast Hotel, and Maui Oceanfront Inn - offer discounts and senior packages. Kaanapali Beach Hotel offers seniors a 10% discount based on room availability and a 30 day advance registration.

Elder Hostel Hawai'i arranges inexpensive housing in college dorms during summer months along with special interest classes and sports activities. Call (808) 262-8942 on O'ahu for information on Maui accommodations. For kayaking and snorkeling, Ron Bass (on Maui) (808) 572-6299 works with them to provide senior excursions addressing their special needs.

Maui Marriott offers a 20% AARP discount (food only) at all their restaurants (Moana Terrace, Nikko, Lokelani and Kau Kau Grill) as well as their luau ($50 instead of $62.50); SharRon's in Paia has senior-priced versions of the regular menu items; Mango Cafe & Pie Shop will take off 10% and Cascades at the Hyatt Regency offers seniors 1/2 portions for 1/2 off. Denny's and IHOP also have senior specials. Ask about senior discounts before you book any luau, rental car, or excursion!

Maui movie theaters are $3.50 for seniors anytime; they also have "assisted listening devices" to pump up the volume - or turn it down if it's too loud!

Kaunoa Senior Services in Paia offers programs (line dancing, craft classes, tours) and services for residents and visitors over 55. Call (808) 243-7308 for schedules and more information.

WEDDINGS - HONEYMOONS

If a Hawaiian wedding (or a renewal of vows) is in your dreams, Maui can make them all come true. While the requirements are simple, here are a few tips, based on current requirements at time of publication, for making your wedding plans run more smoothly. We advise you to double check the requirements as things change!

Both bride and groom must be over 18 years of age. (16 years old with written consent from parents or legal guardians.) Birth certificates are not required, but you do need a proof of age such as a driver's license or passport. You do not need proof of citizenship or residence. If either partner has been divorced, the date, county and state of finalization for each divorce must be verbally provided to the licensing agent. If a divorce was finalized within the last three months, then a decree must be provided to the licensing agent.

One wedding agency informed us that your personal vows for a Catholic wedding require special arrangements between your home priest and the Maui priest. If both bride and groom are practicing Catholics, the Church requires that you marry within the church building, unless you are granted special permission from the Bishop in Honolulu.

A license must be purchased in person in the state of Hawaii. Call the Department of Health (808) 984-8210 for the name of a licensing agent in the area where you will be staying. Both bride and groom must appear in person before the agent. The fee is currently $50. There is no waiting period once you have the license, but the license is valid for only 30 days. Check with the Chamber of Commerce in Kahului (808) 871-7711 for information regarding a pastor. Many island pastors are very flexible in meeting your needs, such as an outdoor location, etc. (For $7 you can buy a package with a booklet and information on planning a wedding.)

For copies of current requirements and forms, write in advance to the State of Hawaii, Department of Health, Marriage License Section, PO Box 3378, Honolulu, HI 96801. (808) 586-4545. You can also call the Maui Visitors Bureau (808) 244-3530 for a copy of the requirements as well as information on free public wedding locations at Hawai'i State and National Parks and how to book a marriage ceremony with a judge. (The Courthouse is located at 2145 Main St. in Wailuku.) Call 1-800-525-MAUI for a booklet on "Honeymoons."

As for other wedding items: Arthur's *Limousine Service* is at 296A Alamaha St., Kahului, Maui, HI 96732. Call (808) 871-5555, 1-800-345-4667 or FAX (808) 877-3333. *Classy Taxi* (808) 661-3044 has "gangster-style" limos (circa 1929) and just acquired a 1933 Rolls Royce. Also try *Town & Country* (808) 572-3400 or *Star Limousine* (808) 875-6900. Formal wear rentals for the gents in your party can be obtained from *Gilbert's Formal Wear* at 104 Market St. in Old Wailuku Town, 244-4017. Rental wedding gowns, formal dresses, and bridesmaid dresses are available through *Maui Fashion Center* at 341 N. Market St., Wailuku HI 96793, 244-3875. *Hawai'i Video Memories* will capture your special day on video tape. 343-C Hanamau St., Kahului, HI 96732, (808) 871-5788. If you'd like to have your wedding catered, see "Catering" at the beginning of the RESTAURANT section. For something unusual, call Charle's House of Miniatures (808) 875-1315 for custom cake top wedding dolls that reflect the real bridal couple's looks, costumes or lifestyle accessories!

Over 125 members of the Hawai'i Wedding Professionals Association are listed in their attractive, informative 12-page booklet, the *Maui Wedding Planner*. Features on island locations, leis/flowers, and planning time-lines are offered along with advice on choosing everything from ministers to photographers. For a free copy of the booklet and a brochure, call 1-800-291-0110 or (808) 572-7898; Email: married@maui.net or visit their website at <http://www.maui.net/~married>

A basic package costs anywhere from $300 - $400. Although each company varies the package slightly, it will probably include assistance in choosing a location and getting your marriage license, a minister and an assortment of extras such as champagne, limited photography, cake, leis, and a bridal garter. Videotaping, witnesses, or music are usually extra.

A Dream Wedding Maui Style (808) 661-1777 or 1-800-743-2777 FAX: (808) 667-2042 <WWW> 143 Dickenson St. #201, Lahaina, HI 96761. One-on-one service, from simple to exotic. Vow renewals. Tracy Flanagan, Consultant.

A Romantic Maui Wedding (808) 874-6444 or 1-800-808-4144 FAX: (808) 879-5525. <WWW> PO Box 307, Kihei, HI 96753. Private oceanfront wedding location. (Video available.) Can also provide formal wear.

A Wedding Just for Two (808) 669-4400 or 1-888-JUS-4-TWO (587-4896). FAX: 669-0794; <WWW> 880 Front St., #587, Lahaina, HI 96761 A spiritual wedding experience sponsored by The Living Ministry. Begin with a Hawaiian lei exchange; close with a blessing. Contact Reverend Beverly Powers.

A Wedding Made in Paradise (808) 879-3444 or 1-800-453-3440 US mainland. PO Box 986, Kihei, Maui, HI 96753. <WWW> Contact Alicia Bay Laurel, the "Martha Stewart of wedding planners."

A White Orchid Wedding (808) 242-VOWS(8697), 1-800-240-9336, FAX (808) 242-6853, PO Box 2696, Wailuku, HI 96793. Have your wedding Alone at Sunset, at an Historic Hawaiian Church or where the Lava Meets the Sea. They can also arrange travel, activities and vow renewals. Contact Carolee Higashiro.

John Pierre's Photographic Studio (808) 667-7988, 143 Dickenson St., Lahaina, Maui, HI 96761. Eighteen years of providing wedding photo packages; John Pierre recently won the Fuji Masterpiece award for his photography.

Now and Forever Maui Weddings (808) 661-5583; 1-800-3272436; PO Box 12380, Lahaina 96761. Deluxe packages from $785-1,975 (for a complete Hawaiian-style wedding) or start with a basic Kuuipo Package at $395 and add from a list of additional services (kind of like a wedding pizza!). Owner Theresa Tuipelehake can assist with everything - even hair & makeup.

Royal Hawaiian Carriage Co. (808) 669-1100 has four carriages, six passengers each and eight trained draft type horses which pull the carriages. The company does wedding transportation to and from the ceremony and/or reception and provides pick up island-wide. They are based at The Ritz-Carlton, Kapalua. Minimum charge is $150 per hour, depending on the location and the number of carriages. PO Box 10581, Lahaina, HI 96761. They also provide restaurant transportation, horse-drawn picnics and other romantic excursions.

Royal Hawaiian Weddings (808) 875-8569 or 1-800-659-1866 US or Canada, FAX: (808) 875-0623 <WWW> PO Box 424, Puunene, HI Andrea Thomas and Janet Renner have been putting together ceremonies for the most special occasions since 1977. Choose from dazzling beachside sunsets, private oceanfront settings, tropical gardens, sleek yachts or remote helicopter landings. Name your dream.

Simply Married (Weddings the Maui Way) (808) 877-7711, 2718 Iolani St., Pukalani, HI 96768. Owners Ken & Judy Grimes offer a choice of being "Simply Married" ($150) or taking a helicopter to a secluded waterfall ($3,000). Both are ordained ministers: Ken (Lutheran); Judy (Unity). Ken is also the president of the Hawai'i Wedding Planners Association.

Special Services and Accommodations (808) 244-5811, 252A Awapuhi Place, Wailuku, Maui, HI 96793. Burt and Linda Freeland offer a range of wedding services in traditional or remote locations.

Tropical Gardens of Maui (808) 244-3085, RR 1, Box 500, Wailuku, Maui, HI 96793. They provide a garden area with waterfalls and a gazebo in the Iao Valley. $150-200.

The social directors of the major resorts can assist you with your wedding plans and there are a variety of locations on the grounds of these beautiful resorts to set the scene for your very special wedding:

Grand Wailea (808) 875-1234. The extraordinary Grand Wailea has constructed a seaside wedding chapel on their grounds. The picturesque white chapel features stained-glass windows, designed by artist Yvonne Cheng, that depict a royal Hawaiian wedding. Woods of red oak, teak and cherry dominate the interior which is accented by three hand-crafted chandeliers from Murano, Italy. Outside the chapel is a flower-filled garden with brass-topped gazebos. A beautiful indoor location for your wedding!

Hyatt Regency (808) 661-1234. A wedding gazebo was added as part of an $11 million renovation in 1996. Designed from ohia wood from the Big Island, it is set amid tropical Hawaiian gardens and waterways.

Royal Lahaina Resort (808) 661-3611. Rows of pink and white hibiscus line the walkways leading to the cottage courtyard and wedding gazebo that features six open air windows. The Royal Lahaina resort has also introduced a unique wedding custom: they provide stepping stones engraved with the bride and groom's name and wedding date. Wedding coordinator, Diana Smith, notes that they hope to someday have all of the walkways paved with these stones.

The Westin Maui (808) 667-2525, Kaanapali Beach, has their own resident Director of Romance who will assist you with your wedding and honeymoon plans - even if you want to be married while parasailing or scuba diving! For more traditional romantics, the release of 2 to 40 white wedding doves from white wicker baskets begins at $125. (Their homing instinct returns them safely back Upcountry upon release.)

For a shipboard wedding see information on *American Hawai'i Cruises* at the end of the *Getting There* chapter.

HELPFUL INFORMATION

INFORMATION BOOTHS: Booths located at the shopping areas can provide helpful information and lots of brochures! (Look for the new wallet-size mini-brochures that are purse and pocket friendly.) Brochure displays are everywhere.

MAUI VISITORS BUREAU: 1727 Wili Pa Loop, PO Box 580, Wailuku, Maui, HI 96793. Phone (808) 244-3530, 1-800-525-MAUI or FAX (808) 244-1337.

BANKS: Basic hours are 8:30am-3pm, but some are open until 4 or 5pm. Most will cash U.S. traveler's checks with a picture ID.

CREDIT CARDS: Many small condominiums still do not accept any form of credit card payment, but stores and hotels almost always do. For lost or stolen credit cards phone: American Express 1-800-528-4800. VISA: 1-800-336-8472. Mastercard: 1-800-627-8372.

TIME: You'll find that Hawai'i has not discovered daylight savings time. However, they are in a different time zone. During "standard time" in the continental U.S. (November thru March) Hawai'i is two hours behind the Pacific time zone. Because they don't switch to daylight savings time, from April-October they are three hours behind Pacific time. You may refer to "Hawaiian Time" or "Maui Time" -- these local phrases often refer not to the hour, but the lack of punctuality!

SALES TAX: A sales tax of 4.167 is added to all purchases made in Hawai'i. There is an additional room-use tax added onto your hotel or condominium bill.

HOLIDAYS: Holidays unique to the state of Hawai'i are: March 26 Prince Kuhio Day. June 11th Kamehameha Day. August 21 Admissions day.

RADIO: Our favorite, KPOA 93.5FM/92.7FM, plays great old and new Hawaiian music. If you have an audio card for your computer, you can listen anywhere in the world at < www.mauigateway.com\koa > and catch the local disk jockeys "talking story"! KLHI ("The Point") at 101.1FM offers adult alternative rock; KKUA 90.7AM has Hawai'i Public Radio and classical music; KDLX 94.3FM has country; KAOI(FM) on either 95.1 (or Upcountry 96.7) has contemporary rock; KPMW 105.5 FM plays Philippine music; KMVI 98.3FM has classic rock; KNUI 99.9 FM offers light rock; and KNUQ ("Q") 103.7 has contemporary hits. On the AM dial, KMVI has oldies at 550; KNUI 900 plays adult contemporary; KAOI 1110 AM has news, talk, and sports; and KUAU 1570 AM - news & information. KONI 104.7 FM not only has "Hot" adult contemporary music, but offers a bit of trivia: The station is owned by Ivan Dixon who was a regular on *Hogan's Heroes* and directed both *Rockford Files* and *Magnum P.I.*!

TELEVISION: The Paradise Network, shown island-wide on Channel 7, is designed especially with visitors in mind. Information is provided on recreation, real estate, shopping, restaurants, history, culture, and art. Channel 6, the Golf Channel, features golf information, interviews with pros, video lessons, and special events and tournaments. A service of Hawaiian Cable Vison, it is broadcast only in West Maui.

PERIODICALS: Some of Maui's free visitor publications have self-explanatory titles (*MENU, Maui Menus, Best Things to do on Maui, Lahaina Historical Guide, 101 Things to do on Maui, Homes & Land, Real Estate Maui Style, "The Best" Guidebook*, and the regional "Beach Resort Guides"); peruse the others (*This Week, Maui Gold, Guide to Maui, Maui Quick Guide, Maui Magazine, Today,* and *Maui Visitor*) to find maps, shuttle schedules, entertainment calendars, shopping tips, activity directories, etc. They all offer lots of advertising, but most do have coupons which will give you discounts on everything from meals to sporting activities to clothing. It may save you a bit to search through these before making your purchases. *Maui No Ka Oi* is Maui's only "real" magazine- a glossy quarterly ($3.25) with columns and features on people, politics, business, lifestyles, current events, environment, history & culture.

There are also a number of newspaper-style publications which offer helpful and interesting information: *The Maui Bulletin* - This is a free newsprint booklet with classified ads and television listings. *South Shore Weekly* - Free weekly. Less touristy, more local stories. *Haleakala Times* - Free regional newspaper serving the Upcountry area. *Maui Time* - Free bi-weekly on music, sports & art (Surfing and live entertainment are highlighted, dude!) *Lahaina News* - A small weekly newspaper. It contains local and West Maui news, columns and lots of advertisements. Fee is 25 cents. *Maui News* - This is the primary Maui newspaper, published Monday-Friday and Sunday, available for 50 cents, and $1.50 for the larger Sunday edition. A good source of local information. The Thursday *Scene* supplement has entertainment and dining news.

WEBSITES: As cyberspace continues to boom, this is a new category for our guide! We have intermingled some websites throughout the text. However, we have determined it impossible to list the website for every business. Instead, we are using the code <WWW> to indicate that they do have a website. Either searching the net or calling the business for their website address are two options if you are interested in viewing it. For rental agents, check the RENTAL AGENT listing at the end of the Accommodation chapter for websites of those that offer them. E-mail addresses, however, are more difficult to find. So, we have included e-mail addresses throughout the text for some business as space allows. Following are some general websites that might be of interest to you! These will have links to assist you with other information.(One that we know will be helpful is <http://www.infomaui.com> a website directory with detailed descriptions and over 500 links to Maui web pages. It's kind of an on-line guidebook that includes Things To Do, Places to See, Shopping and an interactive Q&A section.) The "<" ">" indicates the beginning and end of a URL.

Haddon Holidays is one of many companies that offer packages to Hawaii. You can visit their website at <http://www.haddon/com> *Pleasant Hawaiian Holidays* has a site at <http://www.2hawaii.com> or *Hawaiian Hotels & Resorts* at <http://www.HawaiiHotels.com> And you can reach *Marc Resorts* at <http://www.marcresorts.com>

Concierge Connection offers complimentary advice, information, and recommendations on all aspects of your Maui vacation. Email them with your questions at <connect@maui.net>. From the mainland phone 1-800-961-9196. When on Maui reach them at 875-9366. <WWW>

Here are some additional Maui related websites:
Maui Online home: < http://maui.net/ ~ mol/ >
Maui Net home: < http://www.maui.net/home.html >
Tom Barefoot's Tours: < http://www.maui.net/ ~ barefoot >
Jon's Maui web page: < http://members.aol.com/Derm1/index.html >
Hawaii Pans and Picks: < http://screenmagic.com/hawaii/ >
Jack's Maui Fun page: < http://www.maui.net/ ~ sizzle/mauifun.html >
Activity Owners Organization: < http://www.maui.org >

You might be interested in checking airline flight schedules and prices on the internet. With some, you can even book your reservation.

American Airlines: < http://www.americanair.com >
Continental Airlines: < http://www.flycontinental.com >
Delta Airlines: < http://www.delta-air.com >
Northwest Airlines: < http://www.nwa.com >
United Airlines: < http://www.ual.com >
Aloha Airlines: < http://www.alohaair.com/aloha-air/ >
Hawaiian Airlines: < http://www.hawaiianair.com

EMERGENCIES: There are several clinics around the island which take emergencies or walk-in patients. Your condominium or hotel desk can provide you with suggestions, or check the phone book. Kaiser Permanente Medical Care Facilities are located in Wailuku (243-6000); Lahaina (661-7400) and now Kihei (891-3000). Doctors on Call (Hyatt, Westin or Ritz: 667-7676) and Dr. Ben Azman, (Whalers Village: 667-9721) all specialize in visitor care. See the section on Helpful Information for additional numbers. Calling 911 will put you in contact with local fire, police and ambulances.

SUN SAFETY: The sunshine is stronger in Hawai'i than on the mainland, so a few basic guidelines will ensure that you return home with a tan, not a burn. Use a good lotion with a sunscreen, reapply after swimming and don't forget the lips! Be sure to moisturize after a day in the sun and wear a hat to protect your face. Exercise self-control and stay out a limited time the first few days, remembering that a gradual tan will last longer. It is best to avoid being out between the hours of noon and three when it is the hottest. Be cautious of overcast days when it is very easy to become burned unknowingly. Don't forget that the ocean acts as a reflector and time spent in it equals time spent on the beach.

FOR YOUR PROTECTION: Do not leave valuables in your car, even in your trunk. Many rental car companies urge you to not lock your car as vandals cause extensive and expensive damage breaking the locks. Many companies also warn not to drive on certain roads (Ulupalakua to Hana and the unpaved portion of Hwy. 34) unless you are willing to accept liability for all damages.

TELEPHONE BASICS: The area code for the entire state is (808). Calls anywhere on Maui are considered local calls. At a pay phone it will cost you twenty-five cents. If you are calling another island, you must do so by dialing 1-808-plus the phone number and it is long distance. Note that most resorts charge between seventy-five cents and one dollar for each local call you make and an additional surcharge for long distance.

HELPFUL PHONE NUMBERS:

EMERGENCIES: Police - Ambulance - Fire 911

NON-EMERGENCY POLICE:
    Lahaina 661-4441
    Hana 248-8311
    Wailuku 244-6340

Civil Defense Agency 243-7285
Poison Control (on O'ahu) 1-800-362-3585
Helpline (suicide & crisis center) 244-7407
Red Cross 244-0051
Consumer Protection 984-8244
Concierge Connection 875-9366
Visitor Complaint Hotline (Activity Owners Association) . 871-7947
Directory Assistance:
    Local . . . . (1) 411
    Inter-island . . . . 1-(808)-555-1212
    Mainland . . . . 1-(area code)-555-1212
Hospital (Maui Memorial):
    Information 242-2036
    Switchboard 244-9056
Camping Permits:
    State Parks 984-8109
    County Parks 243-7389
Maui Visitors Bureau 244-3530
Time of Day 242-0212
Information - County of Maui (Gov't info & complaint) . . 243-7587
Haleakala National Park Information (recording) 572-4400
Ohe'o Headquarters Ranger Station (10am-4pm) 248-7375
Lahaina Town Action Committee 667-9175
Baldwin Home (9am-5pm) 661-3262
Weather:
    Maui 877-5111
    Marine (also tides, sunrises, sunsets) 877-3477
    Recreational Area (Haleakala) 871-5054

For toll-free access to state agencies on O'ahu (numbers beginning with 586), dial 984-2400 then the last 5 digits of the O'ahu number (beginning with 6) followed by the # sign.

Check the *Aloha Pages* in the front of the phone book for various hotline numbers to call for community events, entertainment, etc. on Maui. While the call is free, the companies pay to be included, so information is biased.

GETTING THERE

ARRIVAL AND DEPARTURE TIPS! During your flight to Honolulu, the airline staff will provide you with a visitor information sheet. This is used by the Hawai'i Visitors Bureau to track the number of visitors and their island destinations. This is also where you must report any animals, fruits, vegetables or plants that will need to be inspected upon arrival in Honolulu.

AGRICULTURAL INSPECTION: You haven't even arrived, but we'd like to advise you of this to ensure you'll be prepared when you return to the airport to head home. On your return, you will have to take your checked as well as carry-on baggage through agricultural inspection. Where your luggage will be inspected will depend upon your travel plans. If you are checking baggage at the Kahului airport which will be transferred directly to your connecting flight in Honolulu, then you will need to go through the agricultural inspection at the main entrance of the airport before proceeding to the airline ticketing counter to check in. Don't bother checking your carry-on baggage at this point, as you will just have to do it again in Honolulu. When you arrive in Honolulu and begin trekking from your inter-island flight to your mainland carrier, almost mystically an agricultural inspection center will appear. Don't bother looking, they seem to just find you! (In case this is your first trip, they look like a "regular" airport baggage security center.) At this point you will need have your carry-on baggage inspected. You'll be amazed to see the apples, oranges, and other fruits stacked up on the agricultural inspection centers. Even though they may have originally come from the mainland US, they will not pass inspection to get back there! Okay items include: Maui onions, pineapples, and preinspected protea, anthurium starts, ti plants and orchids. But forget taking any kind of citrus, fresh mangos, and certain flowers. Fruit can be purchased in inspected and sealed cartons from reputable island retailers. Generally, you will not have trouble with most flowers and/or leis. If you are unsure what is transportable, contact the U.S. Department of Agricultural at (808) 871-5656.

AIRLINE INFORMATION: The best prices on major air carriers can generally be arranged through a reputable travel agent who can often secure air or air-with-car packages at good prices by volume purchasing. Prices can vary considerably so comparison shopping is a wise idea. Be sure to ask about senior citizen and companion fare discounts. Another alternative is to book a package trip through one of several agencies which specializes in Hawai'i travel. While some use major airlines, others use charter services.

"Airfare Only" is available through *Sunquest* (on their Sun Country Charters). These prices are incredibly good values, but on the downside you have to depart from their westcoast gateway, Los Angeles 1-800-357-2400. *Pleasant Hawaiian Holidays* also offers air only and uses commercial carriers including Delta Airlines, Hawaiian Airlines, United Airlines and American TransAir.

Creative Leisure 1-800-426-6367, (808) 778-1800. While you may not find the most inexpensive packages, Creative Leisure utilizes moderate to more expensive, higher end condominiums and hotels with about 30 properties available on Maui. They offer the advantage of traveling any day you choose and the option of staying as long as you want. Rates are for the entire unit, not per person.

Year-round discount airfares are available on United and you will receive full Mileage Plus credit for all United Airlines and Aloha Airlines travel booked through them. TravelGuard insurance is also available. Sample prices include accommodation plus rental car and taxes:

Pleasant Hawaiian Holidays 1-800-242-9244. Founded in 1959 as Pleasant Travel Service in Point Pleasant, New Jersey, Edward Hogan and his company have grown and expanded to provide a range of airfare, air only and land only options. They work in conjunction with American TransAir direct to Maui and Honolulu from L.A. and San Francisco. They also utilize Hawaiian Airlines, United and Delta. Rental cars also available. < www.2hawaii.com > They work with the following properties: Kahana Beach Condos, Kamaole Sands, Maui Park, Paki Maui, Maui Eldorado, Kaanapali Beach Hotel, Royal Kahana, Maui Lu, Maui Islander, Kaanapali Shores, Lahaina Shores, Mahana, Marriott, Napili Shores, Papakea, Royal Lahaina Resort, Sheraton Maui, Aston Wailea, Embassy Vacation Resort, Hyatt Regency Maui, Kaanapali Alii, Kea Lani, Kapalua Bay Hotel and Villas, Whaler, Maui Prince, Renaissance, Ritz Carlton, Grand Wailea, and Four Seasons. Pleasant has just started packaging suites ($115-5,000!) and their new Concierge Service can arrange anything from fruit baskets to tee times. Escorted 3 and 4 day tours are available. A $35 fee will waive any cancellation or penalties should you have to adjust your travel plans. Their "Last Minute Desk" is for those of you trying to find space on short notice.

Sunquest Holidays 1-800-357-2400 - isn't the new kid on the block, but they are new to serving Hawai'i bound vacationers. If you are from the midwest, you might be familiar with Sun Country which began in 1983 and has been flying to exotic Caribbean destinations. In the spring of 1997 they added Hawai'i, utilizing Los Angeles as their gateway to the Pacific. This means that if you live in the Southern California area you might get a great deal, but the rest of us have to make our own travel arrangements to the LAX airport. They do, however, fly (DC-10's) every day of the week which allows you to customize the length of your vacation stay. Land only, air only and combination packages including rental cars are available for O'ahu, Maui, Kaua'i and The Big Island. They offer some unique and intriguing incentives! By booking early you can take an extra $20 off the published airfares. Sunquest Holidays also offers FREE children's holidays for youngster up to 19 years of age. You get one free child per two full-paying passengers, when sharing a room and using existing bedding. A minimum seven night stay is required. Other children qualify for package discounts, which are still a good deal! Travel protection insurance, in the event you have to cancel at the last minute, is available as is travel insurance. Dollar Rent a Car handles the ground transportation (Hawai'i Rental Vehicle Surcharge of $2 per day not included in prices) and Aloha Airlines is the carrier used for inter-island flights. Single or multiple island packages are available. For airfare only, rates are staggered based on the day of the week you depart and the time of the year. Current prices are for seven night stays, not including US Departure Tax, to Honolulu with connection onto Maui. Call for free catalog.

Remember! Be sure to check all the air carriers. Experience has taught us that a little leg work pays off! Sometimes the best deals may be through one of these agencies, but if you have the time, it may be worth a thorough investigation (and you may be pleasantly surprised). We have discovered that United Airlines may offer promotional specials that far and away beat these packages and even the charters!! Always make sure you let the airline know if you are flexible on your arrival and departure days. You may be able to squeeze into some price cut promotion "window" that offers an even better value on your flight dollar.

FLIGHTS TO THE ISLANDS

Most of the airlines have their own websites. These are especially handy for getting an idea of flight schedules. (See websites in preceding section for their world wide web addresses.) The major American carriers that fly from the mainland to The Honolulu International Airport on O'ahu or to Kahului Airport on Maui are:

AMERICAN AIRLINES - 1-800-433-7300; (808) 833-7600 in Honolulu, or on Maui: (808) 244-5522. Direct from Los Angeles or from San Francisco connecting in Honolulu.

CANADIAN AIRLINES INTERNATIONAL - 1-800-426-7000; Nineteen weekly flights from Vancouver to and from Honolulu. Then connecting inter-island carriers to Maui.

CONTINENTAL AIRLINES - 1-800-525-0280; Mainland to Honolulu with connecting service to Maui only via inter-island carriers.

DELTA AIR LINES - 1-800-221-1212; Flight information 1-800-325-1999. Their flights out of Atlanta stop in Los Angeles, then fly direct to Maui. They also have one direct flight from Atlanta and one from Dallas-Fort Worth to Honolulu.

HAWAIIAN AIRLINES - 1-800-367-5320; in Honolulu (808) 838-1555; on Maui (808) 871-6132. Flies DC10's with regularly scheduled flights servicing Tahiti, Samoa and the Mainland: Los Angeles, Las Vegas, San Francisco, Portland and Seattle. Hawaiian is proud of their *"Mea Ho'okipa"* service which includes award wining Hawaiian Regional Cuisine (in First Class), innovative in-flight audio selections which feature Hawaiian musicians and singers (also an award winning service), and cultural narratives by flight attendant shared in "talk story" style. Loosely translated, *Mea Ho'okipa* means to "act as a good host to guests." If you plan to do a lot of island hopping, Hawaiian's "Island Pass" offers unlimited travel on all islands for 5, 7 or 14 days. (Approximately $299-409). Coupon books are available through your travel agent at about $53 for a one way ticket.

NORTHWEST AIRLINES - 1-800-225-2525; Flies into Honolulu (808) 955-2255.) No direct Maui flights. No Maui phone number.

PLEASANT HAWAIIAN HOLIDAYS ★ - 1-800-242-9244. People seem to be very pleased by the Pleasant Hawaiian service and they just added a non-stop flight from San Diego to Honolulu!

TWA - Call 1-800-221-2000 from Hawai'i or the Mainland. To Honolulu (direct from St. Louis) only.

UNITED AIRLINES ★ - United has more flights to Hawai'i from more U.S. cities than any other airline. UAL Reservations 1-800-241-6522. Flight information 1-800-824-6200. They have a number of direct flights to Maui from Los Angeles and San Francisco as well as through (but not direct) flights from Denver, Chicago and Philadelphia. No local Maui phone number. United Airlines offers a free round trip ticket on Aloha Airlines for 5,000 mileage plus miles. If you have miles to use, check United for the price of their O'ahu flight.

AIRLINE TIPS!! The direct flights available on United, Delta, and American Airlines save time and energy by avoiding the otherwise necessary stopover on O'ahu. Travel agents schedule at least an hour and a half between arrival on O'ahu and departure for Maui to account for any delays, baggage transfers, and the time required to reach the inter-island terminal. If you do arrive early, check with the inter-island carrier. Very often you can get an earlier flight which will arrive on Maui in time to get your car, and maybe some groceries, before returning to pick up your luggage when it arrives on your scheduled flight.

INTER-ISLAND FLIGHTS

Hawai'i is unique in that its intrastate roads are actually water or sky. For your travel by sky, there are several inter-island carriers that operate between Honolulu and Maui. If you plan on doing frequent inter-island excursions, some allow you to purchase a coupon book of six or so tickets that work out to being a small discount per ticket over a single ticket purchase.

Travel agents schedule at least an hour and a half between arrival on O'ahu and departure for Maui to account for any delays, baggage transfers, and the time required to reach the inter-island terminal. The flight time from O'ahu to Kahului on Maui is just 35 minutes. When returning from Maui to Honolulu, make sure you have plenty of time before your connecting flight to the mainland. Otherwise you might make your flight, but your baggage won't! Traveling from the main carrier to the inter-island terminal can be rather exhausting and confusing. You will probably need to take one Wiki Wiki bus to a drop-off point and then pick up another to take you to the inter-island terminal. If you do arrive early, check with the inter-island carrier. Very often you can get an earlier flight which will arrive on Maui in time to get your car before returning to pick up your luggage when it arrives on your scheduled flight. If you are traveling "light" and have only brought carry-on luggage with you, be advised that what is carry-on for the major airlines may **NOT** be carry-on for the inter-island carriers. For example, those new small suitcases with wheels and long handles that extend out to pull along behind you MUST be checked by many of the inter-island carriers. Knowing this in advance, you may be able to pack those items that are more fragile in a smaller tote bag.

Most visitors arrive at the *Kahului Airport*, via direct or inter-island flights. The Kahului Airport is convenient with accessible parking, an on-site rental car area, even a restaurant that offers runway views (although the walk from the United Airlines gate to the baggage claim area can be quite a distance!) From the airport it is only a 20-30 minute drive to the Kihei-Wailea-Makena areas, but a 45 to 60 minute drive to the Kaanapali/Kapalua areas. However, If your destination is West Maui from O'ahu, Kaua'i, or Hawai'i, it might be more convenient to fly into the ***Kapalua West Maui Airport***. This small, uncrowded airport is serviced by Island Air.

INTERISLAND CARRIERS:

ALOHA AIRLINES ★ - They fly only jets - all 737s. 1-800-367-5250 U.S.; 1-800-235-0936 Canada. Their Honolulu number is (808) 484-1111; on Maui (808) 244-9071. Aloha offers First Class service, Drive-Thru Check-In at Honolulu and daily non-stop service between Maui-Kaua'i (2X); Maui-Hilo (2X); Maui-Hilo (3X). This airline keeps on schedule and has always had one of the lowest passenger complaint records of all U.S. Airlines. They fly over 1,200 flights weekly with their fleet of seventeen Boeing 737s. Also weekly charter service to Midway, Johnson, and Christmas Islands, and long range charters upon request.

When making reservations, you might inquire about any special promotions, AAA membership discounts, passes, or coupon books that are currently available. During slower times of the year they offer assorted discounts. If you have a family or plan lots of inter-island excursions, you can purchase a coupon book through your travel agent which can reduce the standard $86 one-way fare to as low as $51. They also have a 7 pass which allows unlimited travel on both Aloha and Island Air to all islands. (Sort of Hawai'i's version of a Eurail Pass!) If you are an AAA member and have your membership card, you can purchase a ticket for $65. For 5,000 United Mileage Plus miles, you can receive a free round trip ticket! Be sure to check into their Fly/Drive packages for rental cars - especially during slow season. Current flight schedule is available on the world wide web < www.alohaair.com/aloha-air/ >

ISLAND AIR - The sister airline to Aloha specializes in serving Hawai'i's smaller community and resort destinations. Their fleet consists of three 18 passenger twin engine De Havilland Dash 6 Twin Otters (Turbo-prop) aircraft and three 37 passenger DH Dash 8's. They fly 80 flights daily servicing Kahului and Hana and are the only airlines that currently fly in and out of the Kapalua West Maui Airport to Lana'i City, Moloka'i and Honolulu. From Hawai'i, the toll free number is 1-800-652-6541. From the U.S. Mainland call 1-800-323-3345; in Honolulu, (808) 484-2222 Charters available. < www.alohaair.com/aloha ~ air >

HAWAIIAN AIRLINES - They fly McDonnel Douglas DC9's between Honolulu and Maui. If you plan to do a lot of island hopping, Hawaiian's "Island Pass" offers unlimited travel on all islands for 5, 7 or 14 days. (Approximately $299-409). Coupon books are available through your travel agent, cost is about $53 for a one way ticket. Toll free from the mainland 1-800-367-5320. (808) 245-1813.

PACIFIC WINGS - Scheduled flights, charter service and scenic air tours, they service Kahului to Hana (Maui), Moloka'i and Kamuela (Big Island) in their 8 passenger, twin engine Cessna 402C. Call them toll free 1-888-675-4546, Email: info@pacificwings.com or website < www.pacificwings.com >

If you are traveling to Lana'i, you can take an inter-island commuter flight or you can also shuttle there by water: ***Expeditions*** (808) 661-3756 departs from Lahaina five times daily. Cost is $50 round trip adults, $40 children.

CRUISELINES

One pleasant way to see the Hawaiian islands is aboard the **American Hawai'i Cruises** ship *Independence,* operated by The Delta Queen Steamboat Co. This comfortable 700-foot (800 passenger) ship provides accommodations and friendly service during the seven day sail around the islands. Hawaiian costumes, onboard hands-on Hawaiian museum exhibits, cabins with Hawaiian names, traditional Hawaiian church services, menus filled with Hawaiian specialties, and tropical flowers in every room are among the touches which bring the essence of Hawai'i on board. American Hawai'i has on board Kumus (Hawaiian teachers) to teach passengers about the culture and history of Hawai'i. A Kumu's Study with historic artifacts has been developed off the central lounge. Fully handicapped-accessible suites are available. Direct cellular telephone service from each cabin. American Hawai'i also offers half day or full day shore excursions which include opportunities for passengers to discover the "hidden" Hawai'i. Shore excursions provide the opportunity to visit Lahaina, attend a luau, bike down Haleakala or experience a submarine ride.

Wedding ceremonies can be performed on board with the purchase of a special wedding package ($595). The package includes photography service, souvenir wedding album, two-tiered wedding cake, chilled champagne in etched champagne glasses, Hawaiian-style music performed by onboard musicians and an official to perform the ceremony. See Weddings - Honeymoons in this section for information on tests and licenses.

They offer three, four and seven day cruises, plus the option of extending your stay on land before or following your cruise. The idea of a cruise is to give you a taste of each of the islands without the time and inconvenience of traveling by plane in-between islands. In fact, it would be impossible to see all the islands in a week in any other fashion.

A seven day package begins with a Saturday, 9pm departure from Honolulu, Sunday is spent at sea. On Monday the Independence visits Nawiliwili on Kaua'i, on Tuesday and Wednesday it is in port at Maui, on Thursday it arrives in Hilo on the Big Island and the next day you'll be on the Big Island's east shore at Kona, returning to Honolulu on Saturday morning at 7:15 am.

For additional information contact American Hawai'i Cruises at 1-800-765-7000 or FAX (504) 585-0690. Or write American Hawai'i Cruises, Robin St. Wharf, 1380 Port of New Orleans Place, New Orleans, LA 70130-1890.

GETTING AROUND

FROM THE AIRPORT: After arriving, there are several options: Taxi cabs, because of the distances between areas, can be very costly (i.e., $50) from Kahului to Kaanapali), but there are also several bus/limo services available. What little around-the-island public transportation that does exist is very limited and expensive ($10-15 one way) although there are some local area shuttles. The best option may be a rental car unless your resort provides transportation. For cab service, try *Alii Cab*, (808) 661-3688 or *Executive Cab*, (808) 667-7770.

Transhawaiian 1-800-533-8765 U.S., 1-800-231-6984 inter-island, (808) 877-7308, provides service from Kahului Airport to Lahaina-Kaanapali-Kapalua for $13 one-way, $19 round trip. (Should you need one-way transportation *from* your hotel to the airport, the charge is only $7.) No charge for first two bags; $1 per bag for additional. Currently departs every half hour from 9am to 4pm. (Call to verify current schedules and price.) Check in by baggage claim area #3. *Airport Shuttle* offers door-to-door airport service that fits your schedule. Pick up anytime to any location in their 7 or 15 passenger vans. Individual fares - from $16 (Kihei) to $26 (Kaanapali) - are far less expensive than a cab and an even better deal if there are two or more of you ($18-28 for two, $20-30 for three, etc.) Especially economical for a family! Call ahead for reservations (1-800-977-2605 from the mainland); (808) 661-6667 on Maui; or just press #15 from the airport courtesy phone board. (In addition to airport service, they also offer transportation to or from anywhere on the island.) *SpeediShuttle* also offers door-to-door airport service. (808) 875-8070. Travel in style with one of the *limousine services*. Rates between them are competitive, $50 and up per hour plus tax and gratuity. Minimum 2 hours. (They also do tours and weddings.) *Arthur's Limousine Service* currently commutes to most resorts from the Kahului airport (1-800-345-4667 or (808) 871-5555 ($88.05 per hour, 2 hour minimum!). *Classy Taxi* (808) 661-3044 has "gangster-style" limos (circa 1929) and just acquired a 1933 Rolls Royce. Also try *Town & Country* (808) 572-3400 or *Star Limousine* (808) 875-6900. Some companies offer chauffeurs as drivers for your own car.

LOCAL TRANSPORTATION: If you don't choose a rental car, you will find Maui offers no public transportation. Transhawaiian, however, has just introduced three custom-built trolleys to provide daily service between South (Makena) and West (Kapalua) Maui. The open-air "blue" trolleys of the West Maui Shopping Express shuttle between Lahaina and Kaanapali with an alternate route that continues on to Kapalua (stopping at condos and shopping centers along the way.) Fare is $1 each way. The South-to-Whalers/Maui Ocean Center route (air-conditioned "red" trolley) runs from the Kihei/Wailea resorts to Whalers Village in Kaanapali for $15 one way (free return with any purchase there); the reverse Kaanapali to South Maui trip is $15 each way. Maui Ocean Center is $7 in either direction and free return with admission. (As you can probably tell, these are not part of a public system, but subsidized by the various shopping centers and businesses. Both the free *Maui Quick Guide* and *Lahaina Historical Guide* list several of the schedules or you can call Transhawaiian at 877-7308.

The free Kaanapali Trolley services the resort area operating only between the area hotels and golf course. Kapalua has a shuttle running 6am to 11pm between the condos and the hotel. Call the front desk to request it. Most van tours offer pickup at your hotel or condo. There is also a free shuttle in Wailea that offers transportation between the hotels, restaurants, and shopping. Check with the front desk or concierge at the property at which you stay.

RENTAL CARS AND TRUCKS: It has been said that Maui has more rental cars per mile of road than anywhere in the nation. This is not surprising when you realize that Maui has a population of well over 100,000 (1996 figure-see web at < www.hawaii.gov/dbedt > for current statistics), 2.3 million visitors per year - and no mass transit. (Although the local area shuttles above have been initiated to help alleviate this problem.) So, given the status of public transportation on

Maui, a rental car is still the best bet - sometimes the only way to get around the island and, for your dollar, a very good buy. A choice of more than 20 car rental companies offer luxury or economy and new or used models. Some are local island operators, others are nation-wide chains, but all are very competitive. The rates vary, not only between high and low season, but from week to weekend and even day to day! (One rate we were quoted on a Wednesday had gone up $8 by Saturday!) The best values are during price wars, or super summer discount specials. Prices vary as much within the same company as they do between companies and are approximated as follows: Vans, Jeeps, and Convertibles are all in the high-end range from $50-90, Full-size $35-50, Mid-size $30-$45, Compacts $25-$40. The least expensive choice is a late-model compact or economy. Often these cars are only 2 - 3 years old and in very good condition. Rental car discounts are few and far between. You might be able to use some airline award coupons, but they are often very restrictive. If you are a member of AAA you can receive a discount with some rental companies. Check with Aloha Airlines for some great slow-season rates with their inter-island fly and drive packages. Also available from specialty car rental agencies are a variety of luxury cars. Vans are available from a number of agencies, but camping in them is not allowed. We advise that you bring your own camping equipment.

Many of the rental companies have booths next to the main terminal building at the Kahului Airport. There is also a large courtesy phone board in the baggage claim area. This free phone is for those rental agencies not having an airport booth, or for regular shuttle service, so that you can call for a pick up. A few agencies will take your flight information when your car reservation is made and will meet you and your luggage at the airport with your car. The policies of all the rental car agencies are basically the same. Most require a minimum age of 21 to 25 and a maximum age of 70. All feature unlimited mileage with you buying the gas ($1.75-$2 per gallon so check for "discount days" in Wailuku/Kahului!) Be sure to fill up before you return your car, the rental companies charge about $2.60 or more per gallon to do it for you. A few require a deposit or major credit card to hold your reservation.

Insurance is an option you may wish to purchase which can run an additional $14-20 a day. A few agencies will require insurance for those under age 25. Most of the car rental agencies strongly encourage you buy the optional collision damage waiver (CDW) which provides coverage for most cars in case of loss or damage. We suggest you check with your own insurance company before you leave to verify exactly what your policy covers. Some credit cards now provide CDW coverage for rental cars if you use that credit card to charge your rental fees (usually a practice with Gold Cards). This does not include liability insurance, so you need to check to see if your own policy will cover you for liability in a rental car. Add to the rental price a 4% sales tax and a $2 per day highway road tax. A few of Maui's roadways are rough and rugged. The rental agencies recommend that cars not traverse these areas (shown on the map they distribute) and that if these roads are attempted, you are responsible for any damage. Some restrict driving to Haleakala due to drivers riding the brakes down the steep road.

In addition to the rental agency's *Maui Drive Guide* magazine and maps, you can pick up a free *Maui Driving Map* at most brochure racks. The front section of the phone book also has some excellent detailed street maps.

RENTAL CAR LISTING:

ACCESSIBLE VANS OF HAWAII
(Handicapped Accessible Vans)
1-800-303-3750
(808) 879-5521

ADVENTURES
RENT A JEEP
1-800-701-JEEP
(808) 877-6626

ALAMO
1-800-327-9633
Kahului (808) 871-6235
Lahaina (808) 661-7181

ANDRES
Kahului (808) 877-5378

AVIS
1-800-331-1212
Kahului (808) 871-7575
Kaanapali (808) 661-4588
Kihei (808) 874-4077
Kapalua (808) 669-5046

BUDGET
1-800-527-0700
Kaanapali (808) 661-8721
Wailea (808) 874-2831
Kahului (808) 871-8811

DOLLAR
1-800-800-4000
Kahului 877-2731
Kaanapali (808) 667-2651
Interisland 1-800-342-7398

HERTZ
1-800-654-3131
Kahului (808) 877-5167
Kaanapali:
(Marriott) (808) 667-1966
(Westin) (808) 667-5381

ISLAND RIDERS
Lahaina (808) 661-9966
Kihei (808) 874-0311
Harleys, sport cars, boats &
mountain bikes

KIHEI RENT-A-CAR
1-800-251-5288
Kihei (808) 879-7257

LTAR Auto Rental
(808) 874-4800
Weekly rentals only (from $99!)

MAUI MOUNTAIN CRUISERS
Wailuku (808) 249-2319
Older Toyotas, Hondas, Nissans

NATIONAL
1-800-227-7368
Kahului (808) 871-8851
Kaanapali (808) 667-9737

SEARS
contracts with Budget
1-800-451-3600

SURF RENTS TRUCKS
(flat beds, pick-ups)
Wailuku (808) 244-5544

THRIFTY CAR RENTAL
1-800-367-2277
Kahului (808) 871-2860

THE TOY STORE
(808) 661-1212 <WWW>
Exotic cars, jeeps,
and Harleys

WHEELS ARE US
Lahaina (808) 667-7751
Kahului (808) 871-6858
Cheap but you get what you pay for

WORD OF MOUTH
RENT A CAR
1-800-533-5929
Kahului (808) 877-2436

GROCERY SHOPPING

Grocery store prices may be one of the biggest surprises of your trip. While there are some locally grown foods and dairies, most of the products must be flown or shipped to the islands. The local folks can shop the advertisements and use the coupons, but it isn't so easy when traveling.

To give you an idea of what to expect at the supermarket, here are some grocery store prices. Bread $2.39, Bananas $.99 lb., baby food $.55-69 per jar, Chicken $1.69 per pound, hamburger $1.99 lb., mayonnaise $3.79, Bumble Bee Tuna $1.29 per can, diapers $6.69 in the 12-24 count size, ketchup $2.29, skim milk $4.59 per gallon.

The three major grocery stores in Kahului are Foodland, Safeway and Star Market (all accept Visa or Mastercard).

In Wailuku, at the Wailuku Towne Center, you'll find Sack N Save, a warehouse store that also has a large seafood selection, flowers and leis, plus an instore bakery.

In Lahaina you can choose between the brand-new, expanded Foodland or the Safeway at Lahaina Cannery Mall. Look for a new Star Market in Honokowai.

In Kihei, the major markets are Foodland and Star Market with a new Safeway scheduled to open by early '99. These larger stores offer the same variety as your hometown store and the prices are better than at the small grocery outlets.

In Hana there is Hasegawa's and the Hana Ranch Store. Longs Drug Stores carry some food items as do Kmart and Costco.

Azeka's Market (Kihei) is now an Ace Hardware, but with a take-out window on the outside where you can still get their famous ribs - as well as teriyaki beef and chicken. (879-0611)

GRATED RIPE COCONUT

The Farmers' Market of Maui is a group of people who bring produce down from the Kula area. They set up roadside shopping, and you can't find it fresher. Their locations seem to change periodically, but currently the Honokowai Market is set up Mon & Thurs 6:30-11:30 am; Kihei (in front of Suda's Store) on Tues & Fri from 1-5:30pm. Just look for the green sandwich board signs that are set up roadside. Ohana Farmers & Crafters Market (572-1934) meets at Kahului Shopping Center every Wed, 7:30am-1pm, offering fresh produce plus everything from malasadas to massage! Kaenae Open Market (248-7858) comes to the Kaenae Ball Park the second Sat of the month from 8am-2:30pm. Fresh produce, Hawaiian arts & crafts, baked goods - and a view! VIP Foodservice (871-2535) now has a produce market, Mon-Wed-Fri, 10am-4pm. (Their retail store is open to the public, but most of the products are sold in bulk. Check them out if you're staying a while!)

The *Maui Swap Meet* held Saturday mornings in Kahului, also has some good food values, although not always a very diverse selection. Usually you can pick up papayas, pineapple and coconuts as well as some vegetable items. Lots of flowers here, too! Admission is 50¢ for adults.

Take Home Maui (661-8067) is located just off Front Street in Lahaina and offers a selection of fruits and vegetables for shipment home. The *Nagasako Fish Market* on Lower Main Street in Wailuku has what may be the most diverse selection of fresh seafood from reef fish to live clams and crabs.

Local grocery shopping is a little more adventuresome. The largest local stores are in Wailuku and Kahului. In addition to the regular food staples they often have deli sections which feature local favorites and plate lunches. *Takamiya's* at 359 N. Market St. in Wailuku has a huge deli section with perhaps more than 50 cooked foods and salads as well as very fresh meats. *Ah Fook's* at the older Kahului Mall has a smaller deli section with plate lunches running about $3. *Ooka* is the largest of the three. The packed parking lot and crowded aisles prove its popularity and low prices. Besides the usual sundry items, they have a fascinating and unusual array of foods. How about a tasty fresh pig ear ($4.99 lb.), pig blood ($4 lb.), tripe ($5), calf hoof or tongue? In the seafood aisle check out the Opihi ($25 lb.), cuttlefish ($13 lb.), Tobikko (Flying Fish Roe, $23.16 lb.), lomi salmon ($6 lb.) and whole or filets of fresh island fish like catfish ($6 lb.) or Onaga ($10-15 lb.). They even have some reef fish, such as parrot fish.

You'll find the highest concentration of health food stores in Makawao and Paia, but for one closer to your hotel there's also *West Side Natural Foods* in Lahaina, *Hawaiian Moons* in Kihei and *Down to Earth* in Kahului. (Each has a hot food buffet and salad bar.)

ANNUAL MAUI EVENTS

JANUARY/FEBRUARY
- "Whales Alive" Celebration of the Whales at the Four Seasons Wailea
- Chinese New Year celebrations with Lion Dancers in Lahaina and Wailea. (Many restaurants offer special holiday meals.)
- Professional surfing at Honolua Bay
- Hula Bowl at War Memorial Stadium, Wailuku
- Black History Month: Annual Soul Food Dinner & Celebration (573-0370)

MARCH
- WhaleFest - Week-long events and activities in Lahainatown and West Maui
- Annual Maui Marathon from Kahului to Lahaina, sponsored by the Valley Isle Road Runners
- Annual Kukini Run along the Kahakuloa Valley Trail
- The 26th is Prince Kuhio Day, a state holiday
- East Maui Taro Festival in Hana with entertainment, exhibits, demonstrations and samplings
- St. Patrick's Day Parade - Kaanapali Parkway
- "Wild and Wonderful" Whale Regatta/Whale Day
- Just Desserts fundraiser for Maui Humane Society

APRIL
- David Malo Day at Lahainaluna High School includes Hawaiian entertainment and local food
- Hui No'eau Visual Arts Center, "Art Maui" - an annual juried show with works by island artists. Free admission
- Budlight Triple Crown Softball Tournament - teams from Hawai'i and the mainland compete in Wailuku and Kihei
- Annual Maui Marathon, 10K Run in Iao Valley, Valley Isle Road Runners
- The Ritz-Carlton, Kapalua "Celebration of the Arts" music & art festival
- "The Ulupalakua Thing" is an Agricultural Trade Show with Maui product booths, entertainment, cooking contests, chef's demonstrations and lots of free samples. Held at Ulupalakua Ranch/Tedeschi Winery
- Kihei Sea Fest at Kamaole Beach Park

MAY
- Lei Day celebration in Lahaina and Wailea (check with hotels for their events)
- Pineapple Jam on Lana'i - a two-day festival with arts, crafts, entertainment, cooking contests and samplings
- Seabury Hall in Makawao sponsors an annual craft fair the Saturday prior to Mother's Day
- Annual Lei Festival at Aston Wailea Beach Resort
- Annual Hard Rock Cafe World Cup of Windsurfing at Ho'okipa Beach Park
- The Moloka'i Ka Hula Piko, a celebration of the birth of hula on Moloka'i
- Tedeschi Vineyard 10K run through Upcountry Maui. Entry fee
- Annual Bankoh Kayak Challenge, Moloka'i to O'ahu, 41 mile kayak race
- Maui Music Festival - Memorial Day weekend celebration of jazz and contemporary music, Kaanapali
- "In Celebration of Canoes" parade, booths, and canoe displays on Front Street

JUNE
- Maui Chamber Music Festival (formerly Kapalua Music Festival) - a week of Hawaiian and classical music at Sacred Hearts Mission Church in Kapalua
- Obon Season (late June through August) - Bon Odori festivals are held at the many Buddhist temples around the island. They are announced in the local newspapers and the public is invited
- King Kamehameha Day Celebration - Front Street parade with *pa'u* riders and floral floats
- Maui Upcountry Fair, Eddie Tam Center, Makawao
- Hard Rock Cafe Rock N Roll, 10K run
- Makeke Fair at the Hana Ballpark - Hawaiian music, hula, crafts, food & games
- Kapalua Wine and Food Symposium - seminars and tastings culminating in the Kapalua Seafood Festival, a one day event featuring goodies from the best chefs from the best restaurants from all the islands (Sometimes in July)
- Taste of South Maui - Kihei and Wailea chefs offer their best at this food festival to raise money for the Kihei Youth Center
- Earth Maui Nature Summit Environmental Festival, Kapalua - 4 days of seminars, films & exhibits, plus a 5K run, wildlife tours, hikes, golf tournament, swim challenge, *hukilau* and Harvest Festival

JULY
- All-American Fourth of July celebration with fireworks at Aston Wailea Beach Resort
- Independence Day fireworks display over Black Rock at Kaanapali Beach
- Annual 4th of July Rodeo & Parade in Makawao
- Pineapple Festival - Kaahumanu Center, free tastings, games, entertainment and historic photo and label displays from Maui Pineapple Co.
- Canoe races at Ho'okipa State Park
- Maui Jaycees Carnival at Maui War Memorial Complex, Wailuku
- Annual Sausa Cup races in Lahaina, sponsored by the Lahaina Yacht Club
- Victoria to Maui Yacht Race
- Keiki Fishing Tournament at Kaanapali
- Annual Wailea Open Tennis Championships at the Wailea Tennis Club

AUGUST
- "Maui Calls" (a celebration of Hawaii's "boat days" at the Maui Arts & Cultural Center
- Run to the Sun Marathon, a grueling trek from sea level up to the 10,000 foot level of Haleakala Crater
- Ice Cream Festival at Maui War Memorial Complex, Wailuku
- Maui Onion Festival at Whalers Village, Kaanapali
- The 21st is Admissions Day, a state holiday

SEPTEMBER
- Maui County Rodeo in Makawao
- Aloha Festivals (events stretch into October)
- Labor Day Fishing Tournament
- The Annual Maui Writers Conference and Retreat, Labor Day Weekend at The Grand Wailea Resort
- Maui Academy of Performing Arts annual Garden Party

SEPTEMBER (Continued)
- "Taste of Lahaina" Friday Chef's Dinner followed by two-day Food Festival at Lahaina Cannery Mall. Maui's biggest food event with over 30 participating restaurants. Proceeds from the festival donated to designated charity each year
- Haku Mele O Hana sponsored by the Hotel Hana-Maui. Traditional song & dance
- Terry Fox Run and "Under the Stars" dinner raises funds for cancer research. Sponsored by Four Seasons Wailea

OCTOBER
- Hawaiian Sailing Canoe Regatta at Aston Wailea Beach Resort
- Maui County Fair at the War Memorial Complex in Wailuku
- Invitational Pro-Am Golf Championship
- Polo Season Begins at the Olinda Polo Field (808) 572-2790
- Parade and Halloween festivities in Lahaina, "The Mardi Gras of the Pacific"
- Lahaina Coolers Historic Fun Run. A 5K run/walk through Lahaina's history with entertainment and re-enactments at each landmark.
- Hawai'i Winter League Season opens at Wailuku Baseball Stadium (242-2950)

NOVEMBER
- Queen Kaahumanu Festival at the Maui High School
- Hawai'i International Film Festival at Maui Arts & Cultural Center
- Thanksgiving weekend - The Moloka'i Ranch Rodeo, a statewide event held on the island of Moloka'i combined with the Great Moloka'i Stew Cook Off
- Santa arrives at Kaahumanu Center
- La Hoomaikai - Thanksgiving luau celebration at Aston Wailea Beach Resort

DECEMBER
- Santa arrives by outrigger canoe at Wailea Beach - First part of December, Maui's Largest Gala Treelighting Ceremony at The Ritz-Carlton Kapalua honors people around the world and raises funds for the homeless
- Boar's Head Feast, an Elizabethian Madrigal Dinner with Renaissance costumes & food (242-7469)
- Kapalua/Betsy Nagelsen Pro-Am Tennis Invitational
- Bridges Family/Whales Alive Pro-Celebrity Tennis Tournament at Wailea Tennis Club raises funds for Whales Alive.
- The Na Mele O Maui Festival celebrates Hawai'i's music heritage throughout the Kaanapali Resort. Children's song contest, hula festival, arts and crafts fair.
- Old Fashioned Holiday Celebration on Front Street, - Santa Claus, carolers, holiday treats.
- Christmas House at Hui No'eau, near Makawao, a non-profit organization featuring pottery, wreaths, and other holiday artwork and gifts
- First Night Maui at Maui Arts & Cultural Center - alcohol-free, family festival to celebrate the New Year

For the exact dates of many of these events, write to the Hawai'i Visitor & Convention Bureau, 2270 Kalakaua Avenue #801, Honolulu, HI 96815, and request the Hawai'i Special Events Calendar. The calendar also gives non-annual information and the contact person for each event. A more complete listing for Maui events can be obtained from the Maui Visitors Bureau, PO Box 580, Wailuku, HI 96793. Check the local papers for dates of additional events.

WEATHER

When thinking of Hawaii, and especially Maui, one visualizes bright sunny days cooled by refreshing trade winds, and this is the weather at least 300 days a year. But what about the other 65 days? Most aren't really bad - just not perfect.

Although there are only two seasons, summer and winter, temperatures remain quite constant. Following are the average daily highs and lows for each month and the general weather conditions.

January	80/64	May	84/67	September	87/70
Feb.	79/64	June	86/69	October	86/69
March	80/64	July	86/70	November	83/68
April	82/66	Aug.	87/71	December	80/66

Winter: Mid-October through April, 75-80 degree days, 60-70 degree nights. Tradewinds are more erratic, vigorous to none. Kona winds are more frequent causing wide-spread cloudiness, rain showers, mugginess and even an occasional thunderstorm. 11 hours of daylight.

Summer: May through mid-October, 80-85 degree days, 70-80 degree nights. Tradewinds are more consistent keeping the temperatures tolerable. When the trades stop, however, the weather becomes hot and sticky. Kona winds are less frequent. 13 hours of daylight.

Summer type wear is suitable all year round. However, a warm sweater or light-weight jacket is a good idea for evenings and trips to cooler spots like Haleakala.

If you are interested in the types of weather you may encounter, or are confused by some of the terms you hear, read on. For further reference consult *Weather in Hawaiian Waters*, by Paul Haraguchi, 99 pages, available at island bookstores.

TRADE WINDS: Trade winds are an almost constant wind blowing from the northeast through the east and are caused by the Pacific anti-cyclone, a high pressure area. This high pressure area is well developed and remains semi-stationary in the summer causing the trades to remain steady over 90% of the time. Interruptions are much more frequent in the winter when they blow only 40 to 60% of the time. The major resort areas of South and West Maui are situated in the lee of the West Maui Mountains and Haleakala respectively. Here they are sheltered from the trades and the tremendous amount of rain (400 plus inches per year) they bring to the mountains.

KONA WINDS: The Kona Wind is a stormy, rain-bearing wind blowing from the southwest, or basically from the opposite direction of the trades. It brings high and rough surf to the resort side of the island - great for surfing and boogie-boarding, bad for snorkeling. These conditions are caused by low pressure areas northwest of the islands. Kona winds strong enough to cause property damage have occurred only twice since 1970. Lighter, non-damaging Kona winds are much more common, occurring 2 - 5 times almost every winter (Nov-April).

KONA WEATHER: Windless, hot and humid weather is referred to as Kona weather. The interruption of the normal trade wind pattern brings this on. The trades are replaced by light and variable winds and, although this may occur any time of the year, it is most noticeable during the summer when the weather is generally hotter and more humid, with fewer localized breezes.

KONA LOW: A Kona low is a slow-moving, meandering, extensive low pressure area which forms near the islands. This causes continuous rain with thunderstorms over an extensive area and lasts for several days. November through May is the most usual time for these to occur.

HURRICANES: Hawai'i is not free of hurricanes. However, most of the threatening tropical cyclones have weakened before reaching the islands, or have passed harmlessly to the west. Their effects are usually minimal, causing only high surf on the eastern and southern shores of some of the islands. At least 21 hurricanes or tropical storms have passed within 300 miles of the islands in the last 33 years, but most did little or no damage. Hurricane season is considered to be July through November. Hurricanes are given Hawaiian names when they pass within 1,000 miles of the Hawaiian islands.

Hurricane Dot of 1959, Hurricane Iwa of 1982 and Hurricane Iniki in 1992 caused extensive damage. In each case, the island of Kaua'i was hit hardest, with lesser damage to southeast O'ahu and very little damage to Maui, except for the beaches. Kaua'i has been much slower to recover from the damage caused by the September 1992 Hurricane Iniki, and more than four years following the devastation, there are still several major island resorts that have not yet begun restoration. Some of the difficulties in restoring real estate have been collecting on insurance and finding new companies to insure against future natural disasters.

TSUNAMIS: A tsunami is an ocean wave produced by an undersea earthquake, volcanic eruption, or landslide. Tsunamis are usually generated along the coasts of South America, the Aleutian Islands, the Kamchatka Peninsula or Japan and travel through the ocean at 400 to 500 miles an hour. It takes at least 4 1/2 hours for a tsunami to reach the Hawaiian Islands. A 24-hour Tsunami Warning System has been established in Hawai'i since 1946. When the possibility exists of a tsunami reaching Hawaiian waters, the public will be informed by the sound of the attention alert signal sirens. This particular signal is a steady one minute siren, followed by one minute of silence, repeating as long as necessary. If you hear it, turn on a TV or radio immediately; all stations will carry CIV-Alert emergency information and instructions with the arrival time of the first waves.

Do not take chances - false alarms are not issued. Move quickly out of low lying coastal areas that are subject to possible inundation.

The warning sirens are tested throughout the state on the first working Monday of every month at 11 am. The test lasts only a few minutes and CIV-Alert announces on all stations that the test is underway. Since 1813, there have been 112 tsunamis observed in Hawai'i with only 16 causing significant damage.

Tsunamis may also be generated by local volcanic earthquakes. In the last 100 years there have been only six (the last one was November 29, 1975) affecting the southeast coast of the island of Hawaii. The Hawaiian Civil Defense has placed earthquake sensors on all the islands and, if a violent local earthquake occurs, an urgent tsunami warning will be broadcast and the tsunami sirens will sound.

However, a locally generated tsunami will reach the other islands very quickly. Therefore, there may not be time for an attention alert signal to sound. Any violent earthquake that causes you to fall or hold onto something to prevent falling is an urgent warning, and you should immediately evacuate beaches and coastal low-lying areas.

For additional information on warnings and procedures in the event of a hurricane, tsunami, earthquake or flash flood, read the civil defense section located in the forward section of the Maui phone book.

TIDES: The average tidal range is about two feet. Tide tables are available daily in the Maui News or by calling the marine weather number, 877-3477.

SUNRISE AND SUNSET: In Hawaii, day length and the altitude of the noon sun above the horizon do not vary as much throughout the year as at the temperate regions because of the island's low latitude within the sub-tropics. The longest day is 13 hours 26 minutes (sunrise 5:53am, sunset 7:18pm) at the end of June, and the shortest day is 10 hours 50 minutes (sunrise 7:09am and sunset 6:01pm at the end of December). Daylight for outdoor activities without artificial lighting lasts about 45 minutes past sunset.

WHERE TO STAY
WHAT TO SEE

INTRODUCTION

Maui has more than 18,000 hotel rooms and condominium units in vacation rental programs, with the bulk of the accommodations located in two areas. These are *West Maui*, a 10-mile stretch between *Lahaina* and *Kapalua*, and the South shore of *East Maui*, which is also about ten miles of coastline between Ma'alaea and Makena, and includes *Kihei* and *Wailea*. On the northern side, in the *Kahului/-Wailuku* area, as well in *Upcountry* Maui, accommodations are more limited. In *Hana* there are a number of agencies that provide homes for rent and a few condominiums. This chapter contains a list of essentially all of the condominiums that are in rental programs, as well as the island's hotels. Bed and Breakfast homes are sprinkled around the island, and we have included a few of these along with agencies that have additional listings.

If you are physically impaired, please see our section in the GENERAL INFORMATION chapter. While many accommodations do have facilities to accommodate the physically impaired, you may encounter difficulty with some of the tourist attractions. Access to many of them is limited.

HOW TO USE THIS CHAPTER: For ease in locating information, the properties are first indexed alphabetically following this introduction. In both South and West Maui, the condominiums have been divided into groups that are geographically distinct and are laid out (sequentially) as you would approach them arriving from the Kahului area. These areas also seem to offer similar price ranges, building style, and beachfronts. At the beginning of each section is a description of the area, sights to see, shopping information, best bets and a sequential listing of the complexes. For each complex, we have listed the local address and/or PO Box and the local, FAX and toll-free phone numbers. We have included Email addresses and indicated if they have a website by the abbreviation <WWW>. Often times the management at the property does reservations, other times not.

In many cases there are a variety of rental agents handling units in addition to the on-site management and we have listed an assortment of these. We suggest that when you determine which condo you are interested in that you call all of the agents. Be aware that while one agent may have no vacancy, another will have several. The prices we have listed are generally the lowest available (although some agents may offer lower rates with the reduction of certain services such as maid service on check in only - that means your room is clean when you arrive - rather than daily maid service). Unfortunately, we've had at least one occasion where the cheaper rate resulted in a condo that needed not only a good cleaning, but complete renovation. On the other hand, a reputable rental agent will not let a unit fall into disrepair. We can recommend *Maui & All Island Condominiums*. Be sure to ask about their seasonal specials! *Kihei Maui Vacations* is a also very good with their broad range of properties in South Maui, and *Whalers Realty* in West Maui offers moderate to expensive properties at rates lower than the posted rack rates. At the end of the accommodations chapter is an alphabetical listing of rental agents and the properties they handle. Prices can vary, sometimes greatly, from one agent to another, so we suggest again that you contact them all.

Prices are listed to aid your selection and, while these were the most current available at press time, they are subject to change without notice. As island vacationers ourselves, we found it important to include this feature rather than just giving you broad categories such as budget or expensive. After all, one person's "expensive" may be "budget" to someone else!

For the sake of space, we have made use of several abbreviations. The size of the condominiums are identified as studio (S BR), one bedroom (1 BR), two bedroom (2 BR) and three bedroom (3 BR). The numbers in parenthesis refers to the number of people that can occupy the unit for the price listed and that there are enough beds for a maximum number of people to occupy this unit. The description will tell you how much it will be for additional persons over two, i.e. each additional person $10/night. Some facilities consider an infant as an extra person, others will allow children free up to a specified age. The abbreviations o.f., g.v., and o.v. refer to oceanfront, gardenview and oceanview units.

The prices are listed with a slash dividing them. The first price listed is the high season rate, the second price is the low season rate. A few have a flat yearly rate so there will be only be a single price.

All listings are condominiums unless specified as a (Hotel). Condos are abundant, and the prices and facilities they offer can be quite varied. We have tried to indicate our own personal preferences by the use of a ★. We felt these were the best buys or special in some way. However, it is impossible for us to stay in or view all the units within a complex, and since condominiums are privately owned, each unit can vary in its furnishings and its condition.

WHERE TO STAY: As for choosing the area of the island in which to stay, we offer these suggestions. The Lahaina and Kaanapali areas offer the visitor the hub of the island's activities, but accommodations are a little more costly. The beaches are especially good at Kaanapali.

The values and choice of condos are more extensive a little beyond Kaanapali in Honokowai, Kahana (Lower Honoapiilani Highway area) and further at Napili. However, there are fewer restaurants here with slightly cooler temperatures, and, often times, more rain. Some of the condominiums in this area, while very adequate, may be a little overdue for redecorating. While many complexes are on nice beaches, many are also on rocky shores.

Kapalua offers high class and high price condominium and hotel accommodations. Ma'alaea and Kihei are a half-hour drive from Lahaina and offer some attractive condo units at excellent prices and, although few are located on a beach, there are plenty of easily accessible public beach parks.

Many Maui vacationers feel that Kihei offers better weather in the winter months, and this may be true with annual rainfall only about 3" on Maui's southern shore.

There are plenty of restaurants here and an even broader selection by driving the short distance to Wailuku to sample some local fare.

The Wailea and Makena areas are just beyond Kihei and are beautifully developed resort areas. The beaches are excellent for a variety of water activities, however, it is significantly more expensive than the neighboring Kihei. The introductory section to each area offers additional information.

HOW TO SAVE MONEY: Maui has two price seasons. High or "in" season and low or "off" season. Low season is generally considered to be April 15 to about December 15, and the rates are discounted at some places as much as 30%. Different resorts and condominiums may vary these dates by as much as two weeks and a few resorts are going to a flat, year round rate. Ironically, some of the best weather is during the fall when temperatures are cooler than summer and there is less rain than the winter and spring months. (See GENERAL INFORMATION - Weather for year round temperatures). For longer than one week, a condo unit with a kitchen can result in significant savings on your food bill. While this will give you more space than a hotel room and at a lower price, you may give up some resort amenities (shops, restaurants, maid service, etc.). There are several large grocery stores around the island with fairly competitive prices, although most things at the store will run slightly higher than on the mainland. (See GENERAL INFORMATION - Shopping.)

Money can be saved by using the following tips when choosing a place to settle. First, it is less expensive to stay during the off or low season. Second, there are some areas that are much less expensive. Although Kahului has some motel units, we can't recommend this area as a place to headquarter your stay. The weather is wetter in winter, hotter in summer, generally windier than the other side of the island, and there are few good beaches. Two renovated old hotels in Wailuku now offer serviceable, basic and affordable accommodations for the budget minded, and they should especially appeal to the windsurfing community with nearby Ho'okipa Beach. There are a couple of hostel type accommodations also in this area. There are some good deals in the Ma'alaea and Kihei areas, and the northern area above Lahaina has some older complexes that are reasonably good values. Third, there are some pleasant condo units either across the road from the beach or on a rocky, less attractive beach. This can represent a tremendous savings, and there are always good beaches a short walk or drive away. Fourth, hotel rooms or condos with garden or mountain views are less costly than an oceanview or oceanfront room. We find the mountainview, especially in Kaanapali, to be, in fact, superior. The mountains are simply gorgeous and we'd rather be on the beach than look at it!

Most condominiums offer maid service only on check-out. A few might offer it twice a week or weekly. Additional maid service may be available for an extra charge. A few condos still do not provide in-room phones or color televisions, and fewer still have no pool. (A few words of caution: condominium units within one complex can differ greatly and, if a phone is important to you, ask!) Many are adding microwaves to their kitchens. Some may also add up to $1 per in-room local call, others have no extra charge for local calls. Some units have washers and dryers in the rooms, while others do not. Many have coin-operated laundry facilities on the premises.

Travel agents will be able to book your stay in the Maui hotels and also in most condominiums. If you prefer to make your own reservation, we have listed the various contacts for each condominium and endeavored to quote the best price generally available. Rates vary between rental agents, so check all those listed for a particular condominium. We have indicated toll free 800 or 888 numbers when available. Some may not be accessible from Canada, so for those, check the rental agent list at the end of this chapter. Look for an 808 or 888 area code preceding the non-toll free numbers. You might also check the classified ads in your local newspaper for owners offering their units, which may be a better bargain. We've provided Email addresses where possible.

Although prices can jump, most go up only 5-10% per year. Prices listed do not include the sales tax which is over 9%.

GENERAL POLICIES: IMPORTANT! Condominium complexes require a deposit, usually equivalent to one or two nights stay, to secure your reservation and insure your room rate from price increases. Some charge higher deposits during winter or over Christmas holidays. Generally a 30 day notice of cancellation is needed to receive a full refund. Most require payment in full either 30 days prior to arrival or upon arrival, and many do not accept credit cards.

The usual minimum condo stay is three nights with some requiring one week in winter. Christmas holidays may have steeper restrictions with minimum stays as long as two weeks, payments 90 days in advance and heavy cancellation penalties. It is not uncommon to book as much as two years in advance for the Christmas season. ALL CONDOMINIUMS HAVE KITCHENS, TV'S., AND POOLS UNLESS OTHERWISE SPECIFIED.

Monthly and often times weekly discounts are available. Room rates quoted are generally for two people. Additional persons run $8 - $15 per night per person with the exception of the high class resorts and hotels where it may run as much as $25 to $35 extra. Many complexes can arrange for crib rentals. (See GENERAL INFORMATION - Traveling with Children.)

We have tried to give the lowest rates generally available, which might not be through the hotel or condo office, so check with the offices as well as the rental agents. When contacting condominium complexes by mail, be sure to address your correspondence to the attention of the manager. The managers of several complexes do not handle any reservations so we have indicated to whom you should address reservation requests at these properties. If two addresses are given, use the PO Box rather than street address.

BED AND BREAKFAST

An alternative to condominiums and hotels are the Bed and Breakfast organizations. They offer homes around the island, and some very reasonable rates. *Bed & Breakfast Hawai'i* is among the best known. To become a member and receive their directory (which also includes the other islands) contact: *Bed and Breakfast Hawaii*, Directory of Homes, Box 449, Kapaa, HI 96746.

Linda Little runs *Affordable Accommodations Maui* and can be reached at or (808) 879-7865 or FAX (808) 874-0831 or Email: llittle@maui.net In addition to assisting with Bed and Breakfast accommodations, she also offers homes ($159-750) and cottages price $75-150. *Go Native Hawai'i* also features Bed and Breakfast vacation accommodations. Contact them at PO Box 13115, Lansing, MI 48901, phone (517-349-9598). Following are just a few of the Bed and Breakfast selections offered on Maui. (You can book them all directly).

Aloha Lani, 13 Kauaula Rd., Lahaina, Maui, HI 96761. (808) 661-8040. 1-800-57-ALOHA, FAX (808) 661-8045. Email: tony@maui.net <WWW> Located at the corner of Kauaula Rd. and Front Street. This four bedroom Hawaiian-style home offers a casual atmosphere. Two bedrooms are located on either side of the home with a shared bath between the two rooms. Complimentary Kona coffee each morning, continental breakfast $4.50. Tax included $59 single, $69 double. Two night minimum stay. Visa and mastercard accepted.

Ann & Bob Babson's B & B Vacation Rentals, 3371 Keha Drive, Kihei, Maui, HI 96753. (808) 874-1166, FAX (808) 879-7906 or toll free from the mainland 1-800-824-6409. E-mail: babson@mauibnb.com or <www.mauibub.com> The Babson's offer four vacation rentals with panoramic Pacific Ocean views in Maui Meadows, a residential area located above Wailea on the Southwest side of Maui. Rentals include cable TV, telephone, and washer/dryer. Four day minimum stay and breakfast is served on Monday through Saturday. The main house is situated on a half acre and offers a Bougainvillea Suite (bedroom with private bath), Molokini Master Suite (Master BR with private bath & jacuzzi) or Hibiscus Hideaway Apartment (1 BR 1 BTH w/ kitchen) $80-95. 2BR 2BTH cottage w/kitchen $115 single/double, each additional person $15 up to maximum of 6 persons. (Weekly discounts)

Bambula, 518 Ilikahi St., Lahaina, HI 96761. (808) 667-6753, FAX (808) 667-0979. <Email: bambula@maui.net> <WWW> Host Pierre Chasle, his wife, and daughter offer two Bed and Breakfast options. The Makai studio is adjacent to the house. It has a ceiling fan and comfortable, clean furnishings. The kitchen & living room area adjoin, with a television and a sofa which makes into a futon-type bed. The separate bedroom has a double bed. The Mauka studio is a separate 500 sq ft cottage with air conditioning. Seasonally Pierre even takes guests aboard his sailboat, *"Bambula"* for a bit of whale watching. The property is walking distance to Lahaina and located in a residential area. Lots of extras are provided, including boogie boards, snorkel gear and even bikes. The drawback is the noise from the nearby highway, and neighborhood dogs which seemed to make themselves known at all hours of the day and night. We'd recommend ear plugs. Mauka studio $95, Makai $85.

Eva Villa, 815 Kumulani Drive, Kihei, HI 96753. Hosts Rick and Dale Pounds invite you to their home at the top of Maui Meadows, just above Wailea. Guests can use their pool, jacuzzi and barbecue facilities. They offer three accommodations: The Studio, The Apartment, or The Cottage. Price range $95-120.

George's Place, 718 Pakanu St., Haiku. (808) 573-0284, FAX (808) 573-1610, Email: <alohahtw@maui.net> We haven't toured this place, but George Simon tells us he wants quiet, clean, responsible guests only. (No drugs or alcohol or meat or cigarettes!) Ocean and mountain views, vegetarian, clothing optional, magnetic sleep systems, free arrival massage, hot tub and trampoline. He has two individual rooms with a shared bath at $50 a night or $300 per week. A two bedroom, one bath *ohana* and kitchen is $100 per night or $600 per week. Master bedroom is $68 or $400 per week.

Hale Huelo Bed & Breakfast, PO Box 1237, Haiku, HI 96708. (808) 572-8669 or FAX (808) 573-8403, Email: <halehuel@maui.net> Doug Barrett is your host. Rooms have modern bathrooms and small convenient mini-kitchens. The oceanview is spectacular from all the suites. The atmosphere is "Country Hawaiian" with a touch of Japanese. Other amenities include a swimming pool, secluded hot tub and a bathroom shower than can be entered from inside or straight from the outdoor patio - no need to shower off just to get to the shower! Rates are $100 off-season, $125 high season or rent the whole three bedroom house!

Halfway to Hana House, PO Box 675, Haiku, HI 96708. (808) 572-1176. FAX (808) 572-3609, Email: <gailp@maui.net> <WWW>. Located 20 minutes from Paia on the Hana Road, they offer a studio with breakfast $70 double, $60 single, or without breakfast $60 double, $55 single. Three night minimum. The studio has a private entrance, bathroom, double bed, mini-kitchen and patio.

House of Fountains, 1579 Lokia Street, Lahaina, HI 96761. (808) 667-2121, 1-800-789-6865, <WWW> Email: <private@maui.net>. Located three blocks from the beach. Accommodations in their 7,000 square foot home. Air conditioned rooms furnished with queen bed, private bath. German breakfast. $85-125.

Kula Cottage, Write: 380 Hoohana St., Kahului, HI 96732. (808) 871-6230 or (808) 878-2043. FAX (808) 871-9187. Email <gilassoc@maui.net> Cecilia and Larry Gilbert offer an upcountry one bedroom cottage with a queen size bed. Other amenities include a wood-burning fireplace (yes!), a full kitchen, TV and VCR, private driveway, and barbecue. Two night minimum stay. One night deposit. $85 per night.

Kula View B & B, PO Box 322, Kula, HI 96790. (808) 878-6736. Located on two acres in the cool Upcountry region on the slopes of Haleakala. They offer private room, bath, and deck with own entrance. $85 single or double occupancy. Your host, Susan Kauai, is descended from a *kamaaina* Hawai'i family.

Kula Lynn Farm, PO Box 847, Kula, HI 96789. (808) 878-6176 or FAX (808) 878-6320. Your hosts are a part of the Coon family (Trilogy Excursions) and they offer several rooms, two full baths, kitchen (with a refrigerator stocked with breakfast fixings) and living room, on the ground level of their home. The home is located on the slopes of Haleakala, in lower Kula. $85 single or double, $10 each additional person, max. 6 persons. Three night minimum.

Maluhia Hale, PO Box 687, Haiku, HI 96708. (808) 572-2959. Located at Twin Falls, about 25 miles past the airport. Diane Garrett rents a private plantation style cottage. The cottage is furnished with a king-size bed and additional double bed in the sitting room. The furnishings are antiques that reflect the plantation era. There is a kitchenette stocked with coffee and tea and they serve a light breakfast of fruit and muffins on your first morning. There is a glassed-in sitting room and a screened veranda for indoor/outdoor sitting and relaxing. $85 double $105 triple, two night minimum. No charge cards.

Old Lahaina House Bed & Breakfast, PO Box 10355, Lahaina, HI 96761. (808) 667-4663, 1-800-847-0761, FAX (808) 667-5615. Hosts John and Sherry Barbier offer rooms in their home in the historic Lahaina area. They feature two rooms, each with king size bed, air conditioning, phone, private bath at $95. Two rooms each with two twin beds, air conditioning, phone, private bath at $69. Breakfast is included except on Sundays. Swimming pool. They are across the street from a neighborhood beach and four blocks from Lahaina Harbor.

Old Wailuku Inn at Ulupono 2100 Kahoʻokele Street, Wailuku, HI 96793. (808) 244-5897, Toll free 1-800-305-4899, FAX (808) 242-9600, or e-mail: < Maui BandB@aol.com > Your hosts are Janice and Tom Fairbanks. Built in 1924 by a wealthy island banker as a wedding gift for his daughter-in-law, this historic Wailuku home has been lovingly restored. In fact, they just won the Kahili "Keep it Hawaiian" Award for Accommodations (from the Hawaiʻi Visitors & Convention Bureau) for "saluting the former 1920 plantation home for blending a nostalgic ambiance while at the same time providing all comforts and conveniences for the modern day traveler." The rooms and overall theme of the inn are a tribute to Hawaiʻi's famed poet of the 1920's and 30's, Don Blanding. All rooms have 10-foot ceilings, wide crown molding, hardwood floors, but all the comforts provided by cable television, VCR, ceiling fans, private baths and heirloom Hawaiian quilts. Daily afternoon tea is served as well as breakfast. Fax machine, photocopier and computer are available for guest use. Not an inexpensive alternative, this fits into the luxury section of B&B accommodations. Seven rooms available, prices based on double occupancy run $120-180 per night. Two night minimum. Additional person is $20.

Silver Cloud Upcountry Guest Ranch RR2 Box 201, Kula, Maui, HI 96790. (808) 878-6101, FAX (808) 878-2132, website at: < www.maui.net/ ~ slvrcld > or Email: < slvrcld@maui.net >. Silver Cloud Ranch was originally part of the Thompson Ranch, which had its beginnings on Maui in 1902. The nine-acre ranch is located at the 2,800 ft. elevation on the slopes of Haleakala. Owners Mike and Sara Gerry offer 12 rooms, suites and cottages, each with private bathrooms and most with private lanais and entrances. The King Kamehameha and Queen Emma suites are located in the main house with a private lanai and view of the lush Upcountry. The Lanaʻi Cottage offers total privacy with a complete kitchen, clawfooted bathtub, and woodburning stove surrounded by a lovely flower garden and lanai. The Paniolo Bunkhouse has studios that are furnished in Hawaiian motif. They offer kitchenettes and lanais. The Bunkhouse's Haleakala suite is a larger facility with a bedroom, separate living area, fireplace and complete kitchen. All room rates include breakfast and use of the main house and kitchen. Rates $105-150.

Wai Ola, PO Box 12580, Lahaina, HI 96761. (808) 661-7901 (FAX/phone) or 1-800-492-4652. Host Julie Frank offers a 500 sq. ft. studio and a one bedroom apartment. Both include full kitchens, queen bed. Pool, jacuzzi, air conditioning, and private phone. Located two blocks to beach. Rates $75-100.

PRIVATE RESIDENCES, HOMES & COTTAGES

For a large family, a couple of families, or a group of friends, a vacation home rather than a condo, may be a more spacious and cost effective option. Homes are available in all areas of the island. Following are a list of owners and agents. Cottages might run $100 or less a night, with luxury homes reaching more than $1,000 per night.

Hale Alana, PO Box 160, Kihei, HI 96753. 1-800-871-5032. FAX (808) 879-6851 <WWW> Email: <kstover@maui.net> Located in Maui Meadows. There are two master bedrooms and a third bedroom with two double beds. Great ocean vistas from the private deck and beautifully appointed all around. Rates vary based on length of stay and number of guests. Also available are several cottages at $75 per night. Contact: Karen & Ken Stover.

Bello Realty-Maui Beach Homes, PO Box 1776, Kihei, Maui, HI 96753. (808) 879-2598. 1-800-541-3060 U.S. & Canada. E-mail: pam@bellowmaui.com. Website: <www.bellomaui.com> Condos and homes rented by the day, week or month. Specializing in the Kihei area. Their rates look pretty competitive. Check them out!

Elite Properties Unlimited, PO Box 5273, Lahaina, Maui, HI 96761. 1-800-448-9222 U.S. & Canada, (808) 665-0561), FAX (808) 669-2417, Email: elite!@maui.net, <www.maui.net/~elite>. Family homes and luxury estates (3-7 bedrooms) available on all four major islands. Weekly and monthly rentals. One week minimum. Maid service, chefs and concierge services available.

Hale Hawaiian Apartment Leasing Enterprise, 479 Ocean Ave., Suite B., Laguna Beach, CA 92651. 1-800-854-8843 U.S. and Canada. 150 plus homes and 90 condominium properties on all islands.

Hana Alii Holidays, PO Box 536, Hana, Maui, HI. 1-800-548-0478 or (808) 248-7742, Email <info@Hanaalii.com>. They handle rental homes in Hana, Maui.

Hana AAA Bay Vacation Rentals, Stan Collins offers homes in the Hana area. Contact Hana Bay Vacation Rentals, PO Box 318, Hana, Maui, HI 96713. (808) 248-7727.

Hana Plantation Houses, PO Box 249, Hana, Maui, HI 96713. 1-800-228-HANA. (808) 248-7868. They offer rental houses on Moloka'i and in Hana, Maui.

Kathy Scheper's Maui Accommodations, (808) 879-8744, 1-800-645-3753, FAX (808) 879-9100. Email: <vacation@maui411.com> Kathy offers a beach cottage and studio located on her property in Kihei. The rates are hard to beat! The cottage sleeps four. The studio is suited for one or two on a budget. It includes a small refrigerator, microwave oven, color TV and a half bath. A private tropical garden patio has a private outdoor shower. The beach is a short walk away. She also rents units at the Kai Nani Beach Condo. *Beach Cottage $80/65, Studio $49/39.*

Kihei Maui Vacations ★ , 1-800-542-6284 US, 1-800-423-8733 ext. 4000 Canada (808) 879-7581. In addition to condos they offer homes and cottages in the Kihei, Wailea, and Makena areas.

Maui and All Island Condominiums and Cars ★ , PO Box 1089, Aldergrove, BC V4W 2V1. U.S. Mailing address PO Box 947, Lynden, WA 98264. 1-800-663-6962 from U.S. and Canada. FAX (604) 856-4187. In Canada phone (604) 856-4190. Approximately 25,000 condos and homes rented weekly, bi-weekly and monthly on Kaua'i, Hawai'i, O'ahu and Maui. (71 properties on Maui!) The office is open (Pacific Time) Mon. to Fri. 9am-8pm and Saturday 11am-5pm.

Maui Condo and Home Realty, PO Box 1840, Kihei, Hi 96753. 1-800-822-4409, (808) 879-0028, FAX (808) 875-1769. < www.mauicondo.com >. Homes & condos in the Kihei-Wailea area.

Maui Dream Cottages, 265 W. Kuiaha Rd., Haiku, HI 96708. (808) 575-9079, FAX (808) 575-9477, Email: < gblue@aloha.net > Gregg Blue offers two dream cottages. Both are equipped with washer/dryer, phone, TV/VCR and sleep 2-5 people. There are oceanviews from inside both houses. Rates are $490 per week for two and $10 per night for each additional person.

Maui Visions, 1680 Makawao, Ave. Makawao, HI 96768. (808) 572-2161. Email: < visions@maui.net > website: < garden.maui.net/visions > They are customized, full-service travel planners. They can arrange family reunions and honeymoons as well as provide help with airfare, lodgings, and even eco-tours, wellness/rejuvenation vacations, and other off-the-beaten-path options.

My Wai Beach Cottage, located at 2128A Iliili Road in Kihei. Booking agent: Linda R. Owen, 3538 207th SE, Issaquah, WA 98029. Toll free 1-800-882-9007 or Email < lro@ix.netcom.com > Linda offers a deluxe one bedroom, two bath oceanfront cottage. It is located 500 yards from Kamaole Beach #1 and the front lawn area also adjoins a small beach. The cottage has a TV, VCR, stereo with CD, full kitchen microwave, 3 telephones, ceiling fans. There is a dual king in the bedroom and a queen size Murphy bed in the living room. Minimum stay of 5 nights or $75 cleaning fee for less. Rates are $170 per night plus tax for 2; extra persons up to maximum of 4 are $10 each.

Windsurfing West, Ltd., PO Box 1359, Haiku, HI 96708 1-800-782-6105. (808) 575-9228, FAX (808) 575-2826, Email: < windsurf@maui.net >. They have continued to broaden and diversify their list of rental condominiums to cover the North Shore, South Shore, and Upcountry properties. Along with condos they have rental homes and cottages. Rates range from $55 to $1000 per night. Even if you're not a windsurfer, you might want to check into their "Accommodations Only" packages! For their windsurfing guests, they can also arrange equipment rentals and lessons.

LONG-TERM STAYS

Almost all condo complexes and rental agents offer the long term visitor moderate to substantial discounts for stays of one month or more. Private homes can also be booked through the agents listed above.

CONDOMINIUM & HOTEL INDEX

LAHAINA

INTRODUCTION

As you leave the Kahului area on Hwy. 38, you plunge immediately into Maui's central valley. The rugged and deeply carved valleys of the West Maui mountains are on the right, and on the left is the dormant volcano, *Haleakala*. Its broad base and seemingly gentle slopes belie its 11,000 foot height and no hint of its enormous moon-like crater is discernible from below. On a clear day the mountains are so distinct and sharp-edged they appear to have been cut out with giant scissors. The drive across the isthmus ends quickly as you pass Ma'alaea Harbor where the gently swaying sugar cane gives way to rugged sea cliffs and panoramic Pacific vistas. Across the bay is the South Maui coastline and in the distance the islands of Kaho'olawe and Lana'i. Construction of this road was to accommodate the new resort developments at Kaanapali that began in the 1960's. Traffic must have been far different on the old road which is still visible in places along the craggy cliffside of the pali. The pull-off along the roadside offers an ideal vantage point from which to do a little whale watching December through May. A hiking trail over the pali (the Old Lahaina Pali Trail) is continually being refurbished and improved. The tunnel, built in 1951, is the only one on Maui. Just beyond it are enormous metal chain blankets hanging along the rocky cliffs above the road. Termed a protective measure by some and an eyesore by others, they were installed in 1987.

As you descend from the cliffs, the first glimpse of the tropical and undeveloped West Maui coastline is always a thrill. Stretching as far as the eye can see are sugar cane fields hugging the lower slopes of the mountains and a series of narrow, white sand beaches lined by kiawe trees and coconut palms. For several miles the constant stream of traffic is the only clue to the populated areas ahead. The first sign of civilization is Olowalu, a mere hamlet along the roadside and an unusual location for one of the island's best restaurants, Chez Paul. Public beaches line the highway and the unobstructed view of the ocean is a visual feast.

A few homes to the left and the monolithic smoke stack of the Pioneer Mill announces your arrival to *Lahaina*, the bustling tourist center of Maui. It has maintained the aura of more than a century ago when it was the whaling capitol of the world. Located about a 45 minute drive from the Kahului Airport (depending on traffic), this coastal port is noted for its Front Street, which is a multiblock strip of shops and restaurants along the waterfront. The Lahaina Harbor is filled with boats of varying shapes and sizes, eager to take the visitor aboard for a variety of sea excursions.

The oldest accommodation on the island, Pioneer Inn, is located here. Still popular among many a visitor, it offers a nostalgic and rustic atmosphere, and reasonable prices. Other accommodations include a luxuriously expensive condominium complex, several priced in the moderate range, two charming country-style inns and a number of Bed & Breakfasts. Although several complexes are located oceanfront, the beaches in Lahaina are fronted by a close-in reef which prohibits swimming. Only Puamana has a beach suitable for swimming. If you want to be in the midst of the action on Maui, you might want to investigate staying in this area.

Old Lahaina Town

Historical Sites are numbered to correspond with signs on the Lahaina Restoration Foundation Walking Tour (There are 31 in all).

1. Masters' Reading Room
2. Baldwin Home
7. *Carthaginian*
8. Pioneer Inn
9. Banyan Tree
10. Courthouse
11. Remnants of Old Fort
16. Malu ulu o lele Park
21. The Old Prison
26. Maria Lanakila Church
27. Seamen's Cemetary
31. Jodo Mission
A. Lahaina Inn
B. Plantation Inn
C. Dickenson Square
D. Lahaina Center-
   Hale Kahiko
E. Industrial Center
F. Sugar Cane
   Train Depot
G. Lahaina Square
H. Old Lahaina Center
I. Wharf Cinema
   (Shopping) Center
J. Kamehameha III School
K. Maui Medical Group
L. Kamehameha Iki Park
M. 505 Front Street
   Shops & Restaurants
N. Lahaina Shores
   Beach Resort

Parking Lots

WHAT TO DO AND SEE

There is much to see and do in busy Lahaina Town. The word **Lahaina** means "merciless sun," and it does tend to become quite warm, especially in the afternoon, with little relief from the tropical trade winds. Parking can be somewhat irksome. Several all-day lots are located near the corner of Wainee and Dickenson (only a couple of blocks off Front Street) and the charge is about $6 for all day. One nearer to Front Street charges $8 per day. The inexpensive lots fill up early in the day. The Old Lahaina Center (formerly Lahaina Shopping Center) has a three hour (free) parking area, but it is always very crowded. The "new" Lahaina Center across the street has pay parking, validated with a movie ticket or purchase from one of the stores. If you don't mind a short walk, parking is available across the road from the 505 Front Street shops. Other paid parking lots are primarily on side streets off Front Street. On-street parking is very limited and if you are fortunate enough to find a spot, many are only for one hour. BEWARE: the police here are quite prompt and efficient at towing. There is no longer any free shuttle service. Transhawaiian, aka the Maui Shopping Express (877-7308), offers transportation between Lahaina and Kaanapali or Kapalua for $1 with lots of stops at resort areas and shopping centers. The "two-new-blue" open-air trolleys began service in April, 1998 and operate daily between 8am and 9:20pm. The trolley's are named *Ho'okipa* (Hospitality), *Kamahele* (The Traveler) and *Alahele I Ka La* (Pathway to the Sun).

Now that you have arrived, let's get started. Historical memorabilia abounds in Lahaina. The Lahaina Restoration Foundation has done an admirable job restoring and maintaining many historical landmarks. If you have questions, contact their office at 661-3262. The historical landmarks have all been identified by numbered markers. A free walking tour map of Lahaina can be found in a copy of the Lahaina Historical Guide. Look for free copies of this pocket-size guide on corner display racks in Lahaina Town. Then enjoy your walking tour of the Baldwin House, the *Brig Carthaginian*, Masters Reading Room, and Wo Hing Temple. The LahainaTown Action Committee recently initiated a "Walking Museum" featuring building plaques with photos and stories depicting the history of that building's colorful past. You can pick up a brochure to identify the sites as you walk along. (And while you walk, the recent Front Street Improvement project hopes you will notice the wider sidewalks with handicapped curb cuts and rest areas, newly paved roads, and better street lights.)

The Banyan Tree is very easy to spot at the south end of Lahaina adjacent to Pioneer Inn on Front Street. It was planted on April 24, 1873, by Sheriff William Owen Smith, to commemorate the 50th anniversary of Lahaina's first Protestant Christian Mission. You may find art shows or other events happening under the cool, shady boughs of this magnificent arbor. With its long, heavy limbs supported by wood braces and 12 solid trunks that have re-rooted themselves over a 200-foot area, visitors find it hard to believe that this is all one tree! The stone ruins of **The Old Fort** can be found harborside near the Banyan Tree. The fort was constructed in the 1830's to protect the missionaries' homes from the whaling ships and the occasional cannonball that would be shot off when the sailors were too rowdy. The fort was later torn down and the coral blocks reused elsewhere. A few blocks were excavated and the corner of the fort was rebuilt as a landmark in 1964. On the corner near the Pioneer Inn is a plaque marking the site of the

1987 Lahaina Reunion Time Capsule, which contains newspapers, photos and other memorabilia.

Pioneer Inn is the distinguished green and white structure just north of the Banyan Tree. It was a haven for inter-island travelers during the early days of the 20th century. Built back in 1901, it managed to survive the dry years of prohibition, adding a new wing, center garden and pool area in 1966. Two restaurants operate here and accommodations are available. The history of Pioneer Inn is an interesting one and is discussed under the accommodation information which follows. (See RESTAURANTS - Lahaina and WHERE TO STAY - Lahaina for additional information.)

You'll find the *Lahaina Courthouse* nearby, across from the Lahaina Harbor. It was built in 1859, at a cost of $7,000, from wood and stone taken from the palace of Kamehameha II. In 1925 the building was extensively remodeled to serve as Courthouse, Post Office, Police Station, and Tax Office. It is being restored by the County of Maui to match its 1925 appearance with fire safety, handicapped access, and other improvements. Specifics as to just who will use the facility once it reopens (Spring 1999) have not been determined as we go to press. Lahaina Arts Society has expressed interest in returning, but the Lahaina Visitor Center is currently negotiating for a new building/restroom facility to be built on the Front Street side of the library lawn.

The *Lahaina Harbor* is in front of the Pioneer Inn and the Courthouse. You can stroll down and see the boats and visit stalls where a wide variety of water sports and tours can be arranged. (See RECREATION AND TOURS) *The Brig Carthaginian,* anchored just outside the harbor, is a replica of a 19th century square rigger, typical of the ships that brought the first missionaries and whalers to these shores. The first *Carthaginian* sank on Easter Sunday, April 2, 1972. It had been built in 1921 in Denmark as a schooner and the 130 foot vessel had sailed the world as a cargo ship. She was purchased by Tucker Thompson and sailed to Hawai'i in 1964. Her original name was *Wandia,* but was rechristened *Carthaginian* in Honolulu with a bottle of passion fruit juice. The ship was used for a time in the South Pacific later was restored to resemble a whaling vessel for

PIONEER INN

81

the movie version of Michener's *Hawai'i*. The Lahaina Restoration Foundation worked to acquire the *Carthaginian* for $75,000. The ship found a home at the Lahaina wharf, becoming its definitive exhibit of the whaling era. On June 20, 1971 it was discovered by the ship's skipper, Don Bell, that the vessel was sinking. The ship was pumped and a large hole was patched, the cause seeming to be dry rot. It was decided the following year to tow her to Honolulu for repairs in dry dock. However, 150 yards from dock she became lodged on the reef and valiant efforts to save her were not successful. An immediate search began for a replacement and it was found in the Danish port of Soby. The ship was a 97 foot steel hulled freighter that had originally been a schooner, but had been demasted. The ship called *Komet* had been built in the shipyards in Germany in 1920 and was purchased for $20,500. An all-Lahaina crew sailed via the Panama Canal and arrived in Hawai'i in September, 1973. Volunteers set to work transforming the ship to the proud vessel it is today and it was christened *Brig Carthaginian* on April 26, 1980. Today the ship features video movies and recorded songs of humpback whales, and an authentic 19th century whale boat. All items are on display below deck. The ship is open daily from 10am-4pm. Admission $3 adults, seniors $2 and children free. Whale watching is always an exciting pastime in Lahaina. The whales usually arrive in December to breed and calve in the warm waters off Maui for several months. There is also a number to call to report any sightings you make: WHALE WATCH HOTLINE at 879-8811. (See RECREATION AND TOURS for whale watching excursion information.)

Adjacent to the *Carthaginian* is the Lahaina Harbor Lighthouse - recently adopted (1998) by the Lahaina Restoration Foundation to add new railings and a connecting ramp - which predates any along the Pacific. "It was on this site in 1840 that King Kamehameha III ordered a nine-foot wooden tower built as an aid to navigation for the whaling ships. It was equipped with whale oil lamps kept burning at night by a Hawaiian caretaker who was paid $20 a year." In 1866 it increased to 26 feet in size and was again rebuilt in 1905. The present structure of concrete was dedicated in 1916. (Information from an engraved plaque placed on the lighthouse by the Lahaina Restoration Foundation.)

The Hauola Stone or Healing Rock can be found in front of the Lahaina Library next to the harbor. Look for the cluster of rocks marked with a Visitors Bureau "warrior" sign. The rock, resembling a chair, was believed to have healing properties which could be obtained by merely sitting in it with feet dangling in the surf. Here you will also find remnants of the **Brick Palace** of Kamehameha the Great. Vandals destroyed the display which once showed examples of the original mud bricks.

The Baldwin Home is across Front Street from Pioneer Inn. Built during 1834-1835, it housed the Reverend Dwight Baldwin and his family from 1837 to 1871. Tours of the home, furnished as it was in days gone by, are given between the hours of 10am and 4pm. Adults are $3, seniors $2, no charge for children or a family rate of $5. The empty lot adjacent was once the home of Reverend William Richards, and a target of attack by cannonballs from angry sailors during the heyday of whaling. On the other side of the Baldwin Home is the Masters' Reading Room. Built in 1833, it is the oldest structure on Maui. Its original purpose was to provide a place of leisure for visiting sea captains. It is not open to the public at this time.

Hale Paahao (The Old Prison) on Prison Street just off Wainee is only a short trek from Front Street. Upon entry you'll notice the large gate house which the Lahaina Restoration Foundation reconstructed to its original state in 1988. Nearby is a 60-year-old Royal Palm, and in the courtyard, an enormous 150-year-old breadfruit tree. The cell block was built in 1852 to house the unruly sailors from the whaling vessels and to replace the old fort. It was reconstructed in 1959. In 1854 coral walls (the blocks taken from the old fort) were constructed. The jail was used until the 1920s when it was relocated to the basement of the Lahaina Courthouse next to the Harbor. While you're at Hale Paahao be sure to say hello to the jail's only tenant, George. He is a wax replica of a sailor who is reported to have had a few too many brews at Uncle Henry's Front Street Beer House back in the 1850's, then missed his ship's curfew and was tossed into jail by Sheriff William O. Smith. George will briefly converse with you by means of a taped recording. The grounds are open to the public daily, no charge.

The construction of the *Waiola Church* began in 1828 on what was then called the Wainee Church. The original church was made of stone and was large enough to accommodate 3,000 people. Hale Aloha was built in 1858 as a branch of the Wainee Church and was used as a school. It's name, "House of Love," was a way of giving thanks that the citizens of Lahaina did not suffer in a smallpox epidemic that ravaged the island of O'ahu during 1853. The Waiola Church is now a United Church of Christ with worship in Hawaiian and English.

In 1951 a fierce wind, called a Kaua'ula wind, seriously damaged the church and Hale Aloha. The wind is named for a narrow valley in the mountains above Lahaina called Kaua'ula, through which the wind blows and gains force. Legend has it that the wind blows when the ali'i die. Among the damage incurred during the wind of 1951 was the loss of the Hale Aloha belfry. Hale Aloha and the church were both sold to the county in the 1960s. In 1996 the bellfry was restored as a result of efforts of the Lahaina Restoration Foundation. (But they're still looking for a bell!) *Hale Aloha* is now fully restored and used as a framing shop for Lahaina Printsellers. In the neighboring cemetery you will find tombs of several notable members of Hawaiian royalty, including Queen Keopuolani, wife of Kamehameha the Great and mother of Kamehameha II and III. The church is located on Wainee and Shaw Streets. The *Maria Lanakila Church* is on the corner of Wainee and Dickenson. Built in 1928, it is a replica of the 1858 church. Next door is the Seamen's Cemetery.

The *Hawai'i Experience Domed Theatre* ★ at 824 Front Street occupies what was once the site of the old Queen's Theatre and has been recycled into a theatre once again. The 180 degree screen curves up and to the sides of the auditorium, offering an unobstructed view for the 150 seats. The history of the islands is narrated as the viewer is thrilled to a bird's eye view of the remote Hawaiian leeward islands of Tern, Nihoa and Necker. Travel through the jungles and volcanoes of the major islands as well as the underwater world of the Pacific. The adults in our group found the show realistic enough to cause an occasional "seasick" sensation (especially the bike ride down Haleakala), but the kids were riveted and motionless for the 40 minute show. The film, "Hawaii: Island of the Gods," is an informative show and the air-conditioned comfort is a pleasant break from the warm sidewalk shopping in Lahaina. The show is offered hourly from 10am-10pm. $6.95 adults, children (4-12) $3.95, under 3 free. (808) 661-8314.

The Wo Hing Temple on Front Street opened following restoration in late 1984. Built in 1912, it now houses a museum which features the influence of the Chinese population on Maui. Hours are 10am-4:30pm with a $1 admission donation appreciated. The adjacent cook house has become a theater which features movies filmed by Thomas Edison during his trips to Hawai'i in 1898 and 1906. In 1993 a Koban information booth was added near the Wo Hing Temple.

A small, but interesting **Whaling Museum** is located in the Crazy Shirts shop on Front Street. No admission is charged.

Follow Front Street towards Kaanapali to find **The Seamen's Hospital**. This structure was once a hideaway for King Kamehameha III and a gaming house for sailors of Old Lahaina. Now it houses The Paradise Television Network, a local television station.

Hale Pa'i is on the campus of Lahainaluna school. Founded in 1831, Lahainaluna is the oldest school and printing press west of the Rockies. You will find it located just outside of Lahaina at the top of Lahainaluna Road. The hours fluctuate depending on volunteers, so call the Lahaina Restoration office at 661-3262 for current schedule. No admission fee. Donations welcomed.

The Lahaina Jodo Mission is located on the Kaanapali side of Lahaina, on Ala Moana Street near the Mala Wharf. The great Buddha commemorated the 100th anniversary of the Japanese immigration to the islands which was celebrated at the mission in 1968. The grounds are open to the public, but not the buildings. The public is welcome to attend their summer O'Bon festivals, usually in late June and early July. Check the papers for dates and times.

WHERE TO SHOP

Shopping is a prime fascination in Lahaina and it is such a major business that it breeds volatility. Shops change frequently, sometimes seemingly overnight, with a definite "trendiness" to their merchandise. It was a few years back that visitors could view artisans creating scrimshaw in numerous stores. The next few years saw the transformation to T-shirt stores. There still are plenty of clothing stores and a little price comparison can be worthwhile. The next theme was art, art, and more art. Galleries sprang up on every corner. It was a wonderful opportunity to view the fine work of many local artists and international ones as well. Original oils, watercolors, acrylics, carvings and even pottery, were all on display. Rather like a museum without any admission fee! Since the last edition of this guide, we have seen a decline in art galleries. With the prices on these original pieces of artwork in the $$$$$$ figures, perhaps there were more lookers than buyers. Unfortunately, the transition we now see are the eruption of numerous tour and activity book agents. We find that they have infiltrated every nook and cranny, even a corner of one ice cream shop. While some are pleasant enough, others are obnoxious and extremely pushy. More editorial opinion on this in the RECREATION AND TOURS section. In thinking back, only a few of the same shops have remained in operation along Front Street since we began this book some 15 years ago!

Here are a few shops that we feel are worth the mention:

Environmental awareness has arrived at the *Endangered Species Store* at 707 Front St. It's filled with T-shirts, collectibles, books, and toys that all focus on endangered wildlife worldwide. Next door is a fun store with a novel idea that certainly makes this shop memorable from the many others that line Front Street. Step through the door of *The Gecko Store* and take a look at what is under your feet! We'll let you be surprised!

The best representation of local artists may be found at *Lahaina Galleries* located at 728 Front Street in Lahaina and at the Kapalua Shops at 123 Bay Drive. Begun in 1976, their art falls in the $500-$30,000 (and up) range.

A number of "retired" movie and television stars have turned artist and you'll see the work of Tony Curtis, Red Skelton, Anthony Quinn, Buddy Ebsen, and Richard Chamberlain at some of the larger galleries in town. Rock stars like John Lennon, Ron Wood, Miles Davis, Jerry Garcia, and Bob Dylan are represented at Celebrités Gallery of Fine Art at 764 Front Street. Originals, numbered lithographs and poster prints by popular Hawaiian artists Pegge Hopper, Diana Hansen-Young and others can be found at The Village Galleries; David Lee Galleries, Galerie Lassen, Robert Lyn Nelson Studio, and Kingwell Island Arts Collection feature the works of their namesake artists. The Lahaina Arts Society is a non-profit organization featuring work by local Maui artists. Due to the renovation of the Lahaina Courthouse, their Old Jail Gallery and Banyan Tree Gallery have closed. They still feature arts and craft shows under the Banyan Tree on Saturday, but the gallery is currently at Lahaina Center (900 Front Street) across from the movie theaters. They are open 9am-5pm daily, till 9pm on Fridays when they offer "strolling" artists and musicians throughout the center. Friday night in Lahaina is ART NIGHT! Participating galleries feature a special event between 6 and 9pm that might include guest artists.

Island Sandals is tucked away in a niche of the Wharf Cinema Center near the postal center at 658 Front Street, Space #125, Lahaina, Maui, HI 96761, (661-5110). Michael Mahnensmith is the proprietor and creator of custom-made sandals. He learned his craft in Santa Monica from David Webb who was making sandals for the Greek and Roman movies of the late 50's and early 60's. He rediscovered his sandal design from the sandals used 3,000 years ago by the desert warriors of Ethiopia. He developed the idea while living in Catalina in the 1960's and copyrighted it in 1978. The sandals are all leather, which is porous and keeps the feet cool and dry, with the exception of a non-skid synthetic heel.

The sandals feature a single strap which laces around the big toe, then over and under the foot, and around the heel, providing comfort and good arch support. As the sandal breaks in, the strap stretches and you simply adjust the entire strap to maintain proper fit (which makes them feel more like a shoe than a sandal). They are clever and functional. His sandals have been copied by others, but never duplicated. So beware of other sandals which appear the same, but don't offer the fit, comfort or function of Michael's! The charge for ladies is $115 for the right shoe and the left shoe is free. Men's sizes are $135 (Slightly higher over size 13). Anyone who gets shoes from Island Sandals becomes an agent and is authorized to trace foot prints of others. Commissions are automatic when your sales reach the "high range." (However, you must like coconuts and bananas.) Michael stresses the importance of good footwear, so stop in upon your arrival! Sandals can also be ordered by sending a tracing of both feet and both big toes, including the spaces in-between (or by having an "authorized agent" do so) along with the purchase price and shipping charge of $8 (US) or $15 (International) to Island Sandals. Michael can also assist with leather repair of your shoes, purses, bags, or suitcases.

A three-screen movie theater is located on the upper level of the *Wharf Cinema Center* with seating capacity for 330 people (matinees before 3:30 and all-day Tuesday prices are currently $4). The *Fun Factory* is located in the lower level with video games and prize-oriented games. Watch artists at work and buy all Maui-made gifts at *Hawaiiana Arts & Crafts*. The novelty of *Magnet Madness* is a new addition, and *Tuna Luna* is a particularly nice gift store with unique jewelry items, candle holders, palm brush animals, ceramics, and petroglyphs in every form. *Island Swimwear* has stood the test of time, although the many restaurants throughout the center seem to be as changeable as they are varied.

Although built nearly a century later, *Dickenson Square* (On Dickenson St. off Front St.) bears a strong resemblance to the Pioneer Inn. The Contemporary Village Gallery, Whalers General Store, Sub Shack Deli and Pizza, and Lahaina Coolers restaurant are located here.

Walking south on Front Street you'll pass the Banyan Tree and Kamehameha III School before you come to *Kamehameha Iki Park* (also known as Armory Park) on your right. *Hui O Wa'a Kaulua* (the assembly of the double hulled canoe) is a nonprofit organization that is working with the County of Maui to develop and maintain it as a Hawaiian cultural park that offers both exhibits and "hands-on" experiences. The focus will be the design, construction, sailing, and maintenance of magnificent Hawaiian double-hulled sailing canoes constructed along traditional lines. Two *Hale Wa'a*, or canoe houses will be constructed. They will be thirty-seven feet tall, forty-one feet wide and one-hundred feet long. The two *Hale Wa'a* will house three double-hulled canoes on the ground floor with room in the

ceiling for smaller or lighter canoes. A 62 foot double-hulled canoe of traditional design with a single sail has already been constructed. The canoe is named *Mo'okiha*, which means sacred lizard/dragon. They also have a 42.5-foot canoe called *Mo'olele*.

Plans also include the construction of a kitchen, as well as a covered picnic area with space for working, teaching, and demonstrating Hawaiian crafts. Landscaping of the park will include vegetation that will serve the Hawaiian activities, such as ti, taro, bamboo, Hawaiian medicinal plants and bananas.

Completion of these projects is anticipated within the next five years. If you would like more information or are interested in membership, contact *Hui O Wa'a Kaulua*, 525 Front Street, Lahaina, HI 96761. Family membership is $50, adult dues $25.

Across the street (at what is now a baseball field and parking lot), is *Moku'ula*, a sacred place for royalty from the early fifteenth century. Once a kapu (forbidden) island in the center of an 11-acre fishpond (*Loko o Mokuhinia*), *Moku'ula* was part of the region known as *Kalua O Kiha* - the center of ali'i residence when Lahaina was capital of the kingdom. Today, the non-profit *Friends of Moku'ula* are continuing the historical and archeological study of the area and hope to restore this private compound of King Kamehameha III along with the natural pond and royal island that once comprised this ancient site. To learn more about the project and/or send a donation, write to: *Friends of Moku'ula*, c/o Akoni Akana, 505 Front St., Suite 234, Lahaina, HI 96761 or visit their website at < www.hookele.com/mokuula >

505 Front Street (across the street and next door to the park) was originally developed as a shopping center; unsuccessfully converted into condominiums; and now restored into shops and restaurants. *Maui Cafe* and *Village Pizzeria* offer a respite for the hungry shopper or there is oceanfront dining at *Hecocks* and *Pacific'O*. A new luau and restaurant were expected to open by the end of 1998. (Shops here change faster than we can keep track!)

Dan's Green House at 133 Prison Street (661-8412) has a variety of beautiful tropical birds for sale as well as an array of plants for shipping home. Their specialty is Fuku-Bonsai "Lava Rock" plants. These bonsai are well packaged to tolerate the trip home.

The old Hamburger Mary's/Tasca building at 608 Front Street (at Prison) is now called *Aloha Avenue*, an arts & crafts center for Maui-made products and gifts. Historic district restrictions required that they keep the facade, but the back has been rebuilt to encompass a garden patio where guest artists will show works-in-progress and offer demonstrations.

Lahaina Center, on the Kaanapali end of Lahaina, is composed of two parts. The Lahaina Shopping Center is newly renovated (which some sections completely razed and rebuilt) and is now called "Old Lahaina Center." New roofing, terra cotta & marble-print walkways, planters, and a new elevator have modernized the existing part of the shopping center. The "new" old center is now anchored by Foodland supermarket which moved from their location across the street at

Lahaina Square after the closing of the more than 30-year-old Nagasako Supermarket. The longtime Kamaaina family now operates the new Nagasako Okazu-ya and Wiki Wiki Mart next to the Nagasako Variety Store. The "New Lahaina Center" located across the street, is a low level structure with pioneer type architecture and a validated parking lot. A free exhibit housed here is the *Hale Kahiko* Hawaiian village which depicts the living quarters of ancient Hawai'i with thatched *hale* (houses) on display. (Open daily with free activities Mon-Fri). There is also a Japanese garden with seating by a bridge-covered pond. The 17,000 square foot *Hilo Hattie* is famous around the islands for its aloha wear. We'd recommend it for its good selection of "touristy" souvenirs, including key chains, jams & jellies, tropical candy, and macadamia nuts. (Hilo Hattie is the only retail establishment ever to win the Kahili "Keep it Hawaiian" Award for "Best Attraction" from the Hawai'i Visitors Bureau!) Another shop/attraction is the Lahaina Gun Club which offers target shooting as well as upscale Western clothes and jewelry. The *Hard Rock Cafe* has always been a popular spot although they may have some competition with the recent arrival of *Ruth's Chris Steak House, Sam Choy's*, and *Maui Brews*. There is also a multi-screen movie theater with $4 bargain matinees before 3:30pm.

An area slightly removed from Lahaina's Front Street is termed the industrial area. Follow Honoapiilani Hwy. and turn by the Pizza Hut. *The Sugar Cane Train* (661-0089) offers a nostalgic trip between Kaanapali and Lahaina. Round trip fare for adults is $14, children 3-12 years is $7.50. They have several package options that combine the train ride with another Lahaina experience. The prices on the packages offer a bit of a discount if you were to price the two activities separately. Make your plans early as space is limited and sometimes the return trips are booked. The red double decker bus will transfer you from the Sugar Cane Depot to the Wharf Cinema Center and in front of Pioneer Inn. You can catch the bus back to the train depot from these same locations.

Also in the industrial area, *The Bakery* is a personal favorite for some really fine pastries and breads. *MGM, Maui Gold Manufacturing* (661-8981), not only does standard repairs, but designs outstanding jewelry pieces. They can design something to your specifications, or choose a piece from one of their many photograph books. A limited number of pieces are ready made for sale as well. *J.R.'s Music Shop* (661-0801), on the back side of The Bakery building, has a large selection of Hawaiian tapes and records as well as just about any other type of music.

Just on the Kaanapali side of Lahaina (a drive of less than a mile) is *The Lahaina Cannery Mall* opened in 1987. The original structure, built in 1920, was used as a pineapple cannery until its closure in 1963, and this new facility was built to resemble its predecessor. It's easy to spot as you leave Lahaina heading for Kaanapali. A large parking area makes for convenient access. This enclosed air-conditioned mall is anchored by *Safeway* and *Longs Drug Store*. Within the mall are several fast food eateries, as well as sit-down dining at *Compadres* restaurant or *Mango Cafe*. Shops include a coffee house, dive shop, jewelry, clothing, and sporting goods stores plus Waldenbooks and Lahaina Printsellers. (A multi-million dollar renovation including expansion of the food court, center stage, and public restrooms along with more kiosks, sliding doors, improved landscaping, brighter colors and lighting, a tropical fruit theme, Compadres upgrade, and an

Lahaina

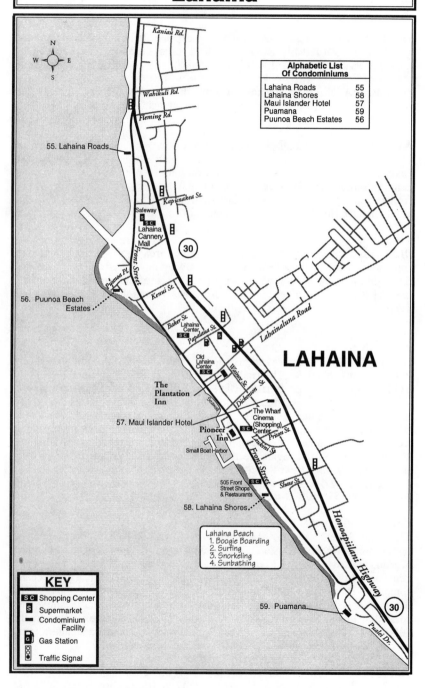

Kaniau Rd.

Wahikuli Rd.

Fleming Rd.

Alphabetic List Of Condominiums

Lahaina Roads	55
Lahaina Shores	58
Maui Islander Hotel	57
Puamana	59
Puunoa Beach Estates	56

55. Lahaina Roads

Kapunakea St.

Safeway
Lahaina Cannery Mall

(30)

Puunoa Pl.

Front Street

56. Puunoa Beach Estates

Kenui St.

Baker St.
Lahaina Center

Papalaua St.

Lahainaluna Road

LAHAINA

Old Lahaina Center

Wainee St.

Dickenson St.

The Plantation Inn

Seawall

57. Maui Islander Hotel

The Wharf Cinema (Shopping) Center

Prison St.

Pioneer Inn

Luakini St.

Small Boat Harbor

Front Street

505 Front Street Shops & Restaurants

Shaw St.

58. Lahaina Shores

Lahaina Beach
1. Boogie Boarding
2. Surfing
3. Snorkeling
4. Sunbathing

Honoapiilani Highway

59. Puamana

(30)

Pualei Dr.

KEY

SC	Shopping Center
S	Supermarket
—	Condominium Facility
G	Gas Station
000	Traffic Signal

overall enhancement and modernization was expected to be completed by the end of 1998.) The *Old Lahaina Luau* is now held across the street (ocean side of the center) at its new, expanded location at *Moa'li'i*.

BE FOREWARNED!!! If you have the time, do a lot of window shopping before you buy. Prices can vary significantly on some items from one store to another.

ACCOMMODATIONS - LAHAINA

Puamana	Plantation Inn
Lahaina Shores Beach Resort	Lahaina Inn
Pioneer Inn	Lahaina Roads
Maui Islander Hotel	Puunoa

BEST BETS: *Puamana* - A nice residential type area of two-plex and four-plex units, some oceanfront. *Lahaina Shores* - A moderately priced colonial style high rise right on the beach and within walking distance of Lahaina shops. *Lahaina Inn* and *Plantation Inn* are both tastefully done with all the elegance of bygone days.

PUAMANA ★
PO Box 11108, Lahaina, Maui, HI 96761. (808) 667-2551, 1-800-628-6731. Rental Agents: Maui & All Island 1-800-663-6962, Hale Hawaiian 1-800-854-8843, Maui Beachfront Rentals 1-888-661-7200, Klahani 1-800-669-MAUI, Whalers Realty 1-800-367-5632. A series of duplexes and four-plexes in a garden setting with 228 units. This large oceanside complex resembles a residential community much more than a vacation resort. The variation in price reflects location in the complex, oceanfront to gardenview. Some rental agents offer per night rates; 3 BR units available through Klahani and perhaps other booking agents. *Weekly rates from Whalers Realty:*
1 BR g.v. $840/770; 1 BR o.f. $1155/1100;
2 BR g.v. $1155/1100; 2 BR o.f. $1500/1350

LAHAINA SHORES BEACH RESORT ★
475 Front Street, Lahaina, Maui, HI 96761. (808) 661-4835 (Hotel only, no reservations). Agents: Classic Resorts 1-800-628-6699. This seven-story building of plantation style offers 200 oceanfront units with air-conditioning, lanais, full kitchens, daily maid service, and laundry facilities on each floor. They recently completed room renovations and resurfacing of the pool and patio areas. The beach here is fair and the water calm due to offshore reefs, but shallow with coral. Lahaina town is only a short walk away, plus this complex neighbors the 505 Front Street Shopping Center which offers several restaurants and a small grocery/convenience store. Car/condo packages also available.
SBR (2;max 3) mt.v.-o.f. $130-160 /120-145;
1BR (2;max 4) mt.v. $180/155; 1BR (2;max 4) o.f. $210/180;
PENTHOUSE(2;max 5) mt.v. $220/190; PENTHOUSE(2;max 5) o.f. $245/215

(BEST WESTERN) PIONEER INN (Hotel)
658 Wharf St., PO Box 243, Lahaina, Maui, HI 96764. 1-800-457-5457, FAX
(808) 667-5708, (808) 661-3636. Website: < www.bestwestern.com > Email:
< pioneer@maui.net >

George Freeland, a robust 300 pound, 6 ft. 5 inch Englishman, had relocated to
Vancouver, Canada and become a Royal Canadian Mountie. He was sent to
Hawai'i in 1900 to capture a suspect, but failing to do so, chose to make Maui
his home. He formed the Pioneer Hotel Co., Ltd and sold $50 shares of stock.
In October of 1901 he constructed the hotel as accommodations for the inter-
island travelers. Similar to the plantation house of the Maunalei Sugar Company
on Lana'i, the total cost of constructing the hotel was $6,000. (Note: On Lana'i
we heard a report that the Maunalei Plantation House was transported to Maui
and became Pioneer Inn, but this was not accurate. Apparently, years ago, the
Honolulu Star-Bulletin printed an article to this effect. George Alan Freeland, son
of Pioneer Inn's founder George Freeland spoke with Lawrence Gay, the owner
of most of Lana'i at the turn of the century, and was told that when the
construction of Pioneer Hotel was completed, the similar-designed building on the
island of Lana'i was still standing.) Soon George Freeland opened the Pioneer
saloon, the Pioneer Grange, the Pioneer Wholesale Liquor Company and in 1913
the Pioneer Theater. The Pioneer Theater ran silent movies to packed crowds and
had stage shows and plays in the theater as well. George Freeland died on July
25, 1925, survived by his wife, a Hawaiian woman, three sons and four
daughters. His eldest son, George Alan Freeland, ran the business until the early
1960's. His grandson, George "Keoki" Freeland, is now the Director of the
Lahaina Restoration Foundation. In the late 1960's the inn was expanded and at
that time the theater was torn down. A complete history of the Pioneer Inn is
available along with their brochure. A guest in 1901 would have been required
to adhere to the following bizarre "house rules:"

> *"You must pay you rent in advance. You must not let you room go one day
> back. Women is not allow in you room. If you wet or burn you bed you going
> out. You are not allow to gamble in you room. You are not allow to give you
> bed to you freand. If you freand stay overnight you must see the mgr. You
> must leave you room at 11 am so the women can clean you room. Only on
> Sunday you can sleep all day. You are not allow in the down stears in the
> seating room or in the dinering room or in the kitchen when you are drunk.
> You are not allow to drink on the front porch. You must use a shirt when you
> come to the seating room. If you cant keep this rules please dont take the
> room."*

With such a colorful history, Pioneer Inn remains a nostalgic Lahaina landmark.
Best Western International took over property management in January of 1998
and began room renovation to include queen beds, tiled modern bathrooms, air
conditioning and ceiling fans, color tv, radio, and direct-dial telephones. A
courtyard swimming pool was also added. Room rates vary seasonally: Two
deluxe units with mini-bar facility and refrigerators are available. One of these
units has two queen beds. Room rates $135-189. The other deluxe unit has one
queen bed and adjoins with another standard single queen making this into a two
room suite with wetbar and refrigerator $169-209. The remaining rooms have
three descriptions. The Banyan Tree Park View overlooks the historic Banyan

Tree. The Front Street View faces directly toward Front Street. The Court-yard/poolside rooms are all non-smoking and face the interior of the property and are the quietest. A total of 50 guest rooms will be available when renovations are complete. *All three room locations have single queen beds and run $90-120.*

MAUI ISLANDER HOTEL
660 Wainee Street, Lahaina, Maui, HI 96761. (808) 667-9766, Aston 1-800-922-7866. Aston assumed the management of this property in 1998, announcing $1 million dollars in planned improvements during 1998 and 1999. The 374-unit property includes 11 two-story buildings set on nearly 10 acres, featuring hotel rooms, studios, deluxe studios and one-and two-bedroom suites. All include full kitchens, except for the hotel rooms which feature mini-refrigerators.Located in the heart of Lahaina town, less than a 5 minute walk to the sea wall, yet far enough away to be peaceful. The back of the building borders the Honoapiilani Hwy., so front units may be a bit quieter. Daily maid service, air-conditioning, laundry facilities, tennis courts, pool. *Hotel Room $82-92; Studio $95-105; Deluxe Studio $104-114; 1 BR $115-125 2 BR Room $172-182*

PLANTATION INN ★
174 Lahainaluna Rd., Lahaina, Maui, HI 96761 (808) 667-9225, 1-800-433-6815, FAX (808) 667-9293. This 18 room building has all the charm of an old inn, while incorporating all the benefits of modernization. Filled with antiques, beautiful Victorian decor, hardwood floors, and stained glass, they also offer air-conditioning, refrigerators and even VCR's. Very quiet, too! We'd recommend the newer wing with patios out to the pool area or balconies on the second floor. Some units even have kitchens and jacuzzi tubs! Located just blocks from the ocean in the heart of Lahaina, it also has a 12 foot deep tiled pool, and a spa. (A great benefit is that the spa is open 24 hours!) An added bonus is the outstanding Gerard's Restaurant, just footsteps away, for your evening dining pleasure. Fresh fruit, outstanding French toast, piping hot coffee all served in their lovely poolside room or around the pool. We were surprised by the number of families with young children who seemed to find this modern inn the ideal family vacation spot. *Room rates range: High season $119-219; low season $104-195.*

LAHAINA INN ★ (Hotel)
127 Lahainaluna Rd., Lahaina, Maui, HI 96761. (808) 661-0577, FAX (808) 667-9480, 1-800-669-3444. The history of this property is an interesting one. Built in 1938 by Tomezo Masuda for his general store, Maui Trading Company, it was apparently a popular place for World War II army men to "hang loose." Dickie, the Masuda's black German Shepherd, became legendary for his mail run. He would make the trip to the Lahaina post office to fetch the store's mail. In 1949, the Tabata family purchased the business from Masuda, but by the early 1960's the business failed and the building was placed at public auction. George Izaki purchased the property and made the street level store into four business spaces and transformed the second floor into a hotel. A fire destroyed the business in the mid 1960's. The interior was reconstructed and the Lahainaluna Hotel was developed in the second story level. There were 19 rooms and three baths. The hotel gradually deteriorated. In the early 1980's when we toured the property for the first edition of this guidebook, the Lahainaluna was renting for $20 a night. And that was a lot for what you got.

In 1986 Rick Ralston, who also owns Crazy Shirts, undertook renovations at this ideally situated location and the transformation was dramatic. Gone are the cheap "rustic" units. The fully air-conditioned hotel has 13 rooms for single or double occupancy only. The hotel has been restored exactly as if it were sent into a time warp between 1860 and 1900. (That means no televisions, too!) No details have been overlooked from the authentic antiques to the ceiling moldings. All the furnishings have come from Rick Ralston's personal collection so each room is different. The headboards and footboards are intricately carved as are the highboy dressers. Each room is unique with lush wallpaper in deep greens, burgundy, blues and golds and offers a small, but adequate private bathroom. Each has its own lanai complete with rocking chairs. Other amenities include in-room bottled water and classical music piped into the rooms if you choose. In-room phones offer free local calls. Considering you are in the center of town, the rooms are surprisingly quiet. The rooms are not only beautifully decorated, but the maintenance of them is superb. In the morning, a few steps down the hall will lead you to the buffet with steaming hot coffee, fresh fruit and muffins or croissants.

If you can do without the oceanview, we can't imagine a more romantic, charming and intimate way to spend your Maui vacation. Adjacent is the David Paul's Lahaina Grill. Parking $5 per day. Honeymoon packages. *Standard rooms with full size bed or two twin-size m.v. $99/89. Harbor view with full-size bed $109/99. Makai Room with full-size bed and harbor view $149/139. Mauka Room, queen-size bed, with Harbor & m.v. $149/139. Lahainaluna Room, m.v., king-size bed $149/139. (6th night free!)*

LAHAINA ROADS
1403 Front St., Lahaina, Maui, HI 96761. (808) 661-3166. No bookings available from the resident manager. Agent: Klahani Resorts 1-800-669-0795. Forty-two oceanview units, covered parking and elevator to upper levels. Microwaves, washer/dryer, cable. A very unpretentious, non-resort looking property. Klahani Rates: *1 BR o.f. (2,max 4) $100, 2 BR (4,max 6) $180*

PUUNOA BEACH ESTATES
45 Kai Pali Place, Lahaina, Maui, HI 96761. Agents: Classic Resorts (808) 667-1400, 1-800-642-MAUI. Amenities include full size swimming pool, jacuzzi, his and hers sauna, and paddle tennis courts. Units include laundry rooms, lanais, master bath with jacuzzi, full bar, and daily maid service. These luxury units are located on Puunoa Beach in a residential area just north of Lahaina. Beautiful and spacious air-conditioned units, convenient to restaurants and shops. The beachfront has a coral reef which makes for calm conditions for children, but swimming or snorkeling are poor due to the shallowness and coral. A full size rental car is included. Three night minimum.
2 BR 2 bath o.f. (4) $580/550, 2 BR with loft (6) $695/580
3 BR o.f $730/605, 3 BR with loft (8) $800/665

KAANAPALI

INTRODUCTION

The drive from Lahaina is quick (unless it's rush hour - or "luau time"). All that is really visible from the highway are a couple of gas stations, the old mill, a few nondescript commercial buildings, and a Pizza Hut. Old Lahaina and the water-front a couple of large blocks off to the left, cannot be seen. The large shopping center on the left is the Cannery, described previously. As you leave Lahaina, the vista opens up with views of the Hyatt Regency and the beginning of the Kaanapali Beach Resort a mile off in the distance. The resort is beautifully framed by the West Maui mountains on the right, the peaks of Moloka'i (appearing to be another part of Maui in the background) the island of Lana'i off to the left, and of course, the ocean. The name Kaanapali means "rolling cliffs" or "land divided by cliffs" and refers to the wide, open ridges that stretch up behind the resort toward Pu'u Kukui, West Maui's highest peak. The beaches and plush resorts here are what many come to Hawai'i to find.

Kaanapali began in the early 1960s as an Amfac Development with the first hotels, the Royal Lahaina and the Sheraton Maui, opening in late 1962 and early 1963, respectively. The Kaanapali Beach Resort, 500 acres along three miles of prime beachfront, is reputed to be the first large-scale planned resort in the world. There are six beachfront hotels and seven condominiums which total more than 5,000 rooms and units, two golf courses, 37 tennis courts, and a shopping village.

The resort boasts the most convention space of any of the neighboring islands, with the Maui Marriott, Westin Maui and the Hyatt Regency being popular locations. All the hotels are located beachfront, although some of the condos are situated above the beach in the golf course area. All are priced in the luxury range. The wide avenues and the spaciousness of the resort's lush green and manicured grounds are most impressive. No on-street parking and careful planning have successfully given this resort a feeling of spaciousness. Nestled between a pristine white sand beach and scenic golf courses with a mountain range beyond, this may be the ideal spot for your vacation.

This may be paradise, but traffic congestion between Kaanapali and Lahaina may have reminded you more of LA in the past few years. Non-synchronized traffic lights, roads designed for 20 years ago, and greatly increased traffic, caused the three mile transit through Lahaina to Kaanapali (or Kaanapali to Lahaina) to consume over an hour during the afternoon rush (most other times there was only light traffic). Of deep concern to the government, residents and business interests alike, this situation was eased considerably with the completion of four lanes from Kaanapali to Lahaina. The two Kaanapali to Lahaina shuttles have also somewhat eased congestion. The major bottleneck is now at the first Kaanapali entrance where the four lanes end. Getting past this point in either direction can be difficult. Hopefully, the four lanes will extend up to at least Napili or Kahana in the near future.

Lahaina and Kaanapali

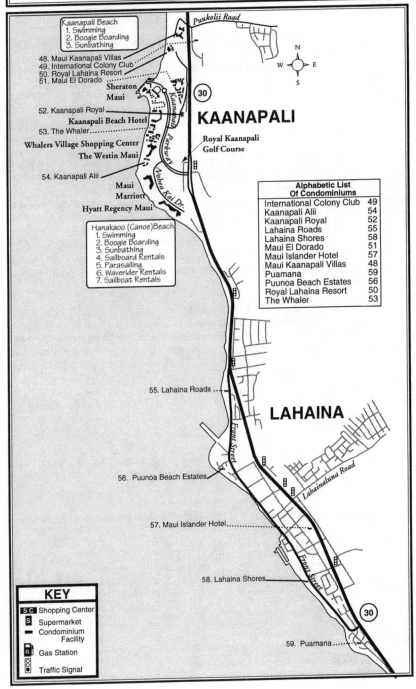

Puukolii Road

Kaanapali Beach
1. Swimming
2. Boogie Boarding
3. Sunbathing

48. Maui Kaanapali Villas
49. International Colony Club
50. Royal Lahaina Resort
51. Maui El Dorado

Sheraton
Maui

52. Kaanapali Royal
Kaanapali Beach Hotel
53. The Whaler
Whalers Village Shopping Center
The Westin Maui

54. Kaanapali Alii

Maui
Marriott
Hyatt Regency Maui

30

KAANAPALI

Royal Kaanapali
Golf Course

Kaanapali Parkway

Nohea Kai Dr.

Hanakaoo (Canoe)Beach
1. Swimming
2. Boogie Boarding
3. Sunbathing
4. Sailboard Rentals
5. Parasailing
6. Waverider Rentals
7. Sailboat Rentals

Alphabetic List Of Condominiums

International Colony Club	49
Kaanapali Alii	54
Kaanapali Royal	52
Lahaina Roads	55
Lahaina Shores	58
Maui El Dorado	51
Maui Islander Hotel	57
Maui Kaanapali Villas	48
Puamana	59
Puunoa Beach Estates	56
Royal Lahaina Resort	50
The Whaler	53

55. Lahaina Roads

LAHAINA

Front Street

Lahainaluna Road

56. Puunoa Beach Estates

57. Maui Islander Hotel

Front Street

58. Lahaina Shores

30

KEY

SC	Shopping Center
S	Supermarket
—	Condominium Facility
G	Gas Station
	Traffic Signal

59. Puamana

Until recently, Kahekili Park was the only development in the former Kaanapali Airport location at the far end of the resort, but Amfac hopes to build a six-story, 280-unit timeshare condominium on an adjacent 14 acres. Construction has been awaiting a number of things, including the aforementioned road improvements, but the more immediate problem is the controversy that this new project has generated.

WHAT TO DO AND SEE

The Hyatt Regency Maui and ***The Westin Maui*** must be put at the top of everyone's list of things to see. Few hotels can boast that they need their own wildlife manager, but upon entry you'll see why they do. Without spoiling the surprises too much, just envision the Hyatt with palm trees growing through the lobby, flamingos strolling by, and parrots perched amid extraordinary pieces of Oriental art. The lagoon and black swans are spectacular. And did we mention there are penquins, too? The pool area occupies two acres and features two swim-through waterfalls and a cavern in the middle with a swim up bar. A swinging bridge is suspended over one of the two pools and a water slide offers added thrills particularly for the young traveler.

To appreciate the Westin Maui, a little background may be necessary. The Maui Surf was the original hotel with the single curved building and a large expanse of lush green lawn and two pools. The transformation has been extraordinary. The pool areas are unsurpassed, with five swimming pools on various levels fed by waterfalls and connected by two slides. There are exotic birds afloat on the lagoons which greet you upon your arrival and glide gracefully by two of the hotel's restaurants. The Oriental art collection surpasses even the Hyatt's. Both resorts feature glamorous shopping arcades - with prices to match, of course! Both developments were designed by the remarkable, champion hotel builder of Hawaii, Chris Hemmeter.

WHERE TO SHOP

Whalers Village shopping center is located in the heart of Kaanapali. Some part or other of this center always seems to be under construction or renovation. It offers a small grocery store, restaurants and a food court. Recent renovations have brought in very "high end" specialty and boutique shops. These designer clothing stores and jewelry stores (including Tiffany's) offer little for the average shopper. There are still a couple of clothing stores, including a Crazy Shirts outlet. Other shops include *Waikiki Aloe, Elephant Walk, The Body Shop, Lahaina Printsellers*, an art gallery, and several novelty stores. The mall is a pleasant place for an evening stroll and shop-browsing, before or after dinner, followed by a seaside walk back to your accommodations on the paved beachfront sidewalk.

Hale Kohola (House of the Whale) is a museum located on the upper level of the shopping center. Admission is free, but donations are welcome. They recently expanded in size and have a wonderful exhibition of the great whales with special emphasis on the Humpback Whale. The information director gives lectures on topics from scrimshaw to the life of a sailor. Call for times at their local number 661-5992. Private group lectures are also a possibility.

Restaurants include *The Rusty Harpoon, Leilani's*, and *Hula Grill*. All are beachfront and good options for breakfast, lunch or dinner. The Food Court offers several additional dining options.

A multi-level parking structure is adjacent to the mall and parking is $1 for the first two hours or fraction thereof, and 50¢ for each additional half hour, with a $10 maximum charge. Restaurants can provide validation or you can find 2-hours free coupons in many of the visitor publications.

ACCOMMODATIONS - KAANAPALI

Hyatt Regency Maui
Maui Marriott Resort
Kaanapali Alii
Westin Maui
The Whaler
Kaanapali Beach Hotel
Sheraton Maui

Royal Lahaina Resort
Maui Kaanapali Villas
Kaanapali Plantation
International Colony Club
Maui Eldorado
Kaanapali Royal

BEST BETS: *Hyatt Regency Maui* - An elegant and exotic setting with a wonderful selection of great restaurants. *Maui Marriott Resort* - Beautiful grounds with a nice pool area and attractively decorated rooms. *Westin Maui* - A gorgeous resort and a pool lover's paradise. *Kaanapali Alii* - One of only three condominiums that are oceanfront. Luxurious, expensive and spacious. (Christie's choice to purchase a unit with future lottery winnings!) *Royal Lahaina Resort* - A beautiful property on sandy Kaanapali Beach. *The Whaler* - Condominiums on the heart of Honokaoo Beach adjacent to the Whalers Village Shopping Center. NOTE: Some resort hotels have begun charging guests a daily parking fee.

HYATT REGENCY MAUI ★ (Hotel)

200 Nohea Kai Drive, Lahaina, Maui, HI 96761. (808) 661-1234, 1-800-223-1234. This magnificent complex is located on 40 beachfront acres and offers 815 rooms and suites. The beach is beautiful, but has a steep drop off. Adjoining Hanokao'o Beach Park offers a gentler slope into deeper water. The pool area is an impressive feature, covering two acres and resembling a contemporary adventure that Robinson Crusoe could only have dreamt. The pool is divided by a large cavern that can be reached on either side by swimming beneath a waterfall. The more adventurous can try out their waterslide. One side of the pool is spanned by a large swinging rope bridge. The kids just love walking back and forth with the swaying motion! Penguins, jewel-toned koi, parrots, swans, cranes, and flamingos around the grounds require full time game keepers. The lobby is a blend of beautiful pieces of oriental art and paths that lead to the grounds. The tropical birds are so at home here that some are reproducing, a rarity for some of these species in captivity! Non-guests should definitely visit the Hyatt for a self guided tour of the grounds, the art, the elegant shops and for an opportunity to enjoy one of this resort's fine restaurants which include Swan Court, Spats, Cascades, Pavilion and the luau show. It's worth coming here just to look around! Parking $8 per day, validated parking for diners. The newest addition is the outdoor wedding gazebo. Made of natural *ohia* wood from the Big Island, it is set amid a tropical Hawaiian garden overlooking the ocean. All rooms offer complimentary access to the health club. A novel and popular activity is the **Hyatt's Tour of the Stars**. Shows are three times nightly on the hotel rooftop. Seating is limited to 10 persons per show, cost is $12 adults, $6 children 12 and under.

The Regency Club at the Hyatt consists of two floors that feature special services, including continental breakfast, evening cocktails, and appetizers. Room rates based on single/double occupancy. Maximum 3 adults or 2 adults/2 children. *Terrace $275; golf/mountain.view $345; partial o.f. $375; o.f. $415; Regency Club partial o.v. $455; regency club o.f. $495; Ocean Suite $660; Deluxe Suite $900; Regency Suite $1,400; Presidential Suite or Palace Suite $3,000*

PARROTS

MAUI MARRIOTT ★ (Hotel)

100 Nohea Kai Drive, Lahaina, Maui, HI 96761. 1-800-228-9290, (808) 667-1200, FAX (808) 667-8300. Marriot website with Maui descriptions at: <www.marriott/hi-070.htm> This 720 room complex has a large, open lobby in the middle featuring an array of fine shops. Although not as exotic as its neighbor, the Hyatt, this is still a very attractive, upscale property. The pool area is large and a keiki (children's) wading pool is a welcome addition for families. Their "Keiki Kamp," a children's activity and adventure program, is offered Monday-Friday for guests aged 6-12 years. Fee includes lunch, transportation, and a camp T-shirt. On-site restaurants are Nikko Japanese Steak House, Lokelani, Moana Terrace and the Kau Kau Grill. "Lobby Bar & Sushi" opened in early 1998, as did a new fitness center located next to the Maui Beach & Tennis Club. Complimentary water aerobics classes as well as low impact aerobics and power walking are available. Inquire regarding their current package plans, one package is their "Maui Grab Bag" which includes an ocean view room, choice of compact car and free parking or full buffet breakfast for two, discounted rates from May-December. *Leisure Rates (single or double): Standard $209, Ocean View $229, Deluxe Ocean $249, Junior Suites $349, Oceanfront Suites $399-595, Presidential Suite $1,000. Plus $7 per day parking fee.*

KAANAPALI ALII ★

50 Nohea Kai Dr., Lahaina, Maui, HI 96761. 1-800-367-6090. Agents: Classic Resorts 1-800-642-MAUI or FAX (808) 661-0147, Whalers Realty 1-800-676-4112, Hale Hawaiian. All 264 units are very spacious and beautifully furnished, with air-conditioning, microwaves, washer/dryer, and daily maid service. Other amenities include security entrances and covered parking. The 1-bedroom units have a den, which actually makes them equivalent to a 2-bedroom. Three lighted tennis courts, pool (also a children's pool), and exercise room. No restaurants on the property, but shops and restaurants are within easy walking distance. A very elegant, high-class and quiet property with a very cordial staff and concierge department. They charge for local phone calls from room, as do most hotels. Rates are through Classic Resorts and require 3 night minimum during high season, no minimum low season. *1 BR (2, max 4) g.v. $270/240; o.v. $330/285 2 BR (4, max 6) g.v. $340/295; o.f. $540/490*

WESTIN MAUI ★ (Hotel)

2365 Kaanapali Parkway, Lahaina, Maui, HI 96761. (808) 667-2525). Westin Central Reservations 1-800-228-3000. Under the direction of Chris Hemmeter, champion hotel builder in Hawaii, this gorgeous resort offers 761 deluxe rooms, including 28 suites. The Westin Maui has an ocean tower of 11 stories with 556 guest rooms and a beach tower with 206 guest rooms and suites. Guest rooms are available for those with disabilities as well as non-smoking floors. The rooms have been designed in comfortable hues of muted peach and beige. The top two floors of the new tower house the Royal Beach Club which offers guests complimentary continental breakfast buffet, afternoon cocktails, evening cocktails and hors d'oeuvres, and a private concierge. Complimentary shuttle service is offered to the Royal Lahaina Tennis Ranch, the largest tennis facility on Kaanapali with 11 tennis courts and 6 courts lit for night play. Conference and banquet facilities are available as well as an array of gift, art, and fashion shops. Eight restaurants and lounges overlook the ocean, waterfalls and pools. The hotel exercise room includes weight rooms, sauna, and whirlpools.

The Westin offers three tours to help guests learn more about their resort. Tour the grounds with a guide to learn more about the Westin's family of birds and their tropical surroundings. This resort's 2.5 million art collection could put a museum to shame and each piece was carefully selected and placed personally by Chris Hemmeter. An art collection tour, as well as a self-guide book, are available. Another option is to take a personalized stroll around the manicured 12-acre grounds of the resort to learn more about the flora and fauna found on this resort property. One of the features we like best are the numerous nooks with comfortable chairs and art work that provide intimate conversation areas.

Parents may enjoy a brief respite while the kids enjoy the resort's Westin Kids Club Keiki Kamp for youth ages 5-12 years. It runs daily from 9am-3pm. The participation fee is $45 for the first child and $30 for additional siblings. A night program is offered evenings. Participation is $20 for the first child and $10 for additional siblings. Another family-friendly amenity is the kid's laundry bag provided at check-in! Bag up your stuff and they'll charge only a flat rate of $12.50. Kids will also enjoy the new "Miracle Slide" which carries guests along a 128 foot ride with a dramatic 23 foot drop and two squeal-inducing 270 degree turns. At the end of the waterslide, vacationers are splashed with a whoosh down 23 feet into the family pool. There are a total of five swimming pools (a total of 55,000 square feet of pool!) with two other waterslides and a grotto with a swim up bar, making a pool day an adventure for the whole family. (Ask about family specials and packages!)

For those planning a wedding on Maui, the Westin has their own Director of Romance to assist you with your wedding or honeymoon plans. On property restaurants include Sound of the Falls (open only for Sunday Brunch), The Villa Restaurant, Sea Dogs, Cook's at the Beach and Sen Ju Sushi Bar.

Rates are based on single or double occupancy. Third person add $25, to Royal Beach Club add $45 (maximum 3 persons to a room). Family Plan offers no extra charge for children 18 or under sharing the same room as parents. A 25% discount is available for additional rooms occupied. Complimentary valet parking. *Terrace $265, garden view $295, golf or mountain view $345, oceanview $375, deluxe ocean view $425, ocean front $445, Royal Beach Club o.v. $495, Suites $800-3,000*

THE WHALER ★
2481 Kaanapali Parkway, Lahaina, Maui, HI 96761. (808) 661-4861. Managed by Village Resorts 1-800-367-7052, FAX (808) 661-8315. Agents: Whalers Realty 1-800-367-5632, Hale Hawaiian 1-800-854-8843, RSVP 1-800-663-1118, Sullivan 1-800-326-9874, Maui Beachfront Rentals 1-888-661-7200. Choice location on an excellent beach front in the heart of Kaanapali next to the Whalers Village shopping center. A large pool area is beachfront and they provide a children's program during the summer. Underground parking. $200 deposit, 2-night minimum except over holidays, balance on check-in. 2-week refund notice. Some units have no low season discounts through Village Resorts:

S BR 1 bath (2) g.v. $195/195,	*o.v. $205*	
1 BR 1 bath (4) g.v. $250/230,	*o.v. $290/255*	
1 BR 2 bath (4) g.v. $260/240,	*o.v. $300/265,*	*o.f. $380/350*
2 BR 2 bath (6) not available	*o.v. $415/360,*	*o.f. $495/470*

KA'ANAPALI BEACH HOTEL ★ (Hotel)

2525 Kaanapali Pkwy, Lahaina, Maui, HI 96761 (808) 661-0011, 1-800-262-8450, FAX (808) 667-5616 guests, or (808) 667-5978 administration. The 430 room Ka'anapali Beach Hotel has earned the reputation as Maui's most Hawaiian hotel. There are four wings to this property which embrace a tropical courtyard that features gardens, walkways, a whale-shaped swimming pool and an outdoor bar and grill. Each room is decorated with airy, island decor and offers a private balcony or lanai, air conditioning, mini-refrigerator, color cable TV, in-room safes and coffee maker. Non-smoking rooms are available. Four rooms are equipped for the disabled traveler. The hotel offers two restaurants plus a poolside grill.

A variety of Hawaiian activities are scheduled daily. Among them are lau printing, ti-leaf skirt making, hula classes, lei making, and lauhala weaving. They have an Aloha Friday crafts fair and special employee entertainment on Monday, Wednesday and Friday. A complimentary sunset hula show is performed nightly in the Tiki Terrace Courtyard. Coin-operated laundry facilities on the property. A seasonal Kalo (Taro) Patch Kids program is offered.

Located on Kaanapali Beach near Black Rock and Whalers Village Shops, this hotel has been welcoming guests since it opened in 1964. And there is no doubt that it continues to be the best hotel value on Kaanapali Beach. A great location, but not a "posh" resort. The hotel could use a bit more freshening up, but then it would also be reflected in the prices! This is Maui's most Hawaiian hotel where the staff are actually instructed in Hawaiiana.

Cribs available at no charge. Roll-away bed $15 per night, additional person $25 per night. Children under 17 free when sharing room with parents using existing bedding. Special package rates include complimentary daily breakfast or complimentary compact rental car. Special 10% on room rates for guests 50 years of age or older based on space available and book 30 days in advance.

Garden $160, Courtyard $180, Partial Ocean View $190, Ocean View $210, Oceanfront $250, Suites $210-585.

SHERATON MAUI (Hotel)

2605 Kaanapali Parkway. (808) 661-0031, 1-800-325-3535. One of the first properties to be built along Kaanapali, the property opened in January of 1963. The resort closed in April 1994 for a $150 million renovation that was completed in December of 1996. The new 510-room resort stretches over 23 beachfront acres. The rooms include 16 luxury suites, 30 junior suites, 15 handicapped accessible rooms, and 10 rooms designated for hearing impaired. The lighting of the torches, the dive off Black Rock, and Hawaiian music still welcome the sunset, but $170 million later, that's about all that remains of Kaanapali's first hotel. Bridges, lagoons and lava rock landscape the extended grounds and there are three new restaurants with three new personalities: Fine dining at the resort's Coral Reef adds island touches to its traditional menu; teppanyaki goes "gourmet" at Teppan-Yaki Dan; while the open-air Kekaa Terrace provides all day dining with a view of the resort's lagoon and oceanfront. Other options include the Lagoon and Sundowner Bars, Reef's Edge Lounge and the Honu Snack Shop.

In making better use of their beachfront property, the garden cottages were replaced with several high-rise structures. Each is named as a *hale*, which is Hawaiian for house. The main structure of the original property remains, but the *makai* wing (nearer the ocean) is now Hale Nalu (House of the Surf) while the *mauka* portion is Hale Anuenue (House of the Rainbow). The Hale Moana (House of the Ocean) is built on the point at black rock. The Hale Lahaina and Hale Ohana are in the middle of the property.

Standard guest rooms feature air conditioning, lanai (patio), small refrigerator, iron and ironing board, along with coffee maker, TV with remote and guest safe.

A 140-yard freshwater swimming pool and kiddie pool are available for resort guests; the area is still the best place to watch the nightly cliff-diving ceremony.

Their Keiki Aloha children's program is available June through August. This program is complimentary for resort guests. Children must be ages 5-12 years.

g.v. $310/310 (no discount); mt. v. $350/330; o.v. $380/360; o.f. $410/390; deluxe o.f. $450/425; suites $600-3,150/575-3,000.

ROYAL LAHAINA RESORT ★
2780 Kekaa Dr., Lahaina, HI 96761. (808) 661-3611, 1-800-44-ROYAL. Managed by: Hawaiian Hotels & Resorts. (1-800-22-ALOHA). <www.2maui.com> 592 units located on excellent Kaanapali Beach just north of Black Rock. Located on 27 tropical acres, all cottage suites have kitchens and are situated around the lush, spacious grounds. Recently, the property added 17 suites, some extra amenities and they are underway with a refurbishment project. Coffee and teamakers are now in-room amenities and their five new Ehu Kai suites are decorated with a Hawaiian style and located beachside. The bedrooms of these include a king size bed with Hawaiian quit spread and a sitting area. The adjoining livingroom features an entertainment center with color television, dining area and daybed. The suite's parlor features a queen size sofa bed. A pair of full bathrooms and a complete kitchen round out this lovely suite which can accommodate 5 guests. Certainly easy to feel at home here!

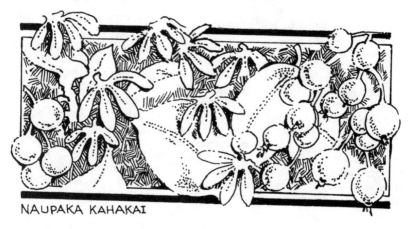

NAUPAKA KAHAKAI

As part of the Royal Lahaina's complimentary "Na Mea Hawai'i" ("Things Hawaiian") program, guests have the opportunity to gain insight into Hawai'i's culture via regularly scheduled activities and demonstrations which include flower lei making, lauhala and coconut weaving, tapa crafts, Polynesian wood carving, and Hawaiian quilting.

A mini-shopping mall is conveniently located on the property. Nearby is the Royal Lahaina Tennis Ranch which also recently underwent major refurbishing. The resorts' 11 courts have been re-surfaced and re-landscaped and new wind guards have been added to the 3,500 seat tennis stadium. The Royal Lahaina also offers three swimming pools. Restaurants on the property are the Royal Ocean Terrace, Basil Tomatoes, and Beachcomber's. Made in the Shade is a poolside restaurant and the Royal Scoop is an ice cream and sandwich shop. Nightly luaus are offered in the luau gardens. Children under 17 sharing parents room in existing beds are free. Additional amenities include beach cabanas for half or full day rental and beach rental equipment. Newly added are the complimentary windsurfing lessons.

The resort offers a wedding gazebo, situated in a courtyard lined with roses of white and pink hibiscus. Each wedding couple is provided with a stepping stone with their name and wedding date engraved. Honeymoon packages are also available. The Royal Lahaina offers some wonderful values and with a location on one of Maui's best beaches, it is a vacation oasis. Inquire about Hawaiian Resorts featured packages.

HH&S offers a complimentary newsletter which features special discounts at all their properties, plus coupons on goodies during your stay. It is well worth a phone call to receive these bonus offers. To subscribe to Essence of Paradise call 1-800-222-5632 or write them at 2404 Townsgate Road, Westlake Village, CA 91361. *Rooms: Garden View $215, Ocean View $295, Ocean Front $335. Cottages: Garden View $295, Ocean Front $385. Suites: $650-1,500.*

MAUI KAANAPALI VILLAS
2805 Honoapiilani Hwy., Lahaina, HI 96761 (808) 667-7791. Agents: Aston 1-800-221-2558, Chase 'N Rainbows 1-800-367-0092, Hale Hawaiian 1-800-854-8843. Located on fabulous, sandy Kaanapali Beach, this was once a part of the Royal Lahaina Resort, and before that the Hilton, prior to being converted into condos. The units are all air-conditioned and have kitchen facilities (except the hotel rooms). The upper floors of the tower unit have wonderful mountain or oceanviews. All privately owned and some units do need updating. Three swimming pools, beach concessions, store nearby. Walking distance to Whalers Village shops and restaurants and adjacent to the Royal Kaanapali Golf Course. *Hotel Room (2) $160/135, Studio w/kitchen (2) $200-230/175-200, 1 BR (4) $g.v. 245/220, o.v. $280/255*

KAANAPALI PLANTATION
150 Puukolii Rd., (PO Box 845) Lahaina, Maui, HI 96761. No rental units available at this time from on-site management. 62-unit one, two and three bedroom units in a garden setting overlooking golf course and ocean.

INTERNATIONAL COLONY CLUB

2750 Kalapu Dr., Lahaina, Maui, HI 96761 (808) 661-4070, FAX (808) 661-5856. For rental information contact Martin Rockwell at (612) 378-3739. Forty-four low-rise single family cottages with lanais and over 1,000 sq. ft of living space. Located on 10 lush acres on the mountain side of Honoapiilani Hwy. Most have washer/dryers; coin-op laundry on site. Two heated swimming pools. It is just a bit of a walk to the beach.
1 BR (1-4) $105, 2 BR (1-4) $125

MAUI ELDORADO

2661 Kekaa Drive, Lahaina, HI 96761. (808) 661-0021, 1-800-367-2967, Canada 1-800-663-1118. Managed by and reservations through Outrigger Resorts: 1-800-OUTRIGGER. Other Agents: Hale Hawaiian 1-800-854-8843, Hawaiian Pacific Resorts 1-800-367-5004. Located on golf course. 204 air-conditioned units with private lanais and free HBO on cable TV. Daily maid service. Three pools. Free shuttle to cabana on nearby beachfront.
S BR (1-2) g.v. $150-175, o.v. $175-200
1 BR (1-4) g.v. $185-220, o.v. $210-250
2 BR (1-6) g.v. $260-285, o.v. $290-325

KAANAPALI ROYAL ★

2560 Kekaa Dr., Lahaina, Maui, HI 96761. (808) 661-8687. Agents: Whalers Realty 1-800-367-5632, Hale Hawaiian 1-800-472-8449, RSVP 1-800-663-1118, Pali Kai 1-800-882-8550. Situated on the 16th fairway of the Kaanapali golf course overlooking the Kaanapali resort and Pacific Ocean, these very spacious condos (1,600-2,000 sq. ft.), offer air-conditioning, lanais, daily maid service, and washer/dryers. Note that while all units have two bedrooms, they may be rented as a one bedroom based on space availability.

Prices quoted from Hale Hawaiian Rental Agency:
2 BR (2,max 6) garden or golf view $180/150

Honokowai, Kahana, Napili & Kapalua

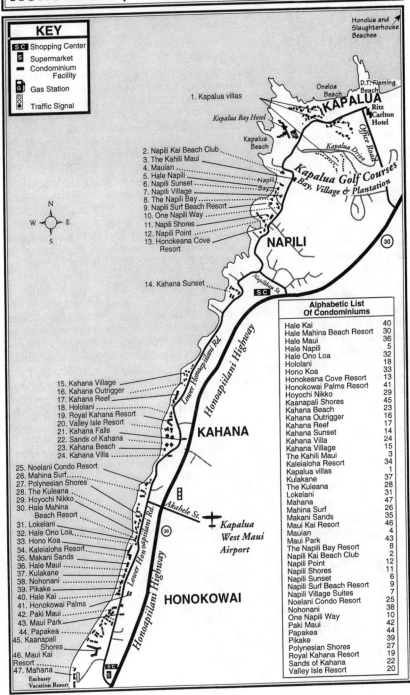

KEY

SC	Shopping Center
S	Supermarket
—	Condominium Facility
G	Gas Station
	Traffic Signal

Honolua and Slaughterhouse Beaches

Oneloa Beach

D.T. Fleming Beach

KAPALUA

Kapalua Bay Hotel

Ritz Carlton Hotel

Office Road

1. Kapalua villas

Kapalua Beach

Kapalua Drive

Kapalua Golf Courses Bay, Village & Plantation

2. Napili Kai Beach Club
3. The Kahili Maui
4. Mauian
5. Hale Napili
6. Napili Sunset
7. Napili Village
8. The Napili Bay
9. Napili Surf Beach Resort
10. One Napili Way
11. Napili Shores
12. Napili Point
13. Honokeana Cove Resort

Napili Bay

NAPILI

30

14. Kahana Sunset

Napilihau St.

SC

Alphabetic List Of Condominiums

Hale Kai	40
Hale Mahina Beach Resort	30
Hale Maui	36
Hale Napili	5
Hale Ono Loa	32
Hololani	18
Hono Koa	33
Honokeana Cove Resort	13
Honokowai Palms Resort	41
Hoyochi Nikko	29
Kaanapali Shores	45
Kahana Beach	23
Kahana Outrigger	16
Kahana Reef	17
Kahana Sunset	14
Kahana Villa	24
Kahana Village	15
The Kahili Maui	3
Kaleialoha Resort	34
Kapalua villas	1
Kulakane	37
The Kuleana	28
Lokelani	31
Mahana	47
Mahina Surf	26
Makani Sands	35
Maui Kai Resort	46
Mauian	4
Maui Park	43
The Napili Bay Resort	8
Napili Kai Beach Club	2
Napili Point	12
Napili Shores	11
Napili Sunset	6
Napili Surf Beach Resort	9
Napili Village Suites	7
Noelani Condo Resort	25
Nohonani	38
One Napili Way	10
Paki Maui	42
Papakea	44
Pikake	39
Polynesian Shores	27
Royal Kahana Resort	19
Sands of Kahana	22
Valley Isle Resort	20

Lower Honoapiilani Rd.

Honoapiilani Highway

KAHANA

15. Kahana Village
16. Kahana Outrigger
17. Kahana Reef
18. Hololani
19. Royal Kahana Resort
20. Valley Isle Resort
21. Kahana Falls
22. Sands of Kahana
23. Kahana Beach
24. Kahana Villa

25. Noelani Condo Resort
26. Mahina Surf
27. Polynesian Shores
28. The Kuleana
29. Hoyochi Nikko
30. Hale Mahina Beach Resort
31. Lokelani
32. Hale Ono Loa
33. Hono Koa
34. Kaleialoha Resort
35. Makani Sands
36. Hale Maui
37. Kulakane
38. Nohonani
39. Pikake
40. Hale Kai
41. Honokowai Palms
42. Paki Maui
43. Maui Park
44. Papakea
45. Kaanapali Shores
46. Maui Kai Resort
47. Mahana

Akahele St.

30

Kapalua West Maui Airport

Lower Honoapiilani Rd.

Honoapiilani Highway

HONOKOWAI

SC
S

Embassy Vacation Resort

105

HONOKOWAI

INTRODUCTION

As you leave the Kaanapali Resort you will pass the site of the old Kaanapali Airport. Resorts and some luxury homes will be stretched along this beach within the next few years. Recent development has created Kaheki'i Park, a terrific day-use facility which offers easy access to this wonderful stretch of beach. Ahead, four large condo complexes signal the beginning of Honokowai, which stretches north along Lower Honoapiilani Highway. Accommodations are a mix of high and low-rise, some new, but most are older. The beachfront is narrow and many complexes have retaining walls. A close-in reef fronts the beach and comes into shore at Papakea and at Honokowai Park. Between the reef and beach is generally shallow water unsuitable for swimming or other water activities. The only wide beach and break in the reef for swimming and snorkeling is at the Kaanapali Shores and Embassy Vacation Resort. In 1987, several condominiums made a major investment in saving the beachfront by building a seawall beneath the sand to prevent winter erosion and it appears to have been successful. A number of the condominiums are perched on rocky bluffs with no sandy beach.

Many people return year after year to this quiet area, away from the bustle of Lahaina and Kaanapali and where condo prices are in the moderate range. The condominiums are individually owned for the most part, and the quality and care of each (or lack of) is reflected by the owner. Perhaps it is the shape of the sloping ridges of Mauna Kahalawai that cause this area to be slightly cooler and cloudier with more frequent rain showers in the afternoon than at neighboring Kaanapali. A couple of small grocery stores are still nearby, but the most recent addition to the area is the Honokowai Marketplace, a Hawaiiana-styled shopping center with green tile roofing which was expected to open in August 1998. Anchored by the 37,500 sq. ft. Star Market, this new shopping complex also offers Leola's Funwear, Oasis Maui Clothing Co., Maui Dive Shop, a video store, and Maui's first Martinizing dry cleaning outlet. Pizza Paradiso & Yogurt and Jean-Marie Josselin's latest - A Pacific Cafe Honokowai - will offer a variety of dining choices along with some fast food outlets. For additional dining out there is the Beach Club restaurant at Kaanapali Shores and The Embassy Vacation Resort has three restaurant options.

COMMON 'AMAKIHI

ACCOMMODATIONS - HONOKOWAI

Mahana Resort
Maui Kai
Embassy Vacation
Resort
Kaanapali Shores
Papakea
Maui Sands
Paki Maui
Maui Parkshore
Honokowai Resort

Hale Kai
Pikake
Hale Maui
Apt. Hotel
Nohonani
Kulankane
Makani Sands
Kaleialoha
Hono Koa

Hale Ono Loa
Lokelani
Hale Mahina
Beach Resort
Hoyochi Nikko
Kuleana
Polynesian Shores
Mahinahina Beach
Mahina Surf
Noelani

BEST BETS: *Kaanapali Shores* - A high-rise surrounded by lovely grounds on the best beach in the area. *Papakea* - A low-rise complex with attractive grounds and pool. *Embassy Vacation Resort* - A mix between a condo and a hotel with breakfast included. Spacious rooms and spacious rooms and a good sandy beach.

MAHANA
110 Kaanapali Shores Place, Lahaina, Maui, HI 96761. (808) 661-8751. Agents: Aston 1-800-922-7866, Whalers Realty 1-800-676-4112, Chase 'N Rainbows 1-800-367-0092, Hale Hawaiian 1-800-854-8843, Pali Kai 1-800-882-8550. Mahana means "twins" as in two towers. All units oceanfront. Two twelve-story towers with two tennis courts, heated pool, central air-conditioning, saunas, elevators, small pool area. Located on narrow beachfront with offshore coral reef precluding swimming and snorkeling. A better swimming area is 100 yards up the beach. We haven't stayed here, but over the years have heard from many of our readers that they wouldn't stay anywhere else. Three night minimum. These rates are through Aston: *S BR 1 bath (1-2) $205-235/165-195;*
1 BR 1 bath (1-4) $265-300/220-250; 2 BR 2 bath (1-6) $400-455/335-390

MAUI KAI
106 Kaanapali Shores Pl., Lahaina, Maui, HI 96761. (808) 661-0002, 1-800-367-5635. < Email: mauikai@worldnet.att.net > Agents: Blue Sky Tours 1-800-678-2787, Classic Resorts 1-800-642-6284, (808) 667-1400, More Hawaii 1-800-967-6687, Maui Beachfront Rentals 1-888-661-7200. A single ten-story building with 79 units. Units offer central air-conditioning, private lanais, full equipped kitchens. Property amenities include swimming pool, jacuzzi, laundry facilities, free parking. Some studio units may be available. Weekly/monthly discounts. 7th night free through on-site management reservations.
SBR (2) o.f. $135-150/120-135; 1 BR (2) o.f. $165-180/150-165
1 BR (2) Corner o.f. $175-190/160-175; 2 BR (4) o.f. $265/245

EMBASSY VACATION RESORT ★

104 Kaanapali Shores Place, Lahaina, Maui, HI 96761. (808) 661-2000. 1-800-669-3155. Agent: Marc Resorts 1-800-535-0085. On 7 1/2 acres, this pink pyramid structure with a three-story blue waterfall cascading down the side can't be missed.

This accommodation blends the best of condo and resort living together. The pool (which is heated) area is large and tropical with plenty of room for lounge chairs. The lobby is open air and their glass enclosed elevators will whisk you up with a view! Atop the resort, families can now enjoy their miniature golf course, open daily 9am-9pm.

Each one bedroom suite is a spacious 820 sq. ft; two bedroom suites are 1,100 sq. ft. Each features lanais with ocean or scenic views. Master bedrooms are equipped with a remote control 20" television and an large adjoining master bath with soaking tub. The living room, decorated in comfortable hues of blue and beige, contains a massive 35" television, stereo receiver, VCR player, and cassette player. Living rooms have a sofa that makes into a double bed. A dining area with a small kitchenette is equipped with a microwave, small refrigerator and sink. Ironing equipment available upon request. One phone in the living room and another in the bedroom connect to a personal answering machine for your own recorded message. Suite rates include complimentary full American breakfasts and daily two-hour Manager's Cocktail Reception.

Their two Presidential Suites are 2,100 sq. ft. and offer two bedrooms, two full baths and a larger kitchen. One features an Oriental theme, the other is decorated with a contemporary California flare.

On property restaurants include North Beach Grille for evening dining, Ohana Bar and Grill for casual lunch and snacks, and the Deli Planet for deli sandwiches and sundries. Video rentals are available.

'ILIMA

Their children's program, Beach Buddies, is dedicated to perpetuating and preserving the heritage of the islands. "As a *Keiki O Ka Aina Ika Pono* (child of the land), let us share with you a 'Hawaiian Experience' rich in culture and tradition." Activities include hula class, lei making, coconut weaving and crafts, beachcombing and pool time. The program is designed for children 4 to 10 years and operates year round, seven days a week, Monday through Friday from 8:30am-2:30pm. The participation fee is $20 per child per day. The fee includes lunch and T-shirt. Their health facility was recently furnished with state-of-the-art exercise equipment. The facilities are open daily from 8am-10pm, seven days a week at no charge to Embassy guests. They also offer salon and spa services. The resort has a gazebo for wedding ceremonies as well as a 13,000 sq. ft. meeting facility. Package plans also available.
1 BR scenic view $(1-4) $270/260, o.v. $345/335, deluxe o.v. $410/400
2 BR suite (1-6) $560/550, Presidential Suite $1,500

KAANAPALI SHORES ★
100 Kaanapali Shores Place, Lahaina, Maui, HI 96761, (808) 667-2211) Agents: Aston 1-800-922-7866, Maui & All Island 1-800-663-6962, Maui Beachfront Rentals 1-888-661-7200, Hale Hawaiian 1-800-854-8843, Whalers Realty 1-800-676-4112. All 463 units offer telephones, free tennis, daily maid service, and air-conditioning. Nicely landscaped grounds and a wide beach with an area of coral reef cleared for swimming and snorkeling. This is the only resort on north Kaanapali Beach that offers a good swimming area. Putting green, jacuzzi and the Beach Club Restaurant located in the pool area. The Aston Kaanapali Shores Resort features a year-round program for children ages 3-10 years. Camp Kaanapali is offered from 8am-3pm, Monday-Friday. A $10 initial registration covers you regardless of the length of your stay and includes a camp T-shirt. Three sessions available each day and the cost is $5 per session. Choose a morning 8-11am session, or a lunch 11am-noon session, or afternoon activities 12-3pm. Activities are all held on property grounds and include hula and crafts. Program for resort guests only.
Hotel Room w/ refrigerator $165/135
S BR (1-2) g.v., partial o.v. $195-215/160-185
1 BR (1-4) g.v. $260/215, o.v. $295/255, family suite (1-5) $310/270
2 BR (1-6) g.v. $365/290, o.v. $415/340, o.f. $465/390
Aloha Oceanfront suite (1-6) $550/500
Penthouse Suite with kitchen (1-6) $750/650

PAPAKEA ★
3543 L. Honoapiilani, Lahaina, Maui, HI 96761. (808) 669-4848, 1-800-367-5037. Agents: Maui Resort Management 1-800-367-5037 (they offer an internet discount on their web page at < www.mauigetaway.com > Maui & All Island 1-800-663-6962, Whalers Realty 1-800-676-4112, RSVP 1-800-663-1118, Chase 'N Rainbows 1-800-367-0092, Hale Hawaiian 1-800-854-8843, Maui Network 1-800-367-5221. Five 4-story buildings with 364 units. Two pools, two jacuzzis, two saunas, tennis courts, putting green, washer/dryers, and BBQ area. The shallow water is great for children due to a protective reef 10-30 yards offshore, but poor for swimming or snorkeling. A better beach is down in front of the Kaanapali Shores. One of the nicer grounds for a condominium complex, Papakea

features lush landscaping and pool areas. A comfortable, and quiet property that we recommend especially for families. No smoking units available. Crib or roll-away $9/day. Christmas holiday 14-day has higher rates and minimum with no refunds after October 1. Cribs available.

Rates shown are through Maui Resort Management:

S BR (2) garden & partial o.v. $100/80 (no o.f. available thru Maui Resort Mgm)
1 BR 1 BTH (4) garden & partial o.v. $120-130/100-110, o.f. $150/135
1 BR 2 BTH LOFT (4) garden & partial o.v. $145/135
2 BR 2 BTH (6) garden & partial o.v. $185/155, o.f. $185/175
2 BR 2 BTH LOFT (6) garden & partial o.v. $185/155

MAUI SANDS

3559 L. Honoapiilani, Lahaina, Maui, HI 96761. Maui Resort Management 1-800-367-5037. All 76 units have air-conditioning and kitchens. Limited maid service. Microwaves, coin-op laundry facility, rollaway & cribs available $9 night. A very friendly atmosphere where old friends have been gathering each year since it was built in the mid-sixties. They feature a large central laundry facility and a large pool area with barbecues. Large boulders line the beach. A good family facility. *1 BR (2,max 3) o.f. $110/90; 2 BR 125/100*

PAKI MAUI

3615 L. Honoapiilani, Lahaina, Maui, HI 96761. (808) 669-8235. Agents: Marc Resorts 1-800-535-0085, Maui & All Island 1-800-663-6962. This complex surrounds a garden and waterfall. No air-conditioning. Daily maid service. S BR (1-2) o.f. $169/159; 1 BR (1-4) g.v. $169.159; o.f. $199/179; 2 BR (1-6) o.f. $249-279/219-249

MAUI PARK

3626 L. Honoapiilani Hwy., Lahaina, Maui, HI 96761. (808) 669-6622. Man-aged by Castle Group: 1-800-367-5004. Agents: RSVP Reservations 1-800-663-1118, Maui Condominiums 1-800-663-6962 US & Canada. Located across the road from Honokowai Beach Park which lacks a sandy shoreline. A quiet area of West Maui with nearby grocery store. All units have complete kitchen. Coin-op laundry facility. Air conditioned with lanais. Originally built as residential apartments, they offer phones, and daily maid service. Because of its original intention, this property does resemble a residential area more than a vacation resort. Some units are now, once again, being rented on a long term basis. All units are garden view. *Rates from Castle Group begin at $99 per night for hotel rooms, studios with kitchen (1-2) $114-135, One bedroom with kitchen (1-4) $125-155, Two bedroom with kitchen (1-6) $169-189.*

HONOKOWAI PALMS RESORT

3666 L. Honoapiilani, Lahaina, Maui, HI 96761. (808) 669-6130. Agent: Klahani 1-800-669-MAUI. Thirty units across road from Honokowai Beachfront Park. Built of cement blocks this property lacks a great deal of ambience as a vacation retreat. Perhaps for the budget conscious it would be suitable, but it is a very basic, functional complex. Klahani Rates:
1 BR (2,max 4) $65, 2 BR (2,max 6) $75.

HALE KAI

3691 L. Honoapiilani Hwy., Lahaina, Maui, HI 96761. (808) 669-6333. 1-800-446-7307. FAX (808) 669-7474. Forty units in a two-story building. The units do have lanais, kitchens, and a pool, but the beach is somewhat rocky. A simple and quiet property. Additional guests $10/night
1 BR (2) $110/95, 2 BR (4) $140-145/125-130, 3 BR (6) $180 year round

PIKAKE

3701 L. Honoapiilani, Lahaina, Maui, HI 96761. (808) 669-6086, 1-800-446-3054. A low-rise, two-story, Polynesian style with only twelve apartments completed in 1966. Private lanais open to the lawn or balconies, with a beach protected by sea wall. Central laundry area. Ceiling fans, no a/c. NO CREDIT CARDS. *1 BR (2,max 4) $80-100, 2 BR (4,max 6) $90-110. $10 extra person.*

HALE MAUI APARTMENT HOTEL

PO Box 516, Lahaina, Maui, HI 96761. (808) 669-6312. All one-bedroom units sleep 5. Lanais, limited maid service, coin-operated washer/dryer, BBQ. Weekly and monthly discounts. Extra persons $10/night. *1 BR (2, max 5) $65-95*

NOHONANI

3723 L. Honoapiilani, Lahaina, Maui, HI 96761. (808) 669-8208, 1-800-822-7368, FAX (808) 822-RENT, Email:alohablu@maui.net. Agent: Klahani 1-800-669-0795. Two 4-story buildings containing 22 oceanfront two-bedroom units and 5 one-bedroom units. Complex has large pool, telephones, and is one block to grocery store. Extra persons $15/night. NO CREDIT CARDS from on-site reservations. *1 BR (1-2) $115/104, 2 BR (1-4) $142/125*

KULAKANE

3741 L. Honoapiilani (PO Box 5236), Lahaina, Maui, HI 96761.(808) 669-6119, FAX (808) 669-9694. 1-800-367-6088. AGENTS: More Hawaii 1-800-967-6687, Chase 'N Rainbows 1-800-367-0092. Forty-two oceanfront units with fully equipped kitchen, laundry facilities. Lanais overlook ocean but no sandy beach. Some 1 BR available. Chase 'N Rainbows rates: *2 BR 2 bath (1-4) $120/115*

MAKANI SANDS

3765 L. Honoapiilani Hwy., Lahaina, Maui, HI 96761. 1-800-227-8223. (808) 669-8223. Thirty units in a three-story building. Dishwashers, washer/dryers, elevator. Oceanfront with small sandy beach. Weekly & monthly discounts.
1 BR (2) $110, 2 BR (4) $150, 3 BR (6) $175

KALEIALOHA

3785 L. Honoapiilani, Lahaina, Maui, HI 96761. Kaleialoha Rental agent - (808) 669-8197, 1-800-222-8688. Agents: Klahani 1-800-628-6731, More Hawaii 1-800-967-6687. Sixty-seven units in a four-story building. *Studio (1-2) mtn.v. $75, 1 BR (1-4) o.v. sup. $105, dlx 95 $85-90*

HONO KOA

3801 L. Honoapiilani, Lahaina, Maui, HI 96761. (808) 669-0979. Timeshare rental only. 28 units in one four-story building.

HALE ONO LOA ★

3823 L. Honoapiilani, Lahaina, Maui, HI 96761. (808) 669-6362. Agents: Klahani 1-800-669-MAUI, Maui Accommodations 1-800-252-MAUI (U.S.) Sixty-seven oceanfront and oceanview units. Maid service extra charge. Beachfront is rocky. The units we toured were roomy and nicely furnished with spacious lanais. The grounds and pool area were pleasant and well groomed. A good choice for a quiet retreat. Grocery store nearby. Some rental agents may offer 2 BR units. Klahani Rates: *1 BR 1 bath (4) g.v. $85/75; 1 BR 1 bath o.v. $95/85*

LOKELANI

3833 L. Honoapiilani, Lahaina, Maui, HI 96761. (808) 669-8110, 1-800-367-2976. Agent: Chase 'N Rainbows 1-800-367-0092. Three 3-story 12 unit buildings with beachfront or oceanviews. The 1 bedroom units are on beach level with lanai, two bedrooms units are townhouses with bedrooms upstairs and lanais on both levels. Washer/dryers. Rates from Chase 'N Rainbows:
1 BR (1-2) $95/85, 2 BR (townhouses) (1-4) $145

HALE MAHINA BEACH RESORT

3875 L. Honoapiilani, Lahaina, Maui, HI 96761. (808) 669-8441, 1-800-367-8047 ext. 441. Agents: Maui Network 1-800-367-5221, Pali Kai 1-800-882-8550, Chase 'N Rainbows 1-800-367-0092, Hale Hawaiian 1-800-854-8843. Hale Mahina means "House of the Pale Moon" and offers 52 units in two, four-story buildings and one two-story building featuring lanais, ceiling fans, microwaves, washer/dryer, BBQ area, jacuzzi. Some 2 BR may be available through different rental agents. Prices from Hale Hawaiian: *1 BR (1-2) $110/89*

HOYOCHI NIKKO

3901 L. Honoapiilani, Lahaina, Maui, HI 96761. (808) 669-8343, 1-800-487-6002, Email: <hoyochi@aol.com> Agents: Klahani 1-800-669-MAUI. All 18 units are one-bedroom, oceanview (on a rocky beachfront) in a two-story building bearing an oriental motif. Underground parking, "Long Boy" twin beds, some with queens, half size washer and dryers in units. They recently added a waterfall that cascades into a pond and have re-tiled their pool with dolphin designs! NO CREDIT CARDS through property. *1 BR $85-105/65-85 $10/extra person*

KULEANA

3959 L. Honoapiilani, Lahaina, Maui, HI 96761. (808) 669-8080 or 1-800-367-5633. Agents: Chase 'N Rainbows 1-800-367-0092. All 118 one bedroom units have queen size sofa bed in living room. Large pool with plenty of lounge chair room and tennis court. A short walk to sandy beaches.
1 BR o.v. $85/80, o.f. 95/90

POLYNESIAN SHORES

3975 L. Honoapiilani, Lahaina, Maui, HI 96761. (808) 669-6065, 1-800-433-6284, from Canada toll free 1-800-488-2179, Email: polyshor@maui.net. Fifty-two units on a rocky shore but nice grounds with deck overlooking the ocean. "Heated" swimming pool!
1 BR 1 bath (2) $100-110/95-105, 2 BR 2 bath (2) $115-125 / $105-115
2 BR 2 Bath End (4) $165/155, 3 BR 3 bath (4) $185/175

MAHINAHINA BEACH
4007 L. Honoapiilani, Lahaina, Maui, HI 96761. Units only through owners.

MAHINA SURF
4057 L. Honoapiilani, Lahaina, Maui, HI 96761 (808) 669-6068, 1-800-367-6086, FAX (808) 669-4534. Agents: Maui Beachfront Rentals 1-888-661-7200. Fifty-six one-bedroom and one-bedroom-with-loft units. Dishwashers. Located on rocky shore, the nearest sandy beach is a short drive to Kahana. Large lawn area around pool offers plenty of room for lounging. AAA and AARP discounts available. No rate information. After a letter and a fax to the resident rental manager with no reply, we called and were *still* asked to call back later!

NOELANI
4095 L. Honoapiilani, Lahaina, Maui, HI 96761. (808) 669-8374, 1-800-367-6030, FAX (808) 669-7904. E-mail: Noelani@maui.net. Fifty oceanfront units in one 4-story building and two 2-story structures. Kitchens with dishwashers and washer/dryers only in 1, 2, and 3-bedroom units. Three bedroom units feature a sunken living room as do the two bedroom units on the third floor. Complex has two pools and maid service mid-week. Located on a rocky shore, nearest sandy beach is short drive to Kahana. 7th night free during low season.
S BR 1 bath (1-2) $97-107, 1 BR 1 bath (1-2) $120
2 BR 2 bath (1-2) $167, 3 BR 3 bath (1-6) $197

KAHANA

INTRODUCTION

To the north of Honokowai - and about seven miles north of Lahaina - is a prominent island of high-rise condos with a handful of two-story complexes strung along the coast in its lee. This is Kahana. The beach adjacent to the high-rises is fairly wide, but tapers off quickly after this point. Several of the larger complexes offer very nice grounds and spacious living quarters with more resort type activities than in Honokowai. The prices are lower than Kaanapali, but higher than Honokowai. In the past we have reported a continuing problem in the Honokowai to Kapalua areas with algae. The algae bloom which clusters in the ocean offshore seems to come and go, causing problems to a greater or lesser degree for reasons yet unknown. State officials continue their investigation but a cause or reason for this condition has not yet been determined. Of late, the problem seems to have improved. The algae doesn't appear to be any health risk, just an annoyance for swimming and snorkeling.

WHERE TO SHOP

There are several shops in the lower level of the Kahana Manor. At nearby Kahana Gateway, outlets include gift and dive shops, a gas station and Whalers General Store, beauty salon, children's fashion store, a laundry, and several eateries - from McDonald's and Ashley's Yogurt & Cafe to Roy's & Roy's Nicolina, the expanded Fish and Games Brew Pub & Rotisserie, and the new Outback Steakhouse.

ACCOMMODATIONS - KAHANA

Kahana Beach Resort
Kahana Villa
Kahana Falls
Sands of Kahana

Valley Isle Resort
Royal Kahana
Hololani
Hawaii Kalani

Kahana Reef
Kahana Outrigger
Kahana Village
Kahana Sunset

BEST BETS: Sands of Kahana - Spacious units on a nice white sand beach.
Kahana Sunset - Low-rise condos surrounding a secluded cove and beach.

KAHANA BEACH CONDOMINIUM HOTEL
4221 L. Honoapiilani, Lahaina, Maui, HI 96761. (808) 669-8611. Management
and Rental Agent: Hawaiian Hotels & Resorts 1-800-22-ALOHA. Agent: Pleasant
Hawaiian Holidays 1-800-242-9244. All units offer oceanview. The studios sleep
up to four and have kitchenettes. The 1 bedroom units have kitchens, 2 lanais,
living room with queen-size loveseat sleeper, bedroom with 2 king beds, 2 full-
size baths, dressing room, and will accommodate 7. Coin-op laundry on premises. Nice, white sandy beach fronting complex.
Studios partial o.v. $125, o.v. $135, o.f. $145; Suites o.f. $225

KAHANA VILLA
4242 L. Honoapiilani, Lahaina, Maui, HI 96761. (808) 669-5613. Agents: Marc
Resorts 1-800-535-0085, Maui & All Island 1-800-663-6962, Whalers Realty 1-
800-367-5632, RSVP 1-800-663-1118. Across the road from the beach. Units
have microwaves, washer/dryers, telephones. Daily maid service. Property also
has sauna, tennis courts, convenience store, and Erik's Seafood Grotto restaurant.
*Studio $149/139; 1 BR 1 bath g.v.(1-4) $159/149, o.v. $179/169, dlx o.v.
$189/179; 2 BR 2 bath g.v. (1-6) $209/189; o.v. $329/219; dlx o.v. $250/239*

KAHANA FALLS
4260 Lower Honoapiilani Hwy., Lahaina, Maui, HI 96761. Thirty-six 2-bedroom
2-bath units and 24 1-bedroom units. This property is time share. No rental units.

WILIWILI

SANDS OF KAHANA ★

4299 L. Honoapiilani, Lahaina, Maui, HI 96761. Agents: Hale Hawaiian 1-800-854-8843, Sullivan 1-800-326-9874, Pali Kai 1-800-882-8550. Ninety-six units on Kahana Beach. Underground parking. If you're looking to be a little away from the hustle of Lahaina/Kaanapali - with quarters large enough for a big family and luxuries such as microwaves and full-size washer/dryers - then this may be just what you seek. Located on a sandy beachfront and only a couple miles from Kaanapali, it is also less than a mile from the West Maui Airport. Four 8-story buildings surround a central restaurant and a dual pool area. Sands of Kahana is family-oriented with the generous size of their rooms and a small putting green to amuse the kids. Spacious 1, 2 or 3 bedroom units have enormous kitchens and beautifully appointed living rooms. Moloka'i is beautifully framed in the large picture windows of the oceanview units, or select among the slightly less expensive garden view units. There was plenty of fun in the sun here with a beachside volleyball court filled each afternoon, and the large three foot deep children's pool was popular as was another larger and deeper pool with jacuzzi, and the three tennis courts.

Most complexes restrict the use of snorkel gear or flotation equipment in the pool, however, here it is allowed to the delight of the children. Parents will appreciate the availability of several garden area charcoal barbecues. Across the street is a full size grocery store and several restaurants are within walking distance. Sullivan Property Rates:
1 BR 1 bath (4) $150-195/110-155; 2 BR 1 bath (6) $195-275/145-225;
3 BR 2 bath (8) $250-340/190-280

VALLEY ISLE RESORT

4327 L. Honoapiilani, Lahaina, Maui, HI 96761. (808) 669-5511 (for brochure only, no reservations) Agents: Klahani (808) 669-5511, More Hawaii 1-800-967-6687, Chase 'N Rainbows 1-800-367-0092, Maui & All Island 1-800-663-6962. Partial air-conditioning. Located on Kahana Beach. Klahani rates:
S BR 1 bath (2) o.f. $100/85; 1 BR 1 bath (2) o.v. $115/100, o.f. $125/110
2 BR 2 bath (4) o.v. available through some rental agents.

ROYAL KAHANA

4365 L. Honoapiilani, Lahaina, Maui, HI 96761. (808) 669-5911, 1-800-447-7783, FAX (808) 669-5950. Agents: Hale Hawaiian 1-800-854-8843, Marc Resorts 1-800-535-0085, Maui Beachfront Rentals 1-888-661-7200. Twelve-story high-rise complex built in 1975 with 236 oceanview units on Kahana Beach. Underground parking and air-conditioning. Daily maid service. A nice pool area with sauna. Tennis courts. Units have full kitchens and microwaves. Nearby grocery stores, restaurants and shops. Rollaways and cribs $6/per day. Garden, oceanview and oceanfront units.
Rates from Marc Resorts:
Studio (1-3) g.v./o.v. $169-189/149-169,
1 BR 1 bath (1-2) $199-219/179-189,
2 BR 2 bath (1-6) $249-319/219-289

HOLOLANI

4401 L. Honoapiilani, Lahaina, Maui, HI 96761. (808) 669-8021, 1-800-367-5032, FAX (808) 669-7682. Agents: More Hawaii 1-800-967-6687, Chase 'N Rainbows 1-800-367-0092. Twenty-seven oceanfront units on sandy, reef protected beach. Covered parking. Children under five free. NO CREDIT CARDS. *2 BR 2 bath (2,max 6) $145-165 / $125-135*

HAWAII KAILANI (POHILANI)

4435 L. Honoapiilani, Lahaina, Maui, HI 96761 (808) 669-6994, FAX (808) 669-4046. Agent: Hawaii Kailani 206-676-1434, Chase 'N Rainbows 1-800-367-0092. Hawaii Kailani is the rental portion of the Pohailani. The Hawaii Kailani offers a mixture of two-bedroom and studio apartments. The larger units are situated around eight park-like acres, while the studio units sit directly on the beach. Walking distance to restaurants and grocery stores. Swimming pool, tennis courts, laundry facilities. TV cable and TV rental are available for each unit, but cannot be requested prior to arrival. Full kitchens in both studio and two bedroom units. Twice weekly maid service. Extra person $5 day. A good value for this area. Chase 'N Rainbows lists Pohailani rates at:
S BR o.f. $75/65, 2 BR g.v. $95/85.

KAHANA REEF ★

4471 L. Honoapiilani, Lahaina, Maui, HI 96761. (808) 669-6491, 1-800-253-3773, FAX (808) 669-2192. Eighty-eight well-kept units. Limited number of oceanfront studios available. Laundry facilities on premises. 15% monthly discounts. Maid service daily except Sunday. NO CREDIT CARDS. Room and car packages. A good value.
Studio $100/95, 1 BR 1 bath (2,max 5) $110/100, 2 BR $200/174

KAHANA OUTRIGGER

4521 L. Honoapiilani, Lahaina, Maui, HI 96761. (808) 669-6550, 1-800-987-8494. Agent: Chase 'N Rainbows 1-800-367-0092, Whalers Realty 1-800-367-5632. Sixteen spacious three bedroom oceanview condo suites in low-rise complex on a narrow sandy beachfront. Units have microwaves, washer/dryers and are appointed with Italian tile. These are rented as a vacation "home" with no on-property service provided.
Rates from Whalers Realty: 3 BR 2 bath o.f. (6) weekly $1995/1890

KAHANA VILLAGE ★

4531 L. Honoapiilani, Lahaina, Maui, HI 96761. (808) 669-5111, 1-800-824-3065. Agents: Maui & All Island 1-800-663-6962, RSVP 1-800-663-1118. Attractive townhouse units. Second level units are 1,200 sq.ft.; ground level three bedroom units have 1,700 sq.ft. with a wet bar, sunken tub in master bath, Jenn-aire ranges, microwaves, lanais, and washer/dryers. They offer a heated pool and attractively landscaped grounds. Nice but narrow beach offering good swimming. 5-day minimum. Bi-weekly maid service. NO CREDIT CARDS.
2 BR o.v. $195/160, o.f. $235/195, 3 BR o.v. $235/195, o.f. $320/260

KAHANA SUNSET ★
PO Box 10219, Lahaina, Maui, HI 96761. (808) 669-8011, 1-800-669-1488, FAX (808) 669-9170. Agents: Village Resorts 1-800-367-7052, FAX (808) 661-8315, RSVP 1-800-663-1118, Sullivan 1-800-326-9874, Hale Hawaiian 1-800-854-8843. Ninety units in 6 two and three story buildings on a beautiful and secluded white sand beach. Units have very large lanais, telephones, and washer/dryers. Each unit has its own lanai, but they adjoin one another, adding to the friendly atmosphere of this complex. One of the very few resorts with a heated pool, heated children's pool and BBQ. You can drive up right to your door on most of the two bedroom units making unloading easy (and with a family heavy into suitcases that can be a real back saver). These are not luxurious units, but it is a location that is difficult to beat.
1 BR 1 bath $160-180, 2 BR 2 bath (2) o.v. $195-205, 2 BR (2) o.f. 265

NAPILI

INTRODUCTION

This area's focal point is the beautiful Napili Bay with good swimming, snorkeling and boogie boarding, and it even has tide pools for children to explore. A new 8-acre park, located *makai* of the highway near Maiha Steet, is scheduled to open by Summer, 1999. The condominium units here are low-rise, with prices mostly in the moderate range, and are clustered tightly around the bay. A number are located right on the beach, others a short walk away. The quality of the units vary considerably, but generally a better location on the bay and better facilities demand a higher price. The complexes are small, most under 50 units, and all but one has a pool. At the nearby Napili Plaza shopping center you'll find a full-size grocery store, restaurants and shops. See the Napili to Kapalua map on page 105.

WHERE TO SHOP

Napili Plaza may be within walking distance, depending on the location of your condominium. It includes Napili Market (a full size grocery store), Subway sandwiches, Stanfield's West Maui Floral, Maui Tacos, The Coffee Store, All Star Video & Dave's Ice Cream, Boss Frog's Dive Shop, Awesome Tee's, Roxana's Hair Affair, First Hawaiian Bank, and Koho Grill and Bar.

ACCOMMODATIONS - NAPILI

Honokeana Cove	Hale Napili
Napili Point	Napili Village
Napili Shores	Mauian
Napili Surf	Napili Gardens
Napili Bay	Napili Kai Beach Club
Napili Sunset	

BEST BETS: *Napili Sunset* - Centered right on the edge of Napili Bay, rooms are well kept. *Napili Kai Beach Club* - A quiet facility on the edge of Napili Bay. Large grounds and a restaurant on site. Resort activities are offered.

HONOKEANA COVE

5255 L. Honoapiilani, Lahaina, Maui, HI 96761. (808) 669-6441, 1-800-237-4948. Agent: Thirty-eight oceanview units on Honokeana Cove near Napili Bay. Attractive grounds - and friendly sea turtles! Weekly and monthly discounts, extra persons (all ages) $10-15 per night.
1 BR 1 bath (2) $ 115, 1 BR 2 bath (2) $120
2 BR 2 bath (4,max 4) $152, 3 BR 2 bath (6,max 6) $180, Townhouse (4) $175

NAPILI POINT

5295 L. Honoapiilani, Lahaina, Maui, HI 96761. Napili Point Resort Rental (808) 669-5611, 1-800-669-6252. Agents: Hale Hawaiian 1-800-854-8843, Maui Beachfront Rentals 1-888-661-7200. Located on rocky beach, but next door to beautiful Napili Bay. Units have washer/dryer, full kitchens including dishwasher, daily maid service. King or queen size beds in one bedroom units. No air conditioning, most units have ceiling fans. Cribs available. Two pools. In some suites the second bedroom is loft-style. Prices from Hale Hawaiian:
1 BR 1 bath (4) o.f. $179/139, 2 BR 2 bath (6) o.f. $239/179

NAPILI SHORES

5315 L. Honoapiilani, Lahaina, Maui, HI 96761. (808) 669-8061, FAX (808) 669-5047. Management & reservations through: Outrigger Resorts Hawaii 1-800-OUTRIGGER, Maui Beachfront Rentals 1-888-661-7200, Hale Hawaiian 1-800-854-8843, RSVP 1-800-663-1118. On Napili Bay. 152 units with lanais; one-bedroom units have dishwashers. Laundry facilities on premises as well as two pools, adult hot tub, croquet, and BBQ area. Restaurants, cocktail lounge and grocery store on property. Extra persons $15/night, no minimum stay, daily maid service. Studios have one queen and one twin bed. Crib $8, rollaway $15 daily.
S BR (2,max 3) g.v. $135-150, o.v. $160-180, o.f. $190-200
1 BR (2,max 4) g.v. $165-185, o.v. $195-210

NAPILI SURF

50 Napili Place, Lahaina, Maui, HI 96761. (808) 669-8002. 1-800-541-0638. FAX (808) 669-8004. Website: <www.napilisurf.com> Fifty-three units on Napili Bay. Two pools, BBQ, shuffleboard, lanais, daily maid service, and laundry facilities. 5 night minimum. NO CREDIT CARDS. Rates based on double occupancy. Children six and under no charge. Add $15 each additional person. Condo-car packages. Weekly discounts.
S BR (2,max 3) g.v. $104, o.v. $142; 1 BR (2,max 5) $184-199.

NAPILI BAY RESORT

33 Hui Drive, Lahaina Maui, HI 96761. (808) 669-6044. Agents: Whalers Realty 1-800-676-4112, Hale Hawaiian 1-800-854-8843, Maui Beachfront Rentals 1-888-661-7200. This older complex on Napili Bay is neat, clean and affordably priced.

Studio apartments offer one queen and two single beds, lanais, kitchens, daily maid service. Coin-op laundromat with public phones. Extra persons $8/night, children under 12 free.
Rates from Whalers Realty: Studio (2,max 4) g.v. $87/77

NAPILI SUNSET ★

46 Hui Rd., Lahaina, Maui, HI 96761. (808) 669-8083, 1-800-447-9229 U.S.A. or 1-800-223-4611 Canada, FAX (808) 669-2730. Forty-one units located on Napili Bay. Daily maid service. Ceiling fans, no air conditioning. These units have great oceanviews and are well maintained. A very friendly atmosphere. Kitchens have microwaves. Full payment for fewer than 4 nights.
Studio (2) g.v. $95/75
1 BR 1 bath (2) o.f. $185/159
2 BR 2 bath (4) o.f. $265/249

HALE NAPILI

65 Hui Rd., Napili, Maui, HI 96761. (808) 669-6184, 1-800-245-2266, FAX (808) 665-0066. Eighteen units oceanfront on Napili Bay. Lanais. Daily maid service except Sunday. Ceiling fans, microwaves, laundry facilities on property. No pool. *Studio (2) g.v. $98, o.f. $128, 1 BR (2) o.f. $155*

NAPILI VILLAGE SUITES

5425 Honoapiilani, Lahaina, HI 96761. (808) 669-6228, 1-800-336-2185, FAX (808) 669-6229. All vacation apartments are 500 sq. ft. and feature king or queen size beds, daily maid service. Laundry facilities on premises. Located a short walk from Napili Bay. *(2) $119/89*

NAPILI GARDENS

5432 Honoapiilani, Lahaina, HI 96761. (808) 661-2648. 1-888-661-7200. Agent: Maui Beachfront Rental 1-888-661-7200. Custom townhouses that offer double car garages, private rear yards, gourmet kitchens, lanais, plus washer/dryer.
Three bedroom and 2.5 baths $250/200

MAUIAN

5441 Honoapiilani, Lahaina, Maui, HI 96761. (808) 669-6205, 1-800-367-5034, FAX (808) 669-0129, website: <www.mauian.com> or Email them at: <mauian@maui.net> 44-Studio apartments on Napili Bay. Kitchen plus microwave, one queen and two twin day beds. BBQ area. Two public phones on property, one courtesy reservation phone. Television only in recreation center. Daily maid service. Three day minimum. Many guests have been returning to vacation at this quiet corner of Napili for 30 years or more. They cannot guarantee any specific room number, however, they will make every attempt to accommodate those guests requesting a particular building location. Check website for special discounts (up to 30%) and on-site events.
Studios are g.v.$145/125, beach $160/140, and o.f. $175/155

NAPILI KAI BEACH CLUB ★

5900 Honoapiilani, Lahaina, Maui, HI 96761. (808) 669-6271, 1-800-367-3030 FAX (808) 669-0086. Units feature lanais, kitchenettes, and telephones. Complimentary tennis equipment, beach equipment, putters, and snorkel gear.

Daily coffee and tea party in Beach Club. Sea House Restaurant located on grounds. Four pools and Hawaii's largest jacuzzi. The key here is location, location, location. The grounds are extensive and the area very quiet. A relaxed and friendly atmosphere, a great beach, and a wide variety of activities may tempt you to spend most of your time enjoying this very personable and complete resort. A popular location for family reunions!

A kids program is offered during the summer months for youth between the ages of six and thirteen. The Napili Kai Keiki Club features an hour or two of free activities daily for children of the resort's guests. Activities include Hawaiian games, hula and lei making, nature/ecology walks, hot dog barbecues, and more. Two night deposit. 14-day refund notice. NO CREDIT CARDS. Christmas rates slightly higher. Group rates available and packages, too!

Hotel Room (2) g.v. $170, o.v. $205
Studio g.v. $185, o.v. $215, beachfront $225, o.f. $265
2 Room Suite g.v. $315, o.v. $285, beachfront $300, o.f. $325-350
3 Room Suite g.v. $475, o.v. $545, o.f. $550

THE RITZ-CARLTON   KAPALUA, MAUI

KAPALUA

INTRODUCTION

The story of **Kapalua** begins in ancient times, for it is said that Mauna Kahalawai, the immense volcano that formed the West Maui Mountains, is the juncture between Heaven and Earth. Hawaiians settled in this region in abundance, they built their *lo'i*, or flooded fields for growing their staple crop, taro. They harvested fish, *'ama'ama*, *moi*, *akule* and *opelo* from the clear waters, never taking more than they needed, and always giving thanks. It was an area rich in blessing, much of it sacred. There was a temple of medicine and one for astronomy. The highest chiefs and their families gathered for sports and games in this place, which they deemed their special retreat and playground. They built *holua* sleds for sliding down the grassy slopes. They rolled lava balls in their game of *ulu maika*, lawn bowling. They wrestled, competed in spear hurling, swam, and surfed the waves at Honolua on giant koa boards. Ruins of ancient temples, fishing shrines and agricultural terraces can still be seen along the streams and shores and people who sometimes find huge lava balls, marvel at the prowess of the ancient bowlers. In earlier times, the Hawaiian lands were divided into *ahupua'a*. These pie-shaped land sections traverse from forest to sea. They give each person access to various elevations for different crops, and an outlet to the ocean for fishing. There were seven beautiful *ahupua'a* called Honolua, Honokahua, Honokawai, Honokohau, Kahana, Mahinahina and Mailepai. Later they were joined to form Honolua Ranch, and parts later became Kapalua resort.

The most important historic site at Kapalua is the Honokahua Burial Grounds which were unearthed when digging began for The Ritz-Carlton, Kapalua. As the significance of the discovery became apparent, the entire hotel was redesigned and moved inland. The mound, which contains over 900 ancient Hawaiian burials dating between 610 and 1800, has been recognized as a sacred site. The mound is now carpeted in lush grass and bordered by native *naupaka* bushes. Also at this site is a portion of the sixteenth century *Alaloa* or King's Trail, a footpath that once encircled the island.

The modern day history of Kapalua dates back to 1836 when the Baldwin family of New England settled on the island of Maui as missionaries. The Baldwin family home is now a historical landmark in Lahaina. After seventeen years of service, Doctor Baldwin was given 2,675 acres, the lands of Mahinahina and Kahana *ahupua'a*, to use for farming grazing. By 1902 the area known as Honolua ranch had grown to 24,500 acres as a result of marriages, purchases, and royal grants. The ranch crops included taro, mango, aloe, and coffee beans. Fishing, along with cattle raising, also took place here. Kapalua became a bustling enclave on the island, with a working ranch that supplied pork and beef to the port of Lahaina. David Fleming arrived from Scotland and became the ranch manager. He experimented with a new fruit, *hala-kahili*, or pineapple, and planted four acres. The ideal environment produced a very sweet pineapple. It was determined that the coffee operation should be moved upland to make room for a pineapple cannery, homes, and bungalows for workers.

The area grew to include a railroad, store, churches, a golf course, tennis courts, and a new house for Fleming. Honolua Ranch became Baldwin Packers, the largest producer of private label pineapple and pineapple juice in the nation. In the years that followed, Kapalua's acres of grassy slopes were transformed into geometric patterns of silver-blue pineapple fields and the first crop of this fruit was harvested in 1914. By 1946 the cattle operation had ceased. In the next two decades, Baldwin Packers merged with Maui Pineapple and in 1969 became Maui Land and Pineapple Company, Inc. Before his death, Colin Cameron, a fifth generation descendent of the Baldwin family, envisioned Kapalua as a sanctuary for man and nature.

In the 1970's a new master plan for Kapalua began to take place when Colin Cameron chose 750 acres of his family's pineapple plantation for the development of this up-scale resort. The result was the Kapalua Bay Hotel (which opened in 1979) and the surrounding resort area that now includes vacation rental villas and homes, a residential community, golf courses, and The Ritz-Carlton, Kapalua resort. Today the resort area encompasses 1,500 acres surrounded by 23,000 acres of pineapple plantation and open fields. In the 1998 *Robb Report*, Kapalua Resort was the only Hawaiian property to rank in the top five "Affluent Communities in the U.S."

Perhaps the most unusual program that Maui Land & Pineapple Company, Inc. has undertaken is to develop a home for Koko, the gorilla. Dr. Francine "Penny" Patterson has been working with Koko for 23 years teaching her communication through sign language. Koko is expected to arrive to her new 70 acre enclosure in the West Maui mountains by the end of 1998. The compound will be called the Allan G. Sanford Gorilla Preserve in memory of the son of Mary Cameron Sanford, chair of Maui Land & Pineapple. Koko will be joined by two male companions, Michael and Ndume. For more information contact The Gorilla Foundation at 1-800-63-GO-APE.

The mood reflected at the Kapalua Bay Hotel and the Ritz-Carlton, Kapalua is serene. Their philosophy of the highest quality food and service in a beachfront resort setting offers the ultimate in privacy and luxury living. Both are set on spacious grounds with manicured lawns amidst an oasis of waterfalls, gardens, and pools. More than 400 condominium units are located in the Ridge, Golf and Bay Villas; over 270 are vacation rentals. Spacious luxury homes and estates are also available as vacation rentals. The resort includes The Bay Course, The Village Course, two 18-hole championship golf courses designed by Arnold Palmer, and the third and newest Plantation Course, designed by Coore & Crenshaw. Two tennis facilities offer twenty plexipave courts (nine lighted) and there is a shopping area with a myriad of boutiques. There are several excellent restaurants in the area from which to choose. Kapalua Bay is a small cove of pristine white sand, nestled at the edge of a coconut palm grove. It has been named among the top beaches in the world. The protected bay offers good snorkeling and a safe swimming area for all ages. This area of Maui tends to be slightly wetter than in neighboring Lahaina, and the winds can and do pick up in the afternoon.

WHAT TO SEE AND DO

Kapalua, "arms embracing the sea," is the most north-western development on Maui. (See the map overview of Kapalua on page 105 at the beginning of the Honokowai section.) The logo for Kapalua is the butterfly, and with a close look you can see the body of the butterfly is a pineapple. One might enjoy a stop at the elegant Kapalua Bay Hotel. The lobby bar is ideally situated for evening refreshment, music, and sunset viewing. The resort has a small shopping mall located just outside the Kapalua Bay Hotel (with the award-winning Sansei Sushi Bar and Restaurant) and there are shops at The Ritz-Carlton, Kapalua.

The road beyond Kapalua is paved and in excellent condition, and offers some magnificent shoreline views. Slaughterhouse Beach is only a couple of miles beyond Kapalua and you may find it interesting to watch the body surfers challenge the winter waves. Just beyond is Honolua Bay where winter swells make excellent board surfing conditions. A good viewing point is along the roadside on the cliffs beyond the bay. Continuing on, you may notice small piles of rocks. This is graffiti Maui style. They began appearing several years ago and these mini-monuments have been sprouting up ever since. There are some wonderful hiking areas here as well. One terrain resembles a moonscape, while another is windswept peninsula with a symbolic rock circle formation. See RECREATION & TOURS - Hiking for more details. There is plenty to see along the way. Some of the cliffs have incredible scenic viewpoints. You will also pass the village of *Kahakuloa*. Some of the residents living here are descendants from the original settlement some 1,500 years ago. It was not many years ago that electricity finally arrived, but much is still done in the way of old Hawai'i. Tours are available. See RECREATION & TOURS - Land Tours. Travel time from Napili to Wailuku in this alternate direction is about 1 1/2 hours. The road beyond is a slow and scenic drive and many parts of the road are windy with room enough for only one car. However, don't venture on if you are in a hurry. On occasion, parts of the road have been washed away, closing it. Some rental car companies may restrict your travel on this route.

Kapalua is home to a number of outstanding annual events. The Kapalua Tennis Jr. Vet/Sr. Championship is held each May. In June both the Maui Chamber Music Festival and the Earth Maui Nature Summit are held at the Kapalua Resort. Presented by Kapalua Nature Society, the event is designed to foster an appreciation of Maui's natural environment. (In 1996 the Kapalua Resort property became the first Audubon Heritage Sanctuary in the world.) AT&T's "Golf in the Environment" tournament is just one of the summit's nature-oriented events. The Kapalua Wine and Food Symposium is offered in July; The Kapalua Open Tennis Tournament in September; and the Kapalua Betsy Nagelson Tennis Invitational is held the end of November and/or the first part of December. The nationally televised Kapalua International is held in November when top PGA golfers try their skills on Kapalua's Plantation Course. In January 1999, Kapalua will be the new home of the PGA TOURS Mercedes Championships. The Ritz-Carlton also sponsors some wonderful events. Every Easter weekend they hold the Celebration of the Arts; throughout the year they host an Artists-in-Residence program; and every December there's a tree-lighting ceremony.

WHERE TO SHOP

The **Kapalua Shops** offers a showcase of treasures. Here you will find *The Kapalua Logo Shop* (669-4172) where everything from men's and women's resort wear to glassware displays the Kapalua butterfly logo. *Kapalua Kids,* features fashions for infants through boys and girls size 7 (808) 669-0033.

ACCOMMODATIONS - KAPALUA

Kapalua Bay Hotel   The Ritz-Carlton, Kapalua
Private Villas and luxury homes

BEST BETS: The Kapalua Bay Hotel and *The Ritz-Carlton, Kapalua* are both outstanding properties, offering quiet elegance, top service and great food with all the amenities. The area's *villas and luxury homes* offer spacious living and complete kitchen facilities. Rentals are located in five different areas, and there are a number of rental agents. Any of the units would be excellent, however, they are not all located within easy walking distance of the beach. A shuttle service is available for all resort guests.

THE KAPALUA BAY HOTEL ★
One Bay Drive, Kapalua, Maui, HI 96761. (808) 669-5656, 1-800-367-8000. FAX (808) 669-4694. Now managed by Halekulani Corporation, the hotel offers 194 hotel rooms and suites in an open-air terraced low-rise. Spacious rooms have service bars, mini-refrigerators, video cassette players, and his-and-her vanities. Recently renovated with new furniture and decor in cool, refreshing shades of light green. Air-conditioning and private lanais in all units. Fifteen "Villa Suites" are also available through the hotel and include all resort and hotel (pool, grounds, services, etc.) amenities.

The Bay Club and the Gardenia Court are the hotel's outstanding restaurants. The Lehua Lounge serves afternoon tea in the open-air lobby. A variety of appetizers and desserts with accompanying piano music are available in the evening. The Plumeria Terrace offers daytime meals poolside. (The pool is butterfly-shaped and located near the ocean.) The resort's three championship golf courses and two tennis facilities (twenty plexipave courts, nine lighted) are all available for guest use. A beauty salon and exercise room are on property and a children's program is available. Lovely grounds, excellent beach and breathtaking bay. The expanse of lawn gives way to lush tropical foliage, waterfalls, pools and gardens. This is elegance on a more sophisticated scale than the glitter and glitz of the Kaanapali resorts. Two children 17 or younger free if sharing room with parent. Extra persons $50. Cribs available at no charge. Three-night deposit high season, one low season. 14-day refund notice. Modified American Plan is available at $65 per person. Room & Car, Golf, and other packages offer value with extra amenities.

g.v. $275, o.v. $325-375-400, o.f. $475-525,
1 BR suite $800-1,200; 2 BR suite $1,275-1,600
Villa Suites: Bay Villa o.f. 1BR $450, 2BR $600

THE RITZ-CARLTON, KAPALUA ★

One Ritz Carlton Drive, Kapalua, Maui, HI 96761. (808) 669-6200. The 550 room oceanfront resort opened in the fall of 1992 at D. T. Fleming Beach and follows in the same quality and high standards set for all of Kapalua. A Hawaiian motif with a plantation feel features native stonework throughout the hotel.

Accommodations include 320 kings, 172 doubles, 58 executive suites, and two Ritz-Carlton suites. Amenities include twice daily made service, in-room terry robes, complimentary in-room safe, multilingual staff, babysitting, and full service beauty salon. Ten tennis courts plus a 10,000 sq. ft., three level swimming pool are among the amenities. Restaurants include The Anuenue Room Restaurant and Lounge, the Terrace Restaurant, and the poolside Banyan Tree. See the Kapalua chapter in RESTAURANTS for further information.

The Ritz-Carlton is certainly another jewel for West Maui. We enjoyed a couple of days at this property and experienced their Club Floor for the first time. These special floors, available at many of the finer properties on Maui, have added security. A special key was required in the elevator to reach your floor. A special "Club" lounge area offered snacks almost continually. The continental breakfast was more than one would expect with some wonderful cereals, pastries, freshly squeezed juices, and fresh fruits. The mid-day snack included sandwiches, and fresh vegetables, or fruits. The early evening hours provided appetizers and wine or mix your own drinks. After dinner (which we missed because we were either too tired or too full) were chocolates and cordials. There were also cold drinks and hot coffee available all day. The lounge/dining room was elegant, yet homey, and the balconies provided entertaining views of golfers playing the course. The kids really enjoyed running down for a snack whenever they felt like it. In fact, they seldom were hungry at mealtimes and probably could have survived for weeks on the goodies served on the Club Floor. While it is more expensive, judging by the number of people in the lounge, it certainly appears to be a popular option and we can see why! This is the way to be pampered in paradise! The guest rooms are spacious and beautifully appointed.

The Ritz-Kids program is a half or full-day program that is distinctly Hawaiian. Geared for ages 5-12 years, with activities including nature walks, scavenger hunts, swimming, beach olympics, Hawaiian games and music, and hands-on science projects. Hotel guests will be delighted at the $15 fee for a full day program 9am-4pm, including lunch. Half day programs - 9am until noon or 1 to 4pm - are complimentary for hotel guests.

Wedding packages can be arranged to include the use of the historic Kumulani Chapel. Construction on the 60-seat New England style plantation church began in the late 1930's, but due to the war, it was not completed until 1951. This lovely chapel was renovated in 1994. Weddings can also be arranged at the Gazebo on the lawn of the chapel, at Lava Point, or on the Beach House lawn. Wedding packages range from $4,000-8,000.

A new feature is the "surfing classes" where you won't get wet! The Computer Center is located in a private room and offers six personal computers with instruction. Cost for surfing lessons is $20 for one hour or private instruction is available. Plenty of annual events are held at Kapalua, ranging from the Earth Maui Nature Summit to Golf and Tennis Championships. See the Calendar of Events in the GENERAL INFORMATION chapter!

Garden $260, golf/mountain/courtyard $280, partial ocean view $330, deluxe ocean view $375, Ritz Carlton Club $450, Executive One Bedroom Suite $495, The Ritz Carlton Club Executive Suite,$595, Ocean Front Suite $675, Ocean Front 2 BR suite $895, The Ritz Carlton One Bedroom Suite $2,500, Ritz Carlton two bedroom Suite $2,700.

VILLAS AND LUXURY HOME RENTALS ★
The Kapalua Villas: 500 Office Road, Kapalua, Maui, HI 96761, Kapalua, Maui, HI 96761. (808) 669-8088, FAX (808) 669-5234, 1-800-545-0018 U.S. mainland and Canada. <www.kapaluavillas.com> OTHER AGENTS: Kapalua Hotel (Villa Suites) 1-800-367-8000. Sullivan Properties 1-800-326-9874, Maui & All Island 1-800-663-6962. There are over 270 vacation rental units in the Ridge, Golf, and Bay Villas and each is spacious and beautifully appointed. Individually decorated and private, they feel much more like a home than a condominium and make wonderful units for a large family or couples traveling together. Rates from The Kapalua Villas include a 24-hour reception center, maid service, concierge, activity desk, and complimentary tennis. (These amenities do not apply if you rent through other agencies.) Their units offer kitchens, washer/dryers, and ceiling fans with 2 tvs, 2 telephones, and a VCR. Recreational facilities include several pools, outdoor barbecues, tropical garden areas, and tennis courts.

The Kapalua Villas also offers luxury homes within the private gated community of Pineapple Hill at Kapalua. With nearly 4,000 sq. ft. of living space, these magnificently furnished homes offer deluxe kitchens, whirlpool and steam baths, private outdoor pools and/or whirlpool spas, and daily maid service. A 5-bedroom, 7,700 sq. ft., multi-million dollar estate is also available at The Plantation Estates. (The oceanview homes of Ironwoods are also beautiful and very expensive, but currently no rentals are available.)

Units at The Ridge are slightly less expensive than the other villas. Although they are equally well-appointed, their location above the hotel in the golf course area makes it quite a walk to the beach. (Ridge Rentals 1-800-326-6284 handles only Ridge villas. However, they told us they weren't interested in sending us any rates and that sometimes they just don't reply to people. So while their rates, in the past, have been great, it doesn't sound like they want your business.)

Prices are reflected by location and view and vary with each agent. A little calling may be worth your while. We'd suggest starting with Kapalua Villas.
1 BR (max 4) fairway v. $185, o.v. $215, o.f. $245
2 BR (4, max 6) fairway v. $250, o.v. $325, o.f. $400
Pineapple Hill luxury homes $995-2,000; Plantation Estates $4,000

MA'ALAEA

INTRODUCTION

Ma'alaea, to many, is just a signpost enroute to Kaanapali, or a harbor for the departure of a tour boat. (Some even think that Buzz's Wharf, with its more visible and prominent sign, is the real name of the town!) However, Ma'alaea (which means "area of red dirt") is the most affordable and centrally located area of the island. A short 10 minutes from Kahului, 25 minutes from Lahaina, and 15 minutes from Wailea makes it easy to see all of the island while headquartered here. You can hop into the car for a beach trip in either direction. Even better is the mere six-mile jaunt to Kahului/Wailuku for some of Maui's best and most affordable eateries. This quiet and relaxing area is a popular living area for local residents. Seven of the ten condominium complexes are located on a sea wall on or near the harbor of Ma'alaea, while the other three are on one end of the three mile long Ma'alaea Bay beach. The two end complexes, Maalaea Mermaid and the Maalaea Yacht Marina are actually within the harbor.

The ocean and beach conditions are best just past the last condo, the Makani A Kai. There is less turbidity providing fair snorkeling at times, good swimming and even two small swimming areas protected by a reef. These are found on either side of the small rock jetty with the old pipe. This length of beach is owned by the government and is undeveloped, providing an excellent opportunity for beach walkers who can saunter all the way down to Kihei. The condominium complexes are small and low-rise with moderate prices and no resort activities. The vistas from many of the lanais are magnificent, with a view of the harbor activity and the entire eastern coastline from Kihei to Makena, including majestic Haleakala, as well as Molokini, Kahoolawe and Lana'i. The view is especially pleasing at night and absolutely stunning when a full moon shimmers its light across the bay and through the palm trees with the lights of Upcountry, Kihei, and Wailea as a backdrop. No other part of the island offers such a tranquil and unique setting. Another plus are the almost constant trade winds which provide non air-conditioned cooling as opposed to the sometimes scorching stillness of the Lahaina area. Summer in Ma'alaea is time for surfing. Summer swells coming into the bay reportedly create the fastest right-breaking rideable waves in the world and are sometimes referred to as "the freight train." The local kids are out riding from dawn to dusk. Winter brings calmer seas with fair snorkeling over the offshore reef. The calm conditions, undisturbed by parasailing and jet-skiing, also entice the Humpback whales into the shallow waters close to shore.

New development is expanding the local area eating options, but one "oldtimer," The Waterfront at the Milowai condominiums, remains constant in its excellent food and service. Buzz's Wharf (another tradition) still sits prominently at the end of the Harbor and is open for lunch, dinner and cocktails. For lighter fare, there are a limited number of snacks available at the Ma'alaea store or you can find sandwiches at the Maalaea Mermaid market.

But, the latest new "buzz" is all about the new *Maalaea Harbor Village*, a shopping and entertainment center on a triangular-shaped plot perched just above the boat harbor. Low-rise buildings and more than 800 free parking stalls are key features in the historic fishing village design. The multi-phased plan calls for nine lots to be sold separately and developed individually - from the moderate Unocal gas station/convenience store site to the expansive Maui Ocean Center which accounts for approximately one fourth of the entire 18-acre project.

Over two dozen shops and restaurants will comprise the almost 4 acres of the northernmost lot which is expected to begin construction in May, 1999. Several galleries, gift shops, activity centers, and clothing stores - along with a coffee bar and yogurt shop - are already set to open. The Pacific Whale Foundation will operate a gift shop, the Blue Marlin will offer a fishing-themed grill & game bar with satellite TV, and Hawaii Regional Chef Peter Merriman will be opening Bamboo Bistro, his second Maui oceanfront restaurant. The next phase will be a 40,000 sq. ft. building that is expected to house a food court, bakery, deli and other shops. Subsequent plans are still in the preliminary stages as we go to press, but we'll keep you apprised of any new developments in our quarterly newsletter!

New developments aside, Ma'alaea is still a quiet and accessible choice. It is not for those seeking the hub of activity or convenient fine dining, but for the independent and modest traveler. We're not sure how all this new development will effect peaceful Ma'alaea. Time will tell.

Note: the mailing address for the Ma'alaea Village condos DOES list the town as Wailuku. Although seemingly far apart, the two towns are actually located directly across from each other on opposite sides of the isthmus - hence they share the same zip code!

Maalaea

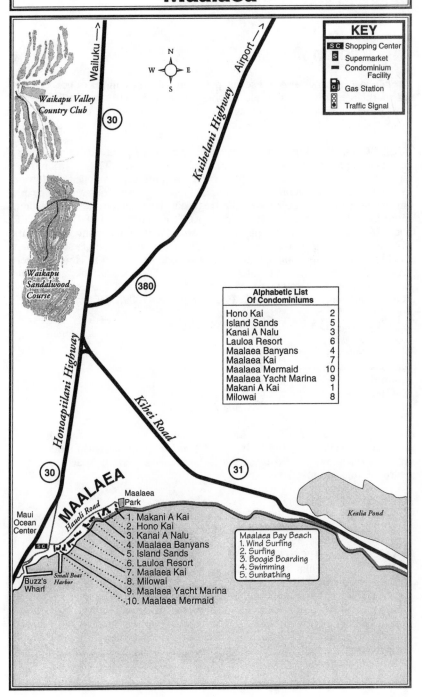

KEY

SC	Shopping Center
S	Supermarket
▬	Condominium Facility
G	Gas Station
🚦	Traffic Signal

Alphabetic List Of Condominiums

Hono Kai	2
Island Sands	5
Kanai A Nalu	3
Lauloa Resort	6
Maalaea Banyans	4
Maalaea Kai	7
Maalaea Mermaid	10
Maalaea Yacht Marina	9
Makani A Kai	1
Milowai	8

Waikapu Valley Country Club

Waikapu Sandalwood Course

Wailuku →

Kuihelani Highway Airport →

Honoapiilani Highway

Kihei Road

MAALAEA

Hauoli Road

Maui Ocean Center

Buzz's Wharf

Small Boat Harbor

Maalaea Park

1. Makani A Kai
2. Hono Kai
3. Kanai A Nalu
4. Maalaea Banyans
5. Island Sands
6. Lauloa Resort
7. Maalaea Kai
8. Milowai
9. Maalaea Yacht Marina
10. Maalaea Mermaid

Kealia Pond

Maalaea Bay Beach
1. Wind Surfing
2. Surfing
3. Boogie Boarding
4. Swimming
5. Sunbathing

WHAT TO DO AND SEE

The Ma'alaea Harbor area is a scenic port from which a number of boats depart for snorkeling, fishing and whale watching. Buzz's Wharf restaurant is still the most prominent landmark, although it has become somewhat dwarfed by the looming Maalaea Harbor Village development project in the background.

In 1998 Coral World International opened their *Maui Ocean Center* as the first and most compelling feature of the Maalaea Harbor Village. The aquarium is the only one of its kind in Hawai'i, but it is the sixth project developed worldwide by Coral World International. Their aim is to inspire appreciation for the ocean's environment and ecology and education regarding the need for reef conservation. More information on the center is in the RECREATION & TOUR CHAPTER under Marine Centers, Museums, and Gardens. Allow a minimum of two hours to visit the Maui Ocean Center which offers tours, films and classes on their exhibits which include an aquarium (the only one of its kind in Hawaii); reef, turtle and ray pools (plus an outdoor "Touch Pool"); a shark tank; and Whale Center. Oceanview restaurant plus kiosk for fast food and snacks. Open 9am-5pm. Admission: $17.50A; $12C. Phone (808) 270-7000.

ACCOMMODATIONS - MA'ALAEA

Maalaea Mermaid	Island Sands
Maalaea Yacht Marina	Maalaea Banyans
Milowai	Kana'I A Nalu
Maalaea Kai	Hono Kai
Lauloa	Makana A Kai

BEST BETS: *Kana'I A Nalu* - Attractive complex with all two-bedroom units on a sandy beachfront, affordably priced. *Lauloa* - Well designed units oceanfront on the seawall. *Makani A Kai* - Located on a sandy beachfront, two bedroom units are townhouse style.

MAALAEA MERMAID
20 Haouli St., Wailuku, HI 96793. No rental information available. Located within the Ma'alaea Seawall. Small market on the ground floor.

MAALAEA YACHT MARINA
30 Hauoli St., Wailuku, Maui, HI 96793. (808) 244-7012. Agents: Maalaea Bay Rentals 1-800-367-6084, Kihei Maui Vacations 1-800-541-6284, Bello Realty 1-800-541-3060. All units are oceanfront, a beach is nearby. The units we viewed were pleasant with a wonderful view of the boats from most units with the added plus of having security elevators and stairways. Many of the units have no air-conditioning; laundry facilities are located in a laundry room on each floor. A postage stamp size grassy area in front and a small, but adequate pool.
Oceanfront Reef Units: 1 BR (2) $85/75, 2 BR (4) $120/80

MILOWAI

50 Hauoli St., Wailuku, Maui, HI 96793. Agents: Milowai Rentals (808) 242-1580), FAX (808) 242-1634, Kihei Maui Vacations 1-800-541-6284, Maalaea Bay Rentals 1-800-367-6084. One of the larger complexes in Ma'alaea with a restaurant on location, The Waterfront. They offer a large pool area, with a BBQ along the seawall. The corner units are a very roomy 1,200 square feet with windows off the master bedrooms. Depending on condo location in the building, the views are of the Ma'alaea harbor or the open ocean. The one bedroom units have a lanai off the living room and a bedroom in the back. Washer/dryer. Weekly/monthly discounts. *1 BR (2) $85/70, 2 BR (4) $120/80*

MAALAEA KAI

70 Hauoli St., Wailuku, Maui, HI 96793. (808) 244-7012). Agents: Maalaea Bay Rentals 1-800-367-6084. Seventy oceanfront units. Laundry facilities, putting green, BBQ, and elevators. Located on the harbor wall, the rooms are standard and quite satisfactory. Most have washer and dryer in the room. Pool area and large pleasant grounds in front along the harbor wall. A few blocks walk down to a sandy beach. Monthly discounts. *o.f.: 1 BR (2) $85/75, 2 BR (4) $120/80*

LAULOA ★

100 Hauoli Street, Wailuku, Maui, HI 96793. (808) 242-6575. Agent: Maalaea Bay Rentals 1-800-367-6084. Forty-seven 2-bedroom, 2-bath units of 1,100 sq. ft. One of the Lauloa's best features is their floor plan. The living room and master bedroom are on the front of the building with a long connecting lanai and sliding glass patio doors which offer unobstructed ocean views. A sliding shoji screen separates the living room from the bedroom. Each morning from the bed you have but to open your eyes to see the palm trees swaying in front of the panoramic ocean view. The second bedroom is in the back of the unit. These two-bedroom units are spacious (only two-bedroom units are currently available in the rental program) and are in fair to good condition (depending on the owner). Each has a washer/dryer in the unit. The pool area and grounds are along the seawall. With a stairway in the sea wall, there often are local fishermen throwing nets and lines into the ocean. Five night minimum; $200 deposit. Maid service extra charge. Monthly discounts. *2 BR 2 bath (4) of. reef $130/95*

ISLAND SANDS

150 Hauoli St., Wailuku, Maui, HI 96793. Island Sands Resort Rentals 1-800-826-7816, (808) 244-0848, FAX (808) 244-5639. Agents: Agent: Maalaea Bay Rentals 1-800-367-6084. Condominium Rentals Hawaii 1-800-367-5242, (808) 879-2778. Eighty-four units in a 6-story building. One of Ma'alaea's larger complexes located along the seawall. Offers a Maui shaped pool, a grassy lawn area, BBQ. Many of these units also have a lanai off the master bedroom, however, the lanais have a concrete piece in the middle of each railing which somewhat limits the view while sitting or lying in bed. (Okay, so we got a little spoiled at the Lauloa!) Washer/dryers, and air-conditioning. Elevators. Extra person $7.50/night. Weekly and monthly discounts. 4-night minimum, $200 deposit with 15-day refund notice. Children under three free.
Studio (2) $80/65, 1 BR 1 Bath (2) 100/85, 2 BR 2 Bath (4) $130/100

MAALAEA BANYANS

190 Hauoli St., Wailuku, Maui, HI 96793. (808) 242-5668. Agents: Maalaea Bay Rentals 1-800-367-6084, More Hawaii 1-800-967-6687, Oihana 1-800-367-5234, Real Hawaii 1-800-967-6687, Maui Condo & Home 1-800-822-4409. Seventy-six oceanview units with lanai and washer/dryer. Weekly and monthly discounts. Oceanfront on rocky shore, short walk to beach. Pool area, jacuzzi, BBQ's. Extra persons $10/night. Seven night minimum. NO CREDIT CARDS. *1 BR Oceanfront Reef (2) $85/75, 2 BR (4) Oceanfront Reef $120/80*

KANA'I A NALU ★

250 Hauoli Street, Wailuku, Maui, HI 96793. Agents: Maalaea Bay Rentals 1-800-367-6084. Eighty units with washer/dryers in four buildings with elevators. No maid service. This is the first of the three condominiums along a sandy beachfront. Its name means "parting of the sea, surf or wave." The complex is V-shaped with a pool area in the middle. Nicely landscaped grounds, a decent beach and only a short walk along the beach to the best swimming and playing area along this section of coastline. While over the last couple of years the high season prices have jumped a bit, the low season rates have consistently remained an excellent value. Overall one of the best values in the Ma'alaea area. Have you wondered where the authors of this guide stay? If we aren't moving around the island, sampling different properties, you'll find us catching our breath here, and enjoying the sunny shores and gentle breezes of Ma'alaea.
5-day minimum, $200 deposit, 30-day refund notice. Weekly discounts.
2 BR (4) o.v. $145/100, o.f. $175/125

HONO KAI

280 Hauoli St., Wailuku, Maui, HI 96793. (244-7012) Agent: Maalaea Bay Rentals 1-800-367-6084. Forty-six units located on the beach. Choice of garden view, oceanview or oceanfront. Laundry facilities, BBQ, pool. This is one of many Ma'alaea properties managed by Maalaea Bay Rentals. This complex is on the beach and bears attention for the budget conscious traveler, but don't expect any frills. Five day minimum stay.
1 BR $80-100/$60-75, 2 BR $110-125/77-88, 3 BR $150/93

MAKANI A KAI ★

300 Hauoli St., Wailuku, Maui, HI 96793. Agent: Maalaea Bay Rentals 1-800-367-6084. These deluxe oceanfront, or oceanview, units are on the beach. Laundry room on property, pool, BBQ. This is the last property along the beach in Ma'alaea. Beyond this is a long stretch of sandy beach along undeveloped state land and about a four mile jaunt down to North Kihei. Great for you beach walkers! The two bedroom units are townhouse style. This is a very pleasant place to headquarter your Maui vacation!
1 BR $95-130 / $70-95, 2 BR $145-175 / $100-125   5-day minimum stay

Kihei North

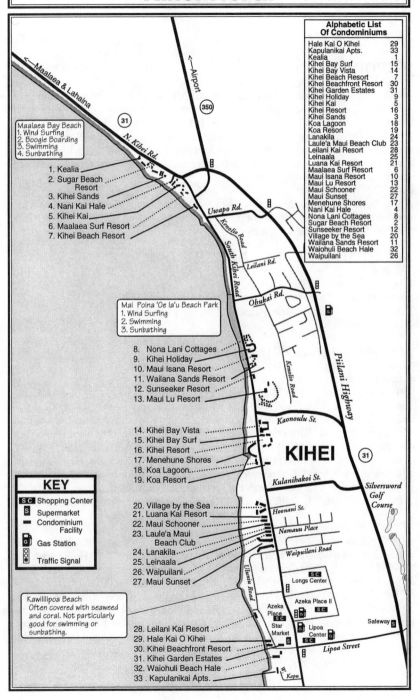

Maalaea & Lahaina ←

← Airport

Maalaea Bay Beach
1. Wind Surfing
2. Boogie Boarding
3. Swimming
4. Sunbathing

N. Kihei Rd.

1. Kealia
2. Sugar Beach Resort
3. Kihei Sands
4. Nani Kai Hale
5. Kihei Kai
6. Maalaea Surf Resort
7. Kihei Beach Resort

Uwapo Rd.

Kenolio Road

South Kihei Road

Leilani Rd.

Ohukai Rd.

Mai Poina 'Oe Ia'u Beach Park
1. Wind Surfing
2. Swimming
3. Sunbathing

8. Nona Lani Cottages
9. Kihei Holiday
10. Maui Isana Resort
11. Wailana Sands Resort
12. Sunseeker Resort
13. Maui Lu Resort

14. Kihei Bay Vista
15. Kihei Bay Surf
16. Kihei Resort
17. Menehune Shores
18. Koa Lagoon
19. Koa Resort

KIHEI

Kaonoulu St.

Kenolio Road

Piilani Highway

Kulanihakoi St.

Silversword Golf Course

20. Village by the Sea
21. Luana Kai Resort
22. Maui Schooner
23. Laule'a Maui Beach Club
24. Lanakila
25. Leinaala
26. Waipuilani
27. Maui Sunset

Hoonani St.

Namauu Place

Waipuilani Road

Ulunia Road

Longs Center

Azeka Place

Azeka Place II

Safeway

Kawililipoa Beach
Often covered with seaweed and coral. Not particularly good for swimming or sunbathing.

28. Leilani Kai Resort
29. Hale Kai O Kihei
30. Kihei Beachfront Resort
31. Kihei Garden Estates
32. Waiohuli Beach Hale
33. Kapulanikai Apts.

Star Market

Lipoa Center

Lipoa Street

Kapu

KEY

S C	Shopping Center
S	Supermarket
—	Condominium Facility
G	Gas Station
▯	Traffic Signal

NORTH KIHEI

INTRODUCTION

North Kihei is 15 minutes from the Kahului Airport and located at the entrance to South Kihei. The condominiums here stretch along a gentle sloping white sand beach. The small Kealia Shopping Center is located between the Kihei Sands and Nani Kai Hale. Another small shopping area is found at the Sugar Beach Condominiums. Several snack shop restaurants can be found along Kihei Road in this area. A little to the south down Kihei Road are additional restaurants, grocery stores, and large shopping areas.

Along with Ma'alaea, this is one of our favorite places to stay because of the good units, central but quiet location, nice beach, cooling breezes and certainly some of the island's best vacation buys.

ACCOMMODATIONS - NORTH KIHEI

Kealia   Kihei Kai
Sugar Beach   Maalaea Surf
Kihei Sands   Kihei Beach Resort
Nani Kai Hale

*BEST BETS: **Kealia** and **Maalaea Surf**.*

KEALIA ★
191 N. Kihei Rd., Kihei, Maui, HI 96753. (808) 879-9159, 1-800-367-5222. Agents: Maui & All Island 1-800-663-6962. Bello Realty 1-800-541-3060. Fifty-one air-conditioned units with lanais, washer/dryers, and dishwashers. Maid service on request. The one bedroom units are a little on the small side, but overall a good value. Well maintained and quiet resort with a wonderful sandy beach. Shops nearby. Extra person $10. 10% monthly discount. $125 deposit, $10 cancellation fee. 100% payment required 30 days prior to arrival. Seven day minimum winter, four day in summer. NO CREDIT CARDS. *Studio (2) $70/55, 1 BR o.v. (2) $90/75, 1 BR o.f. (2) $100/85. Limited number of 2 BR units.*

SUGAR BEACH RESORT
145 N. Kihei Rd. Kihei, Maui, HI 96753. (808) 879-7765. Agents: Maui & All Island 1-800-663-6962, Maui Condo & Home 1-800-822-4409, Hale Hawaiian 1-800-854-8843, Maui Condos 1-800-663-6962 US & Canada, RSVP 1-800-663-1118, More Hawaii 1-800-967-6687, Rainbow Rentals 1-800-451-5366, (808) 874-0233, Condo Rental HI 1-800-367-5242. Bello Realty 1-800-541-3060. Several six-story buildings with elevators. 215 units. Air-conditioning. Jacuzzi, putting green, gas BBQ grills. Sandwich shop and quick shop market on location. A nice pool area and located on an excellent swimming beach. Popular with families, so expect lots of kids around! Prices from Maui Condos: *1 BR o.v. $130/100, o.f. $150/115, 2 BR o.v. $220/165*

KIHEI SANDS
115 N. Kihei Rd., Kihei, Maui, HI 96753. (808) 879-2624, 1-800-882-6284. Thirty oceanfront air-conditioned units, kitchens include microwaves. Shops and restaurant nearby. Minimums: 7 night high season/4 low season, $100 deposit with 20% cancellation fee. 50% of balance due 30 days prior to arrival, balance on arrival. No maid service or room phone. Coin laundry area. NO CREDIT CARDS. Extra persons $6/night. Prices reflect garden view, ocean view or ocean front locations. *1 BR (2) $95-125/$70-98, 2 BR (4) $118-150/$85-110*

NANI KAI HALE ★
73 N. Kihei Rd., Kihei, Maui, HI 96753. (808) 879-9120. 1-800-367-6032. Agents: Maui Condo & Home 1-800-822-4409, Maui & All Island 1-800-663-6962, Hale Hawaiian 1-800-854-8843, Maui Condominiums 1-800-663-6962 US & Canada. 46 units in a six-story building. Under building parking, laundry on each floor, elevator. Patio and BBQ's by beach. Lanais have ocean and mountain views. Prices from Maui Condo: *1 BR 2 bath (2) standard $100/80, o.v. $120/85, o.f. $140/105; 2 BR 2 bath (2) std. $140/105, o.f. $180/150*

KIHEI KAI
61 N. Kihei Rd., Kihei, Maui, HI 96753. (808) 879-2357, 1-800-735-2357. Twenty-four units in a two-story beachfront building. Recreation area, laundry room, units have air-conditioning or ceiling fans. BBQ. On seven-mile stretch of sandy beach, near windsurfing, grocery stores. A good value. NO CREDIT CARDS. Extra persons $5/night. Seasonal weekly discounts. *1 BR (2,max 4) $90-105 / $80-95*

KIHEI BEACH RESORT ★
36 S. Kihei Rd., Kihei, Maui, HI 96753. (808) 879-2744, 1-800-367-6034, FAX (808) 875-0306. Agents: Maui Network 1-800-367-5221, Maui Condo & Home 1-800-822-4409, Maui Condo 1-800-663-6962 Canada. 54 beachfront units with great oceanviews, microwaves, phones. Kihei Beach Resort offers central air-conditioning, recreation area, elevator, limited maid service. Conveniently located in North Kihei, all units are oceanview. The lobby has a pleasant guest lounge with coffee served each morning. Laundry facilities available (coin-op), however, some units have their own washer/dryer. Recent renovations have included sparkling new bathrooms (we love those dimmer switches on the lights!) with attractive taupe-hued tile. The units are cozy and well-maintained. Great location for whale watching and the beach is truly just footsteps away. *1 BR (2,max4) $130/115; 2 BR (4,max 6) $165/145 Weekly and monthly discounts*

MAALAEA SURF ★
12 S. Kihei Rd., Kihei, Maui, HI 96753. (808) 879-1267, 1-800-423-7953. Other Agents: Bello Realty 1-800-541-3060. Sixty oceanview units in 8 two-story oceanfront buildings. These townhouse units have air-conditioning and micro-waves. Daily maid service, except Sundays and holidays. Two pools, two tennis courts, shuffleboard. Laundry facilities in each building. Very attractive and quiet low-rise complex on a great beach. In this price range, these spacious and attractive units, along with five acres of beautiful grounds, are impressive and hard to beat. *1 BR 1 bath (2,max 4) $185/165, 2 BR 2 bath (4,max 6) $252/217*

SOUTH KIHEI

INTRODUCTION

South Kihei began its growth after that of West Maui, but unfortunately with no planned system of development. The result is a six-mile stretch of coastline littered with more than 50 properties, nearly all condominiums, with some 2,400 units in rental programs. Few complexes are actually on a good beach. However, many are across Kihei Road from one of the Kamaole Beach Parks. A variety of beautiful beaches are just a few minutes drive away.

The drive from Maʻalaea to Kihei is but a few miles. There is a mix of sugar cane which blends into the mudflats of Maʻalaea on your right and a rather indistinguishable flatland on your left. The area on your left can best be seen from an aerial perspective. It is the enormous Kealia pond which recently became Hawaiʻi's second-largest national wildlife refuge. The federal government paid $6.9 million for ownership of the 437 acre pond and another 263 acres were donated as a federal wildlife easement by Alexander & Baldwin. Plans are underway to create a boardwalk which will allow visitors to view the endangered wildlife while protecting their habitat. Among the endangered species currently making their home in the pond are the Hawaiian coot and Hawaiian stilt. Kids and adults alike will enjoy a self-guided tour of the coastal wetlands and sand dunes of the *Kealia Pond National Wildlife Refuge*. You'll see turtles (and whales!) from the elevated vantage point - with the aid of interpretive signs along the newly-constructed boardwalk (appx. 3/4 mile) on the tour trail. For more information, call (808) 875-1582.

This section of East Maui has a much different feel than West Maui or Lahaina. There are no large resorts with exotically landscaped grounds, very few units on prime beachfront, and more competition among the complexes making this area a good value for your vacation dollar. (And a good location for extended stays.) Kihei always seemed to operate at a quieter and more leisurely pace than that of Kaanapali and Lahaina, but the last couple of years has seen a significant upsurge of development, not of condos, but of shopping complexes. Sadly, in 1994 what was beginning of shopping in Kihei, the Azeka Market closed its doors. (Although progress pushed out this Kihei institution, it is this same progress that created Azeka Place and Azeka Place II!)

Two new beach parking lots have been created at Kamaole I: the paved and landscaped Charley Young lot along with a temporary gravel pull-off area. Even parts of South Kihei Road have been repaved and regular curbs installed. These changes indicate the increasing tourist activity along with a corresponding loss of Kihei's once laid-back charm. Restaurant selections have expanded as well, giving visitors many options for dining, other than their condominium kitchens. Most needs can be filled locally at one of several large grocery stores or the growing number of mini-malls and shopping centers. Kahului, Wailuku, Wailea, and Lahaina remain an easy drive for additional shopping and dining out.

Kihei South

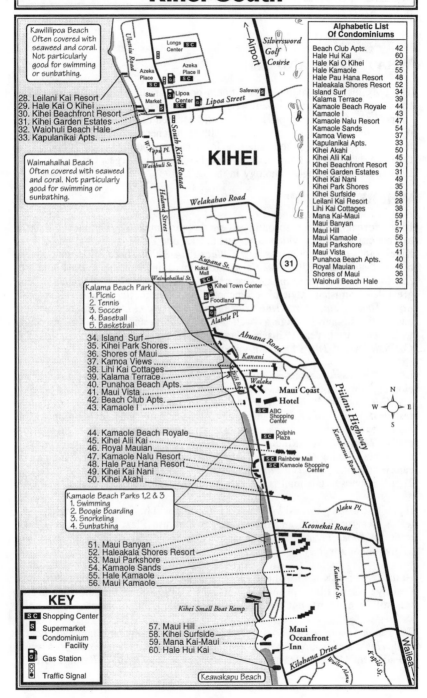

Kawililipoa Beach
Often covered with
seaweed and coral.
Not particularly
good for swimming
or sunbathing.

28. Leilani Kai Resort
29. Hale Kai O Kihei
30. Kihei Beachfront Resort
31. Kihei Garden Estates
32. Waiohuli Beach Hale
33. Kapulanikai Apts.

Waimahaihai Beach
Often covered with seaweed
and coral. Not particularly
good for swimming or
sunbathing.

KIHEI

Kalama Beach Park
1. Picnic
2. Tennis
3. Soccer
4. Baseball
5. Basketball

34. Island Surf
35. Kihei Park Shores
36. Shores of Maui
37. Kamoa Views
38. Lihi Kai Cottages
39. Kalama Terrace
40. Punahoa Beach Apts.
41. Maui Vista
42. Beach Club Apts.
43. Kamaole I

44. Kamaole Beach Royale
45. Kihei Alii Kai
46. Royal Mauian
47. Kamaole Nalu Resort
48. Hale Pau Hana Resort
49. Kihei Kai Nani
50. Kihei Akahi

Kamaole Beach Parks 1,2 & 3
1. Swimming
2. Boogie Boarding
3. Snorkeling
4. Sunbathing

51. Maui Banyan
52. Haleakala Shores Resort
53. Maui Parkshore
54. Kamaole Sands
55. Hale Kamaole
56. Maui Kamaole

57. Maui Hill
58. Kihei Surfside
59. Mana Kai-Maui
60. Hale Hui Kai

Alphabetic List Of Condominiums

Beach Club Apts.	42
Hale Hui Kai	60
Hale Kai O Kihei	29
Hale Kamaole	55
Hale Pau Hana Resort	48
Haleakala Shores Resort	52
Island Surf	34
Kalama Terrace	39
Kamaole Beach Royale	44
Kamaole I	43
Kamaole Nalu Resort	47
Kamaole Sands	54
Kamoa Views	37
Kapulanikai Apts.	33
Kihei Akahi	50
Kihei Alii Kai	45
Kihei Beachfront Resort	30
Kihei Garden Estates	31
Kihei Kai Nani	49
Kihei Park Shores	35
Kihei Surfside	58
Leilani Kai Resort	28
Lihi Kai Cottages	38
Mana Kai-Maui	59
Maui Banyan	51
Maui Hill	57
Maui Kamaole	56
Maui Parkshore	53
Maui Vista	41
Punahoa Beach Apts.	40
Royal Mauian	46
Shores of Maui	36
Waiohuli Beach Hale	32

Silversword
Golf
Course

Longs SC
Center

Azeka
Place II

Azeka
Place

Star
Market

Safeway S

Lipoa
Center

Lipoa Street

Uluniu Road

South Kihei Road

Halama Street

Welakahao Road

Kupana St.

Kukui
Mall

Kihei Town Center

Foodland

Alabele Pl.

Ahuana Road

Kanani

Walaka

**Maui Coast
Hotel**

ABC
Shopping
Center

Dolphin
Plaza

Rainbow Mall
Kamaole Shopping
Center

Alaku Pl.

Keonekai Road

31

Piilani Highway

Kanahena Road

Kawilali St.

Kihei Small Boat Ramp

**Maui
Oceanfront
Inn**

Kilohana Drive

Keawakapu Beach

Wailea Alanui

Kapili St.

Wailea

KEY

SC Shopping Center
S Supermarket
— Condominium
Facility
G Gas Station
Traffic Signal

WHAT TO DO AND SEE

The only historical landmark is a totem pole near the Maui Lu Resort which commemorates the site where Captain Vancouver landed. The scientific "opposite" of the totem pole is The Maui Research & Technology Park located up from the highway on Lipoa Street. Although generally not open to the public, it is worth a mention as their high-performance computing center is one of less than two dozen in the entire nation. It is also one of the largest configurations of IBM super computing technology in the U.S.

WHERE TO SHOP

Every corner of Kihei is sprouting a new shopping mall. The complexes all seem to have quick markets, video stores and at least one T-shirt shop. Traveling down Kihei Road, the first center is *Azeka Place* (874-8400) where Bill Azeka opened his first store in 1950. *Azeka's Market* closed in September 1994 and *Ace Hardware* has relocated in that space. The *Azeka Snack Shop* continues to offer great deals on island style plate lunches. The *International House of Pancakes*, *Royal Thai Cuisine*, *Pizza Hut*, *Home Maid Bakery and Deli*, and *Taco Bell* are among the restaurants here as well as *Crazy Shirts* and assorted tourist shops which vary each year. This is where you'll also find *Old Daze Antiques & Collectibles* and *Tilt*, which is a video arcade.

Located across the street is *Azeka Place II* and there are several jewelry and clothing stores, a baby accessory shop, a bank, an activity center, *In's Eel Skin and Gifts* and *Panda Express*, a Chinese food outlet. *A Pacific Cafe* (a fabulous restaurant), *The Coffee Store* and *Peggy Sue's* seem to form a dividing line in this mall. Beyond these two areas, is another portion of the mall which has a sign that reads *"Longs Drugs Kihei Center."* Here you'll find *Little Polynesians*, a children's clothing store, *Maui Sporting Goods*, and *Mail Boxes Etc* along with eateries that include *Sushi Paradise, Antonio's, Stella Blues*, and *America's Cup Yogurt*. Opposite this mall is the ever popular *McDonald's*.

If you're traveling toward Wailea, on your right will be *Star Market* and on your left a *Chevron* Station and behind this is Paradise Plaza. Behind the service station is *Shaka Pizza*. They have fabulous N.Y. subway style pizza, so be sure to give them a try!

At the corner of Kihei Road and Lipoa is an area that had been trying to become the Royal Kiawe Plaza for several years now. At press time, the construction area was still blocked off, but word is that it's just not going to happen . . .

The *Lipoa Shopping Center* is a block down Lipoa Street and is home to *Hapa*s Brew Haus,* a microbrewery with live music and entertainment six nights a week, the adjacent *Mulberry St.* Italian restaurant as well as *Henry's Bar and Grill*.

Yet another shopping center is being built at the corner of Lipoa Street and the Piilani Highway. Scheduled for completion in 1999, the center is anchored by *Safeway* and will include *Outback Steakhouse* and some other shops, but we have been unable to get anyone to tell us which!

Just past the Kapulanikai condominiums, the **Kukui Mall** at 1819 S. Kihei Rd., (808) 244-8735 gets our vote for the most attractive mall. This large complex is done in Spanish style architecture with a wide assortment of shops. *Waldenbooks* has a great selection of books on just about any subject (and hopefully our Paradise guides!). *Subway* is a handy to pick up sandwiches enroute to one of Wailea's fine beaches or stop by *Coconuts Bakery & Cafe*. *Tony Roma's* is a good dining option here and you can follow up your rib dinner with a cool treat at *I Can't Believe It's Yogurt*. Right next door is the multi-plex *Kukui Mall Theater*. They offer a good selection of first run movies - both mainstream and critically-acclaimed "small" films. The kids might want to spend some time on a rainy afternoon at the *Fun Factory*. They have an assortment of video and arcade games. A number of gift and sundry shops round out this mall.

Across the street from the Kukui Mall is an open air shopping area. *The Aloha Market* is kind of a junky swap meet style tourist trap. Lots of jewelry, T-shirts, and the like. No great deals. It will only remain here until the spring of 1999 when Hawaiian Moons will be expanding their operation to this locale.

A bit farther is the **Kihei Town Center** which offers a selection of shops including sporting goods, novelty items, clothing and the *Foodland* grocery. The restaurants here are *Chuck's*, *Hirohachi* and *Aroma d'Italia*.

On the same side of the street, look for the development of **Kihei Kalama Village**, a cluster of shops, restaurants, and small eateries. Its swap meet-type venue of open air stalls was expected to be transformed and renovated in the summer of 1998 to a bit more formal atmosphere with a large open steel pavilion to shelter the open stalls and shops amid landscaped gardens and monkey pod trees. You'll find affordable menus at *Life's A Beach*, a cute new restaurant bar with burgers, burritos, and sand on the floor, and nearby *Alexander's Fish & Chips* with fish prepared either deep fried or broiled. In addition to island seafood, they import oysters from Puget Sound. *Tokyo Ramen* is a small Japanese restaurant on the corner and towards the back you can "pick your poison" - a drink at the Kahale Beach Club bar or a decadent pastry at the Kalama Village Bakery. The best shave ice in town and a MUST STOP for all visitors is at *Tobi's*. Next door at *Kihei Caffe* you can get a generous meal for a reasonable price; an outstanding spot for breakfast.

The next few shopping areas almost run together. The **Dolphin Plaza**, 2395 S. Kihei Rd., across from Kamaole I Beach is one of the shopping centers. Here you'll find *Senor Taco*, *Koiso Sushi Bar*, *Jack's Famous Bagels* and *Jabooka Juice* for some healthy - but addicting! - fruit smoothies and juices.

Between the Dolphin Plaza and Rainbow Mall is the tiny *Kamaole Beach Center*, 2411 S. Kihei Rd. Here you'll find *Hawaiian Moons Natural Foods*. They offer health foods, vitamins, and organically grown produce. Not quite the same ambiance as the old Paradise Fruits (Hawaiian Moons actually has a floor) but worth a stop anyway. Adjacent is *Hawaiian Moons Salad Bar and Deli*. (Look for Hawaiian Moons to expand to 5,000 sq. ft. when they move their entire operation down the street to the Aloha Marketplace location in September, 1999.) Other eateries at this center are the *Sports Page Grill and Bar* and the popular *Maui Tacos*. Check out *Aloha Books* for used and collectible books.

The Rainbow Mall is a small center also located on the *mauka* side (towards the mountain) of South Kihei Road. They offer jewelry and souvenir stores, a stand that serves shave ice and espresso, and a sub sandwich shop combined with *Premiere Video* rentals. *Haleakala Trading Co.* offers arts & crafts made by local Maui artists - everything from paintings to perfumes! *Steve Amaral's Cucina Pacific* upstairs, is a new fine dining restaurant. *Thai Chef*, towards the back of the mall, is another dining option.

Kamaole Shopping Center is one of the larger malls and offers several restaurant selections including *Denny's*, *Canton Chef*, and *Sandcastle* - which recently relocated from Wailea and has expanded to include a piano bar. The *Cinnamon Roll Faire* has wonderful, huge and decadent cinnamon buns. There is also a *Maui Dive Shop*, *Whalers General Store*, several clothing shops, and the new *King Pin Surf & Skate* (808) 891-1846) for beachwear, boogie, surf and skate boards plus lessons!

The last shopping center in Kihei, across from Kamaole III Beach, is the *Nani Kai Center*. *Kai Ku Ono Bar & Grill*, *Kihei Prime Rib & Seafood*, *The Greek Bistro and Annie's Catering* are the restaurants which make up this complex. There is also a mini-market.

ORCHIDS

ACCOMMODATIONS - SOUTH KIHEI

Nona Lani
Kihei Holiday
Wailana Sands
Maui Isana
Pualani
Sunseeker Resort
Maui Lu Resort
Kihei Bay Vista
Kihei Bay Surf
Menehune Shores
Kihei Resort
Koa Lagoon
Koa Resort
Kauhale Makai
Leinaala
Luana Kai
Maui Schooner
Maui Sunset
Leilani Kai
Kihei Garden
Hale Kai O Kihei
Waiohuli Beach
Kihei Beachfront
Kapulanikai
Island Surf
Kihei Park Shores
Shores of Maui

Punahoa
Beach Club Apts.
Lihi Kai Cottages
Maui Vista
Kamoa Views
Kamaole One
Maui Coast Hotel
Kamaole Beach
  Royale
Kihei Alii Kai
Royal Mauian
Kamaole Nalu
Hale Pau Hana
Kihei Kai Nani
Kihei Akahi
(Aston at the) Maui
Banyan
Haleakala Shores
Maui Parkshore
Kamaole Sands
Hale Kamaole
Maui Kamaole
Maui Hill
Kihei Surfside
Mana Kai Maui
Maui Oceanfront Inn
Hale Hui Kai

BEST BETS: *Maui Hill* - Situated on a hillside across the road from the ocean, some units have excellent ocean views. The three-bedroom units here are roomy and a good value for large families. *Haleakala Shores* - Across from Kamaole III Beach Park. *Mana Kai Maui* - One of Kihei's larger resorts, the units are fair but an extra plus is that they are located on good beaches.

NONA LANI
455 S. Kihei Rd., (PO Box 655) Kihei, Maui, HI 96753. (808) 879-2497, FAX (808) 891-0273. 1-800-733-2688. Eight individual cottages with kitchens, color TV, queen bed plus a rollaway and day bed, full bath with tub and shower, and lanais. Front four cottages now have air conditioning and all were recently refurbished. Large grounds, public phone, two BBQ's, and laundry facilities. Located across the road from sandy beach. NO CREDIT CARDS.
1 BR (2) $68; $455 weekly low season, higher rates December 16-April 1.

KIHEI HOLIDAY
483 S. Kihei Rd., Kihei, Maui, HI 96753. (808) 879-9228. Agents: Kihei Maui Vacations 1-800-541-6284, RSVP 1-800-662-1118. Units are across the street

from the beach and have lanais with garden views. Pool area jacuzzi and BBQ's. Rates from Kihei Maui Vacations: *1 BR $99/79, 2 BR (4) $119/94*

WAILANA SANDS
25 Wailana Place, Kihei, Maui, HI 96753. Ten units, overlook courtyard and pool area, in a two-story structure. Quiet area on a dead end road one block from the beach. No rental rates available.

MAUI ISANA RESORT
515 S. Kihei Road, Kihei, Maui, HI 96753 (808) 879-7800, 1-800-633-3833. Agent: Kihei Maui Vacations 1-800-541-6284. These 51-one-bedroom units are decorated in muted beige and blues and are complete down to an electric rice cooker and china dishes. A spacious pool area is the focal point of the central courtyard. Located across the road from the beach. Washer/dryer. There may be 2 bedroom units available from on-property rental agent.
Price from Kihei Maui Vacations: *1 BR 1 BTH (1-3) $129/104*

SUNSEEKER RESORT
551 S. Kihei Rd. (PO Box 276) Kihei, Maui, HI 96753. (808) 879-1261, 1-800-532-MAUI, FAX (808) 879-1261, Email: < sunseekr@maui.net > Units include studios with kitchenettes, one bedrooms with kitchens. Monthly discounts available. No room phones, no pool. Across street from beach. Popular area for windsurfing. NO CREDIT CARDS. Milt & Eileen Preston are the Owner/Managers. *S BR $60/55, 1 BR $70/65, Extra person $6*

MAUI LU RESORT
575 S. Kihei Rd., Kihei, Maui, HI 96753. (808) 879-5881. Agent: Aston 1-800-922-7866. One of the first resorts in the Kihei area and unusual with its spacious grounds: 180 units on 26 acres. Pool is shaped like the island of Maui. Many of the hotel rooms are set back from South Kihei Road and the oceanfront units are not on a sandy beachfront. The *Ukulele Grill* restaurant is located on site. Ask about the Aston Island Hopper rates if you're planning on visiting multiple islands. *Hotel Room with refrigerator (1-2) g.v. $120/99, superior g.v. $130/110, deluxe o.v. $160/140, o.f. $185/165*

KIHEI BAY VISTA
679 S. Kihei Rd., Kihei, Maui, HI 96753.(808) 879-8866. Agents: Kihei Maui Vacations 1-800-541-6284, Marc Resorts 1-800-535-0085. Built in 1989, this complex offers pool, spa, jacuzzi, putting green, air-conditioning, washer/dryer, lanais, and full kitchens. A short walk across the road to Kamaole I Beach. Over-looking Kalepolepo Beach. Kihei Maui Vacations: *1 BR units $99/79*

KIHEI BAY SURF
715 S. Kihei Rd. (Manager Apt. 110), Kihei, Maui, HI 96753. (808) 879-7650. Agents: Kihei Maui Vacations 1-800-541-6284, Maui Condominiums 1-800-663-6962 US & Canada, Maui & All Island 1-800-663-6962, Maui Network 1-800-367-5221, Hale Hawaiian 1-800-854-8843. Kihei Bay Surf offers 118 studio units in 7 two-story buildings. Pool area, jacuzzi, BBQ, laundry area, tennis. Across the road from Kamaole I Beach. Prices Kihei Maui Vacations: *Studios $74/64*

MENEHUNE SHORES

760 Kihei Rd., Kihei, Maui, HI 96753. (808) 879-0076. Agents: Menehune Reservations, PO Box 1327, Kihei, Maui, HI 96753, (808) 879-3428), 1-800-558-9117 US & Canada, FAX (808) 879-5218. RSVP 1-800-663-1118, Kihei Maui Vacations 1-800-541-6284, Hale Hawaiian 1-800-854-8843, Rainbow Rentals 1-800-451-5366. Six story building; 115 units with dishwashers, washer/dryers and lanais. Recreation room, roof gardens with whale-watching platform, and shuffleboard. The ocean area in front of this condominium property is the last remnant of one of Maui's early fish ponds. These ponds, where fish were raised and harvested, were created by the early Hawaiians all around the islands. Condo and car packages available from Menehune Reservations.
1 BR 1 bath (2) $100/ 80, 2 BR 2 bath (2) $140/110,
3 BR 2 bath (6) $155-175/135-155

KIHEI RESORT

777 S. Kihei Rd., Kihei, Maui, HI 96753. Agents: Kihei Maui Vacations 1-800-541-6284, RSVP 1-800-663-1118. Sixty-four units, two-story building, located across the street from the ocean, BBQ's, pool area jacuzzi. Two bedroom units may be available from some rental agents. NO CREDIT CARDS. Prices quoted from Kihei Maui Vacations for 4-6 day stay. Weekly discounts.
1 BR (2) $ 99-119/74-99

KOA LAGOON

800 S. Kihei Rd., Kihei, Maui, HI 96753. 1-800-367-8030. Agents: Kihei Maui Vacations 1-800-541-6284. These 42 oceanview units are in one six story building. Washer/dryers. Pool area pavilion, BBQ's. Located on a small sandy beach that is often plagued by seaweed which washes ashore from the offshore coral reef. This stretch of Kihei is very popular with windsurfers. $45 cleaning charge for stays of 4 days or less.
1 BR 1 bath (2,max 4) $110/80, 2 BR 2 bath (4,max 6) $130/110

KOA RESORT

811 S. Kihei Rd., Kihei, Maui, HI 96753. (808) 879-1161, 1-800-877-1314, FAX (808) 879-4001. Agents: Kihei Maui Vacations 1-800-541-6284, Bello Realty 1-800-541-3060. There are 54 units (2,030 sq.ft.) on spacious 5 1/2-acre grounds in 2 five-story buildings across the road from the beach. Two tennis courts, spa, jacuzzi, putting green. Units have washer/dryers. Prices from Kihei Maui Vacations for 4-6 day stay, weekly discounts, no credit cards.
1 BR 1 bath (2,max 4) $124/99, 2 BR 2 bath (4,max 4) $149/129,
3 BR 2 bath (6,max 8) $179/159

KAUHALE MAKAI (Village by the Sea)

930-938 S. Kihei Rd. Kihei, Maui, HI 96753. (808) 879-8888. Agents: Maui & All Island 1-800-663-6962, Maui Condominium & Home Realty 1-800-822-4409, Maui Condominiums 1-800-663-6962 US & Canada, RSVP 1-800-663-1118, Kihei Maui Vacations 1-800-541-6284. Two six-floor buildings offer 169 air-conditioned units with phones. Complex features putting green, gas BBQ's, plus children's pool, sauna, and laundry center. The beach here is usually strewn with coral rubble and seaweed, but area condos have taken to "vacuuming" it daily! *Studio (2) $85/75, 1 BR (2) $100/80, 2 BR (4) $95-130/110-150*

LUANA KAI ★
940 S. Kihei Rd., Kihei, Maui, HI 96753. (808) 879-1268, 1-800-669-1127, FAX (808) 879-1455, E-mail: luanakai@mauigateway.com AGENTS: Maui & All Island 1-800-663-6962, Bello Realty 1-800-541-3060, Hale Hawaiian 1-800-854-8843, Kihei Maui Vacations 1-800-541-6284, Rainbow Rentals 1-800-451-5366. Located adjacent to a large oceanfront park with public tennis courts. 113 units on 8 acres with washer/dryers. The grounds are nicely landscaped and include a putting green, BBQ area, pool area, sauna and jacuzzi. The beach, however, is almost always covered with coral rubble and seaweed. Children under 12 free. Three bedroom unit may be available thru some agencies. *1 BR (2) g.v. $109/79, 1 BR (2) o.v. $129/99 2 BR (6) g.v. $139/99, 2 BR (6) o.v. $149/109*

MAUI SCHOONER RESORT
980 S Kihei Rd, Kihei, Maui HI 96753. (808) 879-5247) Reservations 1-800-877-7976 (weekday business hours) These 58 units are fully furnished complete with equipped kitchens, TV, VCR, washer/dryer and private lanai. Only one building has an elevator to the upper floors. Fronting these condos is a public park with 4 tennis courts and a beach (that is seasonally strewn with coral rubble). Swimming pool, sauna, and hot tub. Now a time share resort, but offering rentals as well. Check in is 4pm, check out is an early 10 am. Brochure notes that full payment for all rentals required at booking, all sales are final and non-refundable. *Weekly: 1 BR (4) $750, 2 BR (6) $925, 3 BR $1100* (Nightly rates $120-170)

LEINAALA
998 S Kihei Rd, Kihei, Maui, HI 96753. (808) 879-2235, 1-800-334-3305 U.S. & Canada, FAX (808) 879-8366. Twenty-four one and two bedroom units in a 4-story building. Tennis courts at adjoining park. Pool, cable color TV. Oceanview. The property is fronted by a large park which stretches out to the ocean. Leinaala and Maui Sunset are the only two that have currently hired folks to dredge the seaweed and rubble off the beach in front, making it much more pleasant. Lots of good beach parks a short drive away. Weekly/monthly discounts. AARP and AAA discounts. *1 BR (2) $100/75, 2 BR (4) $115/95*

WAIPUILANI
1002 S. Kihei Rd., Kihei, Maui, HI 96753. (808) 879-1465. Forty-two units in three 3-story buildings. Long term only; no vacation rentals.

MAUI SUNSET
1032 S. Kihei, Rd., Kihei, Maui, HI 96753. (808) 879-0674. Reservation Assistance 1-800-843-5880. Agents: Kihei Maui Vacations 1-800-541-6284, Kumulani 1-800-367-2954, Maui Network 1-800-367-5221, Hale Hawaiian 1-800-854-8843, RSVP 1-800-663-1118, Maui Condo & Home 1-800-822-4409. Two multi-story buildings with 225 air-conditioned units. Tennis courts, pitch and putt golf green,

and sauna. Large pool, exercise facility, barbecues. Located on beach park with tennis courts. Apparently the resolution to their long problem of seaweed and coral rubble on the beach is a daily beach "sweeping." Prices from Kihei Maui Vacations for 4-6 day stay. Weekly discounts. No credit cards.
1 BR $119/99, 2 BR $169/139, Some 3 BR $234/189

LEILANI KAI
1226 Uluniu St., (PO Box 296) Kihei, Maui, HI 96753. (808) 879-2606, FAX (808) 879-0241. Eight garden apartments with lanais. NO CREDIT CARDS. Monthly discounts. *Studio (2) $60, 1 BR (2) $70, 1 BR dlx (4) $80, 2 BR (4) $90*

KIHEI GARDEN ESTATES
1299 Uluniu St., Kihei, Maui, HI 96753. (808) 879-5785, 1-800-827-2786. Agents: Kihei Maui Vacations 1-800-541-6284, Maui Condominiums 1-800-663-6962 US & Canada, Maui & All Island 1-800-663-6962. Eighty-four units in eight 2-story buildings. Jacuzzi, BBQ's. Across road and short walk to beaches. Monthly discounts. NO CREDIT CARDS. Rates for 4-6 nights. Weekly discounts. Prices from Kihei Maui Vacations:
1 BR (2,max 4) $99-119/79-99, 2 BR (4,max 6) $119/94

HALE KAI O KIHEI
PO Box 809, 1310 Uluniu Rd., Kihei, Maui, HI 96753. (808) 879-2757, 1-800-457-7014, FAX (808) 875-8242. Agent: Condo Rentals Hawaii 1-800-367-5242. Fifty-nine oceanfront units with lanais in three-story building. Sandy beachfront. Shuffleboard, putting green, BBQ's, laundry, recreation area.
Condo Rentals Hawaii rates: One bedroom condo plus compact car $98 daily

WAIOHULI BEACH HALE
49 West Lipoa St., Kihei, Maui, HI 96753. Agents: Pali Kai 1-800-882-8550. Also de Beer Realty (808) 879-1971; 1-800-326-5396 (US & Can). Four two story buildings with 52 units. Large pool, gas BBQs. Located on beachfront that is poor for swimming or snorkeling, often covered with coral rubble and seaweed. Spacious park-like lawn area around pool. Weekly/monthly discounts. Four night minimum. Extra guests $10 pre night. Children 6 & under $5.
1 BR o.v. (2) $95/70; 2 BR o.v. (4) $115/100; Dlx 2 BR o.v. (4) $129/114
1 BR o.f. (2) $95/80; 2 BR o.f. $120/110. Weekly and monthly discounts.

KIHEI BEACHFRONT RESORT
Located at end of Lipoa St. Agent: Maui Condos & Homes 1-800-822-4409. Eight oceanview two bedroom units with washer/dryers, microwaves, dishwashers, and air-conditioning in a single 2-story building. Large lawn area fronting units. Lanais on upper level. No elevator. Pool area jacuzzi. Rates from Maui Condos: *2 BR o.v./g.v. $130/110, 2 BR o.f. (4) $170/145*

KAPULANIKAI APTS
73 Kapu Place, PO Box 716, Kihei, Maui, HI 96753. Agent: Bello Realty 1-800-541-3060. Twelve units are oceanview with private lanais or open terraces. Beachfront is poor for swimming or snorkeling. Grassy lawn area in front. BBQ's, laundry facilities, pay phone on property. *1 BR 1 bath $80/65*

ISLAND SURF
1993 S. Kihei Rd., Kihei, Maui, HI 96753. This property once had vacation units and there may still be a few, but now primarily commercial or residential.

KIHEI PARK SHORES
No rental agents seem to handle this property!

SHORES OF MAUI
2075 S. Kihei Rd., Kihei, Maui, HI 96753. (808) 879-9140, 1-800-367-8002. Agent: Leisure Properties 1-800-367-8002. Fifty-unit two-level complex in garden setting offers BBQ's, tennis courts, and spa. Located across the street from a rocky shoreline and 1½ blocks north of Kamaole I Beach Park.
1 BR $94/69, 2 BR $119/94

PUNAHOA
2142 Iliili Rd., Kihei, Maui, HI 96753. (808) 879-2720, 1-800-564-2720. Fifteen oceanview units with large lanais, telephones. No pool. Elevator, laundry facilities, beaches nearby. NO CREDIT CARDS. 5-day minimum or pay $50 service charge. Three seasons May 1-October 31 low season, mid season Nov 1-Dec 14 and April 1-April 30, and high season December 15-March 31.
Studio (2) $93/75/66
1 BR (2,max 4) $127-135/102-108/85-87
2 BR (2,max 6) $130/104/94

BEACH CLUB APARTMENTS
2173 Iliili Rd., Kihei, Maui, HI 96753, (808) 874-6474. Long term rentals only.

LIHI KAI COTTAGES
2121 Iliili Rd., Kihei, Maui, HI 96753. (808) 879-2335, 1-800-544-4524. Nine beach cottages are one bedroom and one bath with kitchen and lanai. Self-service laundromat. Next to Kamaole I Beach. NO CREDIT CARDS. Weekly discounts.
1 BR (2) $69/64

MAUI VISTA
2191 S. Kihei Rd., Kihei, Maui, HI 96753. (808) 879-7966, 1-800-367-8047 ext.330. Agents: Maui & All Island 1-800-663-6962, Kihei Maui Vacations 1-800-541-6284, RSVP 1-800-663-1118, Marc Resorts 1-800-535-0085, Maui Condo & Home 1-800-822-4409, Maui Condominiums 1-800-663-6962 US & Canada. Three 4-story buildings, across from the beach. 280 units. Some have air-conditioning, some have washer/dryers. All have kitchens with dishwashers. The two bedroom units are fourth floor townhouses. Some oceanview units. Six tennis courts, three pools, BBQ's. A great value if you don't mind a short walk to the beach, but we had problem with sound carrying from a neighboring unit. Some air-conditioned. Rates from Maui Condo:
1 BR 1 Bath (2,max 4) $95/75, 2 BR w BTH $130/100.

KAMAOLE ONE

2230 S. Kihei Rd., Kihei, Maui, HI 96753. (808) 879-4811 or (808) 879-2449, FAX (808) 874-3744. Two story building. Twelve units, currently nine are available for vacation rental. No elevators or pool, covered parking. Beachfront. Nice location on Kamaole I Beach. Telephones, microwaves, washer/dryers, air-conditioning, ceiling fans and cable TV.

One week minimum stay. $200 deposit. NO CREDIT CARDS. No swimming pool, but as Jean Simpson, manager, notes in her explanation, "we felt it redundant here on Kamaole #1 Beach."
2 BR ground or second floor $160-170/140-150

MAUI COAST HOTEL   (Hotel)

2259 S. Kihei Rd., Kihei, Maui, HI 96753. (808) 874-MAUI, FAX (808) 875-4731. Reservations: 1-800-426-0670. Owned and operated by West Coast Hotels, they opened in February 1993 and offer 260 rooms -- 114 of them suites. The hotel offers a pool area, two outdoor whirlpools, the Kamaole Bar & Grill in front, two night lit tennis courts and complimentary laundry facilities. We found this to be a great concept, a more affordable hotel with some condominium conveniences. (Although the standard room we had was a little crowded with one king bed and the two kids on a sofa bed.) This is a no frills, but nicely appointed property. The in-room refrigerator was stocked with a couple of complimentary cans of juice daily and there was a coffee maker with the fixings. Located across the road from the Kamaole Beach Parks, the pool area was pleasant and an international mix of people seemed to be staying at the property during our visit.

Standard Hotel room $129-139; alcove suite $149-159; deluxe king $169; Standard 1 BR suite $169; Standard 2 BR suite $225, Deluxe 2 BR Suite $250; Royal Suite $300. Room rate special includes a suite upgrade, complimentary breakfast for two, welcome Mai Tai for two, and free daily rental car: $159

REEF DWELLERS   J. BAYOT

KAMAOLE BEACH ROYALE

2385 S. Kihei Rd., Kihei, Maui, HI 96753. (808) 879-3131, 1-800-421-3661, FAX (808) 879-9163. Sixty-four units with washer/dryers and single or double lanais in a single seven story building across from Kamaole I Beach. Recreation area, elevator, roof garden. 5-day minimum, $200 deposit, balance due 30 days prior to arrival. $25 cancellation service charge. NO CREDIT CARDS.
1 BR 1 bath (2) $ 95/70 Extra person $10 per night
2 BR 2 bath (2) $110-115 / $85-90
3 BR 3 bath (2) $120/95

KIHEI ALII KAI

2387 S. Kihei Rd., Kihei, Maui, HI 96753. (808) 879-6770, 1-800-888-MAUI. Agents: Leisure Properties (PO Box 985, Kihei, 96753) 1-800-888-MAUI, Pali Kai 1-800-882-8550, RSVP 1-800-663-1118, Kihei Maui Vacations 1-800-541-6284. Four buildings with 127 units. All units have washer/dryers. No maid service. Complex features pool, jacuzzi, sauna, two tennis courts, BBQ. Across road and up street from beach. Nearby restaurants and shops. Prices from Leisure: *1 BR (2) $90/65, 2 BR (4) $105-115 / $80-90, 3 BR (6) $145/120*

ROYAL MAUIAN

2430 S. Kihei Rd., Kihei, Maui, HI 96753. (808) 879-1263, 1-800-367-8009, FAX (808) 367-8009. Agent: Maui Condo & Home 1-800-822-4409. Complex has shuffleboard, carpeted roof garden, and is next to the pleasant Kamaole II Beach Park. 107 units with lanai, washer/dryer, in a six story building. Rates from Maui Condo: *1 BR 1 bath or 2 bath o.f.(2) $125/105; 2 BR 2 bath o.f. (2) $180/145; Some 3 BR may be available through other rental agents as well as side wing two bedroom.*

KAMAOLE NALU

2450 S. Kihei Rd., Kihei, Maui, HI 96753 (808) 879-1006, 1-800-767-1497. FAX (808) 879-8693. Agent: Maui & All Island 1-800-663-6962. Thirty-six two bedroom, two bath units with large lanai, dishwasher, and washer/dryer in a 6-story building. Located between Kamaole I and II Beach Parks with all units offering oceanviews. Weekly maid service during high season. $12-15 extra person. Three day minimum. Summer specials.
2 BR 2 bath (2) o.v. $145/110, o.f. $165/130

HALE PAU HANA

2480 S. Kihei Rd., Kihei, Maui, HI 96753. (808) 879-2715, 1-800-367-6036, FAX (808) 875-0238. Agents: Maui Condo & Home 1-800-822-4409, RSVP 1-800-663-1118, Kihei Maui Vacations 1-800-541-6284. Seventy-eight oceanview units in four buildings. Laundry area, elevator, laundry facilities. Located on Kamaole II Beach. NO CREDIT CARDS through on-site reservations. Extra person $10-12. No charge for children 5 years and younger. Inquire about condo/car packages and summer specials.
Tower: 1 BR 1 or 2 Bath (2,max 4) $165-170/134-140
In the Low Rise: 1 BR 1 bath (2,max 4) $160-165/130-135

KIHEI KAI NANI
2495 S. Kihei Rd., Kihei, Maui, HI 96753. Front desk: (808) 879-1430, reservations 1-800-473-1493. Email:kkndiaz@maui.net Agents: Maui Condominiums 1-800-663-6962 US & Canada, Rainbow Rentals 1-800-451-5366. This complex is one of the older ones along Kihei Rd. comprised of 180 one-bedroom units with lanai or balcony in a two and three story structure. Laundry room and recreation center. Across from Kamaole II Beach. Senior discount low season. NO CREDIT CARDS thru front desk reservations. Car/condo packages and weekly discounts available thru front desk office. *1 BR (2) $85/65*

(ASTON AT THE) MAUI BANYAN
2575 S. Kihei Rd. Managed by Aston Resorts: 1-800-922-7866. Agents: Maui & All Island 1-800-663-6962, Kihei Maui Vacations 1-800-541-6284, Kumulani 1-800-879-9272, Maui Condo & Home 1-800-822-4409, Maui Condominiums 1-800-663-6962 US & Canada. Overlooking Kamaole II Beach Park, these suites feature kitchens, washer/dryer, lanai, air-conditioning, cable TV and telephone. Facilities include tennis court, pool and jacuzzi. Upgrades in 1998 have renovated the lobby area and a putting green and BBQ area have been added. Hotel rooms have no kitchens. Daily maid service.
Hotel Room (1-2) std $130/115; 1 BR (max. 4) std. $180/145, sup. $200/165
2 BR (max. 6) standard $230/190, superior $255/215
3 BR (Max. 8) suite with kitchen, deluxe $305/270

KIHEI AKAHI
2531 S. Kihei Rd., Kihei, Maui, HI 96753. (808) 879-1881. Agents: Maui Condominiums 1-800-663-6962 US & Canada, Kihei Maui Vacations 1-800-541-6284, Maui & All Island 1-800-663-6962, RSVP 1-800-663-1118, Hale Hawaiian 1-800-854-8843. Across from Kamaole II Beach Park. 240 units with washer and dryers. 2 pools, tennis court, BBQ's. NO CREDIT CARDS. Studios and 2 bedroom units may be available through some rental agents.
Prices quoted Kihei Maui Vacations: *1 BR 1 bth (2) $104/84,*

HALEAKALA SHORES ★
2619 S. Kihei Rd., Kihei, Maui, HI 96753. (808) 879-1218, 1-800-869-1097. Seventy-six, 2-BR units in two four story buildings. Located across the road from Kamaole III Beach. Washer/dryer. Covered parking. A good value! NO CREDIT CARDS. *2 BR 2 Bth (1-4) $120/90*

MAUI PARKSHORE
2653 S. Kihei Rd., Kihei, Maui, HI 96753. (808) 879-1600. Agents: Maui & All Island 1-800-663-6962, Maui Condo & Home 1-800-822-4409, Oihana Properties (808) 244-7685. Sixty-four, two bedroom, two bath oceanview condos with washer/dryers, and lanais in a 4-story building (elevator) across from Kamaole III Beach. Pool area sauna. Rates from Maui Condo: *2 BR 2 bath (4) $120/90*

KAMAOLE SANDS
2695 S. Kihei Rd., Kihei, Maui, HI 96753. (808) 874-8700, FAX (808) 879-0666. Managed by Castle Resorts Reservations 1-800-367-5004 US & Canada Agents: Kihei Maui Vacations 1-800-541-6284, Hale Hawaiian 1-800-854-8843,

Kumulani 1-800-367-2954, Maui Condo & Home 1-800-822-4409, Castle Group 1-800-367-5004, Hawaiian Pacific Resorts 1-800-367-5004, Maui Condominiums 1-800-663-6962 US & Canada, Kihei Maui Vacations 1-800-541-6284. Maui & All Island 1-800-663-6962. Ten 4-story buildings totaling 315 units. Includes daily maid service. 4 tennis courts, wading pool, babysitting services, 2 jacuzzi's and BBQ's. Located on 15 acres across the road from Kamaole III Beach. Three price seasons from Castle Resorts: *Studio w/ kitchen $105-130*
1 BR (1-4) Standard, Superior, Partial Ocean View $135-190
2 BR (1-6) Standard, Garden View, Partial Ocean View $185-265
3 BR (1-7) Garden View, Partial Ocean View $275-300

HALE KAMAOLE
2737 S. Kihei Rd., Kihei, Maui, HI 96753. (808) 879-2698, 1-800-367-2970. Agents: Maui & All Island 1-800-663-6962, More Hawaii 1-800-967-6687, Maui Condo & Home 1-800-822-4409, Maui Condominiums 1-800-663-6962 US & Canada. 188 units in 5 buildings (2 & 3-story, no elevator) across the road from Kamaole III Beach. Laundry building, BBQ's, 2 pools, tennis courts. Some units have washer and dryers. *1 BR (2) $100/80, 2 BR 2 bath (4) $130/100*

MAUI KAMAOLE
2777 S. Kihei Rd., Kihei, Maui, HI 96743. (879-7668). Agents: Kihei Maui Vacations 1-800-541-6284, Maui Condo & Home 1-800-822-4409, Maui & All Island 1-800-663-6962, Pali Kai 1-800-882-8550, Hale Hawaiian 1-800-854-8843, Maui Condominiums 1-800-663-6962 US & Canada. Located on a bluff overlooking the ocean and across the street and a short walk down to Kamaole III Beach Park or Keawakapu Beach. 1 BR units are 1,000-1,300 sq.ft. and 2 BR units are 1,300-1,600 sq.ft. Some have oceanviews. This four phase development is located on 23 oceanview acres. All are low-rise, four-plex buildings grouped into 13 clusters, each named after Hawaiian flora. Rates from Maui Condo: *1 BR 2 BTH g.v. $140/110; 1 BR 2 BTH o.v. $150/120, 2 BR 2 BTH g.v. $170/140; 2 BR/2 BTH o.v. $185/150.*

MAUI HILL ★
2881 S. Kihei Rd., Kihei, Maui, HI 96753. (808) 879-6321. Agents: Aston Hotels 1-800-922-7866, RSVP 1-800-663-1118. Twelve buildings with a Spanish flair clustered on a hillside above the Keawakapu Beach area. 140 attractively furnished units with washer/dryers, air-conditioning, microwaves, dishwashers, and large lanais. Daily maid service. There is a moderate walk down and across the road to the beach. Upper units have oceanviews. The 3-bedroom units are very spacious. Large pool and tennis courts. *1 BR (1-4) o.v. $210/175, 2 BR (1-6) o.v. $240/205, 3 BR o.v. $295/260*

KIHEI SURFSIDE
2936 S. Kihei Rd., Kihei, Maui, HI 96753. (808) 879-1488. 1-800-367-5240. Agents: Maui Condo & Home 1-800-822-4409, More Hawaii 1-800-967-6687, Hale Hawaiian 1-800-854-8843. Eighty-three units on rocky shore with tidepools, a short walk to Keawakapu Beach. Large grassy area and good view. Coin-op laundry on premise. Prices from Maui Condo:
1 BR 1 bath (2) $125/95, 2 BR 2 bath (4) $185/145

MANA KAI ★

2960 S. Kihei Rd., Kihei, Maui, HI 96753. (808) 879-1561, 1-800-525-2025, FAX (808) 874-5042. Agents: Condo Rentals Hawaii 1-800-367-5242, Hale Hawaiian 1-800-854-8843, Maui & All Islands 1-800-663-6962 and Kumulani 1-800-367-2954. Eight story building with 132 rooms. The studio units have a room with an adjoining bath. The one bedroom units have a kitchen and the two bedroom units are actually the hotel unit and a one bedroom combined, each having separate entry doors. The Mana Kai now offers hotel-like services, no minimum stay and daily maid service. Condominium Rentals Hawaii renovated the hotel rooms in the summer of 1997 with fresh carpeting, wallpaper, refrigerator, coffee maker and air conditioning. The one bedroom condo units completed renovations in the summer of 1998. This complex has laundry facilities on each floor, an oceanfront pool, and a restaurant off the lobby. The Mana Kai is nestled at the end of Keawakapu Beach, and offers a majestic view of the blue Pacific, the 10,000 foot high Haleakala and Upcountry Maui. It is the only major facility in Kihei on a prime beachfront location. Keawakapu Beach is not only very nice, but generally very under used. Prices quoted from management company, Maui Beachfront Rentals. Ask about condo/car packages and summer discounts.
Hotel Room (2) $ 80; 1 BR 1 bath (2) o.v. $150, o.f. $160
2 BR 1 bath (2) o.v. $180, o.f. $190

MAUI OCEANFRONT INN

2980 S. Kihei Rd., Kihei, Maui, HI 96753. (808) 879-7744. Managed by & reservations through: Castle Group 1-800-367-5004. Eighty-eight units. Located on Keaweakapu Beach, but only the front unit has an oceanview. No pool. Several two-story buildings, no lanais. *Hotel room rates from $85*

HALE HUI KAI

2994 S. Kihei Rd. Kihei, Maui, HI 96753. On-site property rental agent (808) 879-1219, FAX (808) 879-0600, 1-800-809-MAUI. Oceanfront on Keawakapu Beach. Five night minimum or cleaning fee charged. Rates double occupancy. Additional person $15-20. NO CREDIT CARDS.
All 2 BR 2 bath: O.f. $180-200/145-170, side o.v. $35/105, g.v. $120/95.

WILIWILI

WAILEA

INTRODUCTION

Wailea is a well planned and well manicured resort on 1,500 acres just south of Kihei developed by Alexander and Baldwin. In addition to a selection of outstanding luxury resorts and condominiums, there are a fine selection of championship golf courses, a large tennis center, and a shopping village. (Currently undergoing expansion and major renovation.) The spacious and uncluttered layout is impressive, as are its series of lovely beaches. There is a shoreline paved trail that travels between the Kea Lani up to the Grand Wailea Resort, making it a wonderful option for a stroll, day or night. Besides visiting resorts and beaches, there isn't much to do until the new "Shops at Wailea" complete renovation sometime in late 1999. Currently, on Tuesdays at 1:30pm they feature a free Hawaiian show in the central courtyard of the Wailea Shopping Center that is quite good. Bring a towel or mat to sit on. You can pick up a cold drink, an ice cream cone, or a sandwich to enjoy during the show. This may be discontinued once construction begins. The first two resort hotels were the 550-room Aston Wailea Resort (they opened as the Maui Inter-Continental Resort and changed management in 1996) which opened in 1976, and the 350-room Renaissance Wailea Beach Resort (formerly the Stouffer Wailea Beach Resort) that originally opened as a Westin in 1978. The Palms at Wailea is located at Wailea's entrance. The Four Seasons Resort opened in the spring of 1990 and was followed by the September 1991 opening of the neighboring, 812-room Grand Wailea Resort & Spa, which was originally a Hyatt. Kea Lani, an all-suites resort, opened in November of 1992 with 450 rooms and 37 oceanfront villas on Polo Beach. The Diamond Resort, a private, primarily Japanese "long-stay" hotel, is located in the foothills above Wailea. The Wailea condominium villages are divided into four locations: two are beachfront while two are adjacent to the golf course. The newest of these villages is the Grand Champion Villas which opened in 1989. The Polo Beach condominiums are located adjacent to Wailea resorts on Makena Road. An exclusive property, Wailea Point, has no vacation rentals.

WHAT TO SEE AND DO

The lovely Wailea beaches are actually well-planned and nicely maintained public parks with excellent access, off-street parking and most have restrooms and rinse-off showers. Ulua Beach is our personal favorite. Don't miss visiting one of Wailea's wonderful beaches! And, be sure you spend some time strolling through the imaginative grounds of the Grand Wailea Resort & Spa.

WHERE TO SHOP

Wailea Shopping Village, located at the southern end of Wailea, is currently undergoing major expansion and renovation (in fact, demolition!) to become *The Shops at Wailea*. The new 150,000 sq. ft. shopping center will offer both fine dining and casual restaurants, brand name lifestyle and specialty shops, and luxury retailers (Louis Vuitton is one of the anchor tenants). Completion is expected by the end of 1999.

Wailea and Makena

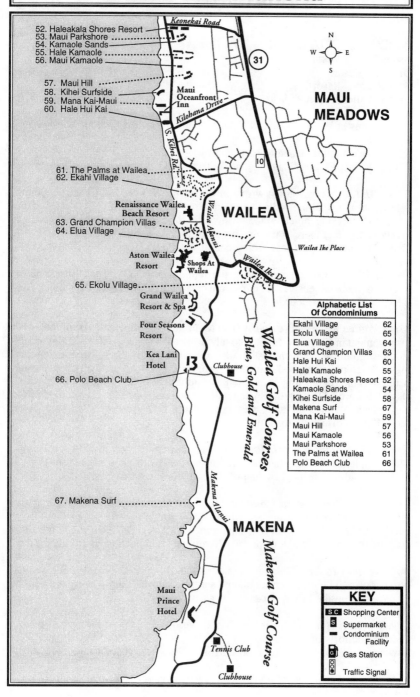

52. Haleakala Shores Resort
53. Maui Parkshore
54. Kamaole Sands
55. Hale Kamaole
56. Maui Kamaole

57. Maui Hill
58. Kihei Surfside
59. Mana Kai-Maui
60. Hale Hui Kai

Keonekai Road

31

N
W — E
S

Maui Oceanfront Inn

Kilohana Drive

S. Kihei Rd.

MAUI MEADOWS

10

61. The Palms at Wailea
62. Ekahi Village

Renaissance Wailea Beach Resort
63. Grand Champion Villas
64. Elua Village

WAILEA

Wailea Alanui

Wailea Ike Place

Aston Wailea Resort
Shops At Wailea

Wailea Ike Dr.

65. Ekolu Village

Grand Wailea Resort & Spa

Four Seasons Resort

Kea Lani Hotel

13

Clubhouse

66. Polo Beach Club

Wailea Golf Courses
Blue, Gold and Emerald

Alphabetic List Of Condominiums

Condominium	No.
Ekahi Village	62
Ekolu Village	65
Elua Village	64
Grand Champion Villas	63
Hale Hui Kai	60
Hale Kamaole	55
Haleakala Shores Resort	52
Kamaole Sands	54
Kihei Surfside	58
Makena Surf	67
Mana Kai-Maui	59
Maui Hill	57
Maui Kamaole	56
Maui Parkshore	53
The Palms at Wailea	61
Polo Beach Club	66

Makena Alanui

67. Makena Surf

MAKENA

Makena Golf Course

Maui Prince Hotel

KEY

SC	Shopping Center
S	Supermarket
▬	Condominium Facility
G	Gas Station
⚬⚬⚬	Traffic Signal

Tennis Club

Clubhouse

ACCOMMODATIONS - WAILEA

Aston Wailea Resort
Diamond Resort
Four Seasons Resort
Grand Wailea Resort & Spa
Kea Lani
(The) Palms at Wailea
Polo Beach Club
Renaissance Wailea Beach Resort
Wailea Villas: Ekolu Village, Ekahi Village, Elua Village, Grand Champion

BEST BETS: It's hard to go wrong in wonderful Wailea. Affordable accommodations are not what the visitor will find here, but there are a variety of excellent condominiums and hotels among which to choose. Each is different, each is lovely and in fact there is not one property that we would not recommend. The choice is up to the personal preference of the guest. Here is a quick synopsis:

Wailea Villas - Our choice among the four areas would be the Elua Village. These are more expensive, of course, but beach aficionados will love having Ulua Beach at their front door.

Aston Wailea Resort - Previously The Maui Inter-Continental, Aston took over management in February 1996. A lovely property featuring a tropical flavor with spacious grounds, excellent restaurants, and two great beaches. They are continuing to develop a wonderful Hawaiiana program. The open-air lobby is exquisite, with charming decor and an ambiance reminiscent of the bygone era of "Boat Days." But we're hoping that Aston will include some guest room renovations in their plans. While very nice, they could use a little freshening up. Ask about second room discounts for kids.

Renaissance Wailea Beach Resort - Formerly Stouffer Wailea Beach Resort. This complex is smaller, and more intimate -- as resorts go -- it has lush, tropical grounds, and it is fronted by one of the island's finest beaches.

The *Grand Wailea Resort and Spa* - This is an enormous resort, but also enormous fun! The pools are incredible, but if you prefer the ocean, there is the excellent Wailea Beach. There is something to do for everyone in the family. Just walking the grounds and touring the $40 million art collection could fill up a day!

Four Seasons Resort - This resort is purely and simply elegant. From it's white porte cochere you enter a tranquil and serene environ. Simply sit by the pool or enjoy a day on the beach. No need to go further!

The *Kea Lani Hotel* - This is an all-suites resort, a blend of the best of resorts and the comforts of a condominium, all on Polo Beach. Want to indulge? Then how about one of their private oceanfront villas with private swimming pool?

Polo Beach - Luxury condominium units with easy access to two small but good beaches.

THE PALMS AT WAILEA

3200 Wailea Alanui Drive, Wailea, Maui, HI 96753 (808) 879-5800. Agents: Outrigger Hotels Hawaii 1-800-OUTRIGGER, Maui Condo & Home 1-800-822-4409, Kihei Maui Vacations 1-800-541-6284. One and two bedroom condominiums on a bluff overlooking the Wailea area with views of the islands of Kaho'olawe and Lana'i. Two-story walk-up, 77 luxury units. Amenities include partial air conditioning, VCR, in-room laundry, light daily maid service, pool and spa. As part of the Wailea Resort Community, this property offers access to the two Wailea golf courses and tennis complex. Daily maid service.
1 BR g.v. (4) $170-185, o.v. $195-210, 2 BR (6) g.v. $190-220, o.v. $225-245

WAILEA VILLAS

3750 Wailea Alanui, Wailea Maui, HI 96753. (808) 879-1595, 1-800-367-5246. Agents: Destination Resorts Wailea (808) 879-1595, 1-800-367-5246, Maui Condo & Home (Grand Champion & Ekolu) 1-800-822-4409, Maui & All Island 1-800-663-6962 (all units), Kumulani (only Ekahi & Elua condos) 1-800-367-2954, Pali Kai (only Ekolu units) 1-800-882-8550. Some agents may have a few units for slightly better prices than those quoted below. The price range reflects location in the complex. Children under 16 free in parent's room.

EKOLU VILLAGE - Located near the tennis center and the Wailea golf course.
1 BR (2) $160-200/140-180, 2BR (4) $190-230/170-210

EKAHI VILLAGE - On the hillside above the south end of Keawakapu Beach, some units are right above the beach. Destination Resorts rates:
S BR (2) $149-189, 1 BR (2) $199-249, 2 BR (4) $279-349

ELUA VILLAGE - Located on Ulua Beach, one of the best in the area. We would recommend these units...expensive though they are!
1 BR (2) g.v.-o.v. $240-295, o.f. $370-395
2 BR (4) g.v.-o.v. $330-385, o.f. $465-495
3 BR (6) g.v. $450, o.f. $575-600

GRAND CHAMPION VILLAS - Located at 155 Wailea Iki Place, Wailea, HI

96753. Agents: Maui Condo & Home 1-800-822-4409, Destination Resorts 1-800-367-5246, Maui Network 1-800-367-5221, Kihei Maui Vacations 1-800-541-6284. Twelve lush acres comprising 188 luxury condominium units with garden view, golf view, or oceanview units. The fourth and newest of the Wailea Villas, this is a sportsman's dream, located between Wailea's Blue Golf Course and the "Wimbledon West" Tennis Center. Bookings through Destination Resorts include daily maid service, grocery delivery, and concierge service. Golf, tennis and/or car packages available. Destination Resorts rates: *1 BR (2) $170-210/150-190, 2 BR (4) $210-240/190-220*

RENAISSANCE WAILEA BEACH RESORT ★ (Hotel)

3550 Wailea Alanui, Wailea, Maui, HI 96753. (808) 879-4900, 1-800-992-4532, FAX (808) 874-5370. This luxury resort (formerly Stouffer Wailea) covers 15.5 acres above beautiful Mokapu Beach with 347 units including 12 suites. Each guest room is 500 sq.ft. and offers a refrigerator, individual air-conditioner, a stocked mini-bar, and private lanai. The rooms are decorated in soothing rose, ash and blue tones. An assortment of daily guest activities are available as well as a year-round children's program called Camp Wailea. The program operates five days per week from 9am-1pm for youth ages 5-12 years. Fee charged.

Fat City is an unusual attraction here. This "multi-colored cat of undetermined lineage" has become the unofficial resort resident. In fact, she has endeared herself to so many guests that she receives mail on a regular basis.

The Mokapu Beach Club is a separate beachfront building with 26 units that feature open beamed ceilings and rich koa wood furnishings, plus a small swimming pool. The resort's restaurants are the Maui Onion, a pool-side gazebo; Palm Court, serving international buffets in an open air atmosphere; and Hana Gion, serving authentic Japanese cuisine in an authentic setting. The Sunset Terrace, located in the lobby area, offers an excellent vantage point for a beautiful sunset and nightly entertainment 5:30pm-8:30pm. The beach offers excellent swimming. The best snorkeling is just a very short walk over to the adjoining Ulua Beach. The grounds are a beautiful tropical jungle with a very attractive pool area which was recently expanded to include additional lounging areas and more jacuzzi pools. They also offer several "breakation" options. These include a combination of room and car, room and golf or honeymoon options.
Terrace $320, Garden $350, Partial ocean view $380, oceanview $435, Mokapu Beach Club $550, One bedroom suite $900, Two Bedroom suite $1,350, Alii Suite $2,200 and Aloha Suite $3,000.

ASTON WAILEA RESORT ★ (Hotel)
3700 Wailea Alanui, Kihei, Maui, HI 96753. (808) 879-1922, FAX (808) 874-8331), 1-800-367-2960. The porte cochere greets your arrival with a grand entry and ocean view. Beautiful koa rockers tempt guests to sit, relax and enjoy the tranquil, gorgeous view. (Pretend you're on the deck of a luxurious cruise ship of the 1930's or 40's!) The lobby design is unpretentious, old Hawaiian and classic. The artwork is subtle. Chests from Japan, huge stone mochi bowls, spirit houses from Thailand, roof finials from New Guinea, and calabashes from the Big Island. Just beyond, the main stairway descends down and winds past a lily pond (a popular wedding site) to the central pool area. The oceanview, 34,000 sq. ft. conference pavilion is topped with a rooftop observatory. Take the elevator or walk up for a panoramic view and a perfect vantage point for whale watching. Located on 22 acres they have 1/2 mile of oceanfront property and access to two great beaches, Ulua and Wailea. There are three pools, a seven-story tower and six low-rise buildings. The wonderful layout of this resort allows 80% of all guest rooms to have an ocean view and the grounds are spacious and sprawling. No "packing them in" feel here! The main pool area has two pools. One deeper and one a 4 1/2 foot depth all over. There is also a pint-size slide into a small pool that is perfect for the pint size members in your family. Nothing exotic or fancy, just plain good water fun. A separate pool in the luau area is often uncrowded. The units located nearest the beach afford wonderful private ocean views. The restaurants in this lovely resort include Hula Moons which serves lunch and dinner, live entertainment, and the islands's only "Chocoholic Bar!"

Lea's serves breakfast and features nightly selections of fresh fish caught in local waters. A very good Sunday Champagne Brunch can be found in the Makai Room, and for nightly fun and games, there's "Pa'ani - a game bar" (for guests ages 21 and older) with board and table games, jukebox, a big screen tv, cigar & cognac lounge - and sunsets! Laundry facilities are coin-op and located in several areas on property. The resort offers the excellent *Hoolokahi* program which are a series of Hawaiian classes available to guests and non-guests for a nominal fee. This is also home to one of the Maui's best luaus. Live entertainment from 5:30-7:30 in the Kai Puka Bar. A number of exciting annual events are sponsored by the resort. Golf, tennis and honeymoon package plans also available.

We have a small complaint regarding their $8 "resort fee." We surveyed the other Wailea resorts and many of the amenities in this resort fee are complimentary at neighboring resorts, including free parking. In addition, they list items such as complimentary shuttle to golf courses and shopping centers. This isn't a service of this hotel, it is a service of the Wailea area and is provided at no charge to all hotels. If you make use of the items, it is a good deal, if not, it isn't! Aston has begun to freshen up the guest rooms. They've ordered new bedspreads which should liven up the rooms.

Rates single/double occupancy are one rate all year: Garden View $219; Mountain View $259; Ocean View $299; Oceanfront $339; Deluxe Oceanfront $399; Junior Suite $499; Ocean Suite $699, Executive Suite $799, Presidential Suite $899. Rates do not include the $8 per room per day "resort service fee." Extra person charge $30 daily (maximum 4)

DIAMOND RESORT (Hotel)
555 Kaukahi St., Wailea, Maui, HI 96753. (808) 874-0500) This private resort, an extension of the Diamond Resort Corporation which manages a chain of 20 resorts throughout Japan, is located just above the Wailea Golf Course. The spa facility which includes a men's and women's daiyokujo (traditional Japanese bath), a waterfall to gently massage your neck and shoulders as well as a soothing Finlandia sauna is one of the resort's highlights. Previously this was a resort for Japanese guests which belonged to the resort chain. However, Diamond Resort has recently launched a program to target mainland visitors. The 72-suite resort comprises 18 two-store buildings on 15 acres. Each suite is 947 sq. ft. and includes a master bedroom, dining area, kitchenette, sitting area, lanai and bath. Suites are ocean view, golf course view or views of Mount Haleakala. Two of their suites have been designed for physically challenged guests and four suites are non-smoking. Their Restaurant Taiko and Le Gunji are both fine dining restaurants. Bella Luna is open evenings for casual dining or cocktails and live entertainment. *Suites are $240 per night.*

WAILEA POINT
4000 Wailea Alanui, Wailea, Maui, HI 96753. There are 136 luxurious oceanview and oceanfront condominiums arranged in four-plexes which are laid out in a residential plan on 26-oceanfront acres. Privacy is maintained by a gate guard at the entrance. Unfortunately, no rental properties available here!

GRAND WAILEA RESORT & SPA ★

3850 Wailea Alanui Drive, Wailea, Maui, HI 96753 (808) 875-1234, Reservations only 1-800-888-6100, FAX (808) 879-4077, Email: info@garndwailea.com. < WWW > The Grand opened their 767 room resort in September 1991 at a cost of $600 million with an additional $30 million in fine artwork. This beautifully appointed resort is a must-see, even if you aren't lucky enough to stay! In fact, make at least two trips... a second at night to enjoy dinner and tour the grounds when they are alight like a twinkling fairy land.

The sea remains the theme throughout the resort. Guests are greeted by a huge waterfall flowing down from Mt. Haleakala as they arrive. Look closely for the Hawaiian sea spirits which are hidden amid this interesting aquatic cascade. Each of the many Hawaiian sculptures has a legend or history -- King Kamehameha stands out near the entry and was created by Herb Kane, a noted specialist on Polynesian culture and history. He also created many of the mermaids, dancers and fisherman found by the resort's lagoons and streams. Inside the resort you'll find Hena, the mother of the demigod Maui. In the open air walkway of the Molokini Wing there are 18 bronzes around the grounds that were sculpted by world-famous artist Fernard Leger. Jan Fisher sculpted ten life-size pieces for the resort including the maidens bathing and the two-trios of hula dancers at the entry of the atrium. Be sure to take note of the beautiful relief painting on the walls of the Grand Dining Room. The murals were painted by Doug Riseborough and depict his version of the legend of the demigod Maui. In the center of the dining room is a sculpture done by Shige Yamada, entitled "Maui Captures the Sun." Just outside the dining room is a small stage with a fabulous Hawaiian mosaic. The resort offers a complimentary art tour twice weekly led by an island art expert. The center courtyard is called the Botero Gallery. These sculptures seem to be getting the most discussion - both good and bad! Fernando Botero is a contemporary artist from Colombia and his work is "oversized." The huge Hawaiian woman reclining on her stomach (smoking a cigarette in the buff) weighs 600 pounds and is appraised at $2 million. If you're on the upper levels, be sure to look down to see her from another.... uh, interesting, perspective!

Over $20 million was spent on the waterfalls, streams, rapids, slides, reflecting pools, swimming pools, river pool, scuba pool, salt water lagoon and spa features. This is one of the most high-tech aquatic systems in the state. Strikingly beautiful, the formal reflecting pool leads you to the sweeping Wailea Beach. Beyond this pool is a formal swimming Hibiscus pool made of Mexican glass tile with gold leaf. This adults only pool is lined with wide Mediterranean-style cabanas. The "action pool" (The Wailea Canyon Activity Pool) is a million gallon, 23,500 square foot pool with five large, free-form pools at various levels beginning at a height of 40 feet and dropping to sea level. Painted tiles depicting turtles & tropical fish in varying shades of green and blue line the bottom and sides, while huge rocks and landscape features line the pools. At one end of the pool is an incredible waterslide, a 225 foot twisting ride that drops three stories. The "jungle pool," another part of the Wailea Canyon Activity pool, offers a rope swing. The pools are connected by a 220 foot river which carries swimmers at varying current speeds, ranging from white water rapids to a lazy cruise.

Along the way are hidden grottoes, whirlpools and saunas, six slides, six water-falls and a bumpy white water rapids that has been created by the use of special aquatic devices. At the bottom of the river is a one-of-a-kind water elevator which lifts the swimmers back up to the top again. Below the rocky waterfall is the scuba pool which gets prospective divers in the mood with an underwater mural featuring a coral reef, and sea life made of tiles. Streams and pools also meander through elaborate gardens in Hawaiian and Japanese themes throughout the resort. It takes 50,000 gallons of water a minute to sustain their aquatic system.

Spa Grande is Hawai'i's largest spa, and spans 50,000 square feet in the atrium wing of the resort. It is designed with Italian marble, original artwork, Venetian chandeliers and inlaid gold. It provides a blend of European, Japanese and American spa philosophies. Hawaiian therapies include a ti leaf wrap, limu (seawood) bath and a lomi lomi massage. The "Terme Wailea" is a 30-minute circuit on the spa's "wet" level which begins with a loofah scrub, followed by a trip to the Roman tub for a cool dip followed by a choice of specialty baths. The masso, thermo and hydrotherapy treatments are available in 42 individual rooms. Also available are a sonic relaxation room, cascading waterfall massage, authentic furo soaking tubs and white and black sand body treatments. An aerobics studio, weight room, plus cardiovascular room, racquetball and squash court (the only ones on Maui), a full-service beauty salon, and game room are among the many spa options.

The *Tsunami Nightclub* (what a great name!) offers 10,000 square feet of high tech lounge with black marble. Five restaurants give guests plenty of choices. Kincha features authentic and very expensive Japanese cuisine and is set amid a beautiful Japanese Garden. The Grand Dining Room Maui, situated 60 feet above sea level, offers a panoramic view of the Pacific, the gardens and Molokini Island from inside or on a lovely outdoor eating veranda. Currently it can only be enjoyed at breakfast. Cafe Kula features family-style foods. The Humuhumu-nukunukua'pua'a restaurant (Humuhumu for short!) is named for the Hawaiian state fish. It sits surrounded by a saltwater lagoon filled with tropical fish. It is definitely worth a stop just to see this restaurant which serves expensive Pacific Rim/seafood cuisine. Bistro Molokini serves California and Italian items and the Volcano Bar provides light dining and snacks. There is also a swim up bar!

Now the rooms! There are 787 oceanfront rooms each 650 square feet and 53 suites. The Presidential suite (5,500 sq. ft.) is priced at a mere $8,000 per night and features what is lovingly referred to as the Imelda Marcos shoe closet, a private sauna, a room-sized shower with ocean view in one bathroom and a black marble and teak soaking tub in the other. Lots of marble is used throughout all the rooms with subtle marbleized wallpapers in earthen hues. The resort was designed so that each room would provide an ocean view.

This may be the one resort that your kids will INSIST you come back to again and again. After you visit the kids' camp you will, at least momentarily, wish you could pass for a 10 or 11 year old. The 20,000 square foot Camp Grande also takes older kids and operates year-round. A huge area is designed with crafts complete with pottery kiln. Adjacent is a kid's dining dream, resembling a 1950's style soda fountain. An outdoor area offers a toddler-size whale-shaped pool, cushy soft grass-like play yard and playground equipment. Another room houses the computer center and another the video arcade. We guarantee that your kids will not be glad to see you upon pickup time.

We are fascinated by the blend of mega resort glitz and Hawaiian themes tempered with outstanding craftsmanship. It seems to work. There is actually a great deal of fine craftsmanship (notice the twisted ohia wood rails that line the pathways) and we especially like the attention to the Hawaiiana aspects.

The resort is visually very stimulating and each time you stroll the grounds you're sure to see something new. The chapel, set in the middle of the grounds is a popular spot for weddings. The woodwork and stained glass windows are absolutely beautiful, and take note of the chandeliers: original cost $100,000 each! The 28,000 sq. ft. ballroom is a convention planner's dream, with concealed projection screens, specialized audio equipment -- the works! The ballroom also has three huge, beautiful and unique artworks in gold and silver leaf which depict the story of Pele, the fire goddess, and her two sisters. Don't neglect a look up at the 29,000 pound Venetian glass chandelier imported from Italy.

All-in-all, if you're seeking an action-packed resort vacation, you'll find it all here. Not everyone wants the activity of a resort, but this one certainly has something for everyone.

Terrace $380, Premier $445, Deluxe Ocean $495, 1 BR suites 1,100-$1,600. Napua Tower: This is a private tower with two private lounges, complimentary continental breakfast, afternoon tea, and cocktails: Suites $580-$10,000

THE FOUR SEASONS RESORT WAILEA ★
3900 Wailea Alanui, Wailea, Maui, HI 96753. (808) 874-8000. (National reservations 1-800-332-3442). Website: < www.fourseasons.com > This gorgeous property offers 380 over-sized guest rooms (600 sq. ft) on eight floors encompassing 15 beachfront acres on the beautiful white sand Wailea Beach. A full service resort featuring two pools, (one large, one smaller lava pool) and a jacuzzi on each end of the main pool, one of which is set aside for children only. The layout of the grand pool provides shelter from the afternoon breezes. In addition there are two tennis courts at the resort, a croquet lawn, health spa, beauty salon, three restaurants and two lounges. The public areas are spacious, open and ocean oriented. (If we had a category for "Best Bathrooms," These would be the winners. They are elegantly decorated and each stall is like a "mini" suite!) A very different atmosphere from other Maui resorts, the blue tiled roof and creamy colored building create a very classical atmosphere. Even the grounds, although a profusion of colors with many varied Hawaiian flora, are more structured in design with a vague resemblance to a Mediterranean villa. The focus of the resort is water. Throughout the resort's gardens and courtyards are an array of attractive formal and natural pools, ponds, waterfalls, and fountains.

Their guest policy features real aloha spirit, with no charge for use of the tennis courts or health spa and complimentary snorkel gear, smash or volleyball equipment. Guest services, which distinguish the Four Seasons from other properties, include their early arrival/late departure program. These guests have their luggage checked and are escorted to the Health Club where a private locker is supplied for personal items. The resort makes available for these guests an array of casual clothing from work-out gear to jogging suits or swim wear.

For the meeting planner, the Four Seasons features a 7,000 square foot ballroom, two banquet rooms and five conference areas situated adjacent to a 3,000 square foot hospitality suite. The suite offers a large living room, two bedrooms, another living space designed for private meetings, kitchen, and a 1,000 square foot lanai.

The *Four Seasons Resort* is peaceful and elegant. No glitz here, just what you come to Paradise for. A "children's only" hot tub allowed the second adult hot tub to be a quiet respite. There are plenty of complimentary cabanas around the pool area and on the beach to enjoy the day while staying out of the sun. Pool and beach staff are on their toes providing prompt attention for guests in setting up their lounge chairs with towels and providing chilled towels or spritzers to cool the face. Seaside, the poolside restaurant and bar (it becomes Ferraro's at night for Italian dining) makes it easy to spend the entire day without leaving your lounge chair. The snorkeling is best out to the left near the rocky shoreline, but go early in the day. Like clockwork, about noon the wind picks up and the water clarity rapidly deteriorates.

Another plus for the Wailea area is the walkway that spans along the shoreline between resorts. It is a pleasant walk over to the neighboring southern resort, the Kea Lani, and the Grand Wailea, to the north, is definitely worth a stroll (go during the day and again at night for a very different experience). The Four Seasons is truly geared for the family. A full-time, year-round children's program is complimentary to hotel guests. Milk and cookies are delivered to the room for those young guests upon arrival.

Numerous special package offers include a room and car, golf, romance, and family packages. (Note: The Golf package offers play at the exclusive and private Waikapu course.) Complimentary, year-round "Kids for All Seasons" program designed for hotel guests aged 5 - 12 years. Restaurants include Pacific Grill, Ferraro's, and Seasons. Amenities for guests on the Club Floor* include a private lounge, 24 hr. concierge, complimentary breakfast, afternoon tea, evening cocktails, and after dinner liqueurs. Under age 18 complimentary when sharing same room with parents, except on club floor, add $60 per night per child ages 5-17. Adjoining children's room is available for $300 when parents pay standard room rate, except on club floors. Suites $710-5,500.

*Mountain Side $295, Garden View $345, Partial Ocean View $405, Ocean View $485 (Club floor $625), Ocean View Prime $550 (*Club Floor $690), Four Seasons Executive Suite, Garden View $545, Four Seasons Executive Suite Ocean View $700, Ocean View Prime $800 (*Club Floor $945). *Club floors include added amenities. Third adult in room $90 night.*

KEA LANI HOTEL, SUITES & VILLAS ★

4100 Wailea Alanui Drive, Wailea, HI 96753. (808) 875-4100 or 1-800-882-4100. There are 413 suites plus 37-one, two and three bedroom oceanfront villas. Designed after Las Hadas in Manzanillo, the name means "White Heavens." Its Mediterranean-style architecture received many mixed reviews when it opened years ago. It seems to us that perhaps this might be the home of a Sultan with a dramatic style set on 22 acres and a bit out of place in Wailea. However, the tropical lushness has grown and softened the look of the resort. You enter a drive lined with Norfolk pines and beyond the porte cochere there is a large open lobby area with a fountain covered by nine domes. Decorations are in Hawaiian florals, with mosaic tile ceilings and floors.

The 413 spacious (840 sq. ft.) one-bedroom suites, each have a private balcony. Views are garden, partial ocean, and deluxe ocean view. Each has a sunken marble tub, an enormous walk-in shower, king or two double beds, two closets, decorated in hues of cream and white. A cotton kimono is provided for guests. The living room features a state of the art compact and laser disc system, 27 inch television and video cassette player. Fresh ground coffee and coffee maker is provided daily in the suite and a mini-kitchen offers a microwave, a small sink, and mini-bar. An iron and ironing board are also available in each room. The exercise room is complimentary for guests. Massage, body treatments, facials, and fitness programs are available in their brand new luxury spa facility. (See RECREATIONS & TOURS - Spas - for more information.)

Caffe Ciao Deli & Bakery is open from 11am-10pm offering both indoor and alfresco seating. The casual Italian deli menu includes pastas and pizzas - baked to order in an outdoor brick oven fired by kiawe wood. The Kea Lani Restaurant serves breakfast then becomes Nick's Fishmarket in the evening for dinner. The indoor and outdoor dining room overlooks the formal pool. The 22,000 sq. ft. pool area is a series of pools connected together. At the upper level pool, Polo Beach Grille & Bar offers a casual, poolside menu and swim-up bar.

In addition to the suites, there are also 37 townhouse style villas which overlook Polo Beach. A 100 sq. ft. one bedroom villa costs $795-895, a 1,800 sq. ft. two-bedroom villa runs $895-995 a night, and a 2,200 sq. ft three-bedroom unit runs $1,095-1,195. A little spendy, but it would be easy to feel at home here! Each has a private lanai, huge walk-in closets, full size kitchen and washer and dryer, and are decorated in very muted mauves. Each has a generous living room and eating area. If you don't want to make that walk to the beach, you can just meander out onto the lanai and take a dip in your private swimming pool. That's right. Each villa has its own pool!

Complimentary daily golf clinics or for those who prefer to be "Beach Bound" they offer beach rental equipment, everything from a single kayak to a pool float. Beach Butlers are on hand to ensure you have a great day at the beach. For a fee the resort offers "Keiki Lani" (Heavenly Kids) for youths aged 5 to 11 years of age. Offered year-round 9am until 3pm includes snack and lunch. Children's menus available in the restaurant.

Honeymoon, wedding, family, and golf packages are available.
1 BR suite scenic view (4) 265, o.v. (4) $350, deluxe o.v. (4) $450
1 BR villa (1-4 persons) o.v. $795, o.f. $895
2 BR villa (1-6 persons) o.v. $895, o.f. $995
3 BR villa (1-8 persons) o.v. $1,095, o.f. $1,195

POLO BEACH CLUB ★
20 Makena Rd., Wailea, Maui, HI 96753. (808) 879-8847. Agents: Destination Resorts 1-800-367-5246 is the on-site rental agent, Hale Hawaiian 1-800-854-8843. Seventy-one apartments in a single 8-story building located on Polo Beach. The units are luxurious and spacious. Underground parking, pool area jacuzzi. This once very secluded area is soon to be "discovered." Located next to the Kea Lani Resort. Additional persons (over 4) $20 each. Prices quoted from Destination resorts, no off-season discounts.
1 BR (2) o.v.-o.f. $275-355, 2 BR 2 bath (4) o.v.-o.f. $340-425

MAKENA

INTRODUCTION

Just south of Wailea is Makena which will probably be one of the last resort areas to be developed on Maui. The Makena Resort began with the completion of an 18-hole golf course in 1981, followed by the opening of the Makena Surf condominium and the magnificent Maui Prince Hotel, located at Maluaka Beach. Seibu, the Japanese conglomerate that owns the 310-room hotel, is seeking permission to build a new 500-room resort hotel just south of the Prince sometime in the next decade. Several beaches in this area still have public access. They include Oneloa, Puuolai, Po'olenalena, Palauea and Maluaka beaches. Since the area is not fully developed, the end results remain to be seen.

Captain James Cook may have been the first Western explorer to visit and map the Hawaiian islands, but he failed to even see Maui during his first voyage. On his second trip in 1779 he spotted the northeast coastline of Maui, but a rugged and rocky shore prevented him from landing. It was Admiral Jean-Francois de Galaup, Comte de La Perouse, who was the first western explorer to set foot on Maui. Seven years after Cook had anchored offshore of Maui, Perouse departed from the Easter Island and arrived in the Sandwich Isles in May of 1786. His two frigates, the *Astrolabe* and the *Boussole* sailed around the Hana coast searching for a location to land. Discovering Maui's south shore, he decided to land at Keone'o'io to conduct trading with the Hawaiians. He was greeted by local Hawaiians that were friendly and eager to trade. They exchanged gifts and La Perouse visited a total of four villages. This brief, three hour visit, resulted in the Keone'o'io Bay being called La Perouse Bay.

WHAT TO DO AND SEE

Hiking beyond La Perouse affords some great ocean vistas. You'll see trails made by local residents in their four wheel drive vehicles, and fishermen's trails leading to volcanic promontories overlooking the ocean. You may even spot the fishing pole holders which have been securely attached to the lava boulders. The Hoapili Trail begins just past La Perouse Bay and is referred to as the King's Highway. It is believed that at one time the early Hawaiians made use of a trail that circled the entire island and this is a remnant of that ancient route. The state Forestry and Wildlife Division and volunteers worked together recently putting in place stone barricades to keep the four wheel drive vehicles and motorcycles from destroying any more of the trail.

Another interesting hike is at the Pu'u O La'i cinder cone, the red-earth hillock which juts out to the sea just beyond the cover fronting the Maui Prince Hotel. It is one of Haleakala's craters (under which is a large cave), and is said to be the sacred dwelling place of Mano, the ancestral shark deity. To reach the top of the cinder cone, turn right on the first dirt path after the hotel, then pass giant cacti and dry brush to reach the hiking trail. The short 15-minute hike uphill offers a rewarding sight of the coast - a black sand beach just below the hill, and broad white beaches and black lava contrasting with the lush greens of the Makena Golf Course. Here are the last really gorgeous and undeveloped recreational beaches on Maui.

The paved road (Makena Alanui) runs from Wailea past the Makena Surf and Maui Prince Hotel, exiting onto the Old Makena Rd. near the entrances to Oneuli (Black Sand) Beach and Oneloa (Big Makena)-Puuolai (Little Makena) Beaches. Past Ahihi Kinau Natural Reserve on Old Makena Rd. you will traverse the last major lava flow on Maui, which still looks pretty fresh after some 250 years,and continues to La Perouse Bay (See BEACHES).

The Keawala'i Church, founded in 1832, was once the cultural and spiritual center of the community. The structure, completed in 1854 is 3 feet thick and made of melted coral gathered from the sea. It is surrounded by ti leaf which is planted because of Hawaiian belief that it provides protection and healing. This charming historical church sits quietly along the ocean in Makena and is home to an active Protestant congregation. Services are in both English and Hawaiian.

ACCOMMODATIONS - MAKENA

BEST BETS: The Maui Prince Hotel and *Makena Surf* - Both are first class, luxury accommodations on beautiful beaches.

MAKENA SURF ★
96 Makena Alanui Rd., Makena, Maui, HI 96753, Destination Resorts 1-800-367-5246, Jim Osgood (425) 391-8900 or check out his web page on the internet at < www.officefinder.com/makena.htm >, Hale Hawaiian 1-800-854-8843. Located 2 miles past Wailea. All units are oceanfront and more or less surround Paipu (Chang's) Beach. These very spacious and attractive condos feature central air-conditioning, fully equipped kitchens, washers and dryers, wet bar, whirlpool spa in the master bath, telephones and daily maid service. Two pools, and four tennis courts are set in landscaped grounds. Three historic sites found on location have been preserved. We recently had the opportunity to stay, for the first time, at this property. It was even better than we had imagined.

When it was first built it seemed that the Makena Surf was very out of the way and removed from the rest of the Wailea area. That isn't the case any more, but this property is still very private. The units are well maintained and luxuriously appointed. Looking out from the oceanfront units it is hard to imagine that this isn't your own private island. Pull up a lounge chair, open that bottle of wine and watch the whales frolic as the sun sets gloriously in the Pacific beyond them. It doesn't get any better than this! Destination Resorts is the management company for this property, so they handle most of the rental units. The 1998 rate schedule for Destination Resorts reflects a single, all-season price. Units are oceanview and oceanfront.

1 BR (2) $305-435, 2 BR (2) $385-510, 3 BR (4) $575-600
Maui Condo offers: 2 BR 2 BTH o.f. $375/300

MAUI PRINCE ★
5400 Makena Alanui, Makena, Maui, HI 96753. (808) 874-1111. Reservations: 1-800-321-6284. In sharp contrast to the ostentatious atmosphere of some of the Kaanapali resorts, the Maui Prince radiates understated elegance. Its simplicity in color and design, with an Oriental theme, provides a tranquil setting and allows the beauty of Maui to be reflected. The central courtyard is the focal point of the resort with a lovely traditional water garden complete with a cool cascading waterfall and ponds filled with gleaming koi. The 310 rooms are tastefully appointed with the comfort of the guests in mind. In 1998 they undertook upgrading of the guest rooms to reflect a greater sense of Hawaiiana. The units have two telephones and a small refrigerator. Terry robes are available for use during the guest's stay. A 24-hour full room service adds to the conveniences. They currently offer the Prince Kids Club program year around to youth ages 5-12 years. Three sessions are offered throughout the day. The morning session (9am to noon) is free. Afternoon session (noon to 3pm) includes lunch and is $15, full session (9am-3pm) is $15 and includes lunch.

There is plenty of room for lounging around two circular swimming pools or in a few steps you can be on Maluaka (Nau Paka) Beach with its luxuriously deep, fine white sand and good snorkeling, swimming and wave playing. The resort comprises 1,800 acres including two championship golf courses. Designed by Robert Trent Jones, Jr., the first 18-holes were built in 1981. In 1993, they were divided and each half was combined with nine new holes to create the North and South Courses.

Restaurants include Prince Court serving Hawaiian Regional dishes (and one of the island's best Sunday brunches), al fresco dining in Cafe Kiowai and the Japanese restaurant and sushi bar at Hakone.

Partial o.v. $230, o.v. $290, o.v. prime $330, o.f. $380, Suites $420-820
No charge for third person using existing beds.

Package plans include Single Golfer Package, Room & Meal Package, Sporting Clays Package, Tennis for Life package, Sunset Romance Package, Unlimited Golf Package and more.

WAILUKU AND KAHULUI

INTRODUCTION

The twin towns of Wailuku and Kahului are located on the northern, windward side of the island. Wailuku is the county seat of Maui while Kahului houses, not only the largest residential population on the island, but also the main airport terminal and deep-water harbor. There are three motel-type accommodations around Kahului Harbor, and while the rates are economical and the location is somewhat central to all parts of the island, we cannot recommend staying in this area for other than a quick stopover that might require easy airport access. This side of the island is generally more windy, overcast and cooler with few good beaches. Except for the avid windsurfer, we feel there is little reason to head-quarter your stay in this area. There are many good reasons to linger and explore.

WHAT TO DO AND SEE

Kahului has a very colorful history beginning in the 1790's with the arrival of King Kamehameha I from the big island of Hawai'i. The meaning of Kahului is "winning" and may have had its origins in the battle which ensued between Kamehameha and the Maui chieftain. The shoreline of Kahului Bay began its development in 1863 with the construction of a warehouse by Thomas Hogan. By 1879, a landing at the bay was necessary to keep up with the growing sugar cane industry. Two years later, in 1881, the Kahului Railroad Company had begun. The city of Kahului grew rapidly until 1900 when it was purposely burned down to destroy the spreading of a bubonic plague outbreak. The reconstruction of Kahului created a full-scale commercial harbor, which was bombed along with Pearl Harbor on December 7, 1941. After World War II, a housing boom began with the development of reasonably priced homes to house the increasing number of people moving to the island. The expansion has continued ever since. Wailuku is the county seat of Maui and has been the center of government since 1930. It is now, slowly, experiencing a rebirth. It is often overlooked by visitors who miss out on some wonderful local restaurants and interesting shopping.

WINDSURFING

Wailuku, Kahului & Kahului Terminal

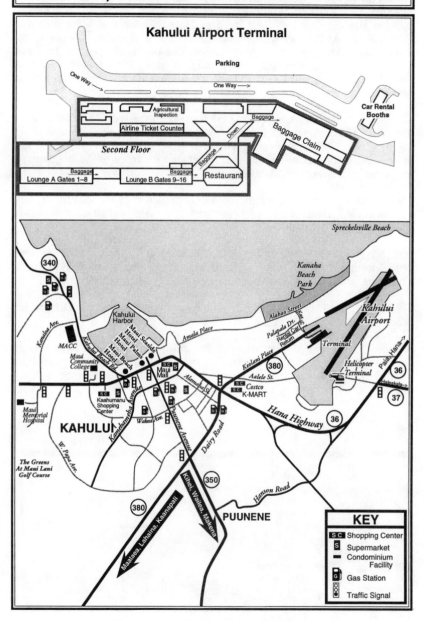

Kahului Airport Terminal

Market Street in Old Wailuku Town is alive with the atmosphere of Old Hawai'i. The area, rich in history, was built on the site of ancient heiaus and has witnessed decisive Hawaiian battles. Later the area hosted the likes of Mark Twain to Robert Redford. It is no wonder that such an area should re-emerge in the modern day with shops of a cultural nature. One-of-a-kind items can be found here, gathered from around the world and eras gone by. Such is the case with Old Wailuku Town and the cluster of interesting antique shops along Market Street.

Set against the lush backdrop of the Iao Valley and the West Maui Mountains, this area offers a quaint alternative to the hustle-bustle vacation centers of Lahaina and Kihei. Surrounding this area is a multitude of wonderful and inexpensive ethnic restaurants. So don't limit your excursion to the few shops on the corner of Market and Main streets.

Emura's at 49 Market Street has consistently proven to be the spot for the best buys of eel skin items from wallets and purses, to shoes and attaches. Pay cash and get an extra discount!

Antique row can be found along Market Street as well: There's *Memory Lane* and adjacent is *Ali'i Antiques* (158 North Market St.) which features Hawaiiana, Christmas items, and military memorabilia, among other antiques items.

The historic *Iao Theatre* is also here with its new eatery, *Applause Cafe*, which is open to the public during the day.

A short drive down Market Street is *Takamiya Market*. They have a large selection of ready-cooked foods. Another grocery store, *Ooka Supermarket* on Main Street, has some of the best grocery values from produce to meats. They also have some interesting local foods!

KAAHUMANU CHURCH

Kaahumanu Church, Maui's oldest remaining church was built in 1837 at High and Main Streets in Wailuku. Hale Hoikeike in Wailuku houses the *Bailey House Museum* (circa 1834). To reach it, follow the signs to Iao Valley and you will see the historical landmark sign on the left side of the road. It's open from 10am-4pm and a small admission is charged. (The third Saturday of the month is Family Day with free admission from 1:30-2:30pm if you call for a reservation at 244-3326.) Here you will find the Bailey Gallery, (once a dining room for the female seminary that was located at this site), with the paintings of Edward Bailey done during the 19th century. His work depicts many aspects of Hawaiian life during earlier days. Also on display are early Hawaiian artifacts and memorabilia from the missionary days. The staff is extremely knowledgeable and friendly. They also have an array of Hawaiian history, art, craft and photographic books for sale. Originally, the Royal Historical Society was established in 1841, but it was not until 1956 that it was reactivated as the Maui Historical Society. The museum was dedicated on July 6, 1957, then closed for restoration on December 31, 1973 and reopened on July 13, 1975. Of special interest are the impressive 20-inch thick walls that are made of plaster using a special missionary recipe which included goat hair as one ingredient. (Talk about recycling!) The thick walls provided the inhabitants with a natural means of air conditioning.

The *Maui Jinsha Mission* is located at 472 Lipo Street, Wailuku. One of the few remaining old Shinto Shrines in the state of Hawai'i, this mission was placed on the National Register of Historic Places in 1978.

The *Halekii and Pihana State Monuments* are among Maui's most interesting early Hawaiian historical sites. Both are of considerable size and situated on the top of a sand dune. These temples were very important structures for the island's early Ali'i. Their exact age is unknown, although one resource reported that they were used from 1765 to 1895. The Halekii monument is in better condition as a result of some reconstruction done on it in 1958. Follow Waiehu Beach Road across a bridge, then turn left onto Kuhio Place and again on Hea Place. Look for and follow the Hawai'i Visitors Bureau markers. Some say the Pihana Heiau (temple) was built by the menehunes (Hawai'i's little people), others believe the construction was done under the guidance of the Maui chieftain, Kahekili.

The Iao Valley is a short drive beyond Hale Hoikeike. Within the valley is an awesome volcanic ridge that rises 2,250 feet and is known as the Iao Needle. A little known fact is that this interesting natural phenomena is not a monolithic formation, but rather what you are viewing is the end of a large, thin ridge. A helicopter view will give you an entirely different perspective! Parking facilities are available and there are a number of hiking trails. The *Tropical Gardens of Maui* is a botanical garden that features the largest selection of exotic orchids in the Hawaiian islands. For a small fee you can stroll the grounds where they grow, and visit their gift shop filled with tropical flowers and Maui made products. Plants can be shipped home. Snack bar and picnic tables available. Phone (808) 244-3085. Open Monday-Saturday; admission is $3.

The Heritage Garden - Kepaniwai Park is an exhibit of pavilions and gardens which pay tribute to the culture of the Hawaiians, Portuguese, Filipinos, Koreans, Japanese, and Chinese. Picnic tables and BBQ's are available for public use. They are located on Iao Valley Road. Free admission, open daily. A public swimming pool for children is open weekends and holidays from 9am-11:45 am and again from 1pm until 4:30pm. The pool is free, but it is cold! Also a popular site for weddings and other functions, it is available for rent from the Maui Parks Dept. A deposit is required. The Wailuku permit office (1580 Kaahumanu Avenue, Wailuku, Maui (808) 243-7389 can provide the forms.

The Hawaii Nature Center at Iao Valley has just opened their new Interactive Science Arcade which houses a towering glass solarium and offers more than 30 hands-on exhibits and experiences focusing on Hawai'i's natural history. Rain forest explorations, dispersal arcade games, live insect and stream animal exhibits along with a dragonfly ride make this a unique, adventuresome and educational attraction. Open 10am-4pm daily, $6 adults, $4 children. Call (808) 244-6500. FAX (808) 244-6525.

Just outside Wailuku on Hwy. 30, between Wailuku and Ma'alaea, is Waikapu, home of the *Maui Tropical Plantation and Country Store*. This visitor attraction has become one of the top ten most heavily visited in the state of Hawai'i. The fifty acres, which opened in 1984, have been planted with sugar cane, bananas, guava and other island produce. A ten-acre visitor center includes exhibits, The Country Store (a marketplace), nursery and restaurant. There is no admission for entry into the store or the restaurant, however, there is an $8.50 adults, $3.50 children (5-12 years) charge for the narrated tram ride around the fields. The tram ride departs every forty-five minutes between 10am and 4pm. The trip includes several stops for samples of fresh fruit. The Country Store is open daily from 9am-5pm.

Baldwin Beach - See the section on BEACHES for Baldwin Beach and others.

HAWAIIAN STILT

In addition to baseball and mini-soccer fields, the new $11 million, 110-acre *Maui Central Park* (*Keopuolani*) offers playgrounds by ages with fifty picnic tables throughout. Proposals are under consideration that the park (or portions) be alcohol and tobacco-free. Go up Kaahumanu to Kanaloa Street and turn by the Wailuku War Memorial Park, now home of the Hula Bowl which is held there in January. The adjoining *Maui Botanical Gardens* is undergoing extensive renovation with complete expansion and revitalization expected by the year 2000. When finished, the Gardens will provide a center for environmental education, plant conservation, Hawaiian cultural expression, biological study, and recreation. During the process, the playground and garden are still open to the public - free. *Keiki Zoo Maui* will also become part of the new park by the end of 1999 when it relocates from Kula.

The Greens at Maui Lani, a challenging new 18-hole golf course and clubhouse designed by Robin Nelson (who also designed Maui's Sandalwood course and the Mauna Lani course on the Big Island) winds from Wailuku through Kahului. Take the newly-constructed Maui Lani Parkway from Wailuku or look for the sign on Kuihelani Hwy. several miles before you approach Kahului.

The Kanaha Wildlife Sanctuary is off Route 32, near the Kahului Airport, and was once a royal fish pond. Now a lookout is located here for those interested in viewing the stilt and other birds which inhabit the area.

A popular Saturday morning stop for local residents and visitors alike is *The Maui Swap Meet* ★ (877-3100) held at grounds around the Christ the King Church, next door to the Post Office off Pu'unene Hwy. 35. You'll find us referring to this event for various reasons throughout this guide. For a fifty-cent admission (children free) you will find an assortment of vendors selling local fruits and vegetables, new and used clothing, household items and many of the same souvenir type items found at higher prices in resort gift shops. We recently discovered one fellow selling "designer" sunglasses and handbags. At one third the price of retail stores, he professed they were the real thing, not knock-offs. The Swap Meet is also a great place to pick up tropical flowers and for only a few dollars you can lavishly decorate your condo during your stay. Protea are seasonally available here, too, for a fraction of the cost elsewhere. This is also the only place to get true spoonmeat coconuts. These are fairly immature coconuts with deliciously mild and soft (to very soft) meat and filled with sweet coconut milk. We stock up on a week's supply at a time. These coconuts are the ones that are trimmed off the trees while still green and far different than the hard brown ones in the supermarkets. One booth we discovered recently had coconuts that could be inscribed with a message and mailed home as a postcard. Plain were around $10 including postage, painted were $15. Another "must purchase" are goodies from Four Sisters Bakery! Hours are 8am-noon.

The *Alexander and Baldwin Sugar Museum* ★ is located at 3957 Hansen Road, in Puunene. Puunene is on Highway 35 between Kahului and Kihei. The tall stacks of the working mill are easily spotted. The museum is housed in a 1902 plantation home that was once occupied by the sugar mill's superintendent.

Memorabilia include the strong-box of Samuel Thomas Alexander and an actual working scale model of a sugar mill. The displays are well done and very informative. Hours are Monday-Saturday 9:30am-4pm. Admission charge: $4 adult visitors, $2 under 18. Children under 6 are free. (808) 871-8058. A *historic tunnel of trees* once lined the Puunene Road between the mill and Kahului. The trees were taken down to make room for state and county road improvements. The earpods and monkeypods were more than 65 years old, but had suffered from time and were frankly rather pitiful. Thirty-five new monkeypods trees have been planted on both sides of the road to replace them.

WHERE TO SHOP

There are three large shopping centers in Kahului, all on Kaahumanu Avenue. The *Maui Mall* is only a two-minute drive from the airport. Across the street from *Safeway* and the *Ross Dress for Less* store, this is where you'll find Star Market and a Longs Drugs that is great for picking up sundry and souvenir items. There are also a variety of small shops and restaurants including *Waldenbooks, M.O.M's Coffee Store*, and a Maui institution: *Tasaka Guri Guri*, a kind of local creamy sherbet you can order with or without beans at the bottom of the cone! The *Paper Airplane Museum* (808) 877-8916) features the unique juice can creations of the Tin Can Man along with aviation model exhibits and pictures depicting the history of aviation in the Hawaiian Islands. In addition, a twelve-screen movie theater with all-new stadium seating is expected to move into the former Woolworth's location by the end of 1998. The older, local style *Kahului Shopping Center* is lined with monkey pod trees and is filled with local residents playing cards. It was recently renovated and freshened up. Check out *Ah Fook's* grocery for their bentos. The largest shopping center is *Kaahumanu Center*, now more than double its original size with a second level which includes a food court. Three major department stores, *Penney's, Sears,* and *Liberty House* anchor this mall with the island's largest selection of clothing and gift shops in between. Here is where you'll find The *Disney Store, Waldenbooks, The Gap, Kids' Footlocker,* two new restaurants by Hawaiian Regional Chef, Sam Choy, and a six-plex cinema operated by Consolidated Theatres - which may expand to twelve by Summer, 1999.

If you don't have accommodations with a kitchen or mini-refrigerator, you might want to pick up a styrofoam type ice chest at one of these centers and stock it with juices, lunch meats and what-not to enjoy in your hotel room and for use on beach trips or drives to Hana and Haleakala. (Check with your hotel regarding small in-room refrigerators.) There is a *Kmart* at the intersection of Dairy Road and the Hana Highway and next door is *Costco*, a wholesale warehouse. Membership is required, but it is good at any of their Hawai'i or mainland stores. Costco has some great deals and some not as great deals. We'd recommend checking out their Hawaiiana CD music and books. Not a complete selection, but good prices on those items that they do stock. Kmart has convenient hours (7am-10pm) and some very good values on everyday items such as sandals. The downside is that the combination of Costco and Kmart has really increased the traffic on Dairy Road!

Adding to the mainland-style congestion is the new *Maui Marketplace* that includes a number of large, mainland-style outlets (e.g. *Eagle Hardware & Garden, OfficeMax, Bugle Boys, Sports Authority*) and the *Kau Kau Market Food Court* with the local/Chinese food combination of *L&L Drive Inn & Chopsticks Express; A Taste of Broadway* (pizza); and the 50's-style *Aloha Grill* diner. This is where you'll also find Borders Books, Music & Cafe and the island's only Starbucks! There's always room for more at this 20-acre development, so look for additional shops and fast-food outlets in the months to come.

Triangle Square (Isn't that an oxymoron?) is located nearby at the intersection of the Hana and Haleakala Highways. *Hi-Tech Surf Sports, Maui Sails, Nevada Bob's*, and *Boomer's* restaurant are here and there is a "Phase II" in the works that is expected to offer additional surf and sports outlets.

Wailuku has no large shopping centers, but as we mentioned earlier, a cluster of shops down their Main Street makes for interesting strolling in a town with old world charm.

ACCOMMODATIONS - WAILUKU

BANANA BUNGALOW MAUI - Hotel & International Hostel
310 North Market Street, Wailuku (808) 244-5090, 1-800-8-HOSTEL. Previously the old Happy Valley Inn and Valley Isle Lodge. They describe their accommodations as an international budget hotel and hostel, with clean and comfortable accommodations and a social atmosphere attracting budget travelers, windsurfers, and international backpackers. Rooms are equipped with closet, chair, mirror, and night stand. Bathrooms are shared. They have recently added a jacuzzi. The lounge offers a cable TV, refrigerator and pay phone. Laundry facilities on property. Free beach or airport shuttle, complimentary coffee and tea. They do take Visa, Mastercard and American Express. *Shared room (sleeps 2-3) $13 per person; Single room with double bed $29 single/35 double*

OLD WAILUKU INN AT ULUPONO ★
2100 Kaho'okele Street, Wailuku, HI 96793. (808) 244-5897, Toll free 1-800-305-4899, fax (808) 242-9600, or e-mail: < Maui BandB@aol.com > Your hosts are Janice and Tom Fairbanks in this circa 1920 plantation home. Detailed description in the Bed & Breakfast section, but it is such a beautiful accommodation, that we felt it was worth noting again. *$120-180 per night.*

NORTHSHORE INN
2080 Vineyard St., Wailuku (808) 242-8999, FAX (808) 244-5004. This hotel offers fifty beds that are used as shared accommodations, with each room sleeping four or six persons. There are several private rooms available for one or two persons. Each room has a ceiling fan and a small refrigerator, some rooms have air-conditioners. The bathrooms are shared by all. A kitchen is available for use by everyone and a TV lounge area offers a VCR. There is a locked storage area for the guests' windsurfing equipment, and a washer and dryer is on the premise. Shuttle trips are provided to and from the airport.

The Inn features an informal, international atmosphere with windsurfers and budget backpackers from around the world staying as guests. Their motto is "Fun is Number 1 - come as guests, leave as friends." The garden in the back of the building is gone, but there are still plenty of great ethnic restaurants up and down the street. Reservations accepted. Weekly discounts. *Shared rooms (sleep 4-6) $15 per night, single $29.70, double $37.50-40.70*

ACCOMMODATIONS - KAHULUI

One advantage to choosing this area for headquarters is its proximity to the Kahului Airport and its somewhat central location to all other parts of the island. The motels are clustered together on the Kahului Harbor.

MAUI PALMS   (Hotel)
170 Kaahumanu Avenue, Kahului, Maui, HI 96732. (808) 877-0051. Agent: Hawaiian Pacific 1-800-367-5004. This property is a 103 unit low-rise hotel with Polynesian decor. Built in 1953, the larger Maui Palms was constructed in 1968. In 1979 the Maui Beach purchased the Palms. The lobby and restaurant were demolished in 1998 to make way for new signage and landscaping, expanded parking stalls, improved lighting, and resurfacing of the parking lot. Renovations planned include a new dining room and room upgrades which won't begin until 1999. Ultimately, the parent company, Elleair Hawaii, hopes to replace the Palms with a 200-room hotel. We wouldn't recommend this property as a vacation stay, but it is convenient if you need a place for a night before an early morning flight from the Kahului Airport. They offer free airport pickup. *Rates (3) $67-80/57-70*

MAUI BEACH HOTEL   (Hotel)
170 Kaahumanu Avenue, Kahului, Maui, HI 96732.(808) 877-0051. Managed by and reservations through: Castle Group 1-800-367-5004. Renovated in 1991, this two story, 152 room hotel is located oceanfront on Kahului Bay. All rooms have air-conditioning, TV, some balconies. Complimentary airport shuttle. The Red Dragon Room and Rainbow Room restaurants just completed renovation that included a new ceiling and sound system plus new carpeting, chairs, draperies and an overall lightening and brightening. Additional lobby renovations (similar to the Maui Palms above) began Summer 1998 with a room-by-room upgrade expected to be completed by the summer of 1999. *Room rates from $93.*

MAUI SEASIDE   (Hotel)
100 Kaahumanu Avenue, Kahului, Maui, HI 96732. 1-800-367-7000 U.S., 1-800-654-7020 Canada, FAX (808) 922-0052. Years ago, the older Maui Hukilau combined with the much newer Maui Seaside to form one property called the Maui Seaside. You might want to inquire when booking here about which of the buildings you will be in. Vi's Restaurant is right across the street. Add $10-15 per day for car. *Rates (2) $85-110/75-100. Extra person $12. Children 17 and under free.*

UPCOUNTRY
and onward to HALEAKALA

INTRODUCTION

The western slopes of Haleakala are generally known as Upcountry and consist of several communities including Makawao and Pukalani. The higher altitude, cooler temperatures and increased rainfall make it an ideal location for produce farming. A few fireplace chimneys can be spotted in this region where the nights can get rather chilly. Accommodations are limited to two small lodges in Kula and a few cabins which are available with the park service for overnight use while hiking in the Haleakala Wilderness Area. (It is actually not a crater, rather an erosional valley.) *Refer to the Maui map at the beginning of the guidebook for the highways and roads discussed in this section.*

WHAT TO DO AND SEE

Enroute to Upcountry is *Pukalani*, meaning "opening to the sky," which is the last stop for gas on the way to Haleakala. There are also several places to enjoy a hearty meal. (See RESTAURANTS.)

Haleakala means "house of the sun" and is claimed to be the largest dormant volcano in the world. While it rises 10,023 feet above sea level, the greater portion of this magnificent mountain lies below the ocean. If measured from the sea floor, Haleakala would rise to a height of nearly 30,000 feet. The volcano is truly awesome and it is easy to see why the old Hawaiians considered it sacred and the center of the earth's spiritual power. The Haleakala National Park was created in 1916, but the first ranger did not arrive until March 1935. In July of 1945 the park, concerned about vandalism of the endangered plants, began checking visitors cars. The park encompasses two districts, the Summit District and the Kipahulu District. The Kipahulu District is on the South Shore near Hana, and will be discussed later. The charge for entry to the summit district is $4 per car. U.S. residents age 62 and older enter free. The most direct route is to follow Hwy. 37 from Kahului then left onto Hwy. 377 above Pukalani and then left again onto Hwy. 378 for the last 10 miles. While only about 40 miles from Kahului, the last part of the trip is very slow. There are numerous switchbacks and bicycle tours doing the 38-mile downhill coast. Two hours should be allowed to reach the summit.

Sunrise at the summit is a popular and memorable experience, but plan your arrival accordingly. Many visitors have missed this spectacular event by only minutes. *The Maui News*, the local daily, prints sunrise and sunset times. The park offers a recording of general weather information and viewing conditions which can be reached by calling locally 572-4400. Be sure you have packed a sweater as the summit temperature can be 30 degrees cooler than the coast and snow is a winter possibility. Early to mid-morning from May to October generally offers the clearest viewing. However, fog (or vog) can cause very limited visibility and a call may save you a trip.

At the park headquarters (open 7:30am-4pm), you can obtain hiking and camping information and permits. Day-hike permits are not required. Keep in mind that this increased elevation may affect your endurance! Short walks include the 1/2 mile Hosmer Grove Nature Trail Lookout, the 1/4 mile trek to the Leleiwi Overlook, the 1/2 mile hike to White Hill and a 2/3 mile hike to the first switchback on the Sliding Sands Trail. Day Hikes include the 2.2 mile hike from Halemau'u to the valley rim, and the Sliding Sands to Ka Lu'u o ka 'o'o, which is a distance of 5 miles with a 1,400 change in elevation each way. For the hiker with more stamina, there is the 10 mile Halemau'u to Silversword Loop and the Sliding Sands to Halemau'u Trailhead which traverses 11 miles. The first stop is Park Headquarters. Here you can see an example of the rare *silversword* which takes up to 20-50 years to mature, then blooms in a profusion of small purplish blossoms in July or August. It then withers and dies in the fall. Some years many silverswords may flower, in other years they may be none. The Hawaiian word for silversword is *'ahinahina.* Hina is the goddess of the moon. Once the silverswords grew in abundance. They were used on floats for parades in the early part of the 1900's and wild cattle, goats and sheep found them so appealing that by the 1930's there were only a few thousand silversword plants remaining. Keep your eye out for the many nene geese which inhabit the volcano.

Exhibits on Haleakala history and geology are in the Haleakala Visitors Center located at an elevation of 9,745 feet. It is open daily from sunrise to 3pm, hours may vary. A short distance by road will bring you to the Summit Building located on the volcano rim. This glassed-in vantage point (the Puu Ulaula outlook) is the best for sunrise and is the highest point on Maui.

The rangers give morning talks here at 9:30, 10:30 and 11:30. The view, on a good day, is nothing short of awesome. The inside of the volcano is seven miles long, two miles wide, and 3,000 feet deep. A closer look is available by foot or horseback (see RECREATION AND TOURS - Horseback riding). A 2 1/2 hour hike down Sliding Sands Trail into the Haleakala Volcano is offered by the park service regularly. Check bulletin boards for schedules. They depart from the House of the Sun Visitor Center. A hike featuring native Hawaiian birds and plants is scheduled regularly. Again, check with the ranger headquarters 572-4400 to verify trips, dates and times.

The park service maintains 30 miles of well-marked trails, three cabins and two campgrounds. All are accessible only by trail. The three cabins are Holua, Kapal-aoa and Paliku, all located within the Haleakala Wilderness Area. The closest cabin is about seven miles away from the observatory. Arrangements for these cabins need to be made 90 days in advance and selection is made 60 days prior to the dates requested by a lottery-type drawing. For more information, write: Superintendent, Haleakala National Park, PO Box 369, Makawao, Maui, HI 96768. Rates are a minimal charge per person. A deposit is required to hold reservations. Maximum cabin occupancy is 12. For current rates call 572-4400.

Short walks might include the three-fourth mile Halemau'u Trail to the volcano rim, one-tenth mile to Leleiwi Overlook, or two-tenth mile on the White Hill Trail to the top of White Hill. Caution: the thin air and steep inclines may be especially tiring. (See RECREATION AND TOURS - Hiking.)

Haleakala Observatories can be seen beyond the visitor center, but it is not open to the public. It houses a solar and lunar observatory operated by the University of Hawaii, television relay stations, and a Department of Defense satellite station. A new public tour program of the *Maui Space Surveillance Complex* began in late 1997. Eight telescopes (located on the top of Haleakala) perform work for the Department of Defense in space surveillance and in optical research and development. Two tours are given the last Friday of the month and last approximately 90 minutes. Groups are limited to 16 people. Due to length of tour and altitude, visitors must be ages 13 and up. For more information call (808) 874-1601 or visit their website at: < www.ulua.mhpcc.af.mil/ ~ det3 >

To get a better visual idea of Haleakala, see the back of the book for ordering information on the full-color, inexpensive, pictorial book on Haleakala.

If time allows, there is more of Upcountry to be seen! The *Kula* area offers rich volcanic soil and commercial farmers harvest a variety of fruits and vegetables. Grapes, apples, pineapples, lettuce, artichokes, tomatoes and, of course, Maui onions are only a few. It can be reached by retracking Hwy. 378 to the Upper Kula Road where you turn left. The protea, a relatively recent floral immigrant from South Africa, has created a profitable business.

The Kula Botanical Gardens (878-1715) charges an admission of $4 for adults; $1 for children 6-12 years to tour their 6-acre facility with over 2,000 plants (including native Hawaiian plants like the Sandalwood tree!) Open 9am-4pm.

The *Enchanting Floral Gardens*, on Hwy. 37 in Kula, charges $5 for adults, $1 for children for a self-guided botanical tour. Open 9-5 daily. 878-2531.

The *Sunrise Protea Farm* (876-0200) in Kula has a small, but diverse, variety of protea growing adjacent to their market and flower stand for shipment home. Dried assortments begin at about $25. Picnic tables available and no charge for just looking!

Be sure and stop in Keokea at *Grandma's Coffee House*. This wonderfully cozy, restaurant is the place for some freshly made, Maui grown coffee, hot out of the oven cinnamon rolls or a light lunch. If you stop in, will you check and see if they've found Christie's coffee cup yet? See RESTAURANTS - Upcountry.

Poli Poli Springs Recreational Area, this state park is high on the slopes of Haleakala, above Kula at an elevation of 6,200 feet. Continue on Hwy. 377 past Kula and turn left on Waipoli Rd. If you end up on Hwy. 37, you've gone too far. The sign indicating Poli Poli may be difficult to spot, so you could also look for the sign indicating someone's home that reads WALKER (assuming it is still there).

It's another 10 miles to the park. Fortunately, the road has been paved making accessibility easy. The 10-acre park offers miles of trails, a picnic area, restrooms, running water, a small redwood forest, and great views. This is an excellent trail for the non-athlete or family. Keep your eye out for earth that appears disturbed. This is an indication of one of the wild boars at work. While not likely, we still advise you to keep your ears alert, you don't want to encounter one. On one occasion we heard them rumbling through the brush near the trail. A single cabin, which sleeps up to 10, is available through the Division of Parks, PO Box 537, Makawao, Maui, HI 96768. Cabin rental is $45 for 1-4 persons per day, $5 each additional person. See the "Hiking" section in the RECREATION AND TOURS chapter for more information.

Approximately nine miles past the Kula Botanical Gardens on Hwy. 37 is the *Ulupalakua Ranch*. *The Tedeschi Winery* (878-6058), part of the 30,000 acre ranch, made its debut in 1974. The king's cottage now houses a new, expanded Tasting Room which provides samples of their pineapple, champagne and red table wines at the mango-wood bar (handcrafted from one of the many trees at the surrounding Ulupalakua Ranch). Free daily guided tours are offered between 10am and 5pm. The tour begins at the Tasting Room, then continues on to view the presses used to separate the juice from the grapes, the large fermenting tanks, the corking and the labelling rooms. It is an interesting behind the scenes tour!

If you continue on past the ranch on Hwy. 37 it's another very long 35 miles to Hana with nothing but beautiful scenery. Don't let the distance fool you. It is a good 3-hour trip (each way), at least, over some fairly rough sections of road, which are not approved for standard rental cars. During recent years this road has been closed often to through traffic due to severe washouts. Check with the county to see if it is currently passable. We'd recommend doing just the first part of the road, driving as far as Kaupo. (See Hana section for more information.)

TEDESCHI WINERY

If you are not continuing on, we suggest you turn around and head back to Pukalani and Makawao. Unfortunately, the Ulupalakua Road down to Wailea has been closed for years due to a dispute between the Ranch and the county. It is hoped that this or some other access between Upcountry and the Kihei/Wailea area will someday be developed. On the way down you can go by way of Makawao, the colorful "cowboy" town, and then on to Paia or Haliimaile. Both have several good restaurants. (See RESTAURANTS - Upcountry).

WHERE TO SHOP

The town of Makawao offers a western flavor with a scattering of shops down its main street, along with a few restaurants and grocery stores. We recommend the **Komoda Store** for its popular bakery, but get there early if you want any of their famous cream puffs! *Olas's* and *Gallery Maui* on Makawao Avenue offer an intriguing selection of gifts (like "obi sash" wall hangings and stained glass screens) and just up the street is the Maui School of Therapeutic Massage (572-2277) where you can treat yourself to a relaxing massage for just $20!

The Courtyard at 3620 Baldwin Avenue houses *Viewpoints Gallery* (572-5979), a fine co-operative gallery featuring local artists, and a cluster of interesting gift shops including *Hot Island Glass*, a glassblowing studio and gallery -- a must see in Makawao.

Nearby *Pukalani Shopping Center* has a grocery store, and some small shops and restaurants. A number of good restaurants will allow for a diverse selection of dining options including *Upcountry Toys* - a toy store that has burgers and an old fashioned soda fountain! The new commercial shopping center, Kulamalu Center, will be a shopping and entertainment center with local crafts, restaurants and movie theaters expected to be completed by the first quarter of 2000.

WHAT TO SEE AND DO

The *Hui No'eau Visual Arts Center* may, at first, seem a little out of place, located at 2841 Baldwin Avenue, down the road from Makawao. However, there could not be a more beautiful and tranquil setting than at this estate, called Kaluanui, which was built in 1917 by famous Honolulu architect C.W. Dickey for Harry and Ethel Baldwin. The house was occupied until the mid-1950's and in 1976 Colin Cameron (grandson of Ethel Baldwin) granted Hui No'eau the use of Kaluanui as a Visual Arts Center. A gift shop is open year round and the first part of December they have a special Christmas boutique. Daily 9am-1pm. (572-6560).

Near the entrance to the nine-acre estate are the remains of one of Maui's earliest sugar mills. It utilized mule power and was the first Hawaiian sugar mill to use a centrifuge to separate sugar crystals. What were once stables and tack rooms are now ceramic studios.

Fourth of July weekend is wild and wonderful in Makawao. Festivities include a morning parade through town and several days of rodeo events. Check the local paper for details.

ACCOMMODATIONS - UPCOUNTRY

Accommodations are limited in Upcountry. Five and one-half miles past Pukalani is the Kula Lodge. See listings at beginning of Accommodations section for information on Upcountry Bed and Breakfast facilities.

KULA LODGE
RR 1, Box 475, Kula, Maui, HI 96790 (808) 878-2517, 1-800-233-1535. FAX (808) 878-2518. Five rustic chalet-like cabins located at the 3,200 foot elevation. Restaurant on the property.
Chalet 1 & 2 $150 (queen bed, fireplace, lanai, stairs to loft with 2 twin beds)
Chalet 3 & 4 $120 (queen bed, ladder to loft with two futons)
Chalet 5 $100 (single story with double bed and studio couch)
An additional amount of $30 will be charged for more than two guests

HANA

INTRODUCTION

If you've heard any discussion at all about Maui it has probably included a mention of the Hana Highway. The twisted, narrow route follows the windward shore down to Hana, located on the southern coast of the island. *Hana* is about as far away as you can get from "tourism." More native Hawaiians live in this area than in any other part of Maui. A substantial reason for the isolation of Hana, is the Hana Highway. Hana attracts the average traveler who yearns to get a taste of real Hawai'i as well as the celebrity attempting to find a little seclusion. Leaving Wailuku along Highway 36 you will continue to mile marker 16 and at this point Highway 365, also known as Kaupakulua Road, intersects. This is where the mile markers return to zero, and in our opinion, is the official start of the Hana Highway.

As we discuss later, it is a lengthy drive and will require a full day. (Insider's secret! Hana can best be enjoyed before and after the throngs of visitors who daily make this drive, so try to stay in Hana for a few days!) If you can't plan an extended stay in Hana, you might consider at least an overnight stop at one of the many varied accommodations to break up the long drive to this isolated east coast of Maui. The best travel days are Saturday and Sunday, since road crews are generally not at work and you won't encounter the many delivery trucks which keep Hana supplied with all their goods. Here is a different Maui from the sunny, dry resort areas on the leeward coast. The windward coast here is turbulent with magnificent coastal views, rain forests, and mountain waterfalls that create wonderful pools for swimming. However, DO NOT drink the water from these streams and falls. The water has a high bacteria count from the pigs

Hana

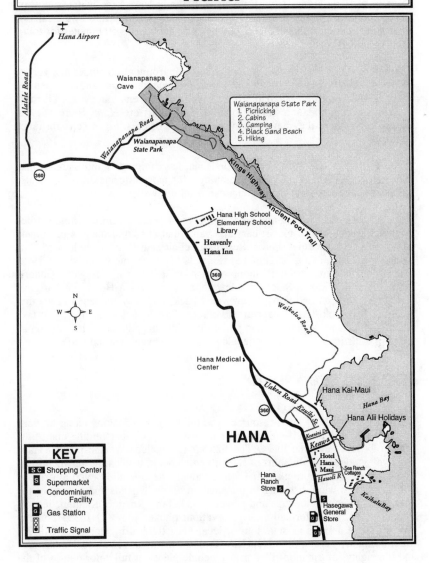

Hana Airport

Alalele Road

Waianapanapa Cave

Waianapanapa Road

Waianapanapa State Park

Waianapanapa State Park
1. Picnicking
2. Cabins
3. Camping
4. Black Sand Beach
5. Hiking

Kings Highway Ancient Foot Trail

360

Hana High School
Elementary School
Library

Heavenly Hana Inn

360

N
W E
S

Waikaloa Road

Hana Medical Center

Uakea Road

Hana Kai-Maui

Hana Bay

360

Kauiki St.

Hana Alii Holidays

Keanini Dr.

Keawa

HANA

Hotel Hana Maui

Sea Ranch Cottages

Hana Ranch Store S

Hauoli R.

Kaihalulu Bay

Hasegawa General Store

which live in the forests above. The beaches along the Hana Hwy. are unsafe for swimming.

The trip to Hana by car from Kahului will take at least three hours, one way, which allows for plenty of time to make some stops, enjoy these waterfalls up close and experience this unique coastline. Add another 45-60 minutes for travel from Lahaina/Kapalua areas.

Accommodations vary from hotel/condo to campgrounds and homes at a variety of price ranges. Several moderately priced condominiums and inexpensive cottages and homes are available from several Hana rental agents. A bit more luxurious accommodation can be found at the 7,000 acre *Hotel Hana Maui* at Hana Ranch where they have achieved their goal of creating an "elegant ranch atmosphere."

Waianapanapa State Park, just outside Hana, has camping facilities and cabins. (See RECREATION & TOURS - Camping - for more information.) Ohe'o also has a tent camping area; bring your own drinking water.

Hana offers a quiet retreat and an atmosphere of peace (seemingly undisturbed by the constant flow of tourist cars and vans) that has lured many a prominent personality to these quiet shores. Restaurant choices are extremely limited. The diversity between eating at Tutu's at Hana Bay and the fine dining of the Hotel Hana Maui is quite striking! Shopping is restricted to the Hasegawa General Store, the Hana Ranch Store or a few shops at the Hana Hotel. The original Hasegawa store burned down a few years back, and they reopened in another location. It is almost as wonderful and cluttered as the old version. (If you take "Hana Time" into account, their plans for rebuilding the store in its original location are running right on schedule - i.e. they haven't started yet!)

WHAT TO SEE AND DO

PAIA - ALONG THE ROAD TO HANA
There are a couple of good resources you might consider taking along on your drive. If you'd like a self-guided, yet narrated tour, consider renting one of the "Best of Maui" cassette tours. The $25 charge includes a tape player, Hana Highway guidebook, blossoms of Hawai'i guide book, tropical flower identification card, detailed route map, and a free video! The tape allows you to drive at your own pace while listening to information on the legends and history of the islands. You pick up the tape and player at 333 Dairy Road, in Kahului, just off Puunene Ave. For information or reservations phone (808) 871-1555. You can also purchase a Hana cassette tour at local tourist and drug stores for $19.95. *Maui's Hana Highway*, by Angela Kay Kepler, runs about $12 at local bookstores and it's eighty information-filled pages include plenty of full color photos of the area -- especially good for identifying the flora and fauna.

A little beyond Wailuku, and along the highway which leads to Hana, is the small town of *Paia*. The name Paia means "noisy," however, the origin of this name is unclear. This quaint town is reminiscent of the early sugar cane era when Henry Baldwin located his first sugar plantation in this area. The wooden buildings are now filled with antiques, art and other gift shops to attract the passing tourist. The advent of windsurfing has caused a rebirth in this small charming town and a number of new restaurants have recently appeared over the last few years with more to come. (See RESTAURANTS for more information.)

The *Maui Crafts Guild*, a group of local artisans own and operate this store. Koa furniture, pottery, weaving, wall sculptures, wood serving pieces, prints and basketry are featured: very lovely, but expensive, hand-crafted items.

Accommodations in Paia are a little scarce. There may be some Bed & Breakfast options and there has been talk now and again of a lodging in the town of Paia, but that is still in the discussion stages.

MAMA'S VACATION RENTALS (FORMERLY KUAU COVE RENTALS)
799 Poho Place, Paia, Maui, HI 96779. (808) 579-9764. FAX (808) 579-8594. < WWW > E-mail: mamas@maui.net. They have a one bedroom apartment with queen bed, kitchen and laundry facilities. Located across the street from the beach at $90 per day. Also available are two-bedroom duplex cottages located on a spacious lawn which faces the beach. Completely equipped kitchens, stereo, TV/VCR, private lanai $225 per night. 20% discount at Mama's Fish House. Minimum 3 night stay. Limited parking. Weekly maid service. Major credit card required for telephone service (to cover long-distance charges.)

HANA
Anyone who endures the three-hour (at least) drive to *Hana* deserves to sport the "I survived the Road to Hana" T-shirts which are sold locally. While it may be true that it is easy to fall in love with Hana, getting there is quite a different story. Even with greatly improved road conditions (as a result of repaving) the drive to Hana is not for everyone. It is not for people who are prone to motion sickness, those who don't like a lot of scenery, those who are in a hurry to get somewhere or those who don't love long drives. However, it is a trip filled with waterfalls and lush tropical jungles (which flourish in the 340-inch average annual rainfall).

Maps are deceiving. It appears you could make the 53-mile journey in much less than three hours, but there are 617 (usually hairpin) curves and 56 miniature bridges along this narrow road. And believe it or not, each of these bridges has its own Hawaiian name! You'll note in places that the road is so narrow there isn't even room to paint a center line! With drivers visually exploring the many scenic wonders, you may find cars traveling in the middle of the road, thus making each turn a potentially exciting experience.

The Hana Hwy. was originally built in 1927 with pick and shovel (which accounts for its narrowness), to provide a link between Hana and Kahului. There can also be delays on the road up to two hours if the road is being worked on.

In days gone by when heavy rains caused washouts, it is said that people would literally climb the mud barricades and swap cars, then resume their journey. Despite all this, 300-500 people traverse this road daily, and it is the supply route for all deliveries to Hana and the small settlements along the way.

Now, if we haven't dissuaded you and you still want to see spectacular undeveloped scenery, plan to spend the whole day (or even better, stop overnight) in Hana. If you are driving, be sure to leave as early in the morning as possible. You don't want to be making a return trip on this road in the dark. Be sure to get gas; the last stations before Hana are in Kahului or Paia. And be sure you pack your own food and drink. With the exception of an occasional fruit stand, there is no place to eat and only limited stops for drinking water. *Picnics* in Paia is a popular stop for a picnic lunch - their newsprint menu even offers a Hana map with points of interest! For something a little more unusual try packing along some local style foods or a bento (box lunch). Takamiya's Market on Lower Market Street has an unbelievable assortment of cooked, pre-packaged food made fresh daily, including fried calamari, tako poki (raw octopus), kalbi ribs, baked yams, and much, much more. If you plan on arriving in Hana after 5pm, make sure you have either dinner plans at the Hotel Hana Maui or some food for your evening meal. The Hana Ranch Restaurant is open only a couple of a nights a week for full dinners. All other local restaurants close by 5pm, as does the *Hasegawa General Store*. Whether you are planning a day or an extended visit in Hana, packing some rain gear and a warm sweater or sweatshirt is a precaution against the sometimes cooler weather and rain showers. Don't forget your camera, but remember not to leave it in your car unattended. We strongly recommend you take along some mosquito repellent.

We also might recommend that if you drive, select a car with an automatic transmission (or else be prepared for constant shifting). Another choice is to try one of the affordable van tours (or splurge with a company such as *Temptation Tours*) which go to Hana and leave the driving to them. Be aware that the driver of your car will be so busy watching the road, they won't have much opportunity to enjoy the spectacular scenery. If you don't wish to retrace your route along the windward shore's Hana Highway, check to see whether the tours are operating their vans around the other, leeward side of the island. This route follows the Piilani Highway and travel will depend on the road conditions. And you thought the Hana Highway was rugged? This route can be traveled in your personal vehicle, but rental car disclaimers warn against or prohibit travel along the Piilani Highway. The exception is some companies which rent four wheel drive vehicles. Check with the rental companies for their guidelines and restrictions. The scenery along the Piilani Highway, on this dry leeward side, is strikingly different from the windward coastal rain forests. Good tour guides will also be able to point out the sights of interest along the way that are easy to miss! Another alternative is to drive to Hana and then fly out of Hana's small airport back to Kahului.

Just past one of the best seafood restaurants on Maui, *Mama's Fish House*, you should be able to spot what appear to be colorful giant butterflies darting along in the ocean offshore. This is *Ho'okipa*, located two miles past Paia, thought by some to offer the world's best windsurfing. There won't be much activity in the morning, but if you are heading back past here in mid to late afternoon when the winds pick up, you are sure to see numerous windsurfers daring both wind and wave. These waves are enough to challenge the most experienced surfers and are not for the novice except as a spectator sport. You'll note that on the left are the windsurfers while the waves on the right are enjoyed by the surfers! A number of covered pavilions offer shaded viewing and the beach, while not recommended for swimming, has some tidepools (of varying size depending on the tidal conditions) for children to enjoy a refreshing splash. This beach is also a popular fishing area for local residents and you may see some folks along the banks casting in their lines.

At mile marker 11 (another turn off is 2.4 miles farther) there is a turn off to Haiku and Makawao. Haiku is a couple of miles inland. *Haiku* is noted for its two canneries that have been converted into local, Hawaiian-style mini-malls. The first is the *Haiku Cannery*, the second is farther up and is the *Pauwela Cannery*. The Hawaiian translation for the word Haiku is "abrupt break." It is not unusual to experience some overcast, rainy weather here. You'll find excellent homemade breakfast and lunch at the *Pauwela Cafe*. Traveling back down to Highway 36, a half mile past milemarker 15 is Ulumalu Road. (A detour up there will take you to *Maui Grown Market* where you can pick up some picnic food fare.) Highway 36 ends just past mile marker 16. At this point Highway 365, also known as Kaupakulua Road intersects. The Hana Highway continues at this point, but it is now Highway 360 and the mile markers begin again at zero! So begins the Hana Highway you have heard and read about!

TARO

Just past the 2 mile marker you will reach the new Hoolawa Bridge. You will probably spot a few cars parked along the roadside. You will need to climb over the gate to begin your trek up the one-mile trail to the waterfall. This area, known as *Twin Falls*, offers a pleasant spot for swimming. The first pool has two waterfalls, but by hiking a little farther, two more pools of crystal clear water created by waterfalls can be easily reached. This is a fairly easy hike, so a good one for the entire family.

Remember, don't drink the stream water, here or in any other fresh water stream or pool! Mosquitos can be prolific so pack bug spray. There are no safe beaches along this route for swimming, so for a cool dip, take advantage of one of the fresh water swimming holes provided.

The picnic area and nature trail 1/3 mile past the roadside marker is *Kolea Koolau State Forest Reserve*. It has no restrooms or drinking water. This area is noted for its stands of majestic bamboo, and you are sure to see wild ginger and huge ferns. Bamboo picking is allowed here with a permit.

Puohokamoa Falls is located near roadside marker #11. There is a pull off area with parking only for a couple of cars. This small picnic area offers one covered (in the event of one of the frequent windward coast rain showers) table. A short tunnel trail through lush foliage leads to a swimming hole beneath the waterfall.

Kaumahina State Wayside is located just past roadside marker #12. Here you'll find a lovely park. This area overlooks the spectacular Honomanu Gulch, the rugged Maui coastline and in the distance a view of the Ke'anae Peninsula. This is a good opportunity to make use of the restroom facilities.

Located a half mile past mile marker 16 is the *YMCA's Camp Ke'anae*. It offers overnight accommodations for men and women (housed separately). The rate is $10 a night. Arrival is requested between 4pm and 6pm. Bring your own food and sleeping bag. On site phone (808) 248-8355. Reservations and information available through the Maui YMCA office at 250 Kanaloa Ave., Kahului, HI 96732 or phone (808) 242-9007.

Just past Camp Ke'anae is the *Ke'anae Arboretum*. This free six-acre botanical garden is managed by the Department of Land and Natural Resources and is home to a myriad of tropical plants. A number of the plants have been labeled for your assistance in identification. Traveling farther up the trail you can view taro patches and beyond, hike into the rainforest.

Just past the arboretum is a dead end which turns off *makai* (to the sea). Follow it down to the ocean and enjoy some spectacular pinnacle lava formations along this peninsula. With the azure Pacific pounding onto the volcanic coastline, it is truly spectacular. The small island off-shore is *Mokumana Island*, a sanctuary for seabirds. Located here is the small *Ke'anae Congregational Church*. The church was built in 1860 of lava and coral and invites visitors to come in and sign their guest book.

The *Ke'anae Peninsula* was formed by a massive outpouring centuries ago from the volcano, Haleakala. The lava poured out of the volcano, flowed down the Koolau Gap and into this valley. Today it is an agricultural area with taro the principal crop. The taro root is cooked and mashed and the result is a bland, pinkish brown paste called poi. Poi was a staple in the diets of early Hawaiians and is still a popular local food product which can be sampled at luaus or purchased at local groceries. Alone, the taste has been described as resembling wallpaper paste, (if you've ever tried wallpaper paste) but it is meant to be eaten with other foods, such as kalua pig. It is a taste that sometimes needs time to acquire. We understand island grandmothers send fresh poi to the mainland for their young grandbabies. Poi is extremely healthy, full of minerals, and well tolerated by young stomachs.

At mile marker 17 you'll find *Uncle Harry's*. The snack shop is named for Harry Kunihi Mitchell and is now operated by his family. Harry was an advocate for Hawaiian Rights. The road just past this stand is Wailua Road. Turn *makai* (left) and you'll reach the main attraction in Wailua, Our Lady of Fatima Shrine, also known as *The Miracle Church*. This historical landmark has a fascinating history. In the mid-1800's the community lacked building materials for their church. The common practice was for men to dive into the ocean and bring up pieces of coral. Obviously, this was very laborious and time consuming. Quite suddenly a huge storm hit and, by some miracle, deposited a load of coral onto the beach. The story continues that following the construction of the church, another storm hit and returned the remaining coral back to the sea. Now painted, the coral church walls are still standing today. Upcoming around a bend in the road near mile marker 19 is the *Wailua Wayside Lookout*. Look carefully for the turnoff on the right. Park and follow the tunnel made by the *hau* plants, up the steps to the Lookout. The short trek up is worth the excellent view. Back up to the highway and a few hundred yards to the next lookout. Here you can take a few photos of the incredible Ke'anae Peninsula. There are no signs, but it is easy to spot this gravel area on the left of the roadside. The *waterfalls* are spectacular along the road, but consider what they are like from the air! We had no idea of the vastness of this tropical forest until we experienced it from a bird's eye view. Almost every waterfall and pool are preceded by another waterfall and pool above it, and above it there are yet others. The slice of this green wonderland seen from the winding Hana highway is just a small piece of the rugged wilderness above. A half-mile past marker 22 is *Pua'a Kaa State Wayside*. This state park offers two waterfalls and pools that are only a short walk from the roadside. This picture-perfect little park is a favorite stop for a picnic lunch. The waterfalls and large pool have combined with this lush tropical locale to make you feel sure a *menehune* must be lurking nearby. Restrooms and drinking water are available here too. Keep your eye out for mongoose. They have been "trained" by some of the van tour guides to make an appearance for a handout at some of these wayside stations. The best place to get a look at them is usually near the garbage cans. Toss a little snack and see if anyone is home. If you don't spot a mongoose, you'll probably meet one of many stray cats. They seem to subsist on the garbage that the visitors leave here.

With a little effort a sharp observer can spot the open ditches and dams along the roadside. These are the *Spreckles Ditches* built over 100 years ago to supply water for the young sugar cane industry. These ditches continue to provide the island with an important part of its supply of water.

Just before mile marker 31, the road begins to straighten out. Look for a flag and flagpole on your left and the turn off to *Hana Gardenland* is on your right. Browse through their gift shop, enjoy their exotic birds and view the flower displays. *The Jungle Cafe at Hana Gardenland* is one of Hana's best eateries. Open for breakfast and lunch, this is a Hana-style cafe - set right in the middle of the Gardenland nursery! Order at the counter and then pick out your favorite picnic table. The plants sold here include the "rare and beautiful" and are available for shipping anywhere. They also have one of the island's best deals for a unique Hawaiian-style postcard. A whole coconut can be shipped to your favorite person with a personalized message. Cost is about $10 for a plain coconut, slightly more for a painted one. Owners of the Gardenland also operate Hana Plantation Houses, so if you are staying in one of their rental units, this is where you will check in and pick up your keys.

The *National Tropical Botanical Garden* operates the *Kahanu Gardens*. The headquarters of the non-profit NTBG is on Kaua'i, where they operate three gardens with another garden in Florida. The 126-acre Kahanu Garden is reached by turning *makai* (toward the sea) on Ulaino Road, just past mile marker 31. It is 1.5 miles to the entrance of the garden. The gardens are located at Kalahu Point, which is also the location of Hawai'i's largest heiau. The Pi'ilanihale Heiau is six centuries old and was constructed by the sons of Maui chief, Piilani, in his honor. Restoration of the heiau is ongoing and two new gardens have recently been added: The Canoe Gardens (plants that were brought to the islands in canoes) and the Coastal Gardens (indigenous plants grown next to the shore-line). Currently tours are available by reservation only at 1pm, Monday-Friday with plans to offer additional tours as demand increases. The tour lasts approximately 2 hours and costs $10. (Children under 12 free.) They host a monthly Open House (free admission) along with a variety of events. They now have a local Maui number to call for more information: (808) 248-8912.

Waianapanapa (pronounced WHY-A-NAHPA-NAHPA) *State Park* is four miles before Hana at mile marker 32. It covers an area of 120 acres. Translated Waianapanapa means "glistening water." This area offers a number of historical sites, ancient heiaus (temples) and early cemeteries. You can spot one of the many lava rock walls used by the early Hawaiians for property boundaries, animal enclosures and also as home foundations. Waianapanapa is noted for its unusual black sand beach made of small, smooth volcanic pebbles. From the rocky cliff protrudes a natural lava arch on the side of Pailoa Bay. This can be reached by following the short path down from the parking lot at the end of the road. The ocean here is not safe for swimming, but there is plenty of exploring! Don some mosquito repellent, tennis shoes are a good idea, and follow the well marked trails to the Waianapanapa Caves. The trail is lined with thick vines, a signal left by the early Hawaiians that this area was *kapu* (off limits).

The huge lava tubes have created pools of cold, clear water. An ancient cave legend tells of a beautiful Hawaiian princess named Popoalaea who fled from Kakae, her cruel husband. She hid in the caves, but was discovered and killed. At certain times of the year the waters turn red. Some say it is a reminder of the beautiful slain princess, while others explain that it is the infestation of thousands of tiny red shrimp.

In ancient times there was a coastal trail that circumnavigated the entire island along a coastal route. Known as the King's Highway, it once traversed 138 miles. Maui is the only island to have had a trail which inter-connected the entire island. Remnants of the King's Highway can be found from here to La Perouse Bay. Examining the King's Highway you can almost imagine the Hawaiians of years gone by traveling over these same smooth stones. The stones were placed on top of the sharp lava rock for obvious reasons. The effort it took to place these many stones must have been tremendous. You can follow this trail east toward Hana, passing a blowhole as well as heiau ruins and ending near Hana town at Kainalimu Bay. The trail also goes north toward the Hana Airport for a short distance.

Camping is allowed at Waianapanapa in their rustic cabins available for rent at a modest charge. (See ACCOMMODATIONS - Hana, which follows).

The Helani Gardens is now closed to the public. It was created by Howard Cooper, and opened in 1970 after thirty years of development. The lower area consists of five acres with manicured grounds and a tropical pool filled with jewel-colored koi. The upper sixty-five acres are a maze of one-lane dirt roads through an abundant jungle of amazing and enormous flowering trees and shrubs. Also closed is *Alii Gardens.*

Now, back in the car for a drive into downtown Hana, but don't blink, or you might miss it. *Hana Cultural Center* (248-8622) opened in August of 1983. It contains a collection of relics of Hana's past in the old courthouse building and a small museum. Open Monday through Sunday 10am-4pm. Located on Uakea Road Street near Hana Bay, watch for signs. *Authors' warning:* Watch out for the little terrier that lives around the corner. He apparently has a hankering for rubber! He dashes out onto the street to run into your car and bites at the tires. He's amazingly proficient at this. We thought the "thud" was the car hitting the terrier, when in fact it was the other way around. It took a year off Christie's life! Amusingly, this terrier seems to be known around Maui for his hobby.

Hana Bay has been the site of many historical events. It was a retreat for Hawaiian royalty as well as an important military point from which Maui warriors attacked the island of Hawaii, and then were, in turn, attacked. This is also the birthplace of Ka'ahumanu (1768), Kamehameha's favorite wife. (See BEACHES for more information.)

The climate on this end of Maui is cooler and wetter, creating an ideal environment for agricultural development. The Ka'eleku Sugar Company established itself in Hana in 1860. Cattle raising, also a prominent industry during the 20th century, continues today. You can still view the paniolos (Hawaiian cowboys) at work at nearby Hana Ranch. There are 3,200 head of cattle which graze on 3,300 acres of land. Every three days the cattle are moved to fresh pastures. Our family was thrilled when a paniolo flagged us to stop on the road outside Hana, while a herd of cattle surrounded our car enroute to greener pastures.

Hana has little to offer in the way of shopping. However, the **Hasegawa General Store** offers a little bit of everything. It has been operated since 1910, meeting the needs of visitors and local residents alike. Several years ago the original structure was burned down, but they reopened in the old Hana Theatre location. Hours are Monday thru Saturday 8am-5pm and Sunday 9am-5pm. This store has even been immortalized in song. You might just run into one of the celebrities who come to the area for vacation. They still have plans for a rebuilding of the store in the original location sometime in the future. The **Hana Ranch Store** is open daily and the Hana Resort has a gift shop and boutique. The oldest building in town, built in 1830, currently houses the laundry facility for the Hana Hotel.

SOME LOCAL HANA INFORMATION:

St. Mary's Church (248-8030) Saturday Mass 5pm, Sunday 9am
Wananalua Protestant Church (248-8040) Established in 1838. Church services are held 10 am Sundays
Hana Ranch Store (248-8261) 7am-7pm daily
Hasegawa Store (248-8231) 8am-5:30pm, Mon.-Sat., Sun. 9am-4:30pm
Hana Community Health Center (248-8294) Emergencies 24 hours. Mon-Thurs 8am-10pm, Fri 8am-8pm, Saturday 8am-5pm. Closed Sunday.
Bank of Hawaii (248-8015) Mon.-Thur. 3-4:30pm and Fri. 3-6pm
(As you can see Hana is the place where they coined the term "Banker's Hours.")
Library (248-7714) Mon. 8am-8pm, Tues.-Fri. 8am-5pm. Closed Saturday and Sunday.
Post Office (248-8258) 8am-4:30pm, Mon.-Fri.

On *Lyon's Hill* stands a 30 foot tall lava-rock cross in memory of Paul Fagan. It was built by two Japanese brothers from Kahului in 1960. Although the access road is chained, the front desk of the Hotel Hana will provide a key. The short

TUTU'S

trip to the top will reward the visitor with a spectacular panoramic view of Hana Bay and the open pasture land of the Hana Ranch. About a quarter of a mile up toward the cross you'll find the beginning of a jogging/walking trail that follows the track of the old narrow-gauge railroad once used on the plantation. The path runs for about 2 1/2 miles.

Kaihalulu Beach (Red Sand Beach) is located in a small cove on the other side of Kauiki Hill from Hana Bay and is accessible by a narrow, crumbly trail more suited to mountain goats than people. The trail descends into a lovely cove bordered by high cliffs and is almost enclosed by a natural lava barrier seaward. (For more details see BEACHES.)

Hamoa Beach is a gorgeous beach that has been very attractively landscaped and developed by the Hotel Hana Maui in a manner that adds to the surrounding lushness. The long sandy beach is in a very tropical setting and surrounded by a low sea cliff. As you leave Hana toward the Pools of 'Ohe'o, look for the sign 1½ miles past the Hasegawa store that says "Koki Park - Hamoa Beach - Hamoa Village." Follow the road, you can't miss it.

You quickly pass fields of grazing world-famous Maui beef cattle and re-enter the tropical jungle once more. Numerous waterfalls cascade along the roadside and after ten curvy, bumpy miles on a very narrow two-lane road (and a 45-60 minute drive) you arrive at one of the reasons for this trip, the *Kipahulu Valley* and *Haleakala National Park*. The Kipahulu Ranger Station offers cultural demonstrations, talks, and guided walks. For more information call 248-7375.

Looking for the Seven Sacred Pools? They don't exist! The National Park Service notes that the term "Seven Sacred Pools" has been misused for this area for more than 50 years. The name was first promoted in 1946 by the social director of a newly developed hotel in Hana to attract visitors to the area. Along the stream there are actually more than 24 large and many small pools along the one mile length of the gulch, so even the term "Seven Pools" is misleading and inaccurate.

For the last few years, these sparkling mountain pools, one of Hana's most sought after tourist sights, fundamentally, had no name. One may properly refer to the area as Kipahulu or Haleakala National Park - Kipahulu. However, a name for these pools has been elusive. Ever since our first Maui guide was published in 1983, this area, for all essential purposes had no real name. Sort of like the artist formerly known as Prince. This area was formerly (and in this case, inaccurately) known as the Seven Sacred Pools.

The term, *'Ohe'o,* refers to the name of the area where the Pipiwai Stream enters the ocean. When the Kipahulu District was acquired by Haleakala National Park in 1969, park rangers interviewed native Hawaiians born and raised in the area to document its history. Without exception all local residents claimed that none of the pools was ever considered sacred. In public hearings in 1974 and 1975, local people strongly expressed that original Hawaiian names be used in place of romantic English terms. Highway signs were changed in 1977 and then in 1982 the incorrect labels were removed by the U.S. Geological Survey from its maps.

In 1996 the confusion was solved when the Haleakala National Park finally settled on a name which will appear in their publications and maps. So now when you head to Kipahulu you can visit the *"Pools of 'Ohe'o."* And imagine that, it only took 50 years to figure out a name!

Waterfalls cascade beneath the narrow bridge (a great place for a photo) flowing over the blue-gray lava to create these lovely lower pools. The pools you see below the bridge are just a few of the more than 20 that have been formed as the water of this stream rushes to the ocean. When not in flood stage, the pools are safe for swimming so pack your suit, but no diving is allowed. Swimming off the black sand beach is very dangerous and many drownings and near-drownings have occurred here. The best time to enjoy the park may be in late afternoon, when the day visitors have returned to their cars for the drive home. (This is another good reason to make Hana an overnight trip.) The bluff above the beach offers a magnificent view of the ocean and cliffs, so have your camera ready.

This area is of historical significance and signs warn visitors not to remove any rocks. A pleasant hike will take you to the upper falls. The falls at *Makahiku* are 184 feet high and there is a fairly easy half mile hike that passes through a forest. *Waimoku Falls* is another mile and a half. Three to four hours should be allowed for this hike which traverses the stream and through a bamboo forest. Heavy rains far above in the mountains can result in flash floods. Avoid swimming in these upper streams or crossing the stream in high water. Check with the park rangers who keep advised as to possible flooding conditions. Also check with the park service (248-7375) to see when the free ranger-guided hikes are available. Cultural demonstrations are given daily; check the bulletin boards for schedules.

Camping at Kipahulu is available at no charge. Be advised there is no drinking water. Bottled water may be available for a minimal cost at the ranger station, but we suggest you arrive with your own supply.

One interesting fact about Kipahulu is that many of the marine animals have evolved from saltwater origins. Others continue to make the transition between the ocean's salty environment and the fresh water of the Palikea stream. One of the most unusual is the rare *oopu* which breeds in the upper stream, migrates to the ocean for its youth and then returns to the stream to mature. After a glimpse of the many waterfalls, this appears to be a most remarkable feat. The ingenious *oopu* actually climb the falls by using its lower front fins as a suction cup to hold onto the steep rock walls which form the falls. Using its tail to propel itself, the *oopu* travels slowly upstream.

The upper *Kipahulu Valley* is a sight visitors will never see. Under the jurisdiction of the park service, it is one of the last fragments of the native rain forests. The native plants in the islands have been destroyed by the more aggressive plants brought by the early Hawaiians and visitors in the centuries which followed. Some rare species, such as the green silversword, grow only in this restricted area. Two miles further on is the *Charles Lindbergh grave*, located in the small cemetery of the 1850 *Kipahulu Hawaiian Church*. He chose this site only a year prior to his death in 1974, after living in the area for a number of years. However, he never envisioned the huge numbers of visitors that would come to Hana to enjoy the scenery and visit his gravesite. A little know fact are the graves behind Lindbergh's that bear a single name. We were told these are the graves of monkeys. Sam Pryor, the President of Pan American Airways was instrumental in encouraging Lindbergh to relocate to Hana following the death of Lindbergh's young child. Pryor apparently had an affection for those primates, and his pets are buried in this churchyard as well. Please respect the sanctity of this area.

It is sometimes possible to travel the back road from Hana through Upcountry and back to Kahului. The trip from Hana to Ulupalakua is a rugged 37 miles. This is Maui's desert region and it is a vivid contrast to the lush windward environs. As your island representatives, we deemed it necessary to attempt the perilous trek around the south coast of Maui on this "primitive" route. You will be following Hwy. 31 (Piilani Hwy.) from Hana along the southern coast until you gradually move inland and begin the ascent up the slopes of Upcountry, joining Hwy. 37 or the Kula Highway.

While some consider this road "an adventure," others term the drive "fool-hardy." In our opinion, they are both correct! Keep in mind the rental car companies have restrictions on travel along this route. Namely, if you get stuck or break down, it is your problem. These restrictions may not apply if you rent a four wheel drive vehicle, but check with the specific rental car company to be sure. It is very important to determine the current condition of the road and the current and future weather is a key factor.

While very parched, this route presents a hazard which can take visitors unaware. Flash floods in the mountains above, which are most likely during November to March, can send walls of water down the mountain, quickly washing out a bridge or overflowing the road. The road is sometimes closed for months due to serious washouts. Check with the county to see the current status of this route. Another good source of road information are the local folks in Hana. Although their viewpoints might differ, they generally seem to be well informed about the road conditions. We checked with no fewer than ten people before ascertaining that we might make it through. Recent rains can cause part of this "road" (that term is used loosely) to become huge oozing, muddy bogs. Currently the road is only seriously eroded for about two or three miles. But travel is reduced to about five miles an hour, or less, over these portions. Another two or three miles are marginally better. The "Drive Slowly" signs that are posted are quite sincere (but hardly necessary)!

The first section of the road past the O'heo area seems easily navigable. However, fairly quickly you may wonder if you made an incorrect turn and ended up on a hiking trail. This section of the unimproved road lasts about 4 1/2 VERY LONG miles. You'll be challenged by steeply dropping cliffs to your left, and the rocky walls on your right, chiseled just enough to let only a single car go by. However, if you have second thoughts at this point, you may be out of luck. There isn't even room to turn around! The most harrowing portions, besides the huge muddy ruts, are the blind corners. During our adventurous trek we heard the rumbling of the huge rock truck before we saw it. It is recommended that you honk as you prepare to navigate these corners. With the sound of the truck pressing down upon as we furiously attempted to find the horn (you know those rental imports) out of sheer panic we started hollering, "honk, honk." (As if that would do any good -- it's one of those things that is probably only funny if you were there.) The area wildlife must have thought these two odd women were absurdly imitating geese. We were successful in locating the horn and eased into a rocky crevice awaiting the rock truck to zoom by. (Apparently, those "drive slowly" signs don't pertain to multi-ton vehicles.) Traffic was very light, and the few cars that passed us, having negotiated the road from Upcountry toward Hana, all seemed to gaze at us with a grin that implied, "Good luck, fools." Obviously, we did make the journey, and we honestly think they need a T-shirt stating "I SURVIVED THE PIILANI HIGHWAY." All in all, we were glad we made the journey, maybe a little amazed at our fortitude, but even with a four-wheel drive vehicle, we couldn't recommend it. The drive from Kaupo to Upcountry is fairly decent, and we would suggest if you want a minor adventure try this. Drive from Upcountry, past the Tedeschi Winery and continue down to Kaupo. The scenery is wonderful and you'll have the opportunity to see Maui from a little different viewpoint and have the opportunity to enjoy lunch and "talk story" with Auntie Jane.

But, we're jumping ahead a little. Returning to "the back road," the condition of the road improves marginally and you'll pass the *Hui Aloha Church*, built in 1859. Continue on to *The Kaupo Store*. It has been operating since 1925 and is open based upon the whim of the management. If they are open, you can head to the back of the store and choose from one of several refrigerators for a cool soda, or the freezer for an ice cream. The walls are lined with an assortment of antiques, none of which are for sale. There are old bottles, an impressive collection of old cameras, radios and antique drug store items. Continue on another 100 yards and visit with Auntie Jane of *Auntie Jane's Fine Foods*. She has her trailer set up in a vacant field with a picnic table or two under a shady tree. She will cook you up a burger "her way," so don't even bother asking for it your way. Her way means something different each day. Perhaps tomorrow it will be fiddle

SPINNER DOLPHINS

ferns or seaweed on the burger, or another day minced onion mixed in with the ground beef. On "our day" it was leaf lettuce and potato salad topping the burger. At $5 they are quite possibly the heartiest and best local-style burgers on the island. She also serves up some great Maui-made ice cream along with floats. If she's in the mood, she might have banana bread or lumpia for sale as well. Auntie Jane has an opinion on most everything, and most of them are pretty sound. One "Auntie-ism" is that in Hawaii you don't eat until you're full, you eat until you're tired. This wonderful woman seems to have lived by that motto. She'll show you her wedding picture and tell you about her husband Charlie who works at Ulupalakua Ranch. However, the love of her life is apparently her stove and she confessed that when she dies, she wants to be buried with it. She reported that Charlie was a little bewildered about where he would be buried. She suggested that if there was room he could go beside her, otherwise he could go in the oven. This lady is what the "real" Hawai'i is all about. Finally, after an hour of laughter talking story with Auntie, it is time to head out and continue your journey to Upcountry.

The scenic attractions are pretty limited for the next few miles. A half mile past Auntie's is *St. Joseph's Church*, built in 1862. Take note of the many lava rock walls along the roadside. This area supported a large native Hawaiian population and these walls served as boundaries as well as retaining walls for livestock, primarily pigs. The walls are centuries old and unfortunately have suffered from visitor vandalism and destruction by the range cattle. Cattle are now the principal area residents. However, more people are gradually moving into this area. You'll note the remnants of an old church on a bluff (*makai*) overlooking the ocean. This is the headquarters of *Ka'ohana O Kahikinui*. This self help organization is attempting to put the Hawaiians back on Hawaiian land. As you enter Upcountry and civilization once more, look for the *Tedeschi Winery*. Located at the Ulupalakua Ranch, it offers tasting daily from 9am-4pm. They began in 1974 and produced only pineapple wine until 1983 when they harvested their first grapes. They also offer a champagne and a red table wine. On the way back down you might stop at *The Kula Botanical Gardens* (before 4pm!) which feature a look at the unusual protea flowers. Admission fee. (See Upcountry)

ACCOMMODATIONS - HANA

Aloha Cottages
Hamoa Bay Bungalow
Hana AAA Bay Vacation Rentals
Hana Alii Holidays
Hana Kai Maui

Hana Plantation Houses
Heavenly Hana Inn
Hotel Hana Maui
Waianapanapa State Park
YMCA Camp Ke'anae

ALOHA COTTAGES
PO Box 205, Hana, Maui, HI 96713 (808) 248-8420. Simple but comfortable furnished 2-3 bedroom cottages in residential areas. Short walk to Hana Bay. No phones; messages will be taken. Phone booths nearby. TV optional. Daily maid service. NO CREDIT CARDS. *Daily rates: $60-90 single/double, $10-20 each additional person.*

HAMOA BAY BUNGALOW

PO Box 773, Hana, HI 96713. (808) 248-7884. FAX (808) 248-8642. This 600 sq. ft. studio cottage has a fully equipped kitchen, including a blender, ice maker and even a coffee maker with grinder. A king-size bed, jacuzzi bath for two, CD/tape player, VCR with mini movie library, microwave, phone, and laundry facilities. One night rate $175 for two, discounts for longer stays.

HANA AAA BAY VACATION RENTALS ★

Stan Collins, PO Box 318 Hana, Maui, HI 96713 (808) 248-7727) FAX (808) 959-7727. They offer cabins, cottages and houses in and around the Hana area. All units have full kitchens, linens and utensils. Some have jacuzzi hot tubs. They offer daily or weekly rates, maid service at extra charge.

HANA ALII HOLIDAYS VACATION RENTALS ★

PO Box 536, Hana, Maui, HI, 1-800-548-0478 or (808) 248-7742. They have a number of homes and cottages. The Popolana Liilii is a tropical one bedroom cottage, with pullout queen size sofa in the living room. Washer/dryer. $100 per night. The Hamoa Hale Kai is a two-bedroom ocean view home within walking distance of Hamoa Beach. Sleeps six. $95 per night for 2, additional persons $10. Hale Hana Bay is a one bedroom oceanfront cottage at $110 per night. Hale Kilohana is available for up to 6 guests, featuring an ocean-front location with three bedrooms, two baths, full kitchen, an ocean facing deck and back deck with hot tub. Five minutes from Hana and a short walk to Hamoa Beach. $200 per night.

HANA KAI MAUI

PO Box 38, Hana, HI 96713. Located at 1533 Uakea Road in Hana. (808) 248-8426 or (808) 248-7506. FAX (808) 248-7482, Mainland toll free 1-800-346-2772. 18 condominiums nestled on Hana Bay. Units are studios and one bedrooms, both have fully equipped kitchens and private lanais. A spring fed pool and barbeque area are amenities.
Studio (2) $125-145, 1 BR (4) $145-195.

HANA PLANTATION HOUSES ★

Blair Shurtleff is once again running this operation and continuing to improve and add to the number of rental properties. Current rental options include: The Hale Kipa, House of Hospitality, located in the town of Hana, a short walk to Hana Bay. This two story plantation style house is located on grounds that include a private spa. Hale Kipa has two separate accommodations, each with its own entrance. The upstairs is a split level that sleeps four with one bedroom, one bath, kitchen, private sundeck, while the downstairs sleeps two. Upstairs rents for $135, downstairs for $100. Their Waikoaloa Beach House is a mile from the town of Hana and this solar-powered home accommodates up to four guests. Rental rate for the Beach House is $160. Other properties available. Full payment is required in advance. PO Box 249, Hana, Maui, HI 96713. 1-800-228-HANA.

HEAVENLY HANA INN

PO Box 790, Hana, Maui, HI 96713. Email: <hanainn@maui.net>, FAX (808) 248-8442. Four units in a Japanese-style inn. Each two bedroom suite has a Japanese style bath, a lanai and a private entrance. Owner Sheryl Murray advises us that the Heavenly Hana Inn was remodeled in 1994 and that they are constantly remodeling the outside.

Due to the economic situation in Hawaii as well as Hana, they have changed the format and the way they operate the inn. They require a minimum stay of 4 days, no exceptions. They also ask that they be contact by mail or Email, they do not take phone reservations. They ask that you fill out an application (profile of the guests) and to obtain an application, send a self addressed stamped envelope to the inn.

There are three private suites with spacious bathrooms including a soaking tub in each bath. The suites also include a small sitting room with cable TV. They are a non-smoking inn and there are no telephones in the suites. There are about 8 guests per week. They provide dinner on Mondays; Tuesday, breakfast and dinner; Wednesday brunch; Thursday, breakfast and dinner; and Friday breakfast. Afternoon tea is served daily. The inn provides healthful gourmet meals and fine wines and beer with dinner and brunch.

Their four day stays, arriving on Monday afternoon and departing on Friday morning, are $2,500 for up to two persons. Additional persons at $1,200. A 50% deposit is required and full payment due 60 days prior to arrival. No credit cards.

HOTEL HANA-MAUI AT HANA RANCH ★

PO Box 8, Hana, Maui, HI 96713 (808) 248-8211, 1-800-321-HANA. FAX (808) 248-7202. This is the most secluded Maui resort, and a Hana landmark that has been called "an island on an island." Five plantations were consolidated when Paul Fagan saw that the end of the sugar industry in Hana was close at hand.

There had been 5,000 residents in Hana in 1946, and only 500 remained when he began the hotel and cattle ranch which rejuvenated Hana. Approximately 1/3 of Hana's population of over 1,000 are employed in some fashion by the hotel, ranch or flower nursery. Hotel Hana Ranch opened for public use in 1947 and was later renamed Hotel Hana Maui.

The 93-room hotel resembles a small neighborhood with the single story units scattered about the grounds. The rooms are simple but elegant with hardwood floors and tiled bathrooms with deep tubs and "walk-in" showers. Wicker and bamboo are also prominent in a harmony of texture and design. The wet bar offers a selection of coffees and teas along with a grinder and cache of fresh beans. The resort prides itself on the fact that it has no televisions or room air-conditioning. Newer additions are the 47 lovely sea ranch cottages located oceanview at Kaihalulu Bay. These resemble the early plantation style houses. These cottages include oceanview and the majority offer private spas on the lanais.

The following are the published rates: Garden accommodations $395, Garden Jr. suites $450, Waikaloa Garden Suites $495; Sea Ranch Cottages $525; Sea Ranch Cottage Suites $795. They also offer a Family and Friends-Suite program. Two night minimum stay is required, maximum of 8 persons including children. Available only in the Waikaloa Garden Suite category. The first room is charged the published rate of $495, the second suite at a special rate of $100. Significant discounts on extended stays. Any guest staying a minimum of five nights is entitled to 33% off the published rate in any category.

The Historic Plantation House has been restored to its original elegance. Built in 1928, the 4,000 square foot building was the home of August Unna, Hana's first plantation owner. The surrounding four acres are filled with beautiful plants and trees that are more than 100 years old. The Plantation House is available as a guest home and offers two bedrooms and baths, a large living room with fireplace, dining room, library, bar and complete kitchen. To provide the latest technology for private business gatherings and meetings, it has been equipped with electronic data transmission equipment and audio-visual equipment that includes a large screen closed circuit television system. An adjacent pavilion and covered deck area add outdoor meeting areas. The site is also the location of the Hotel Hana Maui's weekly Manager's cocktail party.

Hotel Hana Maui activities include a weekly luau, many trails for hiking or horseback riding, or cookouts at Hamoa beach. A shuttle provides convenient transportation for the three mile trip to beautiful Hamoa Beach with private facilities for hotel guests. Tours are also available to 'Ohe'o Stream.

Two swimming pools are located on the hotel grounds. They also offer a dining room as well as an informal dining restaurant. (Restaurant dining and the weekly luau are available to non-hotel guests on a space available basis. Call for reservations.)

Children's activities and overnight sitters are available. A bar with a large fireplace and an open deck with a quiet lounge adjoining invite guests to enjoy a peaceful atmosphere for conversation or reading.

For your fine dining pleasure, the restaurant has a 35-foot ceiling with skylight, hardwood floors and a deck opening to a magnificent oceanview and excellent food.

During the day or in the evening there are some varied adult activities. Enjoy some quiet reading in the library which contains rare volumes of early Hawaiiana as well as popular novels. There is also a small boutique with resort fashions and jewelry in addition to a beauty salon. The "golf adventure" is three holes in the midst of the resort. The Club Room has a television, and evening lectures are sometimes given here. A more tranquil setting is difficult to imagine.

WAIANAPANAPA STATE PARK

54 S. High Street, First Floor, Wailuku, Maui, HI 96793. (808) 243-5354. The State Park Department offers cabins that sleep up to six people. The units have electric lights and hot water, showers and toilet facilities. There is a living room and one bedroom with two bunks in the bedroom and two singles in the living-room. Completely furnished with bedding, bath towels, dish cloth, cooking and eating utensils. Electric range (no oven) and refrigerator.

No pets are allowed and bring your own soap! A five-day maximum stay is the rule and guests are required to clean their units before departure, leaving soiled linens. A 50% deposit is required for reservations and they are booked way ahead (six months to one year). Children are considered those ages 11 and under, adults are counted as being 12 years and above. A pro-rated list of rates will be sent to you by the Parks Department on request.

The beach is unsafe for swimming. However, there are some interesting trails, pools, and lava tubes. The beach is not sand, but actually very small, smooth black pebbles. Mosquito repellent is strongly recommended, even for a short walk through the pool area. Six persons maximum. Following are a few sample prices. *Lodging rates are $45 for 1-4 persons, $5 for each additional person.*

YMCA CAMP KE'ANAE

In Ke'anae. (808) 248-8355. Bring your own sleeping bag and food. Separate facilities for men and women. Accommodations are dormitory style. *$10 a night.* Reservation number (808) 242-9007.

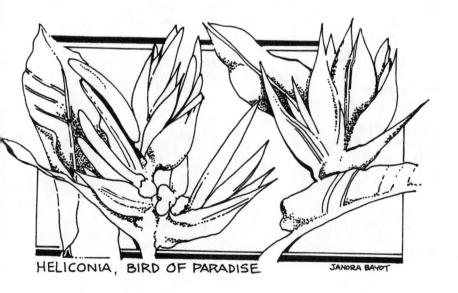

HELICONIA, BIRD OF PARADISE   JANORA BAYOT

ACCOMMODATIONS

RENTAL AGENTS

AA OCEANFRONT CONDO RENTALS
2439 So. Kihei Rd., #102A
Kihei, HI 96753
1-800-488-6004
(808) 879-7288
FAX (808) 879-7500

Cleaning fee for less
than 5 nights.
Focuses on South Shore,
Wailea & Kihei area
properties

ACCESSIBLE VANS OF HAWAII
186 Mehani Circle
Kihei, Maui, HI 96753
(808) 879-5521
1-800-303-3750
FAX (808) 879-0649

Specializes in assisting the
disabled traveler with any
physical limitations.
They can assist with
rental accommodations,
tours, or personal care

AFFORDABLE ACCOMMODATIONS MAUI
(808) 879-7865
FAX (808) 874-0831
Email: <llittle@maui.net>.

Bed & Breakfast as well
as homes and cottages price
$75-150, homes 150-750.
Also good rates on
inter-island car rentals

ASTON HOTELS & RESORTS
2255 Kalakaua Ave. #500
Honolulu, HI 96815
(808) 931-1400; 1-800-321-2558
From Canada 1-800-445-6633
www.aston-hotels.com
(Ask about Island Hopper Rates!)

(Aston at) Maui Banyan
Aston Wailea Resort
Kaanapali Shores
Kaanapali Villas
The Mahana
Maui Hill
Maui Lu Resort

BELLO REALTY
PO Box 1776
Kihei, Maui, HI 96753
1-800-541-3060
(808) 879-3328
FAX (808) 879-3329
E-mail:pam@bellomaui.com
website:www.bellomaui.com

Kapulanikai
Kealia Resort
Koa Resort
Luana Kai
Maalaea Surf
Maalaea Yacht Marina
Palms at Wailea
Sugar Beach Resort
Plus more condos,
also home rentals.

CASTLE GROUP
745 Fort St. Honolulu, HI 96813
1-800-367-5004
Toll free fax 1-800-477-2329
<www.castle-group.com>

Kamaole Sands
Maui Park
Maui Beach
Maui Oceanfront Inn

CHASE 'N RAINBOWS
Lahaina, Maui, HI
1-800-367-6092 U.S. & Canada
(808) 667-7088
Fax (808) 661-8423
Email: CNR@Maui.net
Also car rentals

Hale Mahina
Hololani Resort
Kahana Outrigger
Kulakane
Lokelani
Mahana
Maui Kaanapali Villas
Papakea
Pohilani
Valley Isle

CLASSIC RESORTS
50 Nohea Kai Drive
Lahaina, Maui, HI 96761
1-800-642-6284 (808) 667-1400
FAX (808) 661-1025

Kaanapali Alii
Lahaina Shores
Puunoa

**CONDOMINIUM
RENTALS HAWAII**
362 Huku Li'i Place, #204
Kihei, Maui, HI 96753
(808) 879-2778
1-800-367-5242
Email: crh@amui.net
<www.maui.net/~crh/>

Hale Pau Hana
Hale Kamaole
Island Sands
Kihei Akahi
Mana Kai
Maui Kamaole
Sugar Beach

DESTINATION RESORTS ★
3750 Wailea Alanui
Wailea, Maui, HI 96753
1-800-367-5246 or (808) 879-1595
Email: drh@maui.net
<www.destinationresortshi.com>

Makena Surf
Polo Beach Club
Wailea Ekahi Village
Wailea Elua Village
Wailea Ekolu Village
Grand Champion Villas

ELITE PROPERTIES
PO Box 5273,
Lahaina, Maui, HI 96761.
1-800-448-9222 U.S. & Canada,
(808) 665-0561
FAX (808) 669-2417

Private homes (3-7 bedrooms) and
luxury estates. Maid service, chefs
& concierge services available.

**HALE HAWAIIAN
APARTMENT LEASING**
479 Ocean Avenue, Suite B
Laguna Beach, CA 92651
1-800-854-8843 U.S. & Canada
FAX (949) 497-4183

Hale Mahina
Kaanapali Alii
Kaanapali Royal
Kaanapali Shores
Kahana Outrigger
Kahana Sunset
Kamaole Sands
Kauhale Makai
Kihei Akahi
Kihei Bay Surf
Mahana
Makena Surf
Luana Kai
Mana Kai
Maui Banyans
Maui Kaanapali Villas

**HALE HAWAIIAN
APARTMENT LEASING**
Maui Kamaole
Menehune Shores
Papakea
Palms at Wailea
Polo Beach Club
Royal Kahana
Sands of Kahana
Sugar Beach
Wailea Villas
The Whaler
MORE!

**HANA AAA BAY
VACATION RENTALS ★**
PO Box 318
Hana, Maui, HI 96713
(808) 248-7727

Stan Collins has
a great alternative
to condo vacationing.
Choose one of his
Hana cottages or homes.

**HAWAIIAN HOTELS &
RESORTS**
1-800-22-ALOHA
<www.2maui.com>

Kahana Beach Condominium Hotel
Royal Lahaina Resort

**HAWAIIAN ISLAND
VACATION**
Kahului, Maui
Air, condo and car
vacation packages
(808) 871-4981
FAX (808) 871-4624
1-800-231-6958
<www.hawaiianisland.com>
Email: hisurf@maui.net

HAWAIIAN PACIFIC RESORTS
1150 South King St.
Honolulu, HI 96882

1-800-367-5004
FAX 1-800-477-2329

Kamaole SandsMana Kai
Maui Beach   Maui Eldorado
Maui Palms   Maui Oceanfront

**KATHY SCHEPER'S
MAUI ACCOMMODATIONS**
1587 N. Alaniu Pl.
Kihei, HI 96753
(808) 879-8744
1-800-645-3753
FAX (808) 879-9100.
Private studio & cottage

**HOMES & VILLAS
IN PARADISE**
116 Hekili St. #201
Kailua, HI 96734
1-800-282-2736
FAX (808) 262-4817
Private homes

KIHEI MAUI VACATIONS ★
PO Box 1055, Kihei, HI 96753
(808) 879-7581
1-800-541-6284
FAX (808) 879-2000
Grand Champions
Hale Pau Hana
Kamaole Sands
Kauhale Makai
Kihei Akahi
Kihei Alii Kai
Kihei Bay Surf
Kihei Bay Vista
Kihei Garden
Kihei Holiday
Kihei Kai Nani
Kihei Resort
Koa Lagoon
Koa Resort
Luana Kai
Maalaea Yacht
Maui Kamaole
Maui Banyan
Maui Isana
Maui Sunset
Maui Vista

Menehune Shores
Milowai
Wailea Palms
Wailea Condos
Plus homes and cottages. A good
range of South Maui properties.
Something for every budget.

KLAHANI
PO Box 11108
Lahaina, Maui, HI 96761
1-800-669-6731
1-800-669-0795
(808) 667-2712
FAX (808) 661-5875

Lahaina Roads
Hale Ono Loa
Honokowai Palms
Hoyochi Nikko
Puamana
Nohonani
Valley Isle

KUMULANI
PO Box 1190
Kihei, Maui, HI 96753
1-800-367-2954 U.S. & Canada
(808) 879-9272

Kamaole Sands
Mana Kai
Maui Banyan
Maui Sunset
Wailea Ekahi & Elua

MA'ALAEA BAY RENTALS
280 Hauoli St.
Ma'alaea Village, HI 96793
(808) 244-7012
1-800-367-6084
Email: maalaea@sprynet.com

Hono Kai	Ma'alaea Yacht
Island Sands	Makani A Kai
Kana'i A Nalu	Milowai
Lauloa	
Ma'alaea Kai	

MARC RESORTS
2155 Kalakaua Avenue
7th floor
Honolulu, HI 96815
1-800-535-0085
(808) 992-9700
Toll free fax 1-800-663-5085
Email: marc@aloha.net
< www.marcresorts.com >

Embassy Vacation Resort
Paki Maui at Kaanapali
Kahana Villa Maui
Royal Kahana Resort
Kihei Bay Vista
Maui Vista Resort

MAUI & ALL ISLAND ★ CONDOMINIUMS & CARS
PO Box 1089
ALDERGROVE, BC,
CANADA V4W 2V1
US ADDRESS: PO BOX 947
LYNDEN, WA 98264
Local Canadian # (604) 856-4190
1-800-663-6962 Canada & U.S.
Fax (604) 856-4187
Email: paul@mauiallislands.com
< www.mauiallislands.com >

This is just a partial list of
the 71 properties they
currently book:

Hale Kamaole
Kaanapali Shores
Kahana Village
Kamaole Nalu
Kamaole Sands
Kapalua Villas
Kauhale Makai
Kealia Resort
Kihei Akahi
Kihei Bay Surf
Kihei Garden Estates
Luana Kai
Mana Kai
Maui Banyan

Rental Agents

MAUI & ALL ISLAND
(continued)
Maui Kamaole
Maui Park Shore
Maui Vista
Nani Kai Hale
Paki Maui
Papakea
Puamana
Sugar Beach
Valley Isle
Wailea Condos
Whaler

MAUI BEACHFRONT RENTALS
256 Papalaua Street
Lahaina, HI 96761
toll free 1-888-661-7200
(808) 661-3500
Email: beachfrt@maui.net

Kaanapali Shores   Napili Point
Mahina Surf   Napili Shores
Maui Kai   Puamana
Napili Bay   Royal Kahana
Napili Gardens   Whaler

MAUI CONDO & HOME
PO Box 1840
Kihei, Maui, HI 96753
1-800-822-4409
(808) 879-5445
FAX (808) 874-6144
<www.mauicondo.com>

Grand Champion Maui Banyan
Hale Kamaole   Maui Kamaole
Kamaole Sands   Maui Parkshore
Kauhale Makai   Maui Sunset
Kihei Akahi   Nani Kai Hale
Kihei Beachfront Palms at Wailea
Kihei Surfside Royal Mauian
Makena Surf   Sugar Beach
         Wailea Condos

Specializes in Homes & Condos
in Kihei/Wailea

MAUI NETWORK LTD.
PO Box 1077,
Makawao, Maui, HI 96768
1-800-367-5221 (808) 572-9555
Just about every property on Maui!

MAUI RESORT MGMT.
3600 Lower Honoapiilani Hwy.
Lahaina, HI 96761
(808) 669-1902, 1-800-367-5037
Email: kunisawa@maui.net
<www.mauigetaway.com>

Papakea
Maui Sands
Sands of Kahana

MORE HAWAII FOR LESS
1200 Quail St. #290
Newport Beach, CA 92715
1-800-967-6687 U.S. & Canada
Email: hawaii4less.com

Hale Kamaole   Maalaea Banyans
Honolani   Maui Kai
Kaleialoha   Sugar Beach
Kihei Surfside Valley Isle
Kulakane   And others!

MY WAII BEACH COTTAGE
3537 207th SE
Issaquah, WA 98029
1-800-882-9007
Email: Iro@ix.netcom.com
Great oceanfront cottage:
2128A Iliili Rd., Kihei

NAI'A PROPERTIES, INC.
3823 Lower Honoapiilani Hwy.
Lahaina, HI 96761
1-800-300-5399
(808) 669-0525
FAX (808) 669-0631

Hale Ono Loa
Hololani
Honokeana Cove
Kaleialoha
Kulakane
Makani Sands

OIHANA PROPERTY MANAGEMENT
840 Alua
Wailuku, Maui, HI 96793
(808) 244-7684 or (808) 244-7491
1-800-367-5234 U.S. & Canada
Email: Oihana@maui.net

Kealia
Maalaea Banyans
Maui Parkshore

OUTRIGGER HOTELS HAWAII
2335 Kalakaua Ave.
Honolulu, HI 96715-2941
1-800-OUTRIGGER
(303) 369-7777
<www.outrigger.com>
Email:reservations@outrigger.com

Maui Eldorado Resort
Napili Shores
Palms at Wailea

PALI KAI INC. REALTORS
1993 S. Kihei Rd.
Kihei, Maui, HI 96753
(808) 879-8550
1-800-882-8550
FAX (808) 879-2790

They handle Wailana
Sands and a limited
number of units at
Kihei Alii Kai,
Wailea Ekolu, Kihei
Park Shores, Kaanapali
Royal, Hali Mahina,
Mahana and Sands of Kahana.

PLEASANT HAWAIIAN HOLIDAYS ★
2404 Townsgate Rd.
Westlake Village, CA 91361
1-800-242-9244

Bookings are for package
plans, air or land only.
Aston Wailea Resort

Embassy Vacation Resort
Four Seasons
Grand Wailea
Hyatt Regency Maui
Kaanapali Alii
Kaanapali Beach Hotel
Kaanapali Shores
Kahana Beach Condos
Kamaole Sands
Kapalua Hotel & Villas
Kea Lani
Lahaina Shores
Mahana
Marriott
Maui Eldorado
Maui Islander
Maui Lu
Maui Park
Maui Prince
Napili Shores
Paki Maui
Papakea
Ritz-Carlton Kapalua
Renaissance
Royal Kahana
Royal Lahaina
Sheraton Maui
Whaler

RSVP
1575 W. Georgia St., 3rd Floor
Vancouver, BC Canada V6G 2V3
1-800-663-1118 U.S. and Canada
Following is a partial list of
properties. Ask about specials
they may have for free rental
cars, senior rates etc.

Hale Pau Hana	Maui Hill
Kaanapali Royal	Maui Park
Kahana Sunset	Maui Sunset
Kahana Villa	Maui Vista
Kahana Village	Menehune Shores
Kauhale Makai	Napili Shores
Kihei Akahi	Paki Maui
Kihei Alii Kai	Papakea
Kihei Holiday	Sugar Beach
Kihei Resort	The Whaler

RAINBOW RENTALS
CONDOMINIUM MGNT.
PO Box 1893
Kihei, Maui, HI 96753
1-800-451-5366 U.S. Mainland
(808) 874-0233
FAX (808) 242-0840
Email: polly@aloha.net

Kihei Kai Nani
Luana Kai
Menehune Shores
Sugar Beach
Other Homes and cottages

SULLIVAN PROPERTIES, INC
1-800-326-9874
Email: vacation@maui.net
FAX (808) 669-8409

Kahana Sunset	Papakea
Kapalua Villas	Sands of Kahana
Mahina Surf	Whaler

VILLAGE RESORTS
3478 Buskirk Avenue Suite 275
Pleasant Hill, CA 94523
Reservations: 1-800-367-7052

Kahana Sunset
The Whaler

WHALERS REALTY
MANAGEMENT CO. ★
Kaanapali Professional Center
Suite C
2530 Kekaa Drive
Lahaina, HI 96761
1-800-676-4112
(808) 661-3484
FAX (808) 661-8338
E-mail: Whalers@maui.net

Kaanapali Alii
Kaanapali Royal
Kaanapali Shores
Kahana Outrigger
Kahana Villa
Mahana
Napili Bay
Papakea
Puamana
The Whaler
Plus other Vacation Homes
(They offer high quality
condos at reasonable prices)

WINDSURFING WEST, LTD
PO Box 1359, Haiku, HI 96708
1-800-782-6105. (808) 575-9228
FAX (808) 575-2826,
Email: windsurf@maui.net

Rental condos, homes and cottages
for the non-windsurfer, too!

RESTAURANTS

INTRODUCTION

Whether it's a teriburger at a local cafe or a romantic evening spent dining next to a swan lagoon, Maui offers something for everyone. We're confident that you will enjoy exploring Maui's diverse dining options as much as we have!

The majority of restaurants in the Ma'alaea to Makena and Lahaina to Kapalua areas have been included and for the adventurer or budget conscious traveler, take special note of the wonderful local dining opportunities in Kahului and Wailuku.

Needless to say, we haven't been able to eat every meal served at every restaurant on Maui, but we do discuss with a great many people their experiences in order to get varied opinions. As we go to press there are nearly a dozen new restaurants due to open so we have only been able to give you a general preview of what's in store. Many others have disappeared, only to reappear with new owners, names and menus -- just before they closed again! We've done our best to keep track and to inform you of all the new places that we think will become a permanent part of the Maui dining scene. Look for a lot of new small, local eateries in Wailuku! We look forward to hearing your comments on these newcomers, as well as your experiences with some of the old favorites.

Following this introduction, the restaurants are first indexed alphabetically and then also by food type. The restaurants are then divided by geographical area, separated by price range, and listed alphabetically in those price ranges. These are: "INEXPENSIVE" mostly under $15, "MODERATE" most items $15 to $25, and "EXPENSIVE" $25 and above. As a means of comparison, we have taken an average meal (usually dinner), excluding tax, alcoholic beverages and desserts, for one person at that restaurant. The prices listed were accurate at the time of publication, but we cannot be responsible for any price increases.

For quick reference, the type of food served at the restaurant described is indicated in *Italic* type next to the restaurant name. Sample menu offerings are also included as a helpful guide.

An important postscript here is to reiterate the rapidity with which some island restaurants open and close, change names and raise prices. Our quarterly newsletter, THE MAUI UPDATE, will keep you abreast of these changes although there are times when we even have to issue updates to our Updates!

There are numerous fast food/chain restaurants, but we have only included the larger, more "restaurant-like" ones in key locations. We have also tried to include all the locally-owned places; the inexpensive little "finds" you won't see back home. Among those *not* listed are Subway, McDonald's, Pizza Hut, Taco Bell, KFC, and Dairy Queen. The only Wendy's and Arby's are in Kahului as is the

Little Caesar's mini pizza station inside Kmart. They all serve the same food you'd expect, but most have slightly higher prices than the mainland. Keep an eye out for special offers and promos as they tend to be the same price as the mainland. The Burger King in Lahaina has a very good location on Front St. with patio seating across from the Banyan Tree and a view of the ocean beyond it. The McDonald's have the usual fare, but with some unusual items added in: for breakfast you can have Portuguese sausage with rice and chase it down with a chilled guava juice; then for lunch, try a big bowl of saimin!

Dinner cruises are covered in the Recreation and Tour section of this book.

Our favorite restaurants are generally either a real bargain for the price, serve a very high quality meal, or just have something special to recommend them, and are indicated by a ★.

OUR BEST BETS

TOP RESTAURANTS
Our criteria for a top restaurant are excellence of food preparation and presentation, a pleasing atmosphere, and service that anticipates or responds promptly to one's needs. While the following exemplify these criteria, they are also all "deep pocket" restaurants, so expect to spend at least $70-100 or more for your meal, wine and gratuity for two. Generally, anything you have will be excellent. Remember, even the best restaurants may have an "off" night, but these are seldom. Also, chefs and management do change, rendering what you may have found to be excellent on one occasion to be quite different the next. However, the following have proven to be consistent through the years. Enjoy your meal, enjoy being a little bit spoiled, and remember that muu muus are great for covering up all those calories!!

David Paul's Lahaina Grill
Hakone, Maui Prince Hotel
Koele Lodge - Island of Lana'i
Prince Court, Maui Prince Hotel
Spats Trattoria, Hyatt Regency at Kaanapali
Swan Court, Hyatt Regency at Kaanapali
The Anuenue Room, The Ritz-Carlton, Kapalua
Seasons, The Four Seasons Wailea

TOP RESTAURANTS IN A MORE CASUAL ATMOSPHERE
While some of these restaurants are slightly less expensive, it is still easy to spend $60 or more for dinner for two. They serve a superior meal in a less formal atmosphere.

A Pacific Cafe, Kihei
Avalon, Lahaina
Gardenia Court, Kapalua Bay Hotel
Haliimaile General Store, Haliimaile

TOP RESTAURANTS IN A MORE CASUAL ATMOSPHERE
(Continued)

Longhi's, Lahaina
Mama's Fish House, Paia
Plantation House, Kapalua
Roy's Kahana Bar & Grill, Kahana
Roy's Nicolina, Kahana
SeaWatch, Wailea
The Villa, Westin Maui
Waterfront, Ma'alaea
Hula Grill, Kaanapali

RESTAURANTS WITH THE BEST VIEW
Plantation House, Kapalua
SeaWatch, Wailea
Ferraro's/Seaside, Four Seasons, Wailea
Cascades at the Hyatt Regency, Kaanapali
Monroe's or Sandalwood at Waikapu
Kula Lodge

BEST SUNSET AND COCKTAILS
Naturally, the restaurants with the best view are also the best for sunset dining, but for a tropical sunset to go with your tropical drink try the *Lehua Lounge* or *Club Terrace* at the Kapalua Bay Hotel in West Maui; or in South Maui, the *Molokini Lounge* at the Maui Prince Resort.

BEST AMBIANCE
In West Maui, we like the quaint plantation atmosphere at *Gerard's* restaurant in Lahaina or the plush comfort of Kapalua's stately *Plantation House*. The open-air, aquatic elegance of *Sound of the Falls* (open for brunch) and *Swan Court* can only be enjoyed here in Hawai'i. And if you want oceanside dining, it doesn't get any better than *Hula Grill* at Kaanapali. In South Maui, *SeaWatch* is lovely and spacious, while *A Pacific Cafe* offers an artistic look all its own. And *Caffe Ciao* is like eating in an elegant European shop! Or take a drive and eat in a beach house (*Mama's Fish House*), an upcountry General Store (*Haliimaile*), a greenhouse (*Jungle Cafe at Hana Gardenland*), or a "home" designed by Frank Lloyd Wright (*Monroe's*).

LA CUISINE FRANCAISE
Maui's French restaurants fall in the "champagne" price range. Both *Gerard's* in Lahaina and *Chez Paul* in Olowalu offer outstanding fare, although the atmosphere at Gerard's remains one of our favorites.

BEST SEAFOOD / BEST SEAFOOD BUFFET
Among the best seafood restaurants are: *Mama's Fish House* in Paia, *Gerard's* in Lahaina (though not a seafood restaurant, their fresh fish is outstanding) and *Waterfront* Restaurant in Ma'alaea. *The Villa* restaurant at the Westin Maui has an extensive selection of fresh fish each evening and usually a lobster special.

Fish and Games Brewing Company & Rotisserie in Kahana has a fresh oyster bar combined with a fresh seafood market with live lobster and crab and a very good selection of fresh fish. A number of excellent sushi bars are available around the island with sushi and sashimi appearing on most restaurant appetizer menus.

All of the top restaurants have wonderful seafood, but an All-You-Can-Eat buffet is a seafood lover's dream come true! A number of seafood buffets are available around the island: *The Moana Terrace* at the Maui Marriott has a Saturday seafood buffet that may not be as elaborate as the others with it's relatively low price of $24.95. The Westin Maui offers a seafood mixed grill buffet nightly at their *Villa Terrace*. It is served outside in a casual clambake-style setting for $27.95; $22.95 from 5:30-6:30. The Kapalua Bay Resort was one of the first to offer a Friday seafood buffet (5:30-9:30) in their *Gardenia Court Restaurant* ★ now at $32.95. The Friday seafood buffet at The Ritz-Carlton's *Terrace Restaurant* is good as is the one held Tuesdays and Fridays at *Palm Court* at the Renaissance Wailea Beach, but both are a bit pricey at $35. The most expensive is at the Maui Prince: their Friday seafood buffet at *Prince Court* is $36.

BEST SUSHI BAR
At *Sansei Restaurant and Sushi Bar* in Kapalua, sushi and sashimi are served along with Pacific Rim appetizers at the bar or at a table to mix and match - the best of both worlds!

BEST BRUNCH / BREAKFAST BUFFETS
Buffets are a good way to enjoy a great meal with a wide selection of food at a moderate price. Our favorite for breakfast (and ambiance) is the Hyatt's *Swan Court*. There are no "best" Sunday brunches - they're all wonderful! From the *Prince Court* at the Maui Prince Resort in Makena ($34) or the Makani Room at the Aston Wailea Resort ($29) in South Maui up to the *Gardenia Court* at the Kapalua Bay Resort ($27.95/33.95) in West Maui - you can't go wrong! (And you may not have to eat for the next two days. . .) The least expensive ($20.95) and most casual is at the Kaanapali Beach Hotel's *Tiki Terrace*, but for a few dollars more ($24.95) you can go "posh" at the Westin Maui's elegant *Sound of the Falls*.

Daily breakfast buffets:
In South Maui, the *Grand Dining Room* at the Grand Wailea has an outstanding daily breakfast buffet for $19 adult, $9.50 children. Lea's at the Aston Wailea Resort offers a daily breakfast buffet for $17; the keiki buffet is $7. In West Maui, the *Swan Court* ★ (Hyatt Regency Maui) features a lovely breakfast buffet daily, 7-11:30am, till 12:30pm on Sundays. Adults are $16.95, children $7.95. The elegant atmosphere and macadamia nut pancakes earn this one a star. The *Gardenia Court* at the Kapalua Bay Hotel offers a daily breakfast buffet $14.95; continental buffet $11.95.

Sunday brunches:
LAHAINA: Sound of the Falls ★ (Westin Maui, Kaanapali) serves an elegant Sunday champagne brunch in a beautiful atmosphere ($24.95) from 9am-1pm.

Some people come just for the sushi bar! *Swan Court* ★ (Hyatt Regency, Kaanapali) offers their lovely breakfast buffet for an additional hour each Sunday, until 12:30pm. *The Gardenia Court Restaurant* ★ (Kapalua Bay Hotel) features an artistic presentation and unusual variety of gourmet specialties in an open-air setting for Sunday brunch buffet 9:30am-1:30pm. Prices are $27.95 ($33.95 with champagne.) The most Hawaiian (and least expensive) Sunday Champagne brunch is held in the Kaanapali Beach Hotel's *Tiki Terrace* (and adjoining Plantation Room) from 9am-1:30pm. It's an excellent value at $20.95 ($1 per year for children) and there's live Hawaiian music, too!

WAILEA: *The Makani Room* (Aston Wailea Resort) has a fine Sunday Champagne buffet brunch with entertainment in a casual, oceanfront setting. Offered 9am-1pm, $29 adults; children under 12, $14.50.

MAKENA: *Prince Court* ★ (Maui Prince Hotel) features a spectacular display of over 160 food choices at the Sunday Champagne buffet brunch, each arranged as a work of art, and best of all, each tastes as good as it looks! Held 9:30am-1pm. Adults $34, under 12 are $23, under age 5 are free.

UPCOUNTRY: There are no buffets, but you'll find a good selection of innovative, multi-course Sunday brunch menus at *Impromptu Cafe* (Paia), *Abby's Place* (Makawao), *Trattoria Haiku*, and *Haliimaile General Store*.

BEST DINNER BUFFETS
The weekend buffets (5-9pm) at the Marriott's *Moana Terrace* ★ offer some of the island's best dinner values. The Friday night prime rib buffet is one of the most popular and still a great bargain at $13.75. "Italian Pasta and Sundae" Sunday has that and more for just $14.25 and it's Saturday night for hot & cold seafood at $24.95. (All buffets are $9.95 for ages 7-12; $5.95 for 6 and under.)

Friday-Seafood, Saturday-Hawaiian Paniolo, and Sunday-Italian are the $35 buffets at *The Ritz-Carlton, Kapalua*.

Palm Court (Renaissance Wailea Beach Resort) offers a buffet every night: Monday & Saturday-Prime Rib ($30), Sunday & Wednesday-Italian ($28), Thursday-(Either) French or Spanish ($28) and Tuesday and Friday-Seafood ($35).

Embassy Vacation Resorts offers a different buffet each night at their *North Beach Grill*: For $17.95 choose Pacific/Sunday; Polynesian/Monday; Paniolo/Tuesday; American/Wednesday; Italian/Thursday. Seafood/Saturday is $24.95; Prime Rib/Sunday is $19.95.

On Monday nights, Maui Prince offers a Japanese buffet from 6-9pm in their *Hakone* restaurant. A selection of 25 appetizer, salad, sushi, seafood, and meat dishes are $38 adults; $25 children.

BEST FOOD SPLURGE
Any of the lavish island buffets especially the Sunday Brunch at *Prince Court* (Maui Prince Resort in Makena) or *Sound of the Falls* (Westin Maui at Kaanapali) or the sumptuous seafood buffet at the *Gardenia Court* Restaurant at Kapalua.

A fabulous dinner at the Lodge at Koele on the island of Lana'i. On Maui, dinner at *Prince Court*; *Seasons* at Four Seasons Resort Wailea, or at *Swan Court* at the Hyatt Regency in Kaanapali. *Kincha* at the Grand Wailea not only has its own elevator, it has its on category (Mega-expensive) in our restaurant listings!

BEST SALADS/BEST SALAD BARS
The winners are the Chinese chicken and gado gado salads, both available at *Avalon* restaurant in Lahaina. We keep trying others, but we keep coming back for more of these! There's also their signature Tiki Salmon Salad, certainly the "most unusual" but technically, it's more of an entree consisting of a layered "tower" of mashed potatoes, eggplant, salmon, greens, mango and tomato salsa with plum vinaigrette. Salad bars seem to be making a comeback on Maui: *Makawao Steak House*, *Chuck's*, and *Kahului Charthouse* include theirs with your meal, but you can find a more extensive selection at the *Kihei Prime Rib and Seafood House* or *Ukulele Grill*.

TOP "LOCAL" RESTAURANTS (Kahului/Wailuku)
We have delighted in exploring the many small, family-owned "local" restaurants in Kahului, and especially in Wailuku. The food in these establishments is not only plentiful and well prepared, but also very inexpensive. The service is often better and friendlier than at many of the resort establishments.

A Saigon Cafe (Vietnamese) 243-9569
Aki's Hawaiian Food and Bar (Hawaiian) 244-8122
Bangkok (Thai) 579-8979
Fujiya's (Japanese) 244-0206
Mama Ding's (Puerto Rican) 877-5796
Mel's Lunch To You (Local Style) 242-8271
Mushroom (Local style) 244-7117
Saeng's Thai Cuisine (Thai) 244-1567
Sam Sato's (Japanese/noodles) 244-7124
Siam Thai (Thai) 244-3817
Tasty Crust (Home style) 244-0845
Tokyo Tei (Japanese) 242-9630

BEST PIZZA
One of our personal favorites is *Shaka Pizza and Sandwich* in Kihei, a New York subway style pizza that is wonderful and very cheesey. The pizza at *BJ's Chicago Pizzeria* on Front St. has a crust that's thick, yet light, with fresh, flavorful toppings. *Sub Shack* in Lahaina has come up with a delicious "white" pizza with shrimp and garlic, and readers have frequently mentioned that the Lahaina *Pizza Hut* is great! (We'll take their word for it . . .)

BEST HAMBURGER WITH A VIEW
Best hamburger with a view goes to *Cheeseburger in Paradise*. *Kimo's* in Lahaina is another best bet with a view. Neither is inexpensive!

BEST SANDWICHES
Dona's favorite is the Peking Duck sandwich at *Longhi's* or try the lobster salad sandwich at *Pacific Grill* (Four Seasons), or the "wrappers" at *Planet Juice & Java*. *Kamaole Bar & Grill* (Maui Coast Hotel) and *Reilley's* both have interesting and varied selections. We hear really good things about *Mr. Sub* on Lahainaluna and *Maui Grown Market* in Haiku is confident enough to offer the best sandwich or your money back. (Sort of like putting their money where your mouth is!)

BEST DOGGIE BAG!
Charthouse wins on two counts: 1. The attractive and durable doggie "shopping" bag complete with logo and sturdy handles, and 2. The fact that the portions are so big, you almost always need one!

BEST DESSERT
The artistic mastery served in dessert form at *The Ritz-Carlton, Kapalua* is worth savoring even before you eat it; ditto the Hawaiian "sculptures" at Jean Marie Josselin's *A Pacific Cafe*. To-die-for must-trys: the fun and festive "Fruit Fajita" platter with cinnamon tortillas and ice cream at *Planet Hollywood*, "Brownie to Da Max" sundae at Plantation House, or *Lokelani's* signature Chocolate Macadamia Cream Cheese Pie. The apflestrudel at *Nanny's Kitchen* is the real thing and *BJ's Chicago Pizzeria's* own invention, the "pizookie," is a winner!

MOST OUTRAGEOUS DESSERT
The *Hula Moons* Chocoholic Bar at the Aston Wailea Resort is a chocolate lover's dream come true. This dessert buffet features soft serve frozen yogurt with thirty assorted toppings, Milk Chocolate Kahlua Cheesecake, Hana Bay Macadamia Nut Chocolate Mousse Cake flavored with Hana Bay Rum, Milk Chocolate Sacher, Chocolate Mousse Squares, Dark Chocolate Mousse, Milk Chocolate Amaretto Cake, Trio of White, Dark and Milk Chocolate Fudge Torte, White Chocolate Macadamia Nut Torte, plus assorted cookies and brownies! Offered 6-10pm: $5.50 with an entree; $7.50 *as* an entree.

BEST HAWAIIAN
Aki's, located on Market Street in Wailuku, is small, quaint, and very inexpensive and the *Pukalani Country Club Restaurant* offers a Hawaiian plate and several Hawaiian dishes. *Tiki Terrace* at the *Kaanapali Beach Hotel* offers a genuine Hawaiian menu of Kulaiwi Cuisine as well as a set meal modeled after the Native Hawaiian Wainae Diet. Also check into the section on luaus.

GOOD AND CHEAP *(EARLY BIRD)*
Hours vary, but Early Bird dinners usually begin between 5-5:30pm and end by 6-6:30pm. Meals are often the same ones that you would pay more for an hour later, but selections are limited. Some are good values, others are mediocre fare.

RESTAURANTS
Our Best Bets

Discounts may range from expensive to moderate or moderate to cheap. Be sure to check in some of the brochures and booklets around town for dinner specials. The following are ones we recommend. (Generally, you'll find more of these and other specials offered during the summer months with prices that may also reflect the time of year. Call to verify their hours and to make sure they still have a discount.)

China Boat, Kahana 669-5089
Chuck's Steak House, Kihei 879-4488
Erik's Seafood Grotto 669-4806
Kaanapali Mixed Plate, Kaanapali Beach Hotel 661-0011
Kihei Prime Rib and Seafood House ★ 879-1954
Kobe Japanese Steak House 667-5555
Lahaina Fish Company 661-3472
Maui Marriott ★ 667-1200 (Moana Terrace, Nikko, and Lokelani)
Moose McGillycuddy's, Lahaina 667-7758
Orient Express, Napili 669-8077
Sea House at Napili Kai 669-1500

BEST DINNER VALUES
Some of the better Early Bird offerings are at the Maui Marriott, particularly at their award-winning *Lokelani* restaurant. Currently, their 3-course "Hukilau" feast is offered 6-6:45pm, Wednesday-Sunday for $19.95. *Kaanapali Mixed Plate* at the Kaanapali Beach Hotel has an Early Bird (4-7pm) Prime Rib Buffet for $9.95; from 7-9pm it's still only $12.50. (A different themed buffet lunch including salad bar, beverages and dessert is offered daily for $8.50.) We also recommend reading the chapter on dining in Wailuku to get the most for your vacation restaurant dollar and experience wonderful and inexpensive ethnic meals.

BEST FAMILY DINING VALUES
Koho Grill and Bar (Kahului or Napili) is a good stop with plenty of selections on the menu. *Peggy Sue's* in Kihei has a fun, splashy atmosphere like a 50's diner and malt shop.

BEST FAMILY DINING EXPERIENCE, COST IS NO OBJECT: The older
youth will probably insist on a trip to one of the "cool" restaurants, such as *Hard Rock Cafe*, *Cheeseburger in Paradise* or *Planet Hollywood*. Cheeseburger offers great open-air, oceanview dining. Planet Hollywood is just plain neat. (*Bubba Gump Shrimp Company* is the latest theme restaurant with lots to see and plenty to eat.)

BEST SHAVE ICE
"Shave ice" had almost disappeared on Maui, but a few places have revived it. Shaved ice, however, should not, in our opinion, be confused with a "snow cone." Both are cold and sweet, but a shave ice should be fine bits of ice crystals. *Lappert's*, in Lahaina, serves what they call a "shaved ice," but we thought it was more like a snow cone! They aren't the REAL thing. Fortunately, there are a few better options. *Tobi's Shave Ice* ★ in Kihei offers a friendly

atmosphere as does *Ashley's Yogurt* at Kahana Gateway. Also try *No Ka Oi Deli* or the Lahaina *Orange Julius* - they'll make 'em with beans and ice cream! We're also told that *W & F Washerette Snack Bar* at 125 S. Wakea, Kahului has shaved ice. *The Snack Shop* at Suda's Store sells shaved ice only between 1 and 5pm after Suda's main store closes.

BEST BAKERIES

The Bakery in Lahaina, 991 Limahana Place, 667-9062, is a good early morning stop that will ensure you the best selection of their wonderful French pastries or their original stuffed Tongan bread. Cheese and luncheon meats are also available at their deli. In central Maui, don't miss a stop at the *Home Maid Bakery* ★ on Lower Main Street 244-7015. Their bread pudding is fantastic. They recently opened another outlet - with a deli - at Azkea Place in Kihei. And be sure to stop at the *Four Sisters Bakery* ★ at Vineyard St. at Hinano in Wailuku. Melen, Mila, Beth and Bobbie arrived from the Philippines around 15 years ago. Their father had operated a Spanish Bakery in Manila for 15 years before moving the family to Maui. Not a large selection, but the items are delicious and different. One sweet bread is filled with cinnamon pudding, a sponge cake with a thin layer of butter in the middle of two moist pieces. The butter rolls are very good and the Spanish sweet and cinnamon rolls delicious. They sell their items only at this location and at the Swap Meet each Saturday morning. Hours are Monday thru Friday 4am-8pm. 244-9333. The Casey who owns *Casey's BakeHouse* ★ is Casey A. Logsdon, the award-winning pastry chef from Roy's, Kapalua and Four Seasons. His bakery is located in the Kihei Industrial area. 879-7295. *Komoda Store and Bakery* in Makawao is famous for their cream puffs throughout the state and beyond. Arrive past noon and you'll likely not get any! 572-7261. *The Maui Bake Shop* features fancy pastries and cakes and is operated by Jose and Claire Fujii Krall. Jose was previously the executive pastry chef at the Maui Prince Hotel in Makena. Located at 2092 Vineyard, 242-0064.

BEST VEGETARIAN

The Vegan restaurant in Paia probably has the largest strictly vegetarian menu. *The Raw Experience* just up the road is not only vegetarian, but everything is prepared without baking or cooking. Pizza, crackers, soups, cookies, cakes - all "uncooked" - but taste like they are! You'll just have to try it to believe it!

BEST LUAU (See luau section which follows)

The luau at *Aston Wailea Resort* has always had consistently good food and an entertaining show.

BEST LUAU VALUE

Check the Maui newspaper for advertisements listing local luaus that might be held by churches or other community organizations as fund raisers. A terrific value and you're sure to enjoy some great "local" food!

BEST FOOD FESTIVAL / DINING EVENT
Grand Chefs at Kea Lani teams prominent chefs from the mainland and Hawaii for a variety of events and the Lana'i Visiting Artists program at Koele Lodge frequently features guest chefs. April's "Ulupalakua Thing" is an agricultural fair with food samplings; the Kapalua Wine Symposium and Seafood Festival is a highlight in July, and September's Taste of Lahaina offers both a dinner and food festival. (For dates and details on these and other upcoming culinary events call *Interactive Events* 1-800-961-9196 or Email: events@maui.net. They can also help you create your own culinary event, whether it's meeting a favorite chef, adding to a cookbook collection, touring an agricultural farm or food manufacturing company, or attending a cooking class!)

BEST NIGHT SPOTS
Hapa*s in Kihei has some varied and unusual nightly entertainment as does *Maui Brews* in Lahaina. or check out *Tsunami* (the island's biggest nightclub) at the Grand Wailea Resort & Spa. (More nightlife information is listed at the conclusion of the restaurant chapter.) NOTE: As a rule, we do not list cocktail lounges and poolside snack bars in the index, although we have written about (and sometimes indexed) a few that offer more extensive menus.

There are several food courts around the island. We won't be individually reviewing these, but will include them under a general heading of Food Court. For example: For Ganso Kawara Soba, Pizza Paradiso, Maui Yogurt, and Yakiniku Hahn, see *Food Court at Whalers Village*. Edo Japan, Maui Tacos, Panda Express, Papa Romeo, and Yummy Korean BBQ are listed under *Food Court at Kaahumanu Center*. A Taste of Broadway, Aloha Grill, and L&L Drive Inn/Chopsticks Express are in the Kau Kau Food Court at *Maui Marketplace*. Siu's Chinese Kitchen, Restaurant Matsu, and SW Bar-B-Q are the smaller food outlets in the *Maui Mall* listing.

ALPHABETICAL INDEX

FOOD TYPE INDEX

CATERING (Also check with island restaurants!)

ANNIE'S DELI AND CATERING - Pupu or party platters, breakfast or brunch, dinners, desserts, and weddings. Sample menus feature items like shrimp & artichoke pasta salad, Swedish meatballs, oriental sesame chicken, deviled eggs, mini lox & bagels, oven taters, coconut pecan torte, lemon lovenotes, and Mexican wedding cakes. Annie's Deli is at 2511 S. Kihei Rd., Kihei, HI 96753. Phone 875-8647, FAX 879-8334. Email: annie's@maui.net < WWW >

A TABLE FOR TWO - Owner/chef Paul Alkire offers "an intimate dining experience" whether on a romantic beach or in your private condo. Catering service from his set menu of appetizers, salads, pasta, entrees and desserts or request an item you'd like. Sample choices include opakapaka-crab cakes, potstickers, warm goat cheese salad, gnocchi gorgonzola, NY steak with brandy, Maui onion & mushroom sauce, farfale pesto, chicken & crab gruyere, scampi, five preparations of fresh fish plus crepes, bananas or pineapples foster, and poached pears zinfandel. Can accommodate most dietary requirements such as low fat, low sodium, or heart healthy. Picnic baskets, too. 430 Hookahi St. #17, Wailuku, HI 96790. Phone 244-4556, FAX 243-2298.

BENTOS & BANQUETS BY BERNARD - Personal on-site catering or pick up yourself from $8.75-17.75 per person. Local style menus offer kalua pig, chicken long rice, lomi salmon, kalbi ribs, chicken katsu, and, of course, poi! Pupus include BBQ turkey meatballs, tempura ahi sashimi, sweet & sour tofu pork balls, ahi poke spring rolls, and stuffed shrimp or mushrooms. 85 Church St., Wailuku, HI 96793. Phone 244-1124.

CELEBRATIONS
Beverly Gannon of Haliimaile General Store will cater anything from a romantic dinner for two to a local-style baby luau. Plated dinners like Moloka'i prawns & roast duck, coquille St. Jacques or grilled quail with loin of lamb; buffets of prime rib or roast turkey; and pupus that include Bev's famous crab dip as well as coconut chicken bites, boursin profiteroles, stuffed grape leaves, spicy BBQ ribs, and Peking duck rolls. Multi-course set menus for 50 or more from $28-45 per person. Phone 572-4946, FAX 572-2725.

CLAMBAKE HAWAIIAN STYLE, INC.
A full catering service providing breakfast, brunch, lunch, dinner and cocktail parties. Per person breakfasts $7-8.75; lite lunches plus BBQ or clambake $7.50-14.75; meat or seafood pupu platters priced per pound or choose a "theme" bar with oysters, sushi, pasta, crab, Thai chicken, or baron of beef. Pupu parties for 25 people run $210-382.50. Clambake dinners are their specialty with combinations of lobster tails, clams, crab, bouillabaisse, sesame chicken, grilled steaks, and corn on the cob $15.50-21.95 per person. Meals are cooked on location in their self-contained steam cookers and grill. All seafood is cooked in its shell with Hawaiian salt and butter. Prices include paper products, utensils, buffet service, set up and clean up. No delivery charge for a minimum of 20 people. Children's prices available. RR 1 Box 52, Wailuku, HI 96793. Phone (808) 242-5095, FAX 242-9571.

DANI'S CATERING - If you've never been to the Takamiya Market, you're missing a culinary experience. Dani's is the kitchen for Takamiya's and they specialize in American, Japanese, Hawaiian, and Filipino foods. Pupus include won ton, teri meatballs, tempura, and spring rolls plus lomi salmon, kalua pig, and chicken long rice. Sushi, chow mein, pork adobo, and chicken hekka are a few of the entree choices. Catered parties have a 20-person minimum. They also provide Central Maui delivery at no charge. Set menus range from $10.75 to $11.25 per person and include warmers, plates, chopsticks; no beverages or wait service. Takamiya Market has been in business for over 50 years now and the catering operation has been around for more than 12 of those! Takamiya is at 880 Kolu St., Wailuku, HI 96793. Phone 242-6652. (They no longer have take-out or eat-in lunches.)

GLORIOUS FOOD - The catering services of Kathy and Robin Williams range from dinners for two to "theme" corporate dinners for 10,000. Hollywood celebrities, Wailea families, incentive groups, wedding parties and banquets for film crews are some of the diversified clients that use Glorious Food for Pacific Rim and Italian catering. Duck tacos, drunken prawns, Italian spicy sausages, gnocchi, bruschetta, Thai opakapaka, veal parmigiana and apricot dijon chicken are some of the culinary possibilities from Kathy's kitchen. Robin will also take care of the site, theme, props, staff, lighting, florals or music -- depending on your needs. They now have a small take-out outlet at the Kahului Shopping Center. PO Box 329, Paia, HI 96779. (879-1332)

LONGHI'S CATERING - Complete event planning islandwide from BBQ's to banquets. Specializing in Mediterranean, Pacific Rim, Classic French, and American Regional cuisines. Menus feature filet mignon with green peppercorn brandy sauce, grilled ahi with ginger lime butter, opakapaka with red pepper coulis, and lamb chops with raspberry mint sauce. Beluga caviar canapes, shrimp summer rolls, ahi carpaccio, beef sate, duck pate, and fresh baby artichokes are just a few of the appetizers. Their full bakery can create desserts and wedding cakes and they can provide a full service bar with an award-winning wine list. Phone 667-2288, FAX 661-5795.

VASI'S CATERING COMPANY
Vasi brings over 20 year of catering experience with celebrity clients in Los Angeles to Maui offering both catering and take-home meal service. Choose from a Hawaiian luau; brunch buffet (with or without omelette bar); and a variety of dinners: loin or rack of lamb, filet of beef, mahi mahi, breast of duck, Cornish game hen, or BBQ salmon. Select from a list of pupus like duck flautas with apricot sauce; brie, pecans & brown sugar puff pasty cups; feta triangles with curried chicken & mango chutney; polenta with gorgonzola cream & sundried tomatoes, or Vasi's signature torta with cristini bread. From an elegant private dinner for two on the beach to a gourmet meal for 2,000, Vasi's offers full service catering from $16-120 per person. They also coordinate weddings and specializing in custom wedding cakes. They now offer gourmet take-out with limited counter seating at their Makawao kitchen: 1043 Makawao Ave. Phone 573-8057, FAX 573-8309.

A FEW WORDS ABOUT FISH

Whether cooking fish at your condominium or eating out, the names of the *island fish* can be confusing. While local shore fishermen catch shallow water fish such as Goatfish or Papio for their dinner table, commercial fishermen angle for two types. The steakfish are caught by trolling in deep waters and include Ahi, Ono, and Mahi. The more delicate bottom fish include Opakapaka and Onaga which are caught with lines dropped as deep as 1,500 feet to ledges or shelves off Maui's west shoreline.

A'U - The broadbill swordfish averages 250 lbs. in Hawaiian waters is a"steak-fish." Hard to locate, difficult to hook, and a challenge to land.

AHI - The yellow fin tuna (Allison tuna) is caught in deep waters off the Kaua'i coast. The pinkish red meat is firm yet flaky. This fish is popular for sashimi. They weigh between 60 and 280 pounds.

ALBACORE - This smaller version of the Ahi averages 40-50 pounds and is lighter in both texture and color.

AKU - This is the blue fin tuna.

EHU - Orange snapper

HAPU - Hawaiian sea bass

KAMAKAMAKA - Island catfish, very tasty, but a little difficult to find.

LEHI - The silver mouth is a member of the snapper family with a stronger flavor than Onaga or Opakapaka and a texture resembling Mahi.

MAHI - Although called the dolphin fish, this is no relation to Flipper or his friends. Caught while trolling and weighing 10-65 lbs., this is a seasonal fish which causes it to command a high price when fresh. *Beware*, while excellent fresh, it is often served in restaurants having arrived from the Philippines frozen and is far less pleasing. A clue as to whether fresh or frozen may be the price tag. If it runs less than $10-15 it is probably the frozen variety. Fresh Mahi will run more! This fish has excellent white meat that is moist and light. It is very good sauteed.

MU'U - We tried this mild white fish at the Makawao Steak House years ago and were told there is no common name for this fish. We've never seen it served elsewhere in restaurants.

ONAGA (ULA) - Caught in holes that are 1,000 feet or deeper, this red snapper has an attractive hot pink exterior with tender, juicy, white meat inside.

ONO - Also known as Wahoo. ONO means "very good" in Hawaiian. A member of the Barracuda family, its white meat is firm and more steaklike. It is caught at depths of 25-100 fathoms while trolling and weighs 15 to 65 pounds.

'OPAE - Shrimp

OPAKAPAKA - Otherwise known as pink snapper and one of our favorites. The meat is very light and flaky with a delicate flavor.

PAPIO - A baby Ulua is caught in shallow waters and weighs 5-25 lbs.

UKU - The meat of this grey snapper is light, firm and white with a texture that varies with size. It is very popular with local residents. This fish is caught off Kaua'i, usually in the deep Paka Holes.

ULUA - Also known as Pompano, this fish is firm and flaky with steaklike, textured white meat. It is caught by trolling, bottom fishing, or speared by divers and weighs between 15 and 110 pounds.

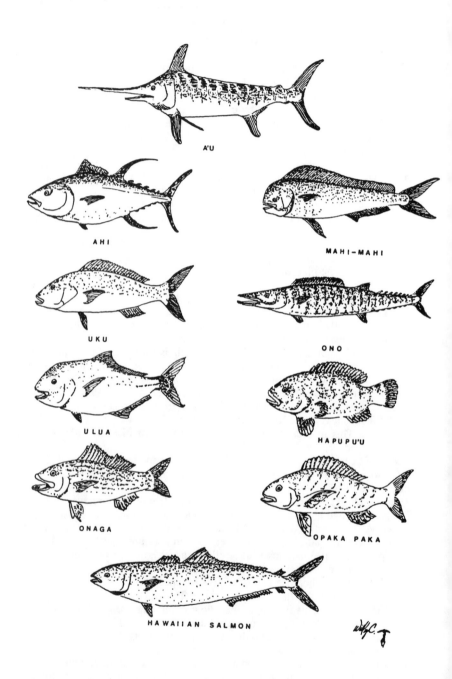

A'U

AHI

MAHI-MAHI

UKU

ONO

ULUA

HAPUPU'U

ONAGA

OPAKA PAKA

HAWAIIAN SALMON

ETHNIC FOODS

The cultural diversity of the Hawaiian islands brings many benefits to visitors and residents alike. As immigrants arrived, they brought with them many varied foods from their native lands. Some may be familiar while others will offer an opportunity to sample something new and interesting.

The restaurants are divided into the same three sections of the island as the accommodations. This should simplify looking for that perfect place for breakfast, lunch or dinner based on the location where you find yourself. A little background on some ethnic foods may tempt you to try a few new foods as a part of your dining adventure on Maui!

CHINESE FOODS

Char Siu: roasted pork with spices
Crack Seed: preserved fruits and seeds, some are sweet, others are sour
Egg Roll: a rolled fried pastry with various vegetables, meat or shrimp inside
Okazuya: this is a style of serving where you select dishes from a buffet line
Won Ton: crispy fried dumpling

FILIPINO FOODS

Adobo: chicken or pork cooked with vinegar and spices
Cascaron: a donut made with rice flour and rolled in sugar
Halo Halo: a tropical fruit sundae that is a blend of milk, sugar, fruits and ice
Lumpia: fried pastry filled with vegetables and meats
Pancit: noodles with vegetables or meat

KOREAN FOODS

Kim Chee: spicy pickled cabbage flavored with ginger and garlic
Kal Bi Ribs: flavored similarly to teriyaki, but with chile pepper, sesame oil and green onions
Mandoo: fried dumplings with meat and vegetable fillings

HAWAIIAN FOODS

Haupia: a sweet custard made of coconut milk
Kalua Pig: roast pig cooked in an underground imu oven, very flavorful
Kulolo: a steamed pudding using coconut milk and grated taro root
Lau Lau: pieces of kalua pig, chicken or fish flavored with coconut milk and mixed with taro leaves, then steamed inside of ti leaves
Lomi Lomi Salmon: diced and salted salmon with tomatoes and green onions
Long Rice: clear noodles cooked with squid or chicken broth.
Opihi: these salt water limpets are eaten raw and considered a delicacy
Poki: raw fish that has been spiced. A variety of types of fish are used and are often mixed with seaweed; for example, tako poki is raw octopus

JAPANESE FOODS

Fish Cake: white fish and starch steamed together
Miso Soup: soup of fermented soy beans
Sushi: white rice with various seafood and seaweed
Sashimi: raw fish
Wasabi: very spicy green horseradish root used to dip sushi into

PUERTO RICAN FOODS

Pasteles: an exterior of grated green banana that is filled with pork and vegetables

LOCAL FAVORITES

Plate lunches: These combinations might include teriyaki chicken, hamburger with gravy or fish, but are always served with rice and a scoop or two of macaroni salad
Loco Moco: a combination of hamburger, rice, fried egg and gravy
Bento: a box lunch
Saimin: Top Ramen -- only better!
Shave Ice: flaked ice that can be topped with a variety of flavored syrups, sometimes available with ice cream

LUAUS AND DINNER SHOWS

For a local luau, check the Maui News. You may be fortunate to find one of the area churches or schools sponsoring a fund-raising luau. The public is welcome and the prices are usually half that of the commercial ventures. You'll see wonderful spontaneous local entertainment.

Most of the luaus are large, with an average of 400-600 guests. Most serve traditional Hawaiian foods. The entertainment ranges from splashy Broadway-style productions to more subtle offerings of authentic Hawaiian dance and song. In general there are a few standard things to be expected at most luaus. These are an imu ceremony (to uncover the cooked pig that will be served that night), the Hawaiian wedding song, poi, haupia (coconut pudding), and mai tais (a Tahitian name meaning "the very best"). Upon arrival there may or may not be some waiting in line before it's your turn to be greeted with a shell lei and a snapshot of your group (available for purchase after the show).

It is very difficult to judge these luaus due to their diversity. While one reader raves about a particular show, another reader will announce their disappointment with the same event. Read the information provided, carefully keeping in mind that the performers do come and go. Luau prices run $57-62 for adults, most have youth prices discounted by about half.

LUAU BEST BETS: *Best Atmosphere, Food and Luau* - Aston Wailea Resort

ASTON WAILEA RESORT ★

The Aston Wailea Resort refers to their luau as "Wailea's Finest Luau" and we'd have to agree. The fabulous outdoor setting in their luau garden is both beautiful and spacious with a sublime ocean view. The stage is set up to offer the ocean and beautiful sunset as backdrop. An open bar is available. Dinner moves swiftly through several buffet lines serving sauteed fish with lemon macadamia nut butter, teriyaki steak, and kalua pig (which was the best of the all the luaus with good flavor, solid but juicy texture and big chunks of meat). Lau lau (pork, beef, & fish with taro steamed in Ti leaf), Hawaiian sweet potatoes, chicken long rice, freshly baked taro rolls, and a variety of salads are just a few of the other offerings. The dessert table (always the best) is now even better with a bigger selection of cream pies and cakes, tropical fruit cobbler, macadamia nut cake, and coconut macaroons.

The show begins just as the sun is setting with the music of Ka Poe o Hawai'i and Paradyse. First is a kahiko hula which is followed by a paniolo number, traditional love songs, Tahitian number and finally the fire-knife dancer, Ifi So'o, who proved to be the best out of all the luaus. He did stunts, somersaults across the stage and even seemed to twirl much faster. After almost a dozen luaus, it is pretty hard to be impressed, but this guy was impressive. (Apparently, we are not alone in our assessment: he has won the World Championship Fire-Knife Dancer competition an unprecedented three times and remains the first and only one *in the world* to do so!) The final song is from an album by Keali'i Reichel, a talented kumu hula and singer who has been getting national recognition. The show features a good range and quality of entertainment with one of the best outdoor settings. And, a truly extraordinary fire-dancer! For overall food, entertainment and setting, this is a great luau which continues to rate in our book as the best overall. And at $58 including tax & gratuity ($26 for children 6-12), it is also one of the least expensive. 5-8pm. Monday, Tuesday, Thursday & Friday. 879-1922.

HOTEL HANA-MAUI AT HANA RANCH

Hamoa Beach Luau is held at Lehoula Beach on Tuesdays at 6pm. Open to non-hotel guests based on availability for $50. Guests of the hotel are transported on horseback or by van to the beachfront luau location. A very local and family-oriented production. Many of those involved in the entertainment are folks you might see working in another capacity around the hotel. Phone 248-8211.

HYATT REGENCY

Hyatt Regency Kaanapali. The "Drums of the Pacific" is more a dinner show than a luau format. It is held on the grounds of the Hyatt, however, there is no ocean view. The show is from 5-8pm and there is usually a bit of a line. Pictures are taken while waiting prior to admission to the grounds, where you are greeted with a lei and taken to a table by your server. The dinner buffet featured mahi mahi with a nice lemon butter sauce and scallion ginger relish. The steaks were cooked to order on the grill and were particularly good. Big slices of Kula potato were unusual and tasty, as was the kim chee. Soba noodles, roasted wedges of

Maui onion, and Polynesian rice with macadamia nuts were other distinctive touches. The desserts were a cut above: the haupia had good texture and coconut flavor, the hot bread pudding was baked with a meringue topping and the macadamia nut cream pie didn't have that awful synthetic taste that cream pies sometimes do. The show starts off with a welcome chant by Cliff Ahue who also does the wonderful free hula show at the Kapalua Shops. His voice is beautiful and enchanting and his choreography has always been very Hawaiian and very authentic. The kahiko hula followed the chant and had a very effective smoke-like mist surrounding the dancers. The imu ceremony was short and nondescript, but did have the "Pig Procession" carrying his piggly majesty through the center aisle of the audience. A separate side stage for solo dances made things visually interesting. Perhaps the best number was the Maui Waltz, a pretty song with girls in high collared white Victorian blouses and colored skirts. Chief Fa'a, the fire dancer, continues to be one of the best. A good, professional, fast-paced production, although the Wayne Newton-like MC may be to your liking or annoyance. All in all, it was a show worth seeing. Prices $62 for adults; teens $39; children $25. Reservations: 667-4420; Hyatt: 661-1234.

MAUI MARRIOTT RESORT
Nightly, $60 for adults, children $27. (Senior discount rate $50) Fruit punch and mai tais are offered from 4:30pm while guests can enjoy and participate in Hawaiian games and crafts from 5-6pm. The regular bar is open from 5-7:30pm while the fruit punch and mai tais are available throughout the show (until 8) from a self-service table. After the games and crafts are "pau," the imu ceremony is held, followed by a narrated fashion show with muu muus, pareaus and the like while guests line up for the buffet. The food lines move quickly past the selection of kalua pig, teriyaki beef steak, sweet and sour chicken, mahi mahi, fried rice and more. The show begins with Barry Kim as MC. The presentation is a lively one, with Fiji warriors doing lots of high jumps, a Hollywood hula segment, Maori men from New Zealand and girls with poi balls doing an effective number. The fire-knife dancer is the finale. Although bordering a little too close Las Vegas, Barry seemed to keep the crowd well entertained. This is one of those luaus that offered nothing truly exceptional or extraordinary, but it certainly had everything you go to for a luau for, so nothing was lacking or disappointing. Reservations: 661-LUAU(5828); Maui Marriott: 667-1200.

OLD LAHAINA LUAU
Before they even opened in their new expanded location, The Old Lahaina Luau started showing signs of becoming the kind of operation we hoped they *wouldn't* be: impersonal, out of touch, and just too big. They built their much-deserved reputation and multi-awarded luau experience on being small, intimate, and authentic, but their new "Hawaiian village" setting belongs more to Disney (Luau Land) than to Hawaiiana. Even so, we were prepared to give them the benefit of the doubt - after all, everything else they have done in the past has been done with style *and* aloha - but after several attempts to get information on the new luau, it was implied that neither we nor our "little" book were important enough to merit the courtesy of a return call, much less to receive the material we needed to let you know about the food, show, new concept or even the most basic day, time, and price information. Obviously, we are disappointed in what we have

always thought of as one of the island's best examples of "aloha spirit." Maybe once they get settled (and are not "too busy" to let interested readers know what they have to offer) they will be more accommodating (and humble?) and will once again treat visitors as welcome guests instead of just a way to pay for the cost of their million dollar plus expansion. (Let us know if you find your experience to be different - in this case, we would be delighted to hear that we were wrong!)

RENAISSANCE WAILEA BEACH RESORT

The Renaissance luau is held every Tuesday, Thursday, and Saturday in the Luau Gardens, a small area that offers an ocean view and pleasant sunset. Seating begins at 5:30 for the 6:00 hosted cocktail reception accompanied by a Hawaiian trio. Followed by the imu ceremony, buffet, and Polynesian show with fire-knife dancer, the evening ends at approximately 8:30. Round tables accommodate 8-10 guests and are covered with fabric tablecloths and matching napkins in tropical print. They take your pictures just above the sand, so you have an appealing ocean backdrop. The opening trio offers a prelude to the diverse Tahitian, Maori, Fijian, and Hawaiian music you'll be hearing during the show. Warren Molina is the master of ceremonies and narrates through the kahiko hula, a poi ball number and a good solo Maori number that is out of the ordinary. The food was surprisingly good, definitely a cut above luau food. The buffet included a variety of salads: Chinese chicken, chow mein, greens, fresh fruit, and macaroni/potato along with poi, lomi lomi salmon, huli huli chicken, char-broiled teriyaki steaks, Hawaiian yams, fried rice, and Portuguese sweet bread. The kalua pig had nice, big chunks, and was moist and tender. The fresh mahi mahi was complimented with a pineapple salsa. The desserts were all bakery quality, from the chocolate macadamia nut bars and banana cake with chocolate frosting to the coconut cream cake, pineapple upside-down cake, and haupia that is served in a mold surrounded by fresh strawberries and whipped cream. And, they were ALL good! (We tried them all, just for you, our readers!) Adults, $57; children 5-12 years $27; under 5 are free. 879-4900.

ROYAL LAHAINA RESORT

In Kaanapali. Nightly at 5:30 or 6pm (changes seasonally), $62 adults, $28 children 5-12 years, under 5 free. (Sunday, Tuesday, Wednesday, and Fridays are family nights - children 12 are under are admitted free with a paying adult.) The ready-made mai tais, fruit punch, open bar and shell leis were the first order of business, but they have a new twist on the photographs. They take two of them, one with your party and male and female greeters, and the other is a circle inset in a picture of the luau performers on stage, making it an effective souvenir. The luau grounds are near the ocean, but without an ocean view (unless you peek over the hedge). Seating is at padded picnic table benches. The imu ceremony was the shortest and some people hadn't even reached the pit before it was over! While people were settling in, hostess Makalapua welcomed guests.

Dinner began at 6:45 with four tables and eight lines allowing people to flow quickly through. Real "glass" glasses for drinks were a pleasant surprise, although the coffee cups were plastic. Large wooden trays offered plenty of room to pile on the teri beef, kalua pig, mahi mahi, pineapple chicken, Hawaiian sweet potatoes, fried rice, lomi lomi salmon, poi, fresh fruit, and a salad bar with an interesting selection. The desserts included haupia, pineapple tart, and the coconut cream cake was particularly good. Frank Hewitt, an award-winning kumu hula and songwriter, is the choreographer and he wrote all the songs in the show (except the Hawaiian Wedding Song). There was just the right amount of audience interaction with Makalapua providing a short hula lesson with instructions about moving and wiggling your papayas and bananas, which was sort of cute. A fashion show followed and the production began with the blowing of the conch shell and kahiko hula, the male dancers making a nice entrance through the audience to be joined by the female dancers on stage. Co-MC Warren Molina (yes, he also appears at the Renaissance) sang a lively tune which was followed by several more very entertaining numbers. The song and hula about the legend of the rain resulted in a very fine water spray reaching the front of the audience. They still have the Hollywood number which is a fun piece, followed by a romantic Hawaiian song. The finale was the fire-knife dance.

Drawbacks at this luau included the gravel covered dirt ground which made annoying crunching sounds as people got up throughout the show to pick up a drink at the bar, which remained open during the show. This is another good, but not great luau. A nice touch is the original music and choreography. Reservations: 661-9119; Royal Lahaina: 661-3611.

Here are some facts and figures you may not want to know!

Luaus are definitely not low-calorie dining options. So eat and enjoy, but just in case you are interested, here is the breakdown! Kalua Pig 1/2 cup 150 calories, Lomi Lomi salmon 1/2 cup 87 calories, Poi 1 cup 161 calories (but who could eat that much!), fried rice 1 cup 200 calories, fish (depending on type served) 150-250 calories, chicken long rice 283 calories, haupia 128 calories, coconut cake 200-350 calories, Mai Tai 302 calories, Pina Colada 252 calories, fruit punch 140 calories, Blue Hawai'i 260 calories, Chi Chi 190 calories.

HAWAIIAN MUSICAL INSTRUMENTS

LAHAINA

INEXPENSIVE

ALOHA BENTO   *Local/ Asian Fast Food*
1036 Limahana Pl. (661-4888) HOURS: 10am-6pm; closed Sunday.
SAMPLING: Plate lunches, stews, soups, and noodles ($6.25-8.50); plus sushi, assorted stir-frys, and a variety of Chinese and Korean specialties ($4.25-8.99) COMMENTS: You can get half-orders of any plate lunch for half price.

ALOHA MIXED PLATE   *Local/Hawaiian*
1285 Front St. across from the Lahaina Cannery (661-3322) HOURS: Breakfast 7:30-10am, lunch/dinner 10am-10pm. Happy Hour 3-6pm & 10pm-midnight.
SAMPLING: Plate lunches, burgers & sandwiches $3.95-6.95. Bentos while they last. COMMENTS: A new wood bar & outdoor sundeck in the old Wiki Wiki Pizza location.

ARAKAWA   *Japanese Fast Food*
736 Front St., at the Wainee St. end of the Kishi Mall. (661-8811) HOURS: 11am-2pm; 5-7:30pm (Closed the 1st, 10th and 20th of every month to do errands!) SAMPLING: Yakitori teriyaki, hekka-tofu, chicken, vegetables, chicken katsu, breaded mahi, chicken katsu curry, katsu don, California roll sushi $4.80-5.09. Fried noodle, fried rice, manapua, vegetable egg roll, macaroni salad, rice, pot sticker, chicken stick $.95-3.50 COMMENTS: This a great little hole-in-the-wall, a little tricky to find, but worth the effort. There are always several locals and a few visitors waiting to order and the general consensus seems to be that the yakitori chicken sticks are the best. A very small counter, so most get their local-style food items to go.

ATHENS GREEK RESTAURANT   *Greek*
Located inside the Lahaina Cannery Mall (661-4300) HOURS: 8am-9pm daily.
A fast food Greek restaurant that features gyros, falafel, sausage, and souvlaki shish kebab sandwiches served on pita bread $5.59; $7.59 with salad. Moussaka and pastichio $6.15-8.15; Greek salad $3.25-5.65; spanakopita $1.99. Baklava $1.99; granitas $3 COMMENTS: Limited seating.

BJ'S CHICAGO PIZZERIA ★   *Italian*
730 Front St. (661-0700) HOURS: 11am-11pm, same menu all day (pizza lunch specials until 4pm). SAMPLING: Start with BJ's bruschetta, toasted ravioli, fried provolone, crab cakes, or their newest invention, the pizza-dilla: quesadilla-like triangles of pizza dough with a creamy topping of artichoke, spinach, and cheese ($5.95-9.95). Then order a basic cheese and tomato $8.95/12.95/14.95 (S/M/L) and add your own toppings or try one of their innovative specialties like "BBQ Chicken or Shrimp Thermidor" ($15.65/20.95/23.55). Calzones for one ($5.95) or two ($9.95), too! BJ's specialty salads include chopped Italian, sesame chicken or chopped BBQ chicken ($4.95-9.70); there are lots of pasta dishes ($8.50-13.95), and homemade sandwiches on BJ's freshly baked rolls offer meatball, Italian sub, and three varieties of chicken: BBQ, Caesar, or Italian for $6.95-7.45. COMMENTS: This Front Street landmark is filled with woodwork, murals,

and historic photographs that recreate the look and feel of its former incarnation as The Blue Max. This ninth restaurant in the BJ's chain came to Maui with a good reputation which has only been improved by local owner Jerry Kunitomo. The deep-dish Chicago-style pizza has a crust that is thick, while surprisingly light, and the toppings are fresh and innovative. Wash it down with a festive Tropitini, a spirited ice cream cooler, or BJ's original-recipe Mai Tai made with Grand Marnier. But leave room for dessert. You won't be able to resist the Pizookie n' Cream: a chocolate chip or white chocolate & macadamia cookie baked fresh in a mini-pizza pan and served warm with vanilla ice cream!

THE BAKERY ★   *French/American*
911 Limahana (turn off Honoapiilani Hwy. by Pizza Hut) (667-9062) HOURS: Mon-Fri 5:30am-3pm; Sat 5:30am-2pm; Sun 5:30am-noon. SAMPLING: Chocolate almond and whole wheat cream cheese croissants; coconut macaroons, palm leaves (the Hawaiian version of elephant ears!), and "real" (water-boiled) bagels. Ham or turkey-stuffed croissants or small sandwiches such as turkey dijon. Huge fresh fruit tortes, fudge, and fresh breads (health, natural grain raisin-walnut, olive rosemary) are made here daily. COMMENTS: There's a small deli case with meats and cheeses, and they have added a few tables in front. Arrive early in the day to insure getting the best selections. They're all delicious and it's well worth the stop if you are a pastry lover. Try their stuffed Tongan bread with savory combinations of mushrooms, onions, and chicken!

BUNS OF MAUI   *Bakery/Deli*
Old Lahaina Center (661-4877) HOURS: Mon-Sat 7am-7pm; Sun 8am-2pm. SAMPLING: Overstuffed sandwiches (chicken macadamia, seafood, turkey, tuna, roast beef) on bagel, white or wheat bun $3.99-4.89; deli or fruit salads $1.99-4.79; soups $2.19-2.99. Cinnamon or caramel buns; muffins (from peanut butter to pineapple); brownies, lemon bars, cookies, and single serving cheesecakes and cupcakes $1.89-3.29. COMMENTS: Limited seating; a few tables inside and out.

CAPTAIN DAVE'S ARCTIC WAVE   *Fish & Chips*
Lahaina Marketplace off Front St. (667-6700) HOURS: 10:30am-9pm. SAMPLING: Ono & chips, prawns & chips, clams & chips, calamari & chips or combination platter $5.95-7.95. Grilled ono or chicken sandwich $5.95-6.95 COMMENTS: All main menu fish items can be ordered fried (in 100% canola oil) or broiled and come with French fries and Maui coleslaw (with pineapple) and homemade tartar or cocktail sauce. If you want to go really lean, order Rosie's Special: broiled fish with Thai chile sauce and cole slaw for $5.95.

CHEESEBURGER IN PARADISE ★   *American*
811 Front St., Lahaina (661-4855) HOURS: Breakfast 8-11am; lunch/dinner 11am-11pm. SAMPLING: Omelettes, eggs benedict, loco moco, fresh fruit, macadamia pancakes, Portuguese sweet bread French toast, and super browns (with bacon & cheese) for breakfast $4.95-7.95. The rest of the day, select a classic BLT, Philly-chicken (with lots of onion, roasted peppers & cheese) or cajun chicken sandwich, jumbo cheese dog, Portuguese turkey burger, the grilled "Maui No Ka *Oink*" (ham & cheese) sandwich, their famous "Cheeseburger in Paradise" and a number of vegetarian dishes including a choice of tofu or garden

burger $6.95-8.50. Entree salads, fish sandwich or coconut shrimp $7.25-9.95; chili cheese or seasoned fries, onion rings, calamari and scallops $3.50-6.50. COMMENTS: A casual and fun atmosphere with open-air dining and wonderful views of the Lahaina Harbor and Front Street from the upstairs loft. You can't go wrong with a cheeseburger and fries, and the other "stuff" is good, too! (A little expensive, but they're all served with that great view at no extra charge!) Live music nightly 4-7pm and 8-11pm. Make sure your try some of their tropical drinks, the Lahaina Sunburn, the Lahainaluna Swirl or Trouble in Paradise. (Or if you want to stay *out* of trouble, try the thick and chunky non-alcoholic Oreo cookie smoothie!) It can be crowded at meal times, but the lines move along pretty quickly. (The same owners as Aloha Cantina a few doors down which, at press time, was about to implement a complete change of menu, concept, and name. Be sure to check the Maui Update for the final result!)

CHOPSTICKS OF MAUI   *Chinese*
Wharf Cinema Center (661-1971) HOURS: 9:30am-9pm. SAMPLING: Chicken, beef, pork, vegetable, and seafood dishes served a la carte ($5.75-9.50) or in a mixed plate lunch ($3.75-7.25) Rice, noodles, and soups ($2.50-7.95) plus breakfast specials ($2.99-3.99) COMMENTS: Chinese and local fast food in the former Song's location.

DENNY'S   *American*
Lahaina Square Shopping Center (667-7898) HOURS: Open 24 hours a day. SAMPLING: Traditional Denny's burgers, sandwiches, and dinners plus island favorites like saimin, mahi sandwich, teri burger, local-style plate lunches, fresh catch, and spam & eggs (would that make it a "spam slam"?). Prices from $5 (pancakes) to $15 (steak & shrimp). Breakfast served anytime. Senior specials and kids meals available. COMMENTS: Wine & beer. Second location in Kihei.

HANAMASA   *Japanese/Sushi*
Behind Planet Hollywood on Luakini St. (661-8838) HOURS: Lunch 11am-2pm; dinner 5-11pm. SAMPLING: Lunch plates, selected sushi items or combinations with both $5-8. Appetizers from tofu to soft shell crab $2.75-8.50; grilled beef or ahi salad $14.95. Shrimp tempura & teri chicken or beef combination bentos $14.95-24.95; Donburi & udon $8.95-17.95. Entrees include assorted tempura, chicken or pork katsu, vegetable stir fry, yakiniku, and steak $8.95-13.95. Sashimi $14.75-17.50. Full sushi menu from cucumber ($2.75) to "swim & turn" shrimp or spider roll ($12.95); Lahaina Rainbow roll $15.95. COMMENTS: Using the same concept that has worked so well for Sansei in Kapalua, they offer sushi and/or Japanese food combinations - both at the sushi bar or at one of the small tables at this attractive sushi "house." Upholstered stools at the counter and colorful tablecloths have a country cottage feel, but look closer and there are Japanese fans in the design. Opened May, 1998.

HARD ROCK CAFE ★   *American*
New Lahaina Center, 900 Front St. (667-7400) HOURS: 11:30am-10pm. SAMPLING: Grilled burgers, turkey pastrami melt, "big" BLT, chicken breast or "pig" sandwiches $7.59-8.99; BBQ chicken, ribs or combo $10.29-15.99; pot roast, fresh fish, or T-bone steak $9.59-17.99 Chicken, beef or combination style

fajitas $11.99. Chinese, Caesar, or Kentucky-fried chicken salads plus spring rolls, onion rings, nachos, chicken & spinach dip $5.99-8.99. Old-fashioned desserts like shakes, malts, sundaes, brownies, cheesecake, and a shareable banana split $3.79-5.59. COMMENTS: A lively atmosphere, if the music isn't too loud for you. Fun and interesting memorabilia on the restaurant walls AND in the bathrooms, too: Guitars owned by Eric Clapton, Slash of Guns N' Roses, the Grateful Dead, and Pearl Jam plus Beatle photos and instruments. Homage is also paid to the Hawaii, surfing, and beach rock and roll era, too. Great prices, good food and a trendy reputation makes this a very popular eatery, so there may be a waiting line to get in during peak dining hours. If the kids (or you!) just want a T-shirt, you'll be happy to know that the merchandise outlet has been expanded to five times its original size with walk-in accessibility from inside or out.

HOUSE OF SAIMIN   *Local*
Old Lahaina Center (667-7572) HOURS: Tues-Thurs 10am-2am; Fri & Sat till 3am. Mon dinner only (5:30pm-2am); closed Sun. SAMPLING: Saimin $3.30-4.10-5.10; with special vegetables $6.55. Portuguese soup $3; with rice $3.50. Hamburgers $2.25; egg salad or tuna sandwiches $2; hot dogs $1.60. Wonton $1, BBQ stick $1.30; Haupia Delite $1.90; Beverages $.80. Monday night dinner specials (meatloaf, chicken curry, beef stew, etc.) $5.50 COMMENTS: One big central counter and late night hours - in the tradition of Kauai's Hamura Saimin - though not quite as funky, so probably not quite as much fun!

IL BUCANIERE   *Italian*
666 Front St. (661-3966) HOURS: Lunch 12-2:30pm, dinner 5:30-9:30pm. SAMPLING: Salads and antipasto $4.25-7.95; pizzas $7.95-8.95; pasta $10.95-13.95 plus a few basic sandwiches ($5.50-7.95) for lunch. Dinner entrees of pork chops, rosemary chicken, steak and fish include scalloped potatoes or rice and vegetable $15.95-18.95. Assorted pastas come with clams, mussels, home-made sausage, mushrooms, or meat sauce $11.95-14.95. Shrimp & spinach risotto $14.95; lasagne $14.95; Assorted antipasto and pizzas $5.95-9.95. COMMENTS: Casual atmosphere upstairs in the old Whale's Tale location overlooking Front Street. Live music nightly. (If you're wondering, Il Bucaniere means "The Navigator")

JACK'S FAMOUS BAGELS   *Bagels/Sandwiches*
West Maui Center, Honoapiilani Highway (667-JACK) <WWW> HOURS: 6am-6pm; Sat & Sun till 4 SAMPLING: Mix and match bagel flavors (garlic, onion, macadamia nut, blueberry, jalapeno, sesame, sundried tomato, spinach, coconut, and pineapple) with gourmet whipped cream cheese (garlic herb, veggie, pesto, lox, strawberry, blueberry, jalapeno, pineapple). Bagelwiches of cream cheese & lox, tuna, egg salad, hummus, PB & J, cheese, and turkey $2.25-7.50. Pat's Pizza Melts: cheese, veggie, jalapeno, pepperoni, Hawaiian $3.95-4.75; Melt Downs with turkey, tuna, or ham $5.95. Salads $2.75; Lunch special: Bagel sandwich of the day with bagel chips & large soda $4.95. Coffee drinks $1.25-3.25. COMMENTS: Authentic water-boiled bagels (freshly-made without fat or oils) from a third generation New York bagel recipe. Kihei and Kahului locations have slightly lower prices.

LOCAL BOY'S DRIVE INN   *Local*
Lahaina Square (661-8830) HOURS: 10am-9pm; Fri & Sat till 10 SAMPLING: Sandwiches & burgers ($1.25-2.95); plate lunches and mini-plates ($3.95-5.65); Stir fry & noodles ($6.25-6.75); Snacks like won ton, chili, saimin, and beef stew($1.40-4.75) They also offer "beach paks" with BBQ chicken, teriyaki beef or BBQ short ribs available raw or cooked ($24.50-28.50) COMMENTS: We didn't drive "in" or sleep over "inn," but still liked the big portions and small prices at this small local outlet in the former Jack-in-the-Box location. The Teriyaki Saimin was a surprise: the BIG chunk 'o meat was a little difficult to negotiate so we tried the Teriyaki Beef sandwich. Yummy! The plate lunch with fried scallops were on the spendy end (about $7!). They have a second location in Kahului that offers a lunch buffet and slightly lower prices.

LOCAL FOOD   *Healthy Hawaiian*
Anchor Square, 888 Wainee St. (667-2882) HOURS: Mon-Fri 10am till whenever they run out of food! SAMPLING: Local dishes like shoyu or roast pork, hamburger steak, and sweet & sour spare ribs $5; Friday Hawaiian Plate with lomi lomi salmon, lau lau, chicken long rice, poi or rice $8.50. COMMENTS: Hawaiian food made healthy for the 90's. Little or no salt, no sugar, light oil.

MANGO GRILL   *Burgers/Sandwiches*
Lahaina Marketplace (661-9085) HOURS: 9:30am-9:30pm. SAMPLING: "Tropical" burgers with mango, pineapple & salsa, Kula onion, or papaya & BBQ sauce $5-5.75. Buffalo wings $4.95-8.75; fried chicken with pineapple-plum sauce, chicken nuggets, grilled chicken sandwich $4.95-5.95; Caesar or garden salads $4.50-6.75; hot dogs; mango iced tea $1.50. COMMENTS: Fast food with interesting island touches; order from the take-out window to sit at one of the outdoor tables at the Marketplace.

MAUI BREWS   *Microbrewery/eclectic menu*
Lahaina Center (667-7794) HOURS: Lunch 11am-3pm; dinner 5-9pm; bistro menu 10pm-1am. SAMPLING: The $7.95 Burger & Brew is their signature lunch special or you can get soups, salads, or pizza ($4.95-10.95) plus Philly cheese steak, chicken, fish, or veggie pita sandwich and almost all the dinner pasta or entree dishes at slightly lower prices $7.95-13.95. Grilled Thai calamari; mac nut crusted brie; ahi, salmon, or beef carpaccio; tri-color nachos; or the Tuscan salad (with prosicutto, peppers, pine nuts, olives & gorgonzola) are some of the more distinctive ways to start your meal ($5.95-9.95) then select from a variety of pizzas (the smoked salmon "White" sounds interesting...); pastas (seafood, smoked salmon, chicken & zucchini, sausage & mushroom); and entrees: spicy garlic prawns, baby back ribs, cioppino, scallops, bratwurst, garlic chicken, or veggies with couscous $8.95-19.95. COMMENTS: Casual, island bistro and nightclub (though "bistro" is more descriptive of the innovative menu rather than the size - it takes up a whole building and the bar is big enough to be its own restaurant!) Thin-crust pizza has surprisingly good texture and taste - no cardboard here! Live entertainment and dancing till 2 am. A variety of tropicals & martinis plus 16 brews on tap. Early bird (2 for 1 entrees) from 5:30-6:30; and a keiki menu with their own beer - a root beer float!

THE MAUI CAFE   *Asian/American*
505 Front St. (667-4051) HOURS: 7am-9pm. SAMPLING: Breakfast sandwiches, French toast, omelets, pancakes, and Pigs in a Blanket ($3.50-5.95) plus assorted pastries and muffins ($1.50-2.50). Caesar, pesto pasta, seafood, and fruit salads ($4.50-7.95) and hamburger, turkey, tuna, ham, and club sandwiches ($5.95-7.95). Their specialty Vietnamese Balé sandwich is made with deli meats (pate, smoked chicken, beef & pork), marinated vegetables, cilantro, and gourmet mayo on a fresh roll $7.95. Spaghetti or lasagna $6.50-7.95 PLUS a full menu of Vietnamese noodles and soups, rice plates, spring & summer rolls, clay pot & fish dishes, and Thai stir frys ($6.50-8.95). Even a kids menu with several options all under $3. COMMENTS: This little cafe and bakery has "grown up" to offer a full menu of Asian cuisine along with their popular sandwiches and salads. Renovation and refurbishing has made this a good restaurant choice for breakfast, lunch, or dinner any time of the day. They offer a good selection of coffee drinks, juices, and Italian sodas and now have a bar with wine and beer. They have expanded their Asian menu, and the Balé sandwich is still a specialty, but the item we still hear most about is the spaghetti and meatballs!

MAUI SWISS CAFE   *Swiss-Continental*
640 Front St. (661-6776) HOURS: 8am-7pm; from 10am Sunday. SAMPLING: Swiss breakfast of sliced ham, cheeses, salami, fruit, hard boiled egg, croissant $5.25; filled croissant with coffee $2-4. Hot and cold sandwiches $5.95-6.95 and Kaseschnitten: open faced hot cheese sandwiches $8.95. Pizzas from $5.95 plus toppings; salads $4.75-6.75. COMMENTS: Hot and iced coffee drinks plus ice cream in a variety of ways: scoops (2 for $2!), sundaes, shakes, smoothies and tropical drinks. Daily lunch specials ($5-5.50) include sandwich, Caesar salad, chips and a drink. Hot sandwiches are served on French baguette (turkey & broccoli with cheese & dijon mustard) or boboli bread (ham & salsa, or spicy roast beef with cheese). A good selection of vegetarian sandwiches, too. Imported swiss chocolates for sale. Limited outdoor seating.

MAUI TACOS   *Healthy Mexican*
Lahaina Square (661-8883) HOURS: 9am-9pm. SAMPLING: Potato enchiladas, hard or soft tacos, quesadillas, chimichangas, nachos, and over a dozen varieties of special hand-held burritos in fish, steak, chicken, beef or vegetarian combinations with black beans $1.65-6.95. COMMENTS: Guacamole and salsa made fresh every day. No lard, no msg -- they use only vegetable oil, fresh beans and lean meats. The complimentary salsa bar offers several choices with jalapenos, onions, cilantro, hot sauce and more. Good values! They also have outlets in Kihei and Kaahumanu Food Court as well as the original in Napili Plaza, all owned and operated by Mark Ellman of Avalon.

MR. SUB   *Sandwiches*
129 Lahainaluna Rd. (667-5683) HOURS: Mon-Fri 7am-5pm; Sat till 4. Closed Sunday. SAMPLING: Sandwiches with one or two items like turkey, tuna, egg salad, roast beef and Danish ham $3.95-5.25. Specialties offer larger combinations with 4-5 meats and cheeses as well as chicken salad, turkey and bacon, garden burger and French dip $4.75-7.25. Caesar, chef's, Chinese chicken, garden, and fruit salads and chicken or tuna in half a papaya priced $3.95-5.75.

Fresh fruit smoothies $3.25. COMMENTS: Great choice of breads, too! We've heard from those who know (guys with hearty appetites who work in the neighborhood) that these are some of the best subs on the island. And now they've added "wraps" - chicken Caesar, Salsa, or Ranch rolled up burrito-style in a tasty spinach or jalapeno cheese tortilla. (We tried the Ranch: Plenty of dressing and chock full of chicken, tomatoes, and lettuce - even avocado - we gotta agree with the guys!) They'll pack up a picnic lunch for $6 (with sandwich, chips, fruit, and a slice of their homemade banana, chocolate, blueberry, or poppy seed bread) and even loan you a free cooler - as long as you bring it back.

NAGASAKO OKAZU-YA (DELI)   *Local*
Old Lahaina Center (661-4108) HOURS: 7am-6pm till 1pm on Sundays. SAMPLING: Local plate lunches like teri beef, chicken long rice, pork adobo, beef broccoli, kalua pig & cabbage $4.25-5.95 with sides (corn, rice, pork hash, salad) 25-75¢. Chow fun $2.25; Burgers and sandwiches $1.50-1.95. COMMENTS: The market is closed, but the family is still here. Small patio with benches and tables outside.

NO KA OI DELI   *Sandwiches & Salads/Local*
222 Papalaua Street (facing Wainee) at Anchor Square (667-2244) HOURS: Mon-Fri 8:30am-5pm; Sat 8am-3pm; Sun 6am-10am. SAMPLING: A good variety of subs (French dip, teri chicken or beef, pastrami, and seafood, tuna, egg, or chicken salad) and salads (Caesar, chef, Chinese chicken) plus daily plate lunch specials ($4.25-5.95). No Ka Oi side specialties include crab potato salad, spinach rolls, and boiled peanuts ($1.25-2.75); fountain drinks from $.85; smoothies and shaved ice (with Li Hing Mui powder or vanilla ice cream) run $1.75-3; homemade cookies $.75. Complete picnic baskets feed 2-4 for $12-28. COMMENTS: "Home of the Famous HOP WO Bread": The Hop Wo Store was a landmark on Front Street from 1917 to its closure in 1985 and now a younger generation of this family has begun what they hope, will be a new Lahaina Landmark. "Ono" baking weekends offer manapua and small pies on Saturdays, Hop Wo bread and biscuits on Sundays or cinnamon rolls and twist donuts, $.70-1. Check out 'Da Wall of Yummies for some crack seed and mochi crunch or just stop by and talk story with Laurie Lei Kam and her mother Carolyn!

ORANGE JULIUS   *American/Sandwiches*
Wharf Cinema Center, lower level (661-1579 or call 661-1423 for a recording of daily specials) HOURS: Daily 8am-9pm. SAMPLING: A variety of hot dogs include the more unusual nacho, pepperoni or bacon & cheese dog $2.25-2.90; chicken, tacos, or turkey salads $5-5.50; teriyaki, chili, western, and other burgers $2.95-5; and 4 kinds of nachos including "Irish" with potatoes, bacon, cheese, onions, and ranch dressing $3-4.75. The grilled chicken sandwich is a favorite as are the pita sandwiches with chicken, turkey or veggies ($2.75-4.25) Seasonal Julius flavors include guava-passion, mango, pina colada, or Tropical Julius. Yum! COMMENTS: Owner Kris Krewson has gone far beyond the usual OJ, so we feel they merit a listing. "Kris' Korner" is right next door with breakfasts of Portuguese sausage, spam, or banana pancakes served until 10:30 ($4-5); local plate lunches and daily specials like beef stroganoff, turkey enchilada, lasagna, corned beef & cabbage, pot roast, lau lau, buttermilk chicken, and

a once-a-month "Thanksgiving" turkey dinner are $5.50-6.50. Kris also has fresh-squeezed lemonade and "real" shave ice: $1.95 or $2.75 with azuki beans and Roselani ice cream!

PANCHO AND LEFTY'S   *Mexican*
Wharf Cinema Center, 658 Front. St. (661-4666) HOURS: 11am-10pm (breakfast 8am-noon) SAMPLING: Breakfast burrito; machaca (eggs, peppers, onions, tomato, and shredded beef); huevos rancheros; chorizo con huevos; and a variety of egg dishes, mac nut pancakes, waffles, and French toast $4.95-8.95. Seafood, taco, or authentic Tijuana Caesar salad $7.95-1095; fajitas, tamales, rellenos, burritos, tacos $5.95-10.95 and specials like carnitas, seafood or steak enchiladas, carne asada, and pechuga pollo relleno (chicken breast stuffed with jack cheese and chiles, dipped in egg batter and fried) $9.95-14.95. Buffalo wings, potato skins, nachos, quesadillas, and a variety of skinny dippers $6.95-8.95. Fried ice cream, macadamia nut pie, cheesecake, or cinnamon crispies $2.95-3.95. COMMENTS: Happy Hour 3-6pm and 10pm-midnight. At the Wharf from 1986-92, Pancho and Lefty's has returned (to the same spot!) with a menu and prices that haven't changed much since. (If it ain't broke . . .)

PANIOLO COFFEE CO.   *Coffee Drinks/Light Meals*
Lahaina Center, 900 Front St. (661-8488) HOURS: Food 8:30am-2:30pm; ice cream, coffee drinks, shave ice, smoothies till 6 (9 on Fridays) SAMPLING: Breakfast wrap (eggs, cheese, tomatoes, and onions with salsa in a flour tortilla), veggie scramble, eggs & bacon or bagels with lox, pesto or tomato & onion $3.50-6.25. Veggie burger or quesadilla; tuna, smoked turkey, or chicken salad sandwich $4.80-5.95. Scones, banana bread and cinnamon buns from $1.95. COMMENTS: Small coffee bar with counter seating. Cowboy-western motif inside with an "awning" of cool mist around the outside.

PIZZA HUT   *Italian*
127 Hinau, Lahaina, (661-3696). HOURS: 11am-10pm daily; Fri and Sat until 10:30pm. Seven locations on Maui from Honokowai to Kihei and from Kahului up to Pukalani. We've heard some good reports on their salad bar and their $7.49 lunch buffet and $9.49 Wed & Thurs dinner buffet. COMMENTS: For years we have driven by, and never stopped. After all, we have Pizza Huts at home, so why eat here? Because we do get letters from our readers telling us that the pizza is great and so is the salad bar.

PLANET JUICE AND JAVA ★ *Juice/Coffee/Light meals*
Lahaina Square Shopping Center (661-8842) HOURS: 7am-6pm; 8am-5pm Sat & Sun SAMPLING: Juiced to order carrot, spinach, celery, apple, orange juice $3-4; wheatgrass juice $1.50-2.50; pineapple, mango, papaya, blueberry smoothies $3.75. Boosters 50¢ each. Espresso, latte, mocha, Italian soda $1.75-3.25. Breakfast served all day. Daily selection of soups, salads, pastas, and pizzas ($3.50-6.95) Pita sandwiches of tuna or chicken curry salad $4.25. Wrappers and rice pots $4.50-6. COMMENTS: Not only are the fresh juices and smoothies wonderful, but so is the food! Their wrappers were the originals on Maui and they are still the ones who do 'em best: these tightly rolled whole wheat

tortillas are filled to the edge with yummy stuff (i.e. rice, vegetables, non-fat yogurt and peanut sauce) and served with an unusual assortment of sweet potato, taro, and other chips. They were also the first to see the juice bar trend and offer it in combination with a coffee house! Dining indoors or out.

SANDWICH ISLAND *Sandwiches*
Lahaina Cannery Mall (661-6128) HOURS: 9:30am-9pm daily. SAMPLING: Ham, turkey, pastrami, roast beef, egg salad, tuna, and vegetarian sandwiches $4.95; Caesar, oriental, somen, and cold pasta salads $4.95-5.25; cheese ravioli, spaghetti, or freshly made pasta of the day $5.25. Clam chowder and saimin $2-3.50; plate lunch specials or spaghetti dinner $6.50.

SIR WILFRED'S ESPRESSO CAFE *Sandwiches/coffee*
Lahaina Cannery Mall, (667-1941) HOURS: 10am-8pm. SAMPLING: Menu includes quiche, lasagna, salads, and a variety of sandwiches including Monte Cristo, turkey & avocado, chicken salad wrap, and Philly steak $4.25-6.95. Bagel with salmon lox or waffle with whipped cream and fresh fruit, both $5.95. Pastries, cookies, cheesecake to enjoy with a great cup of coffee or an espresso drink. COMMENTS: The small, pleasant eatery recently expanded to encompass over half the retail store. Gourmet coffees, Hawaiian name mugs, and tropical jams & jellies available for purchase. Also available is flavored Hawaiian and 100% Kona coffee by the pound. They also have the only walk-in humidor on Maui, so you cigar and pipe smokers will be delighted!

SUB SHACK PIZZA & DELI *Sandwiches plus*
Dickenson Square at Wainee and Dickenson (661-7666) HOURS: 7am-9pm, till 5pm Sundays. SAMPLING: Breakfast burritos, omelettes, egg sandwiches, and French toast ($3.25-5.75). Meatball sub (with Grandmas' sauce and no fillers!), BBQ pork, veggie, Reuben, prime rib, and chicken or eggplant parmesan are the hot sandwiches $4.99-6.35; the corned beef, BLT, and roast beef, tuna, turkey, chicken salad, and Italian subs are served cold $4.75-6.99. Caesar, tortellini, and shrimp Milan salads $4.75-6.50; jumbo vegetable stuffed potato $5.25; lasagna, spaghetti, ravioli or chicken alfredo $6.25-7.75; pizzas $12-16.50. COMMENTS: Daily plate lunch specials; yummy homemade salads; hot, hearty sandwiches and the "pizza-de-resistance," a white pie with fresh garlic, chunks of tomato and big pieces of shrimp on a crust that tastes as good as a loaf of French bread!

SUNRISE CAFE *Sandwiches/Light meals*
693A Front St. (661-8558) HOURS: 6am-6pm. SAMPLING: Pancakes, waffles, or French toast are topped with fresh fruits and choice of syrup $5.95; bakery items; coffee drinks fresh juices, and smoothies $1.95-3. Quiche or savory-topped bagels $6.95; homemade soups $2.95; and salads - Hawaiian, Greek, Caesar, and Chinese chicken - are $6.95. Plate lunches $7.95; gourmet sandwiches (kalua pork, teri chicken, roast beef, turkey, ham, salami, club, vegetarian, and the tangy and delicious mango BBQ chicken breast $5.95. Lasagna, chicken fettucini, eggplant parmesan, and stuffed pasta shells are served with focaccia bread $8.95. COMMENTS: This is a very small, quaint eatery with some nice, outside tables or food available to go. It's all homemade and all good, but the Hawaiian specialties stand out: kalua pork salad with Maui onions, pineapple, steamed cabbage,

and papaya; stuffed pasta shells with macadamia nut pesto; and mango BBQ chicken breast or kalua pork as a plate lunch or a sandwich.

SUSHIYA ★ *Local*
117 Prison Street (661-5679). HOURS: Mon-Fri 6am-4pm, take out available. SAMPLING: Beef teri plate $5.50, chicken teri plate or chicken katsu $5.25, hamburger $3.95, a la carte items include saimin $2.25, kim chee, corned beef hash, macaroni salad from $.60-1.35. Plate lunches and daily specials $3.95-5. COMMENTS: This place is a real find in West Maui. In operation since 1965, Okcha Ito (the daughter-in-law) took over the family business in 1979 - almost 20 years ago! Visitors are discovering what the locals have known for years. Inside you'll find family style tables and benches. It's a clean, comfortable self-service restaurant with no frills. Some interesting selections too -- how about a side order of sweet potato, eggplant, or spam tempura for just 60¢? Escape the hustle and bustle of in-town Lahaina and take a short walk for some local-style dining!

TAKE HOME MAUI *American*
121 Dickenson (667-7056) HOURS: 6:30am-5:30pm. SAMPLING: Bagels and breakfast pastries every morning $1.10-5.95. Fresh fruit smoothies $3.25, sandwiches $4.80-5.95, salads $3.50-5.95, lasagna, quiche, Maui empanada $2.35-4.50. Ice cream and sodas in the freezer. Papayas, pineapples, onions, and Hawaiian coffee are among the items to be shipped or taken home. They offer free airport or hotel delivery. They also do catering. COMMENTS: Limited seating. "Moon Meal" boxed lunch (for that looong road to Hana): sandwich, salad, chips, fruit & cookies $8.95. The staff is helpful and friendly - lots of aloha here! Fruit smoothies are delicious and their sandwiches are good, too!

THAI CHEF *Thai*
Old Lahaina Center (667-2814) HOURS: Lunch 11am-2:30pm Mon-Fri, dinner from 5pm nightly. SAMPLING: Thai crisp noodles, sateh, green papaya salad, Thai toast, Evil Prince, Cornish game hen, honey lemon chicken $5.95-13.95. Seafood saute, Thai scampi, lobster curry, garlic squid $9.95-14.95 COMMENTS: A very lengthy menu ranging from noodle dishes to salads, seafoods, vegetarian fare, and curry dishes. Chef's Suggestions offer combinations for 2, 3 or 4 people. Entrees available in mild, medium or hot (!) - second location at the Rainbow Mall in Kihei.

VILLAGE PIZZERIA *Italian*
At 505 Front St. (661-8112) HOURS: 11am-9pm; Sundays from noon. SAMPLING: Pizza is available in Neapolitan style (thin crust) or Sicilian (thick crust). A 14" plain pizza starts at $12, a combo of 4 items at $17, slices from $2.25. Calzone ($9.95) and pasta entrees (spaghetti, lasagna, ravioli, ziti) with salad $11.95-17.95; a la carte from $9.95. Meatball, sausage & peppers, chicken or veal parmigiana sandwiches served with pasta $6.75-7.95 COMMENTS: The clam and garlic pizza ($17-24.50) is a specialty here along with cannoli, tiramisu and other homemade Italian desserts. Wine and beer.

ZUSHI   *Japanese*
Anchor Square, 888 Wainee St., (667-5142) Lunch 11am-2pm; dinner 5-8pm; COMMENTS: Shrimp and vegetable tempura, chicken and pork katsu, or curry $4.75-6.24. Dinners from $6.72-12.40 include chicken or beef teriyaki, cooked fish, unagi bento, fried chicken or fish, combination dinner or "Zushi Ten." COMMENTS: Located across the street from McDonald's. A little expensive for the fare and atmosphere.

MODERATE

BLUE LAGOON TROPICAL BAR AND GRILL *American*
658 Front. St. on the lower level of the Wharf Cinema Center (661-8141) HOURS: Breakfast 9am-noon; continuous menu 10am-9:30pm. SAMPLING: Omelettes, pancakes, waffles, and full English or American breakfasts $5-8. Sandwiches include French dip, burgers, "volcano chicken" or chicken club, fresh fish, BLT, crab cake, and tuna or avocado melt $7-12 plus Caesar, cobb, papaya boat, or spinach salads $6-11. "British" fish & chips, chicken quesadilla, coconut shrimp, and macadamia-crusted fresh fish are the house specialties $10-18. For appetizers, try the shrimp martini, steamed clams, onion or calamari rings, lumpia, or hot wings $6-12; gourmet pizzas from $8. COMMENTS: Eat in the courtyard of the shopping center (surrounded by waterfalls and koi ponds) at the state-of-the-art bamboo and koa wood bar or off of the colorful, "statement-of-the art" table tops. Additional seating inside in a small recessed area with bamboo and koa wood to make it look like a Polynesian hut.

BUBBA GUMP SHRIMP COMPANY RESTAURANT & MARKET
Seafood & shrimp shack
889 Front Street (661-3111) HOURS: 11am-10:30pm. SAMPLING: Start with Peel 'n Eat SHRIMP; Bubba's Far Out Dip (classic spinach with a twist); Lahaina Wild Wings (spicy, but not too); or All-American Nachos made with French fries instead of tortilla chips $3.59-9.99; sampler trio $11.99. Caesar, SHRIMP or fried-chicken salad $6.99-8.99. Entrees include Lt. Dan's Drunkin SHRIMP, Mama Blue's Crab Pot, Southern Charmed Fried SHRIMP, Alabama SHRIMP Spaghetti (with spicy citrus chile sauce), plus SHRIMP and seafood combination "buckets," rib-eye steak, baby back ribs, and veggies & rice $12.59-17.99. Bread pudding, Dr. Pepper float, and Alabama-style hula pie $2.99-4.75. COMMENTS: Inspired by the award-winning movie *Forrest Gump*, Lahaina is the third in a chain that began in Monterey and San Francisco. "Gumpisms" prevail -- from the "Run Forrest Run" sign that signals for service to the "box of chocolates" (that "life is like") on the dessert menu. Like newspaper is to fish and chips, the funky boat house decor and tin bucket table service is to Bubba Gump's. The friendly service and "fun food" presentations are more than enough to keep you interested, so it's impressive that they offer cut-above extras: tartar sauce with lime and orange rind, cocktail sauce with Tequila, homemade cole slaw, and "real" key lime pie. The all-day menu makes it cheap for dinner, a bit expensive for lunch. Portions can be hit and miss: some are huge; others on the small side, but overall good food and good value. The retail store sells souvenirs and clothing and they plan on a catalog being available soon.

CHART HOUSE ★ *American*
1450 Front St. (661-0937). HOURS: Dinner 5-10pm. SAMPLING: Lobster cakes, coconut shrimp or calamari, steamed artichoke, and sashimi appetizers $6.50-9.95. Steak, prime rib, crab legs, lobster, ginger-citrus shrimp, rack of lamb, ahi, herb-crusted or teri chicken, and fresh ahi, salmon, or catch of the day. Entrees include a particularly good Caesar or fresh garden salad (all you an eat!) and hot squaw bread made with sweet molasses $16.95-25.95. They also offer some good homemade desserts including mud pie, chocolate mousse, and authentic key lime pie. COMMENTS: There is a comfortable atmosphere with lots of wood and lava rock. The limited number of oceanview tables are a hot commodity and require that you arrive when they open. They still have one of the best keiki menus we've seen. "Awesome" prime rib. The adult entree portions are huge and we love their doggie bag! (Trust us, you'll need it.) The coconut calamari was an unusual option; good texture with surprising coconut and calamari tastes. The ahi was a nice thick "steak," cooked on the rare side in ponzu sauce with cilantro lime butter. Additional locations in Kahului and Wailea. Reservations accepted.

COMPADRES ★ *Mexican*
Lahaina Cannery Mall. (661-7189). HOURS: 8am-10pm; breakfast till noon. SAMPLING: Breakfast ($5-10) features chorizo, enchilada, and burrito egg dishes, huevos rancheros, "grande" omelettes, and a Compadres original of carnitas or carne asada with eggs on a large tortilla $5.99-9.99. Gringo specialties include pineapple or macadamia pancakes, and sweet bread French toast $5-6. Quesadillas Internacionales include Baja (Gulf prawns in spicy BBQ sauce), Texas (fajita steak or chicken with Jack cheese) and Thai (chicken, Jack cheese, sprouts, peanuts, shredded carrots and peanut-chili sauce) $7.99-10.50. Mexican pizza, tortilla soup, fajita nachos, chingalinga, six-layer dip, sopes (Mexican bruschetta) and Caesar, cobb, taco and fajita salads are the distinctive starters ($4.75-11.50) while arroz con pollo, camarone (shrimp) rancheros, tequila chicken, seafood enchilada, fish tacos, prawn burrito, and a variety of rellenos are some of the innovative entrees for $8.99-14.99. Mexican club, chicken & guacamole, and Santa Fe chicken are the south-of-the-border sandwiches $7.99-9.50. COMMENTS: We don't usually recommend many chain restaurants, but Compadres earns a star for its innovative menu and all-around good dining fare. Taco bar for $1 chicken or 50¢ beef tacos on Tuesdays from 4-7pm; 50¢ nachos on Fridays.

HECOCKS *American*
505 Front St. (661-8810) HOURS: 7am-10pm, bar 8am-2am. SAMPLING: Omelettes, egg dishes, pancakes, French toast; sandwiches and burgers $4.75-8.95. Dinner entrees of steak, lamb, ribs, chicken, fish & seafood $16.95-22.95; pastas with sausage, clams, or prawns $16.95-20.95. COMMENTS: As you can tell by the hours, it's more bar than restaurant and a waste of the ocean view. You can do better.

HONG KONG SEAFOOD RESTAURANT   *Chinese*
658 Front St., Wharf Cinema Center. (661-1681) HOURS: Open daily for lunch and dinner, 11am-9pm. SAMPLING: Sweet & sour shrimp, lemon chicken, mu shu pork, hot & spicy shrimp, ginger chicken, sweet & sour pork, and shark's fin soup $4.95-29.95. No msg. COMMENTS: The old Harborfront location on the second floor of the Wharf Cinema Center has been completely renovated and decorated with Chinese antiques and artifacts. The same owners also have the Royal King's Garden at the Pukalani Shopping Center. Scheduled to open July, 1998. (Not open as we go to press.)

KIMO'S ★   *American/Seafood*
845 Front St. (661-4811) HOURS: Lunch 11am-3pm. Dinner daily 5-10:30pm, bar until 1am. SAMPLING: Burgers, salads, and sandwich lunches of chicken, steak, reuben, tuna & cheddar, grilled ham, swiss & turkey ($6.50-9.95) plus sashimi, shrimp, veggie plate, and artichoke pupus ($4.95-7.95) are available downstairs daily. Dinner at the bar (limited menu) 5-11pm. Dinner entrees include Kimo's Caesar salad, freshly baked carrot muffins and sour dough rolls, and steamed herb rice. Fresh fish of the day (prepared in one of five ways) is still just $19.95; beef, seafood or island favorites such as seafood rigatoni, kushiyaki, Koloa ribs, and Polynesian chicken $14.95-17.95. Vegetarian pasta $10.95; prime rib (while it lasts) $23.95. Keiki menu $4.50-5.95. COMMENTS: They have a waterfront location and, if you're really lucky, you'll get a table with a view. Our experience has been very good service and well prepared fresh fish. They must be doing something right because they've been doing it since 1977! This is where you find the original hula pie - it's still the biggest and the best and turns heads every time one of the whipped cream skyscrapers comes out of the kitchen. They also have a bar on the lower level and an ocean view which provides a pleasant sunset.

KOBE JAPANESE STEAK HOUSE ★   *Teppanyaki/Sushi Bar*
136 Dickenson (667-5555) HOURS: Dinner 5:30-9:30pm. SAMPLING: Teriyaki chicken $13.90, sukiyaki steak $16.90, teriyaki steak & chicken combo $17.90, hibachi steak $19.90. Seafood & steak combos from $22.90, steak from $23.90. Seafood specials range from $15.90 (orange roughy) to $37.90 (lobster). Dinners include soup, shrimp appetizer, vegetables, rice, and tea. COMMENTS: A sister of the Palm Springs and Honolulu restaurants, they offer teppan cooking (food is prepared on the grill in front of you) and the show is as good as the meal. Keiki menu offers either hibachi steak or chicken teriyaki $6.90-8.90. Sunset specials (served 5:30-6:30pm) $10.90-13.90. Sushi and sashimi items available individually or in chef-selected tray assortments. The sushi bar is popular with local residents and they're very accommodating to visitors. They'll make up your favorite sushi item if it is not on their menu.

LAHAINA COOLERS ★   *American*
180 Dickenson St., Dickenson Square, (661-7082) HOURS: Breakfast 7-11:15 am, lunch 11:30am-5pm, dinner 5pm-midnight. SAMPLING: Four versions of Eggs Benedict plus pancakes, omelettes, and a black bean breakfast burrito are available for breakfast $5.50-8.50. Homemade pastas offered in appetizer or entree

portions ($8.25-14.75) include fettucini with chicken & mushrooms or smoked salmon, shrimp pesto linguini or penne carbonara. The evil jungle pasta with grilled chicken and spicy peanut sauce is their best seller and also comes as a pizza for $10.75. Fresh fish tacos, Moroccan chicken spinach enchilada, and artichoke or sausage pizza combos are available for lunch or dinner ($7.50-9.95). Mini crab cakes, spinach & feta cheese quesadilla, and fried artichoke heart pupus or papaya chicken, Caesar, veggie, and Greek salads run $4.75-8.75. Dinners come in larger sizes and offer additional selections of fresh fish and steak from $16.95. The Riviera banana split of fried banana with ice cream and carmel sauce and their chocolate taco filled with tropical fruit and berry "salsa" are the don't-miss desserts $4.90-5.50. COMMENTS: "Because Life is Too Short to Eat Boring Food", the food items here are always exotic and unique. There's a good kid's menu and an innovative new wine list with all selections available by the glass. At $7.75-10.75, the single-serving pizzas are ample for lunch, but a little small for a hearty dinner eater.

LAHAINA FISH COMPANY   *Seafood-American*
831 Front St. (661-3472) HOURS: Lunch menu served from 11am-midnight; dinner 5-10pm. SAMPLING: Salads, burgers, chicken, fish, and crab cake sandwiches; shrimp, fish, or calamari & chips baskets; cold seafood & sashimi, potstickers, and spring rolls are available all day ($6.95-12.95). For dinner, there are several preparations of fresh fish along with scallops, scampi, oysters and a variety of seafood pastas ($8.95-21.95). Hand carved steaks, stir-fry, or chicken $9.95-22.95. COMMENTS: Pleasant setting on (in fact, right over) the ocean.

MANGO CAFE & PIE SHOP   *American*
Lahaina Cannery Mall (661-5595) HOURS: Breakfast 7:30am-noon, lunch 11am-5pm, dinner 5-9:30pm. SAMPLING: Early bird (7:30-8am) short stack 99¢; fresh pastries, eggs Benedict, omelettes (from pineapple to egg fu young), turkey hash, and a variety of loco moco plus pancakes, waffles or French toast with their special glazed topping of mango (in season) and tropical fruits with caramelized brown sugar and just a touch of brandy! $6.99-8.99. Burgers, hot turkey or meat loaf, corned beef, ahi sandwiches, and daily plate lunch specials $6.99-9.99. A variety of salads: spinach, health, cobb, shrimp, and curried or oriental chicken $3.49-12.99. Dinners include fresh fish, chicken lau lau, liver & onions, mahi & chips, curried shrimp cooked in papaya, turkey pot pie, and roast turkey with all the fixings (both made with "real" turkey!) $9.99-14.99. The new salad bar ($6.99), Polynesian chicken skewers, pineapple shrimp, or their award-winning mango bread are good for starters $3.49-7.99; bread pudding or their special mango, apple & coconut pie make for a nice ending. COMMENTS: If this "tropical Marie Callender's" is not casual enough for you, you can stop by for pastry & coffee at their bakery & pie shop or enjoy a cool treat at Bubbie's Ice Cream Parlor right inside. They also have karaoke Fri & Sat from 8pm-midnight.

MOOSE McGILLYCUDDY'S   *American*
844 Front St., upper level of Mariner's Alley, a small shopping alley at the north end of town (667-7758) HOURS: Breakfast 7:30-11am ($1.99 Early Bird 7:30-8:30), lunch 11am-4pm, dinner 4-10pm. ($8.95 dinner Early Bird special 4-7pm).

SAMPLING: Breakfast meats and unusual egg preparations served in a quesadilla or on potato skins $4.25-8.95. The 21 (count 'em!) omelette options include the 12-egg "Moose" for $19.95. Flavored pancakes, country biscuits and banana muffins $1.50-5.95. A variety of burger and sandwich combinations plus chicken, tostada and garden salads $5.95-8.95. Pupus include wings, nachos, quesadillas, skins, cheesey fries, Maui onion rings, and hot spinach & artichoke dip $4.95-10.95. Dinner entrees include steak, prime rib, coconut shrimp, fresh catch, chicken piccata, fish tacos, BBQ or teri chicken, and shrimp & scallops Yucatan (with vegetables and chipotle cream sauce over pasta) $9.95-15.95. There's chocolate moose for dessert (what else?) and an extensive selection of fun, tropical drinks. COMMENTS: Weekly specials include ribs on Monday; all-you-can-eat crab on Thursday; and steak & lobster on Saturday. The bar is in the center with a dining room on one side; a music & dancing room on the other! This place really gets hopping at night with lots of young adults and live music that may be on the loud side for some.

NANNY'S KITCHEN   *German*
658 Front Street, Wharf Cinema Center (667-5718.) HOURS: 10:30am-2:30pm; dinner 5-10pm ($11.95-18.95). SAMPLING: Hearty omelettes or homemade potato pancakes for a late breakfast $6.75-8.50; bratwurst, kebab, and sauerkraut combinations; and several varieties of schnitzel including a sandwich (with toasted cheese on the *outside!*) $6.95-12.95. Dinners include pork chops, sausage, spaghetti with mushrooms & pork strips, and schnitzel with peppers, wine & mushroom, cream sauce, or tomato $10.95-15.95. A variety of accompaniments like potato salad, spaetzle (noodles), red cabbage, homemade bread, or pan-fried potatoes offer additional German touches. Save room for the *apflestrudel!* COMMENTS: Family-owned German restaurant (the only one on Maui) has seating indoors or outside in their *"biergarten"* patio. The long tables and benches (and keg of draft German beer) make every month look like Oktoberfest!

PIONEER INN BAR & GRILL   *American*
Pioneer Inn (661-3636) HOURS: Breakfast, lunch and dinner. SAMPLING: Macadamia nut pancakes and cinnamon raisin bread French toast $7.25 & $7.95 are the breakfast specialties. Other items include eggs Benedict, fresh fruit, Portuguese sausage, and Belgian waffles $2-9. Lunches offer soups, salads, sandwiches, and "island style plates" $6-11. Seared or traditional ahi sashimi, Caesar salad, spring rolls, or North Pacific butter clams with garlic are a few of the appetizers. Dinners include shrimp scampi with spaghettini, roasted lamb rack Polonaise (fresh mint sauce), choice steaks, veal piccata or parmesan, fresh local fish and shellfish, and a selection of vegetarian entrees $13-24. For dessert they have a fresh tropical fruit banana split. COMMENTS: Dinner is served outside in the central Courtyard accompanied by live Hawaiian music.

PLANET HOLLYWOOD   ★ *California Cuisine*
744 Front St. (667-7877). HOURS: 11am-10pm, bar till 11pm. SAMPLING: Texas nachos, pizza bread, blackened shrimp, parmesan spinach dip, and chicken crunch (breaded with Cap'n Crunch cereal!) are a few of the appetizers $6.50-9.95; pizzas (Hawaiian, spinach & artichoke, NY calzone) run $9.50-10.95; and

Caesar, Hollywood, and Asian salads are $8.95-12.50. Platters with ribs, steak, or teri chicken are $12.95-19.95, burgers $8.50-9.75. Pastas include Thai shrimp, spicy chicken & tomato, penne chicken & broccoli, and L.A. lasagne $9.95-14.50; chicken, beef and shrimp fajitas $12.95-13.95; and sandwiches of steak, smoked turkey, or cajun chicken $8.95-9.75. Be sure to save room for desserts like tiramisu cheesecake, ebony and ivory brownie, or fruit fajitas ($6.50-6.95) COMMENTS: As everyone probably knows by now, shareholders of this project include Arnold Schwarzenegger, Bruce Willis, Sylvester Stallone, and Demi Moore among others. Surprisingly, the food was not just an afterthought and matched the fun with sweet-tasting Cap'n Crunch chicken; L.A. Lasagne (fried like a large egg roll, stuffed with cheese and sauce and "towering" above ordinary pasta dishes!); and desserts like Ebony (dark chocolate) and Ivory (blond) brownie with chocolate and white chocolate ice cream, chocolate and caramel sauces, and their newest: a festive platter of roll-your-own dessert fajitas with fresh strawberries, bananas, and apples, fruit compote, and vanilla ice cream ready to wrap in a cinnamon tortilla and top with chocolate chips, white chocolate shavings, and peanuts! There's also an extensive menu of specialty drinks named after famous films. Similar to Hard Rock Cafe, they feature a collection of movie memorabilia including Cleo, the man-eating plant from *Addams Family Values*, the 5-foot whale model from *Free Willy*, the ship's figurehead from the original *Mutiny on the Bounty*, and Mel Gibson's motorcycle from *Lethal Weapon 3*. There's also Maui-style memories like Keanu Reeves surfboard from *Point Break* and Spencer Tracy's priest costume from *The Devil at 4 o'Clock* (filmed here in Lahaina) along with some recent additions from *Titanic*. The downstairs level is colorful and lively, the upstairs submarine room is very effective with dim lighting and cozy booths. TV monitors show films and videos. And no surprise here, you're also be able to buy T-shirts, watches, sunglasses, varsity & leather jackets, beach towels or bags, and even swim suits in their merchandise shop. The atmosphere alone merits a star, but we liked the food, too!

RED LANTERN   *Chinese*
1312 Front Street. (667-1884) HOURS: Continuous menu from 11am-2am with lunch specials from 11-4. SAMPLING: Lunches (with rice, soup, egg roll and pickle salad) include sweet & sour pork, beef & broccoli plus curry, cashew, lemon, or fragrant chicken $5.99. Beer $1. Vegetable, chicken, beef, pork, noodle, and rice dishes ($7.25-13.95) include fragrant pork or sesame beef, or string beans with minced pork. Duck and seafood dishes are slightly higher ($11.95-18.50) Drunk chicken, thousand-year-old eggs, egg foo young $6.75-11.95. Family dinners served for more than two persons ($10.95/16.95). COMMENTS: Night owls will appreciate the full menu served until 2 am. Live jazz on Sundays from 9pm-midnight. The basic dishes are ok, but it's the Chef's Specials ($12.95-28.95) that really set them apart: seafood in bird's nest, stuffed shrimp & pork in eggplant, sea cucumber with oyster sauce, and honey walnut shrimp that is yummy enough to save for dessert! If it is in your budget, try the Peking duck, abalone in oyster sauce, or minced lobster at $38.95 each.

RUTH'S CHRIS STEAK HOUSE *Upscale Steakhouse*
Lahaina Center, 900 Front St. (661-8815) HOURS: Dinner only. SAMPLING: Steaks, lamb, fresh Hawaiian fish. Extensive wine list. Signature New Orleans-style bread pudding for dessert. COMMENTS: Scheduled to open Summer, 1998. (Not open as we go to press.) Elevated dining room with ocean view. Rated #1 steak house by the Robb Report with 60 locations nationwide including Honolulu.

SAM CHOY'S LAHAINA *"Gourmet Local"*
Lahaina Center, 900 Front St. HOURS: Lunch and dinner 5:30-9pm. SAMPLING: Similar menu to their Kahului restaurant with lunch offerings of fried poke, tripe stew, and "Noodlemania" served with fresh vegetables and edible flowers in a fluted tortilla shell plus good old fashioned meat loaf, roast chicken, beef stew, steak, burgers, sandwiches $6.50-8.95. Appetizers like brie won ton or crab stuffed shrimp $6.50-8.50 followed by dinners of seafood lau lau, lamb chops, roast duck, osso bucco, ahi salad, steak, fresh fish, or tofu lasagna $18.95-26.95; Hawaiian bouillabaisse $31.95. Desserts include bread pudding and frozen espresso pie $4.50-6.95. COMMENTS: Already "big" on the Big Island and on O'ahu, Sam Choy opened his first Maui restaurant in February, 1998. "Firecracker, A Chinese Bistro with Sam Choy" (also at Kaahumanu Center in Kahului) was expected to open in the summer and this two-story West Maui location was scheduled to open soon after with a separate area that will feature a more "specialized" version of Sam's cuisine. Neither were open as we went to press. (For additional information see listing under Sam Choy's Kahului.)

SMOKEHOUSE BAR & GRILL *American BBQ*
1307 Front St., behind The Cannery (667-7005) HOURS: 11am-9pm; till 10 Fri & Sat. SAMPLING: Scallops, calamari or onion rings, zucchini sticks, shrimp $5.95-7.95. Charbroiled burgers, BLT, fresh fish, or breast of chicken, plus smoked ham, turkey, beef or pork sandwiches $5.45-7.95. Grilled meat or fish salads $8.95-12.95. BBQ ribs, chicken, hot sausage combinations or broiled steak, shrimp, fish, chicken or burgers and smoked ribs and chicken are available a la carte $10.95-16.95 or as a complete dinner with corn on the cob, baked potato, cornbread with macadamia honey butter, and choice of steak fries, coleslaw, BBQ baked beans, or rice $12.95-18.95. COMMENTS: Choice of baby back pork ribs or beef ribs. Smoked and charbroiled meats are all from natural Hawaiian kiawe wood. Hula pie or fried ice cream for dessert; full bar. Dining indoors or on their oceanfront patio.

YAKINIKU TROPICANA *Japanese/Korean*
843 Wainee St., Old Lahaina Center (667-4646) HOURS: 10am-10pm, sushi bar noon-1am. SAMPLING: Soup, noodles, stew, broiled & steamed fish, pan-fried octopus, and BBQ beef, tongue, shrimp, chicken, tripe or yakiniku $8.50-18.50. Pot stew $32.50-38.50 (for 2). Lunch specials (served till 3pm) include fish chun, shrimp tempura, beef, pork chop or chicken plate, fried man doo $7.50-9.50. Sushi and sashimi $3.80-6.50; combinations from $12.50. COMMENTS: The menus are printed in English, Korean and Japanese and most of the employees speak Korean as their native language. Yakiniku means table grilled, so you'll be able to enjoy watching your own meal be prepared.

EXPENSIVE

AVALON ★ *Hawaiian Regional Cuisine*
844 Front St., (667-5559) HOURS: Continuous menu 11am-9pm; sushi bar 5-10pm. SAMPLING: Start with seared ahi, chicken satay, fish pot stickers with ponzu sauce, summer rolls with macadamia nut sauce, fresh sugar snap peas with chile sauce, or Maui onion rings with tamarind ketchup $5.95-8.95. Lemon grass or Chinese chicken salad at $11.95. Entrees include luau roasted garlic seafood, mango BBQ mahi, Indonesian lamb chops, pesto macnut opakapaka, spicy charred rare ahi, Asian pasta, or tempura shrimp $22.95-27.95. Cheeseburger, fresh fish, or chicken jack sandwiches served with taro chips $9.95-13.95. Vegetarian selections include lemongrass or Chinese tofu salad, Gado Gado and stir-fried vegetables $9.95-14.95. Caramel Miranda, a fruit and ice cream platter to share, is Avalon's only dessert. COMMENTS: Avalon, was the West Pacific island paradise where King Arthur and other heroes went to in the afterlife - but happily, you don't have to wait that long! Owner/chef Mark Ellman continues to offer the best in traditional and new Hawaiian Regional Cuisine with specialties like Chili Seared Salmon Tiki Style - as much a visual as a culinary experience. A layered "tower" salad of mashed potatoes, eggplant, salmon, greens, island and tomato salsa, it is served with plum vinaigrette for $22.95. The Gado Gado salad ($13.95) comes from the island of Bali and is a tasteful blend of romaine lettuce, cucumbers, tofu, steamed vegetables on a bed of brown rice topped with peanut dressing. Equally delicious is the Chinese tofu salad at $9.95. Both are large portions. Chinese duck with ginger shiitake plum sauce is available on Fri & Sat nights $17.95/23.95. The look here is '40's Hawaiian with antique aloha shirts adorning the walls, ceiling fans whirring and wonderful multi-colored oversized dishes. The original (inside) dining area has been converted to a sushi bar headed up by sushi chef Norio Yamamoto, formerly of Harry's Sushi Bar in Napili. The bar features ten seats and additional seating around a few tables.

CHEZ PAUL ★ *French*
Five miles south of Lahaina at Olowalu (661-3843) HOURS: Two dinner seatings 6:30 and 8:30pm. Closed Sundays May-Nov. SAMPLING: Entrees include fresh fish poached in lobster sauce or champagne, scampi, lobster, sliced loin of lamb, veal, pepper-crusted fresh salmon, and duck $22-36. Dinners include French bread, soup or salad and two vegetables. Escargot, seafood crepe, pate, lobster salad, artichoke, and shrimp are available as appetizers $6-16. Save room for some very special desserts! COMMENTS: This small restaurant -- in what could be a tiny village in France -- opened in 1968 and has maintained its high popularity with excellent food and service for over 30 years! It's not surprising they have won numerous dining awards. They recently expanded their kitchen and now have a "walk-in" wine cellar. The wine list is excellent, although expensive. Wines are also available by the glass. Reservations required. Their menu adds, "no pipes or cigar smoking and keep the cry babies at home."

DAVID PAUL'S LAHAINA GRILL ★ *New American*
127 Lahainaluna at the Lahaina Hotel (667-5117) HOURS: Nightly from 6pm. SAMPLING: The menu is described as New American Grill Cuisine with a flair

for the Southwestern. The menu is constantly changing, but David's popular Tequila Shrimp and Firecracker Rice has become a permanent fixture. Kona coffee roasted lamb, Maui onion crusted seared ahi, roasted squab, seafood risotto or lasagna, and kalua duck are other possible entrees $23-37; eggplant Napoleon, lobster-crab cake and macadamia smoked salmon are good to start with for $8-16. For dessert, try the triple-berry pie, Irish truffle cheesecake, or chocolate crescendo $6.75; sampler dessert selection, $12. COMMENTS: David Paul Johnson has won local and national awards for his innovative cuisine and artistic presentations. The seating area is attractively furnished with a crisp look to it. Black and white floors are contrasted with a beautifully detailed fresco blue/green ceiling and French impressionist art. While beautiful, it somehow lacks the cozy ambiance of one of our favorite restaurants just across the street, Gerard's. It has a masculine look, like the grill room of an elegant European hotel. The original dining area was only half the size and a small annex is now used for private dining and special "Chef's Table" dinners. The bar in the main restaurant is wide and suitable for dining and socializing. You can order appetizers and dinner or enjoy the seafood bar and late night menu until 11pm every evening. The food is excellent and David Paul's has a continually changing menu, which keeps your dining options interesting! (A four-course prix fixe menu offers a good tasting selection for $50 per person.) The last time we were there, we tried the Caesar salad which was excellent and an ample portion for two people. The fresh grilled opakapaka was also a hearty portion accompanied by a tomato/onion zucchini sauce served finely chopped over eggplant. The signature tequila shrimp is available in mild, medium or hot. Medium proved to be plenty warm! David Paul's recently opened a second location on O'ahu.

GERARD'S ★ *French*
In the lobby of the Plantation Inn at 174 Lahainaluna Rd. (661-8939) HOURS: 6-9pm. SAMPLING: The menu changes seasonally with entree selections that might include roasted Hawaiian snapper with orange & ginger butter sauce; seafood ragout, braised beef Burgundy, duck confit with garlic petals, turban of veal sweetbread, or lamb & pork cassoulet $26.50-32.50. Hors d'oeuvres (appetizers to you; pupus to us) offer shiitake and oyster mushrooms in puff pastry; terrine of foie gras, ahi and Hawaiian snapper carpaccio, ravioli with escargots, and sauteed calamari with lime and ginger $8.50-18.50. Salads are just as intriguing with grilled quail and upcountry greens with seasonal fruits and hazelnut oil dressing; Kona lobster & avocado; papaya and grapefruit with smoked salmon; and spinach with grilled scallops $9.50-18.50. Desserts are all priced at $7.50 and include Grand Marnier souffle, strawberry melba, chocolate mousse profiteroles, macadamia nut chocolate cake, and homemade exotic sorbets. COMMENTS: Dining at Gerard's is just as wonderful as it was years ago when it was in its old, small, hole-in-the-wall location up the street. The ambiance is equal to the fine cuisine with old-fashioned cane chairs crisply attired in tropical patterned upholstery. And although (like everyone) we are partial to Maui's sunset ocean views while dining, sitting beneath a mango tree on the veranda of the Plantation Inn while dining at Gerard's is hard to beat. A wine list features a range of moderate to expensive selections from California, France and the Pacific Northwest.

I'O *Pacific Rim*
505 Front St. HOURS: Dinner COMMENTS: Scheduled to open Summer, 1998. (Not open as we go to press.) Pacific'O was expected to open this second restaurant next door in the former Old Lahaina Cafe location with the Old Lahaina Luau providing a nightly Hawaiian revue.

LONGHI'S ★ *Continental*
888 Front St. (667-2288) HOURS: Breakfast 7:30-11:30am, lunch 11:45am-4:45pm, dinner 5-10pm (upstairs from 6) SAMPLING: Fresh fruits, eggs Benedict or Florentine, baked frittata, quiche, and freshly baked cinnamon rolls and pastries are available along with more traditional breakfast fare $3-12. Lunch pastas (canneloni, manicotti and fettucine variations) and entrees include smaller (cheaper!) versions of Longhi's signature dinners: Prawns Venice or Amaretto, shrimp or scallops Longhi, lobster canneloni, and ahi torino $8-16. Among the sandwich offerings is Dona's favorite peking duck for $8.50 and salads feature toppings of chicken, shrimp or lobster $5-16. In addition to the ones already mentioned, a la carte dinner entrees also include filet Longhi, lamb chops, and several Italian preparations of chicken and veal $19-28, pastas from $16, vegetables $6-9. The dessert tray is hard to resist with ever-changing options like chocolate souffle with ganache, lychee sorbet, fresh peach and cardamon pie, strawberry-carrot cake, chocolate zuppa, coconut haupia cream pie, or espresso torte, from $7. COMMENTS: After more than 20 years on Maui, Longhi's has become a legend in Lahaina. Part of the legend is a verbal menu, recited to you by a friendly waiter who will probably pull up a vacant chair to "chat" about the evening's selections. Other Longhi's legends include the to-die-for jalapeno, pizza, and gorgonzola breads served with your meal; the casual setting with lots of windows open to view the bustling Lahaina streets; the accommodating breakfast hours that allow for both early risers (Christie) and the laziest of late sleepers (Dona) to enjoy the fresh baked goods and tasty egg dishes; and of course, Bob Longhi himself, the "man who loves to eat" and hopes you do, too. (As the author of a new cookbook, he also hopes you love to cook!) Longhi's offers espresso and a good wine selection with valet parking nightly.

PACIFIC 'O *Contemporary Pacific cuisine*
505 Front St. (667-4341) HOURS: Lunch 11am-4pm, dinner 5:30-10pm, pupus served until midnight. SAMPLING: Lunch includes Caesar salad with roasted peppers, sashimi, smoked & seared prawns over penne pasta, mahi & chips, Japanese breaded chicken sandwich, and shrimp satay $6.50-11. Dinners start with shrimp won tons, pot stickers, and ahi tartare $8-12; entrees offer sesame seared or coconut macadamia crusted fish, smoked chicken, roast veal chop, kiawe grilled shrimp, sesame crusted lamb, and fresh fish tempura $22.50-29. COMMENTS: Unusual and artistic presentations. Pupus are served on a marble slab with sauces painted in colorful designs. A great ocean front location although the atmosphere is a bit casual for the pricey menu. Unfortunately, the complete disregard for PR and customer service by one of the two owners deprives the good food of a star. Live jazz Thurs-Sat.

SCAROLES ★ *New York Style Italian*
930 Wainee St., Lahaina (661-4466) HOURS: Lunch Mon-Fri 11:30am-2pm; dinner nightly 5:30-9pm. SAMPLING: Lunch items are chicken piccata or marsala, veal or chicken parmesan and meatball sandwiches, homemade sausage lasagna and other pastas, appetizers, soups, and salads $7.95-12.95. Dinners start with stuffed clams, escargot, calamari, steamed mussels, or a selection of salads $6.95-12.95 or pastas prepared with seafood, veggies, mushrooms, gorgonzola, ham or bacon $13.95-16.95. Dinners feature shrimp scampi or fra diavalo; chicken parmigiana and saltimbocca, veal calvados or pizzaiola plus sausage & peppers, raviolis and eggplant parmigiana $19.95-26.95. COMMENTS: Scaroles advertises itself as "The New York side of Lahaina" and we'd tend to agree. Located on the Kaanapali side of Lahaina the restaurant is an open air, smallish, but cozy, dining room for 30 inside and a table or two outdoors. A basic Italian black and white color scheme is the decor here. All entrees are served with homemade soup or salad and fabulous warm-from-the-oven onion rolls. They now have NY style brick oven pizza (like pesto, feta & sundried tomato) from $10.

KAANAPALI

INEXPENSIVE

CASTAWAY CAFE *American with a touch of the islands*
Maui Kaanapali Villas Resort, 45 Kai Ala Dr. (661-9091) HOURS: Breakfast 7:30am-2pm; lunch 11am-5pm, pupus 2-9pm, dinner 5-9pm. SAMPLING: Breakfast burrito, omelettes and egg dishes, Belgian waffle, eggs benedict, loco moco, macadamia, pineapple or banana pancakes, and cinnamon-raisin French toast $4.50-6.95. Caesar, tuna, chicken salads $5.95-8.95; burgers, hot dog, French dip, club, BLT, hot turkey, and fresh fish sandwiches $5.75-7.95. Fish & chips $6.95. Dinners start with calamari, coconut shrimp, crab cakes, artichoke hearts, or steamed vegetables $5.95-8.95 followed by entrees of Chinese pepper steak, BBQ pork chops, tequila prawns, macadamia chicken, shrimp or chicken stir-fry, steak, smoked marlin & prawn pasta, fish tacos, or chicken Cordon Bleu "Hawaiian" (stuffed with ham, pineapple & Swiss cheese then rolled in coconut & herb breading) $12.95-17.95. Desserts include the Chocolate Treasure Chest (brownie, macadamia nut ice cream, chocolate syrup & whipped cream) and "Sosume" (get it?) macadamia nut ice cream pie on an Oreo cookie crust with chocolate fudge, & whipped cream. Lunch salads and sandwiches also available at dinner. COMMENTS: A cozy, poolside restaurant that's reminiscent of a beach cabana, yet it's full-sized with a patio that overlooks the lawn and the ocean. Their Tuesday "2 for 1" Pasta Night is popular and a great value: choose from a variety of pastas priced $12.95-14.95 along with special Italian appetizers of fried mozzarella, grilled zucchini, or bruschetta (priced "1 for 1") at $3.95-5.95. Entertainment Fri-Sun during Happy Hour (3-6pm). They also offer daily chef's specials and can accommodate special meal requirements or preparations.

255

COLONNADE CAFE *American*
Westin Maui, Promenade Level overlooking lagoon of Koi fish with waterfalls and tropical birds. HOURS: 6-11am for continental breakfast; 11am-2pm for sandwiches, salads, and yogurt. COMMENTS: At 5:30pm this becomes the Sen Ju Sushi Bar.

COOK'S AT THE BEACH ★ *American*
Westin Maui, north side of the swimming pool (667-2525) HOURS: Breakfast & buffet 6:30-11am; lunch 11am-2pm and dinner 5:30-9pm. SAMPLING: Daily breakfast buffet $17.95 adults, children $1.50 per year. Other breakfast menu items include Egg Beaters frittata, Continental, fresh fruits, omelettes, eggs benedict, and flavored pancakes $7.25-12. Lunch offers sandwiches, burgers, and pizzas along with chicken quesadilla, poke roll, Thai chicken wings, and summer rolls $5.95-11.95. Caesar, smoked fish, spinach, lobster, and Nicoise salad $6.95-14.50, Dinner features their prime rib buffet with soup, salad bar, baked potato and toppings, fresh catch, vegetable, rice, and corn-on-the-cob, and a very nice dessert cart for $19.95. Regular menu entrees include chicken & Jawaiian spare ribs, pork tonkatsu, shiitake mushrooms (filled with mashed potato); grilled shutome, NY steak, and a variety of appetizers and salads $16-21.95. Pizza & pasta $9.95-11.95. COMMENTS: A good family restaurant with a varied assortment certain to please everyone. Fairly reasonable prices for a resort!

DELI PLANET *American*
Embassy Vacation Resort (661-2000) HOURS: 9am-10pm. SAMPLING: Deli sandwiches include tuna or chicken salad, cheese, hot reuben or build your own with choice of bread, cheese, meat and garnish. Alone or with salad plate or soup $4.95-7.25. COMMENTS: A small store has grocery items and videos.

FOOD COURT (AT WHALERS VILLAGE)
The Food Court at Whalers Village has five outlets on the lower level: *Pizza Paradiso* has pizza, spaghetti, salads, garlic sticks, and submarine sandwiches, and has recently added breakfast. (667-0333); *Ganso Kawara Soba* is a Japanese Noodle Shop (667-0815), *Yakiniku Hahn* serves Korean food (661-9798), *Maui Yogurt* (661-8843) has sandwiches such as cheese and egg salad, turkey or avocado and garden or fruit salads in the $4-5 range, and McDonald's offers its usual fare (667-6674).

GANSO KAWARA SOBA
(See Food Court at Whalers Village)

GARDEN BAR *American*
Westin Maui, located near the beach (667-2525) HOURS: 9am until midnight serving a poolside menu 11am until 6pm. Cocktails. SAMPLING: Club, ahi tuna, deli, or veggie sandwiches. Caesar, spinach, or smoked fish salad. Burgers, pizzas. Thai chicken wings, poke roll, tri-color corn chips with salsa, and vegetarian summer rolls. $4.95-11.95 COMMENTS: Guitar music and Val's Seafood Bar during Happy Hour, 3-7pm. Sashimi, California roll, oysters, shrimp, and crab claws $1.25-5.

HONOKOWAI OKAZUYA & DELI   *Local/Eclectic*
3600 Lower Honoapiilani Hwy., AAAAA Rent-A-Space Mall (665-0512)
HOURS: Mon-Sat 10am-2:30pm; 4:30pm-9pm. Closed Sundays. SAMPLING:
Chicken katsu, Mongolian beef, panko fried mahi, teriyaki steak, veggie frittata,
Schezuan eggplant, egg fu young, Grandma's spicy tofu, pasta primavera,
spaghetti with meatballs or Italian sausage $5.45-6.95. Beef black bean chow fun
$6.95. Hot sandwiches (meatball, Italian sausage, turkey or tuna melt, broiled
chicken, mahi) plus turkey, ham, club, BLT $5.25-6.45. COMMENTS: Former
chefs from Ming Yuen and Buzz's Wharf now offer what they call the "Best
Take-out in Town" - an eclectic selection of local, Italian, Japanese, deli and
vegetarian. Lunch & dinner plates come with rice and a choice of macaroni salad
or fresh, colorful stir-fried vegetables that definitely make these some of the
"healthiest local plates in town."

KAANAPALI MIXED PLATE ★   *American-Hawaiian*
Kaanapali Beach Hotel (661-0011) HOURS/SAMPLING: Breakfast buffet 6-
10:45am for $8.50; Ethnic lunch buffets feature a different theme each day:
American, Japanese, Italian, Chinese, Hawaiian and mixed plate 11am-2pm for
$8.50; prime rib dinner buffet 4-7pm $9.95, 7-9pm $12.50. COMMENTS:
Pleasant coffee shop, decorated with donated mementos that reflect the diverse
ethnic and cultural background of the hotel employees. A description of the
display items and explanation of the cultural foods is featured in a souvenir
booklet given at each table. All buffets include salad bar, beverages, and dessert.
The best value in Kaanapali, especially for the hearty appetite!

KAU KAU GRILL & BAR   *American*
Poolside at the Maui Marriott. (661-1200) HOURS: Early coffee 5:30am; continental breakfast 6am-7am, limited egg dishes until 11am. Lunch and snacks
11am-4pm; bar menu till 5. SAMPLING: Lunch menu includes cheeseburgers,
salads, burgers, and sandwiches. The more unusual offerings include papaya
filled with chicken macadamia salad, roast turkey avocado tortilla roll, grilled
mahi sandwich with spicy aioli, shrimp quesadilla, and veggie pita $6-8.
COMMENTS: Open-air bar and wide-screen tvs. A poolside Pizza Hut kiosk
offers personal to medium-sized pan pizzas for $3.50-16.75 from 11am-7pm
daily. The price of a cup of coffee ($2.25) may be an incentive to give it up, but
the cup (paper) is refillable all day. Or purchase one of their travel cups and it
is refillable with the beverage of your choice during your stay.

LAGOON BAR   *Sandwiches/Pupus*
Sheraton Maui (661-0031) HOURS: 2:30-8pm. SAMPLING: Limited poolside
menu has burgers, hot dogs, sandwiches, and salads $6-9.75 plus assorted sides
and appetizers $2.50-6. Teriyaki, beef or chicken bowl $7.95. COMMENTS:
This is where you can see Sheraton's famous cliff dive ceremony off Black Rock
at sunset followed by live entertainment till 8pm. The Honu Snack Shop also
offers light snacks poolside from 10:30am-2:30pm.

LOBBY BAR & SUSHI   *Sushi/Sashimi*
Maui Marriott lobby (667-1200) HOURS: Thurs-Mon 5-10pm. SAMPLING:
Nigiri sushi $5-7; sashimi $9.95, Maki sushi from $4.75; specials (spicy tuna,

salmon skin, Unakyu, Nikko, and 69 roll) $6.50-11.45. Combinations $18/28. COMMENTS: A casual gathering place to enjoy a variety of sushi and sashimi along with a selection of beverages that includes premium sakes, plum wines, and Japanese beers $3.50-8.

MADE IN THE SHADE *American*
Royal Lahaina Resort (661-3611) HOURS: 11am-4pm. Variety of grilled burgers (including vegetarian) $6.50-7.50 plus teri beef, herb chicken, and fresh fish sandwiches $8.25. (With cole slaw, potato chips, pickle, and beverage $9.50-10.50) Hot dogs $3.75-6.50; Caesar and chicken Caesar pita salads $7-8.50. Chili $1.50; fresh fruit cup $2. COMMENTS: Poolside Hawaiian "hut."

THE MAKAI BAR ★ *American*
Maui Marriott (667-1200) HOURS: 4:30pm-midnight. Located lobby level, Lana'i wing. COMMENTS: Open air cocktail lounge with sweeping ocean view of the island of Lana'i. Great gathering place with nice sunset vistas and live music nightly. Their pupu menu has proven very popular over the years starting with their early night nachos ($1.50) to their late night shrimp fettucine ($6.50). In between the mini-roast beef sandwiches, potato skins, manapua, nachos, quesadillas, tako poke, sushi, sashimi and, ceviche are also affordably priced from $2-6.75.

MAUI YOGURT (See Food Court at Whalers Village.)

OHANA BAR AND GRILL *American-Italian*
Embassy Vacation Resort (661-2000) HOURS: 11am-10pm. SAMPLING: Poolside selections include burgers & sandwiches, salads, pizza, and appetizers. Kalua pork or huli huli chicken sandwich, shrimp quesadilla, tuna croissant, spring rolls, coconut shrimp, nachos, chicken wings, onion, mushroom, or calamari rings, and BBQ baby pork ribs with mango sauce $5.95-9.50. COMMENTS: Full bar & nightly entertainment.

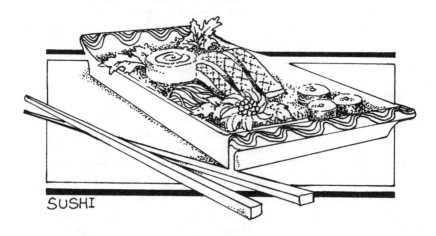

SUSHI

PIZZA PARADISO *Pizza/Italian*
Honokowai Marketplace, 3350 Lower Honoapiilani Hwy. (667-4992) HOURS: Breakfast 7:30-10:30am; lunch/dinner 10:30am-10pm. SAMPLING: Belgian waffles, omelettes, breakfast pastries $2.50-6.75. Gourmet pizza; hot & cold paninis (sandwiches) in traditional meat ball or sausage plus innovative varieties like chicken pesto & sundried tomato, roast vegetable & hummus, or spinach artichoke & gorgonzola; and salads that are equally intriguing: Caesar pasta, penne primavera, tofu & seaweed, broccoli & red pepper, potato & caramelized onion, tabouli, Greek, and Basmati rice $2.50-6.95. Pastas come with a colorful choice of red, creamy white, pesto green or clear olive oil sauces - almost two dozen varieties with everything from shrimp & calamari to artichoke hearts & roasted peppers, $4.95-5.95. Ice cream, smoothies, frozen yogurt, gourmet sundaes, crepes, and pastries: cream caramel with lychee, warm mango crisp, cannoli, tiramisu, Grand Marnier chocolate cake $4.95-5.95; plus coffee drinks, beer & wine. COMMENTS: The original Pizza Paradiso, located in the Whalers Village food court, has gotten accolades for their homemade pies made with fresh herbs, mozzarella and secret sauce. This new, expanded location sounds like a dream come true! Inexpensive gourmet cuisine in a casual setting open both for early breakfast and some sweet & serious nighttime "afters." Scheduled to open summer, 1998. (Not open as we go to press.) Let us know what you think!

REEF'S EDGE LOUNGE *Pupus/Light fare*
Sheraton Maui (661-0031) HOURS: 5:30-11pm; nightly entertainment 8:30am-11pm. SAMPLING: Asian summer rolls, chicken wings, dim sum basket, short ribs, chicken & beef skewers, oysters $6.75-9.50; cobb or chef's salad; chicken or fresh fish Caesar $8.75-12.50. Cheeseburger, turkey club, French dip, or ahi focaccia sandwich $9.95-10.75. Soup, fries, onion rings, nachos $4-6. COMMENTS: Located adjacent to the Keka'a Terrace

ROYAL OCEAN TERRACE LOUNGE *Pupus/Sandwiches*
Royal Lahaina Resort (661-3611) HOURS: Open from 11am-11pm; appetizers and lite meals 4-10pm. SAMPLING: Appetizers of shrimp cocktail, smoked salmon, and sashimi; Chicken cobb or Caesar salad; seafood chowder or baked Maui onion soup 4.25-9.75. Hot pupus offer island crab cakes, buffalo wings, ahi tempura California roll, baked garlic prawns, plus vegetable, four-cheese, or sausage pizza $7.95-10.75. Burger, prime rib or steak sandwich, and pita-style club wrap run $8.50-11.50. They also offer a "grazing menu" of Maui onion soup, Caesar salad, and baked potato for $10.50 plus a shrimp, chicken, teri steak, lobster, or fresh fish kabob priced $2.50 to $6. COMMENTS: Attractive lounge overlooking the pool and the ocean. Sunset torch lighting ceremony at 6:30pm followed by Hawaiian musical entertainment.

ROYAL OCEAN TERRACE RESTAURANT *Buffets*
Royal Lahaina Resort (661-3611) HOURS: Breakfast buffet 6-10am; nightly dinner buffets 5pm-9pm. SAMPLING: Breakfast buffet of fruit, cereal, eggs & meats, oatmeal & cereals, bread pudding, bakery selections, omelette station, Japanese items plus griddle & potato dish of the day $11.50A, $5.75C. Each night, a different selection of themed buffet dishes are added to a basic salad bar

of almost two dozen items and bakery buffet of breads and desserts, all offered at $14.95. Monday-Oriental, Tuesday-Italian, Wednesday-Paniolo, Thursday-South of the Border, Friday-Seafood & Pasta, Saturday-Island Style, and Sunday-Down Home (which has, for example: roast turkey, pot roast, baked ham, mashed potatoes, country gravy, beef vegetable soup, carrots vichy, and biscuits.) COMMENTS: The Royal Ocean Terrace is now housed in the former Alii Terrace, an attractive, oceanfront annex located between the main building and Beachcombers restaurant.

ROYAL SCOOP *American (Sandwiches/Ice Cream)*
Royal Lahaina Resort. (661-3611) HOURS: 6am-10pm. SAMPLING: Limited selection, but a few salad and sandwich items, coffee specialties & espresso, homemade baked goods, and, of course, ice cream! $4-6 COMMENTS: Old-fashioned ice cream parlor, their fresh hot cones are made to order.

SEA DOGS *American*
Westin Maui (667-2525) Poolside snacks at a convenient "quick food" cart between the pool and the beach. HOURS: 10am-5pm. SAMPLING: Pizza, sandwiches, salads and shaved ice.

SUNDOWNER BAR *Sandwiches/Pupus*
Sheraton Maui (661-0031) HOURS: 10am-6pm. SAMPLING: Limited poolside menu has burgers, hot dogs, sandwiches, and salads $6-9.75 plus assorted sides and appetizers $2.50-6. Teriyaki, beef, or chicken bowl $7.95. COMMENTS: The Honu Snack Shop also offers light snacks poolside from 10:30am-2:30pm.

TIKI GRILL *American*
Kaanapali Beach Hotel courtyard HOURS: 11am-8pm. SAMPLING: Teri beef or chicken skewers, Caesar or fruit salads, nachos, turkey or tuna pitas, plus burgers and hot dogs $4.95-6.95. Sunset Pupu (3-8pm) include chicken wings, won ton, spring rolls, calamari rings, and a free hula show beginning at 6:30 on the courtyard stage. The Tiki Bar stays open till 10 serving your favorite tropical drink specials.

YAKINIKU HAHN (See Food Court at Whalers Village.)

MODERATE

BASIL TOMATOES *Italian*
Royal Lahaina Resort (661-3611) HOURS: Dinner 5:30-10pm. SAMPLING: Antipasto selections of stuffed mushrooms, carpaccio, steamed artichoke, and fried calamari, zucchini, or cheese - even fried green tomatoes! $5.99-11.99. Tomato & basil, Caesar, or gorgonzola salads $7.99-12.99; pastas with pesto, herbal, tomato, or Alfredo sauce $14.99-19.99. Entrees include lasagna, seafood ravioli, scampi, veal or eggplant parmesan, chicken manicotti, cheese tortellini, osso bucco, Tuscan steak, stuffed pork chop, or mixed grill $15.99-26.99. Desserts range from Italian ices to banana crepe or tiramisu priced $3.49-5.99.

COMMENTS: Located at the entrance to the Royal Lahaina Resort. Basil Tomatoes' award-winning focaccia bread served with all entrees. Children's menu; coffee drinks; early bird specials 5:30-6:30pm.

BEACHCOMBERS *Oriental-Polynesian*
Royal Lahaina Resort (661-3611) HOURS: Dinner 5:30-9:30pm. SAMPLING: King crab legs $15.95, snow crab legs $13.50, live Kona lobster $16.95, lobster tails $16.95, and prime rib: 1/2 lb. $12.95, "Lahaina" cut $18.95, with crab legs $18.95, with lobster tail $16.95. In addition, they usually features a Friday night, all-you-can-eat prime rib & seafood special (like prime rib & crab legs) served with Beachcombers salad, freshly baked sour dough bread, baked potato, and fresh vegetables from $23.95. COMMENTS: At press time, the Beachcombers menu was being revised and several new items were expected to be added to the entrees listed above: along with appetizers of Ahi Tempura California Roll (with crabmeat & avocado), and basket of dim sum (Asian appetizers) served with watermelon chile sauce $9.50-11, they'll offer their award-winning Beachcombers salad of Kula greens, Hana tomatoes, feta cheese, Maui onions, and bagel chips ($5) as well two entrees that both took first place honors at the yearly "Taste of Lahaina" food festival: Thai Salmon Shioyaki (fresh broiled salmon marinated with kafir lime leaf, lemon grass & fresh basil and served with mango vinaigrette and Moloka'i sweet potato hay), and Olala Rack of Lamb (marinated with soy, garlic, ginger, Maui onion, & chile peppers, garnished with ogo & pohele fern relish, and served with Asian risotto). They were also planning on adding a sampler platter of all three award-winners $19.50-24.95.

CORAL REEF RESTAURANT *Hawai'i-Pacifica*
Sheraton Maui, 2605 Kaanapali Parkway (661-0031) HOURS: Dinner only 5:30-9:30pm. SAMPLING: Appetizer menu offers steamed clams, ahi carpaccio, baby back ribs, potato maki sushi, or seafood cocktail $6.75-11.75; lobster chowder, spinach or Caesar salad $5-7.95. Additional specials might include summer rolls, eggplant Napoleon, lemon grass crab cakes, macadamia nut scallops, or smoked duck soup $5-10. Entrees of steak, roasted chicken, prime rib, fresh fish, seafood linguine, mushroom & asparagus risotto, seared salmon, gourmet pizza, herb crusted prawns, or chicken Cordon Bleu ($13.50-24). Dinner specials might offer nori-wrapped salmon, lobster ravioli, cajun ribeye, veal schnitzel, seafood taco, brie-stuffed filet mignon, or braided salmon Wellington $17-28. Ginger-mocha creme brulee, tiramisu, or Grandma's Baked Apple Pie (served hot from a skillet) are always available for dessert $5.25-7. COMMENTS: This is the same menu (and same prices) they offer in the Keka'a Terrace in their more casual, open-air atmosphere. But if you feel like "dressing up" (in Hawai'i that means no shorts!), Coral Reef offers dining in a more upscale ambiance.

HULA GRILL ★ *Hawaiian Regional/Seafood*
Whalers Village Shopping Center, on the beach (667-6636) HOURS: Dinner 5-9:30pm, Barefoot Bar & Cafe 11am-11pm. SAMPLING: The Barefoot Bar serves a continuous menu for lunch or dinner starting with a selection of dim sum (mac nut & crab won tons, black bean egg rolls, and spicy chicken wings) as well as coconut calamari, Tahitian poisson cru, and smoked marlin $5.95-8.95. Entree-sized Caear, Chinese chicken, shrimp pasta, fruit, and vegetable salads plus

burgers, and assorted sandwiches $7.95-11.95. Fish & chips, fish tacos, and kiawe wood pizzas $8.95-10.95. Additional dim sum appetizers in the dining room include goat cheese & mushroom ravioli, garlic prawns, scallop & lobster potstickers, and poke rolls $6.95-9.95. Entrees offer teriyaki steak or ahi, crab & corn cakes, mac nut roasted opakapaka, shrimp & scallop pasta, crab legs, Hawaiian chicken, firecracker mahi, vegetarian gumbo, BBQ pork spareribs, scampi, and wok-charred ahi, $14.95-24.95. COMMENTS: The Hawaiian Regional Cuisine designed by award-winning Chef Peter Merriman focuses on Hawaiian fish and seafood. The casual oceanfront restaurant, reminiscent of a 1930's Dickey-style beach house, is surrounded by tropical gardens and ponds. The interior has a homey atmosphere with a cozy library room for a waiting area. Each room feels like part of a home and a collection of antique hula dolls are on display throughout. The Barefoot Bar is thatched and surrounded by "indoor" sand. There is an exhibition cooking line in front with a large kiawe grill/BBQ, an imu-style oven for the pizzas and a bar-counter to sit and eat and watch it all. The Hawaiian-style Chinese dim sum is a real treat and the wok-charred ahi is the fantastic. You can order it as an appetizer which means you don't have to miss out on the crusty firecracker mahi mahi - baked with chili and cumin aoili and served with black bean, Maui onion, and avocado relish. Good kids menu, too!

KEKA'A TERRACE   *American*
Sheraton Maui, 2605 Kaanapali Parkway (661-0031) HOURS: Buffet and a la carte breakfast 6:30-11am; Lunch 11am-5pm; dinner 5-10pm. SAMPLING: Buffet breakfast $17.95 ($10.95 continental) and omelettes, corned beef hash, fruit flavored pancakes, Belgian waffle, French toast, eggs benedict $8.75-12; Japanese breakfast $18. Cobb, Caesar, mahi & shrimp, fruit salads $8.50-13; Philly cheese steak, reuben, smoked turkey club, chicken and open-faced turkey or roast beef sandwiches $8.95-12. Appetizers like chicken wings, nachos, soup, or the Hawaiian Quesadilla (with smoked beef, cheese, guacamole, and pineapple mango) $4-6.50; beef curry, spaghetti, or pasta primavera entrees ($8.25-9.95). (See CORAL REEF listing for dinner menu.) COMMENTS: Casual, all day dining with views of the ocean and the resort's tropical lagoons. The dinner menu here is exactly the same as Coral Reef - same menu, same prices - but the ambiance and "dress" there is more upscale.

LEILANI'S ★   *American-Seafood*
Whalers Village Shopping Center, on the beach (661-4495) HOURS: Beachside Grill 11am-11pm, dinner 5-10pm. SAMPLING: The Beachside Grill, located on the lower level beachside of the restaurant, features pupus (shrimp, calamari, buffalo wings, pork-veggie egg rolls, cajun cheese fries, and seafood chowder ($3.50-8.95) and casual menu fare like burgers; salads (cobb, grilled chicken); tuna, veggie, roast beef, or teri chicken sandwiches; pizza; and Hawaiian local plates $6.95-9.95. Seafood fettucine, Malaysian shrimp, ginger chicken, baby back pork ribs, teri chicken & steak brochette, rack of lamb, and prime rib (while it lasts) $15.95-23.95. Catch of the day $19.95. Cheeseburger $8.95, spinach, mushroom & cheese raviolis $10.95. Dinners come with San Francisco sour dough bread, oriental rice, and house salad. Try Kimo's hula pie, chocolate

triple layer torte, or chocolate mousse $3.50-4.95. COMMENTS: The outdoor lounge and terrace dining room are right on the beach offering one of the best sunset viewing spots in Kaanapali. A sister restaurant to Kimo's, Leilani's has been here for years and is a good bet for family dining. Specialties are prepared on lava rock broilers in koa wood ovens. Kids menu. Dinner reservations advised.

LUIGI'S PASTA & PIZZERIA *Italian*
Kaanapali Resort, by the golf course (661-4500) HOURS: Daily 5:30-9:30pm, bar until 2am. SAMPLING: Greek or Caesar salad, seafood stuffed mushrooms, fried calamari, Italian sausage, or fresh asparagus for starters $4.99-8.99. Entree selections of seafood pescatore, mixed grill, veal marsala, scampi, scallops or mahi mahi Alfredo, and eggplant, veal or chicken parmesan $13.99-19.99. Pizza combinations include Hawaiian, cheeseburger and a South Seas special with curry sauce, bananas, onion, peppers, macadamia nuts and shrimp: small $10.99-16.99/large $15.99-27.99. South Seas also available in pasta along with lasagna, manicotti and fettucini Alfredo with chicken and mushrooms $10.99-17.99. COMMENTS: Same owners as Basil Tomatoes and Mango Cafe. (Kaanapali Pizza Pub downstairs delivers Luigi's full menu from 5:30pm-2am.)

MOANA TERRACE ★ *American-Buffet*
Maui Marriott Hotel (667-1200) HOURS: 6:30am-10pm. SAMPLING: Breakfast 6:30-11:30am, lunch 11:30am-2pm, dinner 5-10pm, dinner buffets Fri-Sun (soup and salad bar on other nights) 5pm-9pm. Early Birds 5-7pm. SAMPLING: Breakfast specialties include chicken hash, "crunchy" French toast, macadamia pancakes, and roast vegetable omelette $7.95-12.75. Buffets $13.50/$16.50. Several dinner entrees are available for lunch ($14.95-17.95) along with burgers, Pizza Hut pizza, and sandwiches like grilled chicken on focaccia, mango BBQ imu pork, turkey with mango cranberry relish, mahi on Maui onion bread, and seared ahi BLT $9.25-11.25. Dinner entrees include pesto grilled mahi, roast vegetables & penne pasta, baby back ribs with mango BBQ sauce, grilled sugar cane shrimp, and NY strip steak with crispy Maui onions $14.95-18.95; burgers, sandwiches, salads, and pupus (shrimp & papaya cocktail, potstickers, coconut fried shrimp, smoked chicken quesadilla) $9.25-10.75. Desserts include macadamia nut cheese pie, apple crisp, chocolate truffle cake, and banana papaya split $4.50-5.25. The weekend buffets are legendary for their diversity and value: Friday prime rib $13.75; Saturday seafood $24.95; and Italian pasta & sundae Sunday has even more for $14.95. Children 12 and under have a special menu with a dozen breakfast, lunch or dinner options. COMMENTS: Their set of menus is as long as a book! They have the most varied and changing assortment of meals, buffets, specials, and options of any restaurant on Maui. The good news is that they do a good job on all, making this one of the best family values on the island. Seniors be sure to ask about AARP discounts on the buffets.

LOKELANI ★ *American-Seafood*
Maui Marriott Resort (667-1200) HOURS: Dinner Wed-Sun 6-9pm. SAMPLING: Start with tempura ahi, lobster corn or shrimp risotto cakes, scallop ceviche, or goat cheese lumpia $8-10. Soups and salads (from lobster Caesar to lemon grass saimin) $6-10. Entrees ($18-22), are, by even Maui standards, fairly

inexpensive given the very diverse selection: Mandarin duck, rack of lamb, seafood pasta, filet mignon with Maui onion & wild mushroom ragout, sesame grilled ono, seared tiger prawns, miso-crusted salmon. Each menu item is matched with a suggested wine by the glass priced $5.50-8.50. White chocolate bread pudding, apple banana creme brulee, and chocolate lilikoi souffle are just a few of the dessert offerings ($4.95) COMMENTS: Old Matson menus, menu covers, and photos line the walls; there are almost as many of those on display as the dining awards and ribbons won at food festivals, chef's competitions and fund-raisers! One of the best values on the island is served from 6-6:45 when you can enjoy a complete prix fixe dinner with fish chowder or salad, grilled salmon or filet mignon & sesame crusted chicken breast and macadamia nut cream cheese pie for $19.95. Their innovative coffee service is another special feature: the coffee is freshly brewed at your table and served with a "buffet" of sugars, cinnamon sticks, chocolate shavings and whipped cream - all good enough to eat!

NIKKO JAPANESE STEAK HOUSE   *Japanese*
Maui Marriott Resort (667-1200) HOURS: 6-9pm for dinner only. Samurai Sunset Menu offers complete dinners for $14.50-19.50 from 6-6:30pm. SAMPLING: Mahi mahi, NY steak, and miso shrimp $26.95; chicken $21.95. Tempura dinners $19.95-26.95. Combinations, and sushi & sashimi dinners run $29.95 to 39.95 (for filet & lobster). All are served with shrimp or scallop appetizer, miso or tori soup, Nikko salad, steamed rice, teppan-yaki vegetables, and Japanese green tea. Also included in the price is the "show." The chef works at your table and is adept at knife throwing and other dazzling cooking techniques. COMMENTS: Desserts include the Marriott's signature chocolate macadamia nut pie, fresh fruit in plum and "white chocolate sushi" with ginger mango sauce. (It was yummy, but we're still trying to figure out how they made it!) Children's entrees are half price. The menu notes a 15% service charge is added to your bill.

NORTH BEACH GRILLE   *Pacific Rim*
Embassy Vacation Resort (661-2000) HOURS: Dinner 5-10pm. SAMPLING: Start with seared ahi or tiger prawn cocktail with citrus chile ginger sauce, chicken & vegetable spring rolls, roasted salmon with grapefruit aioli, steamed clams, or their signature "killer bread" $8.50-10.95. Salads from $4.25; salad bar $9.95. Entrees include Polynesian chicken, NY steak, fresh catch, medallion of veal, prime rib, lobster with passion fruit butter, seafood stew, and clam linguine $18.95-34.95. Save room for warm chocolate souffle, orange ricotta cheesecake, banana cream pie with mango & kiwi coulis, or coconut creme brulee $5.25. COMMENTS: North Beach Grille also features several buffet nights offering seafood on Friday $24.95, prime rib on Saturday $19.95, Pacific on Sunday, Polynesian on Monday, Paniolo on Tuesday, American on Wednesday, and Italian on Thursday, all $17.95. They are located right on the ocean - only a sidewalk separates you from the sand!

PAVILION   *Blends Pacifica*
Hyatt Regency Maui, lower level (661-1234) HOURS: Breakfast 6-11:30 am; lunch 11:30am-6pm. SAMPLING: Breakfast buffet $12.95; Focaccia with grilled vegetables, tuna, roast beef, and turkey sandwiches; cobb salads or grilled Asia

chicken salads $6.25-8.75. Hot options of burgers, Buffalo wings, teri chicken or grilled fish sandwich, and chicken quesadilla $5.75-8.25; French fries or onion rings $3-3.50. Keiki meals ($4.50-4.75) include fries and a small drink in a souvenir cup. COMMENTS: Indoor or outdoor seating. The Pavilion Bar offers poolside cocktails and beverage service, 9:30am to dusk.

REILLEY'S   *Steaks & Seafood*
2290 Kaanapali Parkway, overlooking the golf course (667-7477) HOURS: Lunch 11am-4pm, dinner 5-10pm. SAMPLING: Chili, three-onion soup, tuna in papaya, and grilled chicken or seared ahi Caesar salads $5.95-7.95. Bacon & cheese, patty melt, and bleu cheese & onion, are among the burger selections $6.95-8.25. Pupus include calamari, nachos, steamed clams, pot stickers, quesadillas, potato skins, Maui onion "tulip," and Reilley's steak pupu $4.95-8.95. More than a dozen steaks and prime rib preparations are featured for dinner ($16-26) along with fresh fish, seafood fettucine, Alaskan king crab, rack of lamb, and crab & scallop stuffed chicken $14.95-24.95. Steak & seafood combinations $24.95-36. Save room for the apple cobbler, cinnamon creme caramel, brownie sundae, or mint chocolate leprechaun pie $4.25-4.95. COMMENTS: Spacious and attractive pub atmosphere. All-you-can-eat prime rib on Tuesday for $16.95. Award-winning wine list plus beer and a selection of tropical, "Irish" and coffee drinks. Sandwiches are a cut above with a variety that includes teri chicken, grilled ahi, turkey club, chicken BLT, steak, and Reuben $6.50-9.75.

THE RUSTY HARPOON   *American*
Whalers Village (661-3123) HOURS: Breakfast 8-11am; lunch 11am-5pm; dinner 5pm-midnight; bistro menu 10pm-midnight; early bird special 4-6pm. SAMPLING: Their Belgian waffle bar offers coconut, fudge or maple syrups along with assorted fruit toppings, nuts, coconut, granola - even ice cream $7.95. Create-your-own omelette, seafood eggs benedict, and other breakfast items $2.95-9.95. Options for both lunch and dinner include potato skins, crab puffs, stuffed mushrooms, fried calamari, spring rolls, escargot, onion rings, and their signature crispy onion blossom plus shrimp Louie, spinach, tropical chicken and chef's salads $6.95-12.95. Cheese tortellini & ravioli, seafood fettucini and linguini Mediterranean $2-6 over the lunch range of $12.95-16.95. For lunch, build your own gourmet pizza (from $7.95) or opt for a burger, turkey reuben, tuna melt, French dip, cajun chicken, or club sandwich $8.95-9.95. Dinner entrees include rack of lamb, pineapple teri chicken, prime rib, steaks, and fried or stuffed shrimp $19.95-24.95. The sushi & seafood bar is open from 5pm to midnight with roll sushi, cajun ahi sashimi, oysters, and peel & eat shrimp $5.50-19.95. Desserts offer cookies n' cream ice cream pie, white chocolate *amore*, strawberry shortcake, chocolate mousse, cheesecake, and island high macadamia nut cream pie $4.95-5.95. COMMENTS: Pizzas, appetizers and coffee drinks (including flavored cappuccino) are all available on the late night bistro menu. "Jerome E. Metcalfe's Rusty Harpoon and Tavern on Kaanapali Beach" added a lot of words to the old restaurant (along with full sports-satellite large-screen tvs) but the diverse menu and great ocean view remain the same. (Look for the new "Jerome E. Metcalfe's Ale House. . . etc., etc." in Kahului.)

SEN JU SUSHI BAR   *Sushi*
Westin Maui at Kaanapali. (667-2525) HOURS: Daily 5:30-9:30pm. (Happy Hour 5:30-6:30 with selected items at 50% off.) COMMENTS: The name Sen is for the owner of the Westin Maui, but it also means "a thousand" and Ju means happy times. The bar only seats seven, but there are bento-style sushi and sashimi trays that can be taken to the surrounding tables to be enjoyed in the Colonnade. Contemporary or traditional sushi from $5. Special rolls $7-18; combinations $20-30. Also hot sake, American and Japanese wine and beer.

TIKI TERRACE   *American-Hawaiian*
Kaanapali Beach Hotel (661-0011) HOURS: Breakfast 7-11am, Sunday breakfast menu is served 7am-9am followed by Sunday brunch 9am-2pm. Nightly dinner 6-9:30pm. SAMPLING: Philippine-style skewer, calamari steak, sizzling mushrooms, sashimi, Hawaiian smoked salmon & shrimp combo, Maui onion soup, and garden, Caesar, or calamari & fiddle fern salad will start your meal for $3.95-8.95. Dinners include crabmeat stuffed prawns, scampi, mushroom chicken, pasta primavera, or your choice of beef, chicken, steak, or mixed seafood prepared grilled, seared or stir fried ($12.95-22.95) and several preparations for the catch of the day at market price. They also offer a set meal modeled after the Native Hawaiian Wainae Diet with healthy Hawaiian preparations of pohele fern salad, poached chicken breast or filet of fish, and fresh papaya for $17.95. (Vegetable lau lau with tofu & sweet potato is another uniquely Hawaiian dish for $14.95 or try the ahi & sweet potato or Hawaiian chef's salad made with turkey, ham, or pipikaula beef, both $12.95.) Macadamia nut chocolate chip cookie sandwich with mango ice cream; papaya-ginger or guava cheese tartlet, chocolate macadamia tart, or island-style tiramisu $3.95; Creme de Cacao espresso or sweet potato souffle $5.95. COMMENTS: Complimentary hula show nightly with Hawaiian entertainment throughout the evening to enjoy while you dine. For a unique Hawaiian dining experience, Tiki Terrace offers a Chef's Table with a five-course menu of Kulaiwi cuisine. Available on Mon-Wed-Fri with 24 hour advance reservations. menu and prices change each week. Their Sunday champagne brunch (with Hawaiian entertainment) is still a great value and very popular with both visitors and residents.

EXPENSIVE

A PACIFIC CAFE HONOKOWAI   ★ *Hawaiian Regional Cuisine/Rotisserie*
Honokowai Marketplace, 3350 Honoapiilani Hwy. (669-2724) HOURS: 5-10pm. SAMPLING: Skewers of beef, chicken, or lamb over a kiawe wood rotisserie and hearty steaks in addition to A Pacific Cafe signature HRC dishes like Tiger eye ahi sushi tempura with hot mustard sauce; firecracker salmon roll with house kim chee, sweet and sour sauce; wok-charred mahi with garlic sesame crust and lime-ginger beurre blanc $18-27 COMMENTS: The latest in the Jean-Marie Josselin culinary empire will have a more casual, rustic feel and will be the first to have a rotisserie. Scheduled to open summer, 1998 (Not open as we go to press; see Kihei listing for additional information.)

CASCADES GRILLE & SUSHI BAR ★ *American*
Hyatt Regency Maui (661-1234) HOURS: Lunch 11:30am-2pm; dinner 6-10pm;
sushi bar 5-11pm. SAMPLING: Appetizers are served all day: Vietnamese spring
roll, Maui onion rings, crab cakes, Kalbi beef skewers, and (the original and still
best) coconut shrimp $5-10; get them all on a pupu platter for dinner, $19.
Caesar, cobb, roasted chicken, shrimp poke, grilled mahi salads $5-11.75. The
Lahaina club has smoked chicken, avocado and Maui onion or try the grilled fish,
chicken teriyaki, bacon & avocado burger, or crab cake sandwich $8-12.25.
Dinner selections offer seafood mixed grill, steak, prime rib, roasted ginger
chicken, tonkatsu, Szechwan Stir Fry, and a variety of island fish preparations
($19-27) or try the chicken/fish/beef/shrimp sampler, $59 for two. COMMENTS:
The former Lahaina Provision Company has been renovated to reflect its new
name: still cleverly perched above the pool and on the edge of one of the Hyatt's
waterfalls, patio seating has been expanded by extending it into the (formerly
inaccessible) landscaped cliff area that overlooks the ocean. Children and seniors
can order most entrees on the menu at 1/2 price for 1/2 size. The Chocoholic Bar
has been disbanded in favor of the new sushi bar, but what it lacks in chocolate,
the new dessert menu makes up for in artistic presentation: coconut creme brulee
is served in a (partially edible) fresh coconut shell; the chocolate mousse in a
totally edible marbled white chocolate conch shell. The Sushi Bar is intimate, yet
spacious, with attractive wood, pleasant lighting, and Japanese artifacts. It offers
maki & nigiri sushi and sashimi from $5.50; sushi samplers $18-27.

SOUND OF THE FALLS *Sunday Brunch*
Westin Maui (667-2525) This elegant ocean front restaurant no longer serves
dinner, but you can still experience the luxurious ambiance of its grand staircase,
marble floors and cascading waterfalls while enjoying a sumptuous Sunday
Champagne Brunch. HOURS: 9am-1pm. SAMPLING: Salads, yogurt, sushi,
chilled fruit frappe, spiced shrimp, eggs Benedict, smoked fish with mini-bagels

served with cheese, pineapple-papaya blintz, tricolor seafood ravioli, pork ribs with plum sauce, chicken cordon bleu, wok-seared beef with oriental noodles, made-to-order omelettes, sushi & sashimi, breakfast pastries, croissants, strudels, white & dark chocolate fondue, chocolate-dipped strawberries & truffles, petit fours, Hawaiian cheesecake and warm Moloka'i sweet bread pudding. COMMENTS: All-you-can-eat $24.95; $1.50 for every year of age for children under 12. A great price for such an indulgent splurge!

SPATS TRATTORIA ★ *Northern Italian*
Hyatt Regency Maui (661-1234) HOURS: Dinner only 6-10pm. SAMPLING: Deep dish pizza, prosciutto with papaya, mushroom polenta, clams, calamari, and minestrone are some of the appetizers for $5.75-10.25; antipasti for two $14.75. Entrees include seafood grill; veal piccata, marsala, or Romano; beef medallions, scampi, and chicken with porcini mushrooms $20-27. Lasagna, veal & spinach cannelloni, linguine with clams, fettucine carbonara, and other pasta dishes $14.50-19. Tiramisu, amaretto cheesecake, ganache, or chocolate silk torte for dessert $4.75-5.75. COMMENTS: The atmosphere is comfortable and homey, yet very classy, as in the parlor or drawing room of an old Italian mansion. Brass candelabras, sleek wood, beveled glass partitions and plush booths add to the distinctive ambiance. Focaccia, topped with cheese and herbs, arrives with a side of fresh pesto along with olive oil, balsamic vinegar, and herbs for dipping. Kids menu available at 1/2 portion for 1/2 price.

SWAN COURT ★ *Continental*
Hyatt Regency Maui (661-1234) HOURS: Breakfast buffet 6:30-11:30am, till noon on Sunday. Dinner 6-10pm nightly. SAMPLING: Breakfast buffet includes fresh-squeezed orange juice, French toast, crepes, blintzes, bread pudding, cereals, yogurt, breads & pastries, fresh fruits, cheeses, egg dishes, potatoes, breakfast meats, hash, frittata and an omelette station $17.95. Also breakfast a la carte. Dinner appetizers include scallop-potato cannelloni, crispy tangled shrimp, macadamia nut crab cakes, seared ahi, venison carpaccio, prawn martini, lobster ravioli with Tahitian vanilla sauce, and wonton & seafood Napoleon $10-14. Featured entrees are smoked duck with hoison sauce, pepper crusted venison, seafood ensemble, sauteed veal & crab, rack of lamb, filet mignon, and lobster tail $28-36. Classical chocolate souffle $10. COMMENTS: A pond of graceful swans, cascading waterfalls and a landscape of oriental gardens create the atmosphere and view of the Swan Court. Recent renovations added new carpeting, furniture, and Hawaiian murals with an expanded lounge and new dance floor. The ambiance alone is well worth the splurge for breakfast, our "best bet" for a daily breakfast buffet. The dinners are excellent and many unusual preparations are offered. Our only criticism is the proximity of other tables and noise seems to carry. Reservations are advised.

TEPPAN YAKI DAN *Japanese*
Sheraton Maui, 2605 Kaanapali Parkway (661-0031) HOURS: Dinner only 5:30-9:30pm. SAMPLING: Appetizers of sashimi, blackened ahi, green salad, oysters with spinach, oriental pasta with stir fry vegetables, or hot diablo shrimp $4.50-

$10. Entrees of teriyaki chicken, shrimp with pineapple, scallops in macadamia nut crust with watercress pesto, fresh catch, steak, or salmon florentine-style $21-28. Lobster Playpen (chunks of lobster with lemon grass) or steak & seafood combinations $28-42. Ginger garlic fried rice $2 additional. Ice cream cake with coulis of tropical fruits, orange hazelnut cheese cake profiteroles, or lemon grass sorbet $4-5. COMMENTS: "Gourmet teppanyaki" dinners prepared in front of you by a combination chef and showman! All entrees include miso clam soup, tsukemono, fresh Maui vegetables, and white rice.

VILLA RESTAURANT AND VILLA TERRACE ★
American-Seafood/Asian Influences
Westin Maui (667-2525) HOURS: Dinner only 6-10pm; Seafood Buffet at Villa Terrace 6:30-9pm. SAMPLING: Seafood is the specialty! Appetizers have a bit of an Asian influence with their rice paper shrimp and lobster taco, coconut shrimp risotto with Thai curry sauce, and Taste of Lahaina's Best of Show winner, tangled tiger prawns with chili cilantro garlic sauce $7-10. Maui onion soup, lobster, and a selection of salads $4-6. Entrees include Black Angus NY steak, miso glazed shrimp & scallops, eggplant Napoleon, Peking duck, macadamia nut crusted chicken and an excellent selection of fresh fish $16-26. "Maui Style" Lobster Paella for Two $48.95 COMMENTS: One of our best bets for fresh island fish and a beautiful setting. All tables look out onto the lagoon where swans and exotic ducks float along peacefully. They offer a nightly prix fixe menu with choice of ahi salad, black bean soup or steak quesadilla appetizer plus entree of beef tenderloin, pork loin, or mahi mahi, and macadamia velvet cake or truffle ice cream for $28; $22.95 before 6:30pm. Live music 6-9pm. You don't have to wait until Friday to enjoy the seafood buffet in the adjoining Villa Terrace, it's offered nightly for $27.95 from 6-9pm; only $22.95 from 5:30-6:30.

KAHANA - NAPILI - KAPALUA

LOUNGES

(BAY) CLUB TERRACE ★ *tropical drinks/limited lunch service*
Kapalua Bay Resort (669-5656) HOURS: 11:30am-6pm. COMMENTS: Enjoy a fabulous sunset in this elegant setting at the entrance to the Bay Club restaurant. Situated on a promontory overlooking the ocean, it is an idyllic setting from which to enjoy the scenic panorama along with pupus and cocktails. The Bay Club lunch service has been extended to offer a limited selection of menu items out on the terrace or you can just sit back and indulge in one of their ice cream treats, like the Bay Club Delight with Kahlua, Grand Marnier and Amaretto!

LEHUA LOUNGE *appetizers/desserts*
Kapalua Bay Resort (669-5656) HOURS: 7-10pm. SAMPLING: Light appetizers like shrimp cocktail, fruit plate, Caesar salad, baked onion soup, sashimi, seared ahi, and smoked salmon & trout $6-12.50, Dessert menu of chocolate truffle cake, cheesecake, creme caramel, mud pie, and chocolate caramel macadamia nut tart $6.75. On Sundays and Mondays (when the downstairs restaurant Gardenia

Court is closed), they also offer a limited selection of sandwiches and main courses. Burgers, pizza, and club, ahi, and BBQ chicken sandwiches $10.25-14 plus entrees of fresh catch, steak, chicken, stir fry, and pasta $18.50-28. COMMENTS: Panoramic ocean-view in a comfortable open-air living room setting. It's quite the perfect place to enjoy their afternoon selection of teas, eclairs, tarts, chocolate truffles, tea sandwiches, and scones! Piano music nightly (except Friday) from 5:30-8:30pm.

THE LOBBY LOUNGE AND LIBRARY   *Pupus/Sushi bar*
The Ritz-Carlton, Kapalua (669-6200) HOURS: Espresso bar 5:30-10am for coffee drinks and pastries. Noon to midnight for cocktails; pupus from 4:30. SAMPLING: Shrimp cocktail, vegetable crudite, imported cheeses, pizza, and dim sum basket $6.50-15. Wine, cognac, port & cigars. Afternoon tea served in the library (upon request, with advance reservations required.) Finger sandwiches, scones with Devonshire cream, and tea pastries with pot of tea $18.75. Hawaiian entertainment 5-7pm. The Sushi Bar offers seaside sushi and sashimi nightly from 5-10.

THE ANUENUE LOUNGE   *Appetizers/Desserts*
The Ritz-Carlton, Kapalua (669-6200) HOURS: Cocktails 5:30-11pm, appetizers and desserts until 10. Closed Sunday and Monday. Entertainment ranges from solo piano to a jazz duo. Located adjacent to The Anuenue Room restaurant.

RESTAURANTS-INEXPENSIVE

ASHLEY'S   *Sandwiches/Yogurt*
Kahana Gateway (669-0949) HOURS: Breakfast/lunch 8:30am-6pm, store open till 9:30. SAMPLING: Breakfasts include assorted egg dishes and omelettes $3-5 plus bagels, bakery items, juices, and coffee drinks $1.50-3. Deli sandwiches offer turkey, ham, roast beef, tuna, egg salad, or veggie on choice of bread with choice of extras $4.80. Ice cream, yogurt, or shave ice from $2. COMMENTS: Chow fun and crab cole slaw are some of the specials. (Ask Alfred if he's got 'em and while you're at it, find out when he's going to put daughter Ashley's "psghetti sammich" on the menu!) In addition to sandwiches, frozen treats and fountain drinks, they also rent videos and VCR's (no sign-up or membership) and you can rent a Hana audio tape for just $3.99. (Hana picnics available, too.)

(THE) BEACH HOUSE   *American*
The Ritz-Carlton, Kapalua (669-6200) HOURS: Lunch 11:30am-3pm. Bar service 11-5 with daily specialty drinks $5.75. SAMPLING: Lunch selections range from quesadilla, sushi, rib, and chicken appetizers ($8.50-16) to burgers, grilled seafood, Caesar or Chinese chicken salads, fresh fruit, or veggie focaccia sandwich $9-17.50. COMMENTS: Located adjacent to Fleming Beach, this open-air restaurant utilizes more than 40 fully-grown coco palms to offer a natural roof.

(THE) COFFEE STORE   *Coffee/pastries*
Napili Plaza (669-4170) <WWW> HOURS: Daily 6:30am-8pm. SAMPLING: Muffins, cinnamon rolls, sticky buns, and assorted pastries $2.50. Soup, Spinach quiche, lasagna $3.95-6.95. Caesar, tuna, pasta, or Caprese salad $6.95-8.50;

spinach mushroom or turkey, ham & cheese croissant; garden burger, grilled veggie panini on focaccia $5.25-8.25. Cheesecake, pies, brownies, baklava, cookies, and Chocolate Thunder $2.50-4.50. COMMENTS: They also have locations in Kihei and Kahului. Freshly roasted coffee and coffee drinks (with some unusual selections like a banana mocha cooler or an Electric Brown Cow!) $1.50-3.95. Juices and flavored Italian sodas $1.50-2. Smoothies $4.50. Voted "Best Cappuccino" in the "Best of Maui" contest conducted by the Maui News.

DOLLIES *American-Italian*
4310 Honoapiilani Hwy. at the Kahana Manor (669-0266) HOURS: 11am-midnight. SAMPLING: Smoked turkey dip, ham & swiss, BLT, grilled chicken with bacon & cheddar, cajun chicken, garden burger, and grinder sandwiches $6.75-8.25. Quesadilla, nachos, potato skins, cheese bread, chili, and Caesar, chef's, or spinach salads $4.95-6.95. Fettucine with chicken, vegetables, mushrooms, or Alfredo $9.95-11.95. Grilled chicken, Mexican, pesto, spinach & sundried tomato, and Canadian bacon, pineapple & macadamia nut pizzas $13.50-20 or build-your own from $10.95. COMMENTS: Food to go. Good selection of beer, wine and coffee drinks. Popular spot with local residents.

GAZEBO *American*
Napili Shores Resort, 5315 Lower Honoapiilani Hwy., (669-5621) HOURS: Both breakfast and lunch from 7:30am-2pm. SAMPLING: Breakfast offers an assortment of omelettes (from spinach to shrimp) and egg dishes, but they are most popular for their macadamia nut pancakes (pineapple and banana run a close second) $4.25-6.95. Lunch selections include burgers and sandwiches (Monte Cristo, shrimp melt, chicken Monterey, patty melt) plus Caesar, shrimp, tuna, and southwestern chicken salads $5.75-7.95. COMMENTS: It's still "paper-plate" casual (even with real plates) and popular with Maui residents for the friendly atmosphere with a wonderful ocean view.

HONOLUA GENERAL STORE *American*
Past Kapalua as you drive through the golf course. Just above The Ritz-Carlton (669-6128) HOURS: 6am-8pm. SAMPLING: Breakfasts include pancakes, eggs and such. Lunches include four local plate lunches daily which might include stew or teri chicken $4.95-5.50, or a smaller portion called a hobo which is just a main dish and rice for $3.75. Sandwiches and grilled items with fries $5.25-5.75. The spam musubi, a local favorite, is usually sold out by noon. COMMENTS: The Kapalua Hotel refurbished this once funky and local spot. The front portion displays an assortment of Kapalua clothing and some locally made food products as well as gourmet teas and coffees.

MAUI TACOS *Healthy Mexican*
Napili Plaza (665-0222) HOURS: 9am-9pm. SAMPLING: Potato enchiladas, hard or soft tacos, quesadillas, chimichangas, nachos, and over a dozen varieties of special hand-held burritos in fish, steak, chicken, beef or vegetarian combinations with black beans $1.65-6.95. COMMENTS: Guacamole and salsa made fresh every day. No lard, no msg - they use only vegetable oil, fresh beans and lean meats. The complimentary salsa bar offers choices with onions, cilantro,

jalapenos, cilantro, hot sauce and more. Good values! This is the original location with other outlets now in Lahaina Square, Kihei and Kaahumanu Food Court, all owned and operated by Mark Ellman of Avalon.

VILLAGE CAFE *American*
Kapalua Village Golf Course at the first hole. (669-1947) HOURS: Breakfast 7-11am; lunch 11:30am-3pm. SAMPLING: Breakfast sandwiches, quiche, French toast $3.50-4.95. Deli sandwiches plus fish, chicken, dogs, and The Village Cheeseburger $5.50-6.50. Salads $3.95-6.95. COMMENTS: They serve Lappert's Kona Coffee from 6:30 am. The owners also do catering and can arrange events (like a paniolo steak fry, private luau - even a golf-course wedding) here at the cafe.

MODERATE

BANYAN TREE *Mediterranean*
The Ritz-Carlton, Kapalua HOURS: 11:30am-4pm for lunch. SAMPLING: Tropical libations and non-alcohol fruit smoothies. Oysters, ahi, quesadilla, or dim sum basket plus Caesar, spinach, Chinese chicken, and ahi Nicoise salads $9-16. Pizza, calzone, baked clams, and onion soup - all baked in their wood burning oven $9.50-15; entrees of penne pasta, curried rice, steamed moi, sirloin or garden burger, Thai chicken, mahi or ahi club sandwiches $8-21. COMMENTS: Located poolside, they also offer a limited sandwich, salad, and appetizer menu at the Pool Bar from 11-6.

BEACH CLUB *American*
Kaanapali Shores Resort (667-2211) HOURS: Breakfast 7-11am, Lunch 11:30am-3pm, cafe menu (light fare) served 3-9:30pm, dinner 5:30-9:30pm. SAMPLING: Breakfast sandwich, omelettes, pancakes, Portuguese sweet bread French toast, biscuits & gravy, fresh fruit $4.95-7.75. Hot and cold sandwiches, burgers, salads, roast beef dip, cheese quesadillas, and seafood melt $5.25-8.95. Cafe menu has burgers, salads, and appetizers such as seafood stuffed mushrooms, cajun ahi, cheese sticks, kalbi ribs, buffalo wings, and scampi sampler $4.50-9.95. Dinners offer a selection of seafood, chicken, steak, and pasta dishes $11.95-19.95. COMMENTS: Salad bar; Take & Bake pizza for four $19.95. While-they-last specials each evening: $10.95 mahi, chicken, stir fry; $12.95/$15.95 prime rib. Keiki menu available for all meals. Full bar service and an extensive selection of specialty coffee drinks.

CHINA BOAT *Cantonese-Szechuan-Mandarin*
4474 L. Honoapiilani, Kahana (669-5089) HOURS: Lunch 11am-2pm, dinner 5-10pm. SAMPLING: Appetizers feature potstickers, shumai, soft shell crab, minced chicken, thousand-year-old eggs, and chinese pickles $3.75-8.75. Entrees include Kung Pao lobster, green pepper & onion beef, spiced chicken in garlic sauce, shredded pork in Peking sauce, minced scallop with pinenuts, walnut shrimp, Dungeness crab & scrambled egg along with other more familiar Chinese

dishes $8.95-24.95. Peking duck, lobster, abalone, and whole fish up to $42.95. COMMENTS: They specialize in Chinese seafood and have an early bird special every evening from 5-6pm offering several choices that run $8.95-11.75 for a full dinner.

ERIK'S SEAFOOD GROTTO   *Seafood*
4242 Lower Honoapiilani Hwy. on the second floor of the Kahana Villas Condo (669-4806) HOURS: Lunch: 11:30am-2pm; dinner 5-10:30pm. SAMPLING: Lunch offers burgers, club, BLT, shrimp, fish, chicken, and steak sandwiches along with salads like seared ahi, crab, shrimp, chef's, and five kinds of Caesar: chicken, mahi, shrimp, steak, and crab $4.95-10.95. Crab cakes, escargot, stuffed mushrooms, steamers, and oysters are some of the hot appetizers for $5.95-13.95. Dinners include soup or salad, starch and bread with entrees of BBQ shrimp, seafood curry, bouillabaisse, cioppino, lobster thermidor, scampi Olowalu, Coquille St. Jacques, and Chicken Cordon Bleu, along with fresh fish, rack of lamb, steaks, and surf & turf combinations $18.95-26.95. COMMENTS: Lunch allows you to take advantage of that great ocean view from upstairs. Their early bird specials are more creative than most and offer lobster-stuffed boneless chicken breast, crab stuffed prawns, and island mahi "Oscar" in addition to NY steak or fresh fish for $11.95-13.95 from 5-6pm.

FISH AND GAMES BREWING COMPANY & ROTISSERIE
Seafood/Rotisserie & Microbrewery
Kahana Gateway (669-FISH) HOURS: Lunch 11am-3pm; dinner 5:30-10pm; late night menu 10:30pm-1am. SAMPLING: Lunch at the Oyster Bar offers shrimp, sashimi, smoked salmon and, of course, Skookums, Kumamotos, Hama Hama Yearling, Miyagi and Blue Points! ($5.95-10.95) The main menu has clam or oyster chowder, cioppino, seared ahi, steamed clams or mussels, baked oysters, cajun wings, and BBQ rib appetizers for $6.95-9.95 and sandwiches that include oyster po'boy, reuben, steak, shrimp & crab melt, and *real* tuna $7.50-10.95. Salads include Caesar, oriental chicken, and smoked white kipper salmon $5.95-10.95. The dinner menu offers the same appetizer, soup, and oyster bar items with the addition of Oysters Rockefeller, spicy crab cakes, cajun shrimp, ahi carpaccio, and wok-seared scallops; and salads that include a variety of Caesars, grilled scallops, lemon grass shrimp with Maui onion & spinach, and herb & cognac cured salmon on Kula greens $5.95-11.95. Entrees feature pastas with cioppino, scallops, mussels, clams, eggplant, or fresh spinach $13.95-16.95; rack of lamb or angus beef steaks; and live whole crab or lobster, jumbo shrimp, BBQ shrimp, and lobster bouillabaisse $21.95-27.95 (some priced per pound). The new rotisserie and kiawe wood broiler offers entree selections of spice-rubbed chicken, hoison duck, and pork loin (all deliciously moist and flavorful) plus baby back pork ribs and brewer sausage $15.95-22.95. The late night menu offers mini "tapas" versions of their regular menu. COMMENTS: The dining room has an exhibition kitchen, oyster bar, and retail seafood market. The sports bar offers state of the art equipment and satellite system; its elegant wood and brass design is reminiscent of a Gentlemen's club, a concept that has been expanded (literally!) to incorporate a private dining/cigar room, complete with fireplace, leather sofas,

and mahogany humidors filled with a variety of cigars from around the world. A stone hearth rotisserie surrounded by a marble dining counter and gleaming copper tanks of a glass-enclosed microbrewery compete for the most striking new asset of the recent renovation. The atmosphere has a stately, masculine elegance, but with a not-so-hidden agenda of fun, (fish), and games!

JAMESON'S GRILL & BAR AT KAPALUA   *Seafood-American*
200 Kapalua Drive, just across the road from the Kapalua Hotel and a short drive up Kapalua Drive (669-5653) HOURS: Breakfast or lunch 8am-3pm, dinner 5-10pm, cocktails 11am-12:30am. SAMPLING: Omelettes, frittata, cinnamon-raisin French toast, Kapalua parfait (layered with yogurt, fruit & granola); traditional eggs benedict or with beef striploin, crab cakes, or smoked marlin $3.25-11.95. Fish, roast beef, chicken & steak sandwiches, burgers, salads, appetizers, and pizza $4.95-10.95. Dinner appetizers offer crab-stuffed mushrooms, calamari strips, prawn martini, seafood summer rolls, crab cakes, scampi, and Hood Canal steamed clams $7.95-12.95, J.J.'s baked artichoke is still famous and still here for $9.95. Entrees include fresh catch, Angus Beef meats, shrimp & scallop linguine, seared ahi, miso sake prawns, rack of lamb, baked stuffed shrimp, sauteed scallops, prawns & chicken, and roasted vegetable pasta $16.95-27.95. COMMENTS: In 1996, Jameson's-by-the-Sea took over the Kapalua Grill & Bar offering diners the best of both. The award-winning wine list offers everything from the affordable to the impressive. A golf course and ocean view add to the pluses of this restaurant; outdoor on a small patio overlooking the 18th hole. And you can get pretty much eat any time you like: lunch from 8 am, breakfast till 3, and a cafe menu (appetizers, sandwiches, pizza) from 3 to midnight! Dinner reservations suggested.

KOHO GRILL AND BAR ★   *American*
Napili Plaza, 5095 Napilihau St. (669-5299) HOURS: Daily 11am-midnight; lunch from 11am & dinner 5pm-midnight. SAMPLING: Chicken Caesar, oriental chicken, taco, cobb, or fresh catch salads $6.25-7.95. Club, cajun chicken, fresh fish sandwiches, burgers, or plate lunches $5.75-6.75. Sizzling fajitas $7.95-8.95 ($13.95 for two every Tuesday!) Pupus include nachos, chili cheese fries, quesadilla, fish & chips, potato skins, and rib basket $4.95-8.25. Dinner entrees served with soup or salad: fish, steak, chicken stir fry, ribs plus assorted pasta and chicken preparations $8.95-14.95. Cinnamon apple or chocolate sundae, brownie and fried ice cream snow ball for dessert $3.45-4.50. COMMENTS: A diverse menu and affordable prices which boils down to great family dining. They also have a great keiki (kids) menu and knowing how fussy some kids can be, they'll even cut the crusts off the sandwiches! Sports bar & large screen tv. There is another "Koho's" at Kaahumanu Center in Kahului; the same owners also run the Plantation House in Kapalua and the SeaWatch restaurant in Wailea.

ORIENT EXPRESS   *Thai-Chinese*
Napili Shores Resort, one mile before Kapalua (669-8077) HOURS: Dinner 5:30-10pm. SAMPLING: Sizzling Szechuan beef, garlic shrimp, mandarin or spinach duck, honey lemon chicken, mahi lemon sauce, curry, Thai noodles, and seafood in a clay pot are just a few of the options $10.25-14.50. COMMENTS: No MSG. There is a Harry's Sushi Bar here and at Lobster Cove in Wailea. (The

same owner runs both places as well as the legendary Chez Paul). Harry's serves sushi, sashimi and Orient Express pupus and is open till "late." They offer an early bird special from 5:30-6:30pm; five-course dinners from $11.95.

OUTBACK STEAKHOUSE   *Themed Steakhouse*
Kahana Gateway, 4405 Honoapiilani Hwy. (665-1822) HOURS: Mon-Thurs 4-10pm, Fri till 11; Saturday 3-11pm, Sun till 10. SAMPLING: Start with "Aussietizers" of coconut shrimp, cheese fries, chicken wings, grilled shrimp (on the barbie, of course!) and their signature Bloomin' Onion $5.89-7.49, or go for a Bonzer Salad: Caesar with "chook" (chicken!) or shrimp, or the Queensland with chicken, egg, tomato, bacon and two cheeses $7.99-9.99. Entrees include "Down Under Favorites" like pork chops with cinnamon apples, grilled chicken with bacon & mushrooms & cheese, or pastas topped with vegetables and/or chicken and/or shrimp $19.99-13.99. "Land Rover" steaks, rack of lamb, and prime rib come with salad, bread, and choice of potato, rice or vegetable; and the chicken, ribs, and fish are all "Grilled on the Barbie" $14.79-19.79. COMMENTS: And it doesn't stop there, mate! There's still the "Thunder from Down Under" pecan brownie with ice cream & chocolate sauce and "The Wallaby Darned," their specialty drink made with deKuype, Peachtree schnapps, champagne & vodka. They also have a menu of "Cut Lunches" (chook sandwiches & burgers) $6.49-7.49 and a "joey" (that's a baby kangaroo) menu for kids with most items priced "down under" $3.99 (See? *We* got it!) Casual ranch house atmosphere with hardwood floors, wood-framed booths, and plenty of Aussie artifacts. (Dona likes the big koala climbing on the front column!) Opened May 1998 (with a new "joey" expected in Kihei by spring 1999.) No reservations. (We were unable to do a personal review by press time, but given their menu selection, good prices, and "fun" attitude, we think they'll they'll be a "bonzer" new addition to the Maui dining scene - *fair dinkum!*)

PLUMERIA TERRACE RESTAURANT AND BAR   *International*
Kapalua Bay Hotel, poolside (669-5656) HOURS: Open daily noon-3pm. Breakfast on Sunday only 6:30-11am. SAMPLING: Seared ahi, potstickers with tofu & vegetables, fresh fruit plate, hamburger, vegetarian burger, saimin, and grilled medallion of shutome, prawn & zucchini $5.95-13.50. Strawberry, chocolate, or vanilla shakes or malts; homemade sorbets & ice creams; coffee, tea $3-4.50. COMMENTS: The beautiful location of this casual poolside setting features an ocean view from every seat. Limited menu, but with some interesting healthy alternatives like tofu potstickers, vegetarian burger, and seared ahi. Good values, too.

SANSEI RESTAURANT AND SUSHI BAR ★ *Sushi-Japanese-Pacific Rim*
Kapalua Bay Hotel Shops (669-6286) HOURS: 5:30-11pm; Thurs-Fri till 2am with lazer karaoke from 10pm) SAMPLING: Start with Sansei's own nori ravioli of shrimp & salmon, panko-crusted or sizzling sashimi, broiled miso garlic prawns, crab sunomono, tea duck eggroll, or seared ahi salad $4.50-11. Original entrees include their award-winning Asian rock shrimp cake with grilled ahi and ginger-lime chile butter and cilantro pesto; chicken stuffed with gorgonzola and

spinach; and black tea duck in orange-soy-ginger vinaigrette (YIN) and cabernet demi-glaze (YANG) $15-19.75. More traditional (yet still original) offerings include grilled mahi, wok-tossed vegetables, shrimp tempura, macadamia crusted rack of lamb, and appetizers of teriyaki chicken, ahi carpaccio, shrimp & pork gau gee, or kalbi ribs. Sansei sushi selections offer innovative names and combinations like yellow submarine, spider roll with soft shell crab, caterpillar (eel & avocado on the outside), yaki-maki (smoked salmon & dynamite sauce), Kapalua "Butter*fry*" with snapper, smoked salmon, crab & veggies in curry sauce, and the "Kenny G Special" (snapper, garlic, masago, and ponzu) $6.50-12. COMMENTS: Sushi and sashimi, as well as a selection of traditional Japanese and innovative Pacific Rim dishes, are made to share family-style with everyone at the table at this comfortable and inviting sushi bar and small restaurant. The small plates and small portions of these "Asian Tapas" create a friendly, fun atmosphere, not the usual sedate and tranquil ambiance you'd expect from a traditional Japanese restaurant. But as much as we love this innovative and original new dining concept, it's the food that's the ultimate test. We gave it a star our first time out so it's gratifying to know that others agree: Sansei just received the top food rating (for the entire state of Hawai'i!) by the Zagat survey whose participants gave it 98 out of a possible 100 points! As we said before, if you don't like sushi bars, you'll like this one. And if you *love* them, this will probably be your favorite!

SEA HOUSE ★ *American*
5900 Lower Honoapiilani Rd., beachfront at Napili Kai Beach Club (669-1500) HOURS: Breakfast 8-11am, lunch 12-2pm, dinner 6-9pm. SAMPLING: Breakfast croissant, omelettes (Spanish, seafood, vegetarian & lobster), Hawaiian sweet bread French toast, banana macadamia pancakes, Belgian waffle, or Poached eggs Napili Kai (with crab, turkey, or sausage) $4.25-9.95. Luncheon sandwiches include tuna melt, cajun mahi, pastrami, grilled chicken, seared ahi, and turkey roll $5.95-8.95. Caesar, sesame chicken, and Asian noodle salads; seafood platter or pasta, stir fry, wontons $7-11. Dinner entrees are served with vegetable, rice or potato, and walnut flat bread. Maui onion soup, coconut-macadamia shrimp, crab-stuffed mushrooms, ahi-nori tempura, and their award-winning crisp Pacific Rim sushi: crab & avocado rolled in nori and encrusted with macadamia nuts. Prime rib, steak, gingered pork loin chop, seafood pasta, lobster tail, rack of lamb, grilled eggplant, and a variety of fresh fish preparations $15-26. Several items are offered in a light portion and there are keiki menus for lunch and dinner. COMMENTS: Chef Scott Kealoha Lutey has been winning lots of awards lately, especially for his innovative appetizers. It's hard to beat their Thursday's lobster for $18.95 and the open air, right-on-the-beach location is just how you always expected Hawaii to be! Local entertainment most nights in the Whale Watcher's Bar. On Friday evening they offer a Polynesian Dinner Show performed by the children of the Napili Kai Foundation. $35 adults, $20 children.

TERRACE GRILL AND BAR *American*
4299 L. Honoapiilani Hwy., Sands of Kahana Resort (669-5399) HOURS: Breakfast 7:30am-2pm, lunch 11am-5pm, dinner 5-9pm. SAMPLING: Breakfast omelettes and egg dishes $6.50-7.25; cinnamon French toast; waffles; banana,

mac nut, and pineapple pancakes $5-6.50. Lunch menu offers Philly steak, fish, chicken, tuna, BLT, and club sandwiches plus burgers or patty melt $5.95-8.95; Caesar, chicken and pineapple boat salads $5.95-8.95. Dinners start with chicken or calamari strips, crab quesadilla, nachos, or coconut shrimp $6.95-8.95 then entrees of NY steak, liver & onions, shrimp or chicken fettucine, stir-fry, fresh catch, and fish & chips. $9.95-18.95. COMMENTS: Very quiet dining, this restaurant seems to be primarily used by the resort guests. Early bird chicken, steak or mahi ($9.95) from 5-6:30pm. A nice menu selection; lunch items available at dinner too. Live music nightly.

EXPENSIVE

ANUENUE ROOM ★ *Hawaiian Provencal Cuisine*
The Ritz-Carlton, Kapalua (669-6200) HOURS: 6pm-9:30pm; closed Sun-Mon. SAMPLING: Their appetizer menu features Dungeness crab cake, seared duck foie gras, ginger steamed lobster, spicy seared ahi, and fricasse of wild mushroom $16-21. Roasted eggplant. spicy lobster, or Maui onion soups; quail, lobster, and three-cheese souffle salads $8.50-18. Entrees include venison chops, caramelized salmon, sauteed Dover Sole, seared veal, ravioletti Provencale, rare ahi, crusted onaga, beef tenderloin and roasted lamb rack $26-42. The desserts round out a memorable meal. Unique in texture and flavor, they could be considered *objet d'art*! Selections might include banana creme brulee, warm mango Napoleon, pineapple tatin, Hawaiian chocolate tear, and chocolate and Grand Marnier souffles $9-10. COMMENTS: Excellent food and superb service in an elegant, warm and cozy setting, spacious and comfortable, but "ritzy." They recently expanded the dining area to the adjacent lounge so you can enjoy the piano music during dinner and now offer more lanai seating (especially in the summer). Their name has changed from the traditional Grill used in other Ritz hotels to the Hawaiian word for "rainbow."

THE BAY CLUB   *Continental (Hawaiian Influence)*
At Kapalua just before the entrance to the resort (669-8008 after 5pm, 669-5656 before 5pm) HOURS: Lunch 11:30am-2pm, dinner 6-9pm with pianist in the adjoining Club Terrace. SAMPLING: Lunches offer crab cakes; chicken salad in papaya; and sandwiches like roasted vegetables in a pita; grilled ahi on poi bread; fried oyster; turkey, bacon & avocado; BBQ chicken on taro bread; and Monte Cristo $7.50-13.50. Main course cobb, seafood cobb, and Caesar salads $8.50-14. Dinners start with sashimi, grilled tiger prawns, Caesar or goat cheese salad, crab cakes, wild mushrooms & escargot, and lobster sweet potato salad $11.75-14; mosaic of caviar $28. Entrees include prawns or scallop brochette, tenderloin of lamb, NY steak, roasted duckling, seared scallop risotto, grilled pork chop, and fresh fish $25-30; grilled vegetables & pasta $19.50; lobster tail $43. COMMENTS: This Kapalua Hotel restaurant is housed in a separate building on a promontory which overlooks the ocean (and its own pool!) and offers a scenic panorama. A limited lunch menu is now served outside in the adjacent Club Terrace. Lunch dress code in the dining room requires swimsuit coverup and, in the evening, collared shirts or jackets for men. No denim. In the

evening, a pianist in the adjoining lounge adds to the idyllic setting with romantic music. Extensive wine list and yes, Johnny is still there (after 20 years!) to suggest the wines that will best complement your menu choices. The resort (recently sold and now under new management) has been renovating its restaurants and redesigning their menus. Old favorites remain, but it may take a while for all the new ideas to settle in. Dona liked the unusual menu items like Lobster & Okinawan Sweet Potato "Salad," Asparagus-crusted Mahi Mahi with Sundried Cherry Sauce, and Grilled Molasses Pork Chop (with Apricots and Mushroom Bread Pudding); but Christie preferred some of the lighter options (scallops prepared oriental style, and tiger prawns with citrus avocado) and missed some of the more classic offerings from the more traditional Bay Club menu.

GARDENIA COURT RESTAURANT ★ *Island Continental*
Kapalua Bay Resort Hotel (669-5656) HOURS: Open Tues-Thurs & Sat for breakfast (6:30-11am) and dinner (5:30-9:30pm); no lunch. Sun brunch 9:30am-1:30pm; Seafood buffet Fri 5:30-8pm; closed for dinner Sun-Mon. SAMPLING: Breakfast buffet $16.95, continental $12.95, tropical champagnes $6. A la carte fruits, cereals, omelettes, waffles, pancakes, and sweet bread French toast with coconut & macadamia nuts $4.25-12.75. Dinners start with Caesar or tomato & mozzarella salad, sashimi, baked onion soup, crab summer rolls, or prawns & pancetta in crispy lumpia wrappers $7-14. Main courses feature shutome saltimbocca, spicy loin of pork, scampi, NY steak, veal scaloppini, roast chicken, fettucini Alfredo, and fresh fish $15-28. Desserts include chocolate truffle cake, chocolate banana tart with caramel macadamia nuts, and strawberries with almond cream & mint $6-7.50. COMMENTS: Lovely dining room with exotic bamboo furniture and textiles surrounded by koi ponds, hanging vines, and a "waterfall" wall. Each month a different table d'hote dinner is offered: appetizer, entree & dessert for $39. They also have two of the island's best buffets, Sunday Brunch and Friday's Seafood. (See Best Brunches for times and prices.) They're also two of the most popular so reservations are highly recommended.

THE PLANTATION HOUSE ★ *Seafood-Continental*
2000 Plantation Club Drive, Kapalua (669-6299) HOURS: Breakfast/lunch 8am-3pm; dinner 5:30-9:30pm. SAMPLING: The breakfast/lunch menu offers either fare until 3pm. Potato pancakes & lox or Eggs Benedict varieties with spinach, sausage, seared ahi, crab cake, turkey or smoked salmon $7.50-12; plus saimin, omelettes, loco moco, and Moloka'i sweetbread French toast $6-10. Burgers, chicken, tuna melt, club, turkey, crab cake, and their deli-size reuben sandwiches as well as cobb, Caesar, shrimp, goat cheese, taco, and oriental chicken salads $7-10. Honey-guava scallop skewers (also a dinner favorite), fish tacos, crab cakes, stir-fry, or calamari $7-10. Dinners start with curried spinach potstickers, wonton Napoleon, crab-stuffed ahi tempura roll, and scampi plus spinach or macadamia goat cheese salad $6-9. Entrees include sauteed prawns, pork chop with caramelized Maui onion sauce, filet mignon Bernaise, pepper-crusted NY steak (prepared tableside with brandied mushroom sauce, and double cut lamb chops $21-26. The fresh fish preparations are both light & colorful (pan-seared in mirin with crunchy, sweet macadamia nuts and caramelized chili-sesame sauce)

and warm & comforting (sauteed with Maui onion & vegetable stew, or roasted with wild mushrooms). Linguini with chicken, shrimp, or scallops $16-21. Additional appetizer and entree specials nightly. If you have a sweet tooth, don't miss the "Brownie to Da Max." Served warm in a huge brandy snifter with lots of ice cream, whipped cream and macadamia nuts, we've always though of it as the Hula Pie of the '90s. On our last visit, however, we were introduced to the macadamia chocolate torte - chocolate chips and macadamia nuts melted together with Mac Nut liqueur in a shortbread crust with Tahitian vanilla ice cream - which we can ony dub "Torte for a New Millenium". . .COMMENTS: Their location - in the clubhouse of the Plantation Golf Course - provides what is probably the best ocean view dining in West Maui. (Plan to come a half hour or so before sunset for the full experience.) Like the menu, the award-winning wine program is not just a list, but a concept that provides just the right complement, not only in wine to food, but food to ambiance, ambiance to service. The central fireplace evokes warmth quite differently than the Hawaiian sun, yet somehow both are reflected in a restaurant that looks, and feels, and tastes just like it should! Over the years, Chef Alex Stanislaw has evolved to meet the challenge of creating a menu equal to the superb view and the management team has grown right along with him. We liked this restaurant before, but now we really, *really* like it!

ROY'S KAHANA BAR AND GRILL ★ *Euro-Asian-Hawaiian Regional*
4405 Honoapiilani Hwy., Kahana Gateway (669-6999) HOURS: 5:30-10pm. SAMPLING: The menu specials changes nightly, so we really can't tell you what to expect - except a great dining experience! You can usually find individual pizzas like BBQ beef, smoked salmon & goat cheese, Thai chicken, or grilled vegetable; or Chinese chicken, marinated tomato, and rib & black bean salads $6.50-8.50. The fairly constant entrees include Mongolian pot roast, blackened

PLANTATION HOUSE RESTAURANT

ahi, salmon, plum duck, chicken stir-fry, or lemon grass crusted shutome $16.95-24.50. To those, add nightly specials like Tuscan ono cassoulet, crabmeat crusted monchong, cherry & ginger rack of lamb, bacon & spinach crusted salmon, or honey dijon short ribs $18.95-26.95. Special appetizers might include grilled shrimp with lobster pernod, chicken & goat cheese ravioli, BBQ pork & pineapple pizza, fish nacho salad, satay, or Korean mondoo $5.50-8.95. All entrees are a la carte or try their three-course prix menu for $32.95. For dessert, there are plenty of other options besides their signature dark chocolate souffle: Roy's "Snickers" bar, fresh banana creme brulee, fruit cobbler, or homemade ice cream and sorbets $5.50-6.50. COMMENTS: The food is as good as you've heard and Roy's is certainly deserving of its many rave reviews and dozens of national and local awards. He is one of the top chefs in the islands that have made Hawaiian Regional Cuisine (HRC) a trend of the 90's. Unfortunately, the noise from the kitchen combined with the high ceilings make it difficult to carry on a conversation. (But, hey - with its consistently good cuisine, it's worth it to just "shut up and eat" and keep an eye out for celebrity diners who might be dropping by!) Roy's Nicolina Restaurant is (connected) next door and offers a different twist on nightly specials. The "permanent" menu is the same for both so check the listing below for appetizer and entree samplings. Roy's will be opening a banquet room by the end of 1998 and will offer catering for wedding, parties, and private dinners. They are also still planning to open that Kihei outlet and are now looking at a (Maui-time) opening by Spring 1999 for the lucky 13th in their worldwide culinary conquests.

ROY'S NICOLINA ★ *Euro-Asian-Hawaiian Regional*
Kahana Gateway, 4405 Honoapiilani Hwy. (669-5000) HOURS: 5:30-9:30pm.
SAMPLING: Roy's Nicolina offers the same (seasonal) fixed menu as Roy's with additions each night based on what foods are the freshest available. Nightly specials might offer Mediterranean vegetable ravioli, pan-seared calamari with green curry sauce, seared shrimp & scallops, or Caesar salad to start $5-8.95. Entrees might include seafood napoleon, nori seared shrimp, crab crusted ono, grilled pork chops with pear bleu cheese, or filet mignon with wild mushroom cabernet $17.95-26.50. COMMENTS: Named after Roy and Janne Yamaguchi's daughter, Nicole, Roy's Nicolina is located right next door to Roy's and has become just as popular in its own right. Lana'i seating has recently been added affording diners a view of the West Maui Mountains (and an occasional rainbow or two.) This sister (daughter?) restaurant shares its "permanent" menu with Roy's (see listing above), but the nightly specials and preparations are uniquely their own.

THE TERRACE ★ *Pacific Rim Cuisine*
The Ritz-Carlton, Kapalua HOURS: Breakfast 6:30-11:30 am, dinner 5:30-10pm.
SAMPLING: Full American, Japanese and Hawaiian breakfasts $12-17. Dinner appetizers include sashimi, lobster tempura, oysters, shumai, clams, pan-fried tofu & mushrooms plus Caesar, Asian chicken or ahi & prawn salad $8.50-18. Seared mahi, kalbi chicken, sirloin burger, and smoked turkey club sandwiches for a light meal $9-14. Entrees include rare ahi tournedos, steamed onaga, seared salmon, Peking duck, and lamb osso bucco $21-28.50; cheese tortellini, prosciutto calzone, chicken chow mein $12-19. They offer weekend themed buffets

with dozens each of hot and cold items and a selection of desserts for $35 each. There's Seafood on Monday, Hawaiian Paniolo on Saturday, and Italian on Sunday. A little pricey, but the food is excellent and there's plenty of it! COMMENTS: Overlooking the courtyard and pool area with great sunset views. The pleasant, informal atmosphere has been enhanced by an extended patio with awnings that make it look like a "conservatory" or garden room of an elegant stately home.

KIHEI

INEXPENSIVE

ALEXANDER'S FISH, CHICKEN AND RIBS ★ *American*
1913 S. Kihei Rd. (874-0788) HOURS: 11am-9pm daily. SAMPLING: Meals $6.25-9.25; 13 piece baskets 15.75-19.95 Mahi, oysters, calamari, clams, chicken, ono, and shrimp. Fish available by the piece. A la carte items include zucchini sticks, cornbread, french fries, rice, hush puppies, cole slaw, BBQ beans, and onion rings. Broiled items, too: shrimp, ono or chicken sandwich. They also have BBQ ribs. COMMENTS: The first time we came here we thought they did a great job with both the basic fish as well as some of the more unusual offerings. The oysters (like owner Don) were brought in from Puget Sound and they were fresh and tasty. The calamari was tender, not chewy, and the fresh fish really was. But on a recent visit, we found just the opposite: the food was greasy, not cooked properly, and although our ahi was fresh, the portion was tiny and the bitter lettuce made it almost inedible. Since we've mostly heard good reports, we'll consider that this was just an off day and assume that they still deserve their star. They have limited seating at the counter or at a few patio tables, but plan to expand upstairs to offer roof top dining(!)

ANNIE'S DELI & CATERING *American*
2511 So. Kihei Rd. in the Nani Kai Village (875-8647) HOURS: 7am-5pm. SAMPLING: Breakfast served all day featuring pancakes, French toast, lox & bagel, fresh fruit plate, breakfast croissant $3.50-4.95; Annie's Aloha Breakfast (2 eggs with toast, taters or rice, ham, sausage, bacon, or cheese, and iced tea or coffee) $4.99. Sandwiches with choice of bread, cheese or side salad (potato, pasta, bean, or red slaw): turkey, ham, tuna, chicken salad, roast beef, French dip, reuben, pastrami, corned beef, veggie or BLT with avocado, and pita melts $5.95; tuna, chicken, Caesar, chef's, or oriental chicken $3.95-6.95. Daily specials (with entree, rice & salad); soup, spaghetti, chicken teriyaki, and sushi $3.50-5.95. Smoothies and shakes $3.50. COMMENTS: Small cafe with indoor & outdoor seating. Across from Kamaole Beach II.

AROMA D'ITALIA RISTORANTE ★ *Italian*
1881 S. Kihei Rd. at Kihei Town Center next to Foodland (879-0133) HOURS: Dinner Mon-Sat, 5-9pm. Closed Sun. SAMPLING: Antipasto and salads $4.95-7.95. Spaghetti (marinara or with garlic & broccoli), ravioli, lasagna, pasta primavera, linguini with clams, and scampi are some of the pastas. Veal piccata

or marsala, chicken or eggplant parmigiana, and sausage & peppers are a few of the meat offerings that include a side of pasta $6.95-14.95. Tiramisu, pineapple sorbetto, freshly made cannoli, or their special spumoni wedge for dessert $3.75-4.50. COMMENTS: They have now moved to a new location with more seating, but have continued to maintain their casual, homey atmosphere. Seating has increased from 28 to 70, but meals remain mostly under the $10 mark. They have also added a wine list! Dishes are still made from scratch using owner Marie Akina's family recipes. Ample portions, flavorful sauces: the spinach lasagna was GREAT although the sausage lasagna wasn't quite as good. The ravioli was a small portion (more like a side dish) but very inexpensive at $6.50. The side salad was our only real complaint, a disappointing "bag o' lettuce" and not worth the trouble to order which is just as well: you'll need all the room you can get for their WONDERFUL spumoni wedge! Layers and layers of cake and ice cream that we literally couldn't resist. We were too stuffed to have dessert, but Marie put it on the table and it was gone! (Well, you know we ARE eating professionals!) All in all this is still a great and affordable dining option and they keep their star. It's a charming, old-fashioned homestyle restaurant that has a lot of aloha - even if it *is* Italian!

(RESTAURANT) BUNJI *Japanese*
Kihei Kalama Village, 1913 S. Kihei Rd. (879-7051) HOURS: Dinner from 6pm; closed Sunday SAMPLING: Tripe stew, soybean, tofu, teriyaki duck, broiled fish $3-6. Duck noodles, squid, eel $7.50-12.50. Plate dinners $5. COMMENTS: Next to Tokyo Ramen (entrance near the back of Alexander's).

CASEY'S BAKEHOUSE ★ *Bakery/light lunches*
Kihei Commercial Center (879-7295) HOURS: 7am-6pm. SAMPLING: Lunches all under $5: vegetarian lasagna, Caesar or pasta salads, fresh made hummus and roasted turkey, chicken parmesan or vegetarian sandwiches. Specialty breads like Parmesana Tuscana, Maui onion with walnut, red potato with rosemary, Kalamata olive and sundried tomato. Danish, bear claws, sticky buns, muffins, and cranberry scones under $3 plus corn flake & coconut ranger cookies, white & chocolate biscotti and KC's secret recipe chocolate chip macadamia nut cookies. Dessert specialties of white chocolate mousse cake with raspberry glaze, mocha cheesecake, white chocolate pound cake, pear tarts, passion pecan pie, chocolate mousse cake or bars, and chocolate mac nut tart run from $2.50 per slice, $19 for 8" and up. COMMENTS: You're going to have to look a little harder to find their Kihei location. (From the Piilani Hwy., you turn on Ohukai Rd. and drive behind Gas Express.) Casey A. Logsdon is the owner; the bakery is the result of many award-winning years as pastry chef at Roy's (making chocolate souffle), Kapalua Bay Hotel, and Four Seasons.

COCONUTS BAKERY & CAFE *Pastries/light meals*
1819 South Kihei Rd. in Kukui Mall (879-0261) HOURS: 7am-8pm COMMENTS: Emphasis on the use of fresh island fruits in their muffins and pastries, also breads and cakes. A box lunch includes a sandwich, chips, and a cookie for $4.95. They still plan to add a small deli.

(THE) COFFEE STORE   *Coffee/pastries/light meals*
Azeka's Place II, 1279 S. Kihei Rd. (875-4244) <WWW> HOURS: Sun-Thurs 6am-10pm; Fri-Sat 6-11pm. SAMPLING: Muffins, cinnamon rolls, sticky buns, and assorted pastries $2.50. Spinach quiche, tortilla "wrapper" (veggie, chicken, or turkey), selection of quesadillas and sandwiches, lasagna, grilled veggie panini on focaccia; Caesar, tuna, pasta, or Caprese salad $6.95-8.50. Cheesecake, pies, brownies, baklava, cookies, and Chocolate Thunder $2.50-4.50. COMMENTS: They also have locations at Kaahumanu Center and Napili Plaza. Freshly roasted coffee and coffee drinks, flavored Italian sodas $1.50-3.95; smoothies $4.50. Voted "Best Cappuccino" in the "Best of Maui" contest by the *Maui News*.

CYBER CAFE & DELI   *American*
Maui Research & Technology Center (last building) above Lipoa St. (875-2415) <www.Cybercafe@Cybercafemaui.com> HOURS: Mon-Fri, 8:30am-4:30pm. SAMPLING: Danish, muffins, ham & cheese croissant, bagel with turkey or pastrami & cheese $1.60-4.95. Club sandwiches with ham, turkey, tuna, Italian sausage, pastrami, roast beef, or pineapple chicken; veggie burger on focaccia; quesadillas; Caesar, chef's, or Chinese chicken salad $4.95-6.50. Coffee drinks, juices, and desserts: eclairs, chocolate, mousse, and homemade pie or cake of the $3.50. COMMENTS: They're located at the home of Maui's high-performance computing center, so all orders come with a side of free Email and 30 free minutes on the internet!

DENNY'S   *American*
Kamaole Shopping Center (879-0604) HOURS: Open 24 hours. SAMPLING: Traditional Denny's burgers, sandwiches, salads, and dinners plus island favorites like saimin, mahi sandwich, spam & eggs, local-style plate lunches, and fresh catch. Prices from $5 (pancakes) to $15 (steak & shrimp dinner). Breakfast served anytime. Senior specials and kids meals available. COMMENTS: The Good Times Tavern sports bar serves wine, beer and liquor from 8am to midnight and features pool tables, dart machines, foos ball, juke box and NTN Satellite trivia hook up.

DINA'S SAND WITCH   *American*
145 North Kihei Rd., by Sugar Beach Condos (879-3262) HOURS: 11am-10pm. SAMPLING: Turkey, roast beef, club, reuben, spam, tuna egg salad, and hoagie sandwiches plus healthy grilled chicken or garden burger $5.50-6.95. A variety of hot dogs, burrito, saimin, nachos, potato skins, and homemade pasta & potato salads $4.95-6.95. COMMENTS: Flavored teas; milk shakes. Take-out available.

HAPA*S BREW HAUS   *Nightclub/Light meals*
Lipoa Shopping Center, 41 East Lipoa (879-9001; Entertainment hot line 875-1990). <WWW> HOURS: 3pm-1am. SAMPLING: Steamers, calamari, baked artichoke hearts, blackened ahi, and potstickers are a few of the starters $7.95-9.95. Caesar, Greek, or "haus" salad plus burgers, bratwurst, chicken parmesan, ham, turkey, or veggie sandwiches $5.95-7.95. Pasta primavera, fettucini alfredo, and linguini with clams, marinara, or pesto bay shrimp $9.95-11.95. Try pizzas & calzone in combinations of BBQ chicken, veggies, ham & pineapple, Italian

meats, pesto bay shrimp, or "white" with spinach & fresh garlic. (Calzones from $9.95, pizzas from $12.45-15.95 with white or whole wheat crust). COMMENTS: Their own handcrafted brews include Maui Wowee Wheat, Paradise Light, Red Sky Amner, and Black Lava Lager. They offer a good, basic menu, but it is more of an accompaniment to go with the nightly entertainment, live music, satellite sports, game room, and dancing. Mulberry St., the nightclub's new dining "annex," offers lunch and dinner. (Separate listing)

HAWAIIAN MOONS SALAD BAR & DELI   *Healthy/Vegetarian*
2411 South Kihei Rd. (875-4356) <WWW> HOURS: 11am-7pm, Fri-Sat till 9; store open 8am-9pm, till 6pm Sundays. SAMPLING: Salad bar offers organic greens and veggies plus rice and pasta salads, $4.79 lb. Hot entree selections include Third World Macaroni & Cheese, tofu enchiladas, African black-eyed peas, Ulu stew, and curried potatoes, $5.99 lb. Lasagna, homemade soup, and free-range turkey, turkey reuben, and roasted veggie sandwiches are also available with pizzas offered on Friday and Saturdays nights till 9pm. COMMENTS: The Hawaiian Moons Natural Food Store (next door) offers vitamins, herbs, and natural grocery items including fresh organic produce. The juice bar also serves espresso, smoothies, soft serve, and fruit cups. (Look for Hawaiian Moons to move to the open-air Aloha Market location - across the street from Kukui Mall - by the Fall of 1999.)

HENRY'S BAR AND GRILL   *American*
Lipoa Shopping Center (879-2849) HOURS: 10am-1am. SAMPLING: Limited menu: chicken wings, BBQ beef, hamburgers, sandwiches, and peel & eat shrimp $1.50-5.50. COMMENTS: A satellite with four televisions (one a big screen) for sporting events or your favorite soap opera. Dancing Wednesday-Sunday.

HIROHACHI   *Japanese*
Kihei Town Center, 1881 South Kihei Rd.(875-7474) HOURS: Lunch Wed-Thurs-Fri 12-3pm; Dinner nightly 5:30-10:30pm. SAMPLING: Lunch includes oyako Don, chicken katsu don, ten don, una don and tonkatsu or tempura teishoku $8.50-16; soba & udon noodle dishes $10.50-15.50. Set dinner menu offers chicken or pork cutlet and sashimi or tempura assortments $15-28. Sashimi and sushi combinations; vegetable and seafood rolls $4-28.50. COMMENTS: A large selection of sushi and sashimi.

HOME MAID BAKERY & DELI   *Local Bakery*
Azeka Place (874-6035) HOURS: 6:30am-6:30pm. SAMPLING: Sandwiches, soups, turkey, lasagna, and local plates mostly under $5. COMMENTS: Now there's a place in South Maui where you can get their wonderful empanadas, manju, and bread pudding. (Original bakery location in Wailuku.)

INTERNATIONAL HOUSE OF PANCAKES   *American*
Azeka's Place Shopping Center on South Kihei Rd. (879-3445) HOURS: Sunday-Thursday 6am-10pm, Friday and Saturday 6am-midnight. SAMPLING: Breakfast, lunch, and dinner choices served anytime. The usual breakfast fare and sandwiches from $5. "Homestyle" dinners run from $12 and include soup or salad, roll and butter. COMMENTS: Children's menu. Crowded on weekends!

ISANA *Korean/yakiniku/sushi*
Maui Isana Resort, 515 So. Kihei Rd. (874-5700) HOURS: Lunch/dinner 11am-10pm, sushi bar 5-10pm. SAMPLING: Appetizers include "computer spell-checker" favorites like Jhap Chee, Bhin De Duk, Yuk He, He Mulo Jhun, and Fried Man doo $6.50-14.95 plus soup, noodles, and specialties like Yook E Jang, Doenjang Gghige, Kal Bi Tang, Hwe Dup Bhap, Mul Naeng Myun, and Bibhim Bhap. (Luckily, they also have ox tail soup, and shrimp or calamari stir fry!) $9.50-14.95. Yakiniku (table top cooking) offers fish, brisket, beef tongue, kalbi or short ribs, tenderloin, shrimp & vegetable, pork loin, and chicken $12.50-18.50. Nigiri and maki sushi $5.25-13 plus appetizers of baked mussels, ahi poke, spicy fish roe, and Dynamite $5-8.50. COMMENTS: Cocktails upstairs at the Karaoke Club (Karaoke from 9pm-1am). You're on your own to figure out the menu although we do have a few clues (from Korean menus past) to start you out: bul ko gi is thinly sliced BBQ marinated meat, jhun is BBQ meat in egg batter, bi bim naeng myun is cold buckwheat noodles with beef and vegetables, yuk ke jang is spicy beef soup with vegetables and rice noodle, and bi beem bap is made with rice, vegetables, chopped BBQ beef, and fried eggs. (If you mix and match a few words and compare similar spellings, you can probably get a head start on ordering. A word of caution, though: at $26.95 and $34.50 respectively, we recommend you find out for sure about Ghopchang Jungol and He Mul Jungol *before* you order. . . and let us know!)

JACK'S FAMOUS BAGELS *Bagels & Sandwiches*
2395 S. Kihei Rd. at the Dolphin Plaza. (891-2227) < WWW > HOURS: Mon-Fri 6am-6pm; Sat 6:30-5; Sun 7-3 SAMPLING: Mix and match bagel flavors (garlic, onion, macadamia nut, blueberry, jalapeno, sesame, sundried tomato, spinach, coconut, and pineapple) with gourmet whipped cream cheese (garlic herb, veggie, pesto, lox, strawberry, blueberry, jalapeno, pineapple, coconut). Bagelwiches of cream cheese & lox, tuna, egg salad, hummus, PB & J, cheese, and turkey $2.25-7.50. Pat's Pizza: cheese, veggie, jalapeno, pepperoni, Hawaiian $3.95-4.75; Melts with turkey, tuna, or ham $5.95. Salads $2.95; Cheese bagel, bagel dog, bagel chips $1.50-2.95. Coffee drinks, smoothies $1.25-3.25. COMMENTS: Authentic water-boiled bagels (freshly-made without fat or oils) from a third generation New York bagel recipe. Try the pineapple bagel with coconut cream cheese and make your own pina colada! Also in Lahaina and Kahului with slightly different prices.

JOY'S PLACE *Healthy Fast Food*
Island Surf Building (879-9258) HOURS: Mon-Fri 10am-3pm. SAMPLING: Colorful mixed green or hearty pasta, bean, potato, grain, or sea vegetable salads $2.25-3.50; combination plate $4.75. Tuna, hummus & avocado, oven-roasted turkey, avocado & provolone sandwiches served on freshly baked bread in halves or wholes $2.25-5.75. Beef or vegetable chili and rice; vegan vegetable soup $3.25-4.75. Rice wrapper "salad roll" with dipping sauces from $2.50; Big Island Spirulina Smoothie $3.50. COMMENTS: Healthy fast food with organically and locally-grown ingredients. Daily specials might offer curried hummus rolls with quinoa salad, nut spread nori rolls, falafels with tabouleh, or roasted eggplant & feta sandwich ($5.75) and soups like carrot-ginger, yam with lime & ginger or yellow split pea $3.75-4.25.

KALAMA VILLAGE BAKERY   *Sandwiches/Pastries*
Kihei Kalama Village, 1913 So. Kihei Rd. (879-6180) HOURS: 6am-7pm. SAMPLING: Soups, croissant sandwiches, and "pizza" stuffed bread plus a variety of tortes (Linzer, suchard, mocha, lemon, raspberry truffle), Black Forest or carrot cake, key lime tart, and award-winning Maui Mousse. Specialty breads like honey wheat raisin-macadamia nut and a selection of pastries. COMMENTS: Sunny and spacious patio deck with tables & umbrellas.

KAL BI HOUSE   *Korean*
1215 S. Kihei Rd., near Longs Drugs (874-8454) HOURS: 9:30am-9:30pm. SAMPLING: Same menu for lunch and dinner with slightly lower lunch prices. Plate lunch special $5.75 served until 2pm. House special $8.99. Order mixed plate combination meals or separate entrees of BBQ short ribs, fried mandoo dumpling, Bi Beem Bap (Great name! It's rice, vegetables, chopped BBQ and fried eggs), hot spicy chicken, chicken katsu or fried oysters. Stews and soups include some more exotic selections including kim chee, small intestine or cuttle fish stew, seaweed soup and rice or Duk Mandoo Kook $6.99-8.50. (Authors' note: These weird words just drive our computer spell-check system nuts!) COMMENTS: Oriental murals and rugs, Chinese fish bowl planters, Shoji screens and antique fans. All this and Korean music in the background!

KIHEI CAFFE   *Continental*
1945 S. Kihei Rd. (879-2230) HOURS: Breakfast 5am-2pm, Sun. 6am-noon; lunch till 2:30pm. SAMPLING: Breakfast includes Huevos Rancheros, biscuits and gravy, veggie & cheese home fries, French toast, flavored pancakes, muesli, and omelettes $4.25-6.75. Chopped steak, burgers, and sandwiches range from hot pastrami, cajun mahi, and teri chicken to mock chicken tofu, tavern ham, salami, and BLT $5.75-7.95. Couscous, tabouli, Greek, and honey cashew chicken salads $6.25 COMMENTS: A popular restaurant for locals to hang out that visitors have begun discovering as well. Coffee drinks and fresh baked goods made daily. Picnic baskets with sandwiches, drinks, chips, fruit and cookies from $10. COMMENTS: Really yummy breakfasts - not a steal, but a good value. Plan on a bit of a wait as there seem to be plenty of early-to-rise locals and jet-lagged visitors who take advantage of the 5am opening! The French toast is available with cinnamon raisin or Portuguese sweet bread and was light and fluffy. Huevos Rancheros were wonderful as were the omelettes. Heading out to the beach or on a road trip, pick up a Hana Box Lunch to Go for $7.50. We appreciate their keiki breakfast and lunch menu with nothing over $3.25!

KOISO SUSHI BAR   *Sushi*
Dolphin Plaza, 2395 South Kihei (875-8258) COMMENTS: We finally learned the name of this small sushi bar at the Dolphin Plaza, but after repeated phone calls to get information that's still all we know.

LAVA'S BAR & GRILL   *American*
61 South Kihei Rd., next to Suda's Store in Kihei. (879-8855) COMMENTS: Small, funky "alternative" restaurant and bar that is "straight friendly." It's too bad they never sent us any information as they actually offer some surprisingly good "homecooking" - particularly the thick, crusty macaroni & cheese!

LIFE'S A BEACH   *American/Mexican*
Kihei Kalama Village, 1913 S. Kihei Rd. (891-8010) HOURS: 11am-10pm; bar
& selected pupu menu till 2 am. SAMPLING: Salads, burrito, soft tacos,
burgers, hot dogs, nachos, garlic steamers, chili, quesadilla, Italian sausage.
Sandwiches (Roast beef or turkey dip, ham, pineapple chicken, BLT) and tortilla
wraps with choice of five from a dozen ingredients) $5.95-6.95. All-you-can-eat
spaghetti every Wednesday $5.95. COMMENTS: Life's a beach, but if you're
in a hurry they'll get your lunch in 10 minutes or it's free! (Selected items, Mon-
Fri from 11am-2pm) There's real sand at the front entrance with tall tables and
beach umbrellas for outdoor seating. Inside there's a wrap around bar with
several tvs, lots of surfing and sports mementos and bright yellow & white
striped tablecloths. Live entertainment on weekends along with karaoke and
waiters who sing and tell jokes. (Laughing at them is optional.) Mucho cheapo
margaritas and mai tais, and overall good food and good value especially for bar
food. The burritos are a hefty portion, dude.

MAUI TACOS   *Healthy Mexican*
Kamaole Beach Center (879-5005) HOURS: 9am-9pm. SAMPLING: Potato
enchiladas, hard or soft tacos, quesadillas, chimichangas, nachos, and over a
dozen varieties of special hand-held burritos in fish, steak, chicken, beef or
vegetarian combinations with black beans $1.65-6.95. COMMENTS: Guacamole
and salsa made fresh every day. No lard, no msg - they use only vegetable oil,
fresh beans and lean meats. The complimentary salsa bar offers several choices
with jalapenos, onions, cilantro, hot sauce and more. Good values! The original
is in Napili Plaza with other outlets now in Lahaina Square and Kaahumanu Food
Court, all owned and operated by Mark Ellman of Avalon.

OASIS POOL BAR   *American*
Maui Coast Hotel, 2259 S. Kihei Rd. (879-6284) HOURS: 11am-9:30pm. SAM-
PLING: Sashimi, calamari, chicken wings, Caesar, taco, or cobb salad, cheese
and fruit, chicken or fish on a stick, veggie plate, prawn cocktail, burgers, hot
dogs, tuna, turkey, chicken, or fish sandwiches $3.95-8.95. Smoothies $4. COM-
MENTS: Family-owned and operated. Tropical drinks, beer & wine; live
Hawaiian & contemporary music and dancing nightly. Free hula show Thursday
and Sunday, 6:30-9:30pm.

PANDA EXPRESS   *Mandarin Chinese*
At Azeka Place II Shopping Center. HOURS: Daily 10:30am-9pm. SAMPLING:
Combination plates $4.29-8.19 for choice of 1-3 a la carte items (e.g. orange
chicken, chop suey, sweet & sour pork) $3.79-8.49 each. Chef's specials: BBQ
chicken, eggplant in garlic, Szechuan bean curd $3.79-8.49. COMMENTS: A
chain of restaurants started in California. Also at the Kaahumanu Food Court.

PEGGY SUE'S   *Burgers And Such*
Azeka Place II, 1279 S. Kihei Rd. (875-8944) HOURS: 11am-10pm.
SAMPLING: The menu reflects the 50's diner/malt shop theme with sandwiches,
burgers and hot dogs served with "the works" and a side of fries. Go for a Good
Golly Miss Molly (teriyaki burger with pineapple), Earth Angel (garden burger),

Blue Moon (bacon & blue cheese) or Don't Be Cruel (chili-cheese burger) $5.95-7.25; doubles to $8.55. Try a Sea Cruise (tuna), Splish Splash (fish) or Funky Chicken sandwich, or garden, Caesar, or teri chicken salad $3.25-7.95. Plate lunches $5.95-8.95. Ain't Nothing but a Hound Dog is priced at $4.95; other Hot Diggity Dogs run $4.25-5.55. They recently added BBQ spare ribs, $9.95 for half-rack. COMMENTS: They feature an original 1954 Seeburg juke box that operates from the box or by remote from the dining tables. Owners David and Cathy Tarbox relied on David's former occupation as a 1950's soda jerk in planning and decorating their restaurant and it looks like they had a great time doing it! The pink & blue decor gives the malt shop a suitable "Peggy Sue" look and there are plenty of cool, creamy selections including malts, milkshakes, egg creams, phosphates, sundaes, and banana splits to keep the 50's tradition alive in the 90's. They actually do a better job with the chicken dishes and sandwiches than with the burgers, and the French "fries" were oven-baked which took away from their well, "authenticity." (Too healthy?) Cute place - we liked the fun and friendly atmosphere, but the food wouldn't bring us back.

ROYAL THAI CUISINE   *Thai*
Azeka Shopping Center, 1280 S. Kihei Rd. (874-0813) HOURS: Mon-Fri 11-3pm for lunch, daily 5-9:30pm for dinner. SAMPLING: Traditional Thai appetizers, soups, salads plus entrees such as chicken cashew basil, mussels in black bean sauce, Evil Prince shrimp, lemon beef, Thai rice noodle with seafood, sateh broccoli & tofu, and garlic squid $4.95-9.95. Fish in spicy sauce, lobster or crab curry, Thai spicy steak $10-95-13.95. COMMENTS: The prices are pretty decent, but the portions are a little small. Food was good, but nothing outstanding.

SANDPIPER   *American*
Kamaole Sands Resort, 2695 South Kihei Rd. (874-8700) HOURS: Breakfast 8-11am; lunch 11am-3pm; dinner 5-9pm. SAMPLING: Eggs benedict, pancakes, loco moco, sweet bread $4.50-7.25 Lunch sandwiches include beef or veggie burgers, hot dog, BLT, and grilled mahi (with scallion ginger sauce) or grilled chicken (with roast peppers and caramelized onions) $4.25-7.25. Chicken Caesar or Asian chicken salad (with won ton and a tasty ginger dressing), $6.35. Dinners begin with gazpacho, poached salmon salad, shrimp cocktail, or tomato mozzarella salad $4.75-11.95. Fresh fish, rack of lamb (with apricot raspberry compote), BBQ ribs, seafood linguini, chicken stir fry, or rib eye steak are the entrees, $10.75-17.25. COMMENTS: This poolside restaurant for guests of the condominium is now open to the public. Good prices; pleasant, relaxing atmosphere. The same owners also operate a submarine sandwich shop at Rainbow Plaza.

SENOR TACO   *Mexican*
Dolphin Plaza, 2395 South Kihei Rd. (875-2901) HOURS: 10am-9pm. Closed Sunday. SAMPLING: Tacos, enchiladas, tamales $1.80-2.25; tostadas, quesadilla, chile relleno, taco salad, flautas, chimichangas, chilaquiles, sopas, nachos, burritos, and huevos range $3.50-6.50. Combinations dishes run $5.75.

COMMENTS: The usual beef & chicken varieties, with some surprises: mushroom quesadilla, potato chimichanga, chorizo & egg burrito, and a tongue taco! Homecooked "fast food" using authentic Mexican spices with many ingredients imported from Mexico.

SHAKA SANDWICH AND PIZZA ★   *American-Italian*
Paradise Plaza, 1295 So. Kihei Rd. behind Jack-in-the-Box across from Star Market (874-0331) HOURS: 10:30am-9pm; Fri & Sat till 10 SAMPLING: Hot Philadelphia cheese steak (or new chicken cheese steak) with sauteed Maui onions, cold hoagies from $4.10 sm./$8.20 lg. (Supreme $5.10/10.20). All sandwiches are served on their homemade Italian bread from a recipe passed down in the family for years. Pizza available in thin crust or thick square Sicilian pies; $12.95-21.95 for traditional, "white," or their new chicken pesto. Calzone and stromboli $9.95-12.95. COMMENTS: If you like New York subway-style pizza you're in for a real treat. If you have no idea what New York subway-style pizza is, you're also in for a real treat! We've always been partial to their gourmet white cheese pizza with garlic and broccoli. They also have soft pretzels, Caesar salads, fresh-cut fries, homemade garlic bread, and cheesecake $1.85-5.50.

SILVERSWORD GOLF CLUB RESTAURANT   *American*
Located at the Silversword Golf Course (879-0515) HOURS: 11am-2:30pm for lunch daily. SAMPLING: Roast beef, ham, turkey, tuna, corned beef, reuben, pastrami, grilled cheese & bacon sandwiches plus hamburgers, salads, and soups: Portuguese bean, corn chowder, and made-to-order French onion $3-5. Lunch entrees offer beef stroganoff, shrimp Silversword, pasta primavera, mahi mahi, roast pork, chicken piccata, eggplant parmesan, and beef curry - all affordably priced from $6-8. COMMENTS: Located on a lofty setting with a pleasant view of Kihei and beyond Kaho'olawe and Molokini.

SOUTH BEACH CAFE   *Sandwiches/Pastries*
1455 So. Kihei Rd., Maui Dive Shop lot across from St. Theresa's (874-0595) HOURS: 7:30am-7pm. SAMPLING: Breakfast items include cinnamon rolls, chocolate croissants, bagels and fresh Hawaiian fruit plate $1-2.50. Gourmet coffees and coffee drinks; cold beverages; fruit smoothies with boosters $1-3.50. Sandwiches served until 3:30pm: Black Forest ham, roast beef, hickory smoked turkey, prosciutto, tuna, BBQ chicken breast, and prime rib $5; veggie $4. Prime rib dinner with BBQ beans, rice, and cole slaw $9.95 (served 4-7pm). COMMENTS: This would be a hole-in-the-wall (except there's no wall), but it is tiny and has very limited seating outside. They do make a tasty (messy!) BBQ chicken sandwich and it's a good place for a cool drink or bite to eat if you get caught in any of that Kihei Road traffic south of Lipoa - just turn right and wait'll it goes by!

SOUTH SHORE GRINDS   *Healthy food with a local flair*
Kihei Gateway Plaza, 362 Huku Li'i Pl. (875-8472) HOURS: 8am-8pm. Closed Sundays. SAMPLING: Power breakfasts can be ordered with all egg whites, or try the tofu scramble, banana pancakes, breakfast burger, or French toast with

fresh fruit & whipped cream $4.25-6.50. Plate lunches offer shoyu, cashew, or roasted curry chicken; calamari steak, hamburger, fresh catch, or hoison BBQ ribs $4.50-7.95. Burgers range from taro to Thai with Hawaiian, southwestern, and cajun in between $3.25-6.95. Power salads include fresh catch, Indo or lemon lime chicken, or Caesar with hearts of palm plus an innovative selection of pupus (Moloka'i sweet potato chips with banana curry dipping sauce, chicken sate with kiwi salsa and peanut sauce, deep-fried tofu, and coconut calamari) $3.95-8.50. COMMENTS: Opened April, 1998 in the former Boomers location above the highway behind Gas Express. New owners Stefanie Glasser and Chef Rob Wedaa have definitely given the South Shore something good to "grind" with innovative and ono menu selections that give guidebook authors something new and different to write about - and to eat!

SPORTS PAGE GRILL AND BAR *American*
2411 S. Kihei Rd. (879-0602) HOURS: 11:30am-10pm; bar till midnight SAM-PLING: Seattle Supersonics Reuben, Utah Jazz Ham and Cheese, Robby Naish Tuna Salad, Tiger Woods Jr. Club, Pete Rose BLT (Bet, Lose, Trial), and Don King Turkey. COMMENTS: Got the idea? This is definitely the spot for sports aficionados. With confident good humor their menu resembles a newspaper tabloid and reads, "You will be served in 5 minutes...or maybe 10 minutes...or maybe even 15 minutes...relax and enjoy yourself." It may take at least 15 minutes to read over the menu. The front page covers a good selection of domestic and imported beers (plus premium draft) and pre-season games (appetizers), followed on the inside by dugout dogs, champion burgers, sport fishing sandwiches, hot and cold bowl games (otherwise known as soups and salads), and "game favorite" deli sandwiches. Tropical drinks and post-game desserts are on the back. Prices from $2.95-8.45 with only a few items over two digits. Full game room with darts, pool, shuffleboard, video games, and pinball. A big screen TV with remote monitors for college and pro games, championship fights, and satellite subscription events.

SUDA SNACK SHOP *Local Style*
61 S. Kihei Rd. by the gas station along S. Kihei Rd. (879-2668) HOURS: 6am-12:30pm (Closed Sunday). SAMPLING: Burgers $1.95-2.50, hot dogs $1.25-1.65, saimin $2.50-2.75, chow fun $2.75, bentos $4. COMMENTS: We were disappointed that this little "dive" wasn't one of the island's best kept secrets. The burgers were so-so, the french fries were pricey for the portion and the chow fun wasn't a meal, it was snack size. See you in Wailuku!

SUSHI PARADISE *Sushi/Sashimi*
1215 South Kihei Rd., Longs Drugs Kihei Center(879-3751) HOURS: Tues-Sun 6-11pm; closed Monday. SAMPLING: Sushi and sushi rolls $4-8.50; sushi or sashimi combinations, rainbow roll $17.50-25; Dynamite, udon, or sunomono salad $7.50. COMMENTS: Domestic and Japanese beer, hot and cold sake. Karaoke from 9pm.

TASTE OF BROADWAY *New York Italian/Pizza*
Kihei Kalama Village, 1913 So. Kihei Rd. (875-8750) HOURS: 11am-9:30pm. SAMPLING: Brick oven pizza from $5.95M/9.99L plus toppings. Their baked

stromboli ($4.95) or Calzone ($5.55) come in steak, meatball, pepperoni & ham, sausage, spinach, or broccoli; NY sandwiches (steak, hot pastrami, and homemade sausage or meatball) $5.95M/8.95L. Family-recipe pasta meals include salad and garlic bread: Marinara, Arabiata, Putanesca, broccoli & garlic or lasagna $5.95. COMMENTS: Original location at Kau Kau Food Court at the Maui Marketplace.

THAI CHEF *Thai*
Rainbow Mall, 2439 S. Kihei Rd. (874-5605) HOURS: Lunch 11am-2:30pm; Mon-Fri, dinner nightly 5-10pm. SAMPLING: Same menu as their original Lahaina location: Thai crisp noodles, sateh, green papaya salad, Thai toast, Evil Prince, Cornish game hen, honey lemon chicken $4.95-13.95. Seafood saute, Thai scampi, lobster curry, garlic squid $9.95-13.95 COMMENTS: A very lengthy menu ranging from noodle dishes to salads, seafood, vegetarian fare and curry dishes. Entrees available in mild, medium or hot (!)

TOBI'S ICE CREAM AND SHAVE ICE *American-local*
1913 South Kihei Rd. (891-2440) HOURS: 10am-6pm, summers till 9. SAMPLING: Have a quick chili lunch (with rice, nachos or on a hot dog), then dig in to the homemade (Roselani) ice cream pies, special sundaes, smoothies, frozen bananas, and chocolate covered strawberries ($1.50-5). Espresso, coffee drinks, and 30 flavors of "gourmet" shave ice $3.25; with ice cream $3.65. COMMENTS: This started as a family operation: the store was built by Tobi's father and run by Tobi and her mom, Puddie. It features an old woody surfboard that has been made into a table and there is now seating on the lanai. Tobi is busy taking care of twins, so Betty & Nick took over in December of 1997. No credit cards.

TOKYO RAMEN *Japanese noodles*
19113 S. Kihei Rd., Kihei Kalama Village (879-2558) HOURS: Lunch 11am-3pm, dinner 5-9:30pm. Closed Sundays. SAMPLING: Plate dishes of chicken katsu, BBQ pork, chicken or beef teriyaki, meat jhun (beef), tonkatsu (pork), beef bowl, or fried rice $4.75-6.25; kim chee and gyoza $2-4. Ramen flavors of shoyu, miso, vegetable, chicken katsu, char siu, tempura, spicy seafood, and chicken or beef yakisoba $5.25-7.25. COMMENTS: Cute little place located on the side street across from Foodland, just behind Life's A Beach.

MODERATE

BAMBOO BISTRO *Hawaiian Regional Cuisine/Rotisserie*
Ma'alaea Harbor Village (244-7979) HOURS: Scheduled to open Spring 1999 for lunch and dinner. SAMPLING: "Small" plates - like Pacific Rim tapas - to make dining casual, fun - and less expensive! Sesame crusted fish with spicy lilikoi sauce, Kahua Ranch lamb, and wok-charred ahi are just a few of the signature dishes that will be offered by owner/chef Peter Merriman. Chicken, lamb, duck, and even fresh fish will be prepared on the rotisserie or the kiawe wood grill which will also be used for their freshly baked hearth breads. Mostly "small plates" in the $7-14 range; a few complete dinners from $18-25.

COMMENTS: The latest venture from Hawaiian Regional Cuisine Chef Peter Merriman, this 4,500 sq. ft. restaurant will be the Maui version of the original Merriman's on the Big Island. Three levels, all with views of the harbor and the ocean. The rotisserie is new, but Merriman's tradition of using the freshest island produce and locally-raised meats continues. Complete wine list. SCHEDULED TO OPEN SPRING 1999. (NOT OPEN AS WE GO TO PRESS)

BUZZ'S WHARF *American-Seafood*
Ma'alaea Harbor (244-5426) HOURS: Lunch 11am-3pm; Dinner 5-9pm. SAMPLING: Lunches start with escargot, calamari rings, oysters, steamer clams, stuffed mushroom, or artichoke plus Maui onion soup, clam chowder, and Caesar or Tuscan salad $6.95-11.95. Fresh fish, teri steak or chicken, BBQ ribs, seafood pasta, fish or shrimp & chips, and prawns Tahitian $13.95-19.95. French dip, oyster sub, Caesar or cajun chicken, burgers, and tuna sandwiches $6.95-9.95. Dinner menu offers the same starters as lunch - and for the same prices! In addition to the lunch entrees, dinners include shrimp or scallop scampi, ribeye steak, chicken marsala, and seafood medley. $16.95-24.95. For dessert try the mango creme brulee or baked papaya Tahitian - both were chosen first place winners at Taste of Lahaina $4.95. Entrees are served with salad, vegetables and fresh baked rolls. COMMENTS: Offers a scenic view of the Ma'alaea Harbor activities. Bar/lounge. Vegetarian entrees and a full page keiki menu. Be sure to try their house specialty, Prawns Tahitian, as well as their award-winning desserts.

CANTON CHEF *Cantonese-Szechuan*
Kamaole Shopping Center (879-1988) HOURS: Lunch 11-2pm and dinner 5-9pm. SAMPLING: Lunch specials of won ton mein or soup, crispy gau gee mein, lunch plate $5.50-6.25. Set dinners for 2 or more from $22.50. Appetizers, soups, earthen pot courses, Szechuan dishes, and sizzling platters include potstickers, baked shrimp, preserved pickles, abalone soup, black mushrooms & Chinese cabbage, Grandma's shrimp or pork with tofu, sauteed clams, stir fry scallops, steamed pork hash, Mongolian beef, and Canton roast duck $6-14.

CHUCK'S *American*
Kihei Town Center (879-4489) HOURS: Lunch 11am-2:30pm & interim menu 2:30-5pm both served Mon-Sat. Dinner nightly 5-10pm. SAMPLING: Taco or Caesar salad; sandwiches feature turkey, fish, French dip, reuben, and burgers ($4.95-9.95) or you can order a plate lunch, chicken-fried steak, or fresh fish $5.75-10.95. Daily specials like roast turkey, teriyaki shrimp, spaghetti & meat balls, beef stew, stir fry, ravioli, and beef stroganoff $5.95. Escargot, smoked marlin, cheese-stuffed jalapeno peppers, artichoke, scampi, or sauteed maushrooms are available as dinner appetizers $4.95-7.25. Dinner selections include rice or baked potato or fries and salad bar with homebaked seasoned bread. Steaks, prime rib, BBQ ribs, teri chicken or steak, pasta primavera, cajun mahi, lobster, or shrimp $12.95-24.95. If you're still hungry, go for the mud pie, hula pie, chocolate thunder or lemon coconut cake, or strawberry turtle cheesecake $3.50-4.75. COMMENTS: Especially popular for its salad bar which is also available all day from $6.95. (Pretty fair selection with eighteen items and

six dressings.) They have enough daily lunch specials to last for nine weeks with barely a repeat! And they all come with some sort of salad, starch, or vegetable - a great value at $5.95. Early bird BBQ chicken or fish (5-6:30pm) for $10.95. Good children's menu. And now they offer Chuck's Blend coffee - a special blend of sumatra and Hawaiian hazelnut that comes in 1 lb. packages suitable for squishing into the fullest of suitcases!

GREEK BISTRO ★ *Greek*
Kai Nani Shopping Center, 2511 South Kihei Rd. (879-9330) HOURS: Dinner served 5-10pm. SAMPLING: Stuffed grape leaves, pita with tzaiziki, sauteed mushrooms or calamari, Greek salad $3.50-7.95. Lamb, moussaka, pastichio, and spanakopita served a la carte $14.95-16.95 or in combination in the Feast of the Gods platter for $19.95. Mediterranean specialties: shrimp & scallop or lamb kabobs, seafood pasta, leg of lamb, chicken in mandarin orange sauce, steak & prawns, chicken or lamb souvlakia, $14.95-21.95. Cheesecake or baklava for dessert $5. COMMENTS: This little restaurant is a delightful surprise. The Feast of the Gods is excellent and definitely the way to try a little of everything. Renovations have added some classic touches of wood to the bar and around the patio area giving this little garden hideaway the look of a quaint, but elegant European hotel. The seating has also been expanded and they've added an international gift shop. Check this one out!

HAMILTON'S BEACH CAFE *Italian*
760 S. Kihei Rd., at the Menehune Shores Condominiums (879-6399) COMMENTS: The owner never sent us any information and was rather snitty when he told us that he doesn't really care if he's in the book or not. With an attitude like that, we don't really care if you go to his restaurant or not.

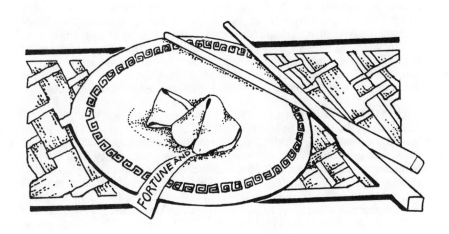

KAHALE BEACH CLUB   *Pupus/Seafood Bar*
1013 So. Kihei Rd; in the rear of Kihei Kalama Village (875-7711)
HOURS:10am-1:30am. SAMPLING: Chicken or jalapeno poppers, taquitos, whole artichoke, buffalo wings, fries, onion rings $2.50-4; 1/2 lb. burger or peel & eat shrimp $4.50. COMMENTS: Funky bar with live music and inexpensive pupus that are even more so during early or late Happy Hours. The "Shuckin' Shack" seafood bar recently opened in the back offering fresh, raw oysters and clams (by the dozen or the bucket) along with steamed shrimp, gumbo, seafood chowder, and cole slaw.

KAI KU ONO BAR & GRILL   *Sandwiches & Pupus*
2511 S. Kihei Rd., at Kai Nani Village (875-1007) HOURS: Breakfast 7:30-11:30am; dinner 5-10pm; sandwiches, salads & pupus 12-12 SAMPLING: All-day menu includes fish & chips, burgers, French dip, grilled chicken, or fish sandwiches plus chicken or ahi Caesar and No Ka Oi salad (made with upcountry greens, apples, walnuts, raisins, & gorgonzola), and steamer clams, spring rolls, pot stickers, pan-fried calamari, and sashimi $6.95-13.95. Dinners offer mango BBQ ribs, ravioli, seared ahi, fresh catch, scampi, stir-fry, NY strip steak, and KKO chicken with ginger-mandarin sauce $12.95-15.95. Breakfast sorbets and smoothies, blueberry pancakes, oatmeal, omelettes, granola and Hawaiian sweet bread French toast $2.95-5.95. COMMENTS: Formerly La Bahia ("The Bay"), Kai Ku Ono means the same in Hawaiian. New owners are now using the nickname "KKO."

KAMAOLE BAR AND GRILL   *American*
Maui Coast Hotel, 2259 S. Kihei Rd. (874-6284) HOURS: Breakfast 7-11am; lunch 11am-4:30pm; dinner 4:30-9:30pm. SAMPLING: Egg dishes, omelettes, biscuits & gravy, banana-macadamia pancakes, and sweetbread French toast $4.95-7.50. Cobb, macadamia chicken, prawn, and Caesar salads or Kalua pork quesadilla, crab won tons, fried calamari, fish & chips, and spicy chicken wings $5.95-7.95. A good variety of sandwiches including Kalua pork, Philly cheesesteak, hot crab melt, Maui Coast club (with Portuguese sausage and turkey) and fresh ahi $5.95-9.95. Dinner entrees include stuffed chicken, fresh fish, steak, seafood marinara, garlic prawns, chicken tortellini, and pasta primavera $10.95-19.95. Hawaiian sweet bread pudding, mud pie, or creme caramel for dessert $3.75-4.25 COMMENTS: Good selection of salads and sandwiches.

MARGARITA'S BEACH CANTINA   *Mexican*
101 N. Kihei Rd., Kealia Village (879-5275) HOURS: Food service 11am-10pm, bar open till midnight. SAMPLING: Quesadillas, nachos, pot stickers, fish & chips, taco or chicken salad, Mexican pizza, tostadas, hot & spicy fried fish plus burgers and sandwiches $5.95-8.95. Combination plates of enchiladas, tacos, chili relleno, tamales, and tostadas $12.95-15.95. Specials include chimichanga, teri chicken, steak or fish tacos, seafood enchiladas, and fajitas $10.95-14.95. From 5pm, dinner items like sweet & sour prawns, mahi Vera Cruz, prawn saute, and NY steak are added to the menu $14.95-16.95. COMMENTS: Outdoor dining on their oceanview deck. Margaritas come in tropical flavors like mango, pineapple, guava, banana, and coconut. And Tuesday is live Maine lobster night:

served with rice and black beans for $12.95 (from 5pm till they run out!) Live music Sunday afternoons from 2:30-5:30pm; Friday "pau hana" (finish work) party with music and live broadcast 5-7pm. Bar features satellite TV and electronic dart boards.

MULBERRY ST. *Italian*
Lipoa Shopping Center, 41 East Lipoa (879-7790) HOURS: Lunch 11am-2:30pm, Mon-Fri., Dinner 5:30-9:30pm. Closed Sundays. SAMPLING: Sauteed mushrooms, fried calamari, fresh mozzarella with grilled eggplant or prosciutto, poached clams, Caesar of the day, and grilled shrimp, fennel & orange salad are a few of the starters $6-9. Pastas like rigatoni with shrimp & cognac, linguini carbonara or with seafood, penne with pancetta or vodka cream sauce, and fettucine with grilled chicken & prosciutto in lemon white wine sauce run $10-18. Fresh fish can be ordered grilled, sauteed in pesto cream, topped with julienne vegetables, or stuffed with crabmeat. Daily specials of steak, chicken, pork chops, and lamb come in a variety of preparations including grilled with mushrooms, pan-seared with peppers, and topped with spinach and pernod sauce $13-25. Many of the same salads, pasta, and entree dishes are offered in smaller portions for lunch $6-10. COMMENTS: This intimate bistro has the look of a small Greenwich Village eatery; its modern black and white color scheme accented by historic photos of turn-of-the century Little Italy. The New York feel is further enhanced by being just steps away from live entertainment from Hapa*s nightclub next door. Opened June, 1998. (Not open as we go to press.)

OUTBACK STEAKHOUSE *Themed Steakhouse*
Safeway Shopping Center at Lipoa & Piilani Hwy. HOURS: (OPENING SPRING 1999) Mon-Tues 4-10pm, Fri till 11; Saturday 3-11pm, Sun till 10. SAMPLING: "Aussie-tizers" include "shrimp on the barbie" and their signature Bloomin' Onion $5.89-7.49; "Bonzer" Salads $7.99-9.99. Complete dinners include "Down Under Favorites" (pork chops, grilled chicken, fresh fish, and assorted pastas) and "Land Rover" steaks, rack of lamb, and prime rib $13.99-19.99. Sandwiches & burgers $6.49-7.49 COMMENTS: The Outback in Kahana opened May 1998 (see separate listing for more detailed menu information) and this "down under" Kihei location was expected to be open by Spring 1999.

SANDCASTLE ★ *American*
Kamaole Shopping Center, upstairs. (879-0606) HOURS: Lunch 11:30am-9pm; dinner from 5pm. SAMPLING: Lunch selections include soup, Caesar, spinach, and cobb salads and tuna, chicken, reuben, Italian meatball, BLT, club, turkey, and prime rib sandwiches $5.50-9.95. Dinner choices of fresh fish, prime rib, pork tenderloin, linguini with chicken, fried shrimp, boboli pizzas, stir-fry, osso bucco, seafood fettucini, spaghetti, and steaks $9.95-21.95. COMMENTS: With the imminent closing of the Wailea Shopping Center, Sandcastle found a new home here in Kihei and added a piano bar and dance floor. They offer a good variety of items and since they serve their lunch menu all day, it is a good afford-able dining option for families. The selection of sandwiches is great and people who used to drive from Lahaina to Wailea just for the Monte Cristo will probably like it even better after the shorter drive!

STELLA BLUES CAFE & DELI   *American*
Longs Center, 1215 S. Kihei Rd. (874-3779) HOURS: Breakfast, 8-11am, Sunday till 2pm; lunch 11am-9pm, dinner 5-9pm. SAMPLING: Scrambled eggs with lox, tofu scramble, banana macadamia pancakes, bagel with lox, onion & tomato; Caesar or cobb salads and corned beef, eggplant, turkey, tofu, and pastrami melt sandwiches $6-8.75. Dinners include crab cakes, eggplant parmesan, BBQ baby back ribs, and fresh catch $11.50-17.95.

TONY ROMA'S   *American-Ribs*
Kukui Mall, 1819 S. Kihei Rd. (875-1104) HOURS: All day menu 11am-11pm; till midnight Fri & Sat. Lunch items until 4pm. SAMPLING: For lunch you can order BBQ chicken teriyaki, BBQ shrimp on a skewer, grilled seafood or sandwiches like grilled sausage, cheese steak or BBQ beef $4.99-10.99. Rib entrees or combos $7.99-12.99; Caesar or oriental chicken salad $5.99-6.99; potato skins, fried cheese, and chicken strips $3.99-4.29. Same salads and appetizers at dinner at slightly higher prices. Baby backs, Carolina honeys, "red hots," and bountiful beef ribs from $10.99-13.99; Roma feast, sampler and combos with BBQ shrimp or chicken, grilled mahi, steak, and chicken $10.99-14.99. COMMENTS: Open 365 days a year. All BBQ, rib and grill entrees come with coleslaw and choice of baked potato, rice, French fries, or ranch beans. They're famous for their ribs, but shrimp and chicken dishes are just as good. Keiki menu available. Tony Roma's began in Florida and they now have locations all over the world. The Maui restaurant has done a nice job with their renovation adapting the previous decor to the brick and dark wood of the Roma's style while incorporating some Hawaiian touches. Separate bar; attractive piano is a focal point.

UKULELE GRILL   ★ *Mid-west/island cuisine*
Maui Lu Resort, 575 South Kihei Rd. (875-1188) HOURS: Dinner only, 5-9pm. SAMPLING: Dinners start with kalua pork lumpia, crab & shrimp cakes, wild mushroom & Maui onion strudel, lobster ravioli, seared ahi, or "Bug" soup (otherwise known as lobsters & crabs!) $6.50-9.95. All-you-can-eat soup & salad bar $12.95 ($5.95 with entree). Entrees include guava-sesame BBQ chicken, trio of fresh fish, pork chop with fuji apple demi-glaze, teriyaki ribeye steak, pasta primavera, coconut shrimp, garlic lamp chops, and Pasta Chouinard, the chef's signature seafood pasta. $15.95-27.95. All-you-can-eat prime rib and salad bar $25.95 ($16.95 between 5-6pm) COMMENTS: From those wonderful folks who brought you the Waterfront restaurant. . . the Smith family brings innovative yet affordable cuisine to the Maui Lu Longhouse. There's something for everyone here: the fish was very good and the combination trio made decision-making easy! The salad bar was great, a very nice assortment with two kinds of soup. Good hula pie, too! Nightly Hawaiian music. Free keiki hula show on Sundays; Hawaiian comedy show Thursdays ($6) - all begin at 6pm. Karaoke Wed-Fri from 9pm. The big room really lends an old Hawaiian air to the ambiance and entertainment - the kind of place you'd see in an old Elvis movie where he would have gotten up to "spontaneously" sing a Hawaiian tune or two!

EXPENSIVE

A PACIFIC CAFE-MAUI ★ *Hawaiian Regional Cuisine*
1279 S. Kihei Rd., Azeka Shopping Center (879-0069) HOURS: 5:30-10pm.
SAMPLING: Tiger eye sushi tempura, grilled asparagus with goat cheese, pan-seared sea scallops with polenta and strawberry-papaya relish, red Thai coconut curry soup (to die for!), ahi-mahi nachos, and firecracker salmon roll are just a few of their "First Tastes" $6.50-12. Kiawe wood grilled entrees include beef filet & crispy shrimp, pork tenderloin, Mongolian BBQ rack of lamb, and swordfish in a candied pecan crust and specialties feature Chinese roasted duck, pan-seared mahi or snapper, rare ahi "popsicle," and halibut "local-style" with bok choy & green onion $24.50-32. After dinner indulgences ($6.50) range from macadamia nut profiteroles to chocolate souffle cake to (our favorite) Toasted Hawaiian: white chocolate cake layered with haupia, white chocolate mousse, macadamia nuts and caramel sauce that looks as distinctively Hawaiian as it tastes! COMMENTS: Jean-Marie Josselin, owner and chef of the highly acclaimed *A Pacific Cafe* in Kaua'i, has also been very successful with this Maui branch garnering more than his share of accolades and awards. (He is one of the twelve acknowledged Hawaiian Regional Cuisine chefs in Hawai'i and is featured in two cookbooks on the market.) They offer two separate dining areas, a wine room (they have an extensive wine list) which seats up to 25, and an island bar. The tables are trimmed in koa wood with a copper inlay and the blonde rattan chairs are covered in tropical brocade. Lots of tables, but you don't feel crushed. As with their Kauai restaurant, the ceramic appetizer plates are one-of-a-kind in varying sizes and shapes designed and hand-made by Chef Josselin's wife, Sophronia. The menu changes regularly to take advantage of the foods as they come into season often featuring a special fruit or vegetable at one of the themed (vintner, guest chef) dinners that are held once or twice a month.

ANTONIO'S *Italian*
Longs Center, 1215 S. Kihei Rd. (875-8800) HOURS: 4:30-9:30pm; closed Mondays. SAMPLING: Antipasti choices include homemade zuppa (soup), sauteed calamari, bruschetta, and mozzarella, tomato & eggplant salad $5.75-7.95. Pasta with meatballs, vegetables, gorgonzola, chicken & mushroom, smoked salmon, wild mushroom, or seafood $8.95-17.95 Entrees (the second course in Italian) of osso bucco, baked eggplant, homemade Italian sausage, seafood or mushroom risotto, lasagna, and ravioli $14.95-21.95. COMMENTS: You'll enter a little piece of Antonio's homeland when you walk through the door. Decor is simple, with bright checkered tablecloths and some amusing memorabilia along the walls. Antonio makes his own bread (baked on the premises) and a to-die-for tiramisu. Weekly specials might offer stuffed artichoke, seafood provencal, or veal parmigiana, or come early (4:30-5:30) for spaghetti and meatballs with salad for just $7.99. The food is excellent (the fourth generation recipes are all made from scratch) and Antonio's enthusiasm for cooking and sharing his food really shines through. (Eating a great tiramisu still makes his knees shake, but don't tell his mama that he has created some Sicilian recipes besides hers!)

CARELLI'S ON THE BEACH   *Italian*
2980 S. Kihei Rd. at the Wailea Oceanfront Inn (875-0001) HOURS: Dinner only 6-10pm, Rocco's Mangia bar menu until 11pm. SAMPLING: Antipasti of seared ahi, steamed clams, beef carpacccio, and oysters $12-18; Pastas include linguini with clams, seafood canneloni with two sauces, mushroom risotto, or seafood ravioli $22-28. Entrees feature cioppino, scampi, rack of lamb, filet mignon, veal, island fish, and chicken breast with white wine & lime juice ("ala Tony's Grandmother") $26-36. They also have pizzas from the wood-fired oven $15-16. COMMENTS: Menu changes seasonally. A minimum food charge of $25 per person at the dining tables seems redundant when you look at the prices. Some of the food was worth it (the seared ahi was excellent; there were both Alfredo and marinara sauces on the canneloni and they used homemade sausage and Maui onions on the pizza), but other dishes were average and uninspiring. In any case, you're not really paying for the food as much as the wonderful ocean view and the equally wonderful view (if that's your thing) of the celebrity diners. They do seem to get more of their share of actors, producers, sports figures, and directors so you're sure to spot at least one familiar face during your meal.

(STEVE AMARAL'S) CUCINA PACIFICA   *Mediterranean*
Rainbow Mall, 2439 S. Kihei Rd. (875-7831) HOURS: Dinner 5:30-10pm; pupus till midnight. SAMPLING: Menu changes seasonally. Winter menu might include seared (on kiawe wood) salmon, spicy elk sausage, black mussels, or Tuscan bean soup to start $6-10 then Spanish seafood stew, ahi pepper steak, veal rib roast, or scallop spanakopita $20-27. In the spring, you might see lobster fettucine, paella, chicken with pancetta, lamb Provencale, or seafood manicotti. Chocolate decadence, creme brulee, ricotta cheesecake, and apple banana flambe. COMMENTS: Southern Europe meets the Pacific in a menu created by former Kea Lani chef Steve Amaral. The expansive restaurant has been divided into smaller, more intimate dining areas with off-the-wall (and on-the-wall) Greek and Roman artwork complete with a mosaic fountain, palm trees, and leopard skin chairs - kind of "Mediterranean kitsch" or "Noveau Bohemian." The circular bar is a focal point and a gathering place for late night pupus. Live music Thurs-Sat.

FIVE PALMS BEACH GRILL   *American*
Mana Kai Resort, 2960 S. Kihei Rd. (879-2607) HOURS: Breakfast Mon-Fri/brunch Sat & Sun 8-11:30am, lunch 11am-3pm, Dinner 5-9pm. SAMPLING: Omelettes, tropical pancakes, French toast, Italian frittata, loco moco, and eggs benedict with crab cakes or fresh spinach include a glass of champagne for brunch $5.95-13.95. Lunches start with clam chowder, calamari, crab stuffed mushrooms, steamed clams, and spinach, Caesar, fruit or cobb salad $6.95-11.95 followed by pizzas, burgers, sandwiches and entrees of pasta, ribs, stuffed shrimp, teri chicken, or prime rib $8.95-14.95. Additional dinner appetizers include crab cakes, chicken quesadilla, escargot, and ahi poke $9.95-11.95 plus entrees of Tahitian lobster, mustard herb crusted rack of lamb, pepper steak, mahi macadamia, and wok-fried whole opakapaka with curry sauce $26.95-32.95. COMMENTS: Children's menu available. Pupus from 3pm. Recent renovation (complete with new furniture, windows, carpets, and wallpaper) has added a more Hawaiian look & feel making one of Kihei's nicest beachfront dining locations even nicer.

KIHEI PRIME RIB AND SEAFOOD HOUSE ★ *American*
2511 South Kihei Rd., in the Nani Kai Village (879-1954) HOURS: Dinner 5-10pm; early bird specials 5-6pm. SAMPLING: Appetizers include baked artichoke, Caccavallo cheese melt, prime rib pupu, sashimi, stuffed mushrooms, sauteed clams, and baked brie $6.95-12.95; sampler $18.95. Entrees come with choice of salad bar, Caesar salad, or soup plus rice or potatoes, vegetables and fresh-baked bread: prime rib, stuffed prawns, fresh fish, huli huli chicken, calamari steak, filet oscar, crab legs, and Tahitian, coconut, or scampi prawns $19.95-22.95. Skillet seafood luau $28.95; seafood linguine with lobster $32.95. Platters for two offer an extensive variety of steak and seafood or whole fresh fish for $79.95. COMMENTS: Live lobster. Fresh fruit tropical drinks. Their early bird is still a great value offering a choice of Huli Huli chicken, prime rib, or fresh fish for $14.95. Keiki menu $6.95 for fish, prime rib, or pasta. Second floor location gives it a good ocean and sunset view. The high-beamed ceilings with hanging plants and wood carvings. A long time Kihei favorite.

SEASCAPE MA'ALAEA RESTAURANT *American*
Maui Ocean Center, Ma'alaea (270-7043) HOURS: Lunch 11am-3pm; cocktails & pupus 2-4pm. SAMPLING: Grilled chicken with mac nut glaze, tempura seafood brochette, garlic roasted NY steak, steamed clams with pasta, and catch of the day are the lunch entrees $10.75-14.75. Caesar, seafood, and fruit salad or burgers, cajun chicken, grilled vegetable, triple fish (ono, mahi & ahi) and lobster salad sandwiches. Desserts offer apple pie, chocolate dream cake, Hana banana cream pie, and "The Lava Tube" $4.25-5.25. Keiki menu has burgers, pizza, and hot dogs priced $4-4.75. Sushi, sashimi, coconut shrimp, jalapeno poppers, teri steak, buffalo wings, and a variety of tropical drinks are available in the afternoon $4.25-7. COMMENTS: Open to the public without admission to the park. Separate entrance on Lahaina side or up from the harbor. Overlooks the Ma'alaea Harbor with large viewing windows into the "Edge of the Reef" tank to watch the tropical fish and reef sharks. Reservations required for lunch.

WATERFRONT ★ *Seafood*
At the Milowai Condo, Ma'alaea (244-9028) HOURS: Lunch Sun-Fri 11:30am-1:30pm, dinner nightly from 5pm. SAMPLING: Fresh fish, BLT, steak, burger, club, shrimp & snow crab, teri chicken, or grilled salmon reuben sandwich $7.95-13.95; Chinese chicken, pan-seared sashimi, or lobster Waldorf salad $12.95-18.95. Pasta, fresh fish, lunch omelette, crab stuffed mushrooms, rock shrimp pot stickers, macadamia-crusted crab cake, or lobster chowder $8.95-11.95. For dinner, fresh island fish is prepared nine uniquely different ways $25-27, or select cioppino, baked prawns Wellington, pan-fried oysters, crab legs, scampi, grilled eggplant, veal scalloppine, teriyaki apple chicken, filet Diane, Szechuan lamb rack, or a daily offering of wild game $18.95-27.95. COMMENTS: A family operation, the Smith's have done a consistently excellent job ever since they opened, winning a number of well-deserved awards and accolades. Fish preparations are particularly innovative offered with shrimp, ginger and coconut milk; salsa, avocado and cilantro butter or "En Bastille": imprisoned in angel hair potato with scallions, mushrooms and tomatoes. Dinner entrees all start with a loaf of onion bread & beer cheese and a garden salad with choice of four homemade dressings. They have a great location to get their fish right off the boat at the Ma'alaea Harbor. Can't get it much fresher than that!

WAILEA - MAKENA

LOUNGES

BOTERO GALLERY
Grand Wailea Resort. HOURS: noon to midnight. The lobby bar is a beautiful setting and they do offer Hawaiian musical entertainment.

GAME IN THE BAR
Grand Wailea Resort, Spa Grande complex. HOURS: Bar service 6pm-midnight. "English" style Gentleman's Club atmosphere where you can play pool, shuffleboard, or sip on a brandy pipe. Library room; imported beer, cognac and Davidoff cigar selection available.

GAMES ROOM
Four Season Resort HOURS: 9:30am-11pm. Pizzas, sandwiches, snacks, desserts, and other food items available all day from the room service menu. Big screen, video games, table shuffleboard, pool tables, and jukebox. Alcohol and smoke-free area on lower level near the health club. Fun for families!

GROTTO BAR
Grand Wailea Resort HOURS: 11-5pm. Dress code *required* here is a swim suit. Set in the midst of waterfalls, rock slides and channels, this is the kind of swim-up bar you've always heard about. They offer a variety of tropical drinks in a volcanic cavern-like setting.

LOBBY BAR AT KEA LANI
Kea Lani Hotel HOURS: 5:30-11pm; entertainment from 8pm. SAMPLING: Start with pupus like kalua chicken with steamed buns, stir-fry fish poke, blackened ahi sashimi, shrimp & crab cakes, and award-winning "Tangled Tiger Prawns" with chili garlic cilantro sauce $8-12. End with desserts like warm mango or chocolate souffle cake, triple chocolate towers, or hand-rolled chocolate cigar with white chocolate and raspberry mousse $7-9.50 COMMENTS: Lounge overlooks the Pacific Ocean and tropical gardens and features a cozy "living room" atmosphere with couches and overstuffed chairs.

LOBBY LOUNGE
Four Seasons Resort HOURS: 5pm-midnight; guitar music 8:30-11:30pm. SAMPLING: Shrimp cocktail, pizza, quesadilla, crab cakes, snail & chicken rolls, sashimi, and selection of cheeses $10.50-15.50; dessert menu of fruit crepes, banana upside down tart, coconut cream cake, citrus creme brulee, fruit cobbler, Kona coffee brownie, and chocolate mousse pyramid $6.50-7. COMMENTS: Terrace adjoining the lobby that overlooks the ocean and West Maui Mountains.

MOLOKINI LOUNGE ★
Maui Prince Hotel, Makena (874-1111) HOURS: 5-9:30pm COMMENTS: Pupu menu $5-12. A wonderful opportunity for a sunset view. Call to check on entertainment available in the lounge or in their lovely outdoor courtyard.

PA'ANI, A GAME BAR
Aston Wailea Beach at the former Inu Inu nightclub (879-1922) HOURS: 6pm-midnight SAMPLING: Dungeness crab cakes, sushi sashimi plate, shrimp cocktail, Maui onion soup $6-12. Chicken or club sandwich, cheeseburger, cheese plate, smoked salmon, pepperoni pizza, marinated chicken, and Caesar salad with chicken, shrimp, or steak $9-17.50. COMMENTS: Juke box, big screen tv, billiards, darts, board games - even a comfortable lounge for cigars and cognac.

SUNSET TERRACE ★
Renaissance Wailea Beach Resort, on the lobby level (879-4900) HOURS: 5:30-11pm COMMENTS: Full service bar with pupu menu that includes onion rings, mushroom fritters, skillet roasted clams, prawn cocktail, ahi sashimi, and goat cheese with focaccia bread $6-10. Create-your-own pizza from $12. Tropical drink menu $6.75.

VOLCANO BAR
Grand Wailea Resort (875-1234) HOURS: Food served 11am-5pm, bar open 10am-6pm. No entertainment. Burgers, hot dogs, nachos, chicken Caesar salad; club, chicken or submarine sandwiches; shrimp, tuna, or turkey in a tortilla wrap, $7.50-13.50. Keiki menu. A choice of almost two dozen smoothie flavors and tropical fruit drinks.

INEXPENSIVE

BEACH WALK JOG 'N' JAVA   *Italian*
Behind Aston Wailea Resort on the Luau Grounds along the Beach Walk (874-7839) HOURS: 6:30am-3pm. SAMPLING: Granola, muffins, bagels, brownies, and quiche $2.50-3; cookies, chips, dried fruits, frozen grapes (great idea!), and other assorted snacks $1-2. Fresh fruit smoothies $$4.50-5; hot or cold coffee drinks $1.85-4. COMMENTS: A quick and easy stop if you're jogging (or walking) along the beach. Cool down with a frosty granita, or buy a bag of their house blend coffee - freshly ground or whole beans.

BELLA LUNA   *Italian/Seafood*
Diamond Resort, 555 Kaukahi St., Wailea (879-8255) HOURS: Open for cocktails Mon-Sat 5:30-9:30pm. Dinner 5:30-8 (winter); 6-8:30 (summer) Closed Sunday. SAMPLING: Start with spinach or Caesar salad with chicken or blackened fish $5.50-10.50. Entrees offer chicken parmigiana, teri chicken, stuffed pork chop, pasta, steak with mushrooms & artichokes, and a variety of seafood dishes including cajun ono, crab stuffed or lemon butter mahi, scampi, and mahi & shrimp $12.50-19.50; lobster tail $24. Creme caramel and NY cheesecake for dessert $3. COMMENTS: Privately owned restaurant on the upper level of the Diamond Resort. Most entrees priced under $15. Great panoramic ocean view from their lanai - which is why they adjust their dinner hours according to the sunset!

CAFE KULA   *Upcountry Farmers Market & Deli*
Grand Wailea Resort (875-1234) HOURS: Breakfast 6am-2pm, lunch 11:30am-2pm. SAMPLING: Breakfasts include a tropical fruit sandwich on banana bread, strawberry crepe, smoked salmon on lava bread, or scrambled eggs & cheese in a tortilla with papaya salsa $6-7.50. Muesli, homemade granola, and baked goods $2-4. Lite lunches offer seafood pasta or soba noodles with chicken & vegetables $8-8.50; and sandwiches of turkey, veggie, ham, or BLT on lava bread; tuna or chicken salad on 7-grain $6.50-8.50. COMMENTS: Open patio setting above flowering gardens with a panoramic view of the ocean. Fresh and healthy fast food. Their original lava bread is slow rising bread, dipped in ice water so that when it bakes it explodes in small bubbles. (Like a volcano?) It also comes in cheese and spicy flavors. Good selection of fruit juices, smoothies, and granitas.

MAKENA RESORT CLUBHOUSE RESTAURANT   *American*
5415 Makena Alanui. At the Golf Course, beyond Wailea and just past the Maui Prince Hotel. (879-1154) HOURS: Coffee express 6:30-8:30am; lunch 10:30am-4pm; limited pupus 4pm to sundown. SAMPLING: Salads include Caesar, ahi Nicoise, chef's cobb, Caesar, chili beef, grilled shrimp soba, and fruit plate $8.50-12. Turkey club, fresh fish, reuben, grilled chicken sandwiches plus burgers, hot dogs, and entrees of beef curry, and saimin bowl $6.50-12. Spring rolls $8; seared ahi $12. COMMENTS: Furnished in a tan and green theme, this open-air restaurant features an outstanding golf course view and one of the few ocean views where you can see Pu'u Ola'i (the rounded hill at the end of the island) up close!

MAUI ONION   *American*
Renaissance Wailea Beach Resort, poolside (879-4900) HOURS: Lunch 11am-6pm, bar open from 10am. SAMPLING: Black Angus burger, turkey "wrap" with cranberry relish, mahi, NY steak, spiced chicken, grilled vegetable burger, and turkey (or classic) BLT $8-12; Caesar, Chinese chicken, seared ahi Nicoise, tropical fruit, and shrimp cobb salads $9-13.50. Maui onion rings, cheese quesadilla, chicken wings, Maui onion soup, or spring rolls $6.50-8.50; pupu platter $12. Ice cream treats $4. Smoothies, tropicals, beer, and wine by the glass $4.50-6.75 COMMENTS: We always hear great things about their onion rings and (some say Maui's best) burgers! Fashion show Wednesdays 12-1pm.

POLO BEACH GRILLE AND BAR   *American*
Kea Lani Hotel, poolside. (875-4100) HOURS: 11am-5pm; SAMPLING: Luncheon menu offers shrimp Louie or Chinese chicken salad, grilled chicken or mahi sandwich, smoked turkey on focaccia, local tuna salad, garden burgers, Maui onion rings, spring & pork rolls, and crab cakes $6.50-13. COMMENTS: Swim up & cocktail bar 11am-6pm. Tropical drinks and smoothies from $6.

MODERATE

CAFFE CIAO ★   *Italian*
Kea Lani (875-4100) HOURS: Lunch 11-5:30pm; Dinner 5:30-10pm. SAMPLING: Full bakery and deli serves coffee drinks, deli salads and sandwiches, homemade sausages, antipasto items, Italian gelatos, breads, pastries, and rich desserts. Salads, minestrone, grilled eggplant or meatball panini (Italian sandwiches), and fried calamari are on the lunch menu $8-12.95 as well as pastas and gourmet pizzas with shrimp, sausage, eggplant, or truffles and a yummy white pizza with roasted chicken, garlic, and Maui onion $15-21. All are baked in the outdoor brick pizza oven as are many of the lunch and dinner entrees. Pizzas are also available for dinner along with pastas like seafood linguine seafood, mushroom or prawn risotto, and salmon farfalle. Entrees of sauteed chicken or prawns, pan-seared veal, grilled steak, macadamia & pistachio crusted snapper $18-26; mixed grill of fish, chicken, lamb, & beef for two $48. COMMENTS: High ceilings, arches, and stone inlays in the sleek black and gold deli which has been expanded to twice the size and now offers antipasti, focaccia sandwiches, gourmet condiments & food products, -- even fresh produce and an exotic, imported olive bar. While dining you can relax by reading one of a variety of complimentary international newspapers either indoors in the classic Art Deco ambiance or on the outside patio that surrounds the brick pizza oven. They cure their own meats and produce their own private label of products to sell: macadamia blossom honey, Maui onion jelly, poha berry butter, pineapple mustard, and mango BBQ sauce. They also have full picnic & gift baskets and a variety of cheeses and other items imported from Italy. You can shop and eat at the same time - the best of both worlds!

CAFE KIOWAI   *Polynesian-American*
Maui Prince Hotel, Makena (874-1111) HOURS: Breakfast 6-10:30am; lunch 11am-3pm. SAMPLING: Hot breakfast buffet $17.95; continental buffet $11.95. A la carte omelettes, eggs Benedict on cornbread, Portuguese sweetbread French

toast, corned beef hash, or vegetable frittata $7-12. Lunches start with ahi Nicoise, shrimp cobb, chicken Caesar, or Chinese chicken salad; coconut prawns, steamed clams, seared ahi, caramelized Maui onion soup, or chilled shrimp in strawberry papaya $5.25-11.50. Sandwiches include grilled NY steak with Maui onions, island mahi, turkey club, hamburger, trio of mini croissants (roast beef, turkey, crab & shrimp) or grilled chicken on focaccia $6.50-12.50. Fresh catch, vegetarian pasta, seafood or chicken curry stew, or saimin $8.50-12. Dessert choices are passion fruit cheesecake, German chocolate cake, creme brulee, fresh fruit tart, and the hotel's signature chocolate macadamia nut brittle flan $5.50-6. COMMENTS: Kiowai pronounced "Key-oh-wy" means "fresh flowing water." A casual, open patio atmosphere. The passion fruit iced tea is a wonderful accompaniment. Good keiki menus for both meals.

CHART HOUSE ★ *American*
100 Wailea Ike Drive (879-2875) HOURS: Dinner 5:30-10pm. SAMPLING: Lobster cakes, coconut shrimp or calamari, steamed artichoke, and sashimi appetizers $6.50-9.95. Steak, prime rib, crab legs, lobster, ginger-citrus shrimp, rack of lamb, ahi, herb-crusted or teri chicken, and fresh ahi, salmon or catch of the day. Entrees include their unlimited fresh garden, spinach or Caesar salad and hot squaw bread (made with sweet molasses) $16.95-25.95. They also offer some good homemade desserts including mud pie, creme brulee, brownie sundae, and authentic key lime pie. COMMENTS: Open-air setting with an ocean view. Other locations in Lahaina and Kahului. They still have one of the best keiki menus we've seen. The adult entree portions are huge and we love their doggie bag! (Trust us, you'll need it.) The coconut calamari was an unusual option; good texture with surprising coconut and calamari tastes. The ahi was a nice thick "steak," cooked on the rare side in ponzu sauce with cilantro lime butter. The tasty spinach salad (with egg, bacon, and poppy seed dressing) had lots of nice extras including Mandarin oranges. A gentleman dining at our neighboring table pronounced the prime rib "awesome." Reservations accepted.

(THE) CLUBHOUSE RESTAURANT *American-Continental*
100 Kaukahi St., at the Wailea (Blue) Golf Course (879-4060) HOURS: Breakfast 7:30-11:30am; lunch 11am-3pm, dinner 6-9pm. Closed Sunday. SAMPLING: Sweet rice waffles, Hawaiian French toast, pancakes, saimin, and a variety of eggs benedict for breakfast plus lunches of beef curry, chicken or fish stir fry; oriental, spinach, or Caesar salad; and French dip, steak, teri chicken, burger, mahi, or club sandwiches $6.50-9. Dinners start with stuffed mushrooms, clam chowder, garlic bread basket, and seared ahi plus Greek and Italian added to the lunch salad selections $5-8; salad bar $9. All entrees come with salad bar and include Kona coffee crusted lamb roast, Cornish game hen, coconut prawns, teri chicken, mahi with lemon butter, NY or pepper steak, along with a variety of fresh fish preparations and cuts of prime rib $13.50-20.50. Children's menu $1 per year up to 8. COMMENTS: Formerly the Fairway. New owner also has Bella Luna (down the road at Diamond Resort) giving him a "lock" on some of the neighborhood's best sunsets!

HARRY'S SUSHI AND PUPU BAR *Japanese*
See Lobster Cove which follows, Wailea-Expensive. (879-7677)

HULA MOONS *Seafood-American*
Aston Wailea Resort (879-1922) HOURS: Lunch 11am-5pm; Dinner 5:30-10pm. SAMPLING: Lunch appetizers include kalua pork spring rolls, Maui onion rings, and tiger shrimp with pineapple cocktail sauce $3.95-9.95. Curried chicken, fresh fish, Caesar, Chinese chicken, and fruit lau lau (in ti leaves) are some entree salads $6.95-10.95. A burger, hot dog, turkey club, grilled chicken, kalua pork, and vegetable or tuna pita are the sandwiches and entrees offer mahi tempura, saimin, grilled catch, or sauteed shrimp in black bean sauce $6-13. Dinner appetizers offer seared ahi, smoked salmon Napoleon, sea scallops, steamed mussels or clams, kalua pork, spring rolls, ahi poke, crab & lobster fritters, oysters, Maui onion soup, and a selection of salads $5-9. Choice of entrees are macadamia crusted mahi, seared ono, chicken & shiitake mushrooms, lilikoi duckling, medallions of beef, lamb or pork chops, steak, and grilled tiger shrimp $18-27; ragout (or stir fry) of vegetables $14-16. COMMENTS: Hula Moons is dedicated to the spirit of Don Blanding, Hawai'i's well known poet, artist and musician. "Hula Moons" was the title of one of his most popular books. The restaurant is located on the pool level; flickering torches and live Hawaiian music add to the ambiance of this ocean view restaurant which may become a favorite if you're a chocolate lover: their nightly (and Maui's only) Chocoholic Bar features soft serve frozen yogurt with thirty assorted toppings, chocolate Kahlua cheesecake, rum & macadamia chocolate mousse cake, chocolate sacher, dark chocolate mousse squares, chocolate Amaretto cake, trio of white, dark & milk chocolate fudge torte, white chocolate macadamia nut torte plus assorted cookies and brownies. It's $5.50 with an entree; $7.50 *as* an entree. Indoor & outdoor seating; live entertainment nightly 5:30-9pm.

LEA'S OCEAN CUISINE ★ *Fresh Fish & Seafood*
Aston Wailea Resort (879-1922) HOURS: Breakfast 6-11am; dinner 6-10pm. (Not open for lunch.) SAMPLING: Breakfast buffet $17; or choose from omelettes, frittatas, smoked salmon, pork & onion hash, Portuguese sweetbread French toast, pineapple upside-down cakes, and banana or macadamia pancakes $7-12. Dinners start with Dungeness crab & pineapple, lobster martini, shrimp lumpia, steamed mussels or asparagus, sashimi, grilled portobello mushroom, seafood chowder, or Maui soup $5-10. Keiki menu available. Entrees of seafood fettucine, seared scallops, seafood "Black Thai" risotto, filet mignon, roast free-range chicken, Szechwan eggplant, fresh fish in a variety of preparations $15.95-25.95. Lobster, crab, or wok-fried whole fish $27.95-37.95. Chocolate-peanut butter mousse cake, tropical fruit trifle, citrus mille feuille, almond tuille cup, or white chocolate cheesecake are all $5.95. COMMENTS: Formerly Lana'i Terrace, the ocean goddess would be proud of her new namesake: more than 80% of the menu is devoted to fresh fish and seafood. Innovative preparations like Oysters Lea (over baby spinach & asparagus with sundried tomatoes), lobster martini (with shallots & brandy), and black Thai risotto (an unusual blend of spicy, Asian & tropical), with Lea's dinner accompaniment of sundried tomato or olive bread are a few of the distinctive touches. Great sunset views, too!

EXPENSIVE

BISTRO MOLOKINI ★   *"Light" Bistro Italian*
Grand Wailea Resort & Spa (875-1234) HOURS: Lunch 11:30am-3pm, light lunch 3-5:30pm; Dinner 5:30-10pm. SAMPLING: Lunches start with minestrone or gazpacho; Greek, Caesar, or fresh fruit salads plus calamari, Maui onion rings, and shrimp cocktail $7-15. Burger, chicken, fish or grilled vegetable sandwiches; lasagna, clam, shrimp, or chicken pasta; choice of pizzas $12.50-18. Dinner menu has the same appetizers as lunch along with seared ahi, baked artichoke, shrimp parmesan, spinach & macadamia nut salad, bruschetta or "red" bread, and antipasto $7-15. Dinner pizzas, a larger selection of pastas (including ravioli, risotto, and cioppino) and entrees of parmesan chicken, veal chops, ahi with lemon coconut aioli, guava lamb chops, baked prawns with mango vinaigrette, NY steak, and opakapaka with prosciutto & red pepper $21-33. Fresh fruit cobbler, chocolate pannacotta, tiramisu, cappuccino creme brulee, and macadamia nut cheesecake $6.50-8. COMMENTS: An open-air bistro overlooking the formal pool and the Pacific Ocean. (Pool service 11am-4:30pm). Exhibition kitchen and wood-burning oven. Casual shorts and shoes are acceptable. The menu is definitely Italian, but very light and innovative. Extensive wine list, beer, coffee drinks, tropicals, smoothies, and Italian sodas. Children's menu.

FERRARO'S   *Italian*
Four Seasons Resort (874-8000) HOURS: Dinner only 6-9pm. Hawaiian entertainment in the evenings. SAMPLING: Antipasto selections of sauteed quail, cold sliced veal, portobello & spinach salad, deep-fried mozzarella, baked country bread with tomato & goat cheese, and seafood salad $8.50-14.50. Pastas include linguini with shrimp, vegetarian penne, gnocchi with eggplant, asparagus & scallop risotto, and pappardelle with veal osso bucco sauce $21.50-23.50. Herb crusted lamb chops, chicken breast in prosciutto, medallions of veal loin, pepper crusted seared ahi, and breaded ehu are some of the entrees $22.50-29.50. Amaretto custard with poached pear, pistachio mousse, dark chocolate roll with biscotti & apricot sauce, rum baba, tiramisu, and strawberries with Galliano are the choices for dessert $6.75-7.50. COMMENTS: There is nothing to encumber the ocean view from this cliffside restaurant located right over the water. (Get there early and you'll be surrounded by sunsets!)

GRAND DINING ROOM ★   *Breakfast only*
Grand Wailea (875-1234) HOURS: Breakfast only 6:30-11am. SAMPLING: Grand Breakfast Buffet $19. A la carte menu offers tropical fruits, a basket of pastries, omelettes, eggs Benedict, banana mac-nut waffles, pancakes with berries, turkey or corned beef hash, homemade granola, Swiss Birchermuesli, sweet bread French toast and a variety of breakfast meats $5.50-18. COMMENTS: Breakfast is now the only meal they serve in this elegant dining room so take advantage and pamper yourself!

HAKONE ★   *Japanese*
Maui Prince Resort, Makena (874-1111) HOURS: Nightly 6-9pm except Monday (Japanese buffet only, 6-9pm) SAMPLING: A dozen dinner selections start at $22

for Haruyama (teriyaki chicken) and range up to the Hakone (their signature bento-style assortment) $42. Grilled or deep fried fish dishes are offered a la carte $7-12; yellowtail with ponzu sauce $18. Tofu or tempura salad; crab, shrimp, or octopus Sunomoto $6-8. Nabemono selections of sukiyaki and sabu shabu are cooked at your table and require a two person minimum by reservation $35. Rakuen Kaiseki (chef's 7-course menu) includes appetizers, sashimi, sushi, one grilled and one fried dish, rice, pickles, dessert, and tea for $58. Hot and cold sake $7.50-12.50. Their new Monday night Japanese buffet ($38A, 25C) offers 25 specially prepared delicacies including sushi, sashimi, shrimp tempura, scallop & vegetable au gratin, kalbi beef, garlic chicken, pork tenderloin, curried beef potato, steamed dumplings, spring rolls, special pupus, miso soup, rice, pickled vegetables, and the chef's weekly dessert. COMMENTS: Authenticity is the key to this wonderful Japanese restaurant, from its construction (the wood, furnishings and even small nails were imported from Japan) to its food (the rice is flown in as well). The food and atmosphere are both wonderful here and, of course, the presentation of the food is artistic! Keiki menu available. There is also a sushi bar, but with only 11 seats, it is definitely on a first-come basis.

HANA GION ★ *Japanese*
Renaissance Wailea Beach Resort (879-4900) HOURS: 6-9pm; closed Thursday. SAMPLING: Set teriyaki & tempura dinners in combinations of chicken, beef, sashimi, or shrimp as well as Nabemono (pot) dishes of sukiyaki, yosenabe, or shabu shabu $24.50-36. Steaks, prawns, scallops, fish, and chicken are prepared Teppanyaki-style at 6 or 8pm dinner seatings (reservations required), $24-31; Hana Gion specials range from $36-38 up to $80 for an eleven course kaiseki meal (24 hour advance reservations requested). A sushi bar is also available. COMMENTS: The decor is as authentic as its cuisine. Woodwork, screens, stone flooring, bamboo trim, and decorative artifacts were all produced in Japan to exacting standards. In fact, parts of the dining area were actually constructed in Japan before dismantling them for shipment to the Renaissance Wailea. The name Gion originates from the Gion district of Kyoto. Traditional Japanese fare emphasizes freshness, subtle flavors and delicate preparations. The restaurant is designed to promote the feeling of privacy and intimacy. There is a main dining area with private dining rooms that seat four or six guests each. The sushi bar accommodates only ten.

HUMUHUMUNUKUNUKUA'PUA'A ★ *Seafood*
Grand Wailea Resort (875-1234) HOURS: Dinner only 5:30-10pm. SAMPLING: Starters include coconut crusted scallops, lobster manapua, spring rolls, BBQ ribs, soba noodle salad, mahi & crab chowder, and one of the best appetizers we've ever had, Ahi Lemon Grass Traps. Appetizers $8-12.50. A la carte entrees: whole sizzling snapper, wok-fired tiger prawns, seared ahi, Hawaiian chicken, NY steak, chateaubriand, and "gourmet" lau lau (crab, lobster, or opakapaka baked with taro & ti leaves) $30-38. Lobster and crab $28-52 per lb. (1½-2 lb. minimum.) Rice, baked potato, or vegetables can be ordered on the side $2-3.50 Desserts feature baked mousse torte with blueberries in chocolate, lady finger & mango cream "volcano" with tropical fruit, rum fudge & banana hula pie, and chocolate coconut tiramisu with mango vanilla sauce $6-8.50. COMMENTS: Are you curious about the "traps"? The appetizer is made with

strips of ahi rolled up with tiny vegetables, "trapped" by stalks of flavorful lemon grass and drizzled with spicy ponzu. There are several traps to an order and the presentation, flavor and texture make this a must-do-pupu! If you're curious about the restaurant's name, it is the Hawai'i state fish, the trigger fish. Since the Hawaiian name is rather a mouthful, the eatery is affectionately and briefly referred to as Humuhumu. Tucked in the front grounds of the resort, it is situated on top of a saltwater pond filled with aquatic life. The huge saltwater tank that divides the bar area is worth stopping by to just admire. The restaurant floats on the lagoon and the thatched-roof and bamboo railings inspire exotic Robinson Crusoe fantasies. Given the prices of the a la carte entrees, the addition of a starter and a side dish or two makes this a little bit more than just expensive fare. The ambiance alone, however, merits a star. They do offer smaller size portions for children 12 and under. Not very affordable family dining, but definitely a place to take the kids (or grownups) to look around. (Or just to order some traps!)

JOE'S BAR & GRILL ★ *Gourmet American*
131 Wailea Ike Place, above the Wailea Tennis Club (875-7767) HOURS: Dinner 5:30-10pm. SAMPLING: Dinners start with grilled bruschetta, salad of field greens (with goat cheese, Maui onion & champagne-papaya vinaigrette), crispy Asian calamari, smoked salmon quesadilla, Joe's gazpacho, spinach & mushroom salad, caprese of tomato & mozzarella, ahi tartare, and Bev's famous crab dip $6-12 and continue with lobster & seafood pot pie, grilled pork chop with dried fruit compote, NY steak with caramelized onions, Joe's meatloaf, rack of lamb, pan-roasted chicken breast, "Pulehu" veal chop, grilled applewood salmon, and pasta with blackened ahi $17-29. Apple or pineapple tartlet with ice cream and warm caramel sauce, lilikoi cheesecake, banana cream pie, creme brulee, mind-bundt cake, or macadamia nut praline mousse cake, chocolate glob are offered for dessert $6. COMMENTS: From those wonderful folks who brought you Haliimaile General, Joe and (Chef) Beverly Gannon. Bev's food is as good as it reads, but nothing is overly-trendy. (She even takes the "goat" out of goat cheese!) Joe's background as a Hollywood producer-director and lighting designer sets the tone with the shiny hardwood floors, 43-foot cooper bar and individual geometric designs on the tables. The theater lighting is soft, yet strong enough to highlight the wall of show-biz memorabilia from Joe's days working with film, tv and music celebrities. All this and an ocean view, too!

KEA LANI RESTAURANT ★ *Breakfast*
Kea Lani Hotel (875-4100) HOURS: Breakfast only 6:30-11am. Becomes Nick's Fishmarket for dinner 5:30-10pm (see separate listing) SAMPLING: Breakfast buffet $19.95A, $10.95C, under 5 free. Cereals including granola and oatmeal with a choice of toppings - from walnuts to wheat germ, pumpkin seeds to pecans; pastries, muffins, and nut breads; bagel & bread station; fresh fruits & yogurts; omelette station; hot breakfast entrees; and Japanese breakfast station. COMMENTS: One traveling family told us that their package stay at the Kea Lani included the daily breakfast buffet and that with their teenage son, the complimentary breakfast saved them huge amounts of money on their food travel budget. They also noted that the breakfast selections were diverse enough to keep their palates interested for the entire week!

LE GUNJI ★ *French-style teppanyaki*
555 Kaukahi St., located at the Diamond Resort (874-0500) HOURS: Two dinner seatings at 6pm and 8pm. Closed Wednesday. SAMPLING: A gourmet teppanyaki restaurant offering set meals. The Diamond Course is $70 and includes appetizer, soup, fresh catch, lobster, wine sorbet, steak, salad, rice, dessert, and coffee; Mini-Diamond courses are the same except for the choice of either fish $45 or lobster $55. All offer a minimum of seven courses. COMMENTS: With $45 as the cheapest entree, this is another on the mega-expensive borderline. The dining room is small and intimate with a beautiful garden courtyard located behind where the chef cooks. This Teppanyaki is a bit different in that it is cooked with a French flair, a style that was introduced to the restaurant by the original chef, Gunji Ito (from Osaka) who had previously cooked French cuisine. Seating hours change in the summer: 6:30 and 8pm from May through August. Reservations required. Shorts and sandals not permitted.

LOBSTER COVE-HARRY'S SUSHI BAR *Seafood-Japanese*
Located next to the Chart House in Wailea (879-7677) HOURS: Dining room 5:30-10pm; Harry's sushi bar till midnight. SAMPLING: Live Maine lobster, live Dungeness crab, king crab legs priced by the pound; lobster tail, roasted scallops, fisherman's stew, linguine with clams, seafood penne pasta, BBQ tiger prawns, filet mignon, and a selection of fresh Hawaiian fish preparations $19.50-26. Steak & seafood combinations $36-41. Lobster, shrimp Caesar, or crab, shrimp & avocado salad $7.50-9.95; sweet & sour crispy shrimp, sashimi, steamed garlic clams or mussels, or lobster cake $9.50-11.50. COMMENTS: Harry's Sushi and Pupu Bar is operated by Harry Okumara and is located at the entrance to Lobster Cove. It always looks busy! The menu offers maki and nigiri sushi with specialties like Dynamite (seafood casserole) and soft shell crab $4-7; sashimi $9-15.50.

NICK'S FISHMARKET MAUI *Seafood*
Kea Lani Hotel (875-4100) HOURS: Dinner 5:30-10pm. SAMPLING: Cajun seared black & blue ahi; Greek Maui Wowie Salad with chopped onion, tomatoes, feta cheese & rock shrimp; grilled ahi steak with eggplant & goat cheese crust topped with sundried tomato pesto; and lobster ravioli (lobster tail, shiitake mushrooms in a light basil cream sauce) are some of the signature items; dinners are expected to average from $30-35. COMMENTS: The Kea Lani Restaurant continues to serve breakfast by day and then becomes Nick's Fishmarket at night for dinner. The fine dining restaurant features 40-foot vaulted ceilings designed in a southern Mediterranean style and offers great ocean views. Shell-design lighting fixtures, fish-shaped chairs, wave-patterned mosaic tabletops, and an 800-gallon aquarium are all part of the blue and white aquatic theme. Private booths; indoor and outdoor seating; plus a glass mosaic bar for cocktails and pupus. Chef Michael Miho (formerly with the restaurant group's Nicholas Nickolas on O'ahu) will continue to utilize the fresh island ingredients from the hotel's own on-site herb and vegetable garden. Scheduled to open summer, 1998. (Not open as we go to press.) Kea Lani will continue to host "Grand Chefs on Tour," a week-long culinary experience pairing a "grand" chef from the mainland with a Hawaiian chef of equal prominence in a series of dinners and cooking demonstrations.

PACIFIC GRILL   *American-Pacific Rim*
Four Seasons Resort (874-8000) HOURS: Breakfast 6-11:30am (buffet 6:30-11, till noon on Sundays), dinner 5:30-9:30pm. (Closed for lunch except during high occupancy at resort) SAMPLING: Breakfast buffet $21.50; Light buffet $17.50. Oatmeal brulee, granola yogurt cocktail, sausage frittata, egg fu young, scrambled egg brioche, vegetable hash, and caramelized apple upside-down pancake with cinnamon cream are some innovative additions to traditional cereal, egg, meat, and fruit choices $5.50-15.75. Pacific Rim appetizers include limu kohu ahi poke, vegan-miso risotto, Thai beef salad with chile, seared ahi, and scallop & goat cheese won ton soup as well as Maui onion soup, gravlax with potato salad, fava beans, steamed clams, or salad of shrimp, peas & avocado $7.50-12.50. Main courses offer seared scallops & shrimp, sesame rack of lamb, chicken or seafood stir-fry, steamed ehu oriental, charred duck breast with citrus glaze, and lemon grass mahi in parchment paper $23-28.50. The "home cooking" options feature roasted chicken, shepherd's pie, mahi & chips, veal casserole, steak, and grilled salmon $19.50-24.50. A wonderful lobster salad & bacon sandwich (available for lunch at their Seaside restaurant), chicken club, burger, and fruit salad are offered for the light eater $12.50-16.75. Tropical fruit crepes, coconut cream cake, chocolate mousse pyramid, citrus creme brulee, coffee brownie, and banana upside-down tart have the final word $6.50-7. COMMENTS: A pleasant dining environment with indoor or lana'i seating overlooking the pool and the ocean. Healthy alternative cuisine selections are indicated on the menu and a full vegetarian menu (with over a dozen items) is available on request. Keiki menu has a good selection priced under $4.50.

PALM COURT ★   *International-Buffet*
Renaissance Wailea Beach Resort (879-4900) HOURS: Breakfast a la carte and buffet 6-11am. Dinner 5:30-9:30pm. SAMPLING: Full breakfast buffets: Full $17, continental $10, cereal bar $8.50. A la carte items include shrimp & crab hash, eggs benedict, buckwheat pancakes, oatmeal with macadamia nut butter, and sourdough French toast with mascarpone cheese and guava jam $5-10.50. Dinner buffet every night: Mon/Sat-Prime Rib ($30), Sun/Wed-Italian ($28), Thurs-(Either) French or Spanish ($28) and Tues/Fri-Seafood ($35). (Children 1/2 price.) A la carte menu has goat cheese napoleon, chilled gazpacho margarita, skillet roasted clams, portobello mushroom fritters, and shrimp & sweet potato ravioli $7-10; pizzas $12-16; salad bar $12.50 ($7.50 with entree). Entrees include chicken tortellini, vegetable lasagna, pasta with shrimp & scallops, seafood risotto, grilled salmon, rack of lamb, filet mignon with gorgonzola & chianti sauce, roast chicken $9.75-25. After dinner visit their dessert bar or indulge in a Grand Marnier or chocolate souffle $6.50-7.50. COMMENTS: This open-air dining hall offers evening breezes and an ocean view.

PRINCE COURT ★   *Hawaiian Regional Cuisine*
Maui Prince Hotel, Makena (874-1111) HOURS: Dinner 6-9:30pm; Champagne Sunday Brunch 9:30am-1pm. SAMPLING: Pan-fried tiger shrimp with hearts of palm, Thai spring rolls, guava glazed ribs, steamed clams & mussels, seared ahi seaweed salad, and lobster bisque are some of the starters $5-12; sampler platter $15. Entrees include a trilogy of fresh fish & seafood on angel hair pasta with lemon butter caper sauce; roasted rack of lamb with Maui onion crust, grilled

chicken with stir fry vegetables, ginger-steamed snapper, pork tenderloin with hoison sauce, NY steak, penne pasta, and taro-crusted mahi with lilikoi butter sauce $17-30. Lilikoi creme brulee, macadamia nut mousse cake, chocolate truffle "Negresco" and chocolate macadamia nut brittle flan are a few of the desserts $5.50-6.50. They now have a Friday seafood buffet ($36) with sashimi, seared ahi, crab legs, chowder, Hawaiian poke, seafood salads, fresh fish (pan-fried to order), seafood curry, steamed clams and selection of desserts. Some of the items on the Sunday brunch buffet include flavored pancakes and crepes, carved meats, chilled crab legs & shrimp, sashimi, smoked seafoods, Russian caviar salad, sweet & sour pork, beef stroganoff and seared ahi. The dessert table is a sumptuous fantasy that tastes as extravagant as it looks. A worthy indulgence for $34 (which is actually very reasonable considering you won't eat again till Tuesday!) Reservations required. COMMENTS: Hawaiian Regional Cuisine continues to be the "buzz" word in dining experiences in the islands. It is simply the opportunity to experience the many varied selections of fresh foods grown, raised or caught in the islands. The culinary cuisine of the Prince Court is an incredible blend of flavors which highlight the best and freshest Hawaiian produce, meats and fish. Beautifully situated, the dining room offers a splendid view of the both the ocean and landscaped hotel grounds. They have an excellent wine list with particularly good prices on champagne and wine selections. The Sunday champagne brunch is still one of the island's best and in fact, one of the few buffets still offered weekly!

(RESTAURANT) TAIKO *Japanese*
Diamond Resort, 555 Kaukahi St., Wailea (874-0500) HOURS: Breakfast 7-11am, lunch 11:45am-1:30pm, dinner 6-9pm. Closed Tuesday. SAMPLING: Set menus for breakfast offer both Japanese (fish, vegetables) or Western (eggs, meats) options at $13 with limited a la carte items $4-6. Lunch also offers both styles with noodles, tempura and teriyaki chicken as well as appetizers, burgers, and sandwiches $5-12 For dinner, appetizers, steamed or vinegar dishes, stir-fry & deep-fried dishes, soup, salad, and rice are offered a la carte for $6-16. Meals feature sliced beef, lobster, teriyaki, tempura, sushi, and sashimi dishes plus sukiyaki, tonkatsu, fresh catch, steak, unagi, sauteed salmon, and broiled cod $18-27; COMMENTS: Diamond Resort is an exclusive property that makes their fine restaurants available to the general public. Large dining hall with cathedral-like ceilings and lots of attractive rockwork. Very simple, elegant decor. Prices here have come way down since our last book; they no longer offer set multi-course meals for dinner. The Plumeria Counter is a small sushi bar that also features a la carte items from 5:30-8:30pm.

SEASIDE *American*
Four Seasons Resort (874-8000) HOURS: Lunch 11:30am-3pm, pupus 3-6pm. SAMPLING: Lunch pupus offer summer rolls and ahi sashimi; in the afternoon you can also get teriyaki beef & chicken sate, coconut shrimp, chicken strips, or goat cheese & eggplant on focaccia $9.50-14.50. Also for lunch are vegetarian or grilled chicken panini, roast turkey club, mahi on nori bread, lobster salad & bacon, mozzarella on bruschetta, or pan bagna tuna salad sandwiches; Cobb, soba noodle, chicken, walnut & apple, or seafood & spinach salads $12.75-16.75. Beef

curry, fresh fish, and herb chicken on mushroom fettucine are the entrees $16.50-18.50. Ricotta cheesecake, cappuccino cup, fruit tart, or island carrot cake $6.25. Good selection of tropical blend smoothies and coffee drinks $5.50-6.50. COMMENTS: You can't get a better ocean view than from this cliffside restaurant located right over the water. Several of the restaurant lunch items are also available poolside (just steps away) from 11:30am-5pm. At night Seaside becomes Ferraro's Italian restaurant.

SEASONS ★ *Contemporary American-Hawaiian*
Four Seasons Resort (874-8000) HOURS: Dinner only 6-9:30pm, pianist 6:30-10:30pm. (Closed Sun-Mon) SAMPLING: As the name implies, the menu changes with the seasons, but you might start with ginger-marinated foie gras, ahi tartare & caviar, sauteed moano with mint tabbouleh salad, rock fish soup, salad of free-range rabbit, seared yellow tail, or charbroiled Keahole lobster & Moloka'i sweet potato puree $15-23 (Beluga caviar, $145). Paprika crusted lamb loin, crisped shutome with pancetta, whole onaga in Hawaiian salt crust, Roasted Keahole lobster with pinot noir & carrots, kumu baked in parchment paper, breast of pheasant, and star anise rotisserie duckling are just a few of the entrees $36-42. Chef's Tasting Menu offers five-course prix-fixe menus $72 & 85; seven courses with selected wines $145. (Forget the caviar, this is a *much* better way to spend that $145!) If you can't make up your mind whether to have the warm strawberry & lemon tart, crusted orange flan, or Hawaiian vintage chocolate surprise, you can order a trio for $19. Other dessert options include sauteed apple crisp (with gingerbread ice cream!), a surprisingly flavorful pineapple custard tart, and selection of souffles $12-15.50. COMMENTS: One of the few fine dining (and dancing!) experiences still to be enjoyed on Maui, this romantic indulgence offers tranquil elegance indoors or on the terrace - both with an ocean view. Famed Hawaiian Regional Chef George Mavrothalassitis brought his reputation from the renowned La Mer restaurant at Honolulu's Halekulani to create all new Maui memories with his diverse menu and classic presentations. Whole onaga baked in a fish-shaped crust; leg and breast of duck served as two distinct courses, carrots that taste as good as the lobster they're served with, and best of all, the invitation to enjoy pairings of half entrees that you can choose yourself. Extensive 16-page wine list, and a delightful selection of complimentary "*mignardes*" - a tiered-tray of tiny desserts served as dessert to your dessert!

SEAWATCH ★ *Island Regional*
100 Wailea Golf Club Drive (875-8080) HOURS: Breakfast/lunch menu served 8am-3pm; pupu menu 3-10pm; dinner 6-10pm. SAMPLING: Breakfast & lunch selections range from fresh fruit, omelettes and eggs benedict, and Moloka'i sweet bread French toast to burgers, pasta, stir-fry, fish tacos and salads like Caesar, cobb, Chinese chicken, seafood papaya, and fruit $6-10. Dinners start with macadamia nut crusted brie, crab cakes, shrimp tempura, yam & char siu pork griddle cakes, and spinach or ahi & sprout salad $8-14. Entrees include miso-glazed tiger prawns, rack of lamb with mango mustard crust, citrus ponzu pork chops, Hawaiian cioppino, kiawe chicken with lychee, plus steaks and fresh fresh fish preparations $22-29. COMMENTS: You can get lunch for breakfast or have breakfast for lunch! An elegant "grand hall" entrance with tall ceilings leads to the restaurant and several distinctive dining areas. The wide lanais offer

the best views of Molokini, Kahoʻolawe, Makena, and Maʻalaea and the grill room is highlighted by giant glass doors and artwork from Arthur Johnson, a Big Island muralist. The lounge has a white baby grand piano as its centerpiece. Spacious seating; descriptive wine list. (Seawatch proprietors also own the two Koho Grill and Bars as well as the Plantation House Restaurant in Kapalua.)

MEGA-EXPENSIVE

KINCHA *Japanese*
Grand Wailea (875-1234) Hours: Dinner only, 6-10pm. COMMENTS: We had to invent the "mega-expensive" category, since just "expensive" really isn't descriptive enough for this very authentic Japanese restaurant. It appears the race is on for which Japanese restaurant in Wailea can charge the most for a meal and Kincha appears to be taking the lead with a per dinner per diner price of $300. No, that is not a typo, and it is dollars, not yen. And believe it or not, the price has actually come down from the $500 dinner of a few years ago! (The $500 Tokubetsu Kaiseki is still available by advance request and includes a tea ceremony, sushi and tempura prepared by a personal chef and served in their private Ozashiki-Tatami Room). Their Royal Kaiseki menu reads, "Set menu of the finest, authentic Japanese food served on individual selected tableware." The Nishiki ("Golden Embroidery") runs $150 and includes homemade fruit wine, sakizuke, appetizer, clear broth soup, sashimi, broiled fish, boiled vegetable course, deep fried course, vinegar course, cold wheat noodles, seasonal fruit, sweet dessert, and the finest green tea. Add a steak course and shokuji for the Aya ("Coloration") $200 and to that, add refreshing hassun and onmono for Miyabi ("Elegance") $300. Multiple-course kaiseki dinners include sushi, tempura, lobster or broiled fish for $80-120. Kamaʻaina Kaiseki, an authentic Japanese full course dinner of eleven items offers sushi, tempura, chicken teriyaki, or steak as an entree for $58. The Osusume Kaiseki has more courses and several intricately designed items per course for $80. Sushi or tempura kaiseki $100; lobster kaiseki $120. A la carte menu ranges from $34-120 with a few minor soup and appetizer offerings under $10. There is also a sushi bar (capacity 17) and a tempura bar (seats 15). Extensive wine list. Their children's menu is called "Keiki Kincha" which is a mini version of those above for $40. COMMENTS: While we may find these prices outrageous, the Japanese visitor may not be in for such a shock. We're told that a fine meal in Japan runs several hundred dollars or more. And although there are a number of food courses, the price is more reflective of the culinary artistry in preparation and display and the gracious ceremony with which it's presented. In any case, when you take the special private elevator to Kincha, you will feel as if you've just arrived in Japan. Created from 350 tons of rock from Mount Fuji, the restaurant features lush gardens and peaceful lagoons. Since the resort's Grand Dining Room is no longer open for dinner, Kincha now serves as the signature fine dining restaurant, offering not only a selection of exquisitely prepared Japanese meals, but a rare and special experience to go with them.

KAHULUI-WAILUKU

Along Lower Main Street in Wailuku are a number of local restaurants which are not often frequented by tourists and may well be one of the island's best kept secrets! Don't expect to find polished silver or extravagant decor, but do expect to find reasonable prices for large portions of food in a comfortable atmosphere. Note that many of these local restaurants may not accept credit cards. Dairy Queen, Pizza Hut, McDonald's, Burger King, and Jack-in-the-Box are a few of the fast food restaurants in and around Kahului and the Maui Mall. These don't require elaboration.

INEXPENSIVE

While not restaurants, two of our favorite haunts bear mention here. The *Home Maid Bakery* at 1005 Lower Main, open 5:30am-9pm daily, is an island institution. Recently remodeled and expanded, they have more than just donuts, you'll find unusual specialties such as empanadas, manju, and bread pudding. They began almost 40 years ago on Maui and do not add any preservatives to their made-from-scratch formulas. They are the home of the original Maui Crispy Manju and noted for their Maui Crunch bread. Some items available at island groceries. 244-7015. Nearby is the *Four Sisters Bakery* on Vineyard and Hinano in Wailuku. It is run by Melen, Mila, Beth and Bobbie who arrived from the Philippines after helping their father run a Spanish Bakery in Manila for fifteen years. Not a large selection, but delicious and different items. One is a sweet bread filled with a cinnamon pudding, a sponge cake "sandwich," as well as cinnamon rolls and butter rolls. The only place you can purchase these goodies is at the bakery or the Kahului Swap Meet. 244-9333. Open daily 5am-8pm.

A SAIGON CAFE ★ *Vietnamese*
1792 Main St. (243-9560) HOURS: 10am-9:30pm; till 8:30 on Sunday. SAMPLING: Spring or summer rolls, shrimp pops marinated and grilled on a sugar cane stick, shredded roast pork rolls $3.75-7.25; rare lemon beef or shrimps, chicken and green papaya salads, saimin, chow fun, or hot & sour soup $6.75-9.95. Pork meatballs; sirloin rolls; lemon grass chicken or beef; stuffed tofu; vermicelli noodle dishes; rice plates; shrimp, catfish, or pork clay pot; wok fried noodles and vegetables; crisp "Garden Party" shrimp; Saigon fondue (cooked at your table) and tofu, fish and chicken entrees $7-9.25. COMMENTS: If you haven't tried Vietnamese food, now is the time and this is the place! Very different from Chinese or Japanese, it is a refreshing combination of flavors that sets it apart. It's all fresh, fresh, fresh . . .right out of owner Jennifer Nguyen's own garden. Lemon grass, cucumbers, sour garlic sauce, daikon pickles, fresh island basil and mint leaves are among the many distinctive ingredients used for seasoning dishes such as Ga Xao Xa Ot (curried chicken with lemon grass) or Bo Lui (grilled beef sirloin rolls). The most fun is Banh Hoi: choose from a variety of meats or seafood to fill with the above ingredients (along with bean sprouts and vermicelli cake noodle) in rice paper that you dip in hot water, then wrap! Thankfully, you don't have to be able to pronounce the food to enjoy it! Located in the old Naokee Steak House location, they still serve steaks on the menu in homage to the former tenant. Try the tapioca for dessert or bring your ID for a

piece of homemade Kahlua cake! A little hard to find (easiest way is from the road behind Ooka's) but well worth it. Simple atmosphere, great food & ample portions, prompt and friendly service -- they deserve all their accolades and awards. A definite best bet!

AJIYOSHI OKAZUYA   *Japanese*
Kahului Industrial Area, 385 Hoohana St. 5-C (877-9080) HOURS: Mon-Sat 6am-2:30pm, Dinner 4-9pm. SAMPLING: Pancakes, waffles, or egg & meat breakfasts $2.95-4.80. Lunch & Dinners: Chicken katsu, teriyaki pork, seafood & vegetable tempura, BBQ beef, udon noodles, chow mein, chow fun, ramen (Japanese style), yakitori or unagi don, and sushi $4.99-8.95. COMMENTS: Entrees come with rice and choice of macaroni salad, stir-fry or Japanese vegetables. Bentos $4.85-5.35; pig feet soup Tues & Sat $7.

AKI'S HAWAIIAN FOOD AND BAR   *Hawaiian*
309 N. Market, Wailuku (244-8122) HOURS: Mon-Sat 11am-9pm, Sunday from 5pm. SAMPLING: Chicken hekka, Hawaiian favorites such as kalua pig with cabbage, pipikaula (beef), saimin, and coconut milk soup $7-12. COMMENTS: Nightly dinners. A good stop if you want to try some local Hawaiian food. (Closed one Sunday each month so that the owner can enjoy her game of golf!)

ALOHA GRILL   *50's Diner*
Maui Marketplace, 270 Dairy Rd., Kahului (893-0263) HOURS: 8am-9pm, till 6pm Sunday. SAMPLING: Regular and large hot dogs (Moon Doggie, Hound Dog, Bo-Didilly Dog) $2.19/2.99-2.79/3.69; Burgers with bacon, teriyaki, ham, chiles, chili and names like Buddy Holy, Gidget, La Bamba, and Great Balls of Fire $4.30-5.85 plus a good variety of vegetarian burgers $4.85. Surfer (sloppy) Joe $3.50; sandwiches $5.75; corndog $1.85, and bite-size menehune burgers 80¢. Fountain treats like sundaes, shakes, malts, floats - even flavored colas $1.75-3.25; banana splits $4.95. COMMENTS: Small (one counter) 50's style soda fountain with stools in the Kau Kau Food Court.

APPLAUSE CAFE   *"Theatrical American"*
68 No. Market St., Wailuku, inside the historic Iao Theatre (244-8680) HOURS: Open for lunch Mon-Fri 11am-3pm and for dinner during performances (Fri-Sun) SAMPLING: Stuffed tomato, spinach, Caesar, and green salads sound SO much better when they're called 42nd Street, I Am What I Am, Et Tu Brute?, and The Secret Garden! ($3.75-6.95) Now that you've got the idea, here are some of the sandwiches: Break a L'egg, Greater Tuna, Bye Bye Birdie, Philadelphia, Catcher in the Rye, and Hamlet $3.50-5.50. (Not to mention: if you want the best of both worlds, Victor, Victoria offers soup or salad & half a sandwich; if you don't want a pound of flesh you can order the Merchant of Venice veggie plate, and if you like your salmon smoked, you can order it a la Smokey Joe's Cafe, $4.50-7.50) COMMENTS: Patio seating around the outside box office makes for a unique atmosphere and good people watching. Dinners reflect the current production with a themed menu (like the King Arthur's feast for *Camelot*) and/or offer food items mentioned in the play! (Note to the theatrically challenged: sandwiches above are egg salad, tuna, chicken salad, Philly cheese steak, pastrami, and ham.)

ARCHIE'S   *American/Japanese*
1440 Lower Main St., Wailuku (244-9401) HOURS: Lunch 10:30am-1pm, dinner 5-8pm. SAMPLING: Noodle dishes are their most popular - saimen, udon, chow fun, somen, and fried noodles $4. Teishoku dinners offer tempura, teriyaki, tofu, and fish dishes $4.50-7.50; combination plates with shrimp, tempura, tonkatsu, BBQ, chicken, and sashimi $6.50-9.50; Hama'ko Teishoku has all of the above for $12.50. They also have an inexpensive selection of American omelettes, salads, chops, and cutlets $4-7; sandwiches $1.70-4. COMMENTS: We found their food good and their prices reasonable, but have always had trouble getting Archie to give us information. After all (as he's told us), he's been in business for over 30 years and is "doing fine" without our book. We finally had a chance to stop by and talk to Hifumi Tanaka (Mrs. Archie) and were able to jot down a few notes from their menu.

ARTIE'S MEXICAN FOOD   *Mexican*
333 Dairy Road, next to Minit-Stop, Kahului (877-7113) HOURS: 10am-6pm. SAMPLING: Chile relleno, taquitos, nachos, tostadas, tacos, enchiladas, burritos, quesadillas, taco salad $3.25-4.95. El Grande burrito with beef, pork & chicken $6.25 Chocolate taco ice cream $1.50. COMMENTS: After years of selling his salsa and chips retail, Artie's Mexican food is now available for lunch and dinner and for take out.

ASIAN CUISINE AND SPORTS BAR   *Yakiniku*
Kahului Shopping Center (877-7776) HOURS: Lunch and dinner or takeout. SAMPLING: Lunch specials $5.50-6. Dinner $6.50-15.95 COMMENTS: Our repeated requests for menu information went unanswered.

BAMBOO RESTAURANT   *Local/Asian*
1032 Lower Main St. (244-1166) HOURS: Mon-Sat 10am-9pm, Half day on Sunday 10am-3pm. SAMPLING: Squid stir-fry, chicken katsu, monk fish, Kal bi ribs $7-14.

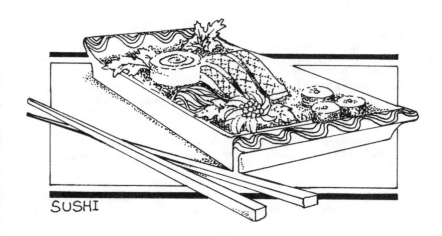

SUSHI

BENTOS AND BANQUETS BY BERNARD   *Local*
85 Church St., Wailuku (244-1124) HOURS: Breakfast 7-10am, lunch 10am-2pm. SAMPLING: Loco moco, hot cakes, veggie & meat lover's omelettes, French toast $3.50-5.75. Turkey burger, teri steak, Caesar salad and noodle dishes (choose two with potato macaroni salad for $5.75.) Weekly specials might include lasagna, mushroom chicken, beef chimichanga, pot roast, Hawaiian plate, Chinese roast pork, and oyster chicken. Salad and sandwich specials, too: deluxe somen salad, reuben or triple club sandwiches $5.75-6.50. COMMENTS: Small take-out shop with limited seating. Good prices, large portions. Their special loco moco-style roast pork with gravy is so popular you can get it for breakfast or lunch. They cater seven days a week offering both local and gourmet food. They also deliver -- for both take-out and catering.

BOOMER'S   *American/Rotisserie*
Triangle Square, Kahului (893-0404) HOURS: 8:30am-8pm, till 9 Fri-Sat; dinners from 5pm. SAMPLING: Boomer burgers or patty melt along with focaccia chicken, ahi melt, fish, reuben and cheese steak sandwiches $5.95-7.75. Tacos and burritos, Hawaiian plate plus Caesar, tuna, and chicken salads $5.50-7.95. Veggie burger or grilled vegetable & goat cheese on focaccia $6.50-6.95. They specialize in freshly roasted rotisserie chicken for lunch ($4.95-7.95) or dinner ($10.95). Other dinner items include sizzling fajitas, cheese ravioli, and tomato penne pasta $8.95-9.95, fresh lemon pesto NY steak 14.95. Keiki menu $4.95. COMMENTS: Located near the airport (down the road apiece from Kmart) so it's handy for a quick bite on the way in or out of Maui. Surf & sports motif (the commercial focus of the Triangle Square outlets) with tables and booths. Self-service (order at the counter); good prices for family dining.

BORDERS CAFE   *Pastries/light meals*
Maui Marketplace, 270 Dairy Rd. (877-6160) HOURS: 11am-9pm. SAMPLING: Chili (with rice & cheese), quiche, spinach feta puff or veggie curry puff, or dilled chicken salad $3.50-7.50. Cheesecake, tiramisu, key lime torte, chocolate mousse cake, apple fritters, lemon bars or monkey bars (with white chocolate chips & banana) plus and assortment of scones, muffins, and cookies with coffees and teas $1.75-4.95. COMMENTS: Small cafe inside Borders bookstore. Coffee bar or tables and chairs. Light meals and/or beverages served with plenty of reading material including out-of-town newspapers.

CALI CAFE   *Vietnamese*
1246 Lower Main St., Wailuku (244-2167) HOURS: 10am-6pm, closed Sunday. SAMPLING: Spring rolls, fresh summer rolls, shrimp pops, crispy calamari, and shrimp or chicken salad $4.95-7.95. Create your own Vietnamese burritos: rice paper wrapped with meat balls, beef sirloin, chicken, or shrimp $8.25-8.95. Beef, seafood and dried noodles soups, vermicelli noodle dishes, rice plate, crispy egg noodles $5.75-7.95. Pork or shrimp in a clay pot; stir fried beef, chicken, seafood, or squid; spicy lemon grass or sweet & sour dishes; and Cali specialties of crispy salted shrimp, fried tofu with vegetables or lemon grass $6.50-9.25. COMMENTS: This is the latest (but probably not the last) Vietnamese restaurant incarnation at this location on lower Main. Owners come

and go faster than we can keep track, but the menu options and food quality seem to remain fairly constant.

CHUM'S   *Local Style*
1900 Main Street, Wailuku (244-1000) HOURS: Breakfast 6:30-11am, Lunch/Dinner 11am-9pm, Fri-Sat till 9:30. Closed Mon-Tues. SAMPLING: Traditional and local breakfasts: eggs, hotcakes and hotcake sandwich, omelettes, sweet bread French toast plus saimin, loco moco, and fried rice $3-6. Homemade soups, and noodle dishes $3-6.25. Local style meals (plate lunches) include pork cutlet, teri chicken, stir fry, chop steak, beef tomato, mahi mahi, roast pork with stuffing, and fried chicken $6-7.25; lasagna, lau lau, spaghetti, kalua pork $6.50-8.50. Burgers, patty melt, Monte Cristo, French dip, and turkey or roast beef sandwiches are served hot; cold selections offer club, BLT, and veggie, ham & cheese $5.50-6.50. Chili dishes $2-5.25; teriyaki beef sticks $1.20 each. COMMENTS: The menu has some nice, friendly little notes that describe the dishes, explain about local plates, and there's even a personal note to Dona (well, actually all late risers) that they understand and will be happy to offer any of their "eggs n things" till 1pm! They have a keiki and senior menu as well as a percentage off daily specials. A good basic menu that's not only reasonable, but friendly and very accommodating!

(THE) COFFEE STORE   *Coffee/Pastries/Light meals*
Kaahumanu Center (871-6860) < WWW > HOURS: Mon-Fri 7am-9pm; Sat 8am-6pm; Sun 8am-5pm. SAMPLING: Muffins, cinnamon rolls, sticky buns, and assorted pastries $2.50. Spinach quiche, tortilla "wrapper" (veggie, chicken, or turkey), selection of quesadillas and sandwiches, lasagna, grilled veggie panini on focaccia; Caesar, tuna, pasta, or Caprese salad $6.95-8.50. Cheesecake, pies, brownies, baklava, cookies, and Chocolate Thunder $2.50-4.50. COMMENTS: They also have locations in Kihei and Napili. Freshly roasted coffee and coffee drinks, flavored Italian sodas $1.50-3.95; smoothies $4.50. Voted "Best Cappuccino" in the "Best of Maui" contest conducted by the Maui News.

CUPIE'S   *American-Local*
134 W. Kamehameha Ave. (877-3055) HOURS: Mon-Sat 9am-9pm for breakfast, lunch and dinner. SAMPLING: $3.99 breakfast served until 10:30; plate lunches (hamburger, omelette, loco moco, kalbi ribs, beef or pork teriyaki, fried ahi) $5.75-6.10. Bento, mini bento, mini-meals, chow fun, fried chicken, burgers, and sandwiches $1.99-5.75. COMMENTS: This used to be one of those places where you sat in your car with the trays on your window, now it is a drive up to order "to go" or seating there. It really is an old-fashioned place -- you can still get a grilled cheese sandwich (or a 32 oz. soda) for 99¢!

DOWN TO EARTH NATURAL FOODS & CAFE   *Vegetarian*
305 Dairy Rd., Kahului (877-7548) HOURS: 8am-7:30pm; store open 7am-9pm, Sun till 7. SAMPLING: Soups and hot vegetarian entrees like bell pepper with couscous, "to fu young," enchilada pie, lasagna, and mock chicken tofu ($5.99 lb.) plus freshly-made sandwiches, burritos, spring rolls, quesadillas, and wraps. Salad bar $4.99 lb. Low-fat, whole grain bakery items include streusel or carrot cake, toffee bars, muffins, baklava, almond walnut & tea cookies, and date bars;

also tofu cheesecake and vegan carob chip cookies 89¢ to $3.29. COMMENTS: The mock chicken is tasty by itself or added to their (or your own) stir fry vegetables. Fruit compote made with blueberries or peaches and coconut baked with crumble topping - yummy! Pleasant seating area upstairs. Retail store has fresh organic produce, bulk items, and packaged vegetarian food products.

EDO JAPAN (See Food Court at Kaahumanu Center)

FOOD COURT (AT KAAHUMANU CENTER)
The Queen's Market Food Court at Kaahumanu Center features seven upstairs restaurants near the main entrance. *Edo Japan* has teppanyaki plate dinners, rice bowls, saimin and sushi. *Yummy Korean BBQ* offers kal bi and BBQ meats, noodle and dumpling soups plus curries. *Panda Express* has Mandarin cuisine like orange chicken, spicy chicken with peanuts, chow mein and eggplant in garlic sauce. *Papa Romeo's Italian* specialties include calzone, pasta, pizza (with gourmet choices like Garlic Chicken or Hawaiian Mango) and sub sandwiches (Italian Combo, Pastrami and more). *Maui Tacos* offers healthy Mexican. (For detailed description see Napili or Kihei listing.) *Maui Mixed Plate* has local food and *McDonald's* offers the usual fare. Prices $4-8 range. Minimum hours in the food court are 11am-9pm daily, although some may open earlier for breakfast and remain open later.

There's also a Cinnabon here and coffee and juice carts are nearby. There is an *Orange Julius/Arby's* downstairs as well. Two local-style restaurants are located inside the Shirokiya department store: *Osamu* offers ramen, saimin, and curry; *Kihata's* has a buffet of hot dishes plus sandwiches, salads, and bentos. Pick up your food at the counter and take it back to your table. (But expect some pretty long lines - the locals know a good thing!) *Island Baking Co.* has a second location here with a limited selection of their breads and pastries. *Koho Grill & Bar, Firecracker Chinese Bistro,* and *Sam Choy's* are also part of the shopping center and are listed individually.

FUJIYA'S ★ *Japanese*
133 Market Street, Wailuku (244-0206) HOURS: Lunch 11am-2pm Mon-Fri, dinner 5-9:30pm Mon-Sat; Closed Sunday. SAMPLING: Lunch: Fried or miso ahi or salmon, teriyaki or salted ika, miso butter fish $6.95-7.95. Noodles $4.25-5.25 Dinner: Tempura, teriyaki, donburi, curry, chicken or pork tofu $4.95-9.95; Sushi $4-8. Five combination dinner choices such as tempura with yakitori, shumai, tsukemono, miso soup and rice. Beer & sake available. COMMENTS: One of our best bets for Japanese food. Sushi lovers will appreciate their sushi bar where a large variety of selections are available at half the usual resort area price. New owners were expected to take over in June, 1998, but planned to keep the menu and prices the same.

(THE) GRILLE AT GRAND WAIKAPU *Lunch*
Grand Waikapu Country Club, just outside of Wailuku. (244-1122) HOURS: 8am-4/5pm. SAMPLING: Omelette or eggs $7-8.50. Curry beef stew, spaghetti, stir-fried noodles, fresh catch, Caesar salad, burgers, and reuben, cajun chicken or club sandwiches $6.50-8.95. A pupu menu offers spring rolls, calamari strips,

cajun wings, and potstickers runs $3-6.25. Sundaes, brownie with ice cream, and apple pie are available for dessert $2.50. COMMENTS: Tiny room "nestled" in the sprawling Frank Lloyd Wright building makes you feel like you're on a cruise ship. Primarily for golfers.

ICHIBAN THE RESTAURANT   *Japanese*
Kahului Shopping Center (871-6977) HOURS: Breakfast 7am-2pm, Saturday 10:30am-2pm. Dinner 5pm-9pm, closed Sunday. SAMPLING: Luncheon menu offers chicken katsu, teriyaki chicken, shrimp tempura, oxtail soup, or donburi and noodle meals $4.50-9.95. Stir-fry dishes and special dinner combination plates $7.95-14.95; steak and lobster $21.95. COMMENTS: Located in the older Kahului Center, this restaurant doesn't stand out as memorable for its food or ambiance.

INTERNATIONAL HOUSE OF PANCAKES   *American*
Maui Mall, Kahului (871-4000) HOURS: Sun-Thurs 6am-midnight; Fri & Sat until 2 am. COMMENTS: A very large facility with a menu that is popular with all family members. Something for everyone and at reasonable prices. Breakfasts begin in the $5 range, dinners from $12.

ISLAND BAKING CO.   *Bakery/Coffee Shop*
150 Hana Hwy, Kahului (873-7746) HOURS: 4:30am-9:30pm. SAMPLING: Open early (or late if you're a night person) for fresh pastries: Danish, apple fritters, cinnamon twists, and fruit squares with a variety of freshly made sandwiches (plus hot turkey or roast beef with gravy) $3.89-4.85; local plates (pork or chicken adobo, meat loaf, hamburger steak, kalua pork & cabbage, and BBQ chicken $5.50; and salads (Caesar, chef's, tofu, somen, seafood, and pasta) $2.95-4.95. COMMENTS: They also sell mochi, manju, pandesal, breads, and rolls. Stop by after 6pm for hot, fresh malasadas or cream-filled puffasadas! Second location inside Shirokiya at Kaahumanu Center.

JACK'S FAMOUS BAGELS   *Bagels & Sandwiches*
333 Dairy Rd., Kahului (871-JACK) <WWW> HOURS: Mon-Fri 5:30am-6pm; Sat 6:30-4; Sun 6:30-3. SAMPLING: Mix and match bagel flavors (garlic, onion, macadamia nut, blueberry, jalapeno, sesame, sundried tomato, spinach, coconut, and pineapple) with gourmet whipped cream cheese (garlic herb, veggie, pesto, lox, strawberry, blueberry, jalapeno, pineapple, coconut, and honey walnut). Bagelwiches of cream cheese & lox, tuna, egg salad, hummus, PB & J, cheese, and turkey $1.95-6.95. Pat's Pizza: cheese, veggie, jalapeno, pepperoni, Hawaiian $2.95; Cheese Melt Downs with turkey, tuna, or ham $5.95. Salads, cheese bagel, bagel dog, bagel chips $1.50-2.95. Coffee drinks $1.25-3.25; smoothies $3.75. COMMENTS: Authentic water-boiled bagels (freshly-made without fat or oils) from a third generation New York bagel recipe. Their pineapple bagel is the first one we've heard of and they now have coconut. (Can pina colada be far behind?) Also in Lahaina and Kihei with slightly different prices.

JACK'S INN   *Local*
(Near Ace Hardware) 312 Alamaha Pl., Kahului (877-3610) HOURS: Mon-Fri 5am-2pm; Sat till 1pm; Closed Sunday. SAMPLING: Egg & meat breakfasts, omelettes, pancakes, French toast, plus local-style miso soup & cabbage, fried rice with egg & hot dog, creamed beef, pancake sandwich, loco moco, and beef stew $2.75-4.25. Burgers, hot open-faced pork, beef, or turkey sandwiches, noodles, curry or beef stew, teri bowl, and local plates $3.95-4.75. Jack's Special with chicken, teriyaki, fish, macaroni salad, hot vegetable, salted cabbage, and "2 scoops rice" $5.50. COMMENTS: They same owners also have Ma-Chan's on Dairy Road, but we were unable to get any menu information.

KIHATA'S
Located inside Shirokiya Store at Kaahumanu Center. See Food Court.

KOHO GRILL AND BAR ★   *American*
Kaahumanu Shopping Center, Kahului (877-5588) HOURS: Breakfast 7-11am, lunch from 11am & dinner 5pm-midnight. SAMPLING: Create an omelette or a breakfast taco with a variety of ingredients or try one of their skillet egg & potato dishes, French toast, loco moco, or pancake sandwich $4.95-6.95. Chicken Caesar, oriental chicken, taco, cobb, or fresh catch salads $6.25-7.95. Club, cajun chicken, fresh fish sandwiches, burgers, or plate lunches $5.75-6.75. Sizzling fajitas $7.95-8.95 ($13.95 for two every Tuesday!) Pupus include nachos, chili cheese fries, quesadilla, fish & chips, potato skins, and rib basket $4.95-8.25. Dinner entrees served with soup or salad: fish, steak, chicken stir fry, ribs plus assorted pasta and chicken preparations $8.95-14.95. Cinnamon apple or chocolate sundae, brownie and fried ice cream snow ball for dessert $3.45-4.50. COMMENTS: A diverse menu and affordable prices which boils down to great family dining. They also have a great keiki (childrens) menu and knowing how fussy some kids can be, they'll even cut the crusts off the sandwiches! Sports bar & large screen tv. One of only a few restaurants in the area open on Sundays, it's a convenient stop for a bite enroute to the airport. There is another "Koho's" at Napili Plaza; the same owners also run the Plantation House in Kapalua and the SeaWatch restaurant in Wailea.

KOKO ICHIBAN-YA   *Japanese*
Dairy Center, 360 Papa Pl., Kahului (871-9108) HOURS: Mon-Fri lunch 9am-2pm, dinner 4:30-8pm; Sat lunch 10am-2pm. SAMPLING: Plate lunches of pork, chicken, and seafood offered tempura, teriyaki, and katsu (breaded) style plus BBQ beef and sauteed salmon $4.80-6.24. Noodles (udon & ramen), bowl dishes (don), and California roll sushi $4.56-4.99; uhagi udon (sea eel) $8.64.

LAS PINATAS OF MAUI   *Mexican*
395 Dairy Rd., Kahului (877-8707) HOURS: Mon-Sat 10:30am-7:30pm; Sun 11am-3pm. SAMPLING: Nachos, tostadas, hard & soft shell tacos, enchiladas, burritos, quesadillas, Mexican salads $2.15-5.95. Combination plates $6.15-7.30. Occasional specials might offer tamales, chille relleno, taquitos, or fish tacos from $2.95 to $7.95 for plates with rice and beans. COMMENTS: A family operation with affordable prices. Everything is made from scratch, from the beans to the salsa (two kinds, blended and smooth or chunky) and they use only

100% cholesterol free oils. Dine in or take out. A small, fast-food sized place; very convenient enroute to the airport. They now take credit cards.

LIWANAG'S   *Filipino*
1276B Lower Main St., Wailuku (242-1636) HOURS: Lunch 10am-6pm, Sunday till 2; breakfast Fri-Sun 6-1am. SAMPLING: More "computer spell-check" favorites like tapa, tosino, and longanisa sinangag for breakfast; kare kare, pinkabet, bulanglang, and pinapaitan plus (luckily), pork & peas, chicken adobo, beef steak, chop suey, menudo, and lumpia priced $3.49/4.99/5.99 for 1, 2, or 3 entrees; a la carte $3.99-9.99. COMMENTS: Small Filipino fast food outlet to dine in or take out. Opened April, 1998.

L&L DRIVE INN / CHOPSTICKS EXPRESS   *Local*
Maui Marketplace, 270 Dairy Road in Kahului (873-0323). There is also a second location (next to Sack N Save) at Wailuku Town Center, 790 Eha St. (242-1880) HOURS: 7am-10:30pm, till 9:30pm Sun (Wailuku); 7am-9pm, till 6pm Sun (Kahului) SAMPLING: At L&L you can get breakfast of omelettes, pancakes, French toast, loco moco, saimin, or fried rice combo until 10am $3.36-5.28. Plate lunches (seafood, chicken, pork, and beef) plus burgers, hot dogs, saimin & ramen, chili, curry, and stew $3.22-5.76. The adjacent Chopsticks Express offers beef, pork, seafood, chicken and vegetarian oriental dishes. Combination plates run $3.84-5.76 for one to three items. Entrees of beef with broccoli, orange chicken, shrimp & vegetables, black pepper chicken strips, or sweet & sour pork $4.80-6.72. COMMENTS: These side-by-side restaurants are both owned by L&L, an O'ahu chain which has branched to Maui with these two locations. With everything under $7, the prices are affordable, but they do seem a little heavy with the rice.

LOCAL BOY'S DRIVE INN   *Local/Chinese*
395F Dairy Road, Kahului (872-9020) HOURS: 10:30am-8pm. SAMPLING: Sandwiches & burgers ($1.25-2.95); plate lunches and mini-plates ($2.75-5.25); Stir fry ($5.75); Snacks like won ton, chili, saimin, curry and beef stew ($1.40-4.75) Buffet served Mon-Fri (11am-2pm) with one, two, or three items: $3.50-4.95-5.59 including noodles or rice. COMMENTS: We didn't drive "in" or sleep over "inn," but still liked the big portions and small prices.The Teriyaki Saimin was a surprise: the BIG chunk 'o meat was a little difficult to negotiate so we tried the Teriyaki Beef sandwich. Yummy! The plate lunch with fried scallops was on the spendy end of the menu (about $7!), but the scallops were good - not huge, but very tender. Their original Lahaina location seems to have slightly higher prices.

LONE STAR COOKHOUSE   *BBQ/Smoked meats*
1234 Lower Main St. (242-6616) HOURS: Mon-Fri 11am-9pm. Sat-Sun noon-8pm. SAMPLING: Smoked BBQ plates of sausage, beef brisket, chicken, and beef ribs with one, two or three meats plus corn on the cob, ranch beans, and cole slaw or potato salad $8.95-12.95. Buffalo wings, jalapeno poppers, chicken strips, chili nachos, or Texas Toothpicks: deep-fried jalapeno & onion strips $3.95-6.95, sampler $9.95; burgers, smoked beef brisket, sausage, grilled chicken, steak hoagie, turkey pita pocket, or ahi BLT sandwiches $5.95-7.95.

Soup & salad bar $5.95; all you can eat $7.95; with meal: soup $1.95, salad bar $2.95. House specialties come with salad bar, and choice of potato or rice: chicken fried steak, pork chops, T-bone steak, and fried chicken $8.95-12.95. COMMENTS: Their meats are seasoned and slow-cooked for 16 hours in custom-built hardwood smokers; orders of ranch style beans are all-you-can-eat. "Buckaroo" menu $3.95-4.95; homemade pie of the day $3.95. Catering and take-out orders. Evening entertainment.

MAMA DING'S PASTELES RESTAURANT ★ *Puerto Rican-Local*
255 E Alamaha St., Kahului (877-5796) HOURS: Breakfast/lunch 6:30am-2:30pm Mon-Fri. You can have lunch at 7am and breakfast at 1pm! SAMPLING: Eggs Bermuda (2 eggs scrambled with cream cheese & onion) served with potatoes or rice and toast, French toast (choice of cinnamon or sweet bread), or Puerto-Rican breakfast with eggs, meat, half pastele, gandule rice, and peach $3.75-5.10. The plate lunch comes with pastele, gandule rice, empanadilla, choice of meat, bacalao salad, and dessert $6.15. Other lunches include teri beef or fried rice plate, saimin, sandwiches, and a homemade chorizo burger $2.50-5.75. COMMENTS: Ready for a different breakfast? Skip IHOP and Denny's and try this cozy restaurant tucked away in the Kahului Industrial Area. Try a pastele which has an exterior of grated green banana and a filling of pork, vegetables and spices that is then steamed. Delicious! We've tried several of their breakfasts, all were good! No credit cards. They also sell specialty breads in Hawaiian flavors like coconut-papaya-pineapple, strawberry guava, and Portuguese sweetbread as well as cinnamon, apple-cinnamon, or potato bread.

MANUEL S. MOLINA'S SPORTS BAR *Hoagie sandwiches*
197 No. Market St., Wailuku (244-4100/244-0141) HOURS: 8am-1am. SAMPLING: Breakfast of two hotcakes, two strips of bacon, one egg and coffee $2.95. Philly cheesesteaks in 8, 12, & 24" sizes $6.75/12/18.75; hoagies come in 4" as well: Italian, American, roast beef, turkey breast, special recipe tuna, veggie, and "Uncle Louie's" sausage from $3.50/5.50/7.50/12.75. Soup $1.50-2.25. COMMENTS: They do one thing and it sounds like they do it well! Hoagies served on a French roll with all the fixins. (They also do catering and can make a forty foot long sandwich for parties.)

MARKET STREET CAFE AND SAIMIN *Local*
318 North Market St., Wailuku (Former location of Sam Sato's) (249-0555). HOURS: Breakfast and Lunch Mon-Sat 5:30am-2pm; Sundays 6am-noon SAMPLING: Belgian waffles with strawberries, sweet bread French toast, loco moco, omelettes or set breakfast $3-4.50. Burgers, tuna, ham & egg, and fried egg sandwiches; beef stew, roast pork, teriyaki, ribs, and saimin or mein noodles $3-5.75. Daily specials include pork tofu, oxtail, kal bi, spaghetti, and roast turkey $5.75-6.25. COMMENTS: Although this was the location of Sam Sato's for many years, you won't be disappointed if you're still looking for good food at low prices. Cute, comfortable, country kitchen look with casual, friendly service.

MAUI BAKE SHOP & DELI ★ *European Pastries-Deli*
2092 Vineyard St., Wailuku (242-0064) HOURS: Mon-Fri 6am-5pm, Sat 7am-2pm. SAMPLING: An early morning arrival assures a greater selection from the many varied goodies: fresh fruit tarts, handmade puff pastry, croissants, cookies, lavosh, fresh breads, and their special novelty desserts shaped like pigs, frogs, rabbits, and chickens! This European style bakery is a combination of efforts between French chef Jose and his wife, Claire Fjuii Krall. They have pizza, quiche, soups, salads, and sandwiches $2.50-6. Specialties include eggplant on focaccia, vegetarian lasagna, grilled chicken salad, and *pain fourre*: chicken, pesto, mushrooms & cheese baked in bread. There are a few ice cream tables and chairs for eating in. The big stone oven is still there, left over from the Yokouchi family that was in this location in the 1930s. Desserts include cakes, napoleons and other very fancy pastries. At Christmas holiday time check out their stollen, gingerbread, and yule logs, at Easter indulge in a marzipan egg. Jose Krall began cooking in 1976 in France and trained in Belgium and France after that. Yum!

MAUI BAKERY & BAGELRY *Light meals*
201 Dairy Rd., Kahului (871-4825) HOURS: Mon-Sat 6:30am-5:30pm; Sun 7am-3:30pm. SAMPLING: Turkey, roast beef, ham, tuna, egg salad, or chicken salad sandwiches on bagel or choice of bread $3.50-5. Also specialty baked goods like focaccia and pesto calzone $3-3.95. Salads include tuna, potato, egg, and curried chicken $3.96-6 lb. Dessert items such as brownies, coffee cake, custard puffs, napoleons, strudel, and chocolate macaroons $1.50-2.25. COMMENTS: Freshly baked bagels come in sixteen flavors with a variety of cream cheese toppings from cinnamon raisin walnut to Maui onion $3-6.

MAUI COFFEE ROASTERS (BEAN'S WORLD) *Light meals*
444 Hana Highway, Kahului (877-CUPS) HOURS: Mon-Fri 7:30am-6pm; Sat 8am-5pm; Sun 9am-3pm. SAMPLING: Fresh-from-the-oven Danish, scones, chocolate croissants, and a variety of fruit and nut flavored muffins $1.75-1.95; granola yogurt parfait $3.95. Bagel specials include veggie, huevos, ham, turkey Benedict, or Florentine bagel plus bagel melts with crab, tuna, turkey, or veggies $4.95-6.50. Veggie burger or homemade soup with focaccia bread $5.95; chicken curry, turkey, focaccia, basmato, falafel pita, or crab salad sandwich plus Caesar, Greek, or Nicky salad (with brown & wild rice blend) $5.95-6.95. COMMENTS: Brightly and whimsically decorated with counter and table seating. Bean's World coffees feature Hawaiian, imported and flavored coffees, freshly roasted or retail sale or to order off the menu. Specialty drinks include granitas, rice milk, Maui juices, flavored teas, and a variety of espressos, lattes and cappuccinos. (You can get anything from a cup of coffee for 50¢ to a latte with espresso chocolate and caramel for $3.40!)

MAUI MALL
Not a food court, but there are several small food outlets in the mall: Restaurant Matsu has Japanese food including plate dishes, tempura, noodles, donburi (in a bowl over rice), sushi and bento lunches. Siu's Chinese Kitchen offers a variety of chicken, beef, pork, and seafood dishes, and combinations plates. There's also SW Bar-B-Q, and Tasaka Guri Guri for a local type of creamy sherbet you can

order with or without beans! (IHOP, Tiffany Luigi's and M.O.M.S. are also at the mall and listed separately.)

MAUI MARKETPLACE *Food Court*
270 Dairy Rd., Kahului. In addition to a Starbuck's and Burger King, their separate Kau Kau Food Court offers three small food outlets - Taste of Broadway, Aloha Grill and L&L Drive Inn/Chopsticks Express. (See individual listings.)

MAUI TACOS (See Food Court at Kaahumanu Center)

MAUI TROPICAL PLANTATION CAFE *Salads/Sandwiches*
Located inside the Maui Tropical Plantation in Waikapu (244-7643) HOURS: 10am-3pm. SAMPLING: Harvest luncheon buffet includes soup, salads (crab with broccoli, three bean, corn, bean sprout, kim chee, daikon, tofu), fresh fruits, roast beef, sauteed fish, chicken curry, rice, vegetables, rolls, desserts (coconut cake, cream tart, pineapple upsidedown cake) and beverage $14.50A; $10.50C. Soup & salad bar (all of the above without the hot entrees) $9.50A, $6.50C. A la carte menu offers cobb, chef's, green, shrimp, or crab salad ($5.95-8.95); a variety of fruit salad presentations ($4.25-7.95); reuben, bay shrimp & curry, tuna melt, turkey & crabmeat club, ham & cheese, eggplant, roast beef sandwiches $5.95-8.50; honey dipped chicken, eggplant parmesan, or mahi & chips (served 11am-2pm) $7.95-8.50. Build your own burger with choice of toppings (from $6.75) or fill a papaya, avocado, pineapple or tomato with tuna, chicken, shrimp or crab salad for $8.95. Homemade cream pies or cake & ice cream with fruit $3.95-4.75. COMMENTS: Pleasant view of the grounds; many of the fruits are plantation-grown. Keiki portions ($4.95) on selected items. Beer, wine, and tropical drinks available.

MEL'S LUNCH TO YOU *Ethnic/Local*
1276 Lower Main St., at the Kanaloa Seafood Market, Wailuku (242-8271) HOURS: Lunch & delivery Mon-Fri 9am-1:30pm. SAMPLING: They have more than 100 dishes overall and feature at least 10 every day on their steam table; some of the daily entrees remain the same, others change weekly. Mel has added some new Vietnamese and Korean dishes to old favorites like chicken yakitori, chow fun, pork tofu, chicken hekka, and Filipino pork with (fresh, local) pumpkin. The Hawaiian plate lunch and Friday seafood platter are popular and Wednesday's roasted turkey special is always a sell-out. They also bring in fresh fish daily. Entrees run $5.50-7. Bento boxes are $6 and you can select the three items to be included. COMMENTS: A little hole-in-the-wall that serves great food. Our readers continue to recommend this as a "real find."

MILLYARD CAFE *Vietnamese*
1764 Wili Pa Loop, Millyard Industrial Park, Wailuku (244-1833) HOURS: 10am-1am. SAMPLING: Spring or summer rolls, shrimp pops, chow fun, dry mein, steak or meat ball soup, green papaya salad $3.50-6.95; rice plates, Chinese wok and vermicelli noodle dishes, clay pot, seafood and vegetarian entrees, hot & sour soup $6.75-8.95. Banh Hoi are "Vietnamese Burritos" that you create yourself: choose from pork meat balls, sirloin rolls, chicken breast or

shrimp pops or spring rolls then add as much as you like of cucumbers, lettuce, bean sprouts, vermicelli noodles, daikon, pickled island basil & carrots, and mint leaves to wrap in softened rice paper and dip in their sweet & sour garlic sauce, $8.25-8.75. Fun to make and delicious to eat! COMMENTS: If the menu sounds a little familiar it's because this is (literally) a "sister" restaurant to A Saigon Cafe: Millyard owner Ann Carpenter is Jennifer Nguyen's sister! We'll have to presume that good taste runs in the family and recommend this as a good place to introduce yourself to the freshness and diversity of Vietnamese cuisine.

M.O.M.S. *American*
Maui Mall, Kahului (877-3711) HOURS: 11:30am-6pm; Fri till 9pm; Sun till 4:30. SAMPLING: Egg or tofu breakfast burritos, Belgian waffles, filled croissants, oatmeal $3.50-6.50. Tofu or garden burger; ham, turkey, chicken, crab, fresh fish, BLT, club, and veggie sandwiches $5.50-7.25. Soup, quiche, tuna, avocado, or pasta salad, chili & rice, or quesadilla $3.50-6.50. COMMENTS: Steamed and iced coffee drinks; Italian sodas; wine & beer. Gourmet teas and coffees available retail. Extensive selection of cigars for sale; monthly Friday night "Smokers" with dinner. Live entertainment Friday nights (6-9pm) with lunchtime piano music Mon-Tues-Wed. Originally Sir Wilfred's, now Myers of Maui (MOM's) as of November, 1997.

MUSHROOM *Local*
2080 Vineyard, Wailuku (244-7117) HOURS: Lunch 10am-2pm, dinner 5-8:30pm. SAMPLING: Chinese pasta, calamari, beef stew, sauteed chicken, shrimp or scallops with mushrooms, veggie stir fry, chicken curry, and roast pork entrees all include rice, salad or soup $5-7.50. "Prepare your own" sandwiches, seafood or oxtail soup, local noodles, special fried rice, and daily specials like meat loaf, fresh salmon or ahi steak, shoyu pork, steak & mushroom, and seared rare ahi $6.75-12.50. COMMENTS: Owner Nagato Kato was with Kobe restaurant in Lahaina and Humuhumu at the Grand Wailea. The shoyu pork is one of their more popular items, tender & juicy, but apparently too big for anyone to finish - they all ask for doggie bags. As Kato says, he's apologized to the farmers for the lack of leftovers to feed the hogs, but "what can I do? Despite the generous portions, the plates come back empty!" This friendly and accommodating restaurant advises that if you're pressed for time you can call in your order 15 minutes before arrival and be served in minutes. They also want you to know that they love kids! Great local fare, one of the best reasons to come to Wailuku is to eat!

NAZO'S *Hawaiian-Local Style*
1063 Lower Main St., Wailuku, at Puuone Plaza (244-0529) HOURS: Lunch 10am-2pm, dinner 5-9pm. (Closed Sunday) SAMPLING: A variety of burgers and sandwiches (ham, tuna, BLT, club, and egg combos) $2.50-4.95; Caesar or Chinese chicken salad or noodles: oxtail or pig feet min, dry mein or won ton mein $3.75-6.50. Plate lunches include chopped steak, hamburger & gravy, loco moco, liver with bacon & onions, pork chops, teri steak or chicken, shrimp tempura, grilled mahi, and chicken katsu $6.25-7.95 with "2 scoops" rice and macaroni salad. Daily specials feature chicken papaya (Mon); pork & squash or pork adobo (Tues); chicken luau stew (Wed); chicken bittermelon (Thurs); pig

feet soup (Sat) $6.50-7.50. Hawaiian, seafood, and roast specials alternate on Aloha Fridays. Mini-plates $4.25. Oxtail soup ($7.95) is their specialty and they now have French fries. COMMENTS: A small, family-owned restaurant. Very affordable; they pride themselves on their home-style cooking. The family's newest venture is Paa's, a "store-front" fast food outlet on Main Street.

NORM'S CAFE *Local style*
740 Lower Main St. (242-1667) HOURS: Breakfast and lunch Tues-Sat 5am-2pm; Sun 6am-2pm. Dinner Wed-Thurs 5-8pm; Fri-Sat 5-9pm. SAMPLING: Local foods with okazuya. Local style "grinds" served with rice, macaroni salad, tossed green salad or coleslaw and includes roast pork, mahi, beef stew, beef tomato, or roast pork $5-6. Dinners $8-13. Norm's sandwiches $3-8. Also noodles and salads.

OSAMU
Located inside Shirokiya Department Store at Kaahumanu Center. See Food Court.

PAA'S LOCAL GRINDS *Local*
2051 Main St., Wailuku (244-5550) HOURS: Mon-Fri 10am-2pm. SAMPLING: Roast pork, loco moco, chicken katsu, grilled mahi, hamburger steak, breaded teri beef, lemon chicken $4.95-5.75; oxtail soup or curry $6.75. Chinese chicken or Caesar salad $5.25. Daily specials offer additional plate lunches like shiitake chicken, Kalbi ribs, chicken papaya, chopped steak, roast turkey or chicken - even lasagna $$5.25-5.50; combos $6.25. COMMENTS: They also do take out, deliver and catering. This is the new fast-food outlet operated by the same family who own Nazo's on Lower Main.

PANDA EXPRESS (See Food Court at Kaahumanu Center)

PAPA ROMEO'S PIZZA & PASTA CO. (See Food Court at Kaahumanu Center)

RAMON'S *Mexican*
2102 Vineyard St., Wailuku (244-7243) HOURS: 10am-9pm, till 10pm Sat-Sun (Breakfast 10am-noon, till 2pm Sat-Sun.) SAMPLING: Pancakes, pancake sandwich, huevos rancheros or con chorizo, Spanish omelette (with rice or beans), and loco moco $5.95. Tostadas, burritos, taco salad, enchiladas, chile relleno, quesdilla, and homemade pork tamales $6.95-9.95 plus burgers, local plates, and beef, pork or chicken combinations dinners $6.95-8.95. Fried ice cream for dessert $3.95. COMMENTS: They plan to add an outside garden patio and a bar/lounge with entertainment, dancing - and a mariachi band - by Fall, 1998.

RAY'S DELI & LOUNGE *Local*
270 Waiehu Beach Road, Wailuku (242-5993) HOURS: 5:30-1:30pm; saimin till 2. SAMPLING: Senior breakfast plus eggs, pancakes, French toast $2.40-3.80. Lunches: local plates, $4.10-6.25; salads, mein & saimin noodles $3.25-5; sandwiches $1.75-2.50. COMMENTS Sports Bar with several tv's.

(RESTAURANT) MATSU (See Maui Mall)

SAENG'S THAI ★ *Thai*
2119 Vineyard St., Wailuku (244-1567) HOURS: Lunch Mon-Sat 11am-3pm; dinner nightly 5-9:30pm. SAMPLING: Mee krob, sateh, spring rolls, and other appetizers $4.95-7.95; coconut, tom yum, or long rice soup, and green papaya, beef, shrimp, and tofu salads $6.50-8.50; entrees of Thai ginger beef, chicken cashew, sweet and sour pork, pad Thai noodles, eggplant tofu, or Evil Prince $6.95-9.50; seafood dishes include honey lemon or garlic shrimps, mahi with black bean sauce, and seafood saute $8.50-12.95; BBQ items include shrimp & pork, Cornish game hen, and dancing prawns stuffed with crabmeat & ground pork; red, green, masman or pineapple shrimp curries $8.95-9.95. COMMENTS: This is one of the most attractive local restaurants in Wailuku. Owners Toh, Tom and Zach Douangphoumy have created a little Eden with lots of plants providing privacy between tables. They also know how to cook Thai. Traveling in India, Laos, Vietnam and Thailand in their youth they had an opportunity to sample a diversity of foods. This is the best of Maui's Thai cuisine. Not only is the service attentive, but the portions generous and every new dish better than the last. (We're especially partial to their peanut sauce.) Don't miss this one!

SAL'S PLACE *Italian/Sushi/Nightclub*
162 Alamaha, Kahului (893-0609) HOURS: Lunch 11am-2:30pm; dinner 5:30-10pm; Pupus 3-5:30pm & 10pm-2am. SAMPLING: Meat or vegetable antipasti, salads (Caprese, Caesar, spinach, or vegetable), beef carpaccio, and prosciutto with ham begin the lunch menu followed by thin-crust Neopolitan style pizzas with spinach & sausage, mushrooms, prosciutto, and pesto plus Italian panini (sandwiches) like Muffaleta, sausage, or chicken on focaccia $5.95-8.95. Pastas with pork & beef, eggplant, Tuscan beans & ham, lasagna, and authentic Spaghetti Carbonara plus entrees of roasted chicken, lamb shanks, and grilled eggplant or sausage run $6.95-11.95. Sushi lunch specials $4.95-9.50. The dinner menu adds a baked sausage appetizer ($5.95), potato & garlic pizza ($8.95), and entrees of grilled pork loin, sirloin, or portobello mushrooms from $12.95-15.95. Daily fresh fish specials. COMMENTS: Opened April, 1998 in the former Ming Yuen location with one from Column A (An Italian restaurant), one from Column B (a sushi Bar) and one from Column C (a nightClub)! The one-room banquet atmosphere has been divided into smaller, more intimate dining areas with an expanded bar and raised "indoor lanai" platform as well as the adjoining sushi bar (that's *"pesce fresco"* in Italian!) Fuji Sushi (877-9417) has lunch specials from 11am-2pm ($4.95-9.50); dinner 5:30-9:30pm. (Closed Sunday) Nightly entertainment includes jazz piano and blues.

SAM SATO'S *Local Style-Hawaiian*
1750 Wili Pa Loop, Wailuku (244-7124) HOURS: Breakfast and lunch 7am-2pm; manju and pastries served until 4pm. Closed Sunday. SAMPLING: Omelettes, hot cakes, or set breakfast $2.25-4. Plate lunches include teriyaki beef, stew, chop steak, spare ribs, or a combination plate of chop suey, egg fu young, char siu, & spare ribs $5.25-5.75; sandwiches and burgers $2.25-2.65. Saimin, chow fun, and other noodle dishes (their specialty!) are served in small or large sizes

$3-5.55. Take out noodles are available for $14-26-46 (to feed 10-15, 25 or 50 people.) COMMENTS: The homemade pastries are wonderful; peach, apple, and coconut turnovers are fragrant and fresh and they also specialize in manju, a Japanese tea cake. It may come as a big surprise when you discover that these tasty morsels are actually filled with a mashed version of lima beans! COMMENTS: Located near the Wailuku post office in the Millyard.

SHIN SHIN CHINESE SEAFOOD   *Northern Chinese*
752 Lower Main St., Wailuku (244-7788) HOURS: 10am-9:30pm; Lunch 10am-2:30pm. Closed Tuesday. SAMPLING: Plate lunch specials offer any two of the following for $5.95: curry beef, Kung Pao chicken, beef with broccoli, sweet & sour pork, eggplant with minced pork, chicken with black bean sauce, or shrimp & vegetables. Lemon, cashew, hot pepper or curry chicken; pork hash with duck egg, bitter melon with beef, bean curd with shrimp, black mushroom with oyster sauce, mu shui pork, Mongolian beef, and Shangai soft chow mein are a few choices for $6.75-7.95. Shrimp, squid, fish, crab, oyster, and scallop dishes ($10.50) plus soup, vegetables, sizzling platters, noodle, and rice dishes.

SIAM THAI   *Thai*
123 N. Market St., Wailuku (244-3817) HOURS: Lunch Mon-Fri 11am-2:30pm; dinner nightly 5-9:30pm. Appetizers include fresh (or fried) spring rolls, sateh, green papaya salad, coconut or spicy soup $5.50-7.95. Eggplant tofu, red, green or yellow curry, Thai broccoli noodles, Siam omelette, deep fried Cornish game hen, Evil Prince, lemon beef or chicken $6.95-8.95. Crispy fish with pepper sauce, fish curry, ahi with ginger sauce, garlic squid $8.50-15.95. COMMENTS: The white table cloths give this restaurant an elegant air. Very good Thai food although the competition is stiff with Saeng's Thai just around the corner. You can't go wrong with any of the currys (just pick your favorite color!) or the Thai tapioca with coconut milk.

SILK ROAD   *Chinese/Korean BBQ*
1951 Vineyard Ave., Wailuku (249-2399) HOURS: Mon-Sat 10am-9pm. SAMPLING: Pot stickers, char siu pork, crispy won ton, fried shrimp $3.29-7.99; soups, noodles, fried rice $2.99-6.99. Chinese pepper steak, moo goo gai pan, sweet & sour pork, shrimp with black bean sauce, kung pao chicken, pork eggplant, and several varieties of egg fu young $5.99; special ginger chicken $6.49. Peking duck (1/2) $13.50; shrimp & seafood combinations $9.99-11.99. COMMENTS: Special dinners $22.50-30.50-49.50 for 2, 3, or 4. Chinese plate specials $3.99-5.99; Korean BBQ plates (ribs, chicken, beef or combination) $5.95-6.50. Everything prepared fresh daily with no MSG. Parking next door at 1939 Vineyard.

SIMPLE PLEASURES CAFE   *Gourmet Vegetarian*
2103 Vineyard St., Wailuku (249-0697) HOURS: Tues-Thurs 11am-3pm. SAMPLING: Homemade soups from coconut curry to carrot bisque; Hawaiian focaccia with macadamia nut pesto, falafel, tofu tandoori, tomato & mushroom quiche, Indian samosas with peanut sauce, timbale, and vegetarian crepes, lasagne, cordon bleu, and veggie burger Wellington in puff pastry plus assorted salads: green bean & potato, chick pea & spinach, black bean & rice, and pasta

with raisins, carrots & almonds all in $3 and $6 sizes. Specialty breads, pastries, and their signature Hawaiian-style desserts: apple strudel, tangy lemon tart, chocolate truffle, coconut haupia pie, Kona coffee tiramisu, and mango-lime cheesecake - all in a macadamia nut crust $3. COMMENTS: Small deli with the look of a European pastry shop. Take out with limited counter seating. This retail outlet began with their Hawaiian Strudel and Creative Catering Concepts companies.

SIU'S KITCHEN (See Maui Mall)

SUB PARADISE   *Submarine Sandwiches*
395-E Dairy Rd., Kahului (877-8779) HOURS: 7am-7pm, Sundays till 2. SAMPLING: Caesar, special Caesar (with tomatoes, olive, onions, mushrooms, & feta), Greek, and chef's salads $6.99 and over two dozen varieties of subs in 6" or 12" sizes: Ham, turkey, pastrami, salami, roast beef, meatball, chicken, vegetarian, egg salad, cheese, and combinations there of from $3.85 small / 6.79 large to $4.45 small / 7.10 large; the Big Kahuna (with eight meats & four cheeses!) runs $7.99-13.59. COMMENTS: Specials include turkey, bacon & avocado ($4.85/8.10) or Chinese chicken salad $3.99-5.99. Hana picnic lunch includes 6" sub, soda, chips, cookie, candy or orange with free cooler ($3 refundable deposit) for $6.99.

SW BAR-B-Q (See Maui Mall)

TASTY CRUST RESTAURANT ★   *Local Style*
1770 Mill St., Wailuku (244-0845) HOURS: 5:30am-1:30pm for breakfast and lunch; 5-11pm for dinner. SAMPLING: Unique and delicious crusty hotcakes are their specialty, two are a meal for $2.40. French toast or waffles $2. Omelettes and egg dishes $3-3.75. Spare ribs, fried shrimp, liver & bacon, pork cutlet, chop suey, stew, roast beef, and several varieties of fried and teriyaki chicken $5.50-5.90 are served with rice and a salad. Sandwiches and hamburgers $1.60-4. COMMENTS: Local atmosphere and no frills, just good food at great prices. (Actually, the pancakes are still good; the coffee is still bad. They also have a very "literal" menu: if you order a mushroom omelette, that's what you'll get - if you want it with cheese . . . well, you'd better say so!) They've been here since 1943, but plan to move to Las Vegas within the next few years -- we're still hoping to get the secret of those legendary pancakes before they go!!

TANYA'S   *Local/Vietnamese*
1322 Lower Main, Wailuku (242-1471 HOURS: 9am-8pm. SAMPLING: Omelettes, pancakes, sweet bread French toast, loco moco, and full breakfasts $3.25-5.50. Vietnamese manapua $1.75; spring or summer rolls, Asian "crepe" with shrimp & pork, and a variety of noodles and noodle soups $3-6.95. Local style or Vietnamese plate lunches (BBQ and curry dishes) $5.25-6.95; Vietnamese Balé sandwiches include lemon grass chicken, teri beef, ham, or tofu $3.25-3.95. COMMENTS: A good selection of local and Vietnamese dishes - their egg noodle soups (with combinations of calamari, shrimp, BBQ duck, and BBQ pork) and Balé sandwiches are a specialty. Eat in or take out.

TASTE OF BROADWAY   *New York Italian/Pizza*
Maui Marketplace, 270 Dairy Road, Kahului (873-7811) HOURS: 9am-9pm, till 6 on Sunday. SAMPLING: Brick oven pizza from $5.95M/9.99S plus toppings. Baked stromboli ($4.95) or calzone ($5.55) come in steak, meatball, pepperoni & ham, sausage, spinach or broccoli; NY sandwiches (steak, hot pastrami, and homemade sausage or meatball) $5.95M/8.95L. Family-recipe pasta meals include salad and garlic bread: Marinara, Arabiata, Putanesca, broccoli & garlic or lasagna $5.95. COMMENTS: Second location at Kihei Kalama Village.

TIFFANY LUIGI'S   *Italian*
Maui Mall, Kahului (871-9521) HOURS: Breakfast 7-11am, Lunch/dinner 11am-10pm; till 5pm on Sun. SAMPLING: Eggs Benedict, omelettes, pancakes, grilled pork chops, loco moco, and saimin, or dry mein for breakfast $4.75-6.99. Buffalo wings, stuffed mushrooms, steamed clams or mussels, calamari steak pupu, fried cheese, several salads, and a variety of potato skins for starters $5.99-7.99. Shrimp Fra Diavolo, veal scallopini, NY steak, scampi, chicken or eggplant parmesan, New Orleans shrimp, and baby back ribs; lasagna, fettucini Alfredo, pasta primavera, pesto, or oriental: $7.99-13.99 a la carte or $10.99-16.99 with soup or salad and garlic bread. Pizzas include clam & garlic, Hawaiian, and veggie $5.99-11.49. Meatball, cajun or roasted pepper chicken, steak, turkey or ham melt, and mahi sandwiches plus a variety of burgers $6.99-8.99. COMMENTS: Hand-tossed pizza dough, homemade sausage and pastas made by their Italian chef. Good selection and large portions. Renovations have lightened and brightened the atmosphere and they now offer a separate banquet room. Entertainment from 10pm-2am Tues-Sat.

TIN YING   *Chinese*
1088 Lower Main St., Wailuku (242-4371) HOURS: Daily 10am-9pm. SAMPLING: Hong Kong or Szechuan style selections offer a variety of duck, chicken, beef, pork, tofu, and seafood dishes $5.75-8.95. Soups and appetizers $3.60-5.50; abalone or scallop soup $9.75-11.95. Rice and noodles $4.95-7.95. Specials include shark's fin or bird's next soup plus abalone & black mushroom dishes $17.95-29.95. Sizzling platter or hot pot are the Chef's specialties. COMMENTS: Family dinners $20.50 for two; $37.95 for four. Eat in or take out.

TOKYO TEI ★   *Japanese*
1063 E. Lower Main St., Wailuku. (242-9630) HOURS: Lunch 11-1:30pm; dinner 5-8:30pm. Open Sunday for dinner only, 5-8pm. SAMPLING: Lunch specials include beef cutlet, sweet sour pork, teriyaki meat, omelettes, and noodles $5.75-6.50. Saimin or fried noodle $3.50-3.75. Teishoku trays include shrimp tempura, sashimi, fried fish, teriyaki pork or steak $9.50-10.50. Dinner selections offer hakata chicken, seafood platter, calamari katsu, somen, yakitori, tempura, teriyaki steak, broiled salmon, sukiyaki, and donburi dishes that include rice, miso soup, ko-ko, and hot tea $6.25-9.25. COMMENTS: Small and cozy atmosphere. Take out meals also available; catering for 50 and over. Cocktails. Popular with both visitors and local residents and deservedly so. (Christie would eat here at least once a week if it wasn't such a long drive from Portland!) Winner of one of our top three awards for best local restaurants. Great food, great value, don't miss this one!

TWO FAT GUYS FROM BOSTON *Pizza*
60 Wakea, Kahului (877-5750) HOURS: 11am-9pm, Sunday till 7. SAMPLING: pizza $10.50-18; calzone, salads, stuffed potatoes $4.99-6.99. Italian slush $1.75.

WAIEHU INN *Local*
Waiehu Golf Course (244-2034) HOURS: 5:30am till 7-8pm daily or later if customers want to stay! SAMPLING: Hamburgers, sandwiches, saimin, local plates (mahi, stew, shrimp - changes daily), ice cream, sodas $2-6. COMMENTS: Lounge serves beer and hard liquor. Also catering. Great find if you can find the golf course - where else can you get a $2 lunch with an ocean view? (Take Market Street to the Kahekili Hwy to Lower Waiehu Beach Road and turn right from Waihee Park into the golf course.)

WEI WEI BARBECUE AND NOODLE HOUSE *Local/Asian*
Millyard Plaza, 21 Imi Kala St., Wailuku (242-7928) HOURS: 10am-9pm. SAMPLING: Local, Chinese, Japanese, and BBQ entrees $4.95-8.50 plus mini-plates and 24 types of noodles $3.95-6.95. Dim sum 99¢ each. Inexpensive selection of American sandwiches $1.30-2.70; breakfasts $3.20. COMMENTS: Really big portions, but maybe we just didn't order the right thing: the duck saimin had little more than bones & cartilage and the lemon grass chicken was a little greasy. We'd recommend going to Sam Sato's or Millyard Cafe - both are just around the corner.

YUMMY KOREAN (See Food Court at Kaahumanu Center)

MODERATE

ALE HOUSE *Steaks & Burgers/Sports bar*
355 E. Kamehameha Hwy., Kahului (877-9001) HOURS: 11am-midnight; breakfast Sat-Sun 7-11am. SAMPLING: Big 1/2 lb. burgers, 4 lb. whole tenderloin, and 8, 12, or 16 oz. steaks. Ten beers on tap. COMMENTS: Pool tables, dart boards, video games, and over two dozen tvs. Karaoke 10pm-1:30am. Open on weekends for breakfast and mainland satellite-feed sporting events. Once again the owner of the Rusty Harpoon gets the award for the longest restaurant name: Jerome E. Metcalfe's Ale House Sports Bar & Restaurant. Scheduled to open June, 1998 in the old Sizzler location. (Not open as we go to press.)

CHART HOUSE ★ *American-Seafood*
500 N. Puunene Ave., Kahului (877-2476) HOURS: Dinner 5:30-9:30/10pm. SAMPLING: Lobster cakes, coconut shrimp or calamari, steamed artichoke, baked brie, and sashimi appetizers $6.50-9.95. Steak, prime rib, crab legs, lobster, ginger-citrus shrimp, rack of lamb, herb-crusted or teri chicken, and fresh ahi, salmon or catch of the day. Entrees include their unlimited fresh garden, spinach, or Caesar salad (or salad bar at this location only) plus hot squaw bread made with sweet molasses $16.95-25.95. They also offer some good homemade desserts including mud pie, chocolate mousse, and authentic key lime pie. COMMENTS: They still have one of the best keiki menus we've seen. And

we can attest to the "Awesome" prime rib. The adult entree portions are huge and we love their doggie bag! (Trust us, you'll need it.) The coconut calamari was an unusual option; good texture with surprising coconut and calamari tastes. The ahi was a nice thick "steak," cooked on the rare side in ponzu sauce with cilantro lime butter. The tasty spinach salad (with egg, bacon, and poppy seed dressing) had lots of nice extras including Mandarin oranges. With additional locations in Lahaina and Wailea, it tends to be less crowded on this side of the island; prices are a few dollars less, too! A pleasant ocean view. Reservations accepted.

THE CLASS ACT ★ *International*
Maui Community College Campus, Kahului (242-1210) HOURS: Lunch only, Wed & Fri 11am-12:15pm. COMMENTS: This is one of Maui's best little finds. Insiders know they are in for a treat when they stop by for a five-course gourmet lunch prepared by the Food Service students of the Maui Community College. At $15 it's become a bit expensive, but not when you know you're supporting such a worthwhile student program (or when you think of it as $3 a course). Students shop, serve, clean, and wait on the tables as well as offering a different menu each week. Each meal represents a different country or region like Italy, New Orleans, Morocco, Austria or Pacific Northwest. A heart healthy alternative, low in sodium and cholesterol, is available at each meal. The program is only offered during the school year, so be sure and call to check on availability and current schedule. They suggest calling for reservations on Wednesday and Friday 8:30-10:30am and reservations are taken up to two weeks in advance. The Class Act is located on the MCC campus adjacent to the upstairs cafeteria. In fact, if a five-course gourmet lunch is too rich for you or your wallet, the cafeteria is open to the public (11am-2:30pm) for hot lunches and local plates for less that $5!

KONA COFFEE   J BAYOT

FIRECRACKER, A CHINESE BISTRO WITH SAM CHOY
Gourmet Chinese/Asian

Kaahumanu Center, 275 W. Kaahumanu Ave. HOURS: Lunch and dinner (Scheduled hours 10:30am-9pm, till 10pm on weekends) SAMPLING: A traditional menu of Asian and Chinese cuisine will be embellished with Sam's own distinctive style along with an on-site microbrewery. They also plan to offer dim sum-type items for lunch and for late night accompaniment to their specially created micro-brews. COMMENTS: Scheduled to open Summer, 1998 (Not open as we go to press.) This will be Sam Choy's second location at the Kaahumanu Center. The 7,200 sq. ft. restaurant (located upstairs next to Penney's) will seat 150 and will feature modern Chinese decor with festive accents of reds, greens, and blacks.

MARCO'S GRILL & DELI   *Italian*

444 Hana Highway (877-4446) HOURS: Breakfast 7:30am-10:45am, Sat-Sun till 1pm. Lunch/dinner daily 10am-10pm. SAMPLING: Large selection of omelettes, Italian breakfast sandwiches plus chocolate cinnamon French toast; granola with strawberries & bananas; and chocolate chip, banana nut, strawberry, or apple cinnamon pancakes $5.95-8.95. Late morning lunches begin with fried mozzarella, bruschetta, scampi, ravioli, gnocchi, calamari & peas, and vodka rigatoni, a house specialty with prosciutto in a garlic pink cream sauce $5.95-9.95. Caesar, Greek, oriental chicken, and stuffed tomato salads plus a choice of pizzas $6.95-10-95. Deli, sub, and grilled sandwiches like chicken or meatball parmigiano, homemade Italian sausage, NY strip steak, hot pastrami, reuben, club, BLT, and burgers $8.95-10.95. Entrees include vodka rigatoni, veggie lasagna, sausage & linguine, veal parmigiano, seafood pasta, grilled salmon, homemade ravioli, mushroom chicken, and Pasta E'Fasio, a house specialty made with smoked ham hock & beans $12.95-22. COMMENTS: They're now twice their original size with more tables and a cocktail lounge with a big screen TV. The menu is diverse and interesting and we hear good reports on the gnocchi and some of the pastas. Although this is a family-run restaurant, there was very little on the lunch and dinner menu appropriate for kids - unless you count some of the new desserts like Reese's peanut butter pie or caramel apple pie!

PAPAS -N- CHILES   *Mexican*

Lono Bldg., 33 Lono Ave. (871-2074) HOURS: Tues-Fri 11am-10pm; Sat-Sun 5-10pm. Closed Sunday. SAMPLING: Caldo seven mares (soup with seven seafoods), enchiladas Mazatlan (with shrimps, bell peppers, mushrooms and guacamole), Pescado frito (a whole red snapper or opakapaka fried), calamari steak, scampi, steak ranchero, shrimp fajita, fish tacos, chile verde or colorado (with pork chunks) $9.95-16.95. Traditional combination plates (taco, burrito, enchilada) served with rice and homemade beans $8.25-10.95. Lite lunches and a la carte items also available $4.95-7.95. COMMENTS: Family-operated restaurant with a menu that emphasizes fish and seafood. The refried beans are homemade with olive oil and chicken stock instead of lard and it really makes a big difference in the flavor! Service is attentive and friendly. Children's menu.

RAINBOW DINING ROOM   *American/Japanese*
Maui Beach Hotel, 170 Kaahumanu Ave., Kahului. (877-0051) HOURS: Breakfast buffet 7-9:30am, lunch buffet 11am-2pm, dinner (a la carte & Japanese buffet) 5:30-8:30pm. SAMPLING: Breakfast buffet with cereal, fruit, baked goods, eggs, bacon, sausage, rice, and miso soup $8.75. All-you-can-eat lunch buffet features a salad bar with miso soup, somen, house noodles, rice, three hot entrees, and cake for $10.75. Dinners start with shrimp cocktail, beef carpaccio, spicy shrimp cake, or salmon $7-10; Caesar, Chinese chicken, or seafood salads $8-13.50. Entrees feature fresh fish, baked Atlantic salmon, broiled shrimp, beef tenderloin, sirloin steak, grilled pork loin, or chef's special chicken stuffed with ground beef, pork, and pineapple $17.50-25.95. COMMENTS: Dinners include soup or salad, rolls and dessert. Children's menu on request. The famous Japanese Imperial Dinner buffet that used to be featured next door is now offered here while the Maui Palms undergoes several years of extensive renovation. Offered nightly from 5:30-8:30pm, the buffet includes teriyaki steak, assorted tempura, chicken yakitori, miso soup, and a salad bar with sushi, sashimi, tofu with ginger, long rice, special house noodles, and other local favorites including Mandarin mousse dessert $25. Both Maui Beach restaurants have recently been renovated; see Red Dragon listing that follows for more details.

RED DRAGON CHINESE RESTAURANT   *Chinese*
Maui Beach Hotel, 170 Kaahumanu Ave., Kahului (877-0051) HOURS: Dinner only 5:30-8:30pm, closed Mon-Tues (At press time they were planning to offer an all-you-can-eat sushi dinner on Tuesday nights.) SAMPLING: Cantonese buffet with over fifteen selections. Shrimp Canton, vegetable chow mein, egg drop or vegetable soup, pickles, Mandarin orange, and lychee dessert are offered nightly. Additional entrees may include Haposai (shrimp, scallops, ika), clams, chop suey (shrimp, chicken, pork, or beef), spare ribs, beef broccoli, spring rolls, sweet and sour pork, beef with oyster sauce, tofu with mushrooms & cabbage, and lemon, ginger or roast chicken $16. COMMENTS: Recent renovations included a new ceiling and sound system plus new carpeting, chairs, draperies and an overall brightening both here and in the Rainbow Room.

SAM CHOY'S KAHULUI   *"Gourmet Local"*
Kaahumanu Center, 275 W. Kaahumanu Ave. (893-0366) HOURS: Breakfast 7-10:30am; lunch 10:30am-3pm; dinner 5:30-9pm, till 9:30 Fri-Sat. SAMPLING: For breakfast choose from several varieties of "loco moco," omelettes (spinach & shiitake mushrooms, poke, beef stew), and pancakes (taro, sourdough blueberry, tropical fruit), plus Belgian waffles (vanilla cream with strawberries, or with bourbon-pecan sauce) and a French toast sandwich filled with ginger sauce $4.75-7.50. (See what we mean about "gourmet local"?) Lunch offerings include fried poke, tripe stew, and "Noodlemania" served with fresh vegetables and edible flowers in a fluted tortilla shell plus good old fashioned meat loaf, roast chicken, beef stew, steak, burgers, sandwiches (and beer by the glass) $6.50-8.95. Dinners are more high-end ($18.95-26.95) and feature seafood lau lau, lamb chops, roast duck, osso bucco, ahi salad, steak, fresh fish, and tofu lasagna; Hawaiian bouillabaisse $31.95. Brie won ton and crab stuffed shrimp are some pupu ($6.50-8.50) and desserts include bread pudding and frozen espresso pie $4.50-6.95. Sam Choy's Brewery selections include Kakaako Cream or Ehu

Ale, Hefe-Weizen, Steamship Lager, and Kiawe Honey Porter. COMMENTS: "Big" is the operative word here: Sam Choy (from the Big Island) is one of the biggest of the Hawaiian Regional Cuisine chefs ("Never trust a skinny chef") and this is the first of his three new restaurants on Maui. ("Firecracker, A Chinese Bistro with Sam Choy" - also at Kaahumanu Center - and "Sam Choy's Lahaina" were scheduled to open Summer, 1998.) This new gateway is already one of the shopping center's biggest successes and his portions are, well - big! ("Never trust a skinny portion. . .")

SANDALWOOD CLUBHOUSE *American*
Grand Waikapu Country Club, just outside of Wailuku. (242-6000/244-1122) HOURS: 10am-3pm; a la carte Sunday brunch 9am-3pm. SAMPLING: Early lunch begins with a pupu menu of fresh baked pizza, Maui onion or calamari rings, hummus dip, shrimp spring rolls, mahi strips, and buffalo wings, $3.95-6.95. Caesar, spinach, cobb, or Chinese chicken salad; burgers, reuben, chicken, club, vegetable, or ahi sandwiches $5.25-7.95. Thai BBQ pork chops, fresh fish & chips, meatloaf, and peanut chicken linguine $7.95-8.95. Warm chocolate banana cake or coconut cream pie $3.50. Lunch buffet (Mon-Sat 11am-2pm) of homemade soups, deli salads & fresh greens, hot entree, a sandwich bar of roasted cold cuts & assorted breads, and desserts $8.95. Sunday brunch offers most of the same lunch items along with a breakfast menu of eggs, omelettes, French toast, and macadamia pancakes $5.75-8.95; champagne or mimosa $2. COMMENTS: Pleasant room set atop the golf course. Seating outside on the wide lanais offers a fantastic, panoramic view of Maui from a slightly different perspective than the usual beach front scenery.

NIGHTBLOOMING CEREUS

EXPENSIVE

MONROE'S   *Dinner & Dancing*
Grand Waikapu Country Club (242-7002) HOURS: Open for dinner Fri-Sat only, 6-9pm; live music in the lounge 7-11pm. Start with Caesar or oriental spiced sushi salad, ginger prawn cocktail, lobster coconut bisque, Maui onion soup, or a "Gourmet Assembly" of sashimi, duck, spring roll, and mushrooms ($7-12); followed by an entree of veal marsala with spinach & portobello mushrooms ($27-35), five-spiced Muscovy duck ($29), fresh fish medley with ginger buerre blanc ($25-32), or one of their signature (and most popular) dishes: herb-crusted rack of lamb with English mustard & mango chutney ($24-31) or whole fresh opakapaka wok-fried with ginger, garlic & peppercorns ($34). Ricotta cheesecake, glazed ginger-orange creme brulee, and strawberry florentine (filled with vanilla cream, mango & pomegranate sauce) are the desserts $8-9. Ports and cognacs from $6. COMMENTS: After five years of private parties, special functions, and much anticipation, Monroe's has finally opened to the public for weekend dinner and dancing (as well as the ultimate in special holiday brunches). Large picture windows offer two ocean views, one on each side of the panoramic Maui scene that surrounds the classic modern building. "The house that Frank (Lloyd Wright) built" was originally designed for Marilyn Monroe and recreated here in the accessible luxury of the Waikapu Country Club. If you want to pay homage to the legend yourself, you can create your own Marilyn menu by ordering the "Blond" Jumbo Scallops with basil mashed potato and ponzu butter ($12), moving on to a timely "Presidential Affair" of beef tenderloin and grilled shrimp with bourbon mushroom ragout ($34) and finish with a cake "For Chocolate Lovers" on raspberry sauce with champagne truffles ($11).

UPCOUNTRY

INEXPENSIVE

ABBY'S PLACE   *Cafe & Bakery*
3620 Baldwin Ave., Makawao (572-0335) HOURS: Breakfast 8-11am, lunch 11am-5pm. Open Sundays till 2; dinner Fri-Sat 5:30-9pm. SAMPLING: Breakfast burrito, open-faced omelette, and waffles, with brunch items like eggs benedict (mahi or cajun), huevos rancheros, or chile relleno served till 2pm on Sunday $3.95-7.95. Lunch sandwiches include tuna, roast beef, burgers, reuben, mahi mahi, turkey (with cranberry mayonnaise), and grilled chicken served with unusually good homemade potato salad or cole slaw $5.75-6.95. Dinners feature a Mexican theme starting with nachos or Caesar salad $5.25-7.45 followed by a selection of burritos, enchiladas, carne asada, chicken fajitas, bistecka (steak) or Camarones (shrimp) Al Queso $6.95-13.25. COMMENTS: New owners have kept the cozy, country feel of the former Courtyard Deli, but freshened it up with a brighter look and expanded seating indoors (on antique tables and chairs) and out in the shady courtyard. It's a great place to sit and relax with an ice cream treat, coffee drink, or cup of tea and one of their specialty baked goods like fruit scones, coffee cakes, Russian tea cookies, or *Heavenly Devil* -- a yummy brownie cookie (or cookie brownie) that is sure to become a signature!

CAFE 808   *Local Style*
Lower Kula Road near Holy Ghost Church (across from Morihara Store) in Kula (878-6874) HOURS: Open 6am-8pm for Breakfast 6-11am; lunch/dinner 11am-8pm. SAMPLING: Belgian waffle, cinnamon French toast, banana pancakes, croissant club, loco moco & veggie moco, frittata, saimin, "brek-burger," omelettes $4-6; green eggs & smoked salmon (not ham?) $6.95. Caesar, cobb, and Chinese chicken salads; burgers, lasagna, and a variety of plate lunches - teri beef, roast pork, chicken katsu, kalbi ribs, curry stew, mahi, or shrimp $5.95-8.95. Deli sandwiches served all day: roast beef, smoked turkey, corned beef, tuna, club, chicken salad, and reuben $3.75-5.50. COMMENTS: Same owners at Upcountry Cafe in Pukalani.

CAFE MAKAWAO   *Gourmet Healthy & International*
3682 Baldwin Ave., corner of Baldwin and Makawao in Makawao town (572-1101) HOURS: Mon-Tues 7am-8pm, till 10 Wed-Sat. Sundays 9am-6pm (brunch till 1) SAMPLING: To start they offer homemade Belgian waffles, fresh fruit, bagels, omelettes, scrambled tofu, ginger-fried rice (with tofu & hijiki), and homemade buttermilk, gingerbread, or cornbread pancakes $4.25-6.50; fresh squeezed orange juice or organic almond milk, and assorted coffees & teas $1.25-2.50. For lunch try the smoked salmon cheesecake, polenta pizza (with macadamias and sundried tomato pesto), nachos plate, or a variety of sandwiches that include oven roasted turkey breast, pita tuna melt, seared ono or mahi (with mango serrano salsa), tempeh burger with ginger-peanut sauce, and a selection of international wraps served in a vegetable tortilla with their own chutneys, salsas, and salad fillings $4-6.25. Dinner specials feature Mediterranean, Indian, African and Asian cuisine with one vegetarian, and one fish or chicken dish nightly $7.25-9.50. For dessert there's vegan carob goddess cake, avocado pie, espresso bean chocolate cake, and NY style cheesecake with maple pecan crust $3.25-3.50. Traditional and vegetarian sushi offered Thurs-Sun nights; all-you-can-eat Sunday brunch (9am-1pm) features a bagel bar (with mix & match flavors of bagels and cream cheese) and a variety of cold brunch items like fresh greens & veggies, homemade salads, tropical fruit, assorted pastries (and even "cool" jazz!) for $12. COMMENTS: Located (literally) at the crossroads of Makawao in a corner building that was once a gas station dating back to the 30's. Smoke-free seating inside in their renovated European-style dining room or outside on their street-side garden lanai. New owners reopened in May, 1998 keeping up the cafe's tradition of using healthy, fresh ingredients while offering some innovative - and intriguing - new touches all their own. Rotating art exhibition, poetry, speakers, and live music add to the upcountry feel and ambiance. BYO wine & beer.

CAFE O'LEI   ★   *Healthy Salads & Sandwiches*
3673 Baldwin Ave. (inside the Paniolo Courtyard), Makawao (573-9065) HOURS: 11am-4pm (Closed Sunday) SAMPLING: Gourmet sandwiches include roast chicken & sweet pepper (or vegetables & goat cheese) on focaccia as well as smoked turkey or prosciutto & provolone $4-5.75; quinoa, Caesar or Asian salads $4.50-5.95. Daily specials might include Thai coconut or won ton soup, somen salad, chicken with ginger or basil cream, curry & vegetables, or tandoori-style chicken. Coffee drinks, lemonade, and mango, passion or Thai iced

tea; chocolate brownies or chocolate chip cookies $1-3. COMMENTS: Good, healthy food with fresh, organic ingredients in a charming setting. The European-style courtyard is lined with flowers and foliage with tables along the brick pathway that make this a "real" sidewalk cafe! The menu is simple, but extra touches make it special: fresh herbs from the garden, lots of garlic in the creamy Caesar dressing, pungent lemon grass in the Asian salad - they even use "real" china and pottery - no paper plates or cups here!

DOWN TO EARTH NATURAL FOODS & CAFE *Vegetarian*
1169 Makawao Ave., Makawao (572-1488) HOURS: Hot food and salad bar noon-7pm; store open 8 to 8. SAMPLING: Soups and hot vegetarian entrees like bell pepper with couscous, "to fu young," enchilada pie, lasagna, and mock chicken tofu ($5.99 lb.) Salad bar $4.99 lb. COMMENTS: The mock chicken is tasty by itself or added to their (or your own) stir fry vegetables. Fruit compote made with blueberries or peaches and coconut baked with crumble topping - yummy! Packaged sandwiches and bakery items from their Kahului outlet. No seating, take out only. Retail store has fresh organic produce, bulk items, and packaged vegetarian food products.

FRENCHY'S BAKERY & CAFE *Pastries/Lite Lunches*
7 Aewa Pl., Pukalani (572-9778) HOURS: Tues-Fri 6:30am-6pm; Sat 7am-4pm; Sun 7am-2pm. Lunch 11am-2pm. (Closed Monday) SAMPLING: Lunch items include quiche, pizza, salads, sandwiches, and homemade clam chowder and Portuguese bean soup $3-5.95. Specialty breads like onion & walnut, olive, sweet potato, honey-nut sunflower, rosemary, jalapeno & cheese, focaccia, and Portuguese sweet bread $2.49-3.49; specialty pastries include malasadas, Linzer tarts, biscotti, rum balls, Berliners (German donuts filled with raspberry, guava, or custard), tiramisu, chocolate or apple pretzels, and old-fashioned lemon cake. Also Danish pastries, cream puffs, eclairs, napoleons, chocolate or coconut mac nut tarts, apple or cherry strudel, and bread pudding. COMMENTS: Located behind Upcountry Cafe; a few tables and chairs inside.

GRANDMA'S COFFEE HOUSE ★ *Local Style*
Located in Keokea (878-2140) HOURS: 7am-5pm daily. COMMENTS: This coffee house is run by Alfred Franco who is encouraging the return of the coffee industry in Upcountry Maui. Born and raised in Upcountry, his grandmother taught him how to roast the coffee beans to perfection. He does this several times a day in his 100 plus year-old coffee roasting machine that was brought from Philadelphia by his great-grandmother. The coffee is sold by the pound in a blend known as "Maui Coffees." Some of the beans used are grown on Moloka'i which is part of Maui County. Prices are high, and there is no decaf available. (Grandmother never taught Alfred how to do that.) A few tables are an invitation to visitors to sit down, enjoy a cup of coffee, espresso, cappuccino, or fresh fruit juice along with cinnamon rolls (get there early!), muffins and more, all fresh from the oven. A bit more of an appetite might require one of their fresh avocado sandwiches, deli salads, or a bowl of chili and rice, pasta, or homemade Portuguese bean soup ($5-7). They also sell their own chocolates, made from Grandma's recipe, of course. With the popularity of this place among locals and visitors alike, it is tough for them to keep up with the demand for these goodies.

They've added a deck for outdoor seating with a great view. Look for Grandma's in Keokea, just five miles before the Tedeschi Winery. (Alfred's goal is to put Keokea on the maps and minds of everyone. And he just may do it!)

KITADA'S KAU KAU CORNER *Local Style*
3617 Baldwin Avenue, Makawao (572-7241) HOURS: 6am-1:30pm daily except Sun. SAMPLING: French toast, eggs, and omelettes $2.50-6.25. Small or large portions of beef teriyaki, hamburger steak, beef or pork tofu, chopsteak, beef stew, pork chops, and spare ribs served with rice, macaroni salad, and salted cabbage $3.75-5.25. Sandwiches and burgers $1.50-2.75; saimin $2.50-3.50. COMMENTS: Owned and operated by the same family for over fifty years! It is still a popular local eatery and with these prices and the variety of local plate lunches, you can see why.

KULA SANDALWOODS RESTAURANT
Haleakala Hwy. (878-3523) Different owners over the years, but one thing has not changed. Really poor communication! We've tried every year to get information from them and every year we have to give up after 4-5 tries.

MIXED PLATE *Local Style*
Pukalani Terrace Center (572-8258) HOURS: Daily 6am-1pm, breakfast and lunch, dinner; Thurs-Fri from 4-8pm. SAMPLING: Any of four breakfast specials $5.25; lunch has an Okazuya daily menu with won ton min, tofu patties, mochiko chicken, chop steak, teriyaki steak and sushi. Specials might include lau lau, chicken hekka, mushroom chicken and kalua pork. Dinners offer curry stew, seafood, sweet sour spare ribs, halemalu chicken, butter fish, and chicken katsu from $5.25.

MAMA-SON'S *Korean BBQ*
Pukalani Terrace Shopping Center, 55 Pukalani St. (572-6213) HOURS: 10am-9pm. Closed Tuesday. SAMPLING: BBQ beef, chicken and pork, kal bi ribs, teri beef or chicken, curry rice, fried mandoo, bibim bap, bibim kook soo and meat jun can be ordered a la carte or in combo plates $6.95-7.95 and come with three scoops rice and three vegetables. Udon or saimin noodles run $3.35-5.95 and soups from oxtail to seaweed are $3.95-6.95. Dinners feature ribs, mahi mahi, and squid or seafood stir-fry $6.95-8.95. COMMENTS: Mama and John (son of Mama) opened their original award-winning restaurant in Hong Kong in 1976.

NATURE'S NECTAR *Healthy Vegetarian*
3647 Baldwin Ave., Makawao (572-9122) HOURS: 10am-6pm, till 4pm Sat-Sun. "Village Feast" dinners, Thursday 6:30-9pm. SAMPLING: Soups like cream of carrot, wild rice mushroom, or Thai coconut ginger plus Caesar, green papaya, seaweed, and marinated beet salads $3.35-5.95; sampler of three $6.55-8.95. Sandwiches include smoked turkey, veggie reuben, bagel veggie, and portobello mushroom or garden burger $3.85-6.95. Three layer vegan pizza $4.75 a slice; Chipoti wraps (Mexican, Thai veggie, or hummus) $3.25. For dessert there's chocolate tofu pie, ginger cake with cardamom sauce, avocado dream pie, or tofu cheese cake $2.95-3.25. Coffee drinks, Chai tea, vegetable, fruit & health juices,

and smoothies. COMMENTS: On Thursday nights, live music and a different ethnic cuisine is featured each week as a "Village Feast." Indian might be coconut curry, baked tofu, Basmati birani, and samosas; and there's also Mediterranean, Mexican, and Thai, $10.95 including dessert.

PIZZA FRESH   *Italian*
1043 Makawao Ave., Unit 103 (572-2000) HOURS: 4-8pm, Fri-Sat till 9. SAMPLING: Pizza varieties include, meat, vegetarian, Hawaiian, clam, scampi, Thai, and their new smoked salmon with capers, red onions & ricotta cheese (small $10.95/medium $16.95/large $20.95/X-large $26.95) or make your own with a base pizza ($6.95-18.95 and choose from more than 50 regular or gourmet toppings priced $.80-3.20. Salads, breadsticks or fresh-baked stuffed bread, lasagne, and a variety of pastas also available $3.95-7.95; calzone (regular or wheat) $10.95; cheesecake $3.50. COMMENTS: All pizzas come with traditional or extra thin crust and choice of traditional, pesto, sundried tomato, or Alfredo sauce plus four cheeses. They've added a lot more to the original concept of Pizza Fresh pizzas you bake yourself and they still offer those, too!

POLLI'S   *Mexican*
1202 Makawao Ave., Makawao (572-7808) HOURS: Lunch 11am-4pm; dinner 4-10pm. SAMPLING: Mexican pizza, taquitos, jalapeno poppers, tacos, tostadas, nachos, chili, steak pupu $4.95-9.95. Chile relleno or tamale plate, stuffed quesadilla, seafood enchilada, chimichanga, sizzling fajitas, burritos supreme, vegetarian chile queso $5.95-14.95. Also burgers, BBQ chicken, steak, and baby back ribs $6.95-10.50). Most items served all day with prices a few dollars less for lunch. Fish or chicken sandwich at lunch $6.95; steak, fish, chicken, or Mexican combination dinners $11.50-15.50. COMMENTS: Black beans and chile verde sauce are two alternative menu options, and vegetarians can request any menu item made with tofu or vegetarian taco mix. Menus for children $3.95; $1 on Tuesdays. Monday is BBQ nite: chicken or ribs $6.95; steak $8.95.

PUKALANI COUNTRY CLUB RESTAURANT   *American-Hawaiian*
360 Pukalani Rd. (572-1325) Turn right just before the shopping center at Pukalani and continue until the road ends. HOURS: Breakfast Mon-Fri 8-10:30am (from 6:30 Sat-Sun); Lunch 10:30am-2pm, dinner 5-9pm. SAMPLING: Omelettes, pancakes, French toast, Belgian waffles or egg dishes with Kalua pig, tripe stew or lau lau and a side of rice or poi $3.35-5.55. For lunch, the Kalua pig, tripe stew, or lau lau are offered as Hawaiian plates or you can get them a la carte along with lomi salmon, pipi kaula, squid, or pulehu ribs $3.85-8.10. More traditional fare includes a tuna melt, jumbo hot dog, burger, club or egg salad sandwich $4.10-6.35. Similar offerings at dinner at slightly higher prices along with steaks, breaded mahi or shrimp, fried chicken and teriyaki beef $7.45-12.70. COMMENTS: Lunch reservations are a must, as this is a popular place with the tour groups. Or eat lunch elsewhere and stop back on the way down from Upcountry for a drink, tropical sunset and a wonderful view. In addition to their authentic Hawaiian menu, they also have nightly specials and a salad bar at dinner. Keiki menu available.

ROYAL KING'S GARDEN   *Chinese*
Pukalani Shopping Center (572-7027) HOURS: Lunch 11am-2pm; Dinner 4pm-9pm. SAMPLING: Lunch specials include two entrees plus rice or chow mein and soda or BBQ teri beef or chicken with rice and salad (served all day) $4.95. Dinners offer pot stickers, char siu, abalone or rainbow tofu soup to start; beef with broccoli, shrimp with ginger & onion, mussels with black bean sauce, sliced fish with oyster sauce, chicken with eggplant, egg fu young, crispy duck, pork hash, steamed mahi, beef with tomato, mu shu chicken, vegetarian chow mein, pork cake noodle, or won ton mein $5.25-9.95. Oysters $12.50; abalone or lobster entrees $24.95. COMMENTS: No MSG. Same owners as the new Hong Kong restaurant in Lahaina.

STOPWATCH SPORTS BAR   *Italian/American*
1127 Makawao Ave. in Makawao (572-1380) HOURS: Daily from 11 am: Monday-Thursday till 9, Friday & Saturday till 10; Sunday till 8. SAMPLING: Onion rings, won tons, cheese sticks, jalapeno poppers $3.75-5.95. Soups, salads, burgers, and chicken, mahi, or roast beef sandwiches $5.75-6.75. Entrees include fish and chips, grilled or fried chicken, mahi, and scampi. $7.25-9 COMMENTS: The apple, banana cream, and coconut cream are just a few of the home-baked pies made from scratch $3.50; Mocha Mudd Pie $4. The architecture was patterned after the old Nashiwa Bakery in Paia that was destroyed by a tidal wave. Upcountry's only sports bar, they offer two big screens and four other TV's with satellite and cable. Daily specials like Monday: Burger Night; Friday: Shrimp Night; Sunday Family Night (fried chicken, fish & chips). Wednesday & Thursday: 2-for-1 entrees (except scampi) 5:30-9pm. Live entertainment Friday & Saturday 9pm-1am.

ULUPALAKUA DELI & GRILL   *Sandwiches*
The Ranch Store at Ulupalakua, near Tedeschi Winery (878-1360) HOURS: 10am-4pm. SAMPLING: Belgian waffles with whipped cream and fresh berries in season. Caesar or chef's salad, stuffed potato, or chili $3.50-5.75. Soup of the day $2.15; spinach, brie & bacon salad $6.75. Hamburger, turkey, or veggie burger $5.50-5.95; taro burger $5.70. Pastrami, turkey, ham & cheese, reuben, BLT, veggie, pita combo, or turkey melt sandwiches along with grilled pizza (veggie & feta or tomato, onion & cheese), and their special muffaletta, BBT (brie, bacon & tomato), and focaccia sandwiches $4.95-6.50. Daily plate lunch $6. Kid's menu $2.95-3.50; shave ice $2.50. COMMENTS: They use local ranch ingredients, sometimes even elk or venison! Picnics available to go. They plan on opening a second deli in South Maui by the end of the year.

UPCOUNTRY CAFE   *Local style*
Andrade Building, 7-2 Aewa Place, Pukalani (572-2395) HOURS: Breakfast/lunch 6:30am-3pm, Sunday brunch until 1pm; dinner 5:30-8:30pm, Fri-Sat till 9. Closed all day Tuesday. SAMPLING/COMMENTS: One step closer! We found out the hours, but - as with our previous edition - we made several attempts and were still never sent any menu information.

UPCOUNTRY TOYS   *Soda Fountain*
Pukalani Terrace Shopping Center (572-7284) HOURS: 10am-4pm Sat & Sun;
till 6 Mon-Wed; till 8 Thurs & Fri. SAMPLING: Mushroom, teriyaki, and taco
burgers $2.70-5.50, with fries and a drink $4.50-5.50. Hot dogs, chili dogs,
Portuguese sausage, and waffle dogs $1-1.75; chili cheese fries, bacon & cheese
potato wedges $3.75. Shakes, sundaes, cones, floats $1.50-2.25, banana split
$5.Shave ice $1.75, with ice cream $2.75. Sodas $.60-1. COMMENTS: An old-
fashioned soda fountain counter inside a big toy store with shelves of toys and
walls covered in balloons. Great place to take the kids after a hard day at
Haleakala!

VASI'S   *Gourmet Take-out*
1043 Makawao Ave., Makawao (573-8056) HOURS: 8am-7pm. Closed Sunday.
SAMPLING: Greek moussaka or spanikopita, crab cakes, crab dip with boboli,
roast chicken, ribs; Chinese chicken, cobb or upcountry salads (with walnuts &
oranges); and mahi, chicken club, turkey, and eggplant on focaccia sandwiches
$6.95. Daily lunch specials might offer chicken or veggie burritos, stuffed
vegetable croissants, turkey pot pie, and cajun or lemon butter shutome $4.75-
8.95. Weekly plate lunches served with kim chee: Shoyu chicken, hamburger
steak, beef stew, and teri beef Monday-Thursday $5.95; Hawaiian Plate on
Friday $6.95. Oriental couscous $4.99 lb. Freshly-baked scones, muffins, and
croissants $2; tropical cheesecake, bread pudding, chocolate chip cookie pie,
chocolate macadamia nut tart, and double chocolate decadence cake $3.50.
COMMENTS: Extension of Vasi's Catering Company that offers gourmet take-
out with very limited counter seating.

MAKAWAO   JBAYOT

MODERATE

CASANOVA ITALIAN RESTAURANT AND DELI   *Italian*
1188 Makawao Ave., Makawao (572-0220) HOURS: Lunch Mon-Sat 11:30am-2pm; dinner nightly 5:30-9:15pm (pizza till midnight Wed-Fri-Sat). Deli open 7:30am-6pm daily. SAMPLING: The deli offers sandwiches with interesting combinations of lemon chicken, smoked salmon, roast peppers, mozzarella, eggplant, smoked ham, brie and pastrami plus Caesar, Greek and pasta salads $3.95-7.95. Breakfast pastries (lilikoi poppyseed cake, corn bread, blueberry scones), waffles, French toast, and omelettes are served until 11:30 for $2-6.50. Coffee drinks include the "Ecoccino" -- a steamed rice dream and grain beverage, caffeine and dairy free. Restaurant lunches start with seared ahi, salmon carpaccio, and fried clams or calamari $6-10. Caesar, Caprese, fresh fish or pear, walnut & gorgonzola salads $6-12. Cannelloni, lasagne and homemade linguini with different sauces $8-10; and turkey, beef tenderloin, chicken, and smoked ham sandwiches with a variety of cheese & sauce combinations come with salad and fried potatoes for $9-10. Dinners offer a larger selection of the lunch appetizers and salads (cioppino, spinach salad & salmon rolls) $5-9 plus fresh fish, steak with gorgonzola cheese or peppercorn sauce, lamb chops, and veal $20-24. Pastas include spinach ravioli, rigatoni with chicken & broccoli, white & green linguini with mushrooms, and gnocchi $10-14; spaghetti Fradiavolo (with spicy seafood) $18. Pizzas and calzone are cooked in their wood-fired authentic Napoli style oven. The burning kiawe wood reaches and maintains a constant temperature of 700 degrees which creates the crispy crust on their pizza $10-16. COMMENTS: One of a few places left to go for dining & dancing. Good food and a variety of entertainment (including special celebrity concerts) have won them accolades - let us know if you agree!

KULA LODGE   *"Kula Cuisine" with locally-grown organic produce*
Five miles past Pukalani on Haleakala Highway (878-1535) HOURS: Breakfast 6:30-11:15am, lunch 11:45-4:45pm, dinner 5-9pm. Sunday brunch 6:30am-1pm. SAMPLING: Breakfasts include stir fry tofu or vegetable omelette, traditional or veggie eggs benedict, multi-grain or banana & macadamia nut griddle cakes, malted Belgian waffle, upcountry granola, exotic fruit sampler with grilled banana, and cinnamon raisin oatmeal $4.50-9.50. Lunches offer Thai summer rolls, Kula onion soup, and a variety of salads including Kula onion & tomato, chicken, avocado & feta, and papaya shrimp $5.50-9.50; burgers, smoked turkey club, or meatloaf sandwich $9-11; and entrees of pasta, fresh fish, grilled chicken, or steak $12-18.50. Several lunch appetizers and salads are served for dinner along with shrimp stuffed ahi, artichoke & mushroom gratinee, and mesquite seared ahi $6.50-12 with entrees of seared salmon, chicken stuffed with shrimp, Japanese tofu steak, rack of lamb Dijon, and fettucini Alfredo or with macadamia nut pesto $19-26. COMMENTS: Breakfast, the most popular meal of the day, has the added benefit of the fireplace (a warming delight after a cold trip to the mountain top), and a spectacular panoramic view. (Sunday brunch offers the same along with a selection of their most popular breakfast & lunch items.) The Garden Terrace boasts a wood burning oven and brick patio amidst the sprawling cliffside garden which is open from 11am to sunset, as the weather

permits, so call ahead to make sure! When it is, they offer a special menu of kiawe-planked fresh fish, tofu steak, mango BBQ steak sticks, grilled Kula vegetable, and a variety of pizzas - all prepared in the outdoor brick oven $11-17.50. Vegetarian specials; children's portions; plus breakfast eye-openers and sunset cocktails (Another way to enjoy that great view!)

MAKAWAO STEAK HOUSE *American*
3612 Baldwin, Makawao (572-8711) HOURS: Dinner only 5:30-9:30pm (winter); 6-10pm (summer) SAMPLING: Artichoke, shrimp cocktail, sauteed mushrooms, teriyaki steak stix, seamed mussels, and calamari strips are the appetizers $5.95-9.95 along with clam chowder or Portuguese bean soup $5.95, and a new salad bar $10.75. Dinners feature steak, prime rib, teriyaki or sauteed shrimp, crab legs, calamari steak, fresh fish, baby back ribs, pork tenderloin, Cornish game hen, and their special chicken Zoie stuffed with spinach in a creamy white wine sauce $15.95-20.95; prime rib 24 oz. cut $26.95. Dinners include salad bar or House salad, baked potato or rice, and selection of breads. Mud pie, hot fudge sundaes or a big piece of old-fashioned rum cake served piping hot with ice cream (yum!) are the desserts $2-3.95. COMMENTS: The original (family) owners are back and have returned this Makawao landmark to its original rustic glory by decorating it with attractive Paniolo Hawaiian artwork, refurbishing the old wood floors, and emphasizing the cozy ambiance with an overall cleaning and freshening of the wood paneling, curtains, and impressive stately fireplace. They've also reinstated the salad bar including it complimentary with dinners taht already offer generous portions. The Steak House Combos are a great way to create your own surf and/or turf entrees; at 19.95 ($22.95 with crab legs or fresh fish) they're also a great value. Dona has waited over 20 years to try their signature Chicken Zoie (yes, they've both been around that long) and found it well worth the wait! Good kids' menu priced $2.50-3.75.

EXPENSIVE

HALIIMAILE GENERAL STORE ★ *Hawai'i Regional & Continental*
Haliimaile Rd., Haliimaile (572-2666) HOURS: Lunch 11am-2:30pm (Mon-Fri), dinner 5:30-9:30pm, Sunday brunch 10am-2:30pm. SAMPLING: Their brunch menu is served a la carte and features Bev's signature boboli with crab dip, crab cakes Benedict, steak and egg hash, French toast, lox & bagel, and omelettes ($6-14) plus selected items from their regular lunch menu. The spinach, Chinese chicken, or Nicoise salad, Seafood Napoleon, ravioli, Thai chicken wrap, grilled eggplant & roasted peppers or BOLT sandwich (BLT with onion) run $7-14. Dinners start with fresh island fish cakes, vegetable "raviloni," Asian pear & duck taco, shrimp & crab lumpia, sushi, and a marvelous brie & grape quesadilla with sweet pea guacamole $7-15. Innovative entrees include Szechuan barbecued salmon, coconut seafood curry, fresh fish with pumpkin seed or sesame crust, lamb Hunan style, blackened chicken enchiladas, and Chinese crispy duck with tamarind & mango sauce $16-28. Signature desserts ($6) are the macadamia nut fudge pie and the pina colada cheesecake. COMMENTS: This restaurant (and Chef Beverly Gannon) have put Haliimaile on the map collecting rave reviews and top ratings since it opened in October, 1988. The original structure dates back to the 1920s when it served as the General Store and hub of this community.

The 5,000 square foot wood building maintains its original high ceiling and the floors are refurbished hardwood. The intricately designed bar in the front dining room is surrounded by tall pine shelves and an exhibition kitchen. The menu changes seasonally, but always features an innovative selection of dishes with unusual and creative preparations. The admirable wine list includes some nice ports, sherrys and cognacs. Because of the wood structure and high ceilings the noise tends to carry, but the food is exquisite and it's well worth the drive across the island.

PAIA/HAIKU

INEXPENSIVE to MODERATE

ANTHONY'S COFFEE CO.   *Coffee/light snacks*
90 Hana Hwy., Paia (579-8340) HOURS: 5:30am-6pm. SAMPLING: Sweet bread French toast, Belgian waffle, granola, yogurt parfait, flavored bagels, or a variety of eggs benedict including veggie and kalua pork $2-4.99. Hot sandwiches include pastrami, chicken, ham & cheddar, turkey or tuna melt, veggie or Mexi-burger ($4.95); cold selections offer turkey, ham, salami, pastrami, roast beef, or veggie $4.25. All come with a choice of bread, cheese, condiments, and veggie garnishings. They feature made-on-Maui ice cream in their cones, shakes, sundaes, floats, and smoothies $2-3.50. COMMENTS: Counter and table seating with plenty of newspapers and magazines to read while you enjoy a variety of hot coffee drinks. They roast their own coffees and offer more than twenty international varieties for sale.

BANGKOK CUISINE   *Thai*
120 Hana Highway, Paia (579-8979) HOURS: Lunch 11am-3pm, dinner 5-9:30pm. SAMPLING: Mee krob, sateh, summer rolls and stuffed chicken wings $5.50-9.50. Calamari, yum yai and green papaya salad; spicy or coconut soups $6.75-9.95. Evil Prince, garlic shrimp, red or green curry, Cornish game hen, chicken cashew basil, zucchini beef, Thai garlic pork, tofu delight with chicken $7.25-11.95, all available in mild, medium or hot. Tapioca, mud pie or white chocolate truffles for dessert $2.95-3.75 COMMENTS: Dinners prepared individually per each request so they ask you to be patient if they take a little longer to serve you! Beer, cocktails and exotic drinks like the Bangkok Itch and the Bangkok Devil. Coffee drinks, too.

CHARLEY'S   *American-Italian*
142 Hana Highway, Paia (579-9453) HOURS: Breakfast 7am-1pm (Sunday till 2:30), lunch 11:30am-2:30pm, dinner 5-10pm. SAMPLING: Breakfast taco or burrito, huevos rancheros, veggie Benedict, cinnamon vanilla French toast, omelettes, pancakes or build-your-own breakfast $4.40-7.45; steak or fish & eggs $10.95. They have "more bennys than any" - poached eggs on an English muffin with over a dozen choices meat, veggies or seafood for $8-8.75. Lunch specials include country fried steak, fish & chips, fried chicken, a variety of chimichanga,

and hamburger steak $6.50-7.95. Sandwiches, salads, soups, burritos, burgers, and chili $3-8.75. Dinners of chicken marsala, seafood fettucine, scampi, lasagna, scampi, BBQ ribs, pizza, calzone, kiawe smoked ribs or marlin, and nightly fresh fish specials $7-15. COMMENTS: Big Screen (72") tv for sporting events by satellite. Charley's was named for the owner's black and white great dane who roamed freely around Front Street when the restaurant began as a small fruit juice stand in Lahaina. Charley and Charley's moved to Paia in 1971 and Charley P. Woofer Restaurant and Saloon was born. Charley, the dog, was named for the movie *Goodbye, Charley* in which Debbie Reynolds was reincarnated as a great dane. Today, the original Charley has been "reincarnated" several times, most recently as a puppy named "C.W." (At least he was still a puppy at press time!) You'll find the story of Charley in its entirety on their menu.

COLLEEN'S HAIKU BAKE SHOPPE & CANNERY PIZZA
Haiku Cannery, 810 Haiku Rd., (575-9211) HOURS: 6am-5pm; pizza & subs 5-9pm. SAMPLING: Breakfast pastries are baked fresh every day: scones, croissants, coffee cakes, honey sticky buns, Santa Fe brownies, and Congo bars along with granola & yogurt, eggs Benedict, muenster croissant stuffed with egg, tomato & ham; and Yuppie Scramble (with spinach, feta, & sun-dried tomato; breakfast burrito, and French toast on their own homemade bread $3.75-5.95. Lunch sandwiches include roast beef, ham & swiss, garden burger, veggie, reuben, eggplant & pepper, parmesan or ginger teriyaki chicken, turkey pesto, and turkey, swiss & sundried tomato on a sourdough baguette $4.75-5.75. Subs and pizzas are on the menu after 5pm: meatball or chicken parmesan, eggplant, ham, and turkey subs $4.50-7.50. Combination pizzas of meat, spinach, veggie, Greek, Hawaiian, and pesto or teri chicken ($13.99/small-17.50/med-20.99/large) or create your own from a basic cheese pizza starting at $9-11-13. COMMENTS: For $2, they offer soy cheese as a topping alternative: this is a REALLY nice addition to the topping choices and is sure to be appreciated by anyone with sensitivity or allergies to dairy products. And those of you with family members that can't tolerate dairy no longer have to avoid pizza!

HAIKU MART *Gourmet Deli & Bakery*
Next to the Post Office on Kokomo Rd., Haiku 575-2028) HOURS: 6am-9pm, from 7am Sat-Sun SAMPLING: Deli specialties like turkey salad with nuts & apples, cole slaw, dill potato salad ($3.50-7 lb.) and sandwiches on freshly-baked bread: smoked turkey, tuna, ham, corned beef, chicken on focaccia with sundried tomatoes plus burgers, garden burgers, and dolmas (stuffed grape leaves) $4.50-5.50. Smothered burritos, fish tacos, chili & rice, biscuits & gravy. Complete dinners (they call 'em "Fat Boy Snacks") like BBQ or roast chicken with mashed potatoes and vegetables from $6.95-8.50; prime rib $13.50. COMMENTS: Smoothies, flavored coffees & coffee drinks. Fresh baked breads, cookies, and pastries: cherry or lemon meringue tarts, brownies, honey cornbread, and their signature chocolate, Kahlua, or Grand Marnier truffles. Mostly for take out and picnics, but they do have limited seating indoors and outdoors on the patio.

IMPROMPTU CAFE ★ *Tropical New American*
71 Baldwin Avenue, Paia (579-8477) HOURS: Breakfast 7:30-11am, lunch 11am-2:30pm, dinner 5:30-9pm. Sunday brunch 8am-2pm. SAMPLING: Omelettes,

pancakes (with berries or chocolate chips), fruit & granola, huevos rancheros, and Hawaiian sweet bread French toast $6-8.95. Mediterranean, spinach, or grilled vegetable salad, mushroom or chorizo quesadilla, smokey bacon pasta, black bean burrito, fresh fish (in orange honey butter), and a bacon cheddar burger on focaccia are some of the lunch items $7.95-9.95. Dinners start with grilled spicy shrimp, pizza, ahi tartare, fried calamari with ratatouille, and "scallops on weed." Most of the lunch pastas and salads are also available at night followed by entrees of rum-seared shrimp, red curry grilled chicken, filet mignon with gorgonzola, rum & pepper painted grilled fish, Caribbean jerk pork tenderloin, and herbed lamb with corn relish $15.95-22.95. Vegetarian offerings include medallions of eggplant & mozzarella and garlic spinach & pinenuts on a bed of mushrooms $11.95-14.95. Sunday Brunch is served a la carte and features selected items from the regular breakfast and lunch menus plus focaccia French toast (with raisins & pine nuts), gorgonzola scramble, banana pancakes, and eggs (with ham or smoked salmon) on focaccia with citrus hollandaise $6.95-9.95. On Thursday through Saturday nights the "bar" bar turns into a sushi bar, complete with sake. COMMENTS: Far from being impromptu, Miles and Lisa Needham have put a lot of thought and imagination into creating a menu that reflects their extensive travel experiences. The rum & pepper painted grilled fish served with mango mojo - a cross between salsa and chutney - is a definitive example of time spent in Barbados, Mexico, Europe - and Hawaii! The Caribbean jerk pork tenderloin is as "Jawaiian" as it comes and their signature "scallops on weed" is an intriguing kind of sushi pizza baked over rice & nori seaweed that well, grows on you! The smoke free environment in the old Ikeda Building seems like it could use a little sprucing up, but its art-accented "funky-sparseness" kind of grows on you, too.

JACQUES' BISTRO *Island/Continental*
89 Hana Hwy., Paia (579-6255) HOURS: Lunch 11:30am-3pm; dinner 5-10pm. SAMPLING: Seafood or pork saimin, ahi poke, teriyaki plate lunch plus mahi, roasted pork, vegetable, teri chicken, or turkey sandwiches $6.50-8.75. Tahitian ceviche, sashimi, Greek or Caesar salad $3.95-6.95. Garlic prawns or seafood linguini $9.95. Dinner entrees (served with purple sweet potatoes and Kula vegetables) include Thai peanut chicken, grilled pork loin, rack of lamb, BBQ ribs, steak, seafood curry, or grilled fresh fish $10.95-19.95; Hawaiian bouillabaisse $24.50. Tomato basil or chicken farfale pasta, Bolognese or seafood linguini $7.50-12.95. Creme brulee, strawberries & cream, or tropical cheesecake $5.25. All wines available by the glass. COMMENTS: Stucco walls and simple furnishings give it a courtyard look, like the patio of a European inn where someone like Hemingway might stop by for a drink. (Or a meal: we've been hearing good things about the food especially the worth-the-drive-from-Kihei creme brulee and the fresh fish - a great value at $12.95!) A new county lot is expected soon which should ease the parking situation at this crossroads of Paia.

LYN'S CAFE *Local*
810 Kokomo Rd., Haiku (575-9363) HOURS: 5am-6pm. SAMPLING: Breakfast, sandwiches, salads, and bentos along with plate lunches like pork lau lau, beef or chicken hekka $3.50-5.50. COMMENTS: Small family operation. Eat in or take out.

MAUI GROWN MARKET   *Sandwiches*

Hana Hwy. and Ulumalu in Haiku (572-1693) HOURS: 6:30am-6pm. SAMPLING: Fresh soup daily and sandwiches ($5.50-6.75) that they claim to be the best on Maui or your money back! We haven't tried 'em yet, but they've got the right idea: all fresh ingredients like Maui onion and Maui sprouts and the condiments are all made from scratch from the mayo to the horseradish to the pesto. Hana box lunches include sandwich, chips, soda, a chocolate coconut "Dream Bar" cookie and some chocolate macadamia nut candy $8.50. COMMENTS: They sound very confident and with all homemade ingredients, they may be justified. The "ono" fish sandwich ($6.75) is the most popular - try it and let us know if you had to ask for your money back!

MILAGROS FOOD CO.   *Tex-Mex*

#3 Baldwin Ave. on the corner of Hana Hwy., Paia (579-8755) HOURS: Breakfast 8-11am, lunch 11:30am-5pm, dinner 5:30-9:30pm. SAMPLING: Breakfast burrito, egg scrambles, huevos rancheros, eggs Benedict, pancakes, waffles, French toast, smoothies, or granola $4.95-7.50. Black bean nachos, burritos, tacos, pesto pasta, cream cheese wrap, burgers, grilled or deli sandwiches; Greek, Caesar, spinach, or taco salads $2.95-6.75. Dinner appetizers include grilled chicken & chipotle quesadilla, tequila butter mussels, taquitos, and black bean feta quesadilla $4.95-6.95; entree menu has chile rellenos, scallop & spinach tacos, blackened ahi, seafood enchiladas, fish tacos, and grilled chicken pasta $9.95-14.95. Mango chimichanga, brownie, or tortilla bowl sundae $4.95. COMMENTS: Outside veranda; coffee drinks and a full bar with margaritas and micro beers. This is the only Maui restaurant with Santa Fe style Mexican food. Huge chicken burritos, but mostly filled with beans and rice. Ahi tacos were way too spicy; our waitress said that the peppers were a little hotter than normal. Sitting outside was good for people watching, but a bit too noisy with the busy road right in front.

NORTHSHORE PIZZA/PAPAYA JOHN'S

105 Baldwin Ave., Paia, The owner was downright rude and nasty. They probably have pizza and maybe even papaya, but they definitely *don't* have any aloha . . .

PAIA FISH MARKET RESTAURANT   *Mexican/Seafood*

101 Hana Highway, on the corner of Baldwin Ave. and Hana Highway in Paia (579-8030) HOURS: Lunch 11am-4:30pm; dinner 4:30-9pm. SAMPLING: Lunch and dinner selections similar to lunch plates with cole slaw, and home fries or rice: teri or charbroiled chicken, soft tacos, quesadilla, chicken pasta, fajitas (lunches $7.95-8.95, dinners $9.95-14.95). Burgers; fish burgers; blackened sashimi; seafood salad; and shrimp, calamari, or fish & chips $5.95-13.95. A blackboard slate recounts the fresh fish offerings selected from the case at market price. Beer and wine. COMMENTS: Order at the counter then pick up your meal and seat yourself at a half-dozen over-sized picnic tables. A dark interior at night with interesting and humorous artifacts lining the walls. The fish (for sale) in the display looks fresh, but our charbroiled mahi and onaga were dried out and came with a pile of fried potatoes that filled up the plate. We were also disappointed in the selections for children.

PAUWELA CAFE ★ *Healthy Homecooking*

Pauwela Cannery, 375 W. Kuiaha Rd., Haiku (575-9242) HOURS: 7am-3pm; Sun 8am-2pm. SAMPLING: Breakfast is served throughout the day and includes hot-out-of-the-oven coffee cake, muffins, scones, breakfast breads, and fruit cobbler $1.75-2.25. Also Eggs Chilaquile (tortillas layered with beans, cheese, chiles and egg custard), Pan Perdu (French bread baked in orange custard), and Belgian waffle (served till 10am) $4.75-5.50. Lunch selections include green leaf, Greek, and Caesar salads; veggie or kalua turkey burrito, and sandwiches of tuna with capers & red peppers, ham & caramelized onion, roasted eggplant & bell pepper, and kalua turkey with green chile pesto $5.75-6. COMMENTS: The lively artwork of Nancy Hoke dresses the walls of this cannery cafe, located on Highway 36 in the old Libby Pineapple Cannery, about 15 miles from Kahului. Built in 1918, it now houses many famous manufacturers of windsurf and surfing gear. The chilaquile is excellent (an innovative alternative to huevos rancheros) and one of these days were going to get there before they run out of the orange custard bread! Their cheesecake is also one-of-a kind made with ricotta, golden raisins, and pinenuts. Daily specials. Coffees, fresh orange or carrot juice, and fruit & yogurt smoothies. Try a Georgio's Cooler - a frothy white beverage in a refreshing minty green glass that's sweet, soothing, and thirst-quenching! Keiki menu and take out available. Everything is made healthy and fresh with unbleached flour and raw sugar in all the baked goods.

PEACHES FOOD CO. *Bakery/sandwiches*

On Baldwin Ave. just off Hana Highway (579-8612) HOURS: 6:30am-6:30pm. SAMPLING: Light meals, sandwiches, and bakery items. Muffins, scones, cake squares, sticky buns, cinnamon knot muffins, fruit-filled puffs, carrot cake, strawberry cheesecake, chocolate mac nut cake, peach cobbler, and "congo bars" (chocolate chips, macadamias & coconut) $1.30-2.60. Pasta salads, spinach feta or vegetable curry puffs, and the huge (dinosaur size?) Barney breakfast biscuit with egg, spinach, mushrooms, onions, and sundried tomatoes on a croissant $3.65. Sandwiches made on their own freshly baked herb bread or fresh croissant $3.95-5.25. Box lunches available. COMMENTS: A few counter seats by the window. Full coffee and cappuccino bar. Formerly (and sort of still called) "Peach's and Crumble" even though there is a new owner.

PICNICS ★ *American-Healthy*

30 Baldwin Ave, a few blocks off the Hana Highway (579-8021) HOURS: Breakfast 7-11am, lunch 11am-7pm. SAMPLING: Breakfast smoothies, banana or blueberry pancakes, omelettes, and egg dishes $4.50-5.75. Plate lunches of teriyaki beef or chicken, roasted chicken, fresh fish, or fish & chips include rice and salad $6.95-7.95. Their specialty is the spinach nutburger, but the mahi mahi supreme is just as good. Other hot sandwiches include teriyaki top round or vegetarian seitan, a variety of burgers, and cajun chicken or fish $4.95-6. Turkey, avocado & swiss, BLT, tuna, veggie, roast beef, and ham sandwiches $4.95-6.25. Chef's, chicken or fish Caesars, and fruit salads $4.95-7.50. Excursion box lunch meals (Picnics!) include choice of sandwich, drink, cookie, chips and fruit: $8.50 for one, $22.95 for two, $52 for 2-4 people - all available in vegetarian. COMMENTS: Coffee drinks and fresh baked pastries plus soft serve ice cream and sundaes. A very popular place to pick up some lunch goodies

for the road to Hana or Haleakala. (In fact, their newsprint menu contains a map, and a Guide to Hana with information about Hana's parks, bridges and points of interest.) Anything on their menu is available to go and everything is ready from 7 am. No need to call ahead, just stop by enroute.

RAW EXPERIENCE   *Raw Organic Vegan*
42 Baldwin Ave., Makawao (579-9729) HOURS: Mon-Sat 10:08am-8:01am ("9" is a godly number); Sunday "cooking" classes from 9:30-11:30am; then open to 3:30. SAMPLING: Nothing they serve is baked, fried, steamed, grilled or in any other manner "cooked." Vegan appetizers of coconut or veggie chips with a choice of dips: carrot almond pate, sprouted hummus, herbed "cheese" spread, guacamole, papaya macadamia salsa, or kim chee $4.50-6.50; sampler of all six for $11. (So, big deal, it's not cooked.) Salads and cold soups $4.50-7. (Uh, huh. Very good, but salads are cold anyway, and cold soup isn't new.) BUT, wait till you try the Pizza in the raw, nori roll deluxe, angel hair pasta, garbanzo falafel, or vegetable pattie Rawitch! Pizza crust is made from sprouted grains and vegetables and topped with choice of sundried tomato sauce & macadamia nut "ricotta" or walnut basil pesto spread. Assorted spreads and vegetables are rolled in the sundried nori roll, and the angel hair pasta is spun from carrots and beets ($5.95-10). Fruit pudding parfait, seven layer Black Forest cake (made with date-nut creme), non-chocolate "moose" or fruit pie, carrot cake, carob hazelnut torte, and raw (but crispy) cookies for dessert or to take home from their new "Sun Bakery" $2-5. Smoothies, juices, non-dairy milk shakes, and health drinks $3-4.20. COMMENTS: Owner Jeremy Safran studied raw foods and "Essene" cuisine in Puerto Rico and has brought this pure, non-toxic way to eat to Maui. Everything is either fresh, dehydrated, sprouted, or fermented which is apparently all you need to make raw foods taste baked, crispy, and frankly, delicious! Your meal starts with an intriguing fire water "shooter" of liquid peppers to aid your digestion (or maybe it's just to hypnotize your palate). It's served with orange segments to cool you down so you can enjoy the truly unique dining experience ahead of you. A few of the items don't quite "work," but most of the menu is a culinary adventure that's almost impossible to describe - so we won't even try! Ho, hum - just another beautiful day in paradise . . . and just another innovative and interesting dining experience on Maui. . .

SHAR-RON'S   *Homecooking/Family dining*
115 Hana Highway, Paia (579-9133) HOURS: Tues-Sat 11am-9pm; Closed Sun-Mon. SAMPLING: Local dishes like stew, hamburger steak with gravy, and meatloaf $4.95-5.95; deep dish beef or chicken, taco, and El Rancho dinners are Southwestern style $5.95-6.95; large combination dinners with choice of any three entrees $7.95-8.95. All dinners come in child-sized portions for $1.99-3.99 (depending on age) and offer a senior discount of 20% off. Dinners are complete with salad, rice or mashed potatoes, jello dessert, and coffee. COMMENTS: Opened May, 1998 in the former Kihata location. Good value - even more so for children and seniors!

TRATTORIA HAIKU   *Italian*
810 Haiku Rd., behind the Old Haiku Cannery (575-2820) HOURS: Dinner 6pm-midnight; Sunday brunch 11am-2pm. (Closed Monday) SAMPLING: Begin with ahi carpaccio, fresh chicken pate, baked artichoke hearts, antipasto, escargot with angel hair pasta plus Caesar or Caprese salad; sauteed spinach or snow peas $6.95-12.95. Pastas include linguine (garlic, carbonara, or pesto with macadamia nuts), smoked chicken sausage & penne, house spaghetti & meatballs, pork tenderloin & eggplant, snow peas & scallions, or lasagna with spinach and pinenuts $12.95-19.95. Entrees feature pork tenders with rosemary-mustard sauce, eggplant parmesan, chicken marsala, and fresh catch with garlic, tomatoes, & capers $15.95-24.95. COMMENTS: In Italy, there is the formal "ristorante" or a family-owned and operated inn like this, a "trattoria." Housed in a cottage (adjacent to the Old Haiku Cannery) that reflects a charming, yet cozy elegance, their press release advises that they offer the "taste and feel of Italy." On Wednesdays, they set up a long table to accommodate 30 guests and serve a traditional family dinner of six courses including wine and dessert. Cost is $39 per person by reservation only. Although it is a family operation, "children are discouraged" as it is an evening dinner house.

(THE) VEGAN RESTAURANT   *Vegetarian*
115 Baldwin Ave., Paia (579-9144) HOURS: 11:30am-9pm. SAMPLING: Salad platters available in small or large portions: garden, tofu, carrot, veggie pate, hummus, or avocado $2.95-4.95. Entree platters include Mexican fiesta, tofu soft taco, and mashed potato, veggie, tofu & salad $6.95-8.95. Vegan or tempeh burger $4.95; Vegan tortilla wraps with hummus, pate, avocado, or carrot salad $2.95-5.95. Lunch burgers, burritos, bacon & egg sandwich, or potato knish $2.95-5.95. Pie, cake, or tapioca for dessert; Thai tea, cashew milk, smoothies, and fruit tahini drinks $1-2.95. Additional entree and dessert specials daily. COMMENTS: Vegan is a non-profit organization that did vegetarian nutrition seminars for more than six years before opening this restaurant in 1989. Their aim was to create foods with tastes and textures to resemble meat, but without the use of animal products or cholesterol in any of their food. Indoor and outdoor seating for a dozen people. Catering also available. The original owner has returned and has kept the menu pretty constant with only a few cents price increase in the last eight years!

EXPENSIVE

MAMA'S FISH HOUSE ★   *Continental-Seafood*
On Highway 36 just 1 1/2 miles past Paia at Kuau, look for the ship's flagpole and the angel fish sign. (579-8488) HOURS: Lunch 11am-2:30pm, pupus 2:30-5pm, dinner 5-9:30pm. SAMPLING: Menu and specials change daily to reflect the day's catch. Lunches might include Szechwan BBQ ahi, ginger teriyaki, fresh fish, NY steak, ahi sandwich, or a luncheon salad with goat cheese, pine nuts, and artichoke hearts $13.95-24.95. Specialties like ono with tropical fruit, baked banana, sweet potato & coconut, and sugar cane shrimp salad run $24.95-26.95. Pupus of crab cakes, steamed clams, fish soup, seafood chowder, smoked fish

mousse, shrimp won tons, grilled portobello mushroom, or seared ahi $9.95-13.95. (Several of the above are also offered on their "transition" menu from 2:30-5pm.) Dinner entrees might include bouillabaisse, Hawaiian chicken, seafood provencal, pepper-grilled venison, and several preparations of fresh fish $24.95-36.95. Meals begin with a warm loaf of fresh poppy seed bread and end with a dessert tray that includes macadamia cheesecake, banana or mango crisp, pineapple almond tart, or Kuau pie: chocolate mousse with melted caramel in graham cracker and Oreo cookie crust. Full bar service, reservations suggested. COMMENTS: Mama's opened in 1973 making it one of the island's oldest restaurants and one of the few that consistently offer an outstanding variety of excellently prepared foods. It really is a beach house, right on the ocean, with just the kind of atmosphere you expect to find in Hawai'i. Mama's mission was "to serve creative seafood dishes with that elusive taste of Maui island cooking." And it appears she has meet her mission! Expensive, but if you're looking for great Hawaiian seafood, put this one on your "must do" list for an only-in-Hawai'i splurge.

HANA

INEXPENSIVE

JUNGLE CAFE AT HANA GARDENLAND *Light and Healthy*
Located just before Hana at the Gardenland Nursery. (248-8975) HOURS: Daily 8:30am-5pm; dinner available for take out. SAMPLING: All day menu of granola or waffles with fresh fruit, steamed eggs and salsa, granola with fresh island fruit, tropical ambrosia, or sunrise "wrap" with spinach, tomato, rice, and eggs with salsa in a flour tortilla ($4.25-5.75); sandwiches of ahi & Maui onion, veggie on red potato & rosemary bread, or smoked turkey with cranberry mayo ($5.75-6.25) plus create-your-own wraps: veggies/smoked turkey/or ahi rolled in a flour/spinach/or sundried tomato tortilla with oriental/pesto-ranch/salsa/or tomato basil sauce! ($6.25). Lighter options include bagels, homemade banana bread, or Thomas' English muffin ($2.50-3). Orange juice, lemonade, or fresh fruit smoothies are sure to quench your thirst after that long drive. (While dining, pick up one of their whole coconuts and send it on home as a postcard.) COMMENTS: Hillary Rodham Clinton and daughter Chelsea visited Maui in 1993 and enjoyed their first meal so much, they came back every day while they vacationed in Hana. (Apparently, steamed eggs and salsa was the First Lady's favorite.) So, follow in the foot steps of the White House family. Good food and a relaxing atmosphere -- inside the nursery!

ALSO IN HANA:

HANA RANCH STORE: Open daily, ready-made sandwiches and hot dogs.

HASEGAWA GENERAL STORE: Open daily, a little bit of everything!! Hasegawa Store still plans to rebuild on the site of the old building that was destroyed by fire, but, well, with Hana-time being even slower than Maui-time . . . They also plan to start a new line of Hana coffee and other Hana products.

TUTU'S: Hana Bay, 8:30-4pm. Sandwiches, plate lunches. (People have been known to drive for miles for their haupia ice cream!)

MODERATE Nothing in Hana qualifies for this price range.

EXPENSIVE

HANA RANCH RESTAURANT *American*
Downtown Hana. (248-8255) HOURS: Breakfast 6:30-10 am, lunch 11am-4pm, light dinner 4-7pm (full dinner menu on Fri & Sat 6-8pm). SAMPLING: Breakfast croissantwich, loco moco, eggs to order, French toast, saimin $2.95-5.25. Late morning (10-11am) hot dogs, chili, salads, or tuna sandwich $2-4.25; add burgers, chicken or beef plate, pasta or Caesar salad, and assorted sandwiches for lunch $4.50-6.50. Buffet lunch (to 3pm) with salad bar, teriyaki chicken, BBQ beef ribs, ranch beans, baked potato, steamed veggies, and beverage $9.95. Most of the lunch menu available for dinner along with lasagne, fried chicken, and mahi mahi $6.50; BBQ ribs $14.25-16.95. Wednesday is Pizza & Pasta night (5:30-8pm) with a special menu of pizzas ($8.50-18.50), spaghetti and lasagne $8.95-9.50 and appetizers of fried calamari, onion rings, buffalo wings, Caesar salad, and salad bar $3.50-10.95. Ice cream desserts or a "Banana Pizza" $3.25-7.50. Weekend dinner entrees include mango BBQ smoked ribs, teriyaki chicken, NY steak, prawns and pasta, prime rib, and fresh catch $21.95-26.95. COMMENTS: Attire is casual; all meals ordered at take-out window to eat inside or out. Wait service for Wed, Fri & Sat dinners only. Reservations recommended: Pizza night is popular with local Hana residents! Full bar service.

HOTEL HANA MAUI DINING ROOM *Continental*
(248-8211) HOURS: Breakfast 7:30-10am, lunch 11:30am-2pm, dinner 6-9pm. Paniolo Bar 11:30am-10:30pm. SAMPLING: Breakfasts ($8.50-12.50) of fruit, eggs, hash, loco moco, waffles, and French toast or try the Mai'a (banana baked in ti leaves with honey and macadamia nuts) or their special recipe taro pancakes. Lunches start with pizza bread, poke salad, or prawn fritters ($9-14.50) followed by entrees of chicken, steak, pasta or fish, $11.50-21. Choose the teriyaki chicken or Po'hole (fern shoot) salad, or a sandwich like the turkey & brie baguette, tuna pita, cajun ahi, or Hawaiian club $9.50-15.95. Dinner appetizers include crab & prawn cakes, nori-wrapped or seared ahi, spinach & grilled eggplant salad, and seared scallop $10-14.50. Entrees offer prime rib, steak, fresh fish, rack of lamb, chicken & pasta, beef medallions, and vegetable curry $21.50-33.50. Desserts ($8.50) include macadamia & date tart, buttermilk charlotte, chocolate truffle cake, or hazelnut, chocolate & orange gateaux. Special buffet and Hawaiian dinner show on Sundays $29.95A, 13.95C. COMMENTS: Dim sum and assorted pupus in the Paniolo Bar from 6-9pm. Children's menu for lunch ($5-12) and a good choice of mini-dinners ($6.50-14.50). Several days a week, the Hotel offers a BBQ lunch at Hamoa Beach from 11:30am-1:30pm. The "beach party" menu includes grilled sandwiches, hot entrees, sides and beverage for $15.95A, $10.95C. Overall, the Hotel serves good, basic food served with light and tasty sauces. Prices are a little high, but when you're the only fine dining place in town, 'guess you're entitled!

SUNSETS AND NIGHTLIFE

With so many activity options during the day, by nightfall you are likely to be ready to unwind (if not head straight for bed!) Here are a few suggestions as to what to do when and after the sun goes down on Maui.

SUNSET WATCHING SUGGESTIONS

Settling down to dinner at The Plantation House in Kapalua
Enjoying pupus from the lobby bar of the Kapalua Bay Resort
On the promontory at the Bay Club, Kapalua
Enroute down from Haleakala, at the Pukalani Country Club
Sitting at a lanai table at the SeaWatch Restaurant in Wailea
Sipping an ice cream drink at The Clubhouse restaurant at Wailea Golf Course
Relaxing in the lobby bar at the Renaissance Wailea Beach Resort
From the sea wall on Front Street
On a sunset cruise as you sail back into Ma'alaea or Lahaina Harbor
Overlooking the valley from Kula Lodge

NIGHT SPOTS & ENTERTAINMENT

The following spots generally offer entertainment, but as everything else, things change very quickly! Call to see what they are offering and which night, as it varies. Check the "Scene" section of the Thursday edition of the *Maui News,* which lists current late night happenings. Other good sources are *Today Magazine*, *This Week,* and *The Maui Bulletin*, all free publications found around town. *Maui Time* also has a good current schedule every two weeks. Karaoke entertainment is still very popular at a number of restaurant/lounges. Karaoke is where a member of the audience selects a song that has music only, no words. They are given a sheet with the words and they sing along. There is usually a fee to entertain. Ukulele Grill, Life's a Beach, Sushi Paradise, Tiffany Luigi's, and Sansei restaurants often have Karaoke.

LAHAINA - KAANAPALI - KAPALUA AREA -- *Lahaina:* Moose McGillycuddy's is always hopping for the young crowd. Kobe Japanese Steakhouse and Il Bucaniere offer musical entertainment. Maui Brews has dancing and offers a variety of live music nightly till 2am. Bubba Gump's and Cheeseburger in Paradise have rock and roll and BJ's Chicago Pizzeria offers Hawaiian music as well. Friday is party night for music & dancing at Longhi's; Compadres offers entertainment on Thursday and Friday; Red Lantern on Sundays. *Kaanapali:* The Makai Bar at the Marriott features entertainment and a very small dance floor. Both Hula Grill and Leilani's offer live Hawaiian music, the Rusty Harpoon offers music and a sports bar at the Whalers Village. The Royal Lahaina Resort, Sheraton Maui, Napili Kai Beach Club, and Kaanapali Beach Hotel also have Hawaiian music. The Beach Club at Aston Kaanapali Shores has entertainment nightly; Castaway Cafe has entertainment on the weekends.

CENTRAL - UPCOUNTRY - HAIKU -- Casanova's in *Makawao* has a dance floor and features blues, jazz, western, disco and a bit of everything else. The Stopwatch in Makawao and the Lounge in *Haiku* have live music primarily on weekends. Entertainment at Sal's Place in *Kahului* includes jazz piano and blues.

KIHEI - WAILEA - MAKENA AREA NIGHT SPOTS -- *Kihei:* Ukulele Grill (Maui Lu) and Hapa*s Brew Haus offer a variety of nightly entertainment including comedy nights. Sports Page offers entertainment and satellite tv; Sandcastle has a piano bar and dance floor. KKO (Kai Ku Ono) has live music; Henry's has dancing and satellite tv. Life's a Beach has entertainment on the weekends. Kahale Beach Club next to Foodland has music; Oasis (Maui Coast) offers poolside entertainment and Hawaiian music. *Wailea:* "Pa'ani, A Game Bar" at the Aston Wailea Resort has a juke box, big screen tv, billiards, darts, and board games; their Hula Moons has live music. Renaissance Wailea Beach and the Kea Lani Hotel also offer entertainment. Tsunami is the high-tech place to be at the Grand Wailea. The 10,000 square foot nightclub features laser and neon lights, video monitors, and hydraulic dance floor. Open Thurs-Sat 9pm-2am; $5 cover charge Fri & Sat. Top 40 music with a disc jockey. *Makena:* The Maui Prince always has something in their Molokini Lounge.

SWEET MAUI MOON
Keola Beamer

Now after the sun goes to sleep,
My Sweet Maui Moon will whisper to me
'cause now that you've gone and said "goodbye,"
My Sweet Maui Moon sings a lullaby

And finding her way to the sea,
She never fails to look down on me
'cause now that you've gone and said "goodbye,"
My Sweet Maui Moon sings a lullaby

CHORUS
And it doesn't matter what mood I am in
Or whether I'm feeling down
Cause sometimes I'm losin' and sometimes I win
And She never lets me down

And rising up into the sky,
My Sweet Maui Moon will kiss me goodnight
'cause now that you've gone and said "goodbye,"
My Sweet Maui Moon sings a lullaby

And it doesn't matter what mood I am in
Or whether I'm feel down
Cause sometimes I'm losin' and sometimes I win
And She never lets me down
Now that you've gone and said "goodbye,"
My Sweet Maui Moon sings a lullaby....

Copyright 1987 Starscape Music.
Our thanks to Keola Beamer for permission to reprint these lyrics.

BEACHES

INTRODUCTION

If you are looking for a variety of beautiful, uncrowded tropical beaches, nearly perfect weather year round, and sparkling clear waters at enjoyable temperatures, Maui will not disappoint you.

With beaches that range from small to long, white sand to black sand or rock, or more exotic shades of green or salt and pepper. Many are well developed, a few (at least for a little longer) remain remote and unspoiled. There is something for everyone, from the lie-on-the-beach-under-a-palm-tree type to the explorer-adventurer. The Maui Visitors Bureau reports that there are 81 accessible beaches, 30 with public facilities, around an island that spans 120 linear miles.

Maui's beaches are publicly owned and most have right-of-way access, however, the access is sometimes tricky to find and parking may be a problem! Parking areas are provided at most developed beaches, but are generally limited to 30 cars or less, making an early arrival at the more popular beaches a good idea. In the undeveloped areas you will have to wedge along the roadside. It is vital that you leave nothing of importance in your car as theft, especially at some of the remoter locations, is high.

We figured we had a story for the television show, *Unsolved Mysteries*. A few years ago we noted the posting of Beach Access signs. Each one was numbered. We decided that this may be of help to the users of this guide and we planned on cross referencing them with the information on each beach. We spoke to no fewer than 16 people in the Department of Land and Natural Resources, State Parks Department, County Parks Department, the Office of Economic Development and a handful more. The first dozen people had never heard of the numbered signs, the next few had heard of them, but didn't know what they were for or who had even placed them. Finally, one individual seemed to be "in the know" and offered to send us a County Shoreline Access Guide 1994. Now this is quite a nice map, and we'd recommend you send for one from The Office of Economic Development, County of Maui, 200 South High Street, Wailuku, HI 96793. While this map tells about facilities and accesses for each beach, the numbers it lists have nothing to do with the access signs, they are just numbers that correspond with the illustration on the map. We speculated as to the reason for these access numbered signs, which by the way, do not follow any sequential order. Perhaps it was for emergency vehicles? To specifically identify which access at which beach might be helpful. At long last we discovered from Jeff Chang that the beaches were numbered to match a 1994 map. However, the map was so popular they ran out and it is now out of print! The only solution seems to be driving the island and manually writing down each sign number. We decided we didn't want to do that, so we aren't going to be able to help you with this one. Actually we decided that the menehunes posted these beach access numbers, just to drive these authors nuts.

At the larger developed beaches, a variety of facilities are provided. Many have convenient rinse-off showers, drinking water, restrooms, and picnic areas. A few have children's play or swim areas. The beaches near the major resorts often have rental equipment available for snorkeling, sailing, boogie boarding, and even underwater cameras. These beaches are generally clean and well maintained. Above Kapalua and below Wailea, where the beaches are undeveloped, expect to find no signs to mark the location, no facilities, and sometimes less cleanliness.

Since virtually all of Maui's good beaches are located on the leeward side of East and West Maui, you can expect sunny weather most of the time. This is because the mountains trap the moisture in the almost constant trade winds. Truly cloudy or bad weather in these areas is rare but when the weather is poor in one area, a short drive may put you back into the sun again. Swells from all directions reach Maui's shores. The three basic swell sources are the east and north-east trade winds, the North Pacific lows, and the South Pacific lows. The trades cause easterly swells of relatively low heights of 2-6 feet throughout most of the year. A stormy, persistent trade wind episode may cause swells of 8-12 feet and occasionally 10-15 feet on exposed eastern shores. Since the main resort areas are on leeward West and East Maui, they are protected.

North Maui and Hana are exposed to these conditions however, along with strong ocean currents. Therefore very few beaches in these areas are considered safe for casual swimming.

Kona winds generated by southern hemisphere storms cause southerly swells that affect leeward Maui. This usually happens in the summer and will last for several days. Surf heights over eight feet are not common, but many of the resort areas have beaches with fairly steep drop offs causing rather sharp shore breaks. Although it may appear fun to play in these waves, many minor to moderate injuries are recorded at these times. Resorts will post red warning flags along the beach during times of unsafe surf conditions. Most beaches are affected during this time causing water turbidity and poor snorkeling conditions. At a few places, such as Lahaina, Olowalu and Ma'alaea, these conditions create good surfing.

MAUI BEACHES

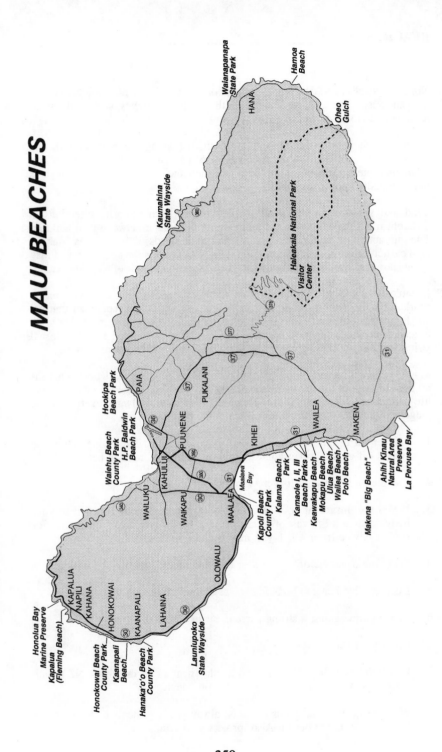

Honolua Bay
Marine Preserve
Kapalua
(Fleming Beach)

Honokowai Beach
County Park
Kaanapali
Beach

Hanaka'o'o Beach
County Park

Launiupoko
State Wayside

KAPALUA
NAPILI
KAHANA
HONOKOWAI
KAANAPALI
LAHAINA
OLOWALU

Walehu Beach
County Park
H.P. Baldwin
Beach Park

Hookipa
Beach Park

Kaumahina
State Wayside

Waianapanapa
State Park

Hamoa
Beach

HANA

Oheo
Gulch

Haleakala National Park

Visitor
Center

PAIA

PUKALANI

PUUNENE

WAILUKU

KAHULUI

WAIKAPU

MAALAEA

Maalaea
Bay

KIHEI

WAILEA

MAKENA

Kapoli Beach
County Park

Kalama Beach
Park

Kamaole I, II, III
Beach Parks
Keawakapu Beach
Mokapu Beach
Ulua Beach
Wailea Beach
Polo Beach

Makena "Big Beach"

Ahihi Kinau
Natural Area
Preserve

La Perouse Bay

Northerly swells caused by winter storms northeast of the island are not common, but can cause large surf, particularly on the northern beaches, such as Baldwin, Kanaha and Hoʻokipa Beach Parks.

Winter North Pacific storms generate high surf along the northwestern and northern shores of Maui. This is the source of the winter surf in Mokuleia Bay (Slaughterhouse), renowned for body surfing, and in Honolua Bay which is internationally known for surfing.

Land and sea breezes are local winds blowing from opposite directions at different times depending on the temperature difference between land and sea. The interaction of daytime sea breezes and trade winds, in the Wailea-Makena area particularly, produce almost daily light cloudiness in the afternoon and may bring showers. This is also somewhat true of the Honokowai to Kapalua region.

Oceanic tidal and trade wind currents are not a problem for the swimmer or snorkeler in the main resort areas from Makena to Kapalua except under unusual conditions such as Kona storms. Beaches outside of the resort areas should be treated with due caution since there are very few considered safe for casual swimming and snorkeling except by knowledgeable, experienced persons.

Maui's ocean playgrounds are probably the most benign in the world. There is no fire coral, jelly fish are rare, and sharks are well fed by the abundant marine life and rarely come into shore. However, you should always exercise good judgement and reasonable caution when at the beach.

1. "Never turn your back to the sea" is an old Hawaiian saying. Don't be caught off guard, waves come in sets with spells of calm in between.

2. Use the buddy system, never swim or snorkel alone.

3. If you are unsure of your abilities, use flotation devices attached to your body, such as a life vest or inflatable vest. Never rely on an air mattress or similar device from which you may become separated.

4. Study the ocean before you enter; look for rocks, breakers, or currents.

5. Duck or dive beneath breaking waves before they reach you.

6. Never swim against a strong current, swim across it.

7. Know your limits.

8. Small children should be allowed to play near or in the surf ONLY with close supervision and should wear flotation devices.

9. When exploring tidal pools or reefs, always wear protective footwear and keep an eye on the ocean. Also, protect your hands.

10. When swimming around coral, be careful where you put your hands and feet. Urchin stings can be painful and coral cuts can be dangerous.

11. Respect the yellow and red flag warnings when placed on the developed beaches. They are there to advise you of unsafe conditions.

Paradise Publications has endeavored to provide current and accurate information on Maui's beautiful beaches. Remember, however, that nature is unpredictable and weather, beach, and current conditions can change. Enjoy your day at the beach, but utilize good judgment. Paradise Publications cannot be held responsible for accidents or injuries incurred.

Surface water temperature varies little with a mean temperature of 73.0 in January and 80.2 in August. Minimum and maximum range from 68 to 84 degrees. This is an almost ideal temperature (refreshing, but not cold) for swimming and you will find most resort pools cooler than the ocean.

BEST BETS
On South Maui our favorite beaches are Makena for its unspoiled beauty, Maluaka for its deep fine sand and beautiful coral, Wailea and Ulua-Mokapu for their great beaches, good snorkeling and beautiful resorts, and Keawakapu and Kamaole II which offer gentler offshore slopes where swimming is excellent. A good place for small children is the park at the end of Hauoli Street in Ma'alaea, just past the Makani A Kai condos. There are two small, sandy-bottomed pools protected by reefs on either side of the small rock jetty.

On West Maui, Kapalua offers a well protected bay with very good swimming and snorkeling. Hanaka'o'o Beach has a gentle offshore slope and the park has lots of parking, good facilities, numerous activities, and is next to the Hyatt. Olowalu has easy access and excellent snorkeling. An excellent place for small children to play in the sand and water is at Pu'unoa Beach, which is well protected by a large offshore reef.

KIHIKIHI

BEACH INDEX

MA'ALAEA TO LAHAINA

The beaches are described in order from Ma'alaea to Lahaina and are easy to spot from Honoapiilani Highway. They are all narrow and usually lined by kiawe trees, however, they have gentle slopes to deeper water and the ocean is generally calmer and warmer than in other areas. The offshore coral reefs offer excellent snorkeling in calm weather, which is most of the time. These beaches are popular because of their convenient access and facilities as well as good swimming and snorkeling conditions.

PAPALAUA STATE WAYSIDE PARK
As you descend from the sea cliffs on your way from Ma'alaea you will see an undeveloped tropical shoreline stretch before you. At the foot of the cliffs at mile marker 11, Papalaua Park is marked by an easily seen sign. There are picnic tables, BBQ grills, and portable restrooms. The beach is long, (about 1/2 mile) and narrow and lined with kiawe trees that almost reach the water's edge in places. The trees provide plenty of shady areas for this beautiful beach. Good swimming and fair snorkeling, popular picnicking area.

UKUMEHAME BEACH PARK
The entrance to the park is near mile marker 12, but there is no identifying sign. There is off-street paved parking for about 12 cars. Five concrete picnic tables. This is also a narrow 1/2 mile long sand beach with lots of kiawe trees providing shade. Good swimming, fair snorkeling.

OLOWALU BEACH ★
About 2/10 mile before and after mile marker 14 you will see a large, but narrow stand of kiawe trees between the road and the beach, followed by a few palm trees, then a few more scattered kiawe trees. Parking is alongside the road. No facilities. This narrow sand beach slopes gently out to water four or five feet deep making it good for swimming and beach playing. There are extensive coral formations starting right offshore and continuing out a quarter mile or more, and a fair amount of fish expecting handouts. The ocean is generally warmer and calmer than elsewhere, making it a popular snorkeling spot.

AWALUA BEACH
The beach at mile marker 16 may be cobble stone or sand depending on the time of year and the prevailing conditions. No facilities. At times when Kona storms create a good southern swell, this becomes a very popular surfing spot for a few days until the swells subside.

LAUNIUPOKO STATE WAYSIDE PARK
This well-marked beach park near mile marker 18 offers a large paved parking area, restrooms, many picnic tables, BBQ grills, rinse-off showers, drinking water, pay phone, and a large grassy area with trees, all of which make for a good picnic spot. There is a large man-made wading pool constructed of large boulders centered in the park. (Sand has accumulated to the extent that even at high tide there is no water in the pool). To the right is a rocky beach and to the left is a 200-yard dark sand beach with fairly gentle slope. It looks nice, but signs

posted warn "Sharks have been seen in the shallow water off this beach. Entry into the water is discouraged." This area is rumored to be a shark breeding ground with shark fishing done here in the past. There is also a "No alcohol" sign posted. For some reason the beach does not seem to be used for much besides picnicking! However, a couple hundred yards offshore is good snorkeling and you may see snorkel excursions visit this shoreline when the weather prohibits a trip to Molokini or Lana'i.

PUAMANA BEACH PARK
Well marked beach park near mile marker 19, just south of the Puamana Resort complex. Parking for 20 cars in paved parking area, with additional parking along the highway. Nice grassy park with seven picnic tables and plenty of shade trees. At the park itself there is no sandy beach, only a large pebble beach. The only beach is a narrow 200 yard long white sand beach just north of the park and fronting Puamana Resort. Fairly gentle slope to shallow water.

LAHAINA TO KAANAPALI

LAHAINA BEACH
There is a large public parking lot across from the 505 Front Street shopping center with easy access to the beach through the mall. There is also on-street parking near the Lahaina Shores with public right-of-way to the beach by the south end of the complex. Public restrooms and showers at 505. This narrow sand beach fronts the Lahaina Shores and 505 Front Street and is protected by a reef 30-50 yards out. The beach is generally sandy offshore with a gentle slope. The water stays fairly shallow out to the reef and contains some interesting coral formations. The area offers fair snorkeling in clear water on calm days. A good place for beginning snorkelers and children, but not good for swimming due to shallow water and abundant coral.

PUUNOA BEACH ★
The beach is at the north end of Lahaina between Kai Pali Rd. and the old Mala Wharf and can be seen as you leave Lahaina on Front Street. Southern access: Take Kai Pali Rd. off Front Street. Parking for about 20 cars along the road which is the entrance for the Puunoa Beach Estates. Public Beach access sign with concrete sidewalk to the beach. Mid beach access: Take Puunoa Place off Front Street at the Public Beach access sign. Parking for about four cars at the end of the road which ends at the beach. A rinse off hose here is the only facility for the beach. North access: Take Mala Wharf off Front Street. Parking for approximately 20 cars along the road just before the entrance to the Mala boat launching parking area.

This narrow, dense, darker sand beach is about 300 yards long and well protected by a reef approximately 100-150 yards offshore. The beach slopes gently to water only 3-4 feet deep. Unfortunately, rock and coral near the surface make swimming unadvised. There are areas of the beach clear of coral 10 - 15 feet out where children can play safely in the calm, shallow water. At high tide there are more fish to see while snorkeling. This continues to be a favorite with our children because of the calm, warm water.

WAHIKULI STATE WAYSIDE PARK
There are three paved off-street parking areas between Lahaina and Kaanapali. Many covered picnic tables, restrooms, showers, and BBQ grills are provided. The first and third parking areas are marked but have no beach. The second unmarked area has an excellent, darker sand beach with a gentle slope to deeper water. There is some shelf rock in places but it's rounded and smooth and not a problem. With the handy facilities, trees for shade, and the nice beach, this is a good (and popular) spot for sunning, swimming, and picnicking.

HANAKA'O'O BEACH PARK ★
Off Honoapiilani Highway, immediately south of the Hyatt Regency, there is a large, well-marked, off-street parking area. The park has rinse-off showers, restroom, and picnic tables. Wide, darker sand beach with gentle slope to deeper water. This is a popular area because of the easy parking, facilities, good beach, shallow water and good swimming, and you are right next to the Hyatt.

HANAKA'O'O BEACH ★ (Kaanapali Beach)
The beach fronts the Hyatt Regency, Maui Marriott, Kaanapali Alii, Westin Maui, Whalers Village shopping center, The Whaler, Kaanapali Beach Hotel, and the Sheraton Maui, and is known as Kaanapali Beach. Access is through the Kaanapali Resort area. Turn off Honoapiilani Highway at either of the first two entrances. Parking is definitely a problem.

A) The Hyatt end of the beach is only a short walk from the large parking area of Hanaka'o'o Beach Park.
B) Public right-of-way with parking for 10 cars at the left of the Hyatt's lower parking lot.
C) Public right-of-way between the Hyatt and Marriott, no parking.
D) Public right-of-way between Marriott and Kaanapali Alii with parking for 11 cars only.
E) Public right-of-way between Kaanapali Alii and Westin, no parking.
F) Public right-of-way between Kaanapali Beach Resort and the Sheraton with parking for 11 cars only.
G) Whalers Village shopping center has a three-story pay parking lot, but with beach access only through the complex.
H) There is no on-street parking anywhere in the Kaanapali Resort complex.

The Hyatt Regency, Maui Marriott, Westin Maui, and Sheraton Maui all have restrooms, showers, bars, and rental equipment. There is a beautiful, long, wide, white sand beach with an abrupt drop-off to deep water. There are small areas of offshore coral from the Hyatt to the Westin Maui at times, but no true offshore reef. Great swimming and good wave playing with the exception of two or three points along the beach where the waves consistently break fairly hard. In the winter, snorkeling can be fair off the Westin when the coral is exposed underwater. The best snorkeling is at Black Rock, fronting the Sheraton. The water is almost always clear and fairly calm, with many types of nearly tame fish due to the popularity of hand feeding by snorkelers. (Bread, frozen peas and packaged dry noodles seem popular.) Not much colorful coral. The best entrance to the water is from the beach alongside Black Rock.

ALII KAHEKILI NUI 'AHUMAHI BEACH PARK ★
Previously we referred to it as KAANAPALI BEACH - South End
This beach begins at the north side of Black Rock and runs for over a mile to the north fronting the Royal Lahaina Resort and the Maui Kaanapali Villas. Turn off Honoapiilani Road at the last Kaanapali exit at the stop light by the Maui Kaanapali Villas. This new beach park has been developed just north of these two resorts.

Kahekili was the last ruler of Maui. This park, which pays tribute to him, is lovely. The park's name, which is quite a mouthful, translates to "Feather Cloaked Nightly Thunderer." Kahekili ruled 1766-1793.

The beach park is open 6am-6:30pm with plenty of paved parking spaces. There are pavilions with dining tables, a very pleasant grassy lawn area dotted with BBQ's and more tables. A rinse off shower is available. There is a gate which is locked nightly. This area was formerly the Kaanapali airport. It has been closed for a number of years now and future hotel and condo development is planned. However, current building and zoning restrictions have put any major development on hold.

This wide, (usually) white sand beach has a steep drop-off to deep water and is usually calm - a good place to swim. Snorkeling around Black Rock is almost always good.

KAHANA - NAPILI - KAPALUA AND BEYOND

KAANAPALI BEACH (North End)
This section of beach fronts the Mahana Resort, Maui Kai, Embassy Vacation Resort, Kaanapali Shores, Papakea, Maui Sands and Paki Maui from south to north, and ends at the Honokowai Beach Park. Access is generally only through the resorts. Most of the resorts have rinse-off showers convenient to the beach, however, no other facilities are available. This is a long, narrow, white sand beach which is fronted by a close-in reef. All the resorts except the Kaanapali Shores and Embassy Vacation Resort have retaining walls along the beach. The Kaanapali Shores has, over the last couple of years, suffered considerable erosion of its once wide beach and has recently completed an expensive new under-the-sand retaining wall in an effort to stabilize and restore it. There is also a cleared area through the coral in front of the resort. This is the only good swimming area on the north section of the beach and is the only good access through the reef for snorkeling.

The reef comes into shore at the south end of Papakea and again at the Honokowai Beach Park. At low tide the reef fronting Papakea can be walked on like a wide sidewalk. (See GENERAL INFORMATION - Travel with Children - for night walking on the reef.) The reef is generally only 10-20 yards offshore and the area between is very shallow with much coral and rock making it undesirable for swimming and snorkeling. The middle section of beach, fronting the old Kaanapali Airport, is slated for future development.

HONOKOWAI BEACH PARK

Turn off the Honoapiilani Hwy. on the first side street past the airport (at the Honokowai sign) and get onto Lower Honoapiilani Hwy. which parallels the ocean. The park is across the street from the Food Pantry (a pay phone is available there). There is paved off-street parking for 30 cars. There are 11 picnic tables, 5 BBQ pits, restrooms, showers, and a grassy park with shade trees. The white sand beach is lined by a wide shelf of beach rock. Between the shelf rock and reef there is a narrow, shallow pool with a sandy bottom which is a good swimming area for small children. There is a break in the reef at the north end of the beach where you can get snorkeling access to the outside reef. Water sport equipment for rent at the Food Pantry.

KAHANA BEACH

In front of the Kahana Beach Condominiums, Sands of Kahana, Royal Kahana, Valley Isle Resort, and Hololani from south to north on Lower Honoapiilani Hwy. There is limited off-road parking at the south end of the beach. Other access would be through the condos. The only facilities available are at the condos, usually rinse-off showers. Kahana Manor Grocery is across the street from Valley Isle Resort and a Whalers General Store is at the nearby Kahana Gateway shopping center. This white sand beach varies from narrow to wide and its offshore area is shallow with rock and sand, semi-protected by reef. Good swimming, fair snorkeling. The beach may be cool and windy in the afternoons.

During the past years, from about 1989, this area has been particularly plagued by the unexplained green algae bloom which tends to concentrate here due to the wind, current and shoreline conditions. The beach is frequently unappealing for swimming and beach use due to the amount of slimy green algae on the beach and in the water. One possible cause of this unsightly mess may be the nitrates and other chemicals which are used for agriculture and golf course maintenance, flowing into the ocean. The county is continuing to investigate and may find it necessary to institute some controls.

KEONENUI BEACH ★

The beach is in front of and surrounded by the Kahana Sunset with no convenient public access. A lovely wide crescent of white sand with a fairly gentle slope to water's edge, then fairly steep slope to deeper water. The beach is set in a small shallow cove, about 150 yards wide, which affords some protection. At times, especially in winter, rough seas come into the beach. When calm (most of the time), this is an excellent swimming and play area with fair snorkeling.

ALAELOA BEACH ("The Cove")

This miniature, jewel-like cove is surrounded by low sea cliffs. The small, approximately 25-30 yard long, white sand beach has a gentle slope with scattered rocks leading into sparkling clear waters. Pavilion and lounge chair area for use by Alaeloa guests. Good swimming and snorkeling with very clear and calm waters except when storm-generated waves come in. Fortunately, or unfortunately, depending on your point of view, this small cove is surrounded by the Alaeloa residential area which has no on or off-street public parking, therefore, public access to this beach is very difficult.

NAPILI BAY ★

There are two public accesses to this beautiful beach. There is a small, easily missed, public right-of-way and Napili Beach sign just past the Napili Shores at Napili Place Street. On-street parking at sign for Napili Surf Beach Resort. The public beach right-of-way sign shows the entrance to the beach. Public telephone in parking lot of Napili Surf. The second entrance is at the public beach right-of-way and Napili Sunset, Hale Napili, and Napili Bay signs on Hui Street. On-street parking and pay phone at entrance to beach walk. This is a long, wide crescent of white sand between two rocky points. The offshore slope is moderately steep. Usually very safe for swimming and snorkeling except during winter storms when large waves occasionally come into the bay. At the south end of the beach are a series of shallow, sandy tide pools which make an excellent place for children, but only under close supervision. Coral formations 30 - 40 yards offshore can provide fair snorkeling on calm days especially at the northern end of the beach and decent boogie boarding with mild swells. No public facilities along the beach. A grocery store is past the second entrance at the Napili Village Hotel.

KAPALUA BEACH ★

Just past the Napili Kai Beach Club you will see a public beach right-of-way sign. Off-street parking area for about 30 - 40 cars. Showers and restrooms. A beautiful crescent of white sand between two rocky points. The beach has a gentle slope to deeper water, maximum about 15 feet. From the left point, a reef arcs toward the long right point creating a very sheltered bay, probably the nicest and safest swimming beach on Maui. Shade is provided by numerous palm trees lining the back shore area. Above the beach are the lovely grounds of the Kapalua Bay Resort. Swimming is almost always excellent with plenty of play area for children. Snorkeling is usually good with many different kinds of fish and interesting coral. It is no surprise that this beach has been selected as one of the top ten beaches in the world. For many years, locals knew this beach as "Fleming's Beach" and called D.T. Fleming Beach, "Stables." *REMEMBER* - parking is limited, so arrive early!

NAMALU BAY ★

Park at Kapalua Beach and take the concrete path along the beach, up through the hotel's grounds, and out to the point of land separating Kapalua Bay from Namalu Bay. This small bay has a shoreline of large lava boulders, no beaches. On calm days snorkeling is very good and entry and exit over the rocks is easy. This little known spot is definitely worth the short walk down the trail.

ONELOA BEACH

Enter at the public right-of-way sign just past the Kapalua Bay Resort. Paved off-street parking for 12 - 15 cars only, no other facilities. Long, straight white sand beach with a shallow sand bar that extends to the surfline. The beach is posted with a warning sign "No swimming at time of high surf due to dangerous currents." This area tends to get windy and cloudy in the afternoons, especially in the winter months. We have usually found this beach deserted.

D. T. FLEMING BEACH PARK
The County maintains a life guard on this beach. The Ritz-Carlton operates The Beach House restaurant. Off-street parking for 70 cars. Public showers. Private restrooms by The Beach House. The long white sand beach is steep with an offshore sand bar which may cause dangerous water conditions when swells hit the beach. This beach was named for David Thomas Fleming (1881-1955), who became manager of the Honolua Ranch in 1912. Under his guidance, the Baldwin cattle ranch was converted to a pineapple plantation. His home later became the now closed Pineapple Hill restaurant at Kapalua. Once called "Stables Beach" as the Fleming family kept their horses at this site into the 1950's.

MOKULEIA BEACH ★ (Slaughterhouse)
On Highway 30, past D. T. Fleming Beach Park, look for cars parked along the roadside and the Mokuleia-Honolua Marine Reserve sign. Park your car and hike down one of the steep dirt and rock trails - they're not difficult. There are no facilities. The wide, white sand beach has a gentle slope to deep water and is bordered by two rocky points and is situated at the foot of steep cliffs. The left middle part of the beach is usually clear of coral and rocks even in winter when the beach is subject to erosion. During the winter this is *THE* bodysurfing spot, especially when the surf is heavy, however, dangerous water conditions also exist. This area is only for the strong, experienced swimmer. The summer is generally much better for swimming and snorkeling. In the past couple of years, this has become a very popular beach. Snorkeling is fair to good, especially around the left rocky point where there is a reef. Okay in winter when the ocean is calm and visibility good. NOTE: The beach is known as Slaughterhouse because of the once existing slaughterhouse on the cliffs above the beach, not because of what the ocean can do to body surfers in the winter when the big ones are coming in! Remember this is part of the Honolua-Mokuleia Bay Marine Life Conservation District - look, but don't disturb or take.

HONOLUA BAY ★
The next bay past Slaughterhouse is Honolua Bay. Watch for a dirt side road on the left. Park here and walk in along the road. There is no beach, just cobble-stone with irregular patches of sand and an old concrete boat ramp in the middle. Excellent snorkeling in summer, spring, and fall especially in the morning, but in winter only on the calmest days. In summer, on calm days the bay resembles a large glassy pond and in our opinion, this is the best snorkeling on Maui. Note: After a heavy rainfall, the water may be turbid for several days before it returns to its sparkling clear condition again. You can enter at the boat ramp or over the rocks and follow the reefs either left or right. Remember, this is a Marine Life Conservation area, so look but don't disturb. There is an interesting phenomenon affecting the bay. As fresh water runoff percolates into the bay, a shimmering boundary layer (usually about three feet below the surface) is created between the fresh and salt waters. Depending on the amount of runoff it may be very apparent or disappear entirely. It is less prevalent on the right side of the bay. Honolua Bay is also an internationally known winter surfing spot. Storm generated waves come thundering in around the right point creating perfect waves and tubes. A good vantage point to watch the action is the cliffs at the right point of the bay, accessible by car on a short dirt road off the main highway.

KIHEI

The Kihei beaches aren't quite as beautiful as Wailea's. They don't have the nicely landscaped parking areas, or the large, beautiful resort complexes (this is condo country). They do offer increased facilities such as BBQs, picnic tables, drinking water, and grassy play areas. The Kamaole I, II and III beaches even have lifeguards. The beaches are listed in order from Ma'alaea Bay to Wailea.

MA'ALAEA BAY BEACH

This gently curving white sand beach stretches three miles from the Ma'alaea boat harbor to Kihei. For the most part, the beach is backed by low sand dunes and large generally wet, sand flats. Public access is from many areas along South Kihei Road. There are no facilities. Casual beach activities are best early in the morning before the strong, mid-morning, prevailing winds begin to sweep across the isthmus. Due to the length of the beach and the hard-packed sand near the water, this has become a popular place to jog. Windsurfing is popular in the afternoons.

The beach begins in front of the last three condominiums in Ma'alaea, the Kana'i A Nalu, Hono Kai and the Makani A Kai. Just past the Makani A Kai on Hauoli Street is a public park and beach access. There is a good section of beach here with a fairly gentle drop off. Also there are two small, sandy-bottomed pools, protected by the reef on either side of the small man-made rock jetty. These are good play areas for kids. The waves remain fairly calm, except at high tide or high surf conditions. The best snorkeling is out from the beach here, but the conditions are extremely variable, from fairly clear to fairly murky, depending on the time of year and prevailing conditions. Snorkeling is usually better in the winter months. The beach from this point to North Kihei is generally fronted by shelf rock or reef and is not good for swimming, but excellent for a lengthy beach walk! The beach becomes excellent for swimming and other beach activities in front of the North Kihei condos. Snorkeling is fair. A beach activity center is located on the beach at the Kealia Beach Center.

MAI POINA OE IAU BEACH PARK

On South Kihei Road, fronting Maui Lu Resort. Paved parking for 8 cars at the Pavilion (numerous other areas to park are along the road). 5 picnic tables, restrooms, showers. This is actually part of the previous beach. In-shore bottom generally sandy with patches of rock, fronted by shallow reef. Swimming and snorkeling are best in the morning before the early afternoon winds come up. Popular windsurfing area in the afternoon.

KAONOULULU BEACH PARK

Located across the street from the Kihei Bay Surf. Off-road parking for 20 cars, restrooms, drinking water, rinse-off showers, picnic tables, and four BBQ grills. Very small beach, well protected by close-in reef.

KAWILIKI POU PARK

Located at the end of Waipulani Street. Paved off-street parking for 30 cars, restrooms, large grassy area, and public tennis courts. Fronts Laule'a, Luana Kai and the Maui Sunset Hotel. Tall, graceful palms line the shoreline. Narrow sandy beach generally strewn with seaweed and coral rubble. (See GENERAL INFORMATION - Travel with Children - for frog hunting information!)

KAWILILIPOA AND WAIMAHAIKAI AREAS
Any of the cross streets off South Kihei Road will take you down toward the beach where public right-of-ways are marked. Limited parking, usually on street. No facilities. The whole shoreline from Kalama Park to Waipulani Street (3 - 4 miles) is an area of uninterrupted beaches lined by residential housing and small condo complexes. Narrow sandy beaches with lots of coral rubble from the fronting reefs.

KALAMA BEACH PARK
Well-marked, 36-acre park with 12 pavilions, 3 restrooms, showers, picnic tables, BBQ grills, playground apparatus, soccer field, baseball field, tennis courts, volleyball, and basketball courts. Lots of grassy areas. There is no beach (in winter), only a large boulder breakwater. Good view of the cinder cone in Makena, Molokini, Kaho'olawe, Lana'i, and West Maui.

KAMAOLE I
Well-marked beach across from the Kamaole Beach Club. Off-street parking for 30 cars. Facilities include picnic tables, restrooms, rinse-off showers, rental equipment, children's swimming area, and lifeguard. Long, white, sandy beach offering good swimming, poor to fair snorkeling. NOTE: The small pocket of sand between rock outcroppings at the right end of the beach is known as Young's Beach. It is also accessible from Kaiau Street with parking for about 20 cars. Public right-of-way sign at end of Kaiau Street.

KAMAOLE II
Located across from the Kai Nani shopping and restaurant complex. On-street parking, restrooms, rinse-off showers, rental equipment, and lifeguard. White sand beach between two rocky points with sharp drop-off to overhead depths. Good swimming, poor to fair snorkeling.

KAMAOLE III ★
Well-marked beach across from the Kamaole Sands Condominiums. Off-street parking, picnic tables, BBQ's, restrooms, rinse-off showers, drinking water, playground equipment, a grassy play area, and a lifeguard. 200-yard long, narrow (in winter) white sand beach with some rocky areas along the beach, and a few submerged rocks. Good swimming, fair snorkeling around rocks at south end of the beach. Kamaole II and III are very popular beaches with locals and tourists because of the nice beaches and easy access.

WAILEA

This area generally has small, lovely, white sand beaches which have marked public access. Parking is off-street in well maintained parking areas, and restrooms as well as rinse-off showers are provided. You won't recognize this area from a few years ago. The Grand Wailea, Kea Lani, and Four Seasons Resorts, along with the renovated Renaissance Wailea Beach and Aston Wailea Resort, have transformed this once under developed area into a world class resort destination rivaling Kaanapali, and even surpassing it in some ways.

KEAWAKAPU BEACH ★
There are two convenient public accesses to this very nice but generally underused beach. There is paved parking for 50 cars across the street from the beach, about 2/10 mile south of Mana Kai Resort. Look for the beach access sign on the left as you travel south. There are two small crescent shaped, white sand beaches separated by a small rocky point. Good swimming, off-shore sandy bottom, fair snorkeling around rocks at far north end. There are rinse-off showers and a restaurant at the Mana Kai which is right on the beach. Access to southern end of beach - go straight at left turn-off to Wailea, road says "Dead End." Parking for about 30 cars. Rinse-off showers. Beautiful, very gently sloping white sand beach with good swimming. Snorkeling off rocks on left. Popular scuba diving spot. Four hundred yards off shore in 80-85 feet of water there is supposed to be an artificial reef of 150 car bodies.

MOKAPU BEACH ★
A public access sign (Ulua/Mokapu Beaches) is near the Renaissance Wailea Beach Resort. Small parking area, restrooms and showers. Rental equipment at nearby Wailea Resort Activities Center at Renaissance. Beautiful white sand beach. Excellent swimming. Good snorkeling in mornings around the rocks which divide the two beaches. The best snorkeling is on the Ulua beach side.

ULUA BEACH ★
A public access sign located near the Renaissance Wailea Beach Resort. Small paved parking area with a short walk to beach. Showers and rest rooms. Rental equipment is only a short walk away at the Wailea Ocean Activities Center. Beautiful white sand beach fronting the Elua Resort complex. Ulua and Mokapu Beaches are separated by a narrow point of rocks. The area around the beaches is beautifully landscaped because of the resorts. The beach is semi-protected and has a sandy offshore bottom. Good swimming, usually very good snorkeling in the mornings around the lava flow between the beaches. Parking is limited!

WAILEA BEACH ★
One half mile south of the Aston Wailea Beach Resort there is a public beach access sign and a paved road down to a landscaped parking area for about 40 cars. Restrooms and rinse-off showers. Rental sailboats and windsurfing boards are available. Beautiful wide crescent of gently sloping white sand. Gentle offshore slope. Good swimming. Snorkeling is only fair to the left (south) around the rocks (moderate currents and not much coral or many fish). The Kea Lani Hotel, Suites & Villas is situated on this beachfront.

POLO BEACH
Just past the Kea Lani Hotel, turn right at the lava rock wall sign (Wailea Golf Club-Blue Course-Restaurant) towards the Polo Beach Resort condominiums. The public access sign is easy to spot. Paved parking area for 40 cars. Showers and restrooms. The beaches are a short walk on a paved sidewalk and down a short flight of stairs. There are actually two beaches, 400 ft. long north beach and 200 ft. long south beach, separated by 150 ft. of large rocks. The beaches' slope begins gently, then continues more steeply off-shore. It is not well protected. This combination can cause swift beach backwash which is particularly concentrated at two or three points with a rough shore break, especially in the afternoons. The beach is dotted with large rocks. Fair swimming, generally poor snorkeling.

MAKENA

This area includes the beaches south of Polo Beach, out to La Perouse Bay (past this point, you either hike or need to have a four-wheel drive). The Makena beaches are relatively undeveloped and relatively unspoiled, and not always easy to find. There are few signs, confusing roads, and some beaches are not visible from the road. Generally, no facilities and parking where you can find it. Currently, the nearest grocery is at the Wailea Shopping Village. (Scheduled for demolition by the end of the year, the new "Shops at Wailea" are not expected to reopen until late 1999.) We hope our directions will help you find these sometimes hard-to-find, but very lovely, nearly pristine beaches.

PALAUEA BEACH
Drive down to the Polo Beach Condos instead, you can continue on Old Makena Road which will loop back to Makena Alanui Road after about a mile. Palauea Beach lays along this road, but is not visible through the trees. There is a break in the fence .35 miles from Polo Beach with a well worn path to the beach. Although this is all private and posted land, the path and the number of cars parked alongside the road seems to indicate that this beautiful white sand beach is getting much more public use than in the past. Good swimming. No facilities. Both Palauea and Po'olenalena beaches have the same conditions as Polo Beach with shallow offshore slope then a steep dropoff which causes fairly strong backwash in places and tends to cause a strong shore break in the afternoon.

PO'OLENALENA BEACH
As you leave Wailea, there is a four-corner intersection with a sign on the left for the Wailea Golf Club, and on the right for the Polo Beach Condos. 8/10 mile past here turn onto the second right turnoff at the small "Paipu Beach" sign. At roads end (about 1/10 mile), park under the trees. Po'olenalena Beach lies in front of you. Walk several hundred feet back towards Polo Beach over a small hill (Haloa Point) and you will see Palauea Beach stretching out before you. A beautiful beach, largely unknown to tourists. The area above the beach at the south end has been developed with pricey residential homes.

This is a lovely wide, white sand beach with a gentle slope offering good swimming. This used to be a popular local camping spot, however no camping signs are now posted.

There is another section of this beach sometimes referred to as Paipu Beach, but it is a continuation of Po'olenalena. Continue another 2/10 to 3/10 miles on Makena Alanui Rd., past Po'olenalena and you will come to Makena Surf (about 1.2 miles from the Wailea Golf Club sign). This development surrounds Chang's Beach, however, there is a public beach access sign and paved parking for about 20 cars. It's a short walk down a concrete path to the beach. A rinse-off shower is provided. There is a small, sandy beach used mostly by guests of the Makena Surf, but there is another public beach access there as well.

ULUPIKUNUI BEACH
Turn right just past the Makena Surf and immediately park off the road. Walk down to the beach at the left end of the complex. The beach is 75-100 feet of rock strewn sand and is not too attractive, but is well protected.

FIVE GRAVES
From the Makena Surf, continue down Old Makena Road another 2/10 mile to the entrance of Five Graves. Limited parking. The 19th century graves are visible from Makena Rd. just a couple hundred feet past the entrance. There is no beach, but this is a good scuba and snorkeling site. Follow the trail down to the shore where you'll see a rocky entrance to the water.

MAKENA LANDING - PAPIPI BEACH
This beach is about 75-100 feet long with gentle slope, sometimes rock strewn. Not very attractive and is used mostly for fishing, but snorkeling can be good if you enter at the beach and follow the shore to the right. Restrooms and showers available. Instead of turning right onto Old Makena Road at the Makena Surf, continue straight and follow the signs to the Makena Golf Course. About 9/10 mile past the Makena Surf there is another turnoff onto Old Makena Rd. At the stop sign at the bottom of the hill, you can turn right and end up back at Makena Landing or turn left and head for Maluaka Beach. 2/10 mile past the stop sign you will see the old Keawalai Church U.C.C. and cemetery. Sunday services continue to be held here. Along the road is a pay phone.

MALUAKA BEACH ★
Lots of changes in the beaches around the Makena area. Past the Maui Prince resort you'll turn right at the first paved dead end road and you'll find a beach park development created by the resort. This public access has plenty of paved parking area. This 200-yard beach is set between a couple of rock promontories. The very fine white sand beach is wide with a gentle slope to deeper water. Snorkeling can be good in the morning until about noon when the wind picks up. There are interesting coral formations at the south end with unusual abstract shapes, and large coral heads of different sizes. Coral in shades of pink, blue, green, purple and lavender can be spotted. There are enough fish to make it interesting, but not an abundance. In the afternoon when the wind comes up, so do the swells, providing good boogie boarding and wave playing.

ONEULI BEACH
The entrance is a non-paved dirt road. The beach is composed of black lava, white cinder and coral combining to form a greyish colored sandy beach. Just past the Maui Prince Resort is a dirt road turnoff. A 4-wheel drive or a high ground clearance vehicle is a good idea for the road can be a rutted, non-paved 3/10 mile to the beach. The beach is lined by an exposed reef. No facilities.

ONELOA BEACH ★ (Makena Beach and also known as "Big Beach")
The entrance for Oneloa is the next paved dead end road. On weekends, particularly Sundays, parking may be almost impossible. There is a second parking area a little farther. Makena's very lovely white sand beach is long (3/4 mile) and wide and is the last major undeveloped beach on the leeward side of the island. Community effort is continuing in their attempt to prevent further development of this beach. The 360-foot cinder cone (Pu'u Olai) at the north end of the beach separates Oneloa from Pu'u Olai Beach. The beach has a quick, sharp drop off and rough shore break particularly in the afternoon. Body surfing is sometimes good. Snorkeling around the rocky point at the cinder cone is only poor to fair with not much to see, and not for beginners due to the usually strong north to south current. Following years of car break-ins, there is now a citizens patrol. Be sure you thank these people for their time and efforts! But still, don't leave any valuables in your car at any beach!

PU'U OLAI BEACH (Little Makena)
Park at Oneloa Beach. From the beach (Big Beach) to your right you will see cindercone and you can hike uphill over the very sharp, steep, and craggy cindercone and down the other side to reach a flat, white sand beach with a shallow sandy bottom which is semi-protected by a shallow cove. The shore break is usually gentle and swimming is good. Bodysurfing sometimes. Snorkeling is only poor to fair around the point on the left. Watch for strong currents. Although definitely illegal, beach activities here tend to be au naturel.

AHIHI-KINAU ★ (NATURAL RESERVE AREA)
Past Makena Beach, a sign indicates the reserve and a short distance past the sign there is a small, 6-foot wide, rock and sandy beach alongside the remnants of an old concrete boat ramp in the water. Although the beach and cove are well protected, the water is shallow and the shoreline is rocky. Not good for swimming, mostly used for snorkeling and scuba. There is also very limited parking here. Up around the curve in the road is a large parking area. It's a short walk to the shore on a crushed lava rock trail that leads to a large "pebble" beach. At the end of this beach you'll find a better entrance than over the slippery rocks. Remember, this is a marine reserve - look, but don't disturb. No facilities.

LA PEROUSE BAY
Past Ahihi-Kinau, over a road carved through Maui's most recent lava flow, is the end of the road unless you have a 4-wheel drive. It is about 1 1/2 miles to the La Perouse Memorial Plaque. From here, if you choose, you can hike. Wear good hiking shoes as you'll be walking over stretches of sharp lava rock. There are a series of small beaches, actually only pockets of sand of various compositions, with fairly deep offshore waters and strong currents.

WAILUKU - KAHULUI

Beaches along this whole side of the island are usually poor for swimming and snorkeling. The weather is generally windy or cloudy in winter and very hot in summer. Due to the weather, type of beaches, and distance from the major tourist areas on the other side of the island, these beaches don't attract many tourists (except Ho'okipa, which is internationally known for wind surfing).

WAIHEE BEACH PARK
From Wailuku take Kahekili Highway about three miles to Waihee and turn right onto Halewaiu Road, then proceed about one-half mile to the Waihee Municipal Golf Course. From there, a park access road takes you into the park. Paved off-street parking, restrooms, showers, and picnic tables. This is a long, narrow, brown sand beach strewn with coral rubble from Waihee Reef. This is one of the longest and widest reefs on Maui and is about one thousand feet wide. The area between the beach and reef is moderately shallow with good areas for swimming and snorkeling when the ocean is calm. Winter surf or storm conditions can produce strong alongshore currents. Do not swim or snorkel at the left end of the beach as there is a large channel through the reef which usually produces a very strong rip current. This area is generally windy.

KANAHA BEACH PARK
Just before reaching the Kahului Airport, turn left, then right on reaching Ahahao Street. The far south area of the park has been landscaped and includes BBQs, picnic tables, restrooms, and showers. Paved off-street parking is provided. The beach is long (about one mile) and wide with a shallow offshore bottom composed of sand and rock. Plenty of thorny kiawe trees in the area make footwear essential. The main attraction of the park is its peaceful setting and view, so picnicking and sunbathing are the primary activities. Swimming would appeal mainly to children. Windsurfing and surfing can be good here. Weekend camping with county permit.

H. A. BALDWIN PARK

The park is located about 1.5 miles past Spreckelsville on the Hana Highway. There is a large off-street parking area, a large pavilion with kitchen facilities, picnic tables, BBQs, and a tent camping area. There are also restrooms, showers, a baseball and a soccer field. The beach is long and wide with a steep slope to overhead depths. This is a very popular park because of the facilities. The very consistent, although usually small, shore break is good for bodysurfing. Swimming is poor. There are two areas where exposed beach rock provides a relatively calm place for children to play.

HO'OKIPA BEACH PARK

Located about two miles past Lower Paia on the Hana Highway. Restrooms, showers, four pavilions with BBQ's and picnic tables, paved off-street parking, and a tent camping area. Small, white sand beach fronted by a wide shelf of beach rock. The offshore bottom is a mixture of reef and patches of sand. Swimming is not advised. The area is popular for the generally good and, at times (during winter), very good surfing. Ho'okipa is internationally known for its excellent windsurfing conditions. This is also a good place to come and watch both of these water sports.

HANA

WAIANAPANAPA STATE PARK

About four miles before you reach Hana on the Hana Highway is Waianapanapa State Park. There is a trail from the parking lot down to the ocean. The beach is not of sand, but of millions of small, smooth, black volcanic stones. Ocean activities are generally unsafe. There is a lava tunnel at the end of the beach that runs about 50 feet and opens into the ocean. Other well marked paths in the park lead to more caves and fresh water pools. An abundance of mosquitos breed in the grotto area and bug repellent is strongly advised.

HANA BEACH PARK

If you make it to Hana, you will have no difficulty finding this beach on the shoreline of Hana Bay. Facilities include a pavilion with picnic tables, restrooms and showers, and also Tutu's snack bar. About a 200-yard beach lies between old concrete pilings on the left and the wharf on the right. Gentle offshore slope and gentle shore break even during heavy outer surf. This is the safest swimming beach on this end of the island. Snorkeling is fair to good on calm days between the pier and the lighthouse. Staying inshore is a must, as beyond the lighthouse the currents are very strong and flow seaward.

KAIHALULU BEACH (Red Sand Beach)

This reddish sand beach is in a small cove on the other side of Kauiki Hill from Hana Bay and is accessible by trail. At the Hana Bay intersection follow the road up to the school. A dirt path leads past the school and disappears into the jungle, then almost vanishes as it goes through an old cemetery, then continues out onto a scenic promontory. The ground here is covered with marble-sized pine cones which make for slippery footing. As the trail leads to the left and over the edge of the cliff, it changes to a very crumbly rock/dirt mixture that is unstable at best.

377

You may wonder why you're doing this as the trail becomes two feet wide and slopes to the edge of a 60 foot cliff in one place. The trail down to the beach can be quite hazardous. Visitors and Hana residents alike have been injured seriously. It is definitely not for the squeamish, those with less than good agility, or for youngsters. And when carrying beach paraphernalia, extra caution is needed. The effort is rewarded as you descend into a lovely cove bordered by high cliffs and almost enclosed by a natural lava barrier seaward. The beach is formed primarily from red volcanic cinder, hence its name. Good swimming, but stay away from the opening at the left end because of rip currents. Although definitely illegal, beach activities here may be au naturel at times. The Hotel Hana Maui has plans to improve the access to this beach sometime in the future.

KOKI BEACH PARK
This beach is reached by traveling 1.5 miles past the Hasegawa Store toward Ohe'o Gulch. Look for Haneo'o Road where the sign will read "Koki Park - Hamoa Beach - Hamoa Village." This beach is unsafe for swimming and the signs posted warn "Dangerous Current."

HAMOA BEACH ★
This gorgeous beach has been very attractively landscaped and developed by the Hotel Hana Maui in a way that adds to the surrounding lushness. The long white sand beach is in a very tropical setting and surrounded by a low sea cliff. To reach it, travel toward Ohe'o Gulch after passing through Hana. Look for the sign 1.5 miles past Hasegawa store that says "Koki Park - Hamoa Beach - Hamoa Village." There are two entrances down steps from the road. Parking is limited to along the roadside. The left side of the beach is calmer, and offers the best snorkeling. Because it is unprotected from the open ocean, there is good surfing and bodysurfing, but also strong alongshore and rip currents are created at times of heavy seas. The Hana Hotel maintains the grounds and offers restrooms, changing area, and beach paraphernalia for the guests. There is an outdoor rinse-off shower for non-hotel guests. Hay wagons bring the guests to the beach for the hotel's weekly luau.

HIBISCUS & PALM

RECREATION
AND TOURS

INTRODUCTION

Maui's ideal climate, diverse land environments, and benign leeward ocean have led to an astounding range of land, sea, and air activities. With such a variety of things to do during your limited vacation time, we suggest browsing through this chapter and choosing those activities that sound most enjoyable. The following suggestions should get you started.

REMEMBER! If you are making your vacation recreation plans from the mainland or another island you'll need to use the (808) area code. This is the area code for all phone numbers unless stated otherwise. When you are on Maui you do not need to use this area code. Wherever possible we have also listed FAX numbers, which also require an (808) prefix. Toll free numbers begin with 800 or 888 prefixes. If you are a person with a disability, see the GENERAL INFORMATION chapter topic on the Physically Impaired for additional information.

Maui is abloom with street corner hawkers selling any and every form of recreational activity. In fact, these authors find it quite unpleasant that every nook has been filled with an activity booth. You should be aware that there are several kinds of activity vendors. Some activity booths are what they appear to be. They explain the various activities and can book you on your choice. Be aware that they may have favorites. This is fine - recommendations are helpful - but if this is based on how much commission they receive from a certain tour operator, then they may not be giving you the full picture. Concierge desks at the major hotels and resort can also book your activities. Most of these (although we'd guess probably all of them) also receive commissions. Those which are affiliated with the resort will no doubt give you the best service since they are a reflection of the resort. However, some activity desks at hotels, condos and the like are merely a concession. They rent the space, just as do the activity booths on Front Street, hence, the educated and informed visitor is ahead of the game in any case. The prices will be about the same, although there are those like Tom Barefoot's Cashback Tours who offer a 10% discount on every tour. (Barefoot's not only offers some great deals, they are also the only activity outlet we know of that DOES NOT sell timeshare! Read on. . .)

The other kind of tour activity broker is the one that *appears* to have the best deal: half price on a helicopter trip; $50 off on a luau. These are the folks that are using the activity as "bait." The "catch" is that you must attend some sort of breakfast meeting or tour of a property. Their aim is to sell you a timeshare unit on Maui. A time share is a week of time which you purchase once each year at a specific property. In a sense, you own 1/52 of a condominium. The cost is in the thousands of dollars. You can put your week into a pool by joining one of several organizations and trade with someone else. In this way you could get a week at some other location around the world. In addition to the purchase price you pay a yearly or monthly maintenance fee. It appears to us that this is a great deal for the condo owner/developer. For example, they charge you $15,000 a week for your one-bedroom oceanview condo. Then they find another 51 folks to do the same and *voila*, they have just made $780,000 for a condo that would sell for perhaps $210,000. A lot of people do own time shares and love them. You may be interested in learning more about them, so you could take advantage of one of these opportunities and have a free meal or save on an activity. If you have plenty of time and more patience than we do, then attending one of these sessions (even if you aren't interested in a time share) may be worth your while to save money on an excursion. However, the time share programs we have attended have proven full of very high pressure sales tactics. The Activity Owners Association of Hawai'i regulates these booths. For information contact them at 1-800-398-9698. Check out their website for additional information and an unbiased activity guide < www.maui.org > or Email: aoa@maui.org. They also offer a "Gold Card" for $20 that entitles you to 10-25% discounts on air, land and sea activities.

The final option is to book the tour yourself by calling one of the numbers listed in this chapter. Ask your questions and inquire if they have any specials or discounts. Since there is not a middle man to take a commission, you might be pleasantly surprised! In any case, it certainly won't hurt to ask. Enough of our editorial comments, now on to why you're reading this chapter: To be an informed and educated visitor! (P.S. We do not get commissions, nor do we sell timeshares!)

BEST BETS

Experience the real Maui, take a hike with guide Ken Schmitt and crew.

For spectacular scenery and lots of fresh air, try the 38-mile coast down the world's largest dormant volcano on a bicycle or take one of several other Upcountry bicycle trips.

On an overcast day, make the drive up to Makawao and enjoy a massage at the Maui School of Massage.

For great snorkeling try Honolua Bay, Namalu, Ahihi Kinau, or Olowalu.

Enjoy a romantic starlight evening sail aboard the *America II*.

Experience the thrill of a real sailing experience aboard *World Class*.

Take a helicopter tour and get a super spectacular view of Maui.

Golf at one of Maui's excellent courses.

Sail to Lana'i and snorkel Hulopo'e Beach on a Trilogy Cruise.

If the whales are in residence, take advantage of a whale watching excursion to view these beautiful mammals a bit more closely. An estimated 1,500 whales winter each year in the waters surrounding Maui.

For an underwater thrill consider an introductory scuba adventure, no experience necessary. Or sample a newer arrival to the Maui aquatic scene, Snuba!

For those who like to stay dry in the water, take a submarine trip to view the underwater sights off Lahaina.

For a wet and wild water tour - plus snorkeling - try a raft trip.

If you're really adventurous, consider parasailing (during the summer when the whales have gone back north!), sea kayaking, or try scuba kayaking at Kapalua.

For great scenery at a great price, drive yourself to Hana and visit the Pools of O'heo at Haleakala National Park-Kipahulu or to Upcountry and Haleakala.

AIRPLANE TOURS

Flightseeing trips are generally available via small plane. There are several charter companies. Trips are arranged by customer request and could include Hana and Haleakala as well as island flights to Mauna Loa on the Big Island, O'ahu, Kaho'olawe, Lana'i or Moloka'i. Small plane trips are less expensive than a helicopter tour, but you won't get as close to the scenery.

GREAT FRIGATE BIRD   JBAYOT

Airwave Aviation - Private tours up to 5 passengers $650. Island of Maui tours and whale watching 1-3 passengers $125. Moloka'i, Maui, and Lana'i tour for 1-5 passengers $350. Introductory flight lessons $50. Cessna rentals. (808) 872-5688. FAX (808) 871-0960. <www.maui.net/~airwave> Email: airwave@maui.net

Big Island Air - Island charters from Kahului and Kapalua to see the active volcano on the Big Island and view Maui by air. (808) 871-8152. Email: mauisle@maui.net

Pacific Wings - Scheduled flights, charter service, and scenic air tours, they service Kahului to Hana (Maui), Moloka'i, and Kamuela (Big Island) in their 8 passenger, twin engine Cessna 402C. Toll-free 1-888-675-4546. <www.pacificwings.com> Email: info@pacificwings.com

Paragon Air - Twenty-four hour charter service to all islands; five and nine passenger planes. Excursions are quite different than those offered on a helicopter tour. Their Kilauea volcano trip is a 2 1/2 hour narrated flight that travels to Hana along the picturesque coastline before traveling the 33 miles across the Alenuihaha Channel to the Big Island of Hawaii. Departs from Kahului, Kapalua and Hana. Combine this with a helicopter tour over the Kilauea Volcano before returning by charter flight to Maui. Or plan a trip to Moloka'i with a tour of the Kalaupapa peninsula or fly to Lana'i for a round of golf. PO Box 575 Kahului, HI 96732. (808) 244-3356 or 1-800-428-1231, FAX (808) 8733-7895. Email: wings@maui.net

AQUARIUM See Maui Ocean Center

ARCHERY

Valley Isle Archers holds weekly meetings Wednesdays at the Kahului Community Center. An annual competitive weekend shoot is held each June on Kamehameha Day. Call John at (808) 875-0770.

ART CLASSES AND ART TOURS

The Aston Wailea Resort offers the *Ho'olokahi Hawaiian Cultural Program*. These activities include lectures and workshops on Hawaiian culture and vary throughout the year. Classes available to guests and non-guests run $5-20 each and include fiber basket weaving, Hawaiian quilting, feather lei making, and other crafts rich with Hawaiian heritage. Lectures and demonstrations are also offered, with reservations required and a small fee charged. Topics might include learning the Hawaiian language, a lecture and demonstration of the lei, or a Learn to Hula session. The *Hana Ka Lima* is an arts and crafts exhibition, currently held every Friday at the resort from 9am-2pm. The exhibition features Maui artisans displaying, demonstrating, and selling their creations throughout the lobby of the resort. It is open to the public free of charge. *Ho'olokahi*, which means "to create unity" was instituted in 1993. The goal of the program is to preserve and perpetuate the Hawaiian culture. (808) 874-7822.

Hui No'eau Visual Arts Center near Makawao offers art classes. Three-hour session every Tuesday explores the ancient art forms of Hawaii. Advanced registration required, $35. Phone (808) 572-6560. The *Art School of Kapalua* also offers art education. Phone (808) 665-0007.

Enjoy a self-guided tour of the wonderful art galleries in Lahaina. *"Friday Night is Art Night"* has many free activities and a chance to meet some of the artists in person. *The Lahaina Arts Society* is a non-profit organization that features work by local Maui artists. They hold arts and craft shows under the Banyan Tree on Saturdays and have a gallery at Lahaina Center.

ASTRONOMY

The rooftop of the Hyatt Regency is home to "Big Blue" the 16-inch recreational telescope. Three times each evening, a maximum of ten people head to the hotel's rooftop for a guided "Tour of the Stars" with the Hyatt's own Director of Astronomy. The cost is $12 for adults, $6 for children 12 and under. For reservations contact the Hyatt Regency Maui at (808) 661-1234 ext. 4727.

A new public tour program of the *Maui Space Surveillance Complex* began in late 1997. Eight telescopes (located on the top of Haleakala) perform work for the Department of Defense in space surveillance and in optical research and development. Two tours are given the last Friday of the month and last approximately 90 minutes. Groups are limited to 16 people. Due to length of tour and altitude, visitors must be ages 13 and up. For more information visit their website at: < www.ulua.mhpcc.af.mil/~det3 > (808) 874-1601

BIKE TOURS
BIKE RENTALS

If you are interested in doing some self exploration on bikes, please use caution on the roadways. There are far too many accidents involving bicyclists and motorists. Remember that a good percentage of those behind the wheel of a car are island visitors that aren't familiar with the area, which perhaps is a contributing factor in these roadway accidents! There is a new Maui County Bicycle Map that might assist you in your pursuits. It highlights all the major roads and rates them as to their suitability or unsuitability. It describes terrain features, elevation and even trade wind directions, and contains a distance guide. The map is available from Maui bike shops or from the Maui Visitors Bureau, 1727 Wili Pa Loop, Wailuku Hi 96793. (808) 244-3530.

The Hawaiian Islands offer an endless array of spectacular air, sea, and land tours, but only on Maui is there an experience quite like the bicycle ride down from the 10,000 foot summit of the world's largest dormant volcano! Bob Kiger, better known as Cruiser Bob, was the originator of the Haleakala downhill.

Cruiser Bob is reported to have made 96 individual bike runs himself to thoroughly test all aspects of the route before the first paying customers attempted the trip. Cruiser Bob's operations are now *pau* (Hawaiian for over), but there are a number of companies still operating Haleakala downhill and upcountry trips.

Each downhill bike tour company differs slightly in its adaptation of the trip, but the principal is the same, to provide the ultimate in biking experiences. For the very early riser (2-3am) you can see the sunrise from the crater before biking down. Later morning expeditions are available as well. Your day will begin with a van pickup at your hotel for a narrated trip to the Haleakala summit along with safety information for the trip down. The temperature at the summit can be as much as 30 degrees cooler than sea level, so appropriate wear would include a sweater or sweatshirt.

General requirements are for riders to wear closed-toe rubber soled shoes, sun glasses, or prescription lenses (not all helmets have visors). A height requirement of about 5 feet is requested by some and no pregnant women are allowed on the trip. Bikers must also sign an acknowledgement of risk and safety consideration form. For the descent, riders are equipped with windbreaker jackets, gloves, helmets, and specially designed bicycles with heavy duty brakes. Dress in layers - the temperature change can be dramatic!

A leader will escort you down the mountain curves with the van providing a rear escort. Somewhere along the way will be a meal break. Some tours provide picnics, others include a sit-down meal at the lodge in Kula or elsewhere. Actual biking time will run about 3 hours for the 38-mile downhill trip. The additional time (about 5 hours for the entire trip) is spent commuting to the summit, meals, and the trip from the volcano's base back to your hotel. Prices for the various tours are competitive and reservations should be made in advance.

We biked down with Maui Downhill and opted for the "late" 7 am trip. We found them to be very careful, courteous, and professional. Unfortunately they don't have control over the weather and the day we chose was clear on the drive up, fogged in and misty at the summit, and there was a torrential downpour for more than half of the 38 miles down. Due to the weather, we couldn't enjoy much of the scenery going down, but probably wouldn't have had much time to gander as it is important to keep your eyes on the road! The leader set a fairly slow pace, not much of a thrill for the biking speedster, but safe and comfortable for most. We were invited to hop in the van at any time, but ours was a hearty group and after a stop to gear up in rain slickers, we all continued on. Our leader also advised that if the weather posed any kind of risk, he would load us on the van. The weather broke just long enough for us to enjoy sandwiches or salads at the Sunrise Market and to bask in the sun's momentary warmth. In radio contact with the group just ahead of us we were advised that the rain promised to await us just a little farther down the volcanic slope. As predicted, the drizzle continued as we biked down through the cowboy town of Makawao. We arrived in Paia only a little wetter for the experience.

Aloha Bicycle Tours - This volcano bike adventure begins at Rice Park in Kula with a continental breakfast before boarding the tour van to the starting area at the entrance to Haleakala National Park. Outfitted with safety gear you begin your descent with a stop at the Sunrise Market and Protea Flower Farm. Other stops at Kokea and the final descent to The Tedeschi Winery for a deli style lunch and time to tour the winery and tasting room. The distance is 33-40 miles, minimum age is 12 years, height is 4'10" Groups are small and they promise that what sets this tour apart is their relaxed pace, stunningly beautiful route, and personal service. 800-749-1564 or (808) 249-09111 Email: marc@mauibike.com

Chris's Adventures-Hike and Bike Tours - They offer some unusual bike expeditions and interesting options. Riders tour around upcountry, not just down it. They use 21 speed mountain bikes and provide helmets, gloves and weather gear. All tours begin in the morning, last 6-8 hours, have a tour host, and include breakfast and lunch. All afternoon tours include a snack and run 4-5 hours. Bike at your own pace. They offer tours which include a unique on or off road trip, a hiking/bike trip, a boat trip and hiking on Lana'i, and a bike/snorkel trip. Trips on Maui and The Big Island. Phone (808) 871-2453

Haleakala Mountain Bikes - 1043 Makawao Ave., Makawao, HI 96768. They have a sunrise special for $59, Haleakala Express $39. These are unguided tours. 1-888-922-2453, (808) 572-2200. Wesite: <www.bikemaui.com>

Matt Schweitzer's Maui Sports Adventures - Dual purpose motorcycles available for dirt biking for experienced riders with valid driving license. Travel to nearby islands by boat for an adventurous off-island trek or tour the trails of Maui. Matt also does fishing, surfing, kayaking and windsurfing! (808) 669-5003. Website: <info@mauisportsadventure.com>

Maui Downhill - Transportation from your hotel/condo. Their 38 mile trips include a sunrise tour with breakfast at Kula Lodge or Kula Sandalwood ($125), day tour with picnic lunch at Sunrise Market ($115), and midday tour with light lunch at Sunrise Market for $110. The 22-mile sunrise tour runs $62. The day trip begins with a stop in their base yard before departure up the mountain. Must be over 12 years. (808) 871-2155 or 1-800-535-2453 in U.S. <WWW> Email: mauidownhill@gte.net

Maui Mountain Cruisers - Pickup provided from Kaanapali, Lahaina, Kahului, and Kihei. Minimum age is 12 years, minimum height is 4'1". Closed-toe shoes and protective eyewear (sunglasses or prescription glasses). Sunrise tour ($99) includes a continental breakfast prior to the tour and breakfast at Kula Sandalwoods. The midday tour runs $86.40 and includes a continental breakfast before the trip with lunch at Impromptu Cafe in Paia. 1-800-232-MAUI or (808) 871-6014, FAX (808) 871-5791. Email: mauicruisers.com

Mountain Riders - They offer a guided sunrise Haleakala Tour for $110.40 and a day tour $105.60 plus tax. 1-800-706-7700 or (808) 242-9739 <WWW>

BIKE SALES AND RENTALS

Bikes and mopeds are an ambitious and fun way to get around the resort areas, although you can rent a car for less than a moped. Available by the hour, day, or week, they can be rented at several convenient locations.

A & B Rentals - 3481 Honoapiilani Hwy. at the ABC store in Honokowai. They have mopeds, bicycles, beach equipment, surfing and boogie boards, snorkel gear, fishing poles, and underwater cameras. (808) 669-0027.

Kukui Activity Center - Kukui Mall, 1819 S. Kihei Rd. Bicycles $12.50 day, $65 week. Delivery $5. Mopeds $27.50 - 24 hours. They also rent used cars, jeeps, and trucks. (808) 875-1151.

South Maui Bicycles - 1983 So. Kihei Rd. #5. They sell and rent mountain, off-road, and road bikes. (808) 874-0068.

BODY SURFING

A number of beaches have good body surfing, depending on the season and daily weather conditions. One of the most popular is Mokuleia (Slaughterhouse) Beach. This is not a place for inexperienced or weak swimmers. When the surf is up, it can be downright dangerous. The high surf after a Kona storm brings fair body surfing conditions (better boogie boarding) to some beaches on leeward Maui. Inquire at local surfing shops where the safest conditions are during your visit.

BOWLING

Aloha Bowling Center in Wailuku is Maui's only alley. Located at 1710 Kaahumanu, Wailuku, they are open daily from 10 am. They have twenty lanes with an automatic scoring system. They also have a room for use for parties and meetings. Rates are $2.75 per person per game (seniors 55 and older $2 between 10am and 5pm.) Shoe rental is $1.50 per pair. The Aloha Bar & Grill has plate lunches, casual snacks and is open the same hours as the bowling alley. (808) 243-9511.

CAMPING

Safe and healthy camping is what it is all about. The Maui Department of Health in Wailuku has a wonderful free booklet called "Healthy Camping in Hawai'i" which outlines some safety tips you should know while enjoying the island's outdoors: surf and currents, flash floods, heat stroke, fungal and bacterial infections, dangerous intersections and pesky critters, as well as diseases such as leptospirosis and giardiasis.

Camp Pecusa is located six miles southeast of Lahaina half way between the 14 & 15 mile markers (behind the sugar cane fields). On the beach tent sites, $5 per person per night. No reservations. Maximum stay 7 nights per month. Toilets, showers, picnic tables, campfire pits, shade trees. No electricity. Managers-in-residence Norman & Linda Nelson advise us that the area is very safe and secure. Camp Pecusa also has a group facility of cabins for groups of 26 or more. (808) 661-4303. <www.maui.net/~norm/pecusa.html> Email: <norm@maui.net> or <linda@maui.net>

MAUI COUNTY PARKS

County permits are available for the three county parks: H.A. Baldwin, Kanaha, and Rainbow Park. The fee is $3 per night (children 50¢) and camping is allowed seven days a week with a maximum of three nights. Camping is limited to weekends only at Kanaha Beach Park. Permits can be obtained by writing the Department of Parks and Recreation, County of Maui, 1580 Kaahumanu Ave., Wailuku, Maui, HI 96793. Phone (808) 243-7389.

H.A. Baldwin Beach Park - This county park is a grassy fenced area near the roadside. It is located near Lower Paia on the Hana Highway and has tent camping space, restrooms, and outdoor showers.

Kanaha Beach Park - Located near the Kahului airport. Picnic tables, restrooms, BBQs, showers.

Rainbow Park - Located in Paia. Facilities: Restrooms.

STATE PARKS

There are only two State Parks on Maui where camping is allowed. A permit is required from the Division of State Parks at 54 South High Street, Wailuku, HI 96793. (808) 984-8109. For information on day use of state parks, see BEACHES.

There is currently no charge for tent camping, but a permit is required. The two campsites on Maui are Polipoli and Waianapanapa. Permits are issued between 8am and 4pm on weekdays only.

The maximum length of stay is five consecutive nights and they do have a limit on the number of campers per campsite.

You will need to provide names and ID numbers of those camping. ID numbers consist of Social Security Number, Driver's License, State ID or Passport.

Poli Poli Springs Recreational Area - Located in Upcountry, this state park has one cabin and offers tent camping. This is a wooded, two-acre area at the 6,200 foot elevation on Haleakala's west slope. The road has been improved, but check to see if you will require a four-wheel drive vehicle to reach the park. Extensive hiking trails offer sweeping views of Maui and the other islands in clear weather. Seasonal bird and pig hunting. Nights are cold, below freezing in winter. No showers. Toilets, picnic tables. The single cabin sleeps 10 and has bunk beds, water, cold shower, kitchenware. Sheets and towels can be picked up along with the key. See additional description in the hiking section which precedes.

Waianapanapa State Park - Located near Hana. Tent camping, 12 cabins. More information on this location can be found under WHERE TO STAY - Hana. Restrooms, picnic tables, outdoor showers. This is a remote volcanic coastline covering 120 acres. Shore fishing, hiking, marine study, forests, caves, blow holes, black sand beach, and *heiau*. The park covers 7.8 acres. BRING MOSQUITO REPELLENT!

NATIONAL PARKS

The most recent information we have received states that a permit is not currently required to camp at either Hosmer Grove or O'heo. A maximum stay of three nights is allowed. For Haleakala Crater camping information write: PO Box 369, Makawao, HI 96768 or telephone (808) 572-4400 for the latest data. For information on use of one of the three cabins located in the Haleakala Crater, please refer to the Upcountry Accommodations section. Haleakala National Park Information (808) 572-4400 (recording); Haleakala Weather 871-5054; Ohe'o Headquarters Ranger Station (10am-4pm) (808) 248-7375.

Hosmer Grove - Haleakala National Park. Tent camping in this wooded area. No permit required. Located at the 7,000 foot elevation on the slope of Haleakala. Cooking area with grill, pit toilets, water, picnic tables.

Kipahulu - Haleakala National Park, Kipahulu District, just outside of Hana. Tent camping. No permit required. Chemical toilets, picnic tables, BBQ grills, bring your own water. Currently there are no rental companies offering camping vehicles. Car rental agencies prohibit use of cars or vans for camping.

DINNER CRUISES - SUNSET CRUISES

Sunset cruises are quite popular on Maui with their free flowing mai tais, congenial passengers, tropical nights, and Hawaiian music which entertains while the boat cruises along the coastline. In the past couple of years, most of the dinner cruises seem to have sunk. In our opinion, this is just as well. Dinner aboard the smaller catamarans is most definitely not *haute cuisine*. The food is generally prepared ahead of time and often tepid by the time it is served. Balancing a plate on your lap is anything but leisurely dining. Several dinner cruises serve a sit down meal on a larger vessel. Dinner cruises typically last about two hours and prices run $60-85. Samples of dinners listed may vary. All in all, don't expect the kind of food quality you'd experience at one of the islands land-locked restaurants. The sunset cruises are far more numerous than dinner cruises and are a pleasant way to enjoy a Maui evening on the water in the $30-40 range.

DINNER CRUISES

Dinner and cruise aboard the 118-foot *Maui Princess*. A tour of the west Maui coastline begins with a 5:15 departure returning at 7:45pm. Their dinner menu currently features boneless chicken breast and filet mignon as entrees along with salad, baked potato, vegetable, rolls, and tropical dessert. It is an all-you can eat, served meal. Open bar and live music compliments the dance floor. The attractive, upscale yacht made this a pleasant cruise with a new menu that seems much improved from our last visit. Adults $78.44/child $37.10 tax included. 1-800-275-6969 or (808) 667-6165. < www.maui.net/ ~ ismarine > Email: ismarine@maui.net

The *Navatek II* offers the smoothest ride with their state-of-the-art vessel and, with an on board kitchen, the most freshly prepared food. Enjoy contemporary live music while dining on a full course dinner. They feature regional cuisine for your two-hour sail along the south Maui coastline enjoying the sunset and live contemporary music. Your dinner includes two drinks. $87 for adults, children 2-11 years $55. Departs about 5:30, times may change slightly seasonally. They serve a glass of non-alcoholic punch as you board and then alcoholic drinks are served after you are out of the harbor. The dining area is nice with tall, wide windows on both sides making it easy to see out either side even across other people and tables. The brass backed chairs have a deco-ish design. The experience was first class, and the food was very good, but again not quite up to restaurant standards.

The technology of this new vessel promises an incredibly smooth ride, another wonderful benefit. If you can live with the price it can be a pleasant evening out (808) 873-3475. Additional description under SEA EXCURSIONS.

Pacific Whale Foundation has a sunset dinner sail aboard the *Manute'a* out of Lahaina Harbor. Live Hawaiian musical entertainment. (Editorial opinion: Good for them! Why go on a Hawaiian sunset or dinner cruise to hear rock & roll?) Beverages and tropical drinks served from an open bar. Several entrees from which to choose. Dessert and Kona coffee follow. Maximum of 17 couples per evening. Departs 5pm, returns 7pm. Adults/children $59.50. (808) 879-8811. 1-800-WHALE-1. < WWW >

Spirit of Windjammer - A 70' three masted schooner which offers an evening of fine dining, romance, and authentic South Seas entertainment. As you cruise with the Hawaiian sunset as a backdrop, you are served an all-you-can-eat buffet dinner which includes prime rib, Alaskan salmon, rice pilaf, green salad, green beans, and fresh Hawaiian pineapple with cheesecake and brownies for dessert.

An open bar services unlimited sodas, juice, cocktails, beer or wine. Adults $73.25, children $36.62. Champagne Brunch Cruise is featured May through November on Fridays and Sundays for $37.10 adults, child under age 12 with paying adult are free. Menu includes prime rib, ham, Portuguese sausage, rice, eggs, potatoes, French toast, fresh fruit muffins, and pastry. Cocktails, juices, and other beverages. (808) 661-8600. 1-800-SEA-HULA.

SUNSET CRUISES

The true sailing enthusiast should investigate the *World Class* and *America II*. The *Gemini* is pleasant and comfortable. It's a really tough choice, but there is a quality trip for any visitor. Several newcomers have joined the sunset cruise fleet since the last edition. Look for more details and reviews on these in future issues of our *Maui Update* newsletter.

Gemini - This 64' glass bottom catamaran is used by the Westin and departs from Kaanapali Beach. They offer a champagne sunset sail nightly from 5-7pm which includes pupus, champagne, mai tais, beer and wine, and non-alcoholic beverages. The sunset cruise costs $42 for adults. This is a glass bottom catamaran with long tables and padded seats inside. The wide passage area is all around, accessible steps and ample headroom make it a comfortable boat. There are viewports on each side (glass bottom windows) and big side windows. No music or entertainment, just a good chance to wind down on a pleasant sail. The *Gemini* also does snorkel sails. (808) 661-2591.

King Kamehameha - A small catamaran, maximum 6 people, with padded seating around the wheel area and a big net out front. You may have recognized it by the big picture of King Kamehameha on the sail! Owner Tom Warren has been sailing on various charter boats since 1969 and purchased the *Kamehameha* in 1977. This is a BYOB with limited snacks provided. $40 per person for a two-hour sail. A good option if you're seeking a smaller boat. (808) 661-4522.

Paragon - Their Sunset Sail departs Lahaina and is a 5-7pm trip with an open bar and appetizers. The vessel is licensed for 49 passengers, but they only take 24 max. $39 adults, 12 and under $29. (808) 244-2087. Email: paragon@maui.net

Scotch Mist - 23 passenger max. Champagne chocolate sunset sail, 2 hours, $35 adults. Seasonal champagne whale watch $35. Private charter. Departs Lahaina Harbor. (808) 661-0386.

Teralani - A 53' catamaran with a champagne sunset sail for $35. Periodically they offer "theme" sails like Italian or Mexican Night, Oktoberfest or a Vintner Sail (from $35). 970 Limahana Place, Suite 204, Lahaina, HI 96761. (808) 661-5500.

Trilogy - Their Kaanapali Sunset sail meets at 3:15 in front of Whalers Village for beach loading. Beverages, snacks are served aboard the *Trilogy IV* before returning to Kaanapali Beach at 5:30pm. Adults $45, children $22.50. 1-800-874-2666. (808) 661-4743. (Authors' comment: Who named this one? The sun doesn't set until after 5:30!)

Whale Mist - 36' monohull sailboat, max. 18, whale watch/sunset cruise, $39 adults. Depart Lahaina, slip #6. (808) 667-2833.

World Class ★ - World Class Yacht Charters is another branch of the Sunshine Helicopter family - a quality operation that sails in luxury and comfort. Their evening sailing cruise aboard the yacht *World Class* includes complimentary beverages, $45 adult. Departures vary according to sunset. This is an opportunity to enjoy a real sailing experience aboard an outstanding yacht, an exciting trip that should appeal to the more adventurous type. The sleek, 65' MacGregor yacht glides through the water making a very fast, but smooth ride! If you enjoy sailing, don't miss this one. (808) 667-7733 or FAX (808) 667-0314.

Zip-purr - Owned by Julie and Mike "Turk" Turkington. Mike built this 47' sailboat and is its captain. While it can carry a maximum of 49 passengers, they prefer to book no more than 35-40. Their two-hour sunset cocktail sail features an appetizer buffet and an open bar. (808) 667-2299.

FISHING

Deep sea fishing off Maui is among the finest in the world and no licenses are required for either trolling or bottom fishing. Fish that might be lured to your bait include the Pacific Blue, Black or Striped Marlin (Au) weighing up to 2,000 lbs., Yellow Fin Tuna (Ahi) up to 300 lbs., Jack Crevalle (Ulua) to 100 lbs., Bonita-Skipjack (Aku) to 40 lbs., Dolphin Fish (Mahi) to 90 lbs., Wahoo (Ono) to 90 lbs., Mackerel (Opelu), Amerjack (Kahala), Grey Snapper (Uku), Red Snapper (Onaga), and Pink Snapper (Opakapaka). Boats generally offer half or full-day fishing trips on a share or private basis. Some are willing to take non-fishing passengers along at half price. Most boats take 4-6 on a shared basis, however several can handle larger groups. All gear is provided.

FINDING A CHARTER: Your local activity center may be able to direct you to a particular boat that they favor, or you could go down to the docks at the Lahaina or Ma'alaea Harbor in the afternoon and browse around. There are also a number of activity booths at both harbors that can be consulted. When reserving a spot, be aware that some boats will give full refunds only if a 48-hour notice is given for cancellation. If you want to take children fishing, many have restrictions for those under age 12. If you are a serious fisherman, you might consider entering one of the numerous tournaments. Some charters offer tournament packages. Following are a list of just some of the charter fishing boats. Since 1972 (thru 1997) *Finest Kind* has been ranked the #1 fishing boat on Maui.

A WORD OF ADVICE: The young man had a grin that reached from ear to ear as he stood on the pier in Ma'alaea, holding up his small ahi for a snapshot of his big catch. The surprise came when the deck hand returned it to the ice chest and continued on with his work. The family all stood, unsure what to do. It appeared that the fish was to remain on board, while the family had envisioned a nice fresh fish dinner. One family member spoke up and a very unhappy crew member sliced a small filet, tossed it into a sack and handed it to the young man. Unlike sportsfishing charters in some parts of the country, the fish caught on board generally remain the property of the boat. The pay to captain and crew is minimal and it is the selling of the boat's catch that subsidizes their income.

Many vacationers booking a fishing excursion are unaware of this fact. There seems to be no written law for how fishing charters in Hawaii handle this, at least everyone we talked to had different answers. Many of the brochures lead one to believe that you keep your fish, but they neglect to mention that it may be only a filet of fish. Occasionally you may find a head boat which operates under a different sort of guideline. In this situation, you pay for your bait, gear, and boat time and then keep the fish. In any case, be sure you check when you book your trip about just what and how much fish will be yours to keep. If the person at the activity desk assures you that you keep your catch, don't leave it there. Also check with the captain when you board. (As thorough editors we checked and Carol Ann of Carol Ann charters told us that on board her vessel, you DO get to keep your fish!) Communication is the key word - and have a mahi mahi day!

SHORE FISHING -- Love to fish, but hate boats? Some new activity companies recently started including Off-Road and Shorefishing Expeditions. David Bloch, long time shoreline fisherman will let you experience shore fishing at proven fishing sites, many of which require their four-wheel transportation to reach. They offer a full day fishing excursion as well as a 24-hour overnight camping and fishing adventure. Customized excursions to fit your experience and physical ability. (808) 572-3470. Kawilani's Unique Tours offers the opportunity to fish with light tackle from the shoreline, or catch your fish by net throwing. A cultural and recreational experience for the true *"lawai'a"* (fisherman). Overnight camping and fishing trips also available. (808) 875-7305.

TROUT FISHING -- Visit a trout farm in the tropical rainforest beyond Kapalua. Five ponds with trout! Transportation provided from West Maui. All fishing gear provided. Full lunch including BBQ trout! $85. (808) 667-0151.

LAHAINA HARBOR

ABSOLUTE SPORTFISHING, *Absolute*, 31' Bertram sportfisher
Charter: 4-8 hr. $450-675, Bottom fishing 4 hr/$350
Westin Maui (808) 661-2591

AERIAL SPORTFISHING, *No Problem*, 37' Merritt, *Aerial III*, 36' Criss-craft
Charters: 8 hr $660-650; 6 hr $550-600, 4 hours $450-500.
(808) 667-9089

FINEST KIND, INC. *Exact*, 31' Bertram; *Finest Kind*, 37' Merritt;
Reel Hooker, 35' Bertram. Charters: $135 full day per person
$120 for 3/4 day per person. Private 6 hr. $650 / 8 hr. $750
PO Box 10481, Lahaina, HI 96761. Maximum 6 people. Ask for Nancy!
(808) 661-0338

HINATEA SPORTFISHING, *Hinatea*, 41' Hataras, Full day $135 shared boat
6 hours $110 shared boat, Slip #27-Lahaina Harbor,
PO Box 5375, Lahaina, HI 96761 (808) 667-7548

ISLANDER II SPORTFISHING, 36' Uniflite, Charters: Private $550-750,
Shared $125-140, Departs Lahaina slip #64
PO Box 12337 Lahaina 96761 (808) 667-6625

KAANAPALI SPORTFISHING, *Desperado* 31' Bertram, Shared boat $110-135
Private charters $500-725, Bring your favorite lunch
and beverage. Alcohol permitted, no bottles or bananas
(bottles can get broken and bananas are bad luck!!) Departs Kaanapali
PO Box 11208 Lahaina (808) 667-5792

LAHAINA CHARTERS, *Broadbill*, 36' Harcraft (max 6), *Judy Ann II,*
43' Delta (max 8), *Alohilani*, 28' Topaz (max 6). Charters: 4 hr $400-450 / 6 hr
$500-600, 8 hours $600-700. Max. 6 people
PO Box 12, Lahaina, HI 96761 (808) 667-6672

LUCKEY STRIKE CHARTERS, *Kanoa*, 31' Uniflite, max. 6, *Luckey Strike II*,
50' Delta, Shared boat: 4 hours $65; 6 hours $120; 8 hours $140
Private charters based on 6: 1/2 day $475-525; full day $675-825
PO Box 1502, Lahaina, HI 96767 (808) 661-4606

MARLIN MISCHIEF, *Marlin Mischief* 47' Buddy Davis. Fish in luxury on this
new one! Shared 6 hr. $150 / 8 hr. $165. Private $675-975. Departs Lahaina slip
#63. 221 Kahoe Place, Kula 96790 (808) 662-3474

OFFSHORE HUNTER, *Offshore Hunter*, 33' Fiberglass Innovater
8 hrs. $130 / 6 hrs. $110, Private $500-700
511 Pikanele, Lahaina, HI 96761 (808) 872-4716

ROBOLO-ONE FISHING, Specialty fishing including fly fishing! Bottom fishing:
1/2 day shared $80. Non-fisher half price. $275 for 4 hour private charter.
Departs Lahaina. PO Box 10253 Lahaina, HI 96761(808) 661-0480

UNREEL SPORT FISHING, 42' Ditmar & Donaldson. $99 4 hours; $119 6
hours; $145 8 hours. Private charters $525-800. Bottom fishing $50 adults.
Departs Slip #72, Lahaina Harbor.
PO Box 12773 Lahaina. (808) 244-2123

MA'ALAEA HARBOR

CAROL ANN CHARTERS, 33' Bertram, max. 6. Private charters: $450-650
Shared boat: 4 hours $100; 6 hours $120; 8 hours $135.
Departs Ma'alaea (808) 877-2181

OCEAN ACTIVITIES CENTER, *No Ka Oi III*, 37' Tolley Craft. Shared: 6 hrs
$115; 8 hrs $140. Private: 6 hrs $535; 8 hrs $635
Departs Ma'alaea (808) 879-4485

RASCAL SPORTFISHING CHARTERS, *Rascal*, Bertram 31'. Shared boat /
private charters. 4 hours $95/425; 6 hours $110/525; 8 hours $135/625
Afternoon bottom fishing $85. Departs slip 13 Ma'alaea.
(808) 874-8633

GOLF

Maui's golf courses have set a high standard of excellence for themselves. Many
are consistently ranked among the top in the United States and the world by
prominent golf magazines. Not only do they provide some very challenging play,
but they also offer distractingly beautiful scenery. Most of the major resorts have
golf packages and for the avid player, this may be an economical plan.

If you are a real golf enthusiast, consider subscribing to *Hawaii Golf*. It details
lots of upcoming golf events on all the islands. The cost is $10 for 12 issues.
Contact Hawaii Golf, PO Box 6107, Honolulu, HI 96818.

Stand-by Golf is a great option for you golfers interested in some serious savings.
They feature discounted rates at public and private courses. They sell unsold tee
times beginning about 6pm until 9pm for the next day of play and after 7 am for
the same day. They book your game at a guaranteed price and time. Discounts
range from 10% on the lowest priced courses up to 33% and more. Prices always
include the cart. They cannot book municipal golf courses. Bookings are handled
by telephone and you pay with a credit card. 1-888-645-BOOK.

Delmar Golf College at Kaanapali Golf Course offers golf instruction for the
beginner or the advanced. Their "curriculum" includes video analysis, half and
all day schools, beginner clinics, private lessons and any of the above paired with
9 or 18 holes of play on the Kaanapali Golf Course. (808) 661-0488.

KAANAPALI

The Kaanapali Resort offers two championship courses. Green fees are $100 for
18 holes, cart included for resort guests. Green fees for non-guests $120.
Twilight rate $65. Kamaaina discounts. The Royal Kaanapali driving range is
located at the Southern entrance to the Kaanapali resort area. Club rental $27.
(808) 661-3691.

The Kaanapali North Course has been attracting celebrities since its inaugural when Bing Crosby played in the opening of the first nine holes. Designed by Robert Trent Jones, this 6,305 yard course places heavy emphasis on putting skills. At par 72, it is rated 70 for men and 71.4 for women.

The South Course first opened in 1970 as an executive course and was reopened in 1977 as a regular championship course after revisions by golf architect Arthur Snyder. At 6,205 yards and par 72 it requires accuracy as opposed to distance, with narrower fairways and more small, hilly greens than the North Course. As an added attraction, the Sugar Cane Train passes by along the 4th hole.

KAPALUA

The Kapalua Resort features the Bay Course, Village Course and Plantation Course. Green fees for the Bay and Village Course: $130 including cart. (Discounts for registered guests of Kapalua Bay Hotel, The Kapalua Villas and The Ritz-Carlton, Kapalua or Maui residents.) Twilight play 2pm-6pm with discounted fees. Green Fees for the Plantation Course: Standard $140. (Discounts for registered guests of Kapalua Bay Hotel, The Kapalua Villas and The Ritz-Carlton, Kapalua.) Replay on any of the courses the same day is $25-30. Club and shoe rentals available. Practice range is open 8am-4:30pm, $5 per bucket. Guests may reserve tee-off times up to 7 days in advance. Non-guest reservations 4 days in advance. Special golf events held at various times throughout the year. One-day golf school available as well as video golf lessons to analyze your swing, and playing lessons are offered. Daily clinics are available Monday-Thursday. (808) 669-8044.

Kapalua recently restored one of the game's lost traditions with the establishment of the Caddie Program. This reflects Kapalua's desire to kindle interest in the game among Maui's youth and restore the player/caddie relationship.

Kapalua has demonstrated its dedication to the land. All three golf courses are Certified Audubon Cooperative Sanctuaries. Kapalua's courses received this Sanctuary designation by meeting the stringent environmental standards set forth by the New York Audubon Cooperative Sanctuary System for water conservation, habitat enhancement, public involvement, integrated pest management and more. An environmental awareness program, "Eagles and Birdies at Kapalua" encourages players to identify the many birds (23 varieties) they are likely to encounter during their rounds at Kapalua.

The Bay Course, under the design of Arnold Palmer, opened in late 1975 and sprawls from sea level to the mountain's edge. This beautiful and scenic 6,600 yard, par 72 course has a distinctly Hawaiian flavor. With its picturesque signature hole extending onto an ocean-framed black lava peninsula, The Bay Course is an excellent example of a premier resort golf course.

The Village Course opened in 1981 and sweeps inland along the pineapple fields and statuesque pine trees. At par 71 and 6,632 yards, designer Arnold Palmer and course architect Ed Seay are reported to have given this course a European flavor. Resembling the mountainous countryside of Scotland, it is reputed to be the most difficult and demanding in Hawaii and one of the most challenging in the world.

The Plantation Course opened in May 1991 and was designed by Coore and Crenshaw of Austin, Texas. The 18-hole championship is situated on 240 acres north of the Village Course. The 7,263 yard course has a par 73 and features expansive greens, deep valleys and expansive fairways.

KIHEI

The Silversword Golf Course, a non-resort course, offers a par 71, 6,800 yard, 18-hole course located off Piilani Highway near Lipoa Street. Green fees, which are currently $70, include shared cart. Rider (non-golfer) $15. Ask about seasonal golf specials from April through mid-December. Twilight (after 1pm; must be in barn by 6pm - no guarantee on 18 holes), $44; Twilight April thru December 18, $42. $15 for same day replay. Rental clubs $22, rental shoes $10. Driving range offers a bucket of balls, open 8am-9pm, except Saturday and Sunday nights, Thursdays noon to 9pm. (808) 874-0777.

WAILEA

The Wailea resort offers the challenging Emerald, Blue, and Gold Courses. Current green fees for Wailea Resort guests are $80 on the Blue Course; $95 on the Gold and Emerald. For the general public they are $110 for the Blue Course and $120 for the Gold and Emerald. The Blue Course has an afternoon rate of $60 for resort guests and $70 for the general public with tee times after 12 noon daily. No afternoon rates available for the Gold or Emerald, but ask about seasonal specials! These include the Wailea Triple Play Pass, good for 3 rounds at Wailea $240 for resort guests or $275 for general public; and a parent-child rate of $90 for resort guests and $105 for the general public. There is also an adult-child twosome play on the Blue Course for tee times after noon. They have added a new, toll-free number, for tee-time reservations 1-888-328-MAUI. Their new computerized reservation system is expected to speed up phone time as well! Locally, call 879-7450 for all three courses. E-mail: info@wailea-resort.com.

The Emerald Course opened in December 1994, and was designed by Robert Trent Jones, Jr. to provide a tropical garden experience. It is a par-72 layout of 6,825 yards. Originally this course was the Orange Course, but was completely revamped and redesigned to be enjoyable for golfers of all caliber. The course also boasts spectacular scenery with an outstanding ocean view on the fourth hole. Definitely worth packing a camera along with your clubs!

Maui Golf Courses

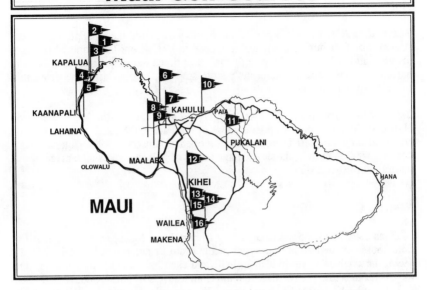

1. **Kapalua Golf Club - Plantation Course**
2. **Kapalua Golf Club - Village Course**
3. **Kapalua Golf Club - Bay Course**
4. **Royal Kaanapali - North Course**
5. **Royal Kaanapali - South Course**
6. **Waiehu Municipal Golf Course**
7. **The Greens at Mani Lani Golf Course**
8. **Waikapu Valley Country Club**
9. **Waikapu Sandalwood Golf Course**
10. **Maui Country Club**
11. **Pukalani Country Club**
12. **Silversword Golf Club**
13. **Wailea Golf Club - Blue Course**
14. **Wailea Golf Club - Gold Course**
15. **Wailea Golf Club - Emerald Course**
16. **Makena Golf Course**

The Wailea Blue Course is par 72 and 6,758 yards from the championship tees. A creation of Arthur Jack Snyder, it opened in 1972. Four lakes and 74 bunkers provide added hazards along with the exceptional scenery. The 16th hole is particularly lovely with numerous people stopping to snap a picture from this magnificent vantage point.

The Gold Course, is par 72, stretching 7,070 yards across the lower slopes of Haleakala and affording exquisite views of the Pacific Ocean. Designed by golf course architect Robert Trent Jones Jr., it opened January 1, 1994. Jones' design concept was to create a classical, rugged style of golf that takes advantage of the natural sloping terrain.

MAKENA

Makena offers two courses designed by Robert Trent Jones, Jr. The original 18-hole course opened at the same time as the Maui Prince resort in 1991-1992. In 1993, the courses were divided in half, and each half was combined with nine new holes to create the North and South Courses. Resort guests $80; twilight $60 (after 2pm). All others $125; twilight $70. Same day replay $35. Fees include cart. King Cobra club rental $35. (808) 879-3344.

The South Course is a more classic open-style course that leads to the ocean. The large cactus which abound in this area were imported to feed the cattle that were once ranched here. This course is 6,168 yards with a par 72.

The North Course is a narrower course that travels along the slopes of Haleakala offering some spectacular panoramic views. The North Course has a par 72 and is 6,151 yards.

WAIKAPU

Sandalwood Golf Course is located at Waikapu, a par 72 course of 5,162 to 6,469 yards - depending on your choice of the blue, white, or red tee-offs. Mandatory cart fee is included. Non-player is extra $15 charge. Regular $75, Rental clubs $30, rental shoes $5, kamaaina discounts. (808) 242-4653 or FAX (808) 242-8089.

The Grand Waikapu Resort Country Club offers a special Golf and Spa package. A $200 all-inclusive package offers a round of 18-holes plus use of the golf course spa facilities. (Special program rate of $120). The course is 6,200 yards, par 71. Nine hole rate is half price. Club rental $30 for 18 holes, $15 for 9 holes. Shoe rental is $5. All green fees include golf cart. The ladies' facilities include jacuzzi, sauna, showers, TV, lounge, and juice bar. The men's features a furo (Japanese bath) sauna, showers, and lounge area. What a way to finish your day of golf! Spa hours daily from 11am-7pm.

In 1949 Frank Lloyd Wright designed a luxury home for the Windfohr family in Fort Worth, Texas. The home was never built. In 1952, Raul Bailleres, a Cabinet

Member of the Mexican Government, had the Windfohr design modified for a site on an Acapulco cliffside. Unfortunately, the Dailleres' suffered the loss of their son, and the project was abandoned. In 1957, Marilyn Monroe and her husband Arthur Miller, requested Mr. Wright design a country home for them in Connecticut. Mr. Wright, being fond of this particular design, again modified the original for Monroe and Miller, and once again the project was abandoned. The design was ultimately purchased for Taliesen West by the Grand Waikapu Country Club owners and has been constructed as the Grand Waikapu Country Club. The Grand Waikapu Country Club clubhouse is tri-level with two thirds of the building underground, and measuring 74,788 square feet. (808) 244-7888.

SPRECKELSVILLE

The Maui Country Club is a private course which invites visitors to play on Mondays only. Call on Sunday after 9 am to schedule Monday tee times. It originally opened in 1925. The front nine holes have a par 37 as do the back nine. Green fees are $45 cart included for 9 or 18 holes. (808) 877-0616.

PUKALANI

Pukalani Country Club and Golf Course is nestled on 160 acres along the slopes of Haleakala and affords a tremendous panoramic view of Central Maui and the ocean from every hole. Designed by Bob Baldock, the first nine holes opened in 1980. Nine additional holes have been added making a 6,692 yard (par 72) course. Green fees are $50, twilight $35, cart included. (808) 572-1314.

KAHULUI / WAILUKU

The Waiehu Municipal Course, which is north of Wailuku, opened with nine holes in 1929 and an additional nine holes were added later. The men's course is 5,330 yards/ par 72, women's course is 5,511 yards/par 71. Green fees are $25 weekdays and $30 weekends and holidays. A cart is optional. $7.50 per person for 9 holes, $15 per person for 18 holes. Inexpensive food and drink at the Waiehu Inn located on the course. (808) 243-7400 or pro shop 244-5934.

The Greens at Maui Lani, a challenging new 18-hole golf course and clubhouse designed by Robin Nelson (who also designed Maui's Sandalwood course and the Mauna Lani course on the Big Island) winds from Wailuku through Kahului. Take the newly-constructed Maui Lani Parkway (near the Maui Memorial Hospital) from Wailuku or look for the sign on Kuihelani Highway, several miles before you approach Kahului at the First Assembly of God on Dairy Road. Still under construction, we don't have word on green fees yet, but they should be in the moderate range. No phone number as we go to press, so check the local Maui phone book or directory assistance. The Clubhouse was expected to open in October; the greens by the beginning of 1999 - or as soon as the grass grows in!

THE ISLAND OF LANA'I

Two 18-hole courses are offered on Lana'i, *The Challenge at Manele* (808) 565-2222 and *The Experience at Koele* (808) 565-4653. Non-guests are charged $175 for either course, resort guests pay $125 per person. Both rates include cart. Reservations can be made from the mainland by calling 1-800-321-4666. A day package which includes round-trip transportation via the Expeditions out of Lahaina, green fees, and Lana'i island transfers is available, (808) 565-7227. Trilogy Excursions can be reached at 1-800-874-2666 or (808) 661-4743. They also offer a golf surf & turf package at The Challenge at Manele course. See the Lana'i section of this guide for course descriptions.

GOLF - MINIATURE

The 18-hole miniature golf course is on the roof of the *Embassy Vacation Resort* in Honokowai. Open from 9am-9pm daily. Adults $5; $2.50 ages 12 & under. Call (808) 661-2000.

HANG GLIDING

Hang Gliding Maui - Motorized and non-motorized hang-gliding flights. Non-motorized hangliding from the top of Haleakala down to the 2,000 ft. level (a vertical drop of 8,000 feet) is $250 including a 24 exposure film from a wing-mounted camera. Maximum 200 lb. weight limit. Flight time varies 25-60 minutes. Non-motorized is $90 for a half hour flight out of Hana. An hour flight is $150. Weight maximum is 230-240 lbs. Extra $25 for camera. Phone or FAX (808) 572-6557.

Proflyght - No experience? Enjoy paragliding via tandem flights with experienced pilots or as a solo venture which includes ground skimming on their bunny slope. Certification Course SPR (solo paragliding rating) available. They also sell new and used equipment. (808) 874-5433. FAX (808) 878-6869. <WWW> E-Mail: gliding@maui.net

HELICOPTER TOURS

The price of an hour helicopter excursion may make you think twice. After all it could be a week's worth of groceries at home. We had visited Maui for 7 years before we finally decided to see what everyone else was raving about. It proved to be the ultimate island excursion. When choosing a special activity for your Maui holiday, we'd suggest putting a helicopter flight at the top of the list. (When you get home you can eat beans for a month!) Adjectives cannot describe the thrill of a helicopter flight above majestic Maui. Among the most popular tours is the Haleakala Crater/Hana trip which contrasts the desolate volcanic crater with the lush vegetation of the Hana area. Maui's innermost secrets unfold as the camera's shutter works frantically to capture the memories (one roll is simply not enough) and pilots narrate as you pass by waterfalls cascading into cool mountain pools. Truly an outstanding experience. Another option is the West Maui to Moloka'i, which affords an incredible opportunity see the whales from a birds eye view between November and April (whale season). Keeping up with the prices is impossible. Listed are standard fares, and we hope you'll be delighted to learn of some special discount rates if you call directly to the helicopter company for reservations. Currently all helicopters depart from the Kahului heliport. Most companies include a video of your trip, some are now charging an additional fee for this service.

In choosing a helicopter tour, you should know that there are several different types of helicopters with different seating configurations. The Hughes 500 is a four-passenger with two passengers in front and two in the back, so each passenger has their own window. The Bell Jet Ranger is a four-passenger with one passenger in front next to the pilot and three in the back seat. The AStar has two passengers in the front and four passengers in the rear seat.

Air Maui - Owners Steven and Penni Eggi relocated to Maui from Kaua'i after Hurricane Iniki and offer flights aboard their six-passenger AStar aircraft. Steve has been flying for 30 years and has logged 20,000 hours flying in a helicopter. A family operation, the office staff and crew range from brothers and mothers to best friends. 45 minute Haleakala/Hana $135, Circle Island 60-65 minutes $179; West-Maui/Moloka'i $189. (808) 877-7005.

Alexair - Features four passenger Hughes 500 helicopters. West Maui Specials begin at $69. A variety of trips include West Maui $99, East Maui $110, Circle Island $175, deluxe circle island with ground stop $240. (808) 871-0792 or 1-888-418-8458 <WWW> Email: alexair@mauigateway.com

Blue Hawaiian - They began on Maui in 1985 and offer a variety of aerial and air-ground tour combinations in their six-passenger AStar. Hana/Haleakala, 45 minutes, $135; West Maui, 30 minutes, $100, Complete Island 65-70 minutes $180, Moloka'i/West Maui 65-70 minutes $180, Sunset Spectacular 60 minutes (with 20 minute ground stop) $195, Complete Island with ground stop $220. Also custom charters and wedding packages. Their multi-million dollar terminal encompasses 9,600 sq. ft. including a customer lounge area with an atrium, waterfalls, and a 1,000 gallon reef aquarium. Blue Hawaiian was chosen to help shoot the aerial photography on such Hawaii-based films as *Jurassic Park, The Lost World, George of the Jungle, Honeymoon in Las Vegas, Crimson Tide, Flight of the Intruder*, and most recently 1998's *Six Days-Seven Nights*. (They'll shoot *your* live video, too, for an additional fee.) The first helicopter tour company in the US to be certified under the national "Tour Operators Program of Safety," they have maintained a flawless safety record since 1985 and have won the 5-Star Diamond Award of Quality, Service and Safety from the American Academy of Hospitality Services for the past three years. (808) 871-8844, FAX (808) 871-6971. Toll free 1-800-745-BLUE. <www.bluehawaiian.com> Email: blue@maui.net.

Hawaii Helicopters Inc. - 6-passenger AStar jet turbine helicopters. Trips include Rainbow Special to East Maui, Haleakala and Hana 40-45 min. $135, Valley Isle Deluxe $179, West Maui/Moloka'i $179, Hana Heli-Trek (5 hours, air and ground) $199. 1-800-367-7095 or (808) 877-3900.

Sunshine Helicopters Inc. ★ - Maui's most experienced pilots fly you with comfort in their "Black Beauties" -- Sunshine's 1993-1994 AStar helicopters featuring state-of-the-art audio and video systems. Three external cameras and one cockpit camera capture live video of your actual flight including passenger reactions. Air-conditioned comfort and recordable CD players on board make for a pleasurable ride into our nation's largest rainforest that is "above the rest." The Hana Grand Adventure ($199) is a combination van tour to Hana with lunch at Hamoa Beach and a swim stop plus a 40-minute helicopter tour of Hana and the rainforest. The five-hour Paniolo Horseback Combination ($229) includes a 30-minute flight with lunch and a horseback ride. Journey into an actual working cattle ranch in the heart of West Maui, then after a western-style open pit BBQ lunch, take off for a full helicopter tour of West Maui. (Weight limit 250 lbs., minimum age 11 years, Western or Hawaiian saddle style.) West Maui Deluxe tour $99; Hana/Haleakala Special $135; Circle Island Special $179; Circle Island Special with beverage stop at Nu'u (an ancient Hawaiian temple ruin overlook) $209; West Maui Moloka'i Tour $179. We've flown with Sunshine on a number of occasions and can recommend their courteous ground crew along with their engaging and informative pilots. (808) 871-0722 or 1-800-544-2520, FAX (808) 871-0682. <www.sunshinehelicopters.com> Email: sales@sunshinehelicopters.com.

Windward Aviation - They fly the McDonnell Douglas Notar, a no tail rotor helicopter that they tell us is the worlds quietest. Sightseeing available on charter basis only. For more information call (808) 877-3368.

HIKING

Maui offers many excellent hiking opportunities for the experienced hiker, or for a family outing. Comprehensive hiking information is available from several excellent references (see ORDERING INFORMATION). Craig Chisholm and his wife Eila were the pioneers in the field of Hawaiian hiking information with the 1975 release of *Hawaiian Hiking Trails*, and it is continually updated. They also publish *Kaua'i Hiking Trails*. The Chisholm's books are attractively done with beautiful color photographs in the frontpiece and easy to follow U.S. Geological maps for each of the hikes. Throughout the text are black and white photos. These books are thoroughly researched by the authors and very accurate. The *Hawaiian Hiking Trails* book has six trails described for Maui.

Robert Smith's *Hiking Maui* was first published in September 1977. He continues to update his book every couple of years, the latest in April, 1997. He also has books for the other islands. The books are compact in size with a color cover and a scattering of black and white photographs and maps. The Maui edition covers 27 trails.

Kathy Morey writes *Maui Trails* which is published by Wilderness Press. There are over 50 trails listed in the hiking table of contents, however, some are really more walks than hikes. It has plenty of easy-to-use maps. Also guides for O'ahu, Kaua'i and The Big Island.

We're not going to even attempt to cover the many hiking trails available on Maui, but would like to share with you several guided and non-guided hiking experiences which we have enjoyed.

There are many interesting and diverse hiking opportunities on Maui. They vary from hiking in a volcanic crater, strolling among a grove of eucalyptus, exploring a rocky shoreline, or walking through a tropical rainforest.

The **Lahaina Pali Trail** was originally built as a foot trail and later used as a horse trail. (While horses were introduced to the islands in 1803, their use was restricted to chiefs or *alii* until the middle of the century.) It traverses from sea level to an elevation on the *Kealaloloa Ridge* of 1600 feet. Portions of the old trail were well preserved. Today, access to the trailhead is possible through the courtesy of the Wailuku Agribusiness Company. An interesting and informative guide for the trail and the area is provided by the Na Ala Hele Statewide Trail and Access Program, a Division of Forestry and Wildlife. It corresponds to markers along the trail and provides some fascinating historical narratives. For example, in by-gone days robbers would wait along the trail, ready to pounce on unsuspecting travelers! If you'd like information on the trail, the free booklet or would be interested in volunteering for trail maintenance call (808) 871-2521.

Another interesting hike is at the Pu'u O La'i Cinder cone, the red-earth hillock which juts out to the sea just beyond the cover fronting the Maui Prince Hotel. It is one of Haleakala's craters (under which is a large cave), and is said to be the sacred dwelling place of Mano, the ancestral shark deity. To reach the top of the cinder cone, turn right on the first dirt path after the hotel, then pass giant cacti and dry brush to reach the hiking trail. The short 15-minute hike uphill offers a rewarding sight of the coast - a black sand beach just below the hill, and broad white beaches and black lava contrasting with the lush greens of the Makena Golf Course.

With permission of Craig Chisholm, the following is one of his favorite hikes. The Waihee Ridge hike requires 3 1/2 hours, round trip and is 4.5 miles. It traverses from an elevation of 1,050 feet to a high point of 2,563. This is just one of a few excellent hikes described in Chisholm's *Hawaiian Hiking Trails* guide.

West Maui's valleys, deeper and more rugged than East Maui's, show that erosion has had a longer time to work without interruption by volcanic building. The Waihee Ridge Trail leads up onto a ridge above such deep valleys, offering spectacular scenery. Waihee Ridge, preserved from erosion by exceptionally durable lava, climbs gradually from pasture land and guava thickets up into wetter areas of West Maui where there is still much native vegetation. There are fine views of the waterfalls in the Makamakaole Valley, the Waihee Valley, central Maui, and, finally, Mount Eke. There is no drinkable water along the route, but the trail is well-marked and in good shape. Choose a dry day. ROUTE: Drive northwest about four miles from Wailuku along the coastline to Waihee. Continue from Waihee Elementary School 2.7 miles farther northwest, to a paved turnoff, on the left, leading to the Boy Scouts' Camp Maluhia. Turn there and drive up 0.9 miles. The trailhead is at a parking area on the left side of the road, before reaching the Scout camp, and is probably marked by a brown "Na Ala Hele" sign. Go through the cattle fence at the first of three stiles, designed, no doubt in Hell's seventh circle for the torment of gluttons. A right of way easement leads for 0.3 miles straight southwest up the hill through private pasture to the boundary of the West Maui Forest Reserve, which is marked by a fence with a second narrow stile. Note the differences in vegetation delineated by the fence. Beyond the fence the shady path, which is also a dirt road, is flanked by planted Norfolk Island pine on the left and invading guava on the right. The road soon disappears as the trail swings right to sidehill up the slope. Just as the trail turns left on a switchback, there is a fine view of a double waterfall in the Makamakaole Valley, to the north. The trail continues a switchbacking ascent along the ridgeline, passing good views of the deep Waihee Valley, Mount Eke, waterfalls, and central Maui across to Haleakala. At about 1.6 miles the trail rounds a corner, passes between Norfolk Island pine, and comes to a small, open swampy area. The trail crosses it and switchbacks up to the top of Lanilili. Note and avoid the deep sinkholes along the trail climbing up Lanilili. The trail ends at the two and a quarter mile mark, a good place for a picnic. There are fine views of Mt. Eke to the southwest and down to wild rain-soaked peat swamps, forested ridges, and steep valleys of the West Maui Natural Area Reserve, Kahakuloa Section. Return as you came. (Hawaiian Hiking Trails is available from Paradise Publications. See ORDERING INFORMATION.

Among the most incredible adventures to be experienced on Maui is one - or more - of the hikes your personal guide *Ken Schmitt* and his staff have available. These hikes (for 4-8 people only) can encompass waterfalls and pools, ridges with panoramic views, rock formations, spectacular redwood forests (yes, there are!), the incomparable Haleakala Crater, or ancient structures found in East Maui. Arriving on Maui in 1979, Ken has spent much of that time living, exploring, and subsisting out-of-doors and experiencing the "Natural Energy" of this island. This soft spoken man offers a wealth of detailed knowledge on the legends, flora, fauna and geography of Maui's many diverse areas.

Ken has traversed the island nearly 400 times and established his eight day-hikes after considerable exploration. His favorites are the 8 and 12 mile crater hikes which he says offer unique, incredible beauty and magic, unlike anywhere else in the world. The early Hawaiians considered Haleakala to be the vortex of one of the strongest natural power points on earth.

Ken has expanded from a one-man operation to a number of experienced guides. John Jasinski specializes in marine biology, and is especially knowledgeable in music and aviation. Lono Hunter is a political science, philosophy, and economics major and his thesis was on the Hawaiian sovereignty movement. Cathy Davenport is an archeologist and is working on her masters in anthropology. Helga Fiederer, from Germany, is a botanist who lived with native tribes of the Amazon for several years studying tropical rain forest plants.

The hikes are tailored to the desires and capabilities of the individual or group and run 1/2 or full day (5-12 hours). They range from very easy for the inexperienced to fairly rugged. These outings are more than mere hikes, however, as Ken and his staff specialize in arranging tours that emphasize the teaching of the natural history of Maui and the Hawaiian islands. Tours run $70-$110 (children are less).

Hikers are supplied with waterproof day packs, picnic lunch, specially designed Japanese fishing slippers, wild fruit and, of course, the incredible knowledge of Ken. Tours include transportation to the trails from their meeting spots in new, air-conditioned tour vans.

Ken and his staff can be reached at *Hike Maui*, (808) 879-5270, FAX (808) 876-0308 or by writing *Ken Schmitt*, P.O. Box 330969, Kahului, Maui, HI 96733. Following is a sample of the excursions you might be able to enjoy with Ken and crew!

HALEAKALA

A hike with Ken Schmitt is a thrill for all the senses. Not only does he pack a great lunch and yummy snacks, but the hike provides beauty for the eyes; cool, fresh air for the lungs; tantalizing scents for the nose; peace and serenity for the ears; and an opportunity to touch and get in touch with Maui's natural beauty.

We chose a trip to Haleakala to see the awesome crater up close. The trip was an 8-mile hike down Switchback (Halemauu) Trail to the Holua cabin and back. The first mile of the trek was over somewhat rocky, but fairly level, terrain. The next mile seemed like three as we descended seemingly endless hairpin twists down the side of the crater with changing panoramic vistas at each turn. Sometimes fog would eerily sweep in, hovering around and obscuring the view completely, only to soon move away. The vegetation (following a period of heavy rains) was exceptionally lush. All the greenery seemed quite out of place in the usually rather desolate crater.

We continued along the crater floor and past the Holua cabin to reach the Holua lava tube. The small opening was not marked and could be easily overlooked. A small sign advised the use of lights inside the cave. We prepared our flashlights and bundled up for the cooler temperatures to be encountered below. A ladder set by the park service provides access. Once at the base of the ladder, the cavern was large, cool and dark. While there were several directions that lead quickly to dead ends, Ken took us further down the main tube. The cavern was so large that seldom did we have to do more than occasionally duck. Once inside we turned out the lights to enjoy a few moments of the quiet darkness. The tube travels about 100 yards with a gradual ascent to daylight. As daylight peeks down through the dark shaft, it appears the end is in sight. Another turn in the tunnel reveals not the end, but a natural altar-like flat rock piled with assorted stones. Light cascading through a hole in the ceiling casts an almost supernatural glow to eyes now accustomed to the darkness. The effect is to create a luminescence on the stones making them appear to be statues set in a natural cathedral. A very awesome experience. Returning to the cabin, we picnicked on the grounds while very friendly nene geese begged for handouts. Ken advised against feeding them as the park rangers prefer these geese not become dependent on human handouts.

After a rest in the warm sun, we retraced our path back up Switchback Trail to the van and continued on to enjoy the summit before heading back to town. Other more strenuous and lengthy crater ventures include the Sliding Sands Trail and one that traverses down the side of the volcano through the Kaupo Gap. Available through Paradise Publications are two excellent photo-filled books from K.C. Publications: *Haleakala* and *Hawai'i Volcanos*. See Order Information.

UPCOUNTRY MAUI

Poli Poli Springs Recreational Area is ideally situated on the leeward slopes of Haleakala. Cool crisp mountain air provides a temperate climate for hiking and the trails are suitable for the entire family. Since the weather can be cool, warm attire and rain apparel should be included in your day or night pack, however, the clouds often clear and treat visitors to a sunny and very mild afternoon. To get to the turn off, go just past the Kula Botanical Gardens and turn on Waipoli Rd., or go 3/10 mile past the junction of Hwy 37 and Hwy 277. Follow the paved, steep and windy road approximately eight miles. The last portion is graded, but rain quickly makes the roads impassable for all but 4-wheel drive vehicles. *WARNING: Rental car agencies are not responsible for damage done to cars that travel this road.*

We have found it passable in a car with high clearance only if the road has been recently graded and is dry. Once you reach the park there is a graveled parking area and a grassy camping area. There are two BBQ's and the luxury of a flush toilet in a small outhouse. Drinking water is available. Trail options include a 0.8 mile trek to the Redwood Forest, a 6 mile Haleakala Trail, 4.8 mile loop trail, 1.0 mile to the cave shelter, and 1.5 miles to Plum Trail.

The 4.8 mile loop is a very easy trail and with frequent snack stops, even our (then) three-year-old was able to make it the entire distance. There is an array of lush foliage and plums may be ripe if you arrive during June and July. The clouds can roll quickly in, causing it to be pleasant and warm one minute and cool the next, as well as creating some interesting lighting effects amongst the trees. The cave shelter, is a bit of a disappointment. It is a shallow cavern and reaching it meant a descent down a steep incline of loose gravel that was too difficult for our young ones. The eucalyptus was especially fragrant as the fallen leaves crunched underneath our tennis shoes. An area along the trail that had been freshly rutted by wild boars demonstrated the incredible power of these animals. On one trip we heard a rustling in the bushes nearby followed by grunting sounds. We have been told that while you definitely want to avoid the wild boars, they are accustomed to being hunted and will also choose to avoid you. Apparently we were down wind of them and since they have poor eyesight we passed by quietly without them noticing us and without seeing them.

HIKING GROUPS

Sierra Club Maui Group of the Hawaii Chapter invites the public to join their guided hikes. This is a wonderful and affordable way to enjoy Maui with a knowledgeable group of people. There are several weekend outings every month. They offer a variety of hikes - introductory, youth, and educational. Donations are accepted. The main office Sierra Club, Hawaii Chapter, is in Honolulu (808) 538-6616. On Maui call (808) 573-4147 for voice mail information and schedules.

The Hawai'i Nature Center at Iao Valley has just opened their new Interactive Science Arcade which houses a towering glass solarium and offers more than 30 hands-on exhibits and experiences focusing on Hawai'i's natural history. Rain forest explorations, dispersal arcade games, live insect and stream animal exhibits along with a dragonfly ride make this a unique, adventuresome and educational attraction. Open 10am-4pm. Admission $6A, 4C. (See "Travel with Children" section for information on their hiking adventures for families.)

The Waikamoi Preserve, Box 1716, Makawao, Maui, HI 96768. For reservations call (808) 572-7849 or FAX (808) 572-1375. On the second Saturday of every month hikes are conducted on this 5,230 acre Nature Conservancy Preserve located on the northeast slope of Haleakala. The preserve was established in 1983 in cooperation with Haleakala Ranch Company and protects this vital habitat for 14 native Hawaiian birds, eight of which are endangered.

Vegetation types range from dense rain forests to open shrub and grasslands to introduced pine tree plantations. The area is remote and very rugged with many steep gulches. The area is named after a stream that runs through the property. Along with a waiver and release form, they will provide you with an information sheet on hiking dates, work party dates as well as background on the native and introduced birds of the area and a brochure on the many island areas throughout the Hawaiian chain that are under their protection. Elevation in the Waikamoi Preserve ranges from 4,400-9,000 feet and annual rainfall varies from 50-200 inches per year. Temperature ranges are 35-70 degrees. The hike begins at Hosmer Grove in Haleakala National Park at 9 am and finishes around 1pm at the same location. They recommend binoculars, cameras as well as warm rain gear and non-canvas shoes. The Nature Conservancy is a non-profit Environmental Awareness Group which has under its protection 13,000 acres of habitat critical to the survival of many of Hawaii's native plants and animals. A donation is appreciated. Reservations are required.

Haleakala National Park offers guided hikes to two different areas twice weekly, 9 am to noon. The hikes are free of charge, but admission to the National Park is $10. Verify by calling their recording at (808) 572-4400.

A reminder! Hiking off established trails without a knowledgeable guide is *definitely* not advised, however, as we mentioned, the following sources will help you find and enjoy many established hikes. *Hawaiian Hiking Trails* by Craig Chisholm, 128 pages, $15.95, has nearly 50 hiking trails throughout the islands, seven of these are on Maui. Robert Smith's book *Hiking Maui* 160 pages, $10.95, will guide you on 27 fairly accessible trails throughout Maui. (See ORDERING INFORMATION).

Big Kahuna Kayak - In addition to surfing and kayaking, they also do rainforest hikes. (808) 875-6395. <WWW>

Maui Cave Adventures, PO Box 40, Hana, HI. Chuck Thorne offers several exciting and unique hiking tours. You have a daily opportunity to trek on a two, four or six hour adventure through Maui's largest lava tube. It traverses miles and miles underground. This is the only Hawaiian cave open to such an activity. (The Hawaii state archeologist has confirmed that this is not a burial cave.) The name of this region in Hana is Ka'eleku, and Chuck recently discovered that the translation is "Standing in a dark hollow cavity." Obviously, the early Hawaiians felt that this cave was a prominent landmark in the area! The two-hour cave tour is open to children 7-17 years at half price with accompanying adult. There is some crawling and ducking as you traverse about 2 miles round trip. $50 plus tax per person. Longer hikes are limited to spelunkers 18 years and older. Call for tour times, rates, and other information. Phone 8am-8pm Hawai'i time: (808) 248-7308. Or visit their website at: <www.maui.net/~hanacave>

Paths in Paradise - Owner/operator Dr. Renate Gassmann-Duvall will explore the Island of Maui with you. Half and full day hikes, waterfalls, rainforests, and family adventure. Adults $75-110, child $55-85. (808) 573-0094 <WWW>

HORSEBACK RIDING

Historically, the first six horses arrived on the islands in 1803 from Baja California. These wild mustangs were named "Lio" by the Hawaiians, which means "open eyes wide in terror." They roamed and multiplied along the volcanic slopes of Maui and the Big Island until they numbered 11,000. They adjusted quickly to the rough terrain and had a reputation for terrific stamina. Today these ponies, also known as Kanaka ponies or Mauna Loa ponies, are all but extinct with fewer than a dozen purebreds still in existence. Lush waterfalls, pineapple fields stretching up the mountain's flanks, cane fields, kukui nut forests, and Haleakala's huge crater are all scenic environs that can be enjoyed on horseback. Beginner, intermediate, or experienced rides can last from 1-2 hours or up to three days. Most stables have age and weight restrictions.

Adventures on Horseback - A 6-hour "Waterfall Adventure Ride" outside Haiku includes lunch and gear. Enjoy the cliffs of North Maui, the slopes of Haleakala, the old Hana Highway, rainforest streams, and secluded waterfalls. Breakfast, picnic lunch, and swimming. Maximum 6 riders. Children 16 years of age or older are welcome provided they have prior riding experience. Reservations (808) 242-7445. Office (808) 572-6211. FAX (808) 572-4996.

Crater Bound - PO Box 265, Kula, HI 96790. Craig Moore offers mule rides into Haleakala Crater with departures from the Visitor Center inside the park. They feature a 2-hour Aloha Ride for $95 which departs 8:45 am and 11:45 am. It descends from 10,000 feet to 8,300 feet in elevation. Their 6-hour Picnic Ride departs at 8:45pm and runs $155. Their Paniolo Ride includes refreshments and lunch and costs $190. This ride descends from 10,000 feet to 7,300 feet in elevation and offers a chance to view scenic points of interest such as central crater, the bottomless pit, Pele's paint pot, and Pele's pig pen. $190. Recorded information (808) 878-1743. Reservations (808) 244-6853.

Hotel Hana Maui - Guided trail rides around the 4,500 acre working cattle ranch on open range, shoreline, rain forest, and mountains. Maximum 10 riders. (808) 248-8211.

Ironwood Ranch - Follow Honoapiilani Highway 11 miles north of Lahaina, entrance near exit for Napili where a van picks you up. Trips are available for beginning, intermediate, or advanced riders in either English or Western style. Rides tour the Honolua Plantation and the West Maui foothills. $75-135. (808) 669-4991 or 669-4702.

Makena Stables - 8299 South Makena Rd., located at La Perouse Bay. Owner operated since 1983 by Patrick and Helaine Borge, their horses were personally raised and trained. They match each person to their horse by ability and offer help and lessons as needed. All of their rides are on Ulupalakua Ranch, a 20,000 acre open range ranch which overlooks the Ahihi-Kinau Reserve, La Perouse Bay, and the lava flows. A two-hour introductory ride goes out in the morning at $99 per person. This ride climbs to Kalua O Lapa, the vent which was the last eruption of Haleakala. It offers panoramic views of the south slopes of Haleakala,

La Perouse Bay, and the islands of Kaho'olawe, Molokini, Lana'i, and Moloka'i. Three-hour rides are designed for the intermediate to experienced rider. This trip continues up the slopes of Ulupalakua Ranch to the cinder hills overlooking La Perouse Bay. The variety and terrain of the trails are more challenging. Sunset (occasional) and morning rides include a break for beverages and snacks $115-130. Their La Perouse Bay Lunch Ride leaves in the morning and tours the south slope of Haleakala through Ulupalakua Ranch. A leisurely picnic lunch is enjoyed at La Perouse Bay. Offered for advanced riders $160. Horseback ride can also can be combined with snorkeling - water and weather permitting. Bring your own snorkel gear. (Due to difficult entry into the water, this is for the experienced snorkeler.) All rides are guided and done Western style. They are all physically strenuous and it is recommended that all riders be in good physical condition. Weight limit is 205 lb. Maximum of six riders. Children 12-14 years with experience are welcome when accompanied by an adult. (808) 879-0244.

Mendes Ranch - Journey into an actual working cattle ranch in the heart of West Maui. After a western-style open-pit BBQ lunch, take off with Sunshine Helicopters for a full tour of West Maui. The Paniolo Horseback Adventure includes lunch, but no helicopter tour $130. With helicopter tour $229. Weight limit 250 pounds, minimum age 11 years, Western or Hawaiian saddle style. (808) 871-5222.

Ohe'o Stables - Morning ride includes continental breakfast, snacks, juice $119. The midday ride includes continental breakfast and lunch $139. Travel around the backslope of Haleakala in the Kipahulu District. Stables located 25 minutes past Hana on County Road 31. (808) 667-2222.

Pony Express Tours - Has trips across Haleakala Ranch (the largest working cattle ranch on Maui) and into Haleakala Crater. Haleakala Ranch treks: one-hour introductory, two-hour intermediate, or Advanced Ranch Rides $40-85. Trips available Monday through Saturday. 7.5 and 12 mile trips into Haleakala Crater $120-150. (808) 667-2200. Website: < www.maui.net/ ~ ponyex >

Seahorse Ranch - Their 3-1/2 hour ride includes lunch at a waterfall and is offered Monday-Saturday for 7 persons or less at $99. Highway 340 Waiehu at 10 mile marker. (808) 244-9862.

Thompson Riding Stables - Located on Thompson Rd. in Kula, the Thompson Ranch was established in 1902. Located at the 3,700 foot elevation, they offer trail and crater tours, sunset and picnic rides. Child under age 4 can ride with adult. 1 1/2 and 2 hour $50-60 with snack & beverage. Sunset rides available on charter basis. (808) 878-1910 or (808) 244-7412.

If you prefer a little something between you and the horse, horse-drawn rides are available on both sides of the island:

Royal Hawaiian Carriages offers romantic evening picnics transported by horse-drawn carriage. Choice of several romantic locations for a gourmet picnic of appetizers (vegetable crudite, fresh tropical fruit, and cheese & crackers), choice of entree (Herb Chicken, Seafood Salad, or try their Plantation Cobb Salad), and cinnamon apple dessert. Narrated tour of the old Honolua Plantation Villages (now the site of The Ritz-Carlton and Kapalua Bay Resorts) includes the Honolua Plantation Store, the oldest park on Maui, and the original residence of D. T. Fleming. Pick up at The Ritz-Carlton or in the Kapalua Resort. Two-hour tours offered at sunset or later. Inclusive prices are $210 for 2, $290 for 3, or $350 for 4. One-hour tour for 2 at $160. (808) 669-1100. (24 hour advance booking required.)

SchinDola Farms can take up to 20 people on a horse-drawn wagon ride through the "wine country" of Ulupalakua to visit the historic Tedeschi Winery. (Kind of like an old-fashioned hay ride - without the hay!) Daily (except Monday) at 9am, 11am, and 1pm. The 1 1/2 hour tours are $45 per person; $55 with breakfast or lunch at the Ulupalakua Ranch Store and Deli. Every third child (under 12) is free when accompanied by a paying adult. (808) 573-9174.

HUNTING / GUN CLUBS   (Also see Sporting Clays)

Contact Bob Caires, owner/guide of *Hunting Adventures of Maui, Inc.*, 1745 Kapakalua Rd., Haiku, Maui, HI 96708. Year round hunting season. Game includes Spanish Goat (*kao*) and Wild Boar (*Pua'a*). Hunting on 100,000 acres of privately owned ranches with all equipment provided. Rates: Goat $450 one person, $375 second and third person each. Boar $500 one person, $400 second and third person each. Non-hunters $100. Three persons maximum. Includes sunrise-sunset hunt, food, beverages, four-wheel drive transportation, clothing, boots, packs, meat storage and packing for home shipment, Kahului airport pick up. Rifle rentals and taxidermy available. Sightseeing safaris also available. A non-resident hunting license is required and you must provide your hunter safety card to purchase the license. Cost is $100. (808) 572-8214.

Lahaina Western Gun Club features an indoor shooting range with 44 magnum and 357 magnum revolver handguns as well as others. Open 7 days a week at Lahaina Center, behind the Hard Rock Cafe near the movie theaters. (808) 661-8833.

JET SKIING

Thrillcraft activities, which include parasailing and jetskiing have been banned during whale season. The "open season" for participating in jet skiing recreation is May 16th-December 14th.

Currently the only jet ski operation, *Pacific Jet Ski Rental*, is at the south end of Kaanapali Beach at Hanaka'o'o Beach Park. They have two and three passenger wave runners. Rental prices are per jet ski, not per person. Super Jet - Wave Runner: 1/2 hr. $45, 1 hr. $65, two people max. Waverunner III: 1/2 hr. $55, 1 hr. $76, three people max. An additional charge of $10 per person is charged if more than two people use the Super Jet or Waverunner and if more than three people use the Waverunner III. Hawaiian law requires a person be 15 years old to operate a machine by himself. Younger persons can ride as a passenger on the waverunner with someone who is at least 15 years of age. All renters are fitted with a life vest. Mon-Sat 9am-4pm (weather permitting). (808) 667-2066.

KAYAKING

Big Kahuna Kayak - Rainforest hikes, surfing school and kayaking tours & rentals. (808) 875-6395. <WWW>

Kaanapali Windsurfing School - Kayak rentals: 1 hour $15 one person, $25 two persons. Kayak tour 9am-noon, $65 includes snorkel, lunch, pickup in Kaanapali or Lahaina. (808) 667-1964.

Keli'i's Kayaking - South Shore of Maui (Turtle Adventure) 2 1/2 hours $55, 4 1/2 hours $85. West Shore 2 1/2 hours $55, 4 1/2 hours $85. North Shore 3 hours $69, 5 hours $99. Maui Sunset 2 1/2 hours $55. Custom tours on request. Call (808) 874-7652.

South Pacific Kayaks - Rainbow Mall at 2439 S. Kihei Rd. They offer introductory paddle and snorkel excursions with short paddling distances combined with offshore snorkeling 2 1/2 - 3 hrs $59. Marine Reserve Explorer trip explores for turtle, dolphin, and whales as it travels along the southern coast with time for snorkeling and a deli lunch. 6 1/2 hours $89. Also available are single and double kayaks as well as car racks, life vests, snorkel gear, and more. (808) 875-4848. 1-800-776-2326.

Tradewind Kayaks - "Wet Your Okole" is a 2 1/2 hour introductory shoreline kayak and snorkel trip $55. Their barefoot special is offered in the winter: "Tharr She Blows," is a 2 1/2 hour whale watching adventure $49. The "Marine Reserve Experience" is a trip to La Perouse along the Kinao lava flow. This 4 1/2 hour excursion runs $75. Their "Exotic Tropical Sunset" is a two-hour trip for $45. (808) 879-2247.

LAND TOURS

Land excursions on Maui are centered upon two major attractions, Hana & the O'heo Valley, and Haleakala Crater. Lesser attractions are trips to the Iao Valley or around West Maui. You can do all of this by car (refer to the WHERE TO STAY - WHAT TO SEE chapter), however, with a tour you can sit back and enjoy the scenery while a professional guide discourses on the history, flora, fauna, and geography of the area. The single most important item on any tour is a good guide/driver and, unfortunately, the luck of the draw prevails here. Another (somewhat expensive) option is a personalized custom tour. A local resident will join you, in your car, for a tour of whatever or wherever you choose. You choose to do the driving or sign on your guide with your rental car company to do the driving. This may allow you the opportunity to linger at those places you enjoy the most, without following the pace of a group. Your guide may also be able to take you to locations the tour vans don't include. **Rent-a-Local** at (808) 877-4042 or 1-800-228-6284. (24 hour advance reservation)

Driving to Hana and back requires a full day and can be very grueling, so this is one trip we recommend you consider taking a tour. A Haleakala Crater tour spans 5-6 hours and can be enjoyed at sunrise (3am departure), midday or sunset. The West Maui and Iao Valley trips are half-day ventures. Only vans travel the road to Hana, however, large buses as well as vans are available for other trips. Prices are competitive and those listed here are correct at time of publication. Some trips include the cost of meals, others do not. Also available are one-day tours to the outer islands. The day begins with an early morning departure to the Big Island, O'ahu or Kaua'i. Some excursions provide a guided ground tour, others offer a rental car to explore the island on your own.

Akina Aloha Tours - This family-owned business has been operating exclusively on Maui for over 80 years. They specialize in ground transportation to groups, charters, and families for tours in their Belgium-made VanHool buses, mini buses, vans, sedans and late vintage limousines. Ecological Tour (Haleakala/Hawaii Nature Center/Maui Ocean Center) $78A, $70C; 8:15-3:15pm. Historical Tour (*Pihana Heiau*/Iao Valley/Bailey House/Lahainatown) $78A, $56C; 9am-2:45pm. Haleakala/Upcountry includes no host lunch at Kula Lodge and guided tour of Tedeschi Winery. $72A, $55C; 9am-2:45pm. Multi-language interpreters. Varying pick up times within the hour before and after above schedule. Admissions included; lunches on own. 1-800-800-3989. (808) 879-2828. FAX (808) 879-0523.

Ekahi Tours - 532 Keolani Place, Kahului, HI 96732. Tours of Hana $75 adult, $60 child, Sunrise Haleakala $60/50 via van. Other areas are arranged by charter at $68.50 per hour. The Kahakuloa Valley tour is an opportunity to enjoy a cultural experience at a Hawaiian *kuleana* (parcel of land) which is part of an *ahupua'a* (land division extending from the uplands to the oceans), located along the northwest coast of Maui. According to background information provided to us from Ekahi Tours, "The Kahakuloa Valley is inhabited by some of the same families of past generations of Hawaiians who were the original settlers 1,500 years ago and is the only village in existence that still has a working *Konohiki.*" A *Konohiki* is the caretaker of the *ahupua'a* and oversees the land and fishing rights. Formerly a policeman, Oliver Dukelow is a Hawaiian who now cultivates taro. Dukelow provides guests with background into the plants, taro farming, and the Hawaiian lifestyle. The half day trip runs $60 adults and $50 children and is only offered Tuesdays and Saturdays. The Hana and Sunrise tours are available to accompanied wheel chair guests. (808) 877-9775. FAX (808) 877-9776. Email: fun@ekahi.com

Kawika's 'Aina Tour Company - 505 Front Street, Suite 231, Lahaina, HI 96761. Tours are offered to Kahakuloa, a remote village on Maui's north shore. Tours are $80 per person. They also offer sunrise and sunset tours to Haleakala, $80 per person, and all day trips to Hana, $100 per person. (808) 667-2204.

RECREATION AND TOURS
Land Tours

Hidden Adventures - Provides ecotourism trips to explore Maui's unique environment. Family or high adventure half day tours to West Maui include exploring bamboo forests, tidepools or waterfalls $65. Full day family or high adventure tours $125. Arnold DeClercq gears his trips for families with children, or high adventure for those of you seeking more excitement. For the latter, you'll go four-wheeling to remote locations and hike into varying adventures. (808) 665-0559 or (808) 264-1423.

Open Eye Tours & Photos - Barry Fried is your guide, customizing a tour with (or without) walking to hidden hideaways around the island. A student of Hawaiian, Barry may guide you to taro patches, offer the opportunity to experience native healing plants, visit churches, monuments, museums, artists' studios, pre-contact Hawaiian sites, wildlife preserves, and other privately guided "off the map" adventures to places seldom seen. Hawaiian educational and environmentally focused. (808) 572-3483. < WWW > Email: openeye@aloha.net

Polynesian Adventure - Haleakala Sunrise $54.69 adult/$36.46 child, includes tax. Haleakala Day trip $57.29/$36.46. Hana $72.40/$46.87. They also offer one day trip to Kaua'i, The Big Island of Hawaii, or O'ahu. These one day, one island trips run $182.29/$177.08. (slightly higher for the O'ahu Circle Island tour). They also do a Hana Grand Adventure which is a land/helicopter tour $114/58/104.17. (808) 877-4242 or 1-800-622-3011 from Mainland U.S.

Rent-a-Local - Discover Maui in your car with an island resident as your guide. Explore the destinations of your choice. $195 for two people, 8 hours (plus your own gas). (808) 877-4042 or 1-800-228-6284.

Robert's Hawaii Tours - Offers land tours in their big air conditioned buses or vans. They depart to all scenic areas from Kahului, Kihei, Wailea, and the West Maui Hotels. Tours include: Kula/Iao Valley/Lahaina; Iao Valley/Lahaina; Haleakala/Iao Valley/Lahaina; Iao Valley/Haleakala Crater; Hana Highlights; Haleakala. Prices vary depending on tour, departure and arrival location. (808) 871-6226 or 1-800-831-5541 U.S. Mainland.

Sugar Cane Train - The Lahaina Kaanapali and Pacific Railroad is affectionately referred to as The Sugar Cane Train. In Lahaina in 1862, the harvesting of sugar cane was one of the island's biggest industries. More than 45,000 tons were produced from 5,000 acres. The Lahaina Kaanapali & Pacific Railroad began in 1882, replacing the slower method (mules and steers) of hauling sugar cane between the harvest area and the Pioneer Sugar Mill. This allowed a greater area of cane to be planted as well. By the 1900's the railroad was also transporting an ever-increasing number of workers to their jobs. In 1970, the Sugar Cane Train was once again brought back to life, but financial difficulties silenced the train whistle once more. In 1973, Mr. Willes B. Kyele purchased the railroad and brought life back to its engines. Currently two trains operate daily on a three foot narrow gauge railroad between 9am and 6pm. The trains are pulled by two steam locomotives, "Anaka" and "Myrtle." The locomotives were built in 1943 and were restored to resemble those that were used in Hawaii at the beginning of the 20th century.

The singing conductor will guide you through history as you wind through the cane fields of Lahaina. The train makes six round trips daily with one way fares for adults $10, round trip $14. Children 3-12 years are $5.50 one way, $7.50 round trip. Their main depot is located just outside of Lahaina (turn at the Pizza Hut sign). The Kaanapali Station is located across the highway from the resort area. The free Kaanapali trolley picks up at the Whalers Village and drops off at this station. The Puukolii boarding platform and parking lot is located on the Kapalua side of Kaanapali. They offer several package options: The Hawai'i Experience is a round trip train ride and Hawai'i Experience Domed Theater movie $19.95 adults and $10.95 children. The Land/Sea Adventure is a round trip train ride plus a one-hour tour on a submarine $41 adults; $21 children. They also offer combinations with helicopters and luaus. Be sure to purchase your return tickets early as they often sell out quickly. Reservations needed for groups of 12 or more. (808) 661-0080 (661-0089 recording) FAX (808) 661-4143.

<www.maui.net//~choochoo/sugrcane.html> Email: choochoo@maui.net

Temptation Tours ★ - If you'd really like to pamper yourself, then enjoy the luxury of a tour by these folks. Working in conjunction with a local helicopter company, they provide a unique option to either Hana or Upcountry Maui. The "Hana Sky-trek" ($199) is their ultimate package that begins with a helicopter trip to Hana, a tour of the town and Waianapanapa in a luxury van, an elegant lunch and then drive back to Kahului. Or the reverse trip where you drive to Hana and fly back. The Hana picnic ($110) is a round trip in their 6-8 passenger limo van, or with the Hana Ultimate, substitute lunch at the Hotel Hana Maui ($139). The Jungle Express ($249) is a Hana tour which includes round trip travel by small airplane from Kahului airport to the Hana airport. Then a van tour of Hana before your flight back to Kahului. The Summit Safari ($159) begins with an ascent up Haleakala in their luxury limo-van, to the eucalyptus

SUGAR TRAIN

forests and pastureland of the Thompson Ranch. An hour and a half to enjoy the view on horseback is followed by an elegant lunch at the Silver Cloud Ranch. Or choose an Upcountry Adventure which offers a trip to the summit of Haleakala, a tour through the Kula area with lunch at Makawao with a chance to visit the galleries there. They also offer a Haleakala Day and Haleakala Sunrise Tour ($115). (808) 877-8888. 1-800-817-1234. FAX (808) 876-0155.

Town & Country Limousine - Enjoy a private Hana tour in their chauffeured limousine. Daily tours begin with hotel pickup, a continental breakfast, open bar and lunch at the Hotel Hana Maui, returning at about 5pm. Price is $169 per person for 2 people/ $145 for 3/ $115 for 4.

Transhawaiian - Reservation number in Honolulu is (808) 566-7333. Haleakala Sunrise tour includes pick up 2:45 to 4:05 am (depending on location) $50A, $37C. Price does not include breakfast or Haleakala National Park entrance fee. Day trip to Hana - pick up 7 to 8:15 am; $68A, $45C (no host lunch) Reservations: (808) 566-7333 (Honolulu); 1-800-533-8765 (mainland); 1-800-231-6984 (neighbor islands). <WWW>

Valley Isle Excursions - Tour to Hana in the comfort of a motorcoach van. Choose between a Hana Picnic trip $99, their Hana Ultra Classic Ranch Buffet $109, or the Ultimate Circle Island Excursion $139. Tours are all-inclusive and they offer $10 discounts for seniors and $20 for children under 12. All tours go around the island. All include continental breakfast and a hot lunch. Special auditory communication is available for the hearing impaired. 1-888-661-8687. (808) 661-8687.

MAUI OCEAN CENTER,

MUSEUMS, AND GARDENS

UPCOUNTRY

The ***Enchanting Floral Gardens***, on Hwy. 37 in Kula, charges $5 for adults, $1 for children for a self-guided botanical tour. Open 9-5 daily. (808) 878-2531.

The Kula Botanical Gardens charges an admission of $4 for adults; $1 for children 6-12 years to tour their 6-acre facility with over 2,000 plants (including native Hawaiian plants like the Sandalwood tree.) Open 9am-4pm. (878-1715)

The ***Sunrise Protea Farm*** (808) 876-0200 in Kula has a small, but diverse, variety of protea growing adjacent to their market and flower stand for shipment home. Dried assortments begin at about $25. Picnic tables available and no charge for just looking!

Hui No'eau Visual Arts Center offers historical tours and art exhibits. Located just below Makawao in the Baldwin plantation home (built in 1917) at 2841 Baldwin Ave. Open 10am-4pm Monday through Saturday. Admission is free, donations welcome. (808) 572-6560. Email: hui@mauinet or visit their website <www.maui.net/~hui>

Haleakala National Park Visitor Center features displays about the wildlife, flora, and geology of this massive dormant volcano. Located one parking lot below the summit, open from sunrise to 3pm daily. Admission is $10 per car.

HANA

Hana Cultural Center opened in August of 1983. It contains a collection of relics of Hana's past in the old courthouse building and a small museum. Open Monday through Sunday 10am-4pm. Located on Uakea Road Street near Hana Bay, watch for signs. (808) 248-8622

The Helani Gardens is now closed to the public. It was created by Howard Cooper, and opened in 1970 after thirty years of development. The lower area consists of five acres with manicured grounds and a tropical pool filled with jewel-colored koi. The upper sixty-five acres are a maze of one-lane dirt roads through an abundant jungle of amazing and enormous flowering trees and shrubs.

The *National Tropical Botanical Garden* operates the *Kahanu Gardens*. The headquarters of the non-profit NTBG is on Kaua'i, where they operate three gardens with another garden in Florida. The 126-acre Kahanu Garden is reached by turning *makai* (toward the sea) on Ulaino Road, just past mile marker 31. It is 1.5 miles to the entrance of the garden. The gardens are located at Kalahu Point, which is also the location of Hawai'i's largest *heiau*. The *Pi'ilanihale Heiau* is six centuries old and was constructed by the sons of Maui chief, *Piilani*, in his honor. Restoration of the *heiau* is ongoing and two new gardens have recently been added: The Canoe Gardens (plants that were brought to the islands in canoes) and the Coastal Gardens (indigenous plants grown next to the shoreline). Currently tours are available by reservation only at 1pm, Monday-Friday with plans to offer additional tours as demand increases. The tour lasts approximately 2 hours and costs $10. (Children under 12 free.) They host a monthly Open House (free admission) along with a variety of events. They now have a local Maui number to call for more information: (808) 248-8912.

SOUTH MAUI

Enjoy a self-guided tour around the grounds of the lavish *Grand Wailea Resort.*

Take a self-guided tour of the coastal wetlands and sand dunes of the *Kealia Pond National Wildlife Refuge* in North Kihei. You'll see turtles and whales from the elevated vantage point - with the aid of interpretive signs along the newly constructed boardwalk (3/4 mile) on the tour trail. For more information (808) 875-1582.

In 1998 Coral World International opened their **Maui Ocean Center** as the first and most compelling feature of the Ma'alaea Harbor Village. The aquarium is the only one of its kind in Hawai'i, but it is the sixth project developed worldwide by Coral World International. Their aim is to inspire appreciation for the ocean's environment and ecology and education regarding the need for reef conservation. Part of the center has been set aside as an educational and research center. This non-profit arm presents tours, films and, classes for groups, schools, and the public. Upon entry to the Reef Building you will view a reef pool with sea water surge which replicates the coastal surf off Maui. The walkway descends and exhibits can be viewed from different levels. There are fascinating turtle and ray pools as well as an outdoor Touch Pool. The Whale Discovery Center features life-sized humpback models and displays focusing on their feeding, migrating, and mating habits. A 600,000 gallon tank in the Pelagic Building is home for tiger sharks, mahi mahi, and tuna. An acrylic tunnel allows visitors to walk through the tank with a 240 degree view of marine life. One portion of the floor is transparent, affording a very realistic in-the-ocean experience. By the time you have toured the facility, you may have worked up an appetite. The oceanview *Seascape Ma'alaea Restaurant* offers California and Pacific Rim items for lunch. A kiosk features fast food and snacks. Plan on spending at least two hours to enjoy all the exhibits. Audio headset recorded tours are available in several languages. Tickets are $17.50 Adults, $12 Children. A morning snorkel cruise aboard Prince Kuhio combined with admission to the Center is available for $89.50 adults, $49.50 children. Round trip shuttle transportation is available for $7 from the Kihei/Wailea resort area or from Whalers Village in West Maui. (808) 270-7000.

CENTRAL MAUI

The **Alexander and Baldwin Sugar Museum** ★ is located at 3957 Hansen Road, in Puunene. Puunene is on Highway 35 between Kahului and Kihei. The tall stacks of the working mill are easily spotted. The museum is housed in a 1902 plantation home that was once occupied by the sugar mill's superintendent. Memorabilia includes the strong-box of Samuel Thomas Alexander and an actual working scale model of a sugar mill. The displays are well done and very informative. Monday-Saturday 9:30am-4:30pm. Admission charge: $4 adult, students and children $2. (808) 871-8058.

Bailey House Museum (circa 1834). To reach it, follow the signs to Iao Valley and you will see the historical landmark sign on the left side of the road. It's open from 10am-4pm, and a small admission is charged. (808) 244-3326

The Hawai'i Nature Center at Iao Valley has opened their new Interactive Science Arcade which houses a towering glass solarium and offers more than 30 hands-on exhibits and experiences focusing on Hawai'is natural history. Rain forest explorations, dispersal arcade games, live insect and stream animal exhibits along with a dragonfly ride make this a unique, adventuresome and educational attraction. Open 10am-4pm daily, $6 adults, $4 children. Call (808) 244-6500. FAX (808) 244-6525.

The Kanaha Wildlife Sanctuary is off Route 32, near the Kahului Airport, and was once a royal fish pond. Now a lookout is located here for those interested in viewing the stilt and other birds which inhabit the area.

The *Maui Botanical Gardens* is undergoing extensive renovation with complete expansion and revitalization expected by the year 2000. During the process, the playground and garden are still open to the public - free. They no longer have a zoo, but it's still a great stop-off so bring along a picnic lunch! For more information see WHERE TO STAY - WHAT TO SEE, Wailuku & Kahului.

The *Maui Military Museum* is currently acquiring their collection and looking for housing for their World War II memorabilia.

Maui Okinawa Cultural Center in Wailuku features artifacts and personal items from first-generation Okinawans. Located at 688 Nukuwai Place. Admission is free, donations welcome. Open 8:30am-noon Monday through Friday. (808) 242-1560.

Maui Tropical Plantation operates a 40-minute narrated tram ride through their tropical plantation. Daily 9am-5pm, $8.50. Admission to the grounds is free. (808) 244-7463. For more information see WHERE TO STAY - WHAT TO SEE, Kahului & Wailuku.

The *Paper Airplane Museum* in the Maui Mall features the unique juice can creations of the Tin Can Man along with aviation model exhibits and pictures depicting the history of aviation in the Hawaiian Islands. Tin can and paper airplane demonstrations, too! Open 9am-5pm Monday through Saturday, 11am-5pm on Sunday. (808) 877-8916.

WEST MAUI

The *Baldwin Home*, built in 1838, was home to early Maui missionaries. It is open to the public daily from 9:30am-5pm. Admission $3 for adults, $2 for seniors, and $5 for family. Located on Front Street in Lahaina. (808) 661-3262.

The Carthaginian, built in 1920, is a steel-hulled freighter restored to the likeness of a whaler. It is the only authentically restored brig in the world and you can enjoy their on-board whale displays. Located at Lahaina Harbor, admission $3 for adults, $2 for seniors, children free with parent. (808) 661-3262.

Hale Kohola (House of the Whale) is a museum located on the upper level at Whalers Village in Kaanapali. Admission is free, but donations are welcome. They feature a wonderful exhibition of the great whales with special emphasis on the humpback whale. The information director gives lectures on topics from scrimshaw to the life of a sailor. Call for times at (808) 661-5992. Private group lectures are also a possibility.

Hale Pa'i is on the campus of Lahainaluna school. Founded in 1831, Lahainaluna is the oldest school and printing press west of the Rockies. You will find it located just outside of Lahaina at the top of Lahainaluna Road. The hours fluctuate depending on volunteers, so call the Lahaina Restoration office at (808) 661-3262 for current schedule. No admission fee. Donations welcomed.

The *Westin Maui* at Kaanapali has an impressive art collection. Take a self-guided tour or call the concierge regarding complimentary art tours led by an island art expert twice weekly.

A small, but interesting *Whaling Museum* is located in the Crazy Shirts shop on Front Street. No admission is charged.

The Wo Hing Temple, built in 1912, now houses a museum which features the influence of the Chinese population on Maui. Hours are 10am-4:30pm with a $1 admission donation appreciated. The adjacent cook house has become a theater which features movies filmed by Thomas Edison during his trips to Hawai'i in 1898 and 1906. Located on Front Street in Lahaina.

PARASAILING

The parasail "season" on Maui is May 16-December 14th due to the restrictions during whale season. For those that aren't familiar with this aquatic experience, parasailing is a skyward adventure where you are hooked to a parachute and attached to a tow line behind a boat and soon are floating high in the air with a bird's eye view of Maui. The flight lasts 8 to 10 minutes which may be either too long or too short for some! Prices $30-$52. Some allow an "observer" (friend) to go along on the boat for an extra fee.

Parasail Kaanapali - Departs from Mala Wharf for a 10 minute ride at 1,000 feet up. Single to triple rides from $30-75. Phone (808) 669-6555.

UFO Parasail - Observers can go for $17. Departs Whalers Village. They use a new wrinkle, a self-contained "winch" boat. You get started standing on the boat and as your parachute fills, you are reeled out 400-800 feet. When it comes time to descend, you're simply reeled back in. $42 standard, $52 deluxe. $37-47 for early bird (before 8:30 am). (808) 661-7836, FAX (808) 667-0373, 1-800-359-4836. <WWW> Email: ufomaui@mauigateway.com

West Maui Para-sail - Lahaina Harbor, Slip #15. Uses "Skyrider," a two passenger aerial recliner as well as harness flights. Dry take-off and landing. Boat departs every 30 minutes with six passengers. They use an 800 ft. line so passengers are over 400 feet above the water. $48 regular or $39 early bird (first flight of the day). Observer $17. The crew is helpful and patient and gives plenty of instructions. They take a roll of pictures for you which you can purchase and develop yourself. (808) 661-4060. Mainland tollfree: 1-800-FLY-4UFO.

POLO

Polo season on Maui is April-November (excluding July). You'll find Polo events every Sunday (during the season) in Makawao with the Maui Polo Club at the arena located at 377 Haleakala Highway. Gates open at noon, games start at 1pm. Tickets are $3 for adults, under age 12 are free. Weekly activities may include a practice, a club game, or events such as the Oskie Rice Memorial Polo Cup or the Annual Rocking Kapalaia Ranch Cup. Call Emiliano at (808) 572-4915 for more information.

RUNNING

Maui is a scenic delight for runners. *Valley Isle Road Runners* can provide up-to-date information on island running events. Events call (808) 871-6441.

SCUBA DIVING

Maui, with nearby Molokini, Kaho'olawe, Lana'i and Moloka'i, offers many excellent diving locations. A large variety of dive operations offer scuba excursions, instruction, certification, and rental equipment. If you are a novice, a great way to get hooked is an introductory dive. No experience is necessary. Instruction, equipment, and dive - all for $70-$100 (averages about $80). Dives are available from boats, or less expensive from the beach. A beginning beach dive may be advisable for the less confident aquatic explorer. For those who are certified but rusty, refresher dives are available.

The mainstay of Maui diving is the two-tank dive, two dive sites with one tank each. Prices depend on location and include all equipment. A trip runs about $100. If the bug bites and you wish to get certified, the typical course is five days, eight hours each day, at an average cost of $350 plus books. One dive shop suggested that visitors with limited time, do "PADI" dive preparation on the mainland and they can then be certified on Maui in just two days. Classes are generally no more than six persons, or if you prefer private lessons, they run slightly more. Advanced open water courses are available in deep diving, search and recovery, underwater navigation, and night diving (at a few shops). If you wish to rent equipment only, a complete scuba package runs $25-30.

The larger resorts also offer complimentary introductory instruction and some can arrange certification courses and excursions. Many of the dive operators utilize boats specifically designed for diving.

Information, equipment, instruction, and excursions can be obtained at the following dive shops and charter operators. As you can see by the number of listings, diving is very popular around Maui.In addition to the following, there are ten Maui Dive Shops plus Ocean Activities and Beach Activities of Maui have outlets in a variety of locations. And believe it or not, there are even some others that we haven't listed!

Scuba friends recommend Mike Severns from their personal experiences diving with his company on numerous occasions. Michael Miller, another Maui scuba instructor is a 5th generation Kamaʻaina, a descendent from one of the early Hawaiian settlers, whaling boat Captain Jacob Brown. Dive sites range in character from lava tubes to caverns or coral gardens and green sea turtle cleaning stations. Shore dives, boat dives, day or night dives are available. Introductory or experienced divers. Check his website (below) for special offers on dive trips plus live weather video and maps.

WEST MAUI

Beach Activities
of Maui-Kaanapali
(808) 661-5552

Beach Activities of Maui
Kapalua Bay Hotel
(808) 669-4664

Boss Frog's
156 Lahainaluna Rd., Lahaina
(808) 661-3333
Napili Plaza
(808) 669-4949
Kahana Manor Shops
(808) 669-6700
Kihei (Dolphin Plaza)
(808) 875-4477

Dive Maui, Inc.
Lahaina, (808) 667-2080
Email: offshore@maui.net

Extended Horizons
Introductory & night dives
P.O. Box 10785
Lahaina, (808) 667-0611
1-888-348-3628
Email: scuba@maui.net

Happy Maui Diving
  & Tours
Michael Miller, instructor
(808) 669-0123
Email: mmiller@maui.net
< WWW >

Island Scuba
Beach scuba & snuba
Scooter dives
(808) 667-4608
Lahaina (808) 661-3369
Email:islndscuba@aol.com

Lahaina Divers
143 Dickenson
Lahaina, (808) 667-7496
1-800-998-3483

Ocean Activities
at Maui Marriott
(808) 661-3631
(808) 667-1200

Tropical Divers Maui
Sands of Kahana
Beach Dives at Black Rock plus
boat dives
& rental equipment
Free West Maui transportation
(808) 667-7709
1-800-994-MAUI
Email: getwet@maui.net

SOUTH MAUI

B & B Scuba
1280 So. Kihei Rd.
(808) 875-2861

Dive & Sea Maui
1975 S. Kihei Rd.
6 passenger boat
(808) 874-1952

Ed Robinson's
Driving Adventures
Kihei, (808) 879-3584
1-800-635-1273

Freelance Scuba
"Geared toward the
Diving Family"
Kihei (808) 879-8606

Makai Scuba
Adventures
Kihei (808) 874-9442

Makena Coast Charters
Kihei, 874-1273
1-800-833-6483

Maui Bubbles Scuba Diving
Beach and boat dives
(808) 879-5070

Maui Diamond II
20 passenger dive boat
Departs Ma'alaea 1-888-477-5484
(808) 879-9119
Email: mcc@maui.net

*Maui Dive Shop
Azeka Center, Kihei
(808) 879-3388
www.mauidiveshop.com

Mike Severns ★
Kihei, (808) 879-6596

Maui Sun Divers
Kihei (808) 879-3337
Email: sundiver@maui.net

Nor'Wester (Day & night dives)
South Maui (808) 879-0004

*Ocean Activities
1847 S. Kihei Rd. #203, Kihei
(808) 879-4485

Pro Diver (Specializes in
back wall Molokini
drift dives) (808) 875-4404

Scuba Connection
(808) 572-5556
1-888-249-8379 ext. 3927
Email: scubacon@maui.net

Scuba Dave's
624 Front Street
(808) 667-6692 < WWW >

Scuba Shack
2349 S. Kihei Rd.
(808) 891-0500
Departs Kihei aboard
the *Jilly Bean*
www.scubashack.com

SCUBA DIVING

AROUND THE ISLAND
*These have multiple locations around Maui. We have listed their main locations.

Kapalua is featuring a **Kayak Scuba Dive** that was developed out of necessity in the summer of 1990. The Kapalua area coastline offers some of the finest diving on the West Coast of Maui, however, entry over lava rock was not feasible. "The Scrambler" offers the means to reach terrific dive spots while not creating the noise or potential anchor damage of a full size dive vessel. "The Scrambler" kayak was designed by Tim Niemier, Olympic kayak coach. It weighs 35 lbs., is approximately 11 feet long, made of recyclable polyurethane and is described as a sit-on-top, self-scupping kayak. The paddler is not tied, strapped or sealed inside the kayak, therefore, if it should roll, the paddler is free to swim to the side, roll the kayak back upright and climb aboard. The term self-scupping refers to the design which allows water to drain free of the topside without any procedures on the part of the paddler. This makes the kayak unsinkable. Departing from Kapalua Bay, each diver paddles his or her own kayak (although a double kayak is available for tight-knit buddy teams) along the rugged and scenic Kapalua coastline for 15 to 20 minutes prior to reaching one of two different dive sites. Trips are limited to a maximum of four divers, price is $89 per person. Also available are Underwater Scooter Dives, night dives, snorkeling, sailing, and windsurfing. Call direct to the Beach Activities of Maui at Kapalua at (808) 669-4664.

SEA EXCURSIONS

Maui offers a bountiful choice for those desiring to spend some time in and on the ocean. Boats available for sea expeditions range from a three-masted schooner, to spacious trimarans and large motor yachts, to the zodiac type rafts for the more adventurous. Your choice is a large group trip or a more pampered small group excursion with a maximum of six people. Two of the most popular snorkeling excursions are to Molokini and Lana'i. Most sailboats motor to these islands and, depending on wind conditions, sail at least part of the return trip. All provide snorkel equipment. Food and beverage service varies and is reflected in the price. Many sailboats are available for hourly, full day or longer private charters. Note: Due to weather conditions, your trip to Molokini may, at the last minute, be altered to another location, usually along the Southern shore of Maui. One of the nicest amenities of a number of boats is the option of a freshwater shower! Some of them even have solar heated their water which provides a refreshing rinse off after your saltwater snorkel/swim.

Excursion boats seem to have a way of sailing off into the sunset. The number of new ones is as startling as the number of operations that have disappeared since our last edition. The new "thing" is the many boat companies now promoting their dolphin watching trips.

As mentioned previously, competition to Molokini has become fierce. Twenty to thirty boats a day now arrive to snorkel in this area. Many more boats now take trips to Lana'i as well.

In the following list, phone numbers of the excursion companies are included in case personal booking is desired, however, most activity desks can also book your reservation. Unless you have a lot of extra time, avoid the time share offers! You may get a discount on an activity, but you'll end up spending at least a portion of a day hearing their sales pitch. The best deal with an activity operator is *Tom Barefoot's Cashback Tours* who can book most boats and offers a 10% refund. (And no timeshare!) Located in Lahaina at 834 Front St. and in Kihei at 2395 So. Kihei Rd. Call (808) 661-8889 <www.maui.net/~barefoot>

PRICES PER PERSON WILL RUN YOU ACCORDINGLY
TAX NOT INCLUDED:

Full day trip to Lana'i $79 - $159
Club Lana'i $89
1/2 day trip to Molokini (3 - 6 hours) $39 - $129
1/2 day Maui coastline (3 - 4 hours) $40 - $65
Full day Maui coastline $80 - $90
Sunset sails (1 1/2 - 2 hrs.) $30 - $50
Whale watching (2-3 hrs/seasonal) $20 - $40
Private charters $100 per hour and up, $400 per day and up
Dinner cruise $70 - $80

SEA EXCURSIONS -

CHARTER LISTING

AMERICA II - Built to compete in the 1987 America's Cup races in Fremantle, Australia, *America II* was skippered by John Kollius. Although she lost to Dennis Connor of the *Stars & Stripes*, Connor did go on to bring the cup home for the U.S. Enjoy a snorkeling and sailing experience on this 12 meter class yacht. They have two morning performance sails (11:30am and 1:30pm) and an afternoon tradewind sail from 2-4pm. Sails include soda, juice, water, and snacks. Beer and wine may be brought on board. Whale watches in season, snorkel/sails during off whale season. Sunset sails available all year. All are two-hour sails: $29.95, $15 for children 6-12 years. (808) 667-2195 or FAX (808) 661-1107.

BEACH ACTIVITIES OF MAUI - In addition to windsurfing lessons, they offer a variety of small boat rentals including Hobie Cat, pedal boats, one and two person kayaks, and UFO floats. Introductory and certified scuba dives are available. They also operate the *Teralani*, a 53' catamaran. They offer daily excursions that include picnic/snorkel sails and sunset cruises. Seasonal whale watches $37. Picnic snorkel sail $69 adults, $35 for children 5-12 years, free for children under age 5. Champagne sunset sail $35 adults, $30 teens, $25 children. Periodically, they also have "theme" sails like Italian or Mexican Night, Oktoberfest or Vintner Sail from $35. PO Box 10056, Lahaina, HI 96761. (808) 661-5500. FAX (808) 661-0448.

BLUE WATER RAFTING ★ - These folks were among the first to initiate ocean rafting on Maui back in 1985. They have two 6-passenger and one 24-passenger high-powered rigid-hulled inflatables. They started their "Kanaio Coast" tour back in 1987 and you'll be amazed at the phenomenal lava formations and sea caves that you'll see on this unique adventure. Lunch and gear provided. The 4-hour Kanaio Coast is $75 adults, children under 12 are $65. Their 5 1/2 hour Kanaio/Molokini Quest is $99 adults, children under 12 are $85. For those of you (like Dona) who like to sleep in, the 2-hour Molokini Express doesn't leave until 11:30 am! Cost is $39. Their seasonal 2-hour whale watch, beverage and gear $39. The 3 1/2 hour Molokini Deluxe includes lunch $55 adults, children $45; the 3 1/2 hour combo snorkel and whale watch $55. Trips depart Kihei. Private charters available. (808) 879-7238. Email: mark@maui.net

CAPTAIN STEVE'S - Snorkel aboard their rigid hull raft and see whales and dolphins. Two-hour tours depart Mala Wharf. (808) 667-5565.

CINDERELLA - A 50' sailing yacht departs from Ma'alaea Harbor to tour coral reefs off the Maui coastline. Hot shower on board. $135 per person, six guests maximum. Private charter $800. Private sunset charter $360. (808) 244-0009. FAX (808) 874-3518. Email: sailmaui@maui.net

CLUB LANA'I - Board one of two large luxury catamarans for their sunset cocktail cruises. Complimentary bar serving Mai Tais, wine, beer, rum/vodka mixers, soda, and juices with live music and dancing. Between mid-December and mid-April they feature a late afternoon whale watching followed by a sunset cruise. Offered four nights a week, departs from Lahaina Harbor, Pier #4. Cost is $39 for adults, children 4-16 are $19, under 4 years are free.

Now this sounds like fun! A new feature is their Ultimate Sunset Beach Party. "Come Calypso Mon" each Thursday evening for a Lobster Feast, Clambake and Beach Party. The four hour event features live Calpyso music throughout the evening performed enroute, as well as on the beach when you reach Lana'i. Open bar featuring their famous Lana'i Tais, Hawaiian tropical drinks, soft drinks and other non-alcoholic beverages. Cost is $99 per person plus tax. Must be 21 with valid ID required for alcoholic beverages.) Cost is $99 plus tax. 1-800-531-5262) or (808) 871-1144.

EXPEDITIONS ★ - Ferry service from Lahaina to Lana'i five times daily. $50 round trip adult, $40 child. If you'd like to explore Lana'i on your own, you can take the early morning ferry boat over and return on the late afternoon trip. From the dock it is a moderate, but easy walk to Manele Bay and the adjacent Manele Bay Resort. There is a shuttle that runs between the dock and the two resorts that charges $15 round trip to Manele Bay and $25 round trip to Koele Lodge. Expeditions offers a day package for two persons, additional persons $50 (4 people maximum for jeep or car and six maximum for the van). Options include boat trip plus car $175, boat trip plus jeep $228, boat trip plus van $255. Lana'i City Service operates a Dollar rental car outlet, from Maui 244-9538. Rental car $60, or Jeep $119-129. On Lana'i call 565-7227. Expeditions (808) 661-3756.

FLEXIBLE FLYER - Molokini Snorkel/Sail 7:30am-1pm $129 includes breakfast/lunch. Two-hour afternoon performance sail $64 includes beverages. Sunset sails 4:30-6:30pm $69 (BYOB). Seasonal whale watching. 6 passengers max. Private charters available. (808) 244-6655. FAX (808) 879-4984.

FRIENDLY CHARTERS - *Lani Kai*, 53' power catamaran. Morning snorkel/cruise $69.95 adults/$49.95 kids ($10 discount if you book direct). Afternoon trips $39.95/$29.95 and $5 discount for booking direct. Snuba available for an extra fee. Seasonal whale watching. Private charters available. Ma'alaea Harbor. (808) 244-1979. Email: Lanikai@maui.net

FROGMAN CHARTERS - Frogman has been in operation since 1986 and offers snorkel and scuba adventures plus seasonal whale watching on their two catamarans, *Frogman* and *Blue Dolphin*. They depart Ma'alaea Harbor each morning for a Molokini Snorkel & Scuba Adventure that includes breakfast, lunch, beverages, equipment, and instruction. Scuba dive from $49.95; Molokini and Turtle Reef $89; two-hour seasonal whale watch $20 adults, $15 youth 4-12 years. They also sell rental equipment from boogie boards to surfboards plus Hana tape tours at their Boss Frog's Dive Shops. Locations at 156 Lahainaluna Rd. in Lahaina; Dolphin Plaza at 2395 So. Kihei Rd. in Kihei; and Napili Plaza. Call 1-888-700-FROG or (808) 661-3333.

GEMINI CHARTERS - The *Gemini* is a 64' catamaran with glass-bottom viewports that departs daily from Kaanapali Beach in front of the Westin Maui. Year round picnic snorkel sails provide snorkel equipment including prescription masks, flotation devices, snorkel instruction, a fresh water shower (this is great!) and a hot buffet lunch. $72 adults, $40 under 12. Champagne Sunset Sail with champagne, beer, wine, mai tais and non-alcoholic beverages $42 adults, $25 under 12. Seasonal morning and afternoon Whale Watch with a Marine Naturalist on board and an underwater hydrophone to listen to the whales singing. They offer a keiki snorkel as a part of their Kamp Kaanapali program at the Maui Westin on Sundays. They can also arrange for private charters. Gemini Charters, PO Box 10846, Lahaina, Maui, HI 96761. (808) 661-2591.

HAWAII OCEAN RAFTING - This family owned and operated business takes 14 passengers aboard their raft for 1/2 day and full day snorkel Lana'i trips. Also by private charter. (808) 667-2191. FAX (808) 878-3574. 1-888-677-7238. Email: ocnraftn@maui.net

HAWAIIAN RAFTING ADVENTURES
DESTINATION PACIFIC - 1223 Front St., Lahaina. In their RAIV (Rigid Aluminum Inflatable Vessels) you can enjoy a full day expedition circumnavigating the island of Lana'i. Includes a BBQ lunch served in a sea cave. Continental breakfast and snorkel gear also provided. Adults $120, $100 children 4-12. Their half-day expedition crosses the Auau Channel and includes continental breakfast, snacks and beverages. Adults $59, $45 children 4-12. Seasonal whale watching. Also available are one-tank introductory dives, two-tank certified dives, one-tank night dive, open water certification. $79-325. Six-hour private charter $1,200. (808) 661-7333. Email: hra@maui.net <WWW>

ISLAND MARINE ACTIVITIES - They offer two vessels that depart from the Lahaina Harbor. The *Lahaina Princess*, a 65' touring yacht (149 passengers maximum) and the *Maui Princess*, a 150 passenger 118' touring yacht. The *Lahaina Princess* is the only boat that offers a Molokini trip from the West Side and the luxurious, stabilized *Maui Princess* is the only yacht that does a trip to Moloka'i. (They are also the only vessel that has a 15' "water trampoline" that deploys on the water for you to jump *on*, jump *from* or just lie around on top *of*!) The *Maui Princess* leaves Lahaina at 6:30 am and arrives at 8 am in Kaunakakai, Moloka'i for your choice of four different tour options: Walking Tour of Kaunakakai town on your own ($69A/$35C); Cruise/Drive, a car rental with courtesy pick-up ($99-109); Alii Tour (van tour of Kaunakakai, Father Damien's Church, Kalaupapa Lookout, and coffee plantation with lunch at Kaluakoi resort), ($129A/$79C); and an overnighter package with golf for $159 per person double occupancy ($259 single). All tours leave Moloka'i at 2pm and arrive back on Maui at 3:30. Their Molokini trip runs $69 adults, $39 children and makes two round trips daily. Dinner and Sunset cruises plus two-hour seasonal whale watches also available. (808) 667-6165.

KAMEHAMEHA SAILS, INC. - *King Kamehameha*, 40' Woody Brown catamaran built in Hawaii for Hawaiian waters. Snorkel/sail, sunset sail, whale watching, private charter from Lahaina Harbor. A small catamaran, maximum 6 passengers, with padded seating around the wheel area and a big net out front. You may have recognized it by the big picture of King Kamehameha on the sail! Owner Tom Warren has been sailing on various charter boats since 1969 and purchased the *Kamehameha* in 1977. A congenial captain, fun casual atmosphere, and small passenger manifest allows for a pleasantly intimate sailing experience. Minimal snacks provided or bring your own. Twice daily seasonal whale watches. Two hour trips are $40 per person, 3 hours are $60, private charters $150 per hour. Seasonal whale watching. (808) 661-4522.

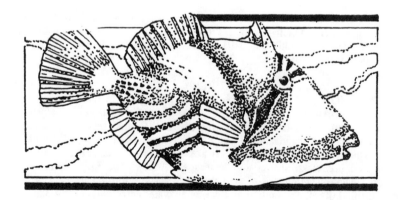

KAPALUA KAI ★ - They now operate out of Whalers Village in Kaanapali. Their 53' wing-masted 49-passenger catamaran offers plenty of shaded area in their open air cabin, a glass bottom viewing area. Snorkel trip includes a buffet lunch catered by Hula Grill which includes smoked turkey and a salad bar featuring Kula greens. Departs 10am-3pm. Adults $79, children $49. The sunset sail offers finger sandwiches, veggie platter, and fresh fruit platter. They sail the whole time through the sunset! $45 adults, $30 children. Both tours have a premium bar and the food is about the best you'll find. Call (808) 665-0344 or 667-5980.

KIELE V - 55' catamaran, 4 hour snorkel/sail; also an afternoon sail. Contact Hyatt Regency, Kaanapali. (808) 661-1234 ext. 3104.

MAKENA BOAT PARTNERS - *Kai Kanani*, 46' catamaran, departs from the Maui Prince Hotel. Molokini picnic/snorkel cruise $65 adults, children $40. Afternoon seasonal whale watching $30 adults, $20 children. (808) 879-7218.

MAUI CLASSIC CHARTERS - *Lavengro*, a 60' Biloxi pilot schooner, was designed for pleasure and owned by a naval captain from Mississippi in the 20's and 30's. It has sailed northwest to Alaska and as far south as Tahiti and during World War II, it served with the Coast Guard, patrolling the waters of the Cajun South. *Lavengro's* daily sail and snorkel to Molokini departs Ma'alaea Harbor for a 7am-1pm trip. The trip includes continental breakfast, deli-style lunch, snorkel gear and instruction, complimentary beer, wine, and soda. On-board restrooms, fresh water showers. Maximum 30 passengers. $59 adult, $40 children any age (not suited for small children). They also offer Molokini snorkel sails aboard *Four Winds*, their new 55' glassbottom catamaran. (The old *Four Winds* was donated to the Marine Biology Dept. of the University of Hawaii and replaced by this bigger, faster vessel in early 1998.) Morning snorkel to Molokini includes continental breakfast, snorkel gear and instruction, BBQ lunch, complimentary bear, wine, and soda. Sport fishing is free. Extra options include Snuba, sea boards, video, underwater camera, prescription masks, wet suits. $69 adults, $45 kids. They also do an afternoon snorkel (1-5pm) to Molokini or Coral Gardens. This includes complimentary beverages; BBQ lunch is optional. $40 Adults, $30 Children. Trips depart from Ma'alaea. (808) 879-8188 or 1-800-736-5740.

MAUI DIVE SHOP - Besides selling scuba and snorkel gear, they also book boating activities. They have a number of shops (10 at this count). Here are a few: Kihei Town Center 879-1919, Azeka II 879-3388, and Lahaina 661-5388.

MAUI-MOLOKA'I SEA CRUISES - *Prince Kuhio*, 92' motor yacht. Whale watching, private charters, 1/2 day snorkel to Molokini / Turtle Town, departs Ma'alaea. This boat has the benefits of a larger vessel with more comforts, but with a bigger capacity, there are a lot more people! Rates are $75 for adults and $40 for children for their snorkel trip. Snuba available for extra fee. Seasonal whale watching runs $30 adults/$20 for children. (808) 242-8777 or 1-800-468-1287. < www.mauigateway.com/ ~prince > Email: prince@mauigateway.com.

MAUI NUI EXPLORER - Royal Hawaiian Cruises offers two very different ocean exploration vessels, one is this 48' rigid hull inflatable supported on large neoprene pontoons. The *Maui Nui Explorer* (and her sister boat on Kaua'i, the *Na Pali Explorer*) are mounted on Scarab ocean racing hulls and powered by twin Volvo turbo supercharged diesels which each generate 230 horsepower. This provides a significantly different kind of boating experience than their other vessel, *Navatek II*. Needless to say, the *Maui Nui Explorer* gets to where it is going pretty quickly, cruising at 25 knots and with the potential of 33 knots. The trip departing from Lahaina and going around Lana'i takes four hours; travel time from Lahaina to Lana'i can be handled in 20 minutes under good weather and ocean conditions. The boat circumnavigates the island of Lana'i with stops for swimming and snorkeling, weather permitting. Trip includes continental breakfast and deli-style lunch. $65 adults, $45.50 for children 5-11 years. They also offer a two-hour afternoon whale watch in season, $29 adults, child 5-11 years $21. Advance booking from the mainland 1-800-852-4183. Locally (808) 873-3475.

NAVATEK II - Royal Hawaiian Cruises described this vessel in their brochure as "travel beyond the usual." This $3 million cruise vessel will definitely catch your eye. The technology provides a revolutionary smooth ride thanks to its SWATH design (Small Water Plane Twin Hull) which is the result of 13 years of research focussed on minimizing ship motions. (According to literature on the *Navatek*, SWATH technology was actually born in the 1800's, but the first patent was not issued until 1942 in the U.S.) The ship rides above the water rather than on it. The main cabin is air conditioned, offers a full service bar, and special viewing area with amphitheater seating. The *Navatek* system was designed by Steven Loui, a Honolulu shipbuilder. *Navatek I* is based in Honolulu, and version II was built in 1994 in the Honolulu shipyard as well. The cruise ship is 82 feet long and 36 feet wide, can carry 149 passengers plus crew, and has a cruising speed of 22 knots. There are two full decks offering 3,250 square feet of space including an enclosed main deck and an open observation deck with amphitheater bow seating, tanning areas, lounge chairs, restrooms, a hot shower, a service bar, and full commercial kitchen. Seasonal two-hour afternoon whale watches along the West Maui coast include a naturalist program with soda, juice, and no-host bar. $39 Adults; $26.50 Children (2-11 years). Sunset Dinner Cruise six nights each week. $87 Adults, $55 Children 2-11 years. (See Dinner Cruises)

"Lana'i Voyage of Discovery" is an adventure to Lana'i (8am-2pm) to visit scenic points around the island including Shipwreck Beach, Pu'u Pehe Rock, and Shark Fin Rock. Guests can also enjoy the naturalist program and Hawaiian arts, crafts, and cultural program. Your day begins early when a tender shuttles you out from the Lahaina Harbor to the Navatek where a waffle bar breakfast is being prepared. The hot Belgian waffles (and pancakes) with fruit toppings (peaches, blueberries and strawberries), syrups (guava, passion strawberry, and cane) whipped cream, nuts, and assorted fruits are breakfast fare. After circumnavigating Lana'i, the boat anchors at Nanahoa (also called Five Needles) about 9 am. Lunch is served about 10:30 am (sounds early, but believe us, you'll be hungry!) and is an American barbecue buffet with grilled chicken, hamburgers and veggie burgers, various salads, chips and dips, and homemade cookies.

If you'd like to sample a cruise ship, then the **Navatek II** comes close. Rates are $125 for adults, $95 for juniors (12-17 years) $75 for children (5-11 years). For you land-lubbers with dreams of the sea, but a stomach for the earth beneath your feet, *Navatek II* may be the one for you! Advance bookings 1-800-852-4183. (808) 873-3475.

OCEAN ACTIVITIES - Departures from Ma'alaea aboard the 37' Tolleycraft *No Ka Oi III* for deep sea sport fishing. Sail aboard the 65' catamaran *Wailea Kai* or power cat *Maka Kai* for Molokini picnic snorkel by charter only. (808) 879-4485 or 1-800-798-0652.

OCEAN RIDERS - "Adventure Rafting" on one of their rigid hull, inflatable rafts, 15-18 people max. They feature unusual destinations (depends on daily weather conditions). Reefs of Kaho'olawe, Moloka'i's cliffs or Lana'i. Seasonal whale watching. Departs Mala Wharf in Lahaina. (808) 661-3586. Email: orders@maui.net <WWW>

PACIFIC WHALE FOUNDATION CRUISES - Eco-adventures with several different vessels to a variety of destinations have departures from Ma'alaea and Lahaina. Whale watching, Lana'i Wild Dolphin and Snorkel Adventure, Molokini Snorkel Crises, and a Sunset Dinner Cruise. Their vessels are *Whale One*, *Whale Two*, *Pacific Whale*, *Manate'a* and *Ocean Spirit*. A variety of options and rates, so call for details. (808) 879-8811. <WWW>

PARAGON SAILING CHARTERS -They have two 47' catamarans built in California with a state-of-the-art rotating carbon fiber masts. The Cabin House offers sunshade and shelter and trampolines offer outside lounging. Their five hour Molokini Sail & Snorkel departs from Ma'alaea Harbor offering a morning snorkel-sail that begins with a 7:30 am departure and a light breakfast as you head toward Molokini. Snorkel gear is provided and they have small size gear for children. A fresh hot/cold water shower is located on top of the swim ladder for refreshment after your swim and before a buffet lunch. Maximum 49 passengers, $68.50 adults. Children 12 and under half price. Their afternoon 3-hour "Speed Sail & Snorkel Coral Gardens" trip includes snorkeling followed by a speed run back. $39 Adults, $19.50 for children under 12. Trip includes appetizers and beverages.

Depart aboard their second vessel from the Lahaina Harbor at 8:30 am for an all day Lana'i Trip. Unloading is done at Manele Bay in Lahaina and guests are provided with snorkel gear, picnic baskets, beach mats and umbrellas for 2 1/2 hours of dining and ocean fun before reboarding the boat. Enroute back they serve desserts, champagne, and have an open bar. Half way back, the captain stops for a deepwater swim before returning to the Lahaina Harbor at 4pm. Cost is $129 adults, $99 children. Their Sunset Sail departs Lahaina and is a 5-7pm trip with an open bar and appetizers. The vessel is licensed for 49 passengers, but they take a maximum of 24. $39 adults, 12 and under $29. Write RR2, Box 43, Kula, HI 96790. Reservations (808) 244-2087 or FAX (808) 878-3933. Email: paragon@maui.net <WWW>

THE PRIDE OF MAUI ★ - 65' catamaran featuring a large indoor cabin and outdoor sundecks. They offer daily departures at 8 am from the Ma'alaea Harbor for morning dives at two destinations. They stop at Molokini and "Turtle Town" (Pu'u O La'i) depending on weather conditions, other snorkel locations may be Olowalu or Coral Gardens. Whale watching seasonally. *The Pride of Maui* has handicap access, freshwater showers, glass bottom viewing, slide, and underwater video cameras available for rent. The boat accommodates up to 135 passengers. The morning snorkel includes breakfast, lunch, beverages, and equipment. Adults $76, Juniors (13-18 years) $69, and $49 for children 4-12 years. Afternoon Molokini Snorkel Cruise (4 hours) includes a meal, beverages, and gear: adults $40, youth $20. (Note: The afternoon sails, on any excursion, can be a rougher and windier trip.) Scuba certified dives are an additional $37 one tank; $57 two tank dives. Snuba available for additional $47. Their other boat, the *Lelani* is a 50' monohull with a maximum of 35 guests. The same trip route & same food, but no slide, no glassbottom viewing, and no certified scuba aboard. (808) 875-0955.

RAINBOW CHASER - Twelve couples maximum for this all day Lana'i snorkel adventure. Departs Lahaina. (808) 667-2270. Email: morefun@maui.net.

ROYAL HAWAIIAN CRUISES - They offer two vessels, see listings under "Navatek II" and " Maui Nui Explorer."

SCOTCH MIST CHARTERS - *Scotch Mist II* is a Santa Cruz 50' sailboat, which takes 23 people max on a 5-hour Lana'i Snorkel sail, $69.95 adults/$49.95 children 5-12 years. Includes continental breakfast and snacks. Two-hour champagne chocolate sunset sail, $35 adults. Seasonal whale watch $35. Departs Lahaina Harbor. (808) 661-0386. FAX (808) 667-2113.

SEA ESCAPE/U-DRIVE BOAT RENTALS - You-drive 16' zodiac raft and 17' Boston whalers for rent by the hour, half day or full day. (808) 879-3721.

SEAFIRE - Two tours daily of Turtle Town, Molokini and the South Maui sea caves from $38 per person. Departs from the Kihei Boat Harbor. An aluminum hull, diesel engine "safe" boat; max 18 passengers. (808) 879-2201.

SILENT LADY - Captain Skip Price is an ex-Navy deep sea diver and master of this 31-ton masted schooner. They take a maximum of 36 passengers for whaling watching seasonally. Molokini & Turtle Reef snorkel sails $88, Sunset sails $44. Book directly and receive a discount. (808) 875-1112.

TRILOGY ★ - *Trilogy I*, 64' Searunner, cutter rigged catamaran max. 55 passengers. *Trilogy II*, 55' sloop rigged catamaran max. 44 passengers, *Trilogy III*, 51' sloop rigged maximum 36 passengers. Their Discover Lana'i excursion is offered Monday-Friday and begins at 6:10 am where you'll meet a Trilogy First Mate at the Trilogy parking lot at the corner of Dickenson and Wainee. Enjoy hot chocolate, coffee, fresh fruit, and those very special 4th generation Mom Coon's homemade cinnamon rolls enroute.

Trilogy arrives at Manele Harbor on Lana'i by 8:30 am which leaves plenty of time for snorkeling and scuba at Hulopo'e Bay Marine Sanctuary before a hot BBQ lunch at their private picnic area. The afternoon affords another opportunity to snorkel and swim or the option of a guided tour of Lana'i City. It is 2pm when you depart Manele Harbor, arriving at Lahaina Harbor at 4pm. Cost is $159 for adults, children 3-12 years $79.50. Scuba is an additional $45-55.

On Saturdays their Lana'i Seafari Snorkel Sail differs in that you snorkel from the vessel off the coast of Lana'i and have only the option of a tour of Lana'i City in the afternoon. They also offer Lana'i Overnight packages Monday-Friday with a stay at the Manele Bay Hotel or Lodge at Koele. (Call for current rates.)

The Trilogy Excursions "Discover Molokini" is aboard *Trilogy V*, a 55' Searunner sloop rigged catamaran with an average load of 54 passengers. Breakfast is the same as on the Lana'i excursion and lunch is hot BBQ teriyaki chicken, green salad, corn on the cob and dinner rolls. Vegetarian selection also available. Price is $89 adults, $44.50 for children 3-12 years. The Trilogy Excursions Kaanapali Snorkel sail meets in front of Whalers Village for a beach loading aboard the *Trilogy IV* at 9:30am - a good choice for those of you who aren't early risers! Their continental breakfast is followed by snorkeling at Honolua Bay and a second site of the Captain's choice. Lunch fare is also the same as above and you'll arrive back at Kaanapali Beach at 2:30pm. Rates are $89 adults, children $44.50. Scuba runs an additional $45-55. The final option is their Kaanapali Sunset sail which meets for beach loading at 3:15. Beverages and snacks are served on board before returning to Kaanapali Beach at 5:30pm. Adults $45, children $22.50. Seasonal whale watching $45. 180 Lahainaluna Road, PO Box 1119, Lahaina, HI 96767-1119. 1-800-874-2666. (808) 661-4743. FAX (808) 667-7766. Email: trilogy@maui.net < WWW >

WHALE MIST - 36' monohull sailboat, Lahaina Harbor. Seasonal whale watching, snorkeling off the Maui coastline. Three-hour coral reef snorkel $38, sunset cruise $38. An interesting specialty cruise is their Introduction to Sailing, $99 per person. This is a six hour, hands-on, primer on sailing under the tutelage of Captain Bill Pritchard with maximum 6 passengers. (808) 667-2833.

WINDJAMMER CRUISES MAUI - *Spirit of Windjammer*, a 70' three-masted schooner offers 2-hour Maui coastline dinner cruise $73.25 adult / $36.62 children. Champagne Brunch Cruise offered May through November on Fridays and Sundays $37.10 adults, children under 12 free. (One free per paying adult, others half price.) Whale Watch cruises $37.10, children under 12 free. Transportation from West Maui and South Maui for additional fee. Departs Lahaina. Maximum 91 passengers. (808) 667-8600, 1-800-SEA-HULA.

WORLD CLASS YACHT CHARTERS ★ - *World Class*, a 65' sleek MacGregor Yacht departs in the afternoon tradewinds for 1 1/2 hours of true sailing. This exciting performance sail departs at 2pm and runs $35. Sunset Sail $45; whale watches during season $25. All tours include complimentary beverages. The four-hour "Captain's Choice" snorkel sail ($59) includes a deli-lunch, ice-cold beverages - and a hot fresh water shower! The captain will choose from one of four locations (depending on the day's weather and visibility) to find the best snorkel spot. All departures from Kaanapali Beach in front of Leilani's restaurant. Private charters and overnight charters are also available and can include catered meals. *World Class* is a real find, but will appeal to a very specific kind of traveler. It's nothing like any of the other visitor boats, this is a yacht! It should appeal to people who REALLY like to sail, and for the more adventurous types. If you enjoy sailing, don't miss this one. It is reportedly the fastest charter yacht in the islands. Feel that wind in your face, Yee Ha! (808) 667-7733, FAX (808) 667-0314. 1-800-600-0959.

ZIP-PURR - This 47' catamaran, departs Kaanapali Beach for a six hour snorkeling trip to Lanaʻi featuring turtles, dolphins and seasonally, whales. The trip includes breakfast, lunch and an open bar with 35 passenger maximum. Built by owner/captain Mike Turkington. They also offer a two hour sunset cocktail sail with an appetizer buffet and an open bar. (808) 667-2299. Email: juliezip@aol.com

MOLOKINI EXCURSION REVIEWS

Molokini Crater - This small semicircular island is the remnant of a volcano. Located about 8 miles off Maʻalaea Harbor, it affords good snorkeling in the crater area. These waters are a marine reserve and the island is a bird sanctuary.

Molokini is usually a 1/2 day excursion with a continental breakfast and lunch provided. Costs are $40-$100 for adults, $25-$60 (plus tax) for children under 12. (You may find rates even lower during a price war.)

MOLOKINI
Molokini is a distinctive landmark off the South Maui coastline. This 10,000 year old dormant volcano reveals only one crescent-shaped portion of the crater rim and serves as a sanctuary for marine and bird life. The inside of the crater offers a water depth of 10-50 feet, a 76 degree temperature and visibility sometimes as much as 150 feet on the outer perimeter creating a fish bowl effect. Molokini has had some turbulent years. Long before tourist boats frequented this sight, it was used as a bombing target for the Navy. Our first snorkeling trip to the crescent shaped crater was in the days when only two or three boats operated trips. But with undetonated bombs an obvious danger, the Navy went ahead and detonated them. Obviously, the aquatic life and the reef system was decimated.

The many tour boats dropping anchors further damaged and destroyed the reef. While it hasn't been restored to the way it was during our first excursions, and likely will never be, it is still a popular snorkeling location. Fortunately, concerned boat operators were granted semi-permanent concrete mooring anchors, thereby preventing further reef damage. Most trips are taken in the morning, some do offer afternoon trips, but expect rougher ocean conditions. On occasion even the morning trips are forced to snorkel at an alternative site, usually La Perouse or another spot off the South Maui coastline.

According to legend, the atoll of Molokini was created as the result of a jealous rage. Pele had a dream lover, Lohiau, who lived in Ma'alaea, located to the north of Makena. Lohiau married a mo'o (lizard) and Pele was so angry she bisected the lizard. The head became Molokini islet and the tail became Pu'u O La'i at Makena. Pu'u O La'i is the rounded hill at the end of Makena. (Dona calls it "the nubby thing" - which probably is not an ancient Hawaiian word.)

We recommend *Blue Water Rafting* ★ for those die-hard snorkelers who would enjoy their early bird arrival to the crater with the opportunity to explore three different Molokini dive locations. They currently offer four small group adventures on their 6 and 24 passenger rafts. They offer a Molokini Express, which is a two hour trip. They arrive at the crater first and snorkel the best spot before the big boats come in. Then it's a stop at the far crater wall for a second snorkeling opportunity. The trip includes beverages and gear for $39. Their Molokini Deluxe trip is 3 1/2 hours. You snorkel at the reef's end, Enenui, and the famous wall on the backside. Trip includes lunch, beverages and snorkel gear $55 adults, $45 youth. (808) 879-RAFT.

The *Four Winds* departs daily from Ma'alaea to Molokini. The half-day morning excursion is 7:30am-12:30pm with a maximum of 112 passengers. Booking directly may save you some money on this one. One of two boats operated by Maui Classic Charters, *Four Winds* is their new 55' glassbottom catamaran that arrived in early 1998. (The old *Four Winds* was donated to the Marine Biology Dept. of the University of Hawaii.) It's faster - and bigger which should alleviate our only previous complaint of being a bit crowded at capacity. They offer a BBQ as compared to a very similar basic (buffet) deli lunch and the breakfast is a varied selection of fresh bagels and cream cheese with jellies, and fresh pineapple and orange slices. A nice change from the old Danish! The BBQ lunch is cooked on board on three grills on the back of the boat. Lunch selections include mahi mahi, burger, vegiburger, or chicken breast. All very good, and a nice selection of condiments for the burgers. Beer, wine and soda included as well. Freshwater showers and an onboard waterslide add to the days fun. There are two decks, one covered and one uncovered and those of you who prefer to stay dry can sample the scenic underwater delights through their submarine-style glassbottom hull. An optional activity is Snuba ($40) which takes six people at a time with air tanks carried on rafts which float at the surface. You can go down to a depth of twenty feet. (808) 879-8188.

A good option for those preferring a larger, more ferry-type boat is the 92' motor yacht *The Prince Kuhio*. (808) 242-8777 or 1-800-468-1287.

The Pride of Maui ★ is a 65' catamaran featuring a large indoor cabin and outdoor sundecks, and hot fresh water shower. They offer daily departures at 8 am from the Ma'alaea Harbor for morning dives at two destinations, Molokini and "Turtle Town" (Pu'u O La'i) or depending on weather conditions, snorkel locations may be Olowalu or Coral Gardens. (808) 875-0955.

435

The Coon family's *Trilogy* operation offers a Molokini snorkel aboard their 55' Searunner *Trilogy V.* Adults $89, Children $44.50 (ages 3-12). They serve breakfast enroute, a snack and then a BBQ chicken lunch. Departs Ma'alaea. (808) 661-4743 or 1-800-874-2666.

LANA'I EXCURSION REVIEWS

Hulopo'e Beach, Lana'i - This is one our favorites. Located on the island of Lana'i, it's worth the trip for the beautiful beach and the abundant coral and fish. We saw a school of fish here that was so large that from the shore it appeared to be a huge moving reef. After swimming through the school and returning to shore we were informed that large predatory fish like to hang out around these schools! Lana'i is usually a full-day excursion with continental breakfast, BBQ lunch and a optional island tour. $79-$149 for adults, $35 and up for youth under age 12. Half-day trips are available on the *Navatek.*

A variety of snorkel/sail/tour options are available for snorkeling along East and West Maui's coastline, Molokini, Moloka'i or Lana'i. Your first decision is choosing between a large or small group tour. Large groups go out in substantial monohull or catamaran motor yachts of 60-90 feet in length. They get you there comfortably and fast, but without the intimate sailing experience of a smaller, less crowded boat. There are also many sleek sailboats (monohull, catamaran or trimaran) that you can share with 4 to 24 people or charter privately. Another option for a Maui sea excursion is a Zodiac type raft that uses 20-23 foot inflatable rafts powered by two large outboards. These rides can be rough, wet and wild. All tours provide snorkel gear with floatation devices, if needed, and instruction. Food and refreshments are provided to varying degrees. *Navatek* provides a state-of-the-art ride on their half-day Lana'i trip. This high-tech boat provides a smooth, even ride making it a good choice for the landlubber! For more detailed information see section on SEA EXCURSIONS.

TRILOGY ★
The Coon family knows better than to mess with a good thing. The morning boat trip over to Lana'i still starts earlier than most would like, but once underway with warm (yes, still homemade by the Coons) cinnamon rolls and a mug (the ceramic kind, no styrofoam here!) of hot chocolate or coffee, it seems all worth the effort. Don't forget to bring the camera! Trilogy boats now bring guests Monday through Friday for snorkeling, sun and fun at Manele Bay. (On Saturdays, snorkeling is off the boat, not at the beach.) Beginning snorkelers are carefully instructed before entering the ocean. If you would prefer, you can skip the tour of Lana'i City and snorkel even longer. The chicken is cooked on the grill by the ship's captain and served on china-type plates. It is accompanied by a delicious stir-fry and fresh rolls, but Mrs. Coon still isn't giving out the secret ingredients for her salad dressing to anyone. The eating area has a series of picnic tables and is pleasantly shaded by an awning. (808) 661-4743 or 1-800-874-2666. Email: trilogy@maui.net < WWW >

CLUB LANA'I

This is a one-of-a-kind operation on Maui and the closest thing the visitor will find to Gilligan's Island. It began operating in 1987, closed and then reopened in the spring of 1992. But the "private island" of Club Lana'i has changed little since it opened originally. The current going rate is $89 adults, $76 for seniors, juniors (13-20 years) $69, children (4-12 years) $29, infants three and under free. Scuba diving available and Snuba for an extra charge. And, if you are feeling a bit tense from all your vacation fun, a massage therapist is on board to provide a 15, 30, or 60 minute massage! Enroute there is a continental breakfast of pastries and coffee and, once you arrive, it is a full day of choosing whatever you want to do. There is biking, horseshoes, ping pong, massage, and kayaking and plenty of time to do nothing at all but enjoy a hammock. For lunch you'll enjoy their outdoor barbecue buffet with Hawaiian entertainment. They serve iced tea and punch and they still offer their special Lana'i Tais at the bar. Most of the guests take advantage of the coastline snorkeling (weather permitting), which leaves plenty of room for the remaining guests to pick out the perfect hammock. Keep an eye out for Mary Ann and the professor! Phone (808) 871-1144.

UNUSUAL SNORKELING EXCURSIONS

BLUE WATER ADVENTURES!

While Molokini continues to be a much touted snorkeling spot, those seeking something a little different should sign up with *Blue Water Rafting* ★ for their *Kanaio Coast of Maui* trip along Maui's southern shore. The area past Makena is geologically one of Maui's youngest and the coastline is only accessible by foot. However, a trip on the zodiac raft will get you up close to see the beautiful and unusual scenic wonders of Mother Nature. Natural lava arches, pinnacles, and caves are explored with the picturesque slopes of Haleakala providing a magnificent backdrop. Our chosen day for the expedition proved to be an exhilarating wet one! The ocean conditions were somewhat rougher than desired, but our hearty group agreed to push forward. With spray from the ocean drenching us, one of the more witty members of our group donned his snorkel and mask which worked admirably at keeping the water out of his eyes! The scenic vistas were fabulous and the boat was able to maneuver through one of the arches and up close to the cliffs which appeared to have been sculpted by a fine artisan. There was a brief stop for some mid-morning nourishment and a snorkel at La Perouse before returning to Kihei. This is the best - and only - way to experience such an exciting adventure! Phone (808) 879-7238.

SNORKELING

Maui offers exceptionally clear waters, warm ocean temperatures, and abundant sea life with safe areas (no adverse water conditions) for snorkeling. If you are a complete novice, most of the resorts and excursion boats offer snorkeling lessons. From the youngest to the oldest, everyone can enjoy this sport that needs little experience and there is no need to dive to see all the splendors of the sea.

If you are unsure of your snorkeling abilities, the use of a floatation device may be of assistance. Be forewarned that the combination of tropical sun and the refreshing coolness of the ocean can deceive those paddling blissfully on the surface, and result in a badly burned backside. Water resistant sunscreens are available locally and are recommended.

Equipment is readily available at resorts and dive shops, and as you can see, much less expensive at the dive shops (even better are the weekly rates). For a listing of dive shops see Scuba Diving. All snorkeling boat trips provide equipment as a part of their package. Some offer prescription masks.

If you plan on doing a lot of snorkeling, the purchase of your own equipment should be considered. Good quality gear is available at all the dive shops. Less expensive sets can be purchased at Longs or Costco.

TYPICAL RENTAL PRICES - MASK-FINS-SNORKEL:

Maui Dive Shop in Kihei - adults $5.95-7.95; silicone $15.95-24.95 per week (kids $1.49 per day)

Boss Frog's in Lahaina, Napili and Kihei - $9 per week; $1.50 per day

Hyatt Regency Resort at Kaanapali - $15 per day, 8am-6pm only

Snorkel Bob's in West Maui and Kihei charges $9 per set per week. Silicon set $19-29 per week, prescription masks $39.

Auntie Snorkel and Uncle Boogie in Kihei (Rainbow Mall) charges $9.95 per week for regular gear, $14.95 for silicon set. Also a "dry set" is $19.95. (879-6263)

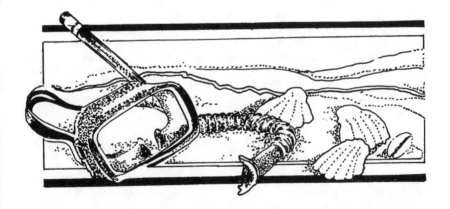

Most major dive shops can fit you with a prescription mask, as long as your vision impairment is not too severe. (Note from Christie: As a contact wearer with a strong prescription, I wear my soft lenses and have no problem with a good fitting mask.)

Good snorkeling spots, if not right in front of your hotel or condo, are only a few minutes' drive away. The following are our favorites, each for a special reason.

WEST MAUI

Black Rock - At the Sheraton in the Kaanapali Resort. Pay for parking at Whalers Village and walk down the beach. Clear water and a variety of tame fish - these fish expect handouts!

Kapalua Bay - Public park with off-street parking, restrooms and showers. A well-protected bay and beautiful beach amid the grounds of the Kapalua Resort. Limited coral and some large coral heads, fair for fish watching. Arrive early as parking is very limited!

Namalu Bay - Park at Kapalua Bay, walk over from Kapalua Bay to the bay which fronts the grounds of the resort. Difficult entry, very good on calm days.

Honolua Bay - No facilities, park alongside the road and walk a 1/4 mile to the bay, but the best snorkeling on Maui, anytime but winter.

Olowalu - At mile marker 14, about 5 miles south of Lahaina. Generally calm and warmer waters with ample parking along the roadside. Very good snorkeling. If you find a pearl earring, let us know, we *STILL* have the match!

EAST MAUI

Ulua-Mokapu Beach - Well-marked public beach park in Wailea with restrooms and showers. Good snorkeling on the Ulua side of the rocky point separating these two picturesque and beautiful beaches.

Maluaka Beach - Located in Makena, no facilities and along the road parking. Good coral formations and a fair amount of fish at the left end of the beach.

Ahihi Kinau Natural Reserve - Approximately five miles past Wailea. No facilities. This is not a very crowded spot and you may feel a little alone here, but the snorkeling is great with lots of coral and a good variety of fish.

Molokini Crater - This volcanic remanent affords good snorkeling, see Molokini See Excursion Reviews: Molokini for additional information.

Generally, the best snorkeling at all locations is in the morning until about 1pm, before the wind picks up. For more information on each area and other locations, refer to the BEACHES chapter.

A good way to become acquainted with Maui's sea life is a guided snorkeling adventure with **Ann Fielding**, marine biologist and author of *Hawaiian Reefs and Tidepools and Underwater Guide to Hawai'i*. She takes small groups (minimum 2, maximum 6) to the best location, but generally Honolua Bay in summer and Ahihi Kinau in winter. These morning (8am-1pm) excursions begin with an introductory discussion on Hawaiian marine life, identification and ecology which is followed by snorkeling. Floatation devices, snorkel gear, and lunch are provided for the $60 fee. Reservations (808) 572-8437 or FAX (808) 572-9769.

You may feel the urge to rent an underwater camera to photograph some of the unusual and beautiful fish you've seen, and by all means try it, but remember, underwater fish photography is a real art. The disposable underwater cameras are fun and inexpensive and available everywhere, but your resulting photos may be disappointing.

There are several video tapes of Maui's marine life available at the island bookstores if you want a permanent record of the fish you've seen. Several of the sea excursions offer video camera rentals.

There are other great places to snorkel, however, you need a boat to reach them. Fortunately, a large variety of charter services will be happy to assist.

SMALL BOAT SAILING

Small boat sailing is available at a number of locations with rentals, usually the 14' - sometimes 16' and 18' - Hobie Cat. Lasers are also available. Typical rental prices are $35-$50 per hour and lessons are available. Most of the resorts have sailing centers with rental facilities on the beaches.

FOR MORE INFORMATION ON SMALL BOAT RENTALS CONTACT:

Beach Activities Pavilion. Rental equipment for windsurfing, kayaking, surfing. Also Hobie Cat, pedal boats, and laser sailboats. (808) 661-5552.

West Maui Sailing School. Also windsurfing, kayak and snorkel equipment. Daily scheduled lessons or personalized lessons. They also have sea cycles: two seaters with two sets of independent pedals. A large snorkeling selection, in-line skates, surfboards, and body boards, too. (808) 667-5545

SNUBA

One of the newer water recreations available is Snuba which is a combination of snorkeling and scuba diving, allowing the freedom of underwater exploration without the heavy equipment of scuba diving. In brief, the snuba diver has a mask and an air hose that is connected to the surface. Some of those currently offering Snuba: *The Pride of Maui* charges $47 in addition to the cruise fee, *Navatek II* is $49, and *The Four Winds* charges $40. *Prince Kuhio*, *Club Lana'i* and *Lani Kai* also offer Snuba.

SPAS, FITNESS CENTERS, HEALTH RETREATS

If you are interested in keeping in shape and you have no fitness center at your resort, here are several that welcome drop in guests:
Gold's Gym, Lahaina Square, (667-7474)
Gold's Gym, Wailuku Industrial Park, (242-6851)
Gold's Gym, Lipoa Shopping Center in Kihei (874-2844)
World Gym, Kihei Commercial Center, 300 Ohukai Rd., (879-1326)

Advanced Aesthetics - Not a spa, but a "a step above a salon," Advanced Aesthetics specializes in skin care from medical & therapeutic treatments to rejuvenating facials and peels, $65-110. Waxing, cosmetic enhancements, and manicures are also offered, but it's the "Ali'i Pedicure" ($45) that visitors are "running" to! Their chair massage system relaxes your body while you soak in a luxurious jacuzzi foot bath, just before your soothing foot and leg massage - and that's before they even start painting your toenails! Open Monday-Saturday from 10 am; closed Sunday. 375 Huku Li'i Pl., #210, Kihei (808) 879-1247

Grand Wailea Resort and Spa invites non-guests to their luxurious spa for $30 admission (use of fitness facilities and specialty baths); an additional $110 per day for a full spa session. Added fees for massage and extras $75-220. (808) 875-1234. If you'd like a sneak peak at what to expect at this grandest of grand spas, here is Dona's first-hand report from the land of Ahhhs: *"As soon as you arrive at the magical, underground, autonomous 'city' of the Grand Wailea Resort Spa, you'll know you're not in Kansas anymore!*

"Spa Grande - designed with Italian marble, original artwork, Venetian chandeliers, mahogany millwork and inlaid gold - offers two full floors of invigorating fitness, rich luxury, soothing relaxation, and stimulating rejuvenation. Whether you need your rusty joints oiled and massaged, your body reshaped and freshened with a honey steam wrap, or you just want to come out with your mane washed and conditioned with the essence of Maui Mist, Spa Grande is the place to point your ruby slippers. This magical city takes you around the globe with a blend of European, Indian, Oriental, and American spa philosophies and treatments, but it's the "Hawaiian Reginal" regime that makes this spa unique.

441

Cleanse with the Hawaiian Salt Glo Scrub, relax with the healing Lomi Lomi massage or Hawaiian Limu Rejuvenator body masque, and soak in a soothing bath of seaweed or fragrant tropical enzymes. Then sit under an indoor waterfall to massage and relieve tired back muscles or refresh under an 'ordinary' shower with extraordinary honey mango bath gel. And what's the password to enter this jewel-like kingdom and enjoy such a multi-faceted experience? Why -- 'Pamper me' -of course!"

Madison Avenue - Full service day spa at Kaahumanu Center offers skin, nail, hair, waxing, and lash & brow services from $10 to $65. Half-hour massage $35, one-hour $65, or a "quickie" chair massage for just $1 per minute! (5-minute minimum.) Sightseers, shoppers, beachgoers - even guidebook authors on deadline - can find time to fit *that* in! Open Monday-Friday 9:30am-9pm; Saturday till 7; Sunday 10am-5pm. (808) 873-0880.

Maui Marriott Beach & Tennis Club - New fitness facility (November, 1997) also offers tennis and a pro shop. Open daily 7am-8pm. Daily fitness pass, $10 per person; 4-day pass, $30 ($60 per couple over a 7-day period); 7-day pass $50 ($100 per couple over a 14 day period). Fitness pass with tennis can also be used at the Sheraton and Royal Lahaina ($15 day, $75 week). Circuit training clinic $15 per person, two people minimum; personal training: $55 per hour private; $35 semi-private (minimum two.) (808) 667-1200.

Maui School of Therapeutic Massage - Whether it is an early morning sunrise at Haleakala or a venture up to the Tedeschi Winery, be sure you include a stop in Makawao at the Maui School of Therapeutic Massage. This is one of the best deals going! The school is located at 1043 Makawao Avenue (upstairs) and appointments are required. The cost for a one-hour massage is an unbelievable $20. There were no complaints from our group of four that stopped in one rainy day! Current clinic hours are Monday, Wednesday, and Friday 5pm-9pm, Tuesday and Thursday 1pm-5pm and Sat. and Sun. 9am-1pm. (808) 572-2277.

Maui Visions Vacations - 1680 Makawao Ave. Makawao, HI 96768. As a part of their customized, full-service planning, they can arrange rejuvenation adventures and retreats. (808) 572-2161.

Spa Kea Lani is the all new spa facility at Kea Lani Hotel, Suites & Villas in Wailea. Experience a variety of massage techniques with their Massage Combo or try a synchronized "double massage" - the ultimate in relaxing massage therapy. Refreshing body treatments, rejuvenating wraps, facials, and waxing services are available individually or as a part of a treatment package ($175-345). Or focus on fitness with a personal training session in their new workout facilities. (808) 875-4100 ext. 229.

Spa Luna in Makawao offers facials, facial and body muscle toning, body wraps, hydrotherapy, massage, sauna, waxing, lymphatic cleansing, reflexology, acupuncture, tai chi classes, yoga classes and wellness workshops. Located at 1156 Makawao Avenue in a remodeled historic building. (808) 572-1300.

SPORTING CLAYS & SHOOTING RANGES

Lahaina Western Gun Club features an indoor shooting range with 44 magnum and 357 magnum revolver handguns as well as others. Open 7 days a week at Lahaina Center, behind the Hard Rock Cafe near the theaters. (808) 661-8833.

Westside Sporting Clays and Pistol Range, located 3.3 miles NE of the entrance to Kapalua, just past Honolua Bay. They have a variety of courses for novice to advanced abilities. (808) 669-7468.

SUBMARINE TOURS

The *Atlantis Submarine* tours the underwater world beyond Lahaina's harbor. Excursions last approximately two hours. The underwater submarine tour lasts about 45 minutes, except the Discover Dive, which is about 30 minutes in length. Children rates apply to those youths 12 years and younger, but they must be at least 36 inches tall to ride aboard *Atlantis*. The *Atlantis* adventures include an ocean cruise out to the dive site (whale watching in season) and complimentary beverages. The dive descends to a depth of 120 feet. They also do Japanese narrated tours. The fully submersible submarine is an 80 ton, 65 foot touring vessel that accommodates 46 passengers. They operate eight dives daily beginning at their Pioneer Inn shop, which also affords you plenty of time to shop for logo items from polo shirts, to visors, beach bottles, jelly beans or beach towels. There is a short boat ride to reach the submarine and quite surprisingly it suddenly emerges out of the middle of the depths of the Pacific. Then you step across from the tender and load onto the submarine. The seats are lined up on both sides in front of 1/2 a porthole. The submarine submerges about 125 feet. The area is a little close, but the temperature is kept cool and comfortable. There are plenty of fish, and fish cards at each station help you identify them. Rocks and coral formations resemble an environ that is somehow extra-terrestrial. The Maui Discover is $69 adults/39 children for this 45 minute submarine ride an 15 minute shoreline excursion to and from the sub. The Maui Odyssey is $79/39. Sub/luau package $99/$49. Whale watch/submarine $89/39, Helicopter/submarine $148/128. (808) 667-2224.

The *Reef Dancer* (formerly *Nautilus*) is a semi-submersible, meaning it only partially submerges, so at any time you feel a bit claustrophobic, you can go up on deck for some fresh air. It departs at least 5 times a day, times change seasonally. The bottom is six feet below the surface and they cruise around the ocean floor off of Puamana. The total trip is an hour, but once you are under-way, you begin viewing, while the *Atlantis* does require some coordinating to get from the dock to the submarine. The *Reef Dancer* seats are more comfortable, allowing for a bit more room to walk around. One of the crew scuba dives out to hold up items for the guests to view. $29.95 adults, $15.95 for children 6-12 years, 5 and under are free. Their new 90 minute tour departs daily at 2:30 and includes a second turtle site. $44.95 adults, $24.95 children. (808) 667-2133 or FAX 661-1107.

The *SeaView* is a 56' semi-submersible vessel that offers 2 hour fully narrated viewing and swim snorkel cruises which depart daily from the Lahaina harbor. This trip offers the opportunity to stay dry in air-conditioned comfort or just jump in for an up-close and personal view. They also have free use of ocean kayaks and viewing boards. Adults $44, $25 for children 4-12 years and children under 4 are free. SeaView Adventure: 661-5550.

THE PROS AND CONS: The *Atlantis* does have clearer viewing since they are down so deep and have infra-red lights. The *Reef Dancer* makes use of sunlight, which at times can be bright, other times cause the water to be hazy. In brief, the *Reef Dancer* is more like dry snorkeling and the *Atlantis* more like dry scuba diving. The *Atlantis* has a smoother, plane-like motion, while the *Reef Dancer* is more like a helicopter, bobbing and rocking as it maneuvers. The *Atlantis* does provide the submarine experience, but you pay the price. The *Reef Dancer* is less expensive than the *Atlantis*, for a few dollars more you can have a two hour trip on *SeaView* (versus one hour on *Reef Dancer*) and a chance to snorkel, too. If you have enjoyed snorkeling on Maui, you won't see much more through the viewing windows on the *Reef Dancer* than you would if you were swimming. But if you are unable or unwilling to get wet, then one of these trips may be an option to consider.

SURFING

(Also see body surfing) Honolua Bay is one of the best surfing spots in Hawaii, and undoubtedly the best on Maui, with waves up to 15 feet on a good winter day and perfect tubes. A spectacular vantage point is on the cliffs above the bay. In the summer this bay is calm and, as it is a Marine Reserve, offers excellent snorkeling.

Also in this area is Punalau Beach (just past Honolua) and Honokeana Bay off Ka'eleki'i Point (just north of the Alaeloa residential area). In the Lahaina area there are breaks north and south of the harbor and periodically good waves at Awalua Beach (mile marker 16).

On the north shore, Hookipa Beach Park, Kanaha Beach, and Baldwin all have good surfing at times. In the Hana area there is Hamoa Beach. There are a couple of good spots in Ma'alaea Bay and at Kalama Beach Park.

Conditions change daily - even from morning to afternoon - around the island. Check with local board rental outlets for current daily conditions.

Alan Cadiz' Hawaiian Sailboarding Techniques - 425 Koloa, Kahului. PO Box 1199 Paia, HI 96779. HST goes "surf-surfari" to wherever the best place for learning happens to be that particular day. Small groups and private instruction available for beginners wanting to cruise the waves their first time out, also intermediate and advanced lessons. Longboard surfing class are two hours, three people per class maximum, includes surfboard for beginner and intermediate lessons. (808) 871-5423. FAX (808) 871-6943. 1-800-968-5423.

Big Kahuna Kayak - Rainforest hikes, surfing school and kayaking tours & rentals. (808) 875-6395. <WWW>

Goofy Foot Surf School ★ - Ever see the old Disney cartoon where Goofy is surfing? Well, standard surfing position is left foot forward, but Goofy has his right forward! (Guess the artists weren't surfers). The resulting term "Goofy Foot" applies to those folks who surf Goofy-style. Tim Sherer, "Board Director" guarantees you'll stand in your first two-hour lesson or the experience is on Goofy Foot. Class sizes are kept small, not more than five students. He promises to make the seemingly difficult remarkably easy. Well, we gave this one a try. Tim and associates begin your 2-hour introduction to surfing at the beach in front of 505 Front Street. The boards are marked with lines to help you position your feet. The first 30 minutes or so is spent learning the different body and foot positions for surfing, and the transitions between. It appeared that it would be a strenuous thigh workout, but we were to be surprised! After that, it is out to the harbor where the waves break small, but are long and consistent. We discovered that surfing isn't the hard part, it is the paddling! But if they called it paddling, rather than surfing, who'd want to do it! Everyone in the class got up at least once or twice. But it was soon obvious, that upper body conditioning was a little lacking in our eager troupe. If there are 5 or more in a class, Tim calls in for reinforcements, so the classes are always very personal.

Another Goofy Foot plus is the opportunity to come back at any time and for a $10 board rental fee, you can join any existing class. Not only does this give you a chance to rest up for a day or two and try again, but you're able to give it a second chance with some supervision on-hand. There isn't any limit to the times you can return. What a deal for those teenagers! (Tim has also just initiated large group surfing beach parties for a full day of surfing, food and games at the beach.) Call (808) 244-WAVE or page Tim locally at 229-6737. <WWW>

Harbor Surf & Dive - Surfboard sales, rental, and repair. Also snorkel, kayak, and boggie board rentals. 113 Prison St., Lahaina. (808) 667-5911.

Maui Surfing School - Andrea Thomas originated the "Learn to Surf in One Lesson" and has taught thousands of people between the ages of 3 and 70. She's been teaching on Maui since 1980 and offers private and group lessons specializing in the beginner and the coward. Board rentals available. Lahaina Harbor. Phone (808) 875-0625.

Nancy Emerson School of Surfing - PO Box 463, Lahaina, HI 96767. Phone (808) 874-1183 or FAX (808) 874-2581.

Surf Lessons with Surf Dog Maui - Private and small groups learn surfing from their mobile surf clinic. Lessons based on wherever surf and weather conditions are the best. Lessons by appointment. PO Box 501, Lahaina, HI 96767. (808) 250-SURF.

TENNIS

Tennis facilities abound on Maui. Many condos and major hotels offer tennis facilities, also, there are quite a few very well-kept public courts. They are, of course, most popular during the cooler early morning and early evening hours.

PUBLIC COURTS

Haliimaile - One court by the baseball park.

Hana - Hana Ball Park, one double lighted court.

Kahului - Maui Community College (Kaahumanu and Wakea Ave.) has 2 unlighted courts. Kahului Community Center (Onehee and Uhu St.) has two lighted courts. The Kahului War Memorial Complex has four lighted courts, located at Kaahumanu and Kanaloa Ave. Phone 243-7389.

Wailuku - Wellspark has seven lighted courts, So. Market St. and Wells St. Local phone 243-7389.

Kihei - Kalama Park has four lighted courts. Six unlighted courts in park fronting Maui Sunset condos. Local phone 879-4364.

Lahaina - Lahaina Civic Center has five lighted courts and there are four lighted courts at Malu-ulu-olele Park. Local phone 661-4685.

Makawao - Eddie Tam Memorial Center has two lighted courts. Local phone 572-8122.

Pukalani - Pukalani Community Center has two lighted courts, located across from the Pukalani Shopping Center. Local phone 572-8122.

PRIVATE COURTS WITH FACILITIES OPEN TO PUBLIC

Hyatt Regency, Kaanapali. Six unlighted courts. 7am-dusk. Guests $15 and $20 for non-guests - per person per day or per court per hour. Lessons $55 per hour private; $65 semi-private. Local phone 661-1234 ext. 3174.

Kapalua Bay Hotel, Kapalua. The *Tennis Garden* has 10 courts, 4 are lighted. Tennis attire required at all times. Local phone 669-5677. The *Village Tennis Center* also has 10 courts, 4 lighted. Local phone 665-0112. Charge for either is $10 per day for resort guests, non-guests $12. Clinics daily.

Makena Tennis Club, 5415 Makena Alanui, Makena Resort. Two lighted courts. Resort guests $18 per hour, non-guests $20 or per person rate of $12 all day. All courts were resurfaced in April, 1998. Local phone 879-8777.

Maui Marriott Beach & Tennis Club, Kaanapali. Five oceanfront courts, three are lighted. New fitness facility and pro shop opened November, 1997. Daily 7am-8pm. Court fees are the same for guests or non-guests: $10 per person per day; with fitness center $15. 4-day pass, $30 ($60 per couple over a 7-day period); 7-day pass $50 ($100 per couple over a 14 day period). Family pass also available. Tennis passes can also be used at the Sheraton and Royal Lahaina. Lessons from $35 for 1/2 hour to $225 for 5-lesson package. Clinics from $15; round robin tournaments $10. Racquets, shoes, balls, ball hopper, and ball machine for rent $2.50-20. Local phone 661-6200 or 667-1200 X689.

Royal Lahaina Tennis Ranch, Kaanapali - Has the largest facility in West Maui with 11 courts, 6 lighted and 1 stadium court. Pro shop and snack bar open 7am-noon and 2-7pm. Tennis passes can also be used at the Maui Marriott and Sheraton Maui. (See Maui Marriott listing for all fees, pass information, and equipment rentals.) Local phone 667-5200 or 661-3611 X2296.

Sheraton Maui Tennis Club, Kaanapali - Three lighted courts and pro shop open daily from 8am-noon and 2-8pm. Tennis passes can also be used at the Maui Marriott and Royal Lahaina. (See Maui Marriott listing for all fees, pass information, and equipment rentals.) Local phone 662-8208 or 661-0031 X8208.

Wailea Tennis Club, Wailea. Has 11 courts, 3 lighted. Rates for Wailea Resort Guests $25 per hour/day; non-guests $30 per hour/day. (The way that works is that your first hour is guaranteed with your reservation and you can play anytime during the rest of the day that the courts are free.) Private lessons $60 per hour. They also offer summer workshops for kids. Pro shop. Local phone 879-1958.

RESORT COURTS RESTRICTED TO GUESTS

Hale Kamaole, Hotel Hana Maui, Kaanapali Alii, Kaanapali Plantation, Kaanapali Shores, Kaanapali Royal, Kahana Villa, Kamaole Sands, Kihei Akahi, Kihei Alii Kai, Kihei Bay Surf, Kuleana, Maalaea Surf, Mahana, Makena Surf, Maui Hill, Maui Islander, Maui Lu Resort, Maui Vista, Papakea, Puamana, Royal Kahana, Sands of Kahana, Shores of Maui, The Whaler.

THEATER, MOVIES, AND THE ARTS

There is a six-plex cinema at the Kaahumanu Center and a four-plex in Kihei's Kukui Mall. In Lahaina, there is a tri-cinema at The Wharf Cinema (Shopping) Center and another set of four theaters at the Lahaina Center. All offer a $4 admission for matinees and all-day Tuesdays. Children and Seniors are $3.75 anytime. At Maui Mall in Kahului, a 12-screen movie theater with all-new stadium seating was expected to move into the former Woolworth's location by the end of 1998. Film buffs will enjoy the Maui Film Festival, a weekly series of award-winning, critically-acclaimed films shown every Wednesday in the state-of-the-art Castle Theater at Maui Arts & Cultural Center. (Call 572-FILM for current schedule.)

The *Maui Arts & Cultural Center* offers everything from local community events to concert performances by internationally known performers. Entertainers as diverse as Tony Bennett, Pearl Jam, Tibetan monks, the Lakota Sioux Indian Dance Theatre, Harry Belafonte, the Doobie Brothers, Santana and the Vienna Boys Choir have performed at the center along with the ballet, symphony, multi-cultural music and dance presentations, the annual Hawaii International Film Festival (November), art gallery exhibits, and weekly tours of the center - 11am every Wednesday. Call 242-SHOW <WWW>

Maui Community Theatre produces a full season of professional quality plays and musicals performing almost every weekend from October through June. Three comedies, two musicals, and one drama are balanced with classic and contemporary theatre. In existence since the 1920's when two theatre groups (the Maui Players and Little Theatre of Maui) joined forces, MCT has continued in varying forms and locations (interrupted only by World War II in the 40's and a fire in the 80's) until settling in their present home at the renovated Historic Iao Theatre on Market Street in Wailuku. Their new sidewalk restaurant, Applause Cafe, serves lunch during the day and show-themed dinners before performances. Call 242-6969 for information or reservations.

Theatre Theatre Maui is a non-profit organization (primarily funded through grants from the County of Maui) that offers a family theatre experience for residents and visitors on the West Side. Three yearly workshops for children; the summer one culminates at the end of July with an annual production held at the Westin Maui. Call 661-1168 for more information.

The Baldwin Performing Arts Learning Center (Baldwin Theatre Guild) offers six main stage productions each year. Generally they do a musical, a children's show, a dramatic presentation, a summer musical and an annual revue. The group was formed in 1964 when interested high school students and adults expressed a desire to organize and perform theatrical productions. Over the years, hundreds of students and adults have been part of this organization - many of whom have gone on to success with national theatre productions and touring companies! Workshops are held at various times during the month and in addition to the performances, the guild also offers its members involvement in other social activities, such as dances or picnics. For information on performances phone (808) 984-5673 or check the local paper.

The *Maui Academy of Performing Arts* clearly has it all when it comes to entertainment. An educational and performing arts organization for youth and adults, the Academy hopes to be fully installed in their new location (The old National Dollar Store on Main St. in Wailuku) by summer, 1999. They offer community theatre performances, special events, ongoing dance and drama classes, and special drama and dance workshops for youth and adults. Visitors welcome. For more information on any of the current programs or daily schedule, call the Academy offices at 244-8760.

WATERSKIING

Hawaii Island Watercraft, Inc. dba *Kaanapali Waterski*. Located at Whalers Village on Kaanapali Beach. Waterskiing runs $25 for 15 minutes, 30 minutes will cost $50, one hour for $80. Also available are the aqua sled (banana boat), private coastal tours, and seasonal whale watching. (808) 667-1964.

Kaanapali Windsurfing School - Beginner lesson 1 1/2 hours $49. Rental equipment $20 per hour, $45 for three hours, $65 for 5 hours. Equipment for beginners to intermediate. They also do Hobie Cat rentals, surfing lessons, waterskiing, and wake boarding. (808) 667-1964.

WHALE WATCHING

Every year beginning December 15 and continuing through May 15 (official whale season - but peak sightings are January-March), the humpback whales arrive in the warm waters off the Hawaiian Islands for breeding, and their own sort of vacation!

The sighting of a whale can be an awesome and memorable experience with the humpbacks (small as whales go) measuring some 40-50 feet and weighing in at 30 tons. The panoramic vistas as you drive over the Pali and down the beachfront road to Lahaina afford some excellent opportunities to catch sight of one of these splendid marine mammals. However, PLEASE pull off the road and enjoy the view. Many accidents are caused by distracted drivers.

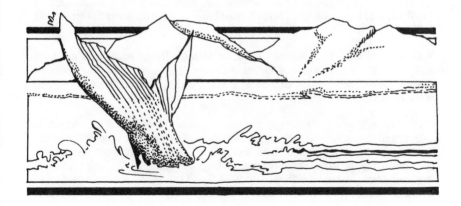

For an even closer view, there are plenty of boat trips (kayaks, too) - almost every boat operator does whale watching tours in season. Many of the tour boats now have a marine biologist onboard to offer insight during your whale watching excursion.

You can report your whale sightings by calling the Whale Watch Hotline at 879-8811. Also refer to SEA EXCURSIONS.

WINDSURFING

Windsurfing is a sport that is increasing (astronomically!) in popularity. Hookipa Beach Park on Maui is one of the best windsurfing sites in the world. This is due to the consistently ideal wind and surf conditions, however, this is definitely NOT the spot for beginners. For the novice, boardsailing beginner group lessons run $40-60 an hour and generally involve instruction on a dry land simulator before you get wet with easy to use beginners equipment. Equipment and/or lessons are available from the following:

Alan Cadiz' Hawaiian Sailboarding Techniques - 425 Koloa St., Kahului. Alan Cadiz and his staff of professional instructors offer a full range of small group and private lessons for beginner or expert. They specialize in one-on-one instruction tailored to each person's ability, travel schedule, budget and goals. (808) 871-5423 or 1-800-968-5423 or FAX (808) 871-6943.

Hawaiian Island Surf and Sport - Pro shop, sales, service, rentals, instruction, and travel (condo & car packages). Three-hour windsurfing group (up to 3 students) beginner lessons or advanced water start at $69. Private instruction begins at $49. 415 Dairy Road, Kahului. 1-800-231-6958 or (808) 871-4981, FAX (808) 871-4624 < www.hawaiianisland.com > Email: hisurf@maui.net

Hi-Tech Surf Equipment - Sales and rentals; they also have lessons. Kahului (808) 877-2111, Paia (808) 579-9297. Also Shapers at Kaahumanu Center. Phone (808) 877-SURF.

Kaanapali Windsurfing School - Beginner lessons. Rental equipment per hour $20, $45 for three hours, $65 for 5 hours. Equipment for beginners to intermediate. They also do Hobie Cat rentals, surfing lessons, waterskiing and wake boarding. (808) 667-1964.

Matt Schweitzer - This young fellow has won 14 world titles, which is understandable as he boasts that his father invented the sport of windsurfing. Matt moved with his family to the Kahana area when he was a teenager. In addition to windsurfing, he can arrange fishing, surfing, dirt biking, or kayaking on Maui or neighbor islands. (808) 669-5003. Or visit his website at: < info@mauisportsadventure.com >

Maui Windsurfari - Offers packages which include accommodations, rental car, windsurfing equipment, and excursions. Many of their vacation rentals are unusual with close proximity to windsurfing locations. (808) 871-7766 or 1-800-736-6284. <http://www.windsurfar.com>

Maui Windsurfing School - Group & private lessons for all levels. Beginning group 2 1/2 hours or private 1 hour $70; three day lesson package $165, five day $250. Also rental equipment via their Maui Windsurf Co. 520 Keolani Place, Kahului. (808) 877-4816 or 1-800-872-0999.

Second Wind - Proshop rental, used and new sales. Private lessons or two hour class. Their travel desk assists with accommodation and car rental plans. (808) 877-7467 or 1-800-936-7787. <http://www.maui.net/~secwind/index.html>

Windsurfing West Maui - Provides windsurfing lessons and equipment. 180 E. Wakea in Kahului. (808) 871-8733. They also operate Maui Vans which offers vans with racks and hangers for boards and equipment. (808) 877-0090 or 1-800-870-4084.

Some resorts offer their guests free clinics. Rental by the hour can get expensive at $20 per hour and $40-$65 per four hours. A better rate is $45 for all day.

BOUGAINVILLEA   J.BAYOT

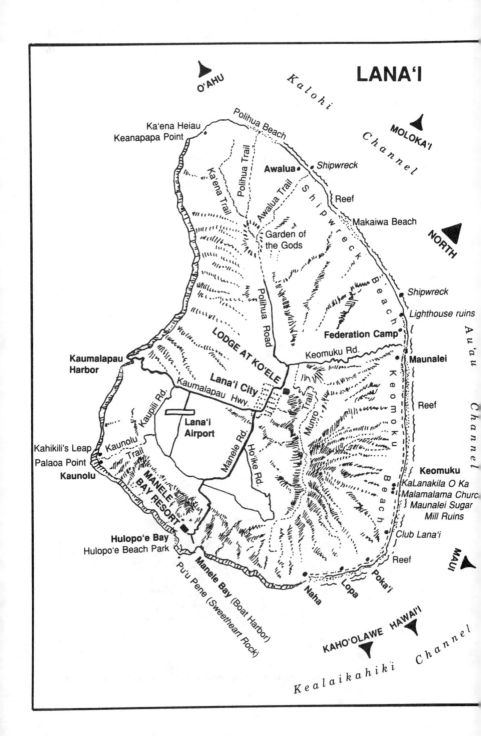

THE ISLAND

OF LANA'I

COUNTY OF MAUI

INTRODUCTION

The meaning of Lana'i seems to be steeped in mystery, at least this was our experience. Several guidebooks report that the name means "swelling" or "hump." In discussions with local residents we were told it meant the obvious interpretation of "porch" or "balcony," perhaps because Lana'i, in a rather nebulous fashion, is the balcony of Maui. So, with no definitive answer we will continue the search, but in the meantime, come enjoy this piece of Paradise.

Just before and immediately following the turn of the century, Lana'i was a bustling sheep and cattle ranch. Beginning in the 1920s, Dole transformed Lana'i into the largest single pineapple plantation in the world. The 1990s have brought Lana'i into the visitor industry with the opening of two new elegant and classy resorts, the country-style Lodge at Koele in Lana'i City and the seashore resort at Manele Bay. Under the helm of David Murdock, the metamorphosis has been a positive one with young people returning to the island to work in the new tourism industry. Cattle are again dotting the landscape as the silver-blue fields of pineapple rapidly fade into extinction.

A few brief island facts and figures: Lana'i has a population of 2,975, its major industries are tourism and agriculture. Two parks, Dole Park in Lana'i City and Hulopo'e Beach Park. Three golf courses. Highest peak is Lana'ihale at 3,366 feet. Most popular visitor attractions are Kanepu'u (Garden of the Gods), Hulopo'e Beach, Lana'ihale, and Kaiolhia Bay (Shipwreck Beach). There are three hotels with a total of 363 rooms and no vacation condominiums. Lana'i has four beaches (with only one accessible via paved road) and there are 47 miles of shoreline which surround the 141 square mile island.

While each isle has its own nickname, it appears that Lana'i has outgrown hers. "The Pineapple Isle" no longer bears much symbolism for an island which has transformed from an agricultural setting to "an oasis within an oasis" for the lucky tourist. In the past it had been a wonderful retreat and happily, much of what was good about Lana'i has not changed. The slow pace of the isle has not been as significantly altered by the arrival of the mega-resort as one might imagine. What new term of endearment will be vested upon the isle? The Isle of Relaxation, Pine Isle, The Island Less Traveled, The Isle of Enchantment? Hawai'i's Most Secluded Island? Time will tell, or perhaps the tourist bureau will! With the continuing construction of luxury homes in the Koele district on 68 acres, and plans for 350 homes at Manele, the rich and famous will very shortly (if not already) be anteing up to purchase a vacation home on Lana'i.

As with each Hawaiian island, Lana'i is unique. The price for a stay at the two resorts may be steep, but if you want to really indulge, read on! A truly luxurious and relaxing island get-away that is only eight miles (but in many ways, 30 years removed) from Maui, Lana'i will simply enchant you.

LANA'I - GEOGRAPHY AND CLIMATE

Lana'i is the sixth largest of the eight major Hawaiian islands. It is situated eight miles to the west of Maui and seven miles south of Moloka'i. It is likely that millions of years ago (when the glaciers were larger and the seas much lower), Maui, Lana'i, Moloka'i and Kaho'olawe comprised one enormous island. This is further substantiated by the fact that the channels between the islands are more shallow and the slopes of the islands visibly more gradual than on the outer coastlines of the islands. The island of Lana'i was formed by a single shield volcano. A ridge runs along the eastern half of the island and forms its most notable feature. This large, raised hump is dotted with majestic Cook Island pines. The summit of the island is Lana'ihale, located at an elevation of 3,370 feet. A rather strenuous hike along the Munro Trail provides access to this summit where you will be treated to the only location in Hawai'i where you can view (on a clear day) five other Hawaiian islands. Maunalei and Hauola are Lana'i's two deepest gulches. Today the Maunalei Gulch continues to supply the island with its water. The center of the island, once a caldera, is the Palawai (basin) which has been used as both farm and ranch land. Lana'i has one city, cleverly dubbed Lana'i City. Located at an elevation of about 1,700 feet, it can be much cooler - and wetter - than the coastline. It is the hub of the island, or what hub there is, and visitors will soon learn that all roads lead to Lana'i City. The island population in 1994 was about 2,600, with almost everyone a resident of Lana'i City. The houses are generally small, mostly roofed with tin, and the yards are abloom with fruits and flowers.

Rainfall along the coastline is limited, only 4 or 5 inches a year. The heart of the island and Lana'i City, however, may have rainfall of 20 inches or more, and the higher slopes receive 45 to 60 inches annually. The weather in Lana'i City might range from 80 degree days in September with lows in the mid-sixties, to cooler January temperatures in the low 70s, dropping an additional 10 degrees at night. The coastline can be warmer by 10 degrees or more. Pineapples and pines, not palms, were the predominant vegetation on the island. At its peak in the 1970s, there were 15,000 acres of pineapple in cultivation. Castle & Cook made the decision in the 1980s to diversify the island and enter the tourist industry in a big way. The pineapple fields have been reduced to only about 100-120 acres, simply enough for local consumption. The production of hay and alfalfa is well underway, and some fields are spotted with Black Angus cattle. Other acreage has been converted to an organic garden for use by the Manele and Koele restaurants. The island flower is very unusual. The Kaunaoa is more a vine in appearance than a flower and there are two varieties. One grows in the uplands and the other near the ocean. The ocean species have a softer vine with more vivid hues of yellow and orange than the mountainous counterparts. Strands of the vine are twisted and adorned with local greens and flowers to make beautiful and unusual leis. The mountain vines make a stiffer lei and, we were told, are used as leis for decorating animals. One of the best places to spot this plant is along the drive down to Keomuku and Shipwreck Beach or along the shoreline. You will note that it is a very arid island. Water supply has always been a problem and most of the greenery is supplied by the Cook Island pines which dot the island.

HISTORY OF LANA'I

The historical tales of the island of Lana'i are intriguing, filled with darkness and evil. As legend has it, in ancient times the island of Lana'i was uninhabited except for evil spirits. It is said that in the olden days, those who went to Lana'i never returned and that the island was tabu (or *kapu* in Hawaiian). Hawaiians banished wrong-doers to Lana'i as punishment for their crimes. The story continues that around the 16th century on West Maui there was a chief named Kaka'alanaeo. He had a son named Kaulula'au who was willful and spoiled. The people became furious with his many misdeeds and finally rebelled and demanded that Kaulula'au be put on trial by the ancient laws. The verdict was guilty and, according to the ancient laws, his punishment was death. His father begged for his life and it was agreed that Kaulula'au would be banished to the island of Lana'i. He was set ashore near the Maunalei Gulch, the only source of potable water on the island. His father promised him that if he could banish the evil spirits from Lana'i, he could then set a bonfire as a signal and his father and the warriors would return for him. And, as luck would have it, Kaulula'au managed to trick the evil spirits and send them over to Kaho'olawe. He signaled his father and returned to Maui, heralded now as a hero. (Be sure you take time to view the beautiful, large murals on either side of the entrance at the Manele Bay Hotel. One depicts the fallen son being taken by canoe to Lana'i. The other shows Kaulula'au, head held high in victory, standing over his signal bonfire.) At this time in history, Maui was reaching its population zenith and Hawaiians relocated to Lana'i with settlements near Keomuku and inland as well.

The first archeological studies were done in 1921 by Kenneth Emory from the anthropology department of the Bishop Museum and he published his work in 1923. (Hardcover reprints of the book are available at Walden bookstores on Maui.) Kenneth Emory found many ancient villages and artifacts which had been, for the most part, undisturbed for hundreds of years. He found the area of Kaunolu to be Lana'i's richest archaeological region filled with house sites and remnants of a successful fishing village. He also ventured to the eastern coastline and explored Naha and Keomuku. He noted eleven *heiaus* (temples), found relics including old stone game boards and discovered a network of trails and petroglyphs. Before the construction on the two new resorts began, the first archeological team since 1921 arrived. Villages were studied and ashes from old fires were analyzed. The findings showed that the ashes dated from 900 A.D., much later than the other islands which were inhabited as early as 40 or 50 B.C. One of the earliest *heiaus*, The Halulu Heiau, is in the Kaunolu area, and it is thought that this region may have been one of the earliest Hawaiian settlements.

While the Hawaiian population increased throughout the archipelago, Lana'i was left largely uninhabited until the 1500s. Two of Captain Cook's ships, *The Discovery* and *The Resolution*, reported a visit to Lana'i. They found the Hawaiians friendly along the windward coastal area where they replenished their supplies of food and water. In talking with the islanders, they estimated that the population was approximately 10,000. They observed and noted that the island was a dry dustbowl and that the people fished and grew some taro. It was about at this same time, chiefs of Maui became worried that the people on Lana'i might become too powerful. So they divided Lana'i into 13 *ohanas* (ohana means family, but this refers more to regions) and put a *konahiki* in charge of each -- this way insuring that no one chief would be too powerful. These district names are still used today. They are Kaa Paomai, Mahana, Maunalei, Kamoku, Kauno-lu, Kalulu, Kealiakapu, Kealiaaupuni, Palawai, Kamao, Pawili and Kaohai.

Six months after the island was visited by Cook's vessels, a tragic event happened that would change life on Lana'i forever. Inter-island battles among the island chiefs were not uncommon, but until this time Lana'i had remained unaffected. In 1778 Kalaniopu'u, the chief on the Big Island, launched an unsuccessful attack on Lahaina, Maui. He retreated, then turned and attacked central Maui. Here again his warriors were overcome. As they returned to the Big Island in great anger, he passed the island of Kaho'olawe, which was loyal to the Maui chief-tains. In retaliation, Kalaniopu'u's warriors massacred the entire population on Kaho'olawe. Bolstered by his victory, Kalaniopu'u turned once again to assault Lahaina and again was defeated. Now enraged, Kalaniopu'u and his warriors chose to strike the leeward coastal villages of Lana'i. Lana'i's warriors were unprepared and retreated to the Ho'okia Ridge to have a better location from which to launch their counterattack. However, without access to food and water, the Lana'i warriors soon weakened and Kalanaiopu'u moved quickly to crush them. The Big Island warriors continued around Lana'i and systematically destroyed all the villages. Kalaniopu'u returned to the Big Island of Hawai'i and there, seven months later, he died and his lieutenant, Kamehameha came to rule.

During the rule of Kamehameha the population increased. The king and his warriors would visit Kaunolu Bay on Lana'i's southwestern coastline. Here Kahekili is said to have leapt from a cliff above the sea into the Pacific waters, proving his loyalty to the king. Other warriors were then challenged to follow his example and the area continues to be referred to as Kahekili's Leap.

The elders from the Church of Jesus Christ of Latter Day Saints acquired land on Lana'i from one of the chiefs in 1855. In 1860 Walter Murray Gibson came to Lana'i with the intent of establishing a Mormon colony called the City of Joseph in the Palawai (basin). Gibson had been instrumental in assisting Kamehameha. He served on his cabinet and was among the advisors for the construction of the Iolani Palace. He purchased 20,000 acres of land on Lana'i and obtained leases on more. By 1863 there were about 600 Mormons living on Lana'i. In 1864, when the church elders arrived to visit, they discovered that Walter had purchased additional lands with the church money, but had listed ownership under his own name, and he wasn't willing to release them. He was quickly expelled from the church and the Mormons went on to develop their church on O'ahu. As owner of 26,000 acres, Gibson first established the Lana'i Sheep Ranch which later became the Lana'i Ranch. In 1867 the population was 394 people (the 600 Mormons had departed earlier), 18,000 goats and 10,000 sheep. In 1870 Gibson attempted a cooperative farm, but this operation soon proved unsuccessful. By 1875 Gibson was controlling ninety percent of the island for ranch or farming operations. In 1874, Gibson's daughter, Talula, married Frederick Harrison Hayselden, formerly of England and Australia, and by the early 1880s Frederick was managing the ranch. Walter Gibson passed away in

San Francisco in 1888 and ownership of the land transferred to his daughter, Talula Hayselden, and his son-in-law Frederick.

By 1894 the Lana'i Ranch now ran 40,000 sheep, 200 horses, and 600 head of cattle in addition to large herds of goats, hogs and wild turkeys. By 1898 the ranch was in debt, but the sugar industry looked promising. The Hayseldens established the Maunalei Sugar Company on the island's windward coast. They began by building three wells and a wharf at Kahalepalaoa for shipment of the cane to Olowalu on Maui for grinding. A railroad was also built between the wharf and Keomuku along with a two-story building, a store, boarding house, camp houses, and barracks.

In 1802, a Chinese entrepreneur spent only one season attempting sugar cultivation in Naha from wild sugar cane. The Maunalei Sugar Company in nearby Keomuku did little better, lasting only a little more than two years. The Hayseldens constructed a six mile train track for transporting their sugar cane. However, they failed to respect the local culture and custom. Stones from an ancient *heiau* (temple) were used to build part of the railroad bed and then the disasters began. Their Japanese workers fell sick and many died. The ever important supply of drinking water went brackish and rain did not fall. Company records show the closure was due to lack of labor and water. The local population knew otherwise: Fred and Talula Hayselden soon left Lana'i. On Lana'i we heard a report that the Maunalei Plantation House was transported to Maui and became Pioneer Inn, but this was not accurate. We did some extensive research with the historical societies to search out the answer. Apparently some years ago the *Honolulu Star-Bulletin* printed an article to this effect. G. Alan Freeland, son of Pioneer Inn's founder George Freeland, spoke with Lawrence Gay, whose family owned most of Lana'i at the turn of the century, and was told that when the construction of the Pioneer Hotel was completed, the similar-designed building on the island of Lana'i was still standing.

In 1902 Charles Gay (a member of the Robinson family from Ni'ihau) and George Munro visited the island of Lana'i and Gay acquired the island at public auction for $108,000. He enlarged his holdings further through various land leases. Gay began making major improvements and bringing cattle from Kaua'i and Ni'ihau to his new ranch on Lana'i. In 1903 Gay purchased the remaining holdings from the Hayseldens and through land leases and other avenues became the sole owner of the entire island. By 1909 financial difficulties forced Charles Gay to loose all but 600 acres of his farmland. On the remaining acres he planted pineapples and operated a piggery while moving his family from Koele to Keomuku. In 1909 a group of businessmen that included Robert Shingle, Cecil Brown, Frank Thompson and others, purchased most of the island from Charles Gay for $375,000 and formed the Lana'i Ranch Company. At that time there were 22,500 sheep, 250 head of cattle, and 150 horses. They changed the emphasis from sheep to cattle and spent $200,000 on ranch improvements. However, because the large herds were allowed to graze the entire island, destroying what vegetation was available, the cattle industry was soon floundering. The island population had dwindled to only 102 at the turn of the twentieth century with fifty people living in Koele (which means farming) and the rest along the windward coastline in Keomuku. There were only thirteen men to work the entire cattle ranch, which was an insufficient number to manage the 40,000 head of beef on land that was overgrazed by the cattle, pigs and goats that roamed freely.

George Munro, a New Zealander by birth who had visited the island in 1902, was asked to return by the new owners to manage the ranch. Soon after arrival he began instituting much needed changes. He ordered sections of the range fenced and restricted the cattle to certain areas while allowing other areas to regrow. He also ordered the wild pigs and goats to be rounded up and destroyed. In 1911 the large three million gallon storm water reservoir - now the beautiful reflecting pond - was built. In 1912 an effort to destroy the goat population began in earnest. The first year 5,000 goats were killed and an additional 3,300 more were destroyed by 1916. (It wasn't until the 1940s that the last pigs and goats were captured.) Sheep dogs were introduced to assist the cowboys.

Water continued to be a major concern. An amateur naturalist, Munro noted that the Norfolk pine tree outside his home seemed to capture the mist that traveled past the island. Today, as in the days of Munro, there is only one Norfolk pine tree on the island. The tree planted in 1875 by Frederick Hayselden is the same one that stood outside Munro's home and has become a noted Lana'i landmark. It remains a stately sight right outside the Lodge at Koele. From that pine an idea was born, and Munro ordered the *paniolos* (Hawaiian cowboys) to carry a bag of Cook Island Pine seeds. They poked a small hole in the sack and, as they traveled the island on horseback, they left a trail of pines. The result is an island of more pine than palm. In 1914 the automobile age arrived on Lana'i in the form of a single 1910 Model T owned by George Munro.

By 1917 there were 4,000 head of cattle and 2,600 sheep, but profits were slim and the Lana'i Ranch Company sold its land to the Baldwin family for $588,000 and George Munro remained as foreman. The ranch slowly became more profitable. In 1920 Axis deer were introduced on Lana'i from Moloka'i and a pipeline was constructed from Maunalei Gulch to provide sources of fresh water.

In 1920 James Dole came to Lana'i, liked what he saw, and purchased the island in 1922 for $1.1 million from Alexander & Baldwin. George Munro was retained as manager. Castle & Cooke acquired one third ownership in the Hawaiian Pineapple Company soon after. The Kaumalapua harbor was dredged and a breakwater constructed in preparation for shipment of pineapple to O'ahu for processing. Lana'i developed into the single largest pineapple plantation in the world, which produced 90% of the United States' total pineapples. The company was called Hawaiian Pineapple Company until 1960 when the name was changed to Dole Corporation. (Today it is called Dole Company Foods.) In 1986 David Murdock became the major stockholder and the chairman of the board of Castle and Cooke (owners of Lana'i Company). The community of Lana'i City also began in the 1920s. The houses were very small, as families were discouraged. The workers arrived from Japan, Korea and the Philippines. The last residents left the Palawai and moved to Lana'i City between 1917 and 1929.

The population of Lana'i soared to 3,000 by 1930. In the 1950s larger homes, located below Fraser Avenue were built to accommodate the workers and their families and in the 1950s employees were given the option of purchasing their homes fee simple. In 1923 Dole realized the need to provide a center for entertaining island guests and had "The Clubhouse" constructed. Today it is known as Hotel Lana'i. The dining room provided meals for guests as well as for the nurses and patients from the plantation hospital. Also constructed in the center of town was *Dole Park*. The building in the middle was once a bowling alley, pool hall and restaurant until the late 1970s when it was made into a meeting hall. As a part of the development of Lana'i, David Murdock had a large new community center built, complete with swimming pool. It's located a block away from the park. Today less than 100 Lana'ians are part- or full-blooded Hawaiian.

The word Manele means "soap berry plant" or is the word used for a hand carried chair, a "sedan." The Manele boat harbor was once a small black sand beach and a fishing shrine found here indicates it was used by the early Hawaiians. You can spot the old *pepe* (cattle) ramp that Charles Gay used for loading his steers onto freighters.

In the 1970s E.E. Black was contracted to build the breakwater. It is traditional for any new project in Hawai'i to be blessed at the onset, but E.E. Black chose to forego the blessing. After only 20 feet of breakwater were constructed, the huge crane fell in the ocean and the people then refused to work. After great effort, another crane was brought over to lift the first from the ocean, but by the time it was recovered, the saltwater had taken its toll and it was worthless. Before resuming construction, E.E. Black held a blessing ceremony, the people returned to work, and the breakwater was completed without further incident.

GETTING THERE

To reach Lana'i you may travel by air or sea. The Lana'i airport is serviced by Island Air and Hawaiian Airlines (See Transportation in the GENERAL INFORMATION Chapter.) Airfare can run $67-89 one way from O'ahu or Maui to Lana'i, but we found out that Hawaiian Airlines offers substantially lower fares (we were quoted $51.50 one way!) when you use one of their new Bank of Hawaii ATM machines to purchase your ticket. On your return, you'll be happy to know that Lana'i Airport has a new Federal agricultural inspection station so you can now check your luggage directly through to the mainland. By boat you can travel a cool and comfortable 45 minutes from the Lahaina harbor aboard *Expeditions*. For a $25 one-way ticket, (children $20), you can have a scenic tour spotting dolphins, flying fish, and whales during the winter season. It is a pleasant way to travel, and much more affordable for a family than air transportation. The boat travels round trip five times daily to Manele Small Boat Harbor where a shuttle van will pick you up for transport to the Manele Bay Hotel and from there up to the Lodge at Koele. Reservations are advised as space is limited. They can also arrange an overnight or golf package. Phone (808) 661-3756.

GETTING AROUND LANA'I

Lana'i City Service offers the only scheduled transportation service available to and from Manele Small Boat Harbor. Their van shuttles between the dock and the resorts for $10 ($15 R/T) to Manele Bay; $15 ($25 R/T) to Lana'i City or the Lodge at Koele, and $15 ($25 R/T) to either golf course. They also provide the island's only taxi service: $20 to the Lodge or Lana'i City, $12.50 to Manele. (Note: If you are a "daytripper" or don't have a lot of luggage, Manele Bay is a relatively short walk from the Harbor.) For guests of the resorts or those with golf reservations, there is a complimentary shuttle every hour from 7 am to midnight between the Lodge at Koele and Manele Bay Hotel. In the evenings and on the weekends (From 3 pm Friday through Sunday afternoon) the schedule increases to every half hour. Depending on how busy they are, they run mini-vans or larger size school type buses. Resort guests can inquire with the hotel van driver regarding a drop off in Lana'i City. (From the Lodge it is a brisk 15-20 minute walk downtown. Bikes are also available for guests.)

For further independent exploration, Lana'i City Service (as a division of Dollar Rent A Car) offers car and jeep rentals. Since many of the island's roads are unimproved and even a small rainshower can render dirt roads impassable, most guests are advised to rent one of the 4-wheel drive Jeeps. A 4 x 4 Wrangler currently costs $119-129 per day and a 15 passenger van will set you back $175. (A Huyandai Excel compact is $60.) Major car repairs require that the unit be transferred by barge to Honolulu, hence the inflated rates. The rental car company notes that given the unique terrain of the island, they are not able to obtain (and therefore cannot provide) insurance of any kind on rental vehicles. Renters take full responsibility for the vehicle whether it is damaged by the renter, a second, or a third party. Contact Lana'i City Service at 1-800-Jeep-808 or Maui: (808) 244-9538; Lana'i: (808) 565-7227. FAX (808) 565-7087.

Red Rover may be the new kid on the block, but not the back roads! They want you to know they are "dedicated to providing the best vehicles and tools available for safely exploring beautiful Lana'i." They have a fleet of 2-to 6-passenger Land Rover Defender 90's at $139 soft top or $149 hard top; their 9-passenger Defender 110 runs $159. They give you lots of cool stuff to use free-like two-way radios, beach gear, cassette tapes, surf and body boards, and a T-shirt! Cell phones are available for a nominal fee with air time charged at prevailing rates. (They'll also come rescue you if you get stuck, but you gotta pay a lot for that.) They offer free delivery (to Hotel Lana'i), but only if you call them and say "Red Rover come on over!" (808) 565-7722. FAX (808) 565-7377. Email: <rover@aloha.net> Website: <www.onlanai.com>

Rabaca's Limousine Service offers hourly charter rates as well as airport transfers. One-way transfers between the resort hotels and the airport run $5-10 per person, two person minimum. Neal Rabaca provides 24-hour limousine service in his seven passenger Mercury Grand Marquis. Charter, hourly rates begin at $73.50 ($147 for the minimum of two hours). Island tours are also available. 1-800-475-6838 or FAX (808) 565-6670. PO Box 304, Lanai City, HI 96763. Email: <rabaca@aloha.net>

461

LANA'I ACCOMMODATIONS

There are currently three choices for hotel accommodations. Lana'i's original Hotel Lana'i and the two luxury hotels, Manele Bay Hotel and the Lodge at Koele. More on these three accommodations in the following sections.

CAMPING ON LANA'I

Tent camping is available at Hulopo'e Bay. Permits are issued by the County of Maui Parks & Recreation Dept. (808) 243-7389 or contact Lana'i Company, Inc., at PO Box 310, Lana'i City, Lana'i, HI 96763. Phone (808) 565-3000.

PRIVATE HOMES

Kay Okamoto offers single family homes in Lana'i City for short and long term vacation rentals. Okamoto Realty (808) 565-7519.

BED AND BREAKFAST

After years of running the only B&B on the island, Lucille Graham has retired. Michael and Susan Hunter still operate *"Dreams Come True"* offering rooms in their home/art studio at 547 - 12th St. Single rate $60, double $75. Price includes continental breakfast. They can also arrange vacation rental homes for one to ten people. Susan provides in-house massages at the rate of $40 per hour! Airport pick up and drop off. A truck and a jeepster are available for rent. PO Box 525, Lana'i City, HI 96763. Phone (808) 565-6961, toll free 1-800-566-6961. Check out their website < www.go-native.com/Inns/0117.html >

You might also try contacting local visitor information at Destination Lana'i, PO Box 700, Lana'i City, 96763 (808) 565-7600, FAX (808) 565-9316.

LANA'I RESORTS, HOTELS AND RESTAURANTS

HOTEL LANA'I
Hotel Lana'i was built in 1923 by James D. Dole as a retreat for Dole Company executives and other important guests. Before the opening of the new resorts, this ten-room hotel had the only accommodations on the island. You'll still find it quiet and comfortable with the ten rooms located in two wings of the original building and connected by a glass-enclosed veranda. After a one half million dollar renovation (in 1994) all rooms have private tiled bathroom facilities with pedestal sinks, hardwood floors, ceiling fans, country quilts, and original pictures of the old plantation days on Lana'i. The hotel and restaurant is now owned and operated by the Richardson family. Rooms range from twins to kings; a few feature four-poster beds. The original "caretakers' cottage" is also available for rent. Rooms run $95-105, $135 for cottage. Children ages eight and under are free in room with parents. You'll want to book as far in advance as possible. For information or reservations write: Hotel Lana'i, PO Box 520, Lana'i City, HI 96763. (808) 565-7211, FAX (808) 565-6450 or toll free 1-800-795-7211.

The Hotel Lana'i staff (family!) can provide you with complimentary inter-resort shuttle service and can arrange a variety of island activities, often with discounted rates. (The hotel works closely with Red Rover and Lana'i Ecoadventure Centre.)

Guests can reserve one of the hotel's ten high quality 21-speed mountain bikes complete with helmets. Or they can book one of the hotel's exclusive Hummers to tour and explore Lana'i in the same kind of rugged vehicle used in "Desert Storm," and ridden by both actor Arnold Schwarzenegger and Hotel Lana'i owner and chef, Henry Clay Richardson! (Don't worry - he always gets back in time to prepare dinner!)

Henry Clay's Rotissiere features the Cajun-influenced cuisine of its talented chef who held executive chef positions at some of Maui's most prestigious hotels and restaurants before he and his family moved to Lana'i in 1996. Always a popular place for island residents (it has the only bar in town!), this Hotel Lana'i dining room has become the island's first "signature" restaurant.

Continental breakfast is provided for hotel guests before the restaurant opens to the public for lunch and dinner. The lunch menu changes monthly, but might include grilled quail or rock shrimp Caesar salad, Cajun seared ahi, steamed clams, rib eye steak "Po-Boy" sandwich, baby back ribs, or Cajun seafood linguini $11.95-14.95. The dinner menu changes twice a year, but always features "free range" chicken roasted on their glass-enclosed French Rotisserie as well as Cajun specialties like Clay's Shrimp and Eggplant Creole. They are also becoming known for their use of game like venison, rabbit, and quail with specials like suckling pig and leg of spring lamb. The stone pizza oven offers handmade pies (like Chicken & Chorizo or Scallops & Shrimp) made to order. They also offer fresh fish caught in Lana'i waters and have a live lobster and crab tank. Grilled Banana Foster and pecan pie are just two of their specialty desserts. Dinners run $16.95-24.95; pizzas from $11.95. Lunch is served 11 am-2 pm, Monday-Friday. Dinner nightly 5:30-9, cocktails served from 5 pm. The bar closes at 9 pm.

THE MANELE BAY HOTEL ★

The resort is spread across the cliffside of Hulopo'e Beach like an enormous Mediterranean villa. It is a strikingly beautiful building with a pale blue tile roof. There are four buildings in the East wing and five in the West wing, and each is slightly different. The rooms line sprawling walkways which meander through five lush courtyard gardens, each with a unique theme. The gardens include The Hawaiian, The Bromelaid, The Chinese, the Japanese, and The Kama'aina Gardens. The original resort plan called for a 450-room hotel directly on the beach, but was revised to the current structure with 250 rooms on the cliff alongside the beach. Behind the resort is the newest 18-hole golf course, The Challenge at Manele, which encompasses 138 acres along the ocean.

The *Hulopo'e Court* is the more casual of the two dining rooms and serves breakfast and dinner with a children's menu available. Breakfasts entrees include Palawai bacon chop with "cocotte" of scrambled eggs, Hulopo'e duck hash with poached egg and ginger green onion hollandaise, open-faced herbed biscuits with scrambled eggs, sundried tomatoes, & goat cheese, taro & macadamia nut pancakes, swiss-style bircher muesli, and icy mango smoothies. $12-22. Their dinner menu is Pacific Rim with Euro-cooking methods and Asian influences and features the culinary talents of new Executive Chef, David Britton. Soups or salads and appetizers run $11 and up and include grilled moana filet, palm heart remoulade and green onion relish or hot smoked ahi tuna with pickled mango and pistachio vinaigrette. Main courses include char grilled Chinese BBQ veal T-bone; crisp duck with Hawaiian vintage mole & almond basmati rice; pan-roasted cured salmon with chic-pea tomato & fennel stew; chili rubbed ahi with pineapple ratatouille; or lamb roast with curried vegetable risotto and minted saffron jus $33-35. Adding a beverage, soup or salad, and dessert will make this elegant dining experience an expensive one.

Chef Britton is also at the helm of *Ihilani*, the formal dining room at the Manele Bay. The menu is Contemporary Mediterranean cuisine or choose a five-course food and wine pairing for $75-95. A sample dinner might be: Foie gras terrine with fresh fig salad, sauteed onaga with almond romesco and champagne grapes, and pan-seared squab breast with crispy salsify and fresh porcini essence. A selection of gourmet cheeses and walnut bread is followed by the dessert of the evening. We haven't had the opportunity to dine here, so let us know if you do!

Hale AheAhe (House of Gentle Breezes) is an indoor lounge located off the upper main lobby that offers nightly entertainment on its outdoor veranda. *The Pool Grill* opens at 11am and serves sandwiches (eggplant pastrami with mozzarella, prosciutto on foccacia), salads (Hawaiian watercress with smoked chicken & blue cheese, shrimp "gado gado"), and gourmet pizzas on whole wheat crust $10-17. *The Challenge at Manele Clubhouse* offers breakfast, lunch, and a pupu-style menu in the evenings: eggplant caviar with flat bread, dim sum, chicken or shrimp satay, vindaloo lamb ribs, ahi with white bean cassoulet, oyster mushroom canneloni, and soba noodle "primavara" with orange curry dressing $8.50-14.

KOELE LODGE

In many of the areas the ceilings have been given very special attention. In the main dining room are huge floral paintings, in the Hale AheAhe lounge you'll see fish and starfish. The resort took advantage of the undiscovered talent of the island residents and much of the artwork was done by local residents.

We enjoyed the proximity to the beachfront, but the pool seemed the place to be and lounges were filled by mid-afternoon. The pool water is slightly warm, yet delightfully refreshing. It seems here on Lana'i, there is no reason to hurry. Attendants from the adjoining restaurant circulate, taking drink and sandwich orders. The poolside restaurant was a little pricey, but the portions were large. We noted with appreciation that they provided a more economical children's menu here as well as in their main dining rooms.

If you're thinking that too much lying in the sun and fine food will affect your waistline, the fitness studio is open from 6am-8pm. There is plenty of equipment for working out then treat yourself to a steam room, massage, pedicure, or facial.

This place is truly an island get-away. If our stay was any indication, then celebrities have quickly found Lana'i to be a convenient and luxurious retreat. Both Kevin Costner and Billy Crystal were guests during our brief stay.

The rooms are spacious, a bit larger than the standard rooms at Koele, and each wing differs slightly in decorating style. Our wing had bright, bold yellow wall coverings and bedspreads accented with very traditional furniture. The bathroom amenities thoughtfully included suntan lotion and moisturizer in a little net bag to take along to the pool or beach. Some rooms have private butler service; all have mini-bars and mini-refrigerators. *Terrace Room $275, Garden Room $300, Partial Ocean View $420, Ocean View $475, Ocean Front $525, *Mauka Mini-Suite $525, *Mauka Suite $650, Ocean Mini Suite $725, Ocean Front Suite $775, *Mauka Corner Suite $900, *Center/Makai Suite $1,300, *Makai Corner Suite $1,500, *Presidential Suite $2,000. *indicates room includes butler service*

LODGE AT KOELE ★

The Lodge at Koele is not what a visitor might expect to find in Hawai'i. Guests arrive via a stately drive lined with Cook Island pines to this Victorian era resort that typifies turn of the century elegance. The inscription on the ceiling of the entry was painted by artist John Wullbrandt and translates "In the center of the Pacific is Hawai'i. In the center of Hawai'i is Lana'i. In the heart of Lana'i is Koele." and Lana'i may quickly find its way into your heart as well.

The rug in the entry is circa 1880, made of Tibetan wool. The Great Hall features enormous natural stone fireplaces that hint at the cooler evening temperatures here in upcountry Lana'i. The twin fireplaces on either side of the lobby are the largest in the state of Hawaii and the Lodge itself sets the record for being Hawai'i's biggest wooden structure. The high beamed ceilings give the room a spacious character, yet the atmosphere is welcoming and the comfortable furnishings invite you to sit and linger. Designer Joszi Meskan of San Francisco spent more than two years securing the many beautiful artifacts from around the world.

A descriptive list is available from the concierge. The Great Hall's rug was handmade in Thailand for the resort and utilizes 75 different colors. Some of the furniture are replicas, but many pieces are antiques, including the huge altar desk where steaming morning coffee awaits the guests. Be sure to notice the two exotic chandeliers, with playful carved monkeys amid the leaves, designed for the great hall by Joszi Meskan. The large portrait on one end of the Great Hall is of Madame Yerken, painted by Belgian artist Jan Van Boern in 1852. An intricately stenciled border runs around the perimeter of the ceiling with antelope, deer and wild turkeys. Another more subtle stenciling is done around the floors. The skylights are beautiful, etched glass. The furnishings are covered in lush brocade tapestries and suede upholstery in hues of burgundy, blues and greens. The room is accented with fresh flowers, many of them orchids grown in the greenhouse located beyond the reflecting pool. The woodwork is finely carved, with pineapples often featured. At the end of an exhausting day of vacationing, there is nothing like curling up in the big overstuffed armchair next to a crackling fire with an after dinner drink to enjoy the evening entertainment, play a game of checkers or visit with local women as they demonstrate Hawaiian quilting. Green is the color theme throughout the resort with the bellman, concierge, and front desk staff crisply attired in pine green suits.

Surrounding the main building is a wonderful veranda with comfortable rattan furniture accented by Hawaiian quilted pillows. (Similar pillows, by the way, are for sale through the concierge at $100 each.) Huge trees hug the building and the view of the horses and fields beyond has a tranquilizing effect. The setting is truly picture perfect.

Several public rooms surround the Great Hall. The library overlooks spacious lawns and offers newspapers from around the world as well as books, backgammon, and chess. The Trophy Room also has an assortment of board games and an interesting, but very uncomfortable, English horn chair. Both of these rooms have fireplaces which can be lit at the request of the guests. The Music Room on the other side of the lobby hosts Afternoon Tea every day between 3-5 pm. A grounds tour is offered daily.

Adjoining the Great Hall is the Terrace Dining Room, open for breakfast, lunch and dinner. The food is excellent and the service outstanding. In fact, the restaurants at the Lodge at Koele could very possibly be the best in all of Hawai'i. (According to the readers of *Conde Nast Traveler*, they are - not only the #1 restaurant in Hawai'i, but also in the top ten in America!) We were also very pleased that they provided a children's menu which offered a varied dinner selection priced $6-8. The formal dining room, open for dinner only, is tucked away in the corner of the resort and requires a jacket for the gentlemen. Executive Chef Edwin Goto makes excellent use of the five-acre organic farm to ensure the freshest ingredients in his meal preparations. Grilled mahi mahi with white bean and foie gras cassoulet, ragout of lamb shank with soft herbed polenta, and pan roasted duck with lemon spaetzle and sundried cranberry jus are just a few examples of Chef Goto's use of Lana'i's local fish, game, and meats $40-58. Herbs, white eggplant, purple turnips, and yellow teardrop tomatoes are among the interesting and varied crops.

Simple, hearty foods with unusual ingredients and elegant presentations are the key to this Rustic American cuisine. Breakfast at the Terrace Dining Room is changeable, but it might include Lana'i Axis deer sausage, Kaunolu bananas on coconut cream, artichoke and asparagus frittata with farm basil and wild tomatoes, or sweet rice waffle $4.75-$12.25. Lunch is another dining experience extraordinaire. Sample the Koele cobb or cilantro pasta salad with grilled scallops, the signature sandwich entree of grilled chicken breast and layered potato with red onion gravy $11.50-14.50. Nightly dinner specials might include veal osso bucco or roast chicken with Portuguese stew or select from their standard menu of a grilled chuck burger with cheddar cheese or grilled lamb and Japanese eggplant sandwich $10-15.25. The Golf Clubhouse at Koele serves both lunch and dinner and has proven popular with the local residents and visitors alike, with their selection of quality meals at prices rather more reasonable than the Lodge. Lunch samples include a grilled fresh fish sandwich, grilled sandwich of three cheeses with vine ripe tomatoes, saimin with char sui, or Chinese chicken salad $5-8. Dinner ($10-18) is offered Friday and Saturday only from 5:30-8:30 pm.

This was once the site of the farming community known as Koele. The pine lined driveway was planted in the 1920s and led to the 20 or 30 homes in this area. Only two remain on the property and are owned by the Richardson family, descendants of the early Lana'i paniolos. The church was moved to the front grounds of the Lodge and a small schoolhouse is being restored and converted into a museum. The grounds of this country manor are sprawling and exquisitely landscaped. More than a mile of lush garden pathways and an orchid house can be enjoyed while strolling the grounds. The large reflecting pond was once the reservoir for the town of Koele. There are plenty of activities to be enjoyed from strolling the grounds to swimming or just relaxing in the Jacuzzi. (See RECREATION & WHAT TO SEE for more information.) In fact, it is so relaxing and so lovely that we didn't even miss the beach. But if you're hankering for some sand and sun, it is only a 25 minute shuttle trip to the shore.

The elegant, uniformed staff are efficient, very friendly and courteous. We were impressed with the quality of service at the Lodge. It is also pleasing to know that the development of the tourist industry on Lana'i has meant a return of many of the island's young people.

There are 102 guests rooms at the Lodge and they are artistically decorated in three different fresh, bright color schemes. The artwork that lines the corridors was done by some of the many talented Lana'i residents and each floor has a different theme. The beds feature a pineapple motif and were custom made in Italy, then handpainted by Lana'i artisans. The floral pictures on each door were painted by the postmaster's wife! The bathrooms have Italian tile floors and vivid blue marble counter tops. Room amenities are thoughtfully packaged and include an array of fine toiletries. There are in-room televisions with video recorders and a couple of beautifully carved walking sticks in the closet tempt the guest to enjoy one of those leisurely walks around the grounds or along the Munro Trail that is accessible from the Lodge. The workout facility by the pool provides free weights and aerobic machines.

Koele Room ($325); Garden Room ($375). The Plantation Rooms ($485) are slightly larger. Plantation Suites ($825) have a wrap around lanai and a separate living and sleeping area with a murphy bed in the living room. The Plantation Room and Plantation Suite can be combined into one large living area. The Norfolk, Terrace Banyan or Plantation Suites ($600-$925) provide separate living room and sleeping areas, and an oversized lanai. Located along the balcony above the Great Hall, these are the only guest rooms that are air conditioned. The Fireplace Suites run $1,100-1,500. They are slightly larger than the regular rooms and just as beautifully decorated. Packages such as Tee Time Golf, 4 X 4 Adventure, Romance/Honeymoon, and 5th Night Free, are some of the available options for extra value and amenities.

As much as we enjoyed the Manele Bay Hotel, we found something very appealing about this Lodge in upcountry. Perhaps it was because the service was so superb, perhaps it was because the air was so fresh, perhaps it was the comfortable and homey quality of the great hall, or perhaps it was because we truly were in the heart of Lana'i. This resort had a special quality, and both kids and adults in our group were enchanted. Our visit will long be a fond memory... that is until we visit once again!

Reservation information for both resorts is available from The Lana'i Company at 800-321-4666, FAX (808) 565-3868. Or write P.O. Box 310, Lana'i City, HI 96763-1310. Email: < reservations@lanai-resorts.com >

SHOPPING - LOCAL DINING

There are three grocery stores from which to choose. ***Richard's***, which has the honor of being on Lana'i since 1946, and the small ***Pine Isle Market***. Since everything must be brought in by barge, prices are steep. Don't be surprised if they are closed for noontime siesta and closed for the day by 6 pm. ***International Food & Clothing*** is the only food store open on Sundays until 1:30. Pineapples are available for sale at all three groceries. We suggest you purchase one and sample the difference between the mainland version of this fruit and the field ripened variety. Pineapples already boxed and ready to take home are at the airport gift shop *"Pineapple Landing."*

One of the limited local style fast food restaurants is ***Tanigawa's***. Open daily for breakfast, lunch, and dinner. You can select sandwiches or burgers $2-4, plate lunches and breakfasts $4-6. The fare is filling and the atmosphere charmingly rustic. Next door is the only other casual dining spot in Lana'i City, the ***Blue Ginger Cafe***, which serves up some of the best, freshly made pastries in town. (The hotel's bakery in Lana'i City delivers ono fresh breads daily to Lana'i grocery stores.) Blue Ginger opens at 6 am for breakfasts which are surprisingly diverse for such an early hour! They offer eggs, pancakes or waffles with blueberries, strawberries, or macadamia nuts. Lunches include sandwiches, local style plate lunches and saimin; dinners include steak, seafood, and pizza. Dinners all under $15 except the lobster at $16.95. HOURS: 6 am-9 pm. Phone: (808) 565-6363. For ***Henry Clay's Rotisserie***, see the listing under the Hotel Lana'i.

Pele's Garden health food store opened in 1995 at 811 Houston Street. Owner Beverly Zigmond (D.N.) offers vitamins, herbs, and homeopathics as well as weight control and baby food products. She also stocks organic groceries and a line of "natural" items including hand-made cotton goods from Guatemala, cards, books, and magazines. Open Mon-Sat 9:30 am-6:30 pm. Phone (808) 565-9629. *Pele's Other Garden* is a "relatively close" deli, pizzeria, and juice bar operated by Beverly's brother Mark and wife Barbara Ann. They offer all natural and organic items on their menu of veggie burgers, black bean & brown rice burritos, cheese quesadillas, salads, and organic pizza. Their New York-style deli sandwiches feature a variety of turkey flavors - from Cajun to cheese smoked! Picnic lunches. Fresh produce. Open Mon-Thurs 11 am-7 pm, Fri-Sat to 9 pm. (808) 565-9628. Sandwiched in between the two "Gardens" is *Gifts with Aloha* offering jewelry, koa products, quilts, clothes, candles, and books. They feature Raku pieces, ceramic ornaments, fusible glass, handmade beads, and island wood creations made by local artists and crafts people from Lana'i. (808) 565-6589. Open Mon-Sat 9:30 am-6 pm.

Across the park is an art gallery called *Heart of Lana'i Gallery* operated by Denise Henig, a water color artist who also teaches classes at the gallery. Work by Lana'i artists and other island artists are on display. (808) 565-6678. (You can also contact Denise about 2-4 week vacation rentals of a nearby house and cottage.) This is the beginning of Lana'i's cultural center. Just one building down is the workshop where island residents can come to pursue their artistic abilities.

The Lodge at Koele and the Manele Bay Hotel both have small sundry gift shops. You can arrange for a day of shopping in Lahaina town from Manele Harbor aboard *Expeditions.* Cost is $25 per person one way.

RECREATION ON LANA'I

ART & CULTURE

If you're a resident or a visitor and interested in pursuing your artistic talents, you can register for the *Lana'i Art Program.* Classes are taught by local and visiting artists and might include a variety of paint medias or even craft classes such as bead making. For registration or other information phone (808) 565-7503. The *Lana'i Visiting Artists Program* offers art and culture to guests of both hotels with a lineup of literary, culinary, and performing artists who come to the island to share their talents in an informal living room setting. Past participants in the program include Chefs Bradley Ogden and Celestino Drago, Dr. Oliver Sacks, actor James Woods, former Presidential Press Secretary Marlin Fitzwater, jazz guitarist Charlie Byrd, producer David Wolper, author Richard Preston (*The Hot Zone*), humor columnist Dave Barry, novelist Paul Theroux, singer Cleo Laine, Pulitzer Prize-winning writer Jane Smiley, humorists Garrison Keillor and Calvin Trillin, authors John McPhee and Susan Isaacs, and pianist Andre Watts.

All events (except dinners) are free of charge. For further information about the program, contact The Lana'i Company at 1-800-321-4666. For history buffs, there is a permanent exhibit of Lana'i artifacts on display at the **Lana'i Conference Center**, the meeting and convention facility perched on a seaside knoll just above the Manele Bay Hotel. These items were returned "home" after their initial discovery and display at Honolulu's Bishop Museum. **Kaupe Culture & Heritage Center** also has frequent cultural exhibits in town.

GOLF

There are a number of selections for the golfer on Lana'i. At Koele there is the 18-hole *Experience at Koele* course, another, older community 9-hole course, and one stupendous 18-hole putting course is also adjacent the Lodge. The *Challenge at Manele* is the newest 18-hole course.

Golfers and non-golfers of all ages will delight in the executive 18-hole putting green at Koele, beautifully manicured course with assorted sand traps and pools lined with tropical flowers and sculptures. No charge. (Putt-putt will never be the same again!) Course rates for the 18-hole Challenge at Manele or Koele Experience is $175 for non-guests and $125 for hotel guests. Reservations for either course can be made from the mainland via their toll free number 1-800-321-4666. Website: < www.lanairesorts.com >

The **Challenge of Manele**, designed by Jack Nicklaus, is the island's newest course and opened on December 25, 1993. Built on several hundred acres of lava out-croppings among natural kiawe and ilima trees, this links-style golf course features three holes constructed on the cliffs of Hulopo'e Bay using the Pacific Ocean as a dramatic water hazard. (808) 565-2222.

The 18-hole **Experience at Koele** was designed by Greg Norman and Ted Robinson. From a golfer's standpoint, Greg Norman assures the golfing guest that this course will require both skill and strategy and adds that it is the only course in Hawaii with Bent grass greens. The beauty of the course, he continues, with its lush natural terrain -- marked by thick stands of Cook Island pines -- and panoramic views will make concentrating on the game difficult for even the most expert golfer. The signature 8th hole of the Experience at Koele has a truly inspired setting. This is a 390 yard, par 4 with a dramatic 200 foot drop in elevation from tee to green. The course is laid out on a multi-tiered plan. The upper seven holes meet the lower eleven at this sublime tee. From the top of the bluff at the eighth tee is a view so stunning that our first thought was that this could be right out of Shangri-la. The mist floats by this enchanted valley, filled with lush vegetation and a lovely lagoon. The lagoon at one time had served as a back up reservoir for the old cattle ranch. Now, while we are not golf aficionados, this single hole was enough to at least consider taking up the sport! The Experience at Koele was recently rated #1 in the world in the 1998 Readers' Poll of the World's Best Golf Courses in *Conde Nast Traveler*. A restaurant at the Golf Clubhouse offers some good luncheon selections. (808) 565-4653.

The Cavendish, a 9 hole, 36 par, 3,071 yard course, is located at the front of the Lodge at Koele and was the island's first. It is a community course, there is no phone, no club house, and no charge! (Donations are suggested.)

HIKING

Walking sticks are provided in all the rooms at the Lodge at Koele for guest usage. It's almost impossible to resist strolling around the pastoral grounds. Near the Lodge at Koele are two small houses. These were originally located where the orchid house is now. The Richardson families live here; their ancestors were among the early Lana'i paniolos. You can stroll around the front grounds to view the enormous Norfolk pine or enjoy watching guests try their hand at lawn bowling, croquet, or miniature golf. Walk down to the horse stables or peek inside the old church. The stables are new, but the church was relocated due to the construction of the Lodge. A small school was also moved and it is currently being restored and perhaps will one day house Lana'i's first museum.

The Munro Trail is a 9-mile arc trek along the ridge of Lana'i. The view from the 3,370 ft. summit of Lana'ihale can be spectacular on a clear day. This route can be tackled by four-wheel drive vehicles, but only during very dry conditions. For the adventurous, there is also the High Pasture Loop, the Old Cowboy Trail, Eucalyptus Ladder or Beyond the Blue Screen. A light to moderate weight raincoat might be a good idea to take along if you're planning on hiking. The concierge can provide you with a map showing the various routes. Picnics can be provided by the hotel.

HORSEBACK RIDING

The Lodge at Koele has an impressive stable. A variety of rides are available from a 15 minute children's ride to one or two hour treks through the plantation, along wooded trails. More experienced riders can enjoy longer trips with a stop for lunch. The two-hour Paniolo Trail ride ($65) travels up through guava groves and patches of Ironwood trees. Here the rider will enjoy the spectacular views of Maui and Moloka'i and have the opportunity to glimpse Axis deer, quail, wild turkeys, and cattle and pass through the dryland forest of Kanepu'u. Also available are the one-hour Plantation Trail Ride ($35) and the Paniolo Lunch Ride which is a three hour trip ($90). Private trail rides can also be scheduled at $70 per hour (2 hours/$120; 3/$180; 4/$280). Riders must wear long pants and sport shoes and children must be at least nine years of age and four feet in height to ride. Riders must be twelve years or older to sign up for the Paniolo rides. Maximum weight of riders is 250 lbs. Safety helmets are provided for all riders.

The horse drawn buggy is another equine activity. Reservations can be made through the concierge at either hotel.

LANA'I ECOADVENTURE CENTRE

In addition to renting snorkeling and kayaking equipment, mountain bikes, and camping gear, this new Lana'i company offers three unique adventure tours: The Keomuku Downhill Road Bike Trek makes stops at the island's most scenic sites including the petroglyphs. The 4x4 Adventure Trekker takes you to the Garden of the Gods, Po'aiwa Gulch, and the Munro Trail via safari van for a beginning level hiking trek that includes refreshments.

The Kayak/Snorkel Adventure provides kayaking gear and instruction for a guided sea kayak and snorkel exploration of Lanai's marine life and sea caves. (Refreshments included.) Half-day tours (4 hours) begin at $69. Combo tours (morning snorkel with afternoon hiking or biking) and shuttle service available.

They can also advise you on inexpensive accommodation and offer the Adventure Hawaii Kayak Bike Hike Club. (The $20 lifetime membership entitles club members to equipment rental discounts, special outing club days, and instructional clinics.)

Contact John or Kris at Lana'i Ecoadventure Centre, PO Box 1394, Lana'i City, HI 96763. Phone/FAX (808) 565-7737. < www.kayakhawaii.com >

LANA'I PINE SPORTING CLAYS

The rustic 14-station course and 6 fully-automated competition high towers are situated within a pine-wooded valley that offers scenic views of Moloka'i and Maui. Skilled and new shooters can choose trap, skeet, compact sporting, or sporting clays. Instruction provided; shotgun and supplies are available for rent. 50 targets $65; 100 for $125. Contact The Lana'i Company 800-321-4666.

MANELE BAY RESORT

RESORT TOURS

Both Manele and Koele offer complimentary tours daily of their resorts. Just sign up at the concierge. The tour of Koele is especially informative and discusses the many unique pieces of art gracing the lobby, making it a worthwhile 30 minutes.

Lawn bowling and both English and American croquet fields surround the Lodge at Koele. Guests can also borrow a mountain bike and ride into town, around the resort paths, or in the early morning or early evening, they are allowed to ride along the golf course paths. One evening we followed one of the garden paths behind the putting green that led to a very steep golf cart track from the lower nine holes to the upper nine. It was so steep, in fact, that it proved quite a challenge to just walk the bikes up. After the journey up, we were delighted to find an ample supply of water and cups that reappeared every couple of holes on the golf course. Once on top, we traveled around a few holes of the golf course which were fairly level. We were pleasantly surprised to find ourselves at the tee off for the 8th hole of the golf course, and as previously described, it was an inspired location. We then attempted to ride down from the tee to the green. The path down was so steep that it required brakes on full force to go slow enough to maintain control! Beyond is another picturesque lagoon and more golf cart trails to follow, again, on flat ground. The walk into town takes about 15 minutes at a fairly brisk pace, but only about 5 minutes by bike. Biking is a good option for seeing Lana'i City or if you just want to sample some of Lana'i's local eateries. Guests who brave the rugged drive can spend the day at Club Lana'i for a reduced rate of $68 adults, $25 youth. (Directions in WHAT TO SEE section that follows.)

Both resorts have wonderful swimming pools. The Koele pool, flanked by two bubbling Jacuzzis was seldom busy. The Manele pool is slightly larger and, at a lower elevation than Koele, became quite hot during the afternoon. The adjacent poolside restaurant provided refreshing drinks and light food fare. Guests at the resorts have pool privileges at both facilities. Scuba diving, fishing expeditions, raft trips, and other ocean excursions can be arranged through the concierge at either resort. Half day raft trips (2 1/2 hr.) run $40-$60. Half day sailing and snorkeling trips are run by Trilogy Excursions. At both resorts, a sheet describing the activities for the next day is left in the room with the evening maid service.

LODGE AT KOELE -- Complimentary coffee and tea are available in the lobby and each of the accommodation wings each morning. The Music Room has an array of interesting musical instruments lining the walls and the grand piano may be used by the guests. This is also where you'll find a delightful Afternoon Tea. In the Trophy Room are board games and the Library has books. Complimentary video tapes are available at the concierge for guests to view in their rooms. A grounds tour is offered daily and at night there is varied musical entertainment in the Great Hall. The twin fireplaces are ablaze and the overstuffed chairs invite you to slow down and relax. The fireplaces are lit, upon request, in the Library, Music, or Trophy room. This may be as close to heaven on earth as you can get.

MANELE BAY HOTEL - Manele also has varied daily activities. A tour of the resort is available and in the evening there is entertainment and complimentary pupus (5-6 pm) at Hale Ahe Ahe. Complimentary video tapes are available for guest use in their rooms and complimentary morning coffee is a pleasurable experience in the Orchid Lounge or Coral Lounge.

TENNIS

There are plexipave courts at both Koele and Manele Bay. These are complimentary for use by hotel guests. Lessons are available at an extra charge. There is also a public court at Lana'i School in Lana'i City.

THEATER

The refurbished Lana'i Playhouse has been Lana'i's movie theater since 1993.

WEDDINGS

Lana'i may well be one of the most romantic places on earth. The Lana'i Wedding is available through the resorts. The wedding package includes a garden setting at Manele Bay Hotel or a gazebo at the Lodge at Koele, minister, bouquet and bridal leis, souvenir book $2,000. An add-on "Touch of Romance" package is available for $200.

WHAT TO SEE

There are only three paved roads on Lana'i outside of Lana'i City, no stop lights, and very few street signs once you leave town. After driving around on even a dry day, we assure you that they aren't kidding when they recommend a four-wheel drive. On rainy days, you can be fairly certain you'll get stuck in the mud and muck! You can pretty much see all of Lana'i in a long day, but if you want to slow down, do some hiking, or simply sit in the sun on a quiet beach, there is plenty to occupy you for days. Either of the resorts can provide you with a map and advice. We were pleased that Pete Agliamo forfeited a day of fishing to act as a tour guide. Born in the Philippines, he has lived on the island for 43 years and has worked for Dole driving pineapple trucks. Besides being an active fisherman, he has hunted around the island for years and was a most knowledgeable guide. Leaving the driving to him was a delight as we cruised along the dirt roads and "talked story." Along the road to the Garden of the Gods we asked him if he was taking a short cut. Judging by the fact that we were zooming between pastures with cattle and abandoned pineapple fields with no street signs at all, we were certain we'd taken the back way, but he assured us we were on the main road. It seemed to us that it wouldn't be all that hard to get lost on Lana'i!

Since there are no local quick-marts, be sure you pack plenty of water and bring along a picnic, because we're sure you'll find the perfect spot to enjoy it.

We headed east and were pleasantly surprised to find the road to the **Garden of the Gods** was smooth, packed dirt that was free of ruts. (However this may not always be the case.) A 20-minute ride took us through a stand of ironwoods before we reached the large carved stone announcing our arrival in the Garden of the Gods, which was named in 1935. (It happened that the stone had been carved by Pete's daughter!) We arrived during mid-day, but the best time to see this lunar-like and rather mystical place is early morning or late evening. In the early morning, on a clear day, you can see the faint outline of Honolulu's sky-scrapers and a sharp eye can observe Axis deer out foraging. The rays of the sun in the early evening cast strange shadows on the amber-baked earth and huge monolithic rocks and your imagination can do the rest.

Interestingly enough, here - in what seems to be the middle of nowhere - with no one in sight, in the peaceful stillness (except for the occasional call of a bird or the wind brushing against your cheek) - are street signs! One indicates Awailua Rd. which is a very rugged and steep dirt path down to the ocean. Most of these roads are used by the local residents for fishing or hunting. Be advised, if you attempt to start down, there may be no place to turn around should you change your mind.

Follow Polihua Road and you'll arrive at a stretch of white sandy beach with rolling sand dunes. According to Lawrence Kainoahou Gay, in his account entitled "True Stories of the Island of Lana'i," the word Polihua means Poli (cover or bay) and hua (eggs). He reports that in this area turtles would visit to lay their eggs above the high water mark. He had seen turtles, in days gone by, that were large enough to carry three people! This beach is not recommended for safe swimming or other water activities. The Kaena Road winds down to a very isolated area called Kaena Iki Point, which is the site of one of Lana'i's largest *heiaus*.

Shipwreck Beach, or *Kaiolohia*, on Lana'i's northeast coast, is about a half hour drive along a paved road from the Lodge at Koele. Enroute down you'll note that there are many little rock piles. At first glance they appear to be some relic of the distant past, however, they began to appear in the 1960s, a product of tourists and/or residents and have no historical or other significance. The road is lined with scrub brush, and as you begin the descent to the shoreline you catch a glimpse of the World War II liberty ship. Be sure to keep an eye out for pheasant, deer, turkeys and the small Franklin partridges.

At the bottom of the road you can choose to go left to Shipwreck Beach or continue straight and follow the coastline on the unpaved, dusty, and very rugged Awalua Road to **Club Lana'i**. Club Lana'i is a day resort that shuttles visitors from Lahaina, Maui to the leeward shores of Lana'i for a day of relaxation and recreation--sort of a Hawaiian version of Gilligan's Island. (See Maui section - WHAT TO SEE for a more detailed description.) It's a bit of a drive and slow going. Four wheel drive vehicles are advised. It is about five miles down the road to Keomuku. There are still remnants of the failed Maunalei Sugar Company near Keomuku, and a Japanese cemetery, also a memento of the failed sugar company.

The beaches are wonderful for sunbathing or picnicking, but not advisable for swimming. Beyond are Naha and Lopa, two uninhabited old villages. The old Kalanakila a ka Malamalama church, located near Keomuku, is still in the process of being renovated. There are also some ancient Hawaiian trails at Naha. The road ends at Naha and you'll have to drive back by the same route.

If you're headed for Shipwreck Beach, go left. (The old sign that said "Federation Camp" is gone.) This is Lapahiki Road, and while dry and bumpy during our drive, we understand a little precipitation can make it impassable except in a four-wheel drive. The dirt road is lined by kiawe trees and deserted little houses. This is a getaway spot for the local residents, although there is no fresh water. The reef along Kaiolohia Beach is very wide, but the surf can be high and treacherous. During a storm, waves come crashing down over the liberty ship that now sits on the reef.

This was one of three Navy L.C.M. ships that were not shipwrecked, but purposely grounded in 1941-1942. The other two have disappeared after losing their battle to the ocean. Barges are also towed over, anchored, and left to rot as well. The channel between here and Moloka'i is called Kolohi, which means mischievous and unpredictable. The channel between Lana'i and Maui is the 'Au'au channel which means "to bathe." There were several ships that were wrecked here or on other parts of the island. In the 1820s the British ship *Alderman Wood* went aground; in 1826 the American ship *London* was wrecked off Lana'i. In 1931 George A. Crozier's *Charlotte C.* foundered somewhere along the beach. The 34 foot yawl called *Tradewind* was wrecked off the mouth of the Maunalei Valley on August 6, 1834 while cruising from Honolulu to Lahaina. There is a remnant of an old lighthouse and also some old petroglyph sites nearby. The concierge desk can give you a list of petroglyphs around the island.

Please respect these sights. The beach is unsafe for swimming, but you might see some people shorefishing. Sometimes after storms, interesting shells, old bottles and assorted artifacts are washed up along the shoreline. One area you probably won't visit is Pohaku "O" which roughly translates to mean "rock." This is in the Mahana region of Lana'i on the island's leeward side. The rocks here resemble tombstones and were avoided by the early Hawaiians as a place of evil. If the breezes are favorable, the wind blowing by the rock creates an "O" sound that changes with the wind, which is the reason this rock received its evil connotations.

For another adventure, leave Lana'i City and follow Kaumalapau Highway past the small airport and continue on another five minutes toward Kaumalapau Harbor. It's paved all the way! The harbor isn't much to see, but the drive down to the water shows the dramatically different landscape of Lana'i's windward coastline. Here you can see the sharply cut rocky shoreline that drops steeply into the ocean, in some places more than 1,500 feet. The Kaunolu Bay can be accessed from the Kaumalapau Highway along a very, very, rugged road. Follow the road just a bit further and you'll reach the harbor. The bulk of the island's materials come in by barge which were also the method used to take the thousands of tons of pineapples to Oʻahu for processing. Each pineapple crate weighed seven tons and a barge could haul 170 crates at a time. Today, pineapple production has become too expensive on Lanaʻi. Hawaiʻi is finding it hard to compete with countries such as the Philippines, where people are willing to work at a much lower daily wage and the fruit can be grown and processed for much less. In the past, freight was brought to Lanaʻi aboard the barges returning from Honolulu after delivering the pineapple. Today the Young Brothers have the contract for freight delivery.

Hulopoʻe Beach is a splendid marine reserve. Along a crescent of white sandy beach is Hulopoʻe Beach which fronts Manele Bay Hotel. It is also Lanai's best swimming beach and was voted "Best Beach in the Country" by the University of Maryland's "Dr. Beach." As with all beaches, be aware of surf conditions. There are attendants at the beach kiosk who can provide beach safety information. Although netting and spearfishing are not allowed, shorefishing is permitted. The best snorkeling is in the mornings before the surf picks up. Across the bay from the Manele Bay Hotel are a series of tidal pools. When the tide drifts down, sea creatures emerge making this a great spot for exploration. The Lodge at Koele and Manele Bay Hotel offer a handy "Tide Pool Guide" prepared by Kathleen Kapalka. It notes that the Hulopoʻe Bay and tide pool areas are both part of a marine life conservation district which was set up in 1976. Also included in the conservation district are Manele Bay and Puʻupehe Cove and as such, all animals and plants (dead or alive) are protected from collection or harm. The color brochure is an easy-to-follow guide to your personal tour of these wonderful tidal areas. Mollusks, arthropods, marine vertebrates, annelids, echinoderms, marine invertebrates, and marine plants are described and illustrated. Safety tips and conservation tips include the fact that suntanning oils are detrimental and should be cleansed from the hands before reaching into the pools. This is an excellent brochure which will make your tidal pool adventure a valuable learning experience. Note: Reef shoes are available at the hotel's beach kiosk for resort guests, a recommended protection when prowling around the rocky shoreline.

Climb up the bluff and you will be rewarded with a great view of Maui and Kahoʻolawe. A large monolithic rock sits off the bluff. This is Puʻupehe (often referred to as Sweetheart Rock) that carries a poignant local legend. As with most oral history, legends tend to take on the special character of the storyteller. Such is the story of Puʻupehe. We asked three people about the legend and heard three different versions. One made the hero into a jealous lover, the other a thoughtful one. So here is our interpretation. There was a strong handsome young Hawaiian man whose true love was a beautiful Hawaiian woman. They made a sea cave near Puʻupehe rock their lover's retreat. One day the man journeyed inland to replenish their supplies, leaving his love in the sea cave. He had gone some distance when he sensed an impending storm. He hurriedly returned to the sea cave, but the storm preceded him and his love had drowned in the cave. He was devastated. Using superhuman strength he carried her to the top of the monolithic rock called Puʻupehe and buried her there before jumping to his death. Whether there is truth to this legend is uncertain, but some years back a scientist did scale the top of the peak, which was no easy task, to investigate. No bones or other evidence was found. However, we were told that in ancient times, the bones were removed and hidden separately away. And so ends this sad tale of lost love.

Manele Bay is a quaint boat port which offers excellent snorkeling just beyond the breakwater. When the surf at Hulopo'e is too strong, Lana'i tour boats often anchor here for snorkeling.

WILDLIFE

You'll notice very quickly that there are many, many birds on Lana'i, a far greater number than on Maui. Fortunately for the birds, Lana'i does not have the mongoose as a predator. Wild turkeys, the last non-native animal to be introduced to Lana'i, are hunted in early November for about two weeks. They are easily spotted, but we understand as soon as the 1st of November appears (the turkeys must have calendars) they disappear until promptly after Thanksgiving. These wild birds look very lean and don't appear to make a very succulent Thanksgiving dinner. The easiest place to spot them is down near the Manele boat harbor where a group of turkeys and a pack of wild cats together enjoy the leftovers from the Trilogy boat's daily picnics.

Pheasant are also hunted seasonally. Wild goats were rounded up and captured years ago. The only island pigs are in the piggery where they are raised for island consumption. Pronghorn antelope, introduced in 1959, have now been hunted to extinction. Twelve Axis deer were introduced by George Munro and have adapted well to Lana'i. It is estimated that there are some 3,000-6,000 animals and, given the fact that they produce offspring twice yearly, the numbers are ever growing.

GARDEN OF THE GODS

In fact deer far outnumber Lana'i's human population. The deer run a mere 110-160 pounds and are hunted almost year round. It is easiest to spot these lean, quick deer in the early mornings or late evenings bounding across fields, but during the day they seek sheltered, shaded areas. There are still a few remaining mouflon sheep, which have distinctive and beautiful curved horns. You'll note many of the houses in Lana'i City are decorated with arrays of horns and antlers across their porch or on a garage wall.

BEACHES

Along Lana'i's northern shore is Polihua. There is an interesting stretch of long sand dunes. This coast is often very windy, and some days the blowing sand is intense. The surf conditions are dangerous and swimming should not be attempted, ever. Also along the northern shore is the area from Awalua to Naha. The beaches are narrow and the offshore waters are shallow with a wide reef. However, the water is often murky. Swimming and snorkeling are not recommended.

Surf conditions can be dangerous. Lopa, on the eastern shore, is a narrow white sand beach that can be enjoyed for picnicking and sunbathing.

Along the western coastline is Kaunola, a rocky shore with no sandy beach and no safe entry or exit. Conditions can be dangerous. Swimming is not advised at any time. Also on the western shore is Kaumalapau Harbor, the deep water harbor used for shipping. Water activities are not recommended at any time.

The southern coastline affords the safest ocean conditions. Manele Bay is the small boat harbor, but water activity is not recommended due to heavy boat traffic. Hulopo'e Bay is the island's best and most beautiful white sand beach. It is located in front of the Manele Bay Hotel. It is popular for swimming, surfing, boogie-boarding and snorkeling. The tidepools make for fun exploration and, although a marine preserve, shore fishing is permitted. On summer weekends the camping area is often filled with local residents. However, large swells, and high surf conditions can exist. During times of high surf, undertows become very strong. Entry is hazardous during these conditions. During these times it is not safe to stand or play even in the shore break, as severe injury can occur. Be aware of water safety signs. There are no lifeguards on duty, however, there are attendants at the resort's beach kiosk who might be able to answer questions you have. Never swim alone and always exercise good water safety judgment.

CHILDCARE

The Manele Bay Hotel and The Lodge at Koele offer the *Pilialoha Adventure Program* for youth aged 5-16 years. Pilialoha means close friendship and beloved companionship. A full day (9am-3pm) includes lunch and runs $60 for one child; $115 for two; and $165 for three. The half-day program, either 9am-12:30pm or 11:30am-3pm, is $40 per child including lunch. ($75 for two children; $105 for three.)

Their evening program is available only on Friday and Saturday and includes dinner (one child/$55; two/$105; three/$150). Additional evening programs may be added during the holidays. Children ages 3-5 years may join the program when appropriate and when accompanied by an attendant. There is an individual care fee of $10 in addition to the regular program rate. Daytime activities include scavenger hunts, exploring petroglyphs, learning about dolphins and whales, putting at the golf course, lawn games, crafts, and tide pool exploration. Evening activities range from a beach party or ice cream social to a luau night or making your own videos. Advanced registration is required; it is suggested that you make your plans with the concierge the day prior. Private babysitting is also available through the concierge at $10 per hour, each additional child at $5 per hour.

There are many activities your child can also enjoy on Lana'i. A Pilialoha staff member can accompany your child for an additional $20 fee. Tennis lessons, half or full hour for youths 12 and younger. Golf lessons at the Challenge of Manele, either private or semi-private. On Saturdays a complimentary golf clinic is available for youths aged 8 and up. Children five and up can enjoy a pony ride for $10, children 9 and up are invited on the one-hour Plantation horseback excursion for $35 and youth ages 12 and up can have private horseback riding lessons or take the two-hour Paniolo ride. A five-hour excursion on Trilogy is offered for $42.50 (aged 11 and younger), $85 for 12 and older. Spinning Dolphin Fishing Charter is available for half day excursions for children 12 and up $85. Scuba and snorkeling lessons at the Manele Bay Pool for those 8 years and up. Hiking, biking, and sporting clays activities also available.

LANA'I RECOMMENDED READING

An excellent account of the history of the island is *True Stories of the Island of Lana'i* by Lawrence Kainoahou Gay, the son of Charles Gay. First published in 1965 and reprinted in 1981 it is available for $12 at the resort gift shops on Lana'i and probably could be obtained through bookstores on the neighboring islands as well.

BREADFRUIT

RECOMMENDED READING

Ashdown, Inez. *Ke Alaloa O Maui. Authentic History and Legends of the Valley Isle*. Hawaii: Kama'aina Historians. 1971.

Ashdown, Inez. *Stories of Old Lahaina*. Honolulu: Hawaiian Service. 1976.

Barrow, Terence. *Incredible Hawaii*. Vermont: Charles Tuttle Co. 1974.

Begley, Bryan. *Taro in Hawaii*. Honolulu: The Oriental Publishing Co. 1979.

Bird, Isabella. *Six Months in the Sandwich Islands*. Tokyo: Tuttle. 1988.

Boom, Bob and Christensen, Chris. *Important Hawaiian Place Names*. Hawaii: Bob Boom Books. 1978.

Chisholm, Craig. *Hawaiian Hiking Trails*. Oregon: Fernglen Press. 1994.

Christensen, Jack Shields. *Instant Hawaiian*. Hawaii: The Robert Boom Co. 1971.

Clark, John. *Beaches of Maui County*. Honolulu: University Press of Hawaii. 1980.

Daws, Gavan. *The Illustrated Atlas of Hawaii*. Australia: Island Heritage. 1980.

Echos of Our Song. Honolulu: University of Hawaii Press.

Fielding, Ann. *Hawaiian Reefs and Tidepools*. Hawaii: Oriental Pub. Co.

Haraguchi, Paul. *Weather in Hawaiian Waters*. 1983.

Hawaii Island Paradise. California: Wide World Publishing. 1987.

Hazama, Dorothy. *The Ancient Hawaiians*. Honolulu: Hogarth Press.

Judd, Gerrit. *Hawaii, an Informal History*. New York: Collier Books. 1961.

Kaye, Glen. *Hawaiian Volcanos*. Nevada: K.C. Publications, 1987.

Kepler, Angela. *Maui's Hana Highway*. Honolulu: Mutual Publishing. 1987.

Kepler, Cameron B. and Angela Kay. *Haleakala, A Guide to the Mountain*. Honolulu: Mutual Publishing. 1988.

Kyselka, Will and Lanterman, Ray. *Maui, How it Came to Be*. Honolulu: The University Press of Hawaii. 1980.

Lahaina Historical Guide. Tokyo: Maui Historical Society. 1971.

Lahaina Restoration Foundation, *Story of Lahaina*. Lahaina: 1980.

"One cannot determine in advance to love a particular woman, nor can one so determine to love Hawaii. One sees, and one loves or does not love. With Hawaii it seems always to be love at first sight. Those for whom the islands were made, or who were made for the islands, are swept off their feet in the first moments of meeting, embrace and are embraced. " Jack London

London, Jack. *Stories of Hawaii*. Honolulu: Mutual Publishing. 1965.

Mack, Jim. *Haleakala and The Story Behind the Scenery*. Nevada: K.C. Publications, 1984.

Mrantz, Maxine. *Whaling Days in Old Hawaii*. Honolulu: Aloha Graphics. 1976.

Na Mele O Hawai'i Nei. Honolulu: University of Hawaii Press. 1970.

Nickerson, Roy. *Lahaina, Royal Capital of Hawaii*. 1980.

On The Hana Coast. Hong Kong: Emphasis Int'l Ltd. and Carl Lundquist. 1987.

Pukui, Mary K. et al. *The Pocket Hawaiian Dictionary*. Honolulu: The University of Hawaii Press. 1975.

Randall, John. *Underwater Guide to Hawaiian Reef Fishes*. Hawaii: Treasures of Time. 1981.

Smith, Robert. *Hiking Maui*. California. 1990.

Stevenson, Robert Louis. *Travels in Hawaii*. Honolulu: University of Hawaii Press. 1973.

Tabrah, Ruth. *Maui The Romantic Island*. Nevada: KC Publications. 1985.

Thorne, Chuck. *50 Locations for Scuba & Snorkeling*. 1983.

Titcomb, M. *Native Use of Fish in Hawaii*. Honolulu: University of Hawaii Press. 1952.

Twain, Mark. *Letters from Mark Twain*. Hawaii: U. of Hawaii Press. 1966.

Twain, Mark. *Mark Twain in Hawaii*. Colorado: Outdoor Books. 1986.

Wallin, Doug. *Exotic Fishes and Coral of Hawaii and the Pacific*. 1974.

Westervelt, H. *Myths and Legends of Hawaii*. Honolulu: Mutual. 1987.

Wisniewski, Richard A. *The Rise and Fall of the Hawaiian Kingdom*. Honolulu: Pacific Basin Enterprises. 1979.

RECOMMENDED READING FOR CHILDREN

Adair, Dick. *The Story of Aloha Bear*. Honolulu: Island Heritage. 1986.

Adair, Dick. *Aloha Bear and the Meaning of Aloha*. Honolulu: Island Heritage. 1987.

Feeney, Stephanie. *Hawaii is a Rainbow*. Honolulu: University of Hawaii Press. 1985.

Feeney, Stephanie and Fielding, Ann. *Sand to Sea: Marine Life of Hawaii*. Honolulu: University of Hawaii Press. 1989.

Kahalewai, Marilyn. *Maui Mouse's Supper*. Honolulu: Bess Press. 1988.

Kahalewai, Marilyn. *Whose Slippers are Those?* Honolulu: Besss Press. 1988.

Knudsen, Eric A. *Spooky Stuffs*. Aiea, Hawaii: Island Heritage Publishing. 1989.

Laird, Donivee Martin. *The Three Little Hawaiian Pigs and the Magic Shark*. Honolulu: Barnaby Books. 1994.

Laird, Donivee Martin. *'Ula Li'i and the Magic Shark*. Honolulu: Barnaby Books. 1985.

Laird, Donivee Martin. *Wili Wai Kula and the Three Mongooses*. Honolulu: Barnaby Books. 1983.

Laird, Donivee Martin. *Keaka and the Lilikoi Vine*. Honolulu: Barnaby Books. 1982.

Land-Nellist, Cassandra. *A Child's First Book About Hawaii*. Hawaii: Press Pacifica. 1987.

McBarnet, Gill. *A Whale's Tale*. Hawaii: Ruwanga Trading. 1988.

McBarnet, Gill. *Fountain of Fire*. Hawaii: Ruwanga Trading. 1987.

McBarnet, Gill. *Goodnight Gecko*. Hawaii: Ruwanga Trading. 1991.

McBarnet, Gill. *The Whale Who Wanted to be Small*. Hawaii: Ruwanga Trading. 1985.

McBarnet, Gill. *The Wonderful Journey*. Hawaii: Ruwanga Trading. 1986.

McBride, Leslie R. *About Hawaii's Volcanoes*. Hilo: Petroglyph Press. 1986.

Pape, Donna L. *Hawaii Puzzle Book*. Honolulu: Bess Press. 1984.

Swanson, Helen. *Angel of Rainbow Gulch*. Honolulu: 1992.

Thompson, Vivian. *Hawaiian Tales of Heroes and Champions.* Honolulu: University of Hawaii Press. 1986.

Tune, Suelyn Ching. *How Maui Slowed the Sun.* Honolulu: University of Hawaii Press. 1988.

Wagenman, Mark A. *The Adventures of Aloha Bear and Maui the Whale.* Honolulu: Island Heritage. 1989.

Warren, Bonnie. *Aloha from Hawaii!* Honolulu: Warren Associates. 1987.

Williams, Julie Stewart. *And the Birds Appeared.* Honolulu: University of Hawaii Press. 1988.

Williams, Julie et. al. *Maui Goes Fishing.* Honolulu: University of Hawaii Press. 1991.

Von Tempski, Armine. *Bright Spurs.* Honolulu: Oxbow Press. 1946

Von Tempski, Armine. *Judy of the Islands.* Honolulu: Oxbow Press. 1941

Von Tempski, Armine. *Pam's Paradise Ranch.* Honolulu: Oxbow Press. 1940.

ORDER INFORMATION

NEWSLETTERS

We offer UPDATE newsletters for Maui and Kaua'i. These quarterly newsletters are published by Paradise Publications and highlight the most current island news and events. Each features late-breaking tips on the newest restaurants, island activities or special, not-to-be-missed events. Each newsletter is available at the single issue price of $2.50 or a yearly subscription (four issues) is $10 per year, $12 to Canada, International subscription is $16 per year.

FREE OFFER: If you'd like to receive a sample issue of either newsletter, send a self-addressed, stamped envelope and we will be happy to forward you a copy of the most recent edition.

The following books are available from Paradise Publications to enhance your travel library. Prices are subject to change without notice.

PARADISE GUIDES

HAWAI'I: THE BIG ISLAND, A Paradise Family Guide by John Penisten
Outstanding for its completeness, this well-organized guide provides useful information for people of every budget and lifestyle. Each chapter features the author's personal recommendations and "best bets." In addition to comprehensive information about island accommodations you will find a full range of water and land activities, plus tours from which to choose. Then enjoy dining at one of the more than 250 restaurants which range from local style drive-ins to fine dining establishments. Sights to see, beaches and helpful travel tips. 300 pages $15.00, 5th edition. Copyright 1999.

KAUA'I: A Paradise Family Guide by Christie Stilson & Dona Early
Completely revised and rewritten since Hurricane Iniki, this information-packed guide describes island accommodations, restaurants, seclude beaches plus recreational and tour options. "If you need a "how to do it" book to guide your next trip to Kaua'i, here's the one." Over 350 pages, multi-indexed maps and illustrations. $15. Copyright November 1997.

MAUI AND LANA'I: A Paradise Family Guide by Dona Early & Christie Stilson.
You're holding this one in your hands, but perhaps you'd like a copy for a friend! Over 500 pages with completely revised, user-friendly island maps! $15. Copyright 1999.

REFERENCE

New Pocket Hawaiian Dictionary
This concise dictionary is fun and useful, too! You'll resolve just what all those Hawaiian words mean and how to pronounce them! $4.95

MAPS & MORE MAPS

A great addition to your travels are full-color topographical maps by cartographer James Bier. Maps are available for $3.95 each for the islands of O'ahu, Maui, Kaua'i, Lana'i plus Moloka'i, and the Big Island of Hawai'i.

The *Hawai'i Volcanoes National Park* and *Haleakala*, Earth Press Topographical maps are a must-purchase if you are planning on enjoying these magnificent parks in depth. Water resistant! Each map $3.95

PHOTOGRAPHIC JOURNALISM

KAUA'I THE UNCONQUERABLE
HALEAKALA
HAWAI'I VOLCANOES
Each of these three fascinating and informative books is filled with vivid full color photographs depicting some of the most incredible scenery in the islands.

VIEWBOOKS
Doug Peebles is quite possibly Hawai'i's best photographer and his finest photography has been showcased in these full-color paperback books. Ideal for the armchair traveler or trip planner, these affordable pictorial guides make wonderful souvenirs and great gifts. Choose from these five: *Hawai'i (The Big Island), Maui, Kaua'i, O'ahu, Volcanoes,* or *Flowers.* Each is paperback, 10x13, 32 pages, $7.95

RECREATION AND EXPLORATION

HAWAIIAN HIKING TRAILS by Craig Chisholm. This attractive and accurate guide details 40 of Hawai'i's best hiking trails. Hikes for every level of ability. Includes photography, topographical maps, and detailed directions. An excellent book for discovering Hawai''s great outdoors. 152 pages. $15.95

DIVERS GUIDE TO MAUI by Chuck Thorne. This easy-to-use guide will give you all the information you need to choose the perfect dive site. $9.95

ROBERT SMITH HIKING GUIDES, each guide is $10.95

Hiking Kaua'i with over 40 trails. 116 pages.
Hiking Maui, 27 hiking areas, 160 pages.
Hiking Hawai'i: The Big Island, 18 hiking areas, 40 hiking trails, 152 pages

DIVING HAWAI'I, featuring 50 dive sites on all the islands. Great photograph. 128 pages. $19.95.

HAWAI'I GOLF GUIDE published by TeeBox, features every island course. Information is comprehensive covering the basics, such as course location, number of holes and phone numbers, as well as in-depth information on golf course features and course strategy. 165 pages. 1994. $10.00

COOKBOOKS

COOKING WITH ALOHA. Discover all the flavors of the Hawaiian Islands in your own kitchen with this easy-to-follow cookbook. Appetizers to desserts are featured. A great and inexpensive guide to cooking your favorite Hawaiian foods. 9x12 paperback. 184 pages. $9.95.

THE FOOD OF PARADISE. Explore Hawai'i's culinary heritage with over 150 recipes, photographs, and a bibliography of Hawai'i's cookbooks. This cookbook is great for cooks, Hawaiiana buffs and food historians. 8x9 paperback, 296 pages, $24.95

HAWAI'I'S SPAM (Registered trademark) COOKBOOK by Ann Kondo Corum records and glorifies the versatility of this unique food, along with sardines, corned beef, and Vienna sausage, which are all favorites in Hawai'i. Humorous illustrations by the author capture some of the local attitudes toward these canned delights. Glossary included. 53 "Spam" recipes, and 44 others. 136 pages. $9.95.

VIDEO

HAWAIIAN PARADISE. Produced by International Video Network. More than a travel log, this is one of the best of many, many videos we have reviewed. The journey covers all six of the major Hawaiian Islands. The narrative begins with the formation of the islands and deviates from the average video by exploring the culture, legend, lore and history of the islands. The lover of Hawai'i will learn new and interesting island facts and points of history and the newcomer will thrill to the visual treats. The next best thing to being there. $29.95. 90 minutes.

FLIGHT OF THE CANYONBIRD. An inspired view of the Garden Island of Kaua'i from a bird's eye perspective, an outstanding 30-minute piece of cinematography. The narration explores the geologic and historic beginnings of the island. A lasting memento or a great gift. $19.95

FOREVER HAWAI'I. This 60-minute video portrait features all six major Hawaiian islands. It includes breathtaking views from the snowcapped peaks of Mauna Kea to the bustling city of Waikiki, from the magnificent Waimea Canyon to the spectacular Haleakala Crater. $24.95

FOREVER MAUI. An in-depth visit to Maui with scenic shots and interesting stories about the Valley Isle. An excellent video for the first-timer or the return island visitor. $19.95. 30 minutes.

KUMUHULA: KEEPERS OF A CULTURE. This 85 minute tape was funded by the Hawai'i State Foundation on Culture and Arts. This beautifully filmed work includes hulas from various troupes on different islands, attired in their brilliantly colored costumes. This film explores the unique qualities of hula as well as explaining its history. $29.95

HULA LESSONS: ONE AND TWO. "Lovely Hula Hands" and "Little Brown Gal" are the two featured hulas taught by Carol "Kalola" Lorenzo who explains the basic steps. A fun and entertaining video for the whole family. 30 minutes $29.95.

SHIPPING: In the Continental U.S. (U.S.P.S. First class priority Mail)

For books or videos:

1-2 items $4
3-4 items $5
5 or more items $6

Maps are $1 shipping each if purchased separately. If purchased in combination with a book or video, there is no additional charge for shipping. If you'd prefer US Mail bookrate or Federal express, please call for a quote.

Canadian Orders
Please add $4 for the first book or tape, $1 for each additional book or tape. No additional shipping charge for maps when ordered with book or tape. For maps ordered separately, please add $2 postage. Orders to Canada are shipped U.S. Small Parcel Airmail.

We accept check, money order, or Visa/Mastercard. Send your order to:

TITLE   QUANTITY   PRICE

_____   _____   _____

_____   _____   _____

_____   _____   _____

ADD SHIPPING   _____

TOTAL   _____

SHIP TO:

_____

_____

_____

Paradise Publications, 8110 SW Wareham, Portland, Oregon 97223-6992
Phone (503) 246-1555
Email at: < Paradyse@worldnet.att.net >

INDEX